History Alive!®
The United States
Through Industrialism

TCi™

Chief Executive Officer: Bert Bower
Chief Operating Officer: Amy Larson
Director of Curriculum: Liz Russell
Managing Editor: Laura Alavosus
Editorial Project Manager: Nancy Rogier
Project Editor: Mali Apple
Copyeditor: Jennifer Seidel
Editorial Associates: Anna Embree, Sarah Sudano
Production Manager: Lynn Sanchez
Art Director: John F. Kelly
Senior Graphic Designers: Christy Uyeno, Paul Rebello
Graphic Designers: Don Taka, Victoria Philp
Photo Edit Manager: Margee Robinson
Photo Editor: Picture Research Consultants, Inc.
Production Project Manager: Eric Houts
Art Editor: Mary Swab

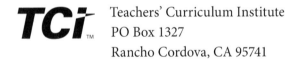

Teachers' Curriculum Institute
PO Box 1327
Rancho Cordova, CA 95741

Customer Service: 800-497-6138
www.teachtci.com

ISBN 978-1-58371-931-2
6 7 8 9 10 11 12 WC 19 18 17 16 15 14

Manufactured by Webcrafters, Inc., Madison, WI
United States of America, October 2014, Job #119262

Program Director

Bert Bower

Program Author

Diane Hart is a nationally recognized social studies textbook author and assessment consultant. She has authored several basal social studies textbooks for students at all levels. She has also written texts for students with special needs that are used in schools, adult literacy, and citizenship classes. In addition to her writing, she consults with state departments of education on the development of standards-based social studies assessments. A former teacher and Woodrow Wilson Fellow, with a master's degree in history from Stanford University, Ms. Hart is deeply involved in social studies education. She is active in the California Council for the Social Studies and serves on the Board of Directors of the National Council for the Social Studies. In both her professional and volunteer activities, she is guided by two passions. The first is engaging students in the social studies curriculum by creating compelling, accessible textbooks. The second is ensuring that all students have opportunities to develop the knowledge, skills, and habits of the heart that they will need to be effective citizens in a complex world.

Creative Development Manager

Kelly Shafsky

Contributing Writers

Laura Alavosus
John Bergez
Susan Buckley
Jill Fox
Christine Freeman
Amy George
Brent Goff
Andrew Goldblatt
David M. Holford
Elspeth Leacock
Tedd Levy
Julie Weiss

Curriculum Developers

Joyce Bartky
April Bennett
Nicole Boylan
Vern Cleary
Terry Coburn
Julie Cremin
Erin Fry
Amy George
Steve Seely
Nathan Wellborne

Reading Specialist

Kate Kinsella, Ed.D.
Reading and TESOL Specialist
San Francisco State University

Teacher Consultants

Melissa Aubuchon
City of Ladue School District
St. Louis, Missouri

Terry Coburn
Brookside School
Stockton, California

Connie Davidson
San Leandro Unified School District
San Leandro, California

Amy George
Weston Middle School
Weston, Massachusetts

Nicolle Hutchinson
Broward County Public Schools
Miramar, Florida

Dawn Lavond
Moreland Middle School
San Jose, California

Julie Peters
Woodstock Community Union School District #200
Woodstock, Illinois

Debra Schneider
Tracy Unified School District
Tracy, California

UNIT 1

Our Colonial Heritage

UNIT 2

Revolution in the Colonies

UNIT 3

Forming a New Nation

UNIT 4

Launching the New Republic

UNIT 5

An Expanding Nation

UNIT 6

Americans in the Mid-1800s

UNIT 7

The Union Challenged

UNIT 8

Migration and Industry

UNIT 9

A Modern Nation Emerges

Maps

Graphs, Diagrams, and Tables

Selected Primary Source Quotations

Political Cartoons

Unit 1

Our Colonial Heritage

Shown here is Plimoth Plantation, a re-creation of what the English colony of Plymouth might have looked like in 1627. Like the original colony, Plimoth Plantation overlooks the Atlantic Ocean.

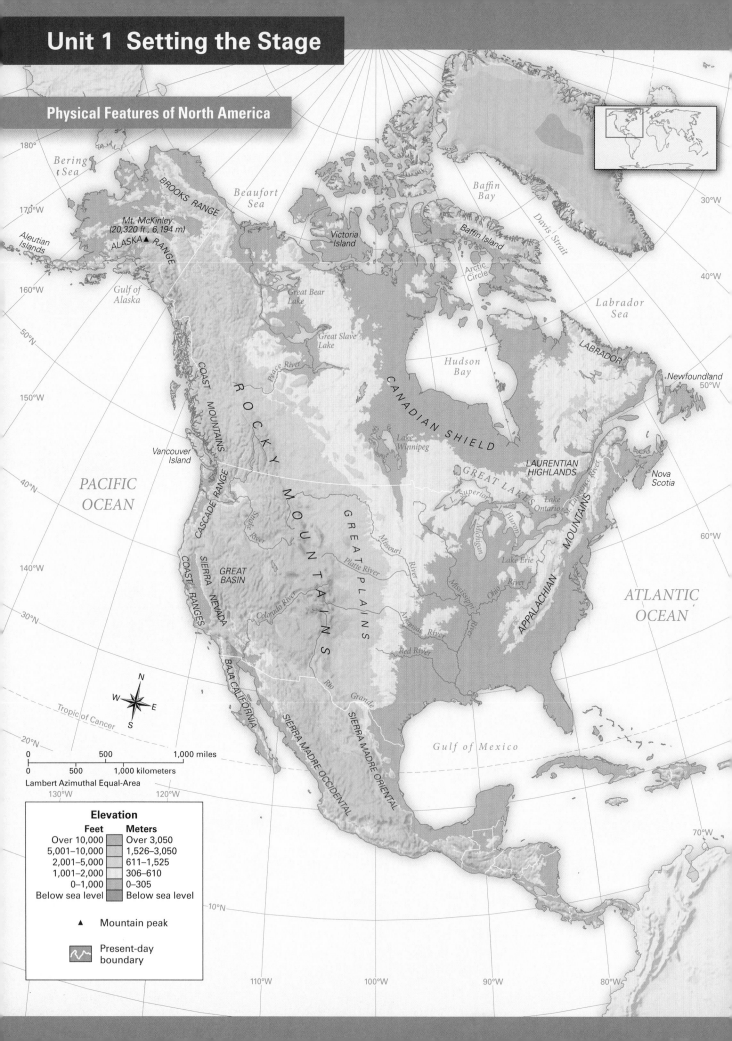

Physical Features of North America

Bering Sea

180°

BROOKS RANGE

Beaufort Sea

Mt. McKinley
(20,320 ft., 6,194 m)
ALASKA RANGE

Aleutian Islands

170°W

160°W

Gulf of Alaska

COAST MOUNTAINS

150°W

50°N

Vancouver Island

40°N

PACIFIC OCEAN

140°W

CASCADE RANGE

COAST RANGES

30°N

SIERRA NEVADA

GREAT BASIN

Colorado River

BAJA CALIFORNIA

20°N

Tropic of Cancer

N
W E
S

130°W

120°W

Peace River

Great Bear Lake

Great Slave Lake

ROCKY MOUNTAINS

Snake River

Platte River

GREAT PLAINS

Missouri River

Arkansas River

Red River

Rio Grande

Victoria Island

Arctic Circle

Baffin Bay

Baffin Island

Davis Strait

CANADIAN SHIELD

Hudson Bay

Lake Winnipeg

LAURENTIAN HIGHLANDS

GREAT LAKES

L. Superior
Lake Michigan
L. Huron
Lake Ontario
Lake Erie

Mississippi River

Ohio River

APPALACHIAN MOUNTAINS

St. Lawrence River

Labrador Sea

LABRADOR

Newfoundland

Nova Scotia

ATLANTIC OCEAN

30°W

40°W

50°W

60°W

70°W

80°W

SIERRA MADRE OCCIDENTAL

SIERRA MADRE ORIENTAL

Gulf of Mexico

110°W

100°W

90°W

10°N

0   500   1,000 miles
0   500   1,000 kilometers
Lambert Azimuthal Equal-Area

Elevation

Feet	Meters	
Over 10,000	Over 3,050	
5,001–10,000	1,526–3,050	
2,001–5,000	611–1,525	
1,001–2,000	306–610	
0–1,000	0–305	
Below sea level	Below sea level	

▲   Mountain peak

〰   Present-day boundary

Our Colonial Heritage

In this unit, you will learn about the first Americans—the American Indian peoples who were here when the first Europeans arrived. You will also learn about the Europeans who colonized North America. The British colonies settled along the Atlantic coast would become the first 13 states in the nation.

Political divisions like colonies and states did not exist before the Europeans arrived. Each American Indian group occupied a territory that had no formal boundaries. As the map on the opposite page shows, the continent's physical geography varies greatly. American Indians lived in harmony with the land. Their different environments gave them different ways of life.

Contact with European colonists changed those ways of life. The map below shows where European nations claimed land in North America. To satisfy French demand for furs, American Indians in regions claimed by France began to hunt more. The Spanish tried to enslave Indians and, along with the English, wanted their land.

Increased hunting, flight from slavery, and loss of land pushed some Indian groups into territory occupied by other Indians. As the British colonies became a nation, and as that nation grew, this population shift continued. Eventually, almost no Indian lands remained. However, the names of many places in North America are reminders of those lands. The Ohio, Mississippi, and Missouri rivers get their names from American Indian words, as do about half the states.

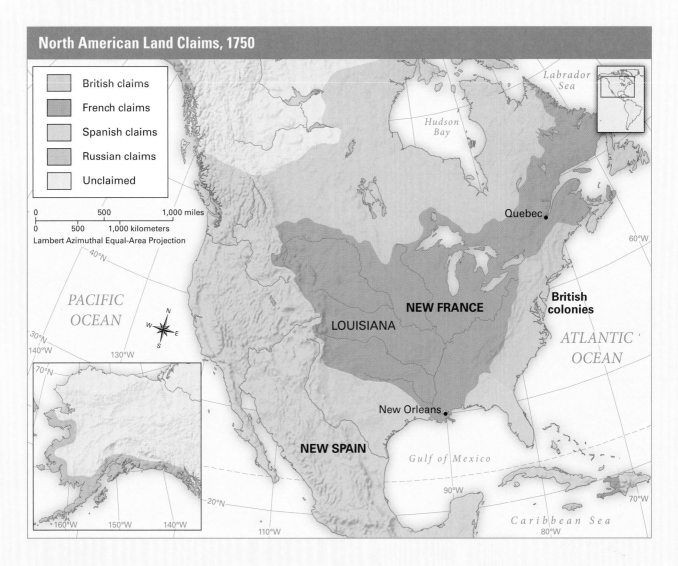

North American Land Claims, 1750

British claims
French claims
Spanish claims
Russian claims
Unclaimed

0   500   1,000 miles
0   500   1,000 kilometers
Lambert Azimuthal Equal-Area Projection

Labrador Sea

Hudson Bay

Quebec

PACIFIC OCEAN

NEW FRANCE

British colonies

LOUISIANA

ATLANTIC OCEAN

New Orleans

NEW SPAIN

Gulf of Mexico

Caribbean Sea

Chapter 1

The First Americans

How did the first Americans adapt to their environments?

1.1 Introduction

As a cold winter wind howls outside, the children huddle under thick fur blankets. They listen to their grandmother's soothing voice. "In the beginning there was the Great Spirit," Grandmother begins, "who ruled over a world of sky and water." Then the Great Spirit, says Grandmother, created land, plants, and animals. Finally, from living wood, the Great Spirit carved people for the new world.

These Abenaki (a-buh-NAH-key) children of New England are learning how their people began. Most groups have beliefs about where they came from. You may have heard stories about how your own relatives first arrived in the United States. But do you know where your ancestors were living 10,000 years ago?

Only if you are American Indian did you have relatives in the United States that long ago. Europeans and other groups did not start arriving in North America until a little more than 500 years ago. For thousands of years, the first Americans had the American continents to themselves. In this chapter, you will learn about these **resourceful** people and the creative ways they adapted to their environments.

Even today, scientists are still trying to find out more about the first Americans. These early people left few written records, so researchers study other items they left behind. Not much has survived except for a few animal and human bones, some stone and metal tools, and bits of pottery. Like detectives, scientists sift through these clues, trying to imagine how these people lived and how their lives changed over time. They come up with ideas about the many ways in which American Indians adapted to their physical surroundings. When scientists find a new object, they try to figure out whether it supports their current ideas or suggests new ones. In your lifetime, we will probably learn much more about how the first Americans adapted to their environments and may **revise** many of our conclusions.

The Anasazi Indians of the southwestern United States made pottery, such as this pitcher, from clay and other materials.

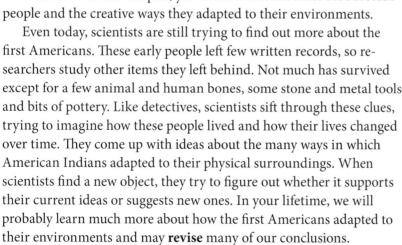

◀ The Anasazi Indians adapted to their environment by building homes in the stone cliffs of the U.S. Southwest.

1.2 Migration Routes of the First Americans

migrate to move from one place and establish a home in a new place. A move of a large number of people is called a migration, and the people who move are called migrants.

Scientists believe that the first Americans migrated on foot from Siberia, in Asia, to present-day Alaska. Today, a strip of ocean called the Bering Strait separates Alaska and Asia. But there was a time when a land bridge connected them.

Across a Land Bridge About 30,000 years ago, the most recent Ice Age began. As temperatures fell, much of Earth was covered by glaciers, sheets of ice up to a mile thick. With water locked up in the glaciers, the level of the oceans dropped 200 feet. This exposed a wide bridge of land between Asia and North America that scientists call Beringia (bear-IN-jee-uh).

In the summer, Beringia's grasslands attracted large Asian mammals, such as mammoths, which are long-haired cousins of the elephant. Over thousands of years, the animals slowly spread eastward. Generations of Siberian hunter families followed. Armed with only stone-tipped spears, they killed these huge, powerful animals for food. Eventually, perhaps between 10,000 and 20,000 years ago, some of the hunters reached America. Other migrants may have traveled along the coast of Beringia by boat to catch fish, seals, and other marine mammals.

Scientists believe that the first Americans migrated from Siberia to Alaska across a land bridge called Beringia. These people were following mammoths and other animals that moved east in search of grazing land.

Migrating East and South Once in America, hunters followed the animals south, where spring brought fresh grasses. Then, about 10,000 years ago, Earth warmed again. As the glaciers melted and the oceans rose, the land bridge disappeared. Mammoths and other traditional prey began to die off, perhaps from disease, overhunting, or the change in climate.

The descendents of Siberian hunters then had to find new sources of food and new materials for clothing and shelter. So these people, now known to us as American Indians, became hunter-gatherers, catching smaller animals, fishing more, and collecting edible plants and seeds. Over thousands of years, they spread across the two American continents, from the Pacific to the Atlantic and from Alaska all the way to the tip of South America.

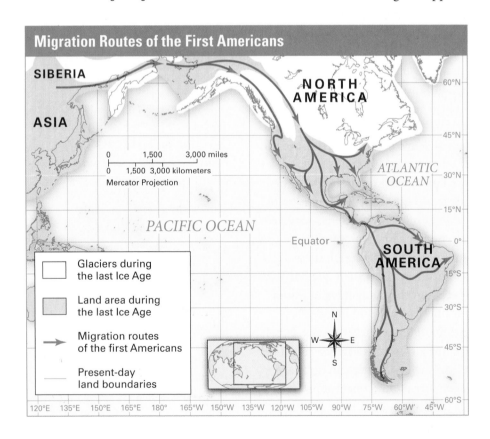

Migration Routes of the First Americans

SIBERIA

ASIA

NORTH AMERICA

PACIFIC OCEAN

ATLANTIC OCEAN

Equator

SOUTH AMERICA

0   1,500   3,000 miles
0   1,500 3,000 kilometers
Mercator Projection

Glaciers during the last Ice Age

Land area during the last Ice Age

Migration routes of the first Americans

Present-day land boundaries

1.3 The First Americans Adapt to the Environment

American Indians lived in a variety of places, from snowy forests to dry deserts and vast grasslands. Each of these kinds of places is an environment. An **environment** includes everything that surrounds us—land, water, animals, and plants. Each environment also has a climate, or long-term weather pattern. Groups of American Indians survived by **adapting,** or changing, their style of living to suit each environment, its climate, and its **natural resources.**

The tents in this Inuit (IN-oo-it) camp in northern Alaska were made from seal and caribou skins. The Inuit used the inflated sealskins, hanging from the poles, as floats.

Using Natural Resources American Indians learned to use the natural resources in their environments for food, clothing, and shelter. In the frigid regions of the far north, early Americans survived by hunting caribou in the summer and sea mammals in the winter. They fashioned warm, hooded clothing from animal skins. To avoid being blinded by the glare of the sun shining on snow, they made goggles out of bone with slits to see through.

The people of the north lived most of the year in houses made from driftwood and animal skins. In winter, hunters built **temporary** shelters called *iglus* (IG-looz) out of blocks of snow.

In warmer climates, American Indians gathered wild plants. Then, about 7,000 years ago, they learned to raise crops such as squash, chili peppers, beans, and corn. Growing their own food enabled them to settle in one place instead of following animals or searching for edible plants in the wild. These early farmers built the first villages and towns in America.

American Indian Cultural Regions Over generations, groups of American Indians developed their own **cultures,** or ways of life. Many became part of larger groupings that were loosely organized under common leaders.

Groups living in the same type of environment often adapted in similar ways. Forest dwellers often lived in houses covered with tree bark, while many desert peoples made shelters out of branches covered with brush.

Using such artifacts (items made by people), historians have grouped American Indian peoples into cultural regions. A **cultural region** is made up of people who share a similar language and way of life.

By the 1400s, between 1 and 2 million American Indians lived in ten major cultural regions north of Mexico. Later in this chapter, you will take a closer look at eight of these regions. They include the Northwest Coast, California, the Great Basin, the Plateau, the Southwest, the Great Plains, the Eastern Woodlands, and the Southeast.

environment all of the physical surroundings in a place, including land, water, animals, plants, and climate

natural resource useful material found in nature, including water, vegetation, animals, and minerals

culture a people's way of life, including beliefs, customs, food, dwellings, and clothing

cultural region an area in which a group of people share a similar culture and language

The first Americans lived through-out the North American continent. Historians have grouped these peoples into cultural regions, based on their shared languages and ways of life. Where American Indians lived also influenced what they wore, the type of housing they built, and the food they ate.

American Indian Cultural Regions

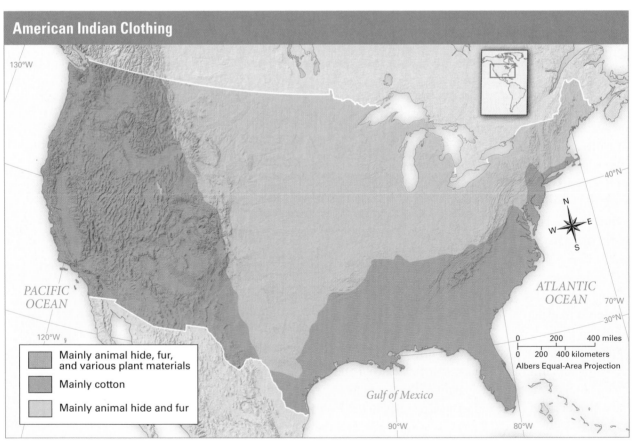

American Indian Clothing

Mainly animal hide, fur, and various plant materials

Mainly cotton

Mainly animal hide and fur

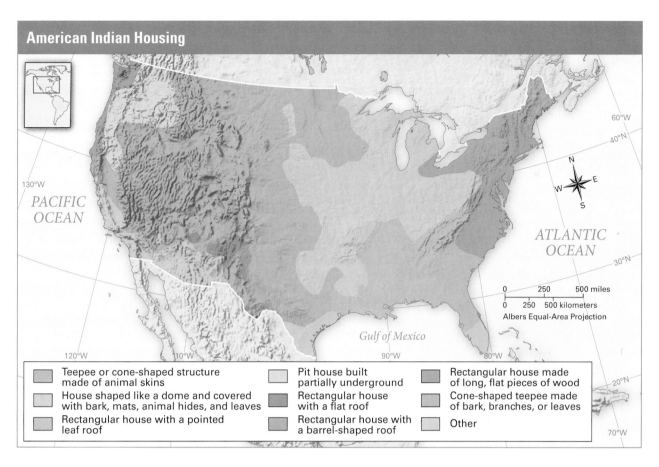

American Indian Housing

Legend:
- Teepee or cone-shaped structure made of animal skins
- House shaped like a dome and covered with bark, mats, animal hides, and leaves
- Rectangular house with a pointed leaf roof
- Pit house built partially underground
- Rectangular house with a flat roof
- Rectangular house with a barrel-shaped roof
- Rectangular house made of long, flat pieces of wood
- Cone-shaped teepee made of bark, branches, or leaves
- Other

PACIFIC OCEAN

ATLANTIC OCEAN

Gulf of Mexico

0   250   500 miles
0   250   500 kilometers
Albers Equal-Area Projection

130°W 120°W 110°W 90°W 80°W 70°W 60°W 40°N 30°N 20°N

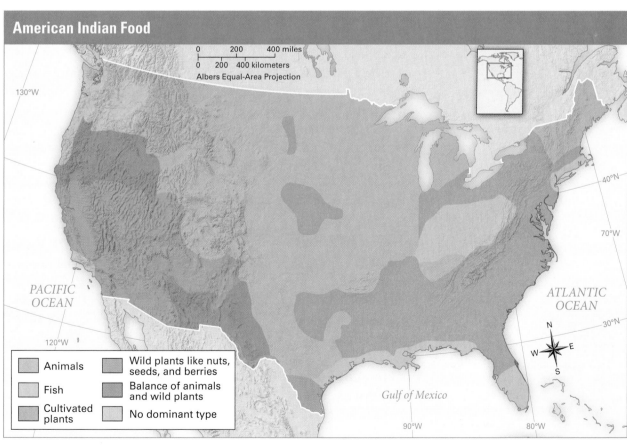

American Indian Food

0   200   400 miles
0   200   400 kilometers
Albers Equal-Area Projection

Legend:
- Animals
- Fish
- Cultivated plants
- Wild plants like nuts, seeds, and berries
- Balance of animals and wild plants
- No dominant type

PACIFIC OCEAN

ATLANTIC OCEAN

Gulf of Mexico

130°W 120°W 90°W 80°W 40°N 70°W 30°N

American Indians believed that humans, animals, plants, and even inanimate objects had their own spirits. Because of this belief, Indians felt related to all parts of nature.

1.4 How American Indians Viewed Their Environment

Wherever they lived, American Indians had a strong connection to their surroundings. They viewed themselves as a part of the community of plants, animals, and other natural objects. As a Sioux (soo) said, "From Wakan Tanka, the Great Spirit, there came a great unifying life force that flowed in and through all things—the flowers of the plains, blowing winds, rocks, trees, birds, animals—and was the same force that had been breathed into the first man."

Nature's Spirits American Indians generally believed that each part of nature had its own spirit. Each person had to maintain a balance with these spirits.

These beliefs were expressed in various customs. Southwest farmers, for example, made corn a part of every ceremony. Hunters gave thanks to the animals they killed.

Using the Land Unlike Europeans, American Indians did not believe that land could be owned as private property. But each group was deeply connected to its homeland—the area where its people lived most of the year. If necessary, American Indians would fight to protect their right to this land.

American Indians modified the land to suit their needs. Woodlands people set fires to clear heavy forest growth so deer could browse and berries could grow. Southwest farmers built ditches to carry water to dry fields.

These practices seldom harmed the environment. As one American Indian historian explains, "We dug our clams here, caught our salmon over there, got . . . seagull eggs on another island . . . By the time we came back here, this place had replenished itself."

American Indians tried not to waste anything taken from nature. A California woman recalled, "When we . . . kill meat, we eat it all up. When we dig roots we make little holes . . . We shake down acorns and pine nuts. We don't chop down the trees."

1.5 American Indians of the Northwest Coast

The Northwest Coast cultural region extends from southern Oregon into Canada. Winters along the ocean are cold but not icy, and summers are cool. To the east, thick forests of fir, spruce, and cedar cover rugged mountains. The mountains trap Pacific storms, so there is heavy rainfall much of the year.

Abundant Food Northwest people found food plentiful, particularly that taken from the sea. They built their villages along the narrow beaches and bays of the coastline and on nearby islands. They gathered clams, other shellfish, and seaweed from shallow waters. They ventured

onto the sea in canoes to hunt seals, sea lions, and whales, as well as halibut and other fish. The forests provided deer, moose, bear, elk, beaver, and mountain goat.

For each kind of creature, hunters developed special weapons. To catch seals, for example, they made long wooden harpoons, or spears. The harpoon had a barbed tip made of bone that held firmly in the seal's hide once it was struck. At the other end, hunters fastened a long rope so that they would not lose either the weapon or their prey.

In early summer, masses of salmon swam from the ocean up the rivers to lay their eggs. Men built wooden fences across the rivers to block the fish, making them easier to net. Women dried salmon meat so that it could be eaten all year long.

Builders and Carvers The forests of the Northwest provided materials for houses and many useful objects. Using wedges and stone-headed sledgehammers, men cut long, thin boards from logs or living trees. They joined these planks to build large, sturdy houses. To keep out the rain, they made roof shingles out of large sheets of cedar bark.

Women cut strips from the soft inner bark and used them to make baskets, mats, rope, and blankets. They even wove the strips of bark into waterproof capes.

With abundant food nearby, the Northwest people had time to practice crafts. Women made decorative shell buttons and sewed them onto their clothing with ivory needles. Men used tools such as wooden wedges, bone drills, stone chisels, and stone knives to carve detailed animal masks and wooden bowls.

The Oregon coast is part of the Northwest Coast cultural region. American Indians of the Northwest relied on the thick forests, abundant seafood, and plentiful game to meet their needs.

1.6 American Indians of California

The California cultural region stretches from southern Oregon through Baja California. Ocean storms bring winter rains to this region. Summers are hot and dry, particularly inland.

The California region includes not only the coast, but also the coastal foothills, an inland valley, deserts, and the western side of the Sierra Nevada mountain range. Over 100 small groups made their homes in these diverse environments, more than in any other cultural region.

Many Sources of Food Groups living along the coast of northern California depended on salmon for much of their food. Farther south, coastal people relied more on shellfish. Away from the coast, groups hunted deer with bows and arrows. They set snares to trap rabbits and used nets to capture ducks. California people also gathered roots, berries, and pine nuts.

Most people in the region relied on acorns from oak trees as a basic food. In the fall, women harvested the acorns, shelled them, and pounded the nuts into meal. Water was rinsed through the meal to remove its bitterness. Women cooked the meal by mixing it with water in tightly woven baskets and then dropping hot cooking stones into the mixture.

Clothing, Houses, and Baskets As they worked, the women wore simple aprons or skirts made from grasses or other plants, or sometimes from leather strips. In colder months, men and women wrapped themselves in animal hides.

Because the climate was mild, California people built simple homes. In forested areas, men used tools made from the antlers of deer and elk to strip large slabs of bark from redwood trees. They draped these into a cone shape to form a house. In marshy areas, people wove thick mats of reeds to drape over a cone-shaped framework of poles.

California people wove plant materials into many useful items. They made cooking baskets, storage baskets, sifters, and fish traps. Women used fine weaving and elegant patterns to make beautiful baskets, decorating their work with clamshells and bird feathers.

The California cultural region contains many different environments. Along the coast, huge redwood trees cover coastal mountains. In the inland areas, oaks and berries grow on rolling hills.

1.7 American Indians of the Great Basin

To the east of California lies the Great Basin, a low area between the Sierra Nevada and the Rocky Mountains. The mountains on either side of this region block the rain, making this land mostly desert.

The types of plants that grow in this area are those that need little water, such as low grasses, sagebrush, and craggy piñon (PIN-yon) trees. Only small animals, such as rabbits and lizards, live in this harsh region.

With limited food and water, only a few families could live in a place at one time. For this reason, people of the Great Basin traveled in small groups and spent much of their time looking for food.

Extreme Heat and Cold Wherever people camped, they made temporary shelters of willow poles shaped into a cone and covered with brush or reeds. Almost all year, they carried water in baskets coated with sap from pine trees.

When winter came, temperatures dropped below freezing. To keep warm, people made robes out of rabbit hides. First they twisted long strips of hide so that only the fur showed. Then they wove these strips on a willow loom. Each adult robe required about 100 rabbit skins.

Searching for Food In this arid (dry) environment, people followed food sources from season to season. In spring, they camped by valley lakes and streams swollen with melted snow. Men attracted migrating ducks with floating decoys made from reeds. When birds landed, the men chased them into nets. Meanwhile, women gathered duck eggs and the tender shoots of cattail plants.

When the streams dried up in summer, Great Basin people enjoyed snakes and grasshoppers as treats. But mostly they ate plants, almost 100 kinds. Women used sharp sticks to dig up roots. They wove flat baskets, called seed beaters, which they used to knock seeds loose from plants. From the mountain slopes, they gathered ripe berries.

In autumn, bands harvested pine nuts and hunted fat jackrabbits. As winter arrived, the Great Basin people bundled into their rabbit robes in the warmer hills. In huts and caves, they lived off food they had dried earlier, waiting for the ducks to return in spring.

Life was difficult for American Indians who lived in the Great Basin. Because of extreme temperatures and sparse rainfall, few plants and animals are able to survive there.

1.8 American Indians of the Plateau

North of the Great Basin lies the Plateau cultural region. This region is bounded by the Cascade Range to the west, the Rockies to the east, and the Fraser River, in present-day Canada, to the north.

The mountains in this area have dense forests. The flatter, central part is drier and covered with grass and sagebrush. Winters are long and cold, while summers remain gentle.

The Plateau people hunted and gathered with the seasons. The cool, wet climate made it fairly easy to find enough to eat. So, too, did the Plateau's two mighty river systems, the Columbia and the Fraser.

Sturdy Houses and Clothing Plateau people built their villages along major rivers. The rivers provided drinking water, fish, and drift-wood to use for shelter and firewood.

Food was so plentiful that some groups were able to live in their villages year-round. To stay cool in summer and warm in winter, they built their homes partly underground. They dug a pit, lined it with a frame of logs, and covered everything with saplings, reeds, and mud.

Plateau people used their weaving skills to create many kinds of baskets, as well as elaborate hats. As the cold months approached, they spent more time making clothes. In the fall, men hunted antelope and deer. Then women scraped and softened the hides for dresses, leggings, and shirts. They decorated their work with designs of seeds and shells.

Camas and Salmon Although hunting usually provided plenty of meat in the fall, most of the time Plateau people relied on fish and plants for food. In spring, they gathered sprouts of wild onions and carrots from the low grass-lands. Their particular favorite was camas, a starchy root related to lilies. Women uprooted it with willow digging sticks for eating raw, for roasting, and for grinding into flour.

The food most important to Plateau people was salmon. When the salmon migrated upstream, men stood on wooden platforms built over the water. From there, they could spear or net fish easily.

The Plateau cultural region features flatlands, rolling hills, and steep gorges. Large rivers provide water.

1.9 American Indians of the Southwest

The Southwest cultural region includes present-day Arizona, New Mexico, southern Utah and Colorado, and portions of Texas, Oklahoma, and California. This region has many environments—canyons, mountains, deserts, and flat-topped mesas. It even has two major rivers, the Colorado and the Rio Grande. But rain seldom falls anywhere.

The heat and lack of water made living in the Southwest a challenge. Yet some American Indians learned to love this arid land. "The whole Southwest was a House Made of Dawn," goes an old Indian song. "There were many colors on the hills and on the plain, and there was a dark wilderness on the mountains beyond."

Survival in the Southwest was a challenge. The area contains mountains, flat-topped mesas, deserts, and canyons, such as the one pictured above. Sparse rainfall prevents the growth of many trees and plants.

Mesa People Different groups found different ways of surviving in the Southwest. Some lived as nomadic (wandering) desert hunters. Along the Colorado River, small groups hunted, gathered, and farmed. Others planted fields of corn, beans, and squash on the tops of high, flat areas called *mesas*.

The mesa people lacked trees for building homes. Instead, they made homes from the earth itself. Using bricks of *adobe* (sun-baked clay), they built thick-walled houses that protected them from summer heat and winter cold. Their villages looked like apartment houses that reached up to four stories high and had hundreds of rooms. A single village, called a *pueblo* (PWEH-blo), might house 1,000 people.

To protect their bodies from the sun, mesa people wore clothes made of cotton that they grew, spun, and wove into cloth. Using plants and minerals, they dyed fabrics with bright colors.

Corn Culture Despite living in a desert, the early mesa people learned to grow corn, beans, and squash. Corn was by far their most important crop.

To make the most of infrequent rain, farmers planted near naturally flooded areas like the mouths of large streambeds or the bases of mesas, where rain runoff flowed. Men dug irrigation ditches from the streams to the fields and built small dams to hold summer rain.

Girls spent many hours a day grinding corn kernels into cornmeal. The women cooked the cornmeal into bread in clay ovens. In clay pots, they cooked stews of corn, rabbit meat, and chili peppers.

1.10 American Indians of the Great Plains

The Great Plains cultural region is a vast area of treeless grasslands. The Great Plains stretch for 2,000 miles from the Rockies to the Mississippi Valley, and from Canada to the Gulf of Mexico. The eastern part of this region has more water and softer soil than the western part. In the drier west, short, dense grasses provided perfect grazing for millions of buffalo.

The Great Plains region is mostly treeless grassland with cold winters and hot summers. Buffalo and other animals grazed freely over a vast territory.

Buffalo Hunters On the eastern Great Plains, various groups took up farming, going on buffalo-hunting trips only a few months each year. On the western Great Plains, American Indians followed buffalo herds much of the year.

In the spring and early summer, small groups lay in ambush where buffalo came to drink. The hunters gripped hardwood bows reinforced with strips of buffalo tendon. Taking aim, each man let loose a wooden arrow tipped with a sharp stone and arrayed with feathers to help it fly straight.

In the fall, huge buffalo herds gathered, and Plains people traveled in larger bands. The men sometimes made a trap for the buffalo by heaping stones into two short walls to form a V-shaped passage. The walls forced the buffalo closer together as they approached a cliff. Behind the herd, people set a grass fire or made loud noises to panic the buffalo. The animals stampeded between the walls and over the cliff edge. Below, waiting hunters finished them off with spears or bows and arrows.

Using the Buffalo Buffalo provided the main food for Plains people. Women and children cut up the buffalo with bone knives. Extra meat was dried and kept for winter.

Plains people used every part of the buffalo. Buffalo hides were turned into shields, waterproof containers, warm robes, and bedding. For clothing and bags, women softened the hides with bone scrapers and rubbed in buffalo brains and fat. Buffalo hair and sinew (tough cords made from the animals' tendons) were twined into bowstrings and rope. Horns and hooves became spoons and bowls or were boiled down to make glue. Dried buffalo dung provided fuel for fires.

Buffalo provided materials for housing as well. Using tendons as thread, women sewed 8 to 20 buffalo skins together. The skins were then fastened around a tall cone of poles to make a *tipi,* a Plains word for "dwelling."

Plains people became even more successful hunters when Spanish explorers introduced horses to the region. With horses, they could bring down more buffalo and move faster and more comfortably to new hunting grounds.

1.11 American Indians of the Eastern Woodlands

The Eastern Woodlands cultural region reaches from the Mississippi River eastward to the Atlantic Ocean and from Canada to North Carolina. Winter snows and summer rains produced endless forests, lakes, and streams.

Two language groups emerged in this cultural region. In most of the territory, people spoke Algonquian (al-GON-kwee-in) languages. In New York and around the southern Great Lakes lived the Iroquois-speaking groups described in this section.

Plentiful Woods The forests provided most of what Iroquois (EER-uh-kwoi) people needed to live. For food, hunters prowled through the forests to track deer. Men also hunted bears, trapped beavers, caught birds in nets, and speared fish. Women gathered fresh greens, nuts, and berries. They made syrup by boiling down sap from maple trees.

Instead of walking through the thick forests, Iroquois often paddled log and bark canoes along lakes and rivers. Because waterways also provided fish and drinking water, Iroquois built their villages nearby.

Each village had dozens of sturdy log-frame houses covered with elm bark. Such longhouses were usually about 20 feet wide and over 100 feet long. Several related families lived in sections of the longhouse.

Women Farmers To clear a space for farming, Iroquois men burned away trees and underbrush. Women did the rest. After hoeing the soil, they planted corn, sometimes several varieties. Around the cornstalks, they let beans twine. Squash grew near the ground, keeping down weeds and holding moisture in the soil.

When the planting was done, women tanned deerskin to make skirts, capes, and moccasins (soft shoes). They scraped corn kernels with bone tools and ground the corn between stones. In the fall, they stored the harvest, often in large bark bins in the longhouses. Iroquois crops included sunflowers, tobacco, and many vegetables that are still planted in American gardens today.

Dense forests, such as this forest in Vermont, are home to deer, beavers, and other wildlife, which provided food, clothing, and shelter for the American Indians of the Eastern Woodlands.

The Southeast cultural region includes river valleys, mountains, coastal plains, and swamps, such as this swamp in Florida. The mild climate allowed American Indians of the Southeast to grow corn, beans, squash, and other crops.

1.12   American Indians of the Southeast

The Southeast cultural region stretches from the southern part of the Ohio Valley to the Gulf of Mexico and from Texas to the Atlantic Ocean. This region's fertile coastal plains, river valleys, mountains, and swamps all have long, warm, humid summers and mild winters. In this green countryside, the people of the Southeast found growing crops fairly easy.

Towns Built Around Mounds Some Southeastern peoples built towns **dominated** by large earthen mounds. The first mounds were burial sites. Centuries later, people made mounds several stories high as platforms for temples.

Building these mounds took months, even years, because people had to move the dirt one basketful at a time. Workers building mounds had no time to help grow or find food. But Southeastern groups had developed a type of corn that grew so fast, they could harvest two crops a year. Farmers raised enough food to feed the people building the mounds.

A single Southeastern town might have had 2 to 12 mounds arrayed around a central town plaza. People clustered their houses around these mounds. They built their homes from strips of young trees woven into a rectangular frame and plastered with clay. Roofs were pointed and made of leaves.

A Fertile Region Beyond their homes, fields lay in all directions. With the region's long growing season, Southeastern people relied on corn, beans, squash, pumpkins, and sunflowers for most of their food.

Women worked the fields with hoes made of stone, shell, or animal shoulder blades fastened to wooden handles. Men sometimes hunted, using blowguns for squirrels, rabbits, and turkeys and bows and arrows for large animals like deer. They even brought home alligators and turtles.

To complete their varied diet, women gathered edible plants like sweet potatoes, wild rice, and persimmons. As they wore simple, short deerskin skirts, they didn't have to spend much time making clothing. Instead, they had time to fashion rings, earrings, arm rings, and hairpins from stones, shells, feathers, pearls, bones, and clay.

Chapter Summary

In this chapter, you read about the first people to settle in North America and the adaptations they made to the environments they found there.

Migration Routes of the First Americans Scientists believe that ancestors of American Indians migrated to America from Asia across a land bridge during the last Ice Age. As their descendants traveled east and south, they adapted to the challenges of living in many different environments.

How American Indians Viewed the Environment Wherever they settled, American Indians had a special relationship with the world around them. They believed they were part of nature, and they treated the environment with respect.

Adaptations to the Local Environment Depending on where they lived, American Indians ate different food, built different kinds of houses, and clothed themselves in different ways. They also practiced many kinds of crafts, making such things as jewelry, fine baskets, and animal masks. American Indians built the first towns and villages in North America, and they were the continent's first farmers.

Languages and Lifestyles American Indians living in different cultural regions developed distinctive ways of life that were suited to their environment's climate and natural resources. Scientists study these ways of life by examining the artifacts America's first people left behind.

This drawing by John White, one of the first English colonists in North America, shows the village life of the Secotan people who lived in North Carolina.

Digging Up the Past

As a boy growing up in southern Illinois in the 1960s, Tim Pauketat loved to explore. There were ancient arrowheads to be found and he collected them. One day, as he rode in his father's delivery truck, he saw a great, flat-topped pyramid. To Tim it looked 100 feet tall, all built of earth. He was instantly hooked on the mysterious mounds of Cahokia.

This serpent mound in Ohio is more than a quarter of a mile long and about 3 feet high. Scholars believe it was built between 1,000 and 1,500 years ago.

Mysteries surround the mounds of Cahokia (kuh-HO-key-uh). As an adult, Tim Pauketat would help solve some of them.

The first mystery was who built the mounds. Tens of thousands of mounds have been discovered in the nation's interior. Some mounds were shaped as tremendous snakes or birds. Others were cone shaped. But the great mound of Cahokia was the most enormous of all. More massive than the pyramids of Egypt, it rose 10 stories high and contained 25 million cubic feet of earth.

Early settlers pushing west in the 1700s first discovered the mounds. Surely, they thought, a lost race of superior beings had built the magnificent mounds. The settlers believed that the American Indians who lived in the area could never have been capable of building such awesome earthworks.

Popular books and poems were written about the "lost race" that had built a great civilization and then vanished. The mystery gripped the public as they looked to Europe, Asia, and Africa for ancient mound builders. Some claimed that the mound builders were Vikings; others were sure they were Phoenicians. Hindus, Greeks, Romans, Persians, and the lost tribes of Israel were each "proven," incorrectly, to be the lost race of mound builders.

The first American to answer the question scientifically was the third president, Thomas Jefferson. Based on the skeletons and artifacts he found when he dug into a mound, Jefferson was certain that American Indians were the builders. And yet, 100 years later, the battle over who built the mysterious mounds still raged. Jefferson was wrong, people claimed.

Finally, in 1881, the Smithsonian Institution hired archaeologist Cyrus Thomas to find out who the mound builders really were. Like most people, Thomas thought the mounds were built by a long-lost race. Over seven years, Thomas and his team unearthed thousands of artifacts. In the end, he disproved his own theory. The mound builders, he declared, were indeed early American Indians.

But many mysteries remained. What culture had built the monumental works, and why had that culture vanished? These are the mysteries that Tim Pauketat got hooked on solving.

Cahokia Uncovered

Today, Tim Pauketat teaches archaeology and brings his students to Cahokia. There, they dig very carefully, looking for clues to the past. What they and other archaeologists have learned helps us imagine what Cahokia might have been like in the year 1150 C.E.

At dawn, the Great Chief might have stood atop what was the greatest earth mound in the Americas. As he raised his arms to welcome the sun, its first rays would have hit his tall-feathered headdress. Slowly, the sun would have lit his jewelry, made of carved shells and copper, and the cape of feathers that hung from his shoulders. The sun was sacred to the people of Cahokia, for it made the corn grow.

The mound the Great Chief called home rose 100 feet from the vast, flat plain that is now southern Illinois. We know it as Monks Mound. From its top, the Great Chief could look down upon a city of some 20,000 subjects. Just beyond the city, thousands more people lived in villages. Altogether, the chief ruled what was probably the largest urban area in the world at the time. He could have seen more than 120 other mounds nearby, and more in the distance (toward what is now St. Louis, Missouri).

A towering wall surrounded the city's center. To the west was a great circle of upright logs—a kind of giant solar calendar that priests used to mark the beginning of spring and fall (the equinoxes) and winter and summer (the solstices).

An artist re-created what Cahokia may have looked like in 1150 C.E. Monks Mound can be seen near the center top.

A huge plaza stretched out over 50 acres from the base of Monks Mound. Here, hundreds or maybe thousands of people gathered for feasts, ceremonies, or a wild game of chunkey. This game of skill, daring, and high-stakes gambling involved two spear-throwing players and a wheel-shaped stone that was rolled across the hardened, flat court. The object was to land a spear closer to the chunkey disk than an opponent did.

The Great Chief ruled all this and more. Cahokia was not only a cultural and spiritual center, it was a trade center for an area stretching a thousand miles in all directions. Cahokia's sphere of influence was enormous. The Great Chief was its most powerful ruler.

The Archaeologist's Toolkit

How did archaeologists figure all this out? The people of Cahokia had no system of writing, so they left no written records. How do we know about the Great Chief and his welcoming of the sun in 1150 C.E.?

People who have no written histories have oral histories—stories that are passed from one generation to the next. Scholars searched for such a story to explain Cahokia but, strangely, never found one. In 1539, however, Spanish explorer Hernando de Soto (ehr-NAN-do day SOH-toh) led an expedition through the Southeast looking for treasure. He didn't find gold or silver, but he did find mound builders much like the people of Cahokia. Written accounts of the expedition describe the mounds and the powerful sun-worshiping rulers who lived atop them.

How do we know the date in the story about the Great Chief? To determine the date of a site, archaeologists look for what they call "black gold"—charcoal. With a process called radiocarbon dating, a piece of charcoal will reveal the date when the wood it was created from burned.

To discover what life in Cahokia was like, archaeologists search for artifacts. When they carefully dug into one small mound at Cahokia, they discovered a wealth of artifacts, along with the remains of a chief. There were thousands of shell beads, fine carvings, copper, and all the things a chief might need in the next life. From these artifacts, we know what the Great Chief wore.

In the mound were fine chunkey disks, too. But if it were not for witnesses—early French explorers who saw the game played and described it in their journals—no one would know what the disks were used for.

Determining the population of Cahokia is harder. One estimate was made by counting the number of laborers it took to build the homes, walls, and especially the mounds of Cahokia. Monks Mound alone required some 14 million baskets of earth dug by hand, carried, deposited, and pounded firmly in place. This number led to an estimate of as many as 43,000 people who had lived in the local region.

Artifacts found at Cahokia include fine pottery, arrowheads, tools, and this figure carved from stone.

How did archaeologists ever figure out there was a solar calendar, given that the logs rotted away hundreds of years ago? They searched for soil stains. As wood rots, it turns the soil a darker color. The researchers searched the soil very carefully to find this clue.

Today, we know all this about Cahokia and a great deal more. However, many mysteries remain.

Cahokia Abandoned

When the first explorers reached Cahokia, the mighty city was completely gone. Only the silent mounds remained. Tim Pauketat says radiocarbon-dating evidence shows that Cahokia was abandoned in the 1300s. He wants to find out why.

There are many theories. Many of them focus on the important relationship of people and the environment. Some scholars say a drought or a change in climate caused crop failure. It took 25,000 to 30,000 pounds of corn a day to feed the Cahokians, so a lack of crops would cause a lot of people to leave the area.

This re-creation shows how the people of Cahokia set up their solar calendar. On the first day of each season, certain poles lined up with the sun. At the spring and fall equinoxes, the sun seemed to rise from Monks Mound.

Others suggest that with so many people packed together in a place without a sewage system, the water became contaminated, causing disease. Still others think that local resources such as wood and game must have grown scarce.

Pauketat agrees these factors would have caused some people to move away. But that is not what happened. By 1350, every last person had fled.

Pauketat thinks that a great power struggle caused a complete failure of government. He and his students are finding evidence of protective walls surrounding the homes of the powerful. This shows the occupants were afraid and felt they needed protection. Pauketat also found several such homes that were burned. Strangely, no one returned to these homes after the fire to gather up the fine tools and baskets of stored food. That's a sign that the occupants had to flee the area.

Tim Pauketat has not found all the answers yet, but he hopes that young people will continue to search for them. He is optimistic that the mysteries that surround Cahokia will one day be solved.

Artists work with archaeologists and other scholars to re-create scenes like this of the Great Chief and his priests greeting the dawn atop Monks Mound.

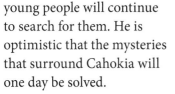

Chapter 2

European Exploration and Settlement

How did Europeans explore and establish settlements in the Americas?

2.1 Introduction

Europeans had no knowledge of the people of the Americas, half a world away, or the land where they lived. When Europeans looked west, they saw only a vast ocean.

Europeans were far more interested in the lands that lay to the east. In the late 1200s, a young man named Marco Polo traveled through Asia with his father, a merchant and trader from Venice, Italy. Marco Polo spent 17 years in China. When he returned to Venice, people flocked to hear his stories of "the Indies," as India and East Asia were then known. He was called "the man with a million stories."

Eventually, a writer helped Marco Polo put his adventures into a book. The book described the wonders Polo had seen in China. It told of rich silks and rare spices, gold and jewels, and luxurious palaces.

When Marco Polo's book was published, very few people in Europe could read. Those who did read it were fascinated by its description of riches to the east. Merchants and traders were eager to find the fastest way to get there. The land route Polo had traveled was long and dangerous. His tales inspired explorers to find an alternative route by sea.

Some explorers would seek a route to China by going around the southern tip of Africa. But a few brave souls looked to the west for another route. Such a trip took courage, because no one knew how far west sailors would have to sail to reach Asia or what monsters and terrors might await them far from Europe's shore.

In this chapter, you will learn how Christopher Columbus faced these dangers and sailed west to find a route to China. As you will see, his unexpected discovery of the American continents led to competition among European nations to explore and profit from these lands. You will also learn how Europeans established settlements in the American continents and, in the process, changed both Europe and the Americas.

In this statue in Barcelona, Spain, Christopher Columbus points toward the Americas.

◄ European explorers confronted many dangers and fears as they voyaged to new lands.

On October 12, 1492, Columbus stepped on land and claimed for Spain an island he named San Salvador. The people he encountered were peaceful, their only weapons being small wooden spears.

2.2 Spain Starts an Empire

Marco Polo's book continued to be read over the next two centuries. This was a time of great change in Europe. The rediscovered writings of ancient Greeks and Romans inspired a new interest in learning and art. This period of lively new thinking has become known as the Renaissance, a word that means "rebirth."

During this time, the invention of the printing press made books, including Marco Polo's, more available. As Europeans learned about the world beyond Europe, they became eager to explore these far-off lands.

Columbus's Discoveries One of the people who was inspired by Marco Polo's writings was an Italian seaman named Christopher Columbus. After studying maps of the world, which at that time did not include the Americas, Columbus became convinced that the shortest route to the Indies lay to the west, across the Atlantic Ocean.

Columbus looked for someone who could pay for the ships and men he needed to test his idea. Eventually, he was able to convince King Ferdinand and Queen Isabella of Spain to sponsor a voyage.

In August 1492, Columbus sailed west with three small ships. After more than a month at sea, his sailors raised the cry of "Land!" The land turned out to be a small island in what we now call the Caribbean Sea.

Columbus was thrilled. In a later letter, he wrote, "I write this to tell you how in thirty-three days I sailed to the Indies with the fleet that the illustrious King and Queen . . . gave me, where I discovered a great many islands, inhabited by numberless people." Mistakenly believing that he had reached the Indies, Columbus called these people Indians.

In reality, the islanders were native people who spoke a language called Taino (TIE-no). The Taino lived in a peaceful fishing community. Never had they seen people like the ones who had suddenly appeared on their shores. Yet they were friendly and welcoming. Columbus wrote, "They are so unsuspicious and so generous with what they possess, that no one who had not seen it would believe it."

Columbus promptly claimed the island for Spain and named it San Salvador, which means "Holy Savior." From there, he sailed on to other islands. Convinced that China lay nearby, Columbus sailed back to Spain for more ships and men.

Columbus made four trips to the Caribbean, finding more islands, as well as the continent of South America. Each time he discovered a new place, he claimed it for Spain. Columbus died still believing he had found Asia. Later explorers quickly realized that he had actually stumbled on a world previously unknown to Europe—the continents of North and South America.

The Columbian Exchange The voyages of Columbus triggered a great transfer of people, plants, animals, and diseases back and forth across the Atlantic Ocean. This transfer, which still continues today, is called the **Columbian Exchange**. The Columbian Exchange brought valuable new crops such as corn, potatoes, and squash to Europe. These foods greatly improved the diet of the average European. Many Europeans also found new opportunities by crossing the Atlantic to settle in the Americas. They introduced crops such as wheat and rice to these lands, as well as **domesticated** animals like horses, cows, pigs, and sheep.

For American Indians, however, the exchange began badly. The Europeans who came to America brought with them germs that caused smallpox and other diseases deadly to Indians. Historians estimate that in some areas, European diseases wiped out 90 percent of the native population.

Slavery Comes to America

This high death rate contributed to the introduction of African slaves to the Americas. Many laborers were needed because some of the Spanish settlers in the Caribbean had started gold mines. Others raised sugar, a crop of great value in Europe. At first, the settlers forced Indians to work for them. But as native people began dying in great numbers from European diseases, the settlers looked for a new workforce. Before long, Africans were replacing Indians.

Slavery had existed around the world since ancient times. Often, people who were on the losing side in wars were enslaved, or treated as the property of their conquerors.

Columbian Exchange the exchange of plants, animals, diseases, and people across the Atlantic Ocean between Europe and the Americas

slavery the treatment of people as property. People who are denied freedom in this way are said to be enslaved.

At first, Spanish settlers relied on the forced labor of American Indians to work their sugar plantations. When disease wiped out this labor force, the Spanish turned to African slaves to perform the backbreaking task of harvesting and refining sugarcane.

The Granger Collection, New York

conquistadors Spanish soldier-explorers, especially those who conquered the native peoples of Mexico and Peru

By the late 1400s, European explorers in West Africa were trading guns and other goods for slaves captured by African traders.

In the 1500s, European slave traders began shipping slaves to the Caribbean for sale. Over the next three centuries, millions of Africans would be carried across the Atlantic in crowded, disease-infested ships. The terrible voyage lasted anywhere from weeks to months. Many died before it was over.

When the Africans arrived in the Americas, they were sold to their new masters at auctions. Many perished from disease and overwork. Those who survived faced a lifetime of forced labor as slaves.

Cortés Conquers Mexico After Columbus's voyages, Spain began sending soldiers called **conquistadors** (kahn-KEES-tah-dors), across the Atlantic. Their mission was to conquer a vast empire for Spain. The conquistadors hoped to get rich along the way.

In 1519, Hernán Cortés (ehr-NAHN kohr-TEHZ) arrived in Mexico with horses and 500 soldiers. There he heard about the powerful Aztecs who ruled much of Mexico. When Cortés and his men reached the Aztec capital of Tenochtitlán (tay-noch-teet-LAN), they could not believe their eyes. A beautiful city seemed to rise out of a sparkling lake. One Spaniard wrote, "Some of our soldiers even asked whether the things that we saw were not a dream."

The Aztecs were unsure what to make of the strangers. They had never seen men dressed in metal armor and riding horses. Some mistook Cortés for the great Aztec god Quetzalcoatl (kwet-zul-kuh-WAH-tul) and welcomed him as a hero. They would soon change their minds.

With the help of Indians who hated their Aztec rulers, and with the spread of smallpox—which killed large numbers of Aztec warriors—

Cortés, shown here with his translator, is trying to convince a group of Native Americans to help him conquer the Aztecs. With the help of Aztec enemies and smallpox, Cortés captured the Aztec capital of Tenochtitlán.

The Granger Collection, New York

Cortés conquered Tenochtitlán. The Spaniards pulled the city down and used its stones to build Mexico City, the capital of a new Spanish empire called New Spain.

Pizarro Conquers Peru Smallpox also helped another Spanish conquistador, Francisco Pizarro (fran-SIS-co pi-ZAR-oh), conquer an empire in South America. In 1532, Pizarro led an attack on the powerful Inca Empire in present-day Peru. Luckily for Pizarro, smallpox reached Peru many months before him, killing thousands of Incas and leaving their empire badly divided.

Pizarro captured the Inca ruler, Atahualpa (ah-tuh-WAHL-puh), but promised to release him in exchange for gold. To save their ruler, the Incas filled three rooms with gold and silver treasures. Pizarro killed Atahualpa anyway and took over the leaderless Inca empire. From there, Spanish conquistadors conquered most of South America.

Explorers from several European countries took various routes to the Americas. Voyages were long and difficult and often involved travel on both land and sea.

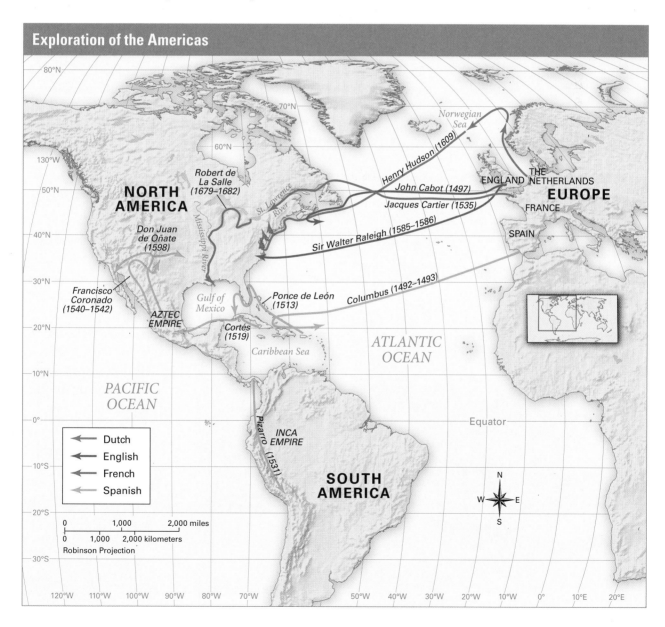

Exploration of the Americas

2.3 The Spanish Borderlands

In both Mexico and Peru, conquistadors found gold and silver riches beyond their wildest dreams. Hoping for still more, they pushed north into lands that are now part of the United States. Because these lands were located on the far edges of Spain's North American empire, they were known as the Spanish borderlands.

Florida One of the first Spanish expeditions into North America was led by a man named Juan Ponce de León (wahn PAHN-suh day lee-OHN). He had sailed with Columbus to the Caribbean and made his fortune by discovering gold on the island of Puerto Rico. Despite his wealth, Ponce de León couldn't stop thinking about Indian rumors of a "fountain of youth" that made old people young again. Restless for more adventure, he set off to find the truth about these tales of everlasting youth.

Ponce de León landed on a sunny peninsula of North America in April 1513. Because he had sighted this lush new land on Easter Sunday, he called it La Florida, meaning "flowery." (The name is short for "flowery Easter.") Eight years later, he returned to Florida with 200 men to establish a Spanish settlement, or **colony**. American Indians in the area used poisoned arrows to drive off the invaders. Instead of finding a fountain of youth, Ponce de León died from a poisoned arrow in his stomach.

The "Seven Cities of Cíbola" Another legend sparked new Spanish expeditions into North America. An old European tale told of the "Seven Cities of Cíbola" (SEE-buh-luh). These cities were said to be so fabulously rich that the streets and houses were decorated with gold and jewels. When the Spanish heard Indians tell similar tales, they became convinced that the Seven Cities of Cíbola were somewhere in North America.

Spanish explorers first looked for the seven cities in Florida and present-day Texas. They found plenty of adventure, but no golden cities. Then a Spanish priest named Marcos de Niza claimed to have seen a shimmering golden city in what is now New Mexico. He raced back to Mexico City with the news.

> **colony** a new settlement or territory established and governed by a country in another land

Although Coronado never found the Seven Cities of Cíbola, his explorations opened a new area for Spanish settlement.

The Coronado Expedition In 1540, a famed conquistador named Francisco Vásquez de Coronado (VAHS-kehz day kohr-uh-NAH-doh) set out from Mexico City with a large expedition and de Niza as his guide. Their goal was to find the legendary golden cities.

After traveling north more than 7,000 miles, the expedition found an American Indian *pueblo*. A pueblo is a village of apartment-like buildings made of stone and adobe rising four and five stories high. To de Niza, this might have looked like a golden city. But to Coronado, it was a "little, crowded village . . . crumpled all up together." The enraged expedition leader sent the priest back to Mexico City.

The Coronado expedition continued north onto the Great Plains before giving up the search for golden cities. Disappointed, Coronado reported to Spain, "Everything is the reverse of what he said, except the name of the cities and the large stone houses . . . The Seven Cities are seven little villages."

Settling the Borderlands As conquistadors explored new territories, they claimed the areas for Spain. By 1600, the Spanish borderlands extended west from Florida across present-day Texas, New Mexico, Arizona, and California.

At first, Spain did little to encourage settlement in these far-flung areas. But when rival European nations also began to show an interest in the land, small bands of soldiers were sent to these regions to protect the claims. The soldiers lived in walled forts called *presidios* (preh-SEE-dee-ohs).

In 1565, for example, a Spanish naval officer named Pedro Menéndez de Avilés (muh-NEN-dez day ah-vuh-LACE) was sent to Florida to protect the area from French explorers. Menéndez successfully drove the French out of their Florida base and built a fort on the peninsula's Atlantic coast. Menéndez named the fort St. Augustine. Over the years, Spanish soldiers based at St. Augustine successfully defended the fort—and Spanish claims to Florida— from both French and English rivals. Today, St. Augustine is the oldest permanent settlement founded by Europeans in the United States.

St. Augustine was originally a *presidio,* or fort, built by the Spanish to protect their claim to Florida. It is the oldest permanent European settlement in the United States.

Missions were established to convert American Indians to Christianity and increase Spanish control over the land. Missions included a church and farmland on which the mission inhabitants produced almost all of what they needed to survive.

Catholic **missionaries** accompanied the soldiers to the borderlands. Missionaries are religious people, like priests, who try to persuade people to **convert** to their religion. The missionaries built settlements, called missions, where they taught local Indians new skills and preached the Christian faith. Each mission grew its own food and produced most of what the inhabitants of the missions needed to survive far from towns and trading centers.

Hardy bands of settlers also moved into the borderlands, where they established towns and farms. Juan de Oñate (own-YAH-tay), who had made a fortune mining silver in Mexico, led the settlement of New Mexico. In 1598, Oñate brought 400 settlers and 7,000 animals from Mexico to New Mexico. The long overland journey took a year and a half to complete.

At first, the Pueblo Indians of New Mexico welcomed the newcomers. Unfortunately, the Spanish repaid the Indians' kindness with cruelty. Indians were made to work for the settlers as slaves. Catholic priests ordered the whipping of Pueblo religious leaders who continued to practice their traditional rituals. Such treatment led the Pueblo people to rise up in **revolt** and drive the Spanish out. Twelve years would pass before Spanish settlers returned to New Mexico.

During the 1600s and 1700s, settlement of the Spanish borderlands proceeded slowly. But in time, the language, religion, and culture of Spain spread across much of the American Southwest.

Impact on American Indians The arrival of Spanish settlers had a great **impact** on the native peoples of the borderlands. The Pueblo people, for example, learned from the Spanish how to use new tools, grow new foods, and raise sheep for wool. In turn, the Indians introduced the Spanish to new **techniques** for growing crops in the desert soil.

From Florida to California, some American Indians converted to the Catholic faith. The converts often lived and worked in and around the missions, growing crops and helping to maintain the churches and other buildings. However, even converts often continued to practice their traditional religious rituals as well.

Unfortunately, wherever the Spanish settled, they brought with them diseases to which native peoples had no resistance. Smallpox, measles, and influenza often wiped out entire villages. Before Coronado's expedition, there had been more than 100 thriving Indian pueblos in New Mexico. By 1700, only 19 remained.

missionaries people who travel to a territory or community in order to make converts to their religion

2.4 New France

As Spanish colonies sent ships loaded with gold and silver home to Spain, all of Europe watched with envy. Every year, Spain seemed to become wealthier and more powerful. Other nations wanted their share of riches from the Americas. But none was strong enough to challenge Spain's American empire. Instead, they would have to seek their fortunes in areas not yet claimed by Spain.

Claiming New France In 1534, France sent Jacques Cartier (zhahk cahr-TYAY) to explore the Atlantic coastline of North America. His goal was to find a Northwest Passage, an all-water route through the North American continent to the Pacific Ocean. Such a passage would provide a shortcut for ships sailing west to Asia.

Cartier failed to find such a passage. But he did claim for France the land we know today as Canada. He later named this land New France. Cartier also discovered something almost as valuable as Spanish gold—beaver fur. Beaver hats were a fashionable item in Europe, and French hatmakers were willing to pay high prices for beaver pelts.

Settling New France The first settlement in New France was founded by Samuel de Champlain (duh sham-PLANE). In 1608, Champlain sailed up the St. Lawrence River and built a trading post he called Quebec (kwuh-BEK). For the next 150 years, Quebec would be a base for French explorers, soldiers, missionaries, traders, and fur trappers.

From Quebec, fur trappers pushed west in search of beaver. They called themselves **coureurs de bois** (kuh-RUR duh BWAH), which means "wood rangers" in French. Catholic missionaries followed the trappers, seeking converts among the native peoples.

Like the Spanish borderlands, New France failed to attract large numbers of settlers. The harsh climate of New France discouraged French farmers from crossing the Atlantic. So did the colony's policy of granting the best land along the St. Lawrence River to French nobles who then planned to rent it out to farmers. The few settlers who did come soon got tired of renting and left their farms to search for furs.

coureurs de bois French fur trappers who learned many skills from the American Indians with whom they worked and lived

Coureurs de bois, or fur trappers, roamed New France in search of beaver pelts. They learned their trapping skills from the American Indians.

The French made friends with the American Indians in New France and often assisted them in battles with their enemies. Here, Samuel de Champlain, in the center, helps the Huron defeat the Iroquois.

American Indian Business Partners Because the French were more interested in furs than farming, they did not try to conquer the Indians and put them to work as the Spanish had done. Instead, the French made American Indians their business partners.

After founding Quebec, Champlain made friends with the nearby Indians, especially the Huron. Fur trappers lived in Huron villages, learned the Huron language, and married Huron women. From the Huron they learned how to survive for months in the wilderness. Unfortunately, the friendship exposed the Huron to European diseases, which swept through their villages and killed many of them.

Champlain even joined the Huron in an attack on their enemy, the Iroquois. He later wrote,

I marched some 20 paces in advance of the rest, until I was within about 30 paces of the enemy . . . When I saw them making a move to fire at us, I rested my musket against my cheek, and aimed directly at one of the three chiefs. With that same shot, two fell to the ground; and one of their men was so wounded that he died some time after . . . When our side saw this shot . . . they began to raise such loud cries that one could not have heard it thunder.

The astonished Iroquois, who had never seen or heard gunfire before, fled in terror. From that day on, the Iroquois would be the bitter enemies of the French.

Claiming Louisiana The search for furs led the French far inland from Quebec. In 1673, two explorers, Father Marquette (mahr-KET) and Louis Joliet (zhal-YAY), explored the great Mississippi River. They hoped this waterway would be the long-sought Northwest Passage. But they discovered that, instead of flowing west to the Pacific Ocean, the river flowed south toward the Gulf of Mexico. Disappointed, the explorers returned to New France.

Nine years later, Robert Cavelier de La Salle explored the entire length of the Mississippi River. On April 9, 1682, he planted a French flag at the mouth of the river and claimed everything west of the Mississippi River for France. La Salle named this vast area Louisiana for the French monarch, King Louis XIV.

2.5 Jamestown: The First English Colony

Columbus's voyages inspired John Cabot, an Italian living in England, to seek his own western route to Asia. In 1497, Cabot, who had moved to England from Venice, sailed west across the Atlantic. He landed in Newfoundland, an island off the coast of Canada. A fellow Venetian living in London wrote of Cabot's brief landing,

> *He coasted for three hundred leagues and landed; saw no human beings, but he has brought here to the king certain snares which had been set to catch game, and a needle for making nets; he also found some felled trees, by which he judged there were inhabitants, and returned to his ship in alarm . . . The discoverer . . . planted on this newly-found land a large cross, with one flag of England and another of St. Mark [the patron saint of Venice] on account of his being a Venetian.*

John Cabot, an Italian exploring for England, sailed to Newfoundland and Nova Scotia, off the coast of present-day Canada. He believed he had reached Asia and claimed the land for England.

Like Columbus, Cabot mistakenly believed he had landed in Asia. Later, however, England would claim all of North America because of the flag planted by Cabot in 1497.

The Lost Colony of Roanoke

Nearly a century later, an English noble named Sir Walter Raleigh tried to start a colony on Roanoke Island off the coast of present-day North Carolina. Indians on the island welcomed the settlers and gave them traps for catching fish. The newcomers, however, were more interested in looking for gold than fishing. When their supplies ran low, they returned to England.

In 1587, Raleigh sent a second group of colonists to Roanoke. Unfortunately, they arrived too late in the season to plant crops. Their leader, John White, sailed back to England for more supplies. While White was in England, however, fighting broke out between England and Spain. As a result, his return to Roanoke was delayed for three years.

When White finally reached the island, the colonists had disappeared. Carved on a doorpost was the word CROATOAN. To this day, both the reason this word was carved and what happened to the lost colony of Roanoke remain a mystery.

The Granger Collection, New York

Settling Jamestown Twenty years went by before a permanent English colony was established in America. In 1607, a group of merchants formed the London Company to start a moneymaking colony in Virginia. The company crammed 105 settlers and 39 sailors into three tiny ships and sent them across the Atlantic. The settlers were to ship back valuable goods such as furs and timber.

When they reached Virginia, the colonists settled on a swampy peninsula they believed could be easily defended against American Indians or Spanish ships. They called their new home Jamestown after King James I. What the settlers didn't know was that the spot they chose to settle would soon be swarming with disease-carrying mosquitoes. It was also surrounded by a large and powerful American Indian group.

To make matters worse, the Jamestown settlers were a mix of gentlemen and craftsmen. None of them knew much about farming. Nor were they willing to work very hard at it. They thought they were in Virginia to look for gold, not to provide for themselves.

As the food the settlers had brought with them disappeared, they began to trade with the Indians, bartering glass beads and iron hatchets for corn and meat. But barter wasn't easy. Many Indians decided they would sooner kill the English—or just let them starve—than trade. Hunger and disease soon took their toll. Every few days, another body was carried off to the graveyard.

John Smith was one of the members of the Jamestown expedition. A natural leader, Smith took control of Jamestown in 1608. "If any would not work," announced Smith, "neither should he eat." They were hungry, so they worked.

The first colonists at Jamestown settled in an area they believed would be easy to defend against American Indians and the Spanish. However, the land was marshy and infested with malaria-carrying mosquitoes.

The Granger Collection, New York

Smith wrote an account of how he met an Indian girl whose help saved the colony from starvation. While scouting for food, Smith was captured by the Indians and brought to a smoky longhouse. Seated at one end, he saw Powhatan, the Indians' powerful chief. The Indians greeted Smith with a loud shout and a great feast. But when the meal ended, the mood changed. Smith was about to be clubbed to death when a young girl leapt out of the shadows. "She got [my] head in her armes and laid her owne upon [mine] to save [me] from death," Smith later wrote.

Smith's savior was Pocahontas, Chief Powhatan's favorite daughter. Historians disagree about the details of how Smith and Pocahontas first met. They do agree, however, that Pocahontas helped Smith save Jamestown by bringing food and keeping peace with her people. "She, next under God," Smith wrote, "was . . . the instrument to preserve this colony from death, famine, and utter confusion."

Pocahontas, the daughter of a powerful Indian leader, brought food to the Jamestown settlers and helped them survive. She later married John Rolfe and visited England with him. This portrait of Pocahontas in European dress is the only authentic painting of her.

The Starving Time Jamestown's troubles, however, were far from over. In the fall of 1609, after being injured in a gunpowder explosion, Smith returned to England. The following winter was the worst ever—so bad that it came to be known as the "Starving Time."

Without the encouragement of Smith and Pocahontas, the Indians refused to trade with the settlers. The English ate dogs, rats, and even human corpses to survive. By spring, only 60 of the 500 people Smith had left in the fall remained alive.

When supply ships came the next spring, the survivors were ordered to abandon their colony. Then three more English ships brought food, 150 new colonists, and 100 soldiers. Jamestown was saved again.

Jamestown Survives Even with more settlers, the people of Jamestown lived in constant danger of Indian attacks. To end that threat, the English kidnapped Pocahontas and held her hostage. For a year, Pocahontas remained a prisoner—but a willing and curious one. During that time she learned English, adopted the Christian faith, and made new friends.

Among those new friends was a widower named John Rolfe. Rolfe had already helped the colony survive by finding a crop that could be raised in Virginia and sold for good prices in England—tobacco. The happy settlers went tobacco mad, planting the crop everywhere, even in Jamestown's streets.

Now Rolfe helped again by making a marriage proposal to Pocahontas. Both the governor of Jamestown and Chief Powhatan gave their consent to this unusual match. Maybe they hoped the marriage would help end the conflict between their peoples.

The union of Pocahontas and John Rolfe did bring peace to Jamestown. In 1616, Rolfe wrote, "Our people yearly plant and reap quietly, and travel in the woods . . . as freely and securely from danger . . . as in England."

Peter Minuit is shown offering American Indians knives, beads, blankets, and trinkets worth about $24 in exchange for Manhattan Island.

2.6 New Netherland: The Short-Lived Dutch Settlement

While John Smith was struggling to save the colony of Jamestown, an English sailor named Henry Hudson was exploring the coastline farther north for the Netherlands. Henry Hudson's voyage was sponsored by Dutch merchants who hoped to find the Northwest Passage. (The people of the Netherlands are called the Dutch.)

In 1609, Hudson discovered a deep river full of fish and thought it might just take him all the way across the continent. It didn't, of course, but he claimed the land along its banks for the Netherlands. The river was later named the Hudson in his honor, and the territory he claimed became known as New Netherland.

In 1621, Dutch merchants formed the Dutch West India Company to start a colony in America. The first Dutch colonists settled along the upper Hudson, where they built Fort Orange, near present-day Albany, New York. The new colonists quickly found that there were good profits to be made in the fur trade. They established trading posts along the Hudson River. The largest was on Manhattan Island at the river's mouth.

Relations with American Indians In 1626, the Dutch West India Company sent Peter Minuit (MIN-yu-what) to New Netherland as the colony's governor. Wanting peaceful relations with the Indians, the company told Minuit that any native peoples on Manhattan Island "must not be expelled with violence or threats but be persuaded with kind words . . . or should be given something."

Following orders, Minuit offered the island's Indians iron pots, beads, and blankets worth about $24 in exchange for their land.

The American Indians didn't believe that anyone could own land. Laughing at the foolishness of the white men, they made the trade.

Dutch traders also made deals with members of the powerful Iroquois Confederacy, an alliance of five Indian groups who lived across the northern portion of New Netherland. The French had long supplied the Huron, the Iroquois's great rivals, with guns in exchange for furs. It made sense for the Iroquois to become partners with the Dutch, who supplied them with the weapons they needed to stand up to the Huron.

This partnership also made sense for the Dutch. The French were their main rivals in the European fur trade. For most of the 1600s, the Iroquois kept the French from moving into the fur-rich Ohio Valley.

New Amsterdam As the fur trade expanded, the Dutch settlement on Manhattan swelled to over 1,000 people. In 1647, the Dutch West India Company hired Peter Stuyvesant (STY-vuh-sunt) as the colony's new governor. When he arrived at Manhattan, Stuyvesant declared that the settlement would be called New Amsterdam, after the capital city of the Netherlands.

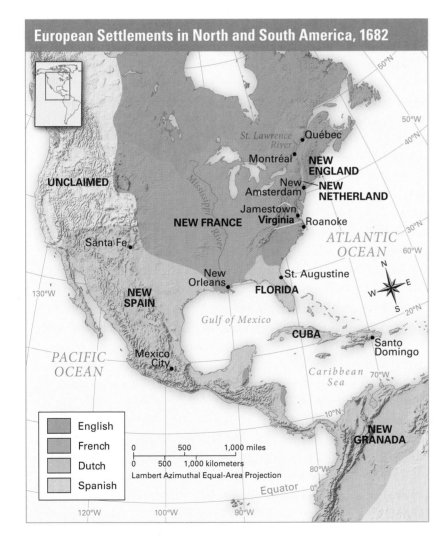

European countries established settlements throughout North and South America. Which European country first settled the area in which you live?

Peter Stuyvesant, the Dutch governor of New Amsterdam, surrendered the settlement to the British without a shot being fired. Outnumbered and out-gunned, Stuyvesant bowed to the pleas of his people to avoid bloodshed and destruction.

Stuyvesant had lost his right leg in battle, and he stomped around on a wooden leg decorated with silver nails. People called him "Old Silvernails" or "Peg Leg Pete." Although he was a strong leader, Old Silvernails was generally disliked. When Dutchmen who had been elected as city councilors disagreed with him, he called them "igno-rant subjects" and threatened to ship them back to the Netherlands in pieces if they gave him trouble.

Despite his reputation as a grouch, Stuyvesant governed New Am-sterdam for 17 years. During this time, he captured a nearby Swedish colony and invited its settlers to live in New Amsterdam. By 1660, the colony had nearly 8,000 people, including Europeans from many na-tions as well as enslaved Africans. New Amsterdam also provided ref-uge for Jews who were seeking a place to practice their religion freely.

New Netherland Becomes New York Stuyvesant's biggest problem was that the English wanted to drive the Dutch out of North America. England's king, Charles II, refused to recognize Dutch claims to New Netherland. In 1664, Charles gave his brother, James, the Duke of York, ownership of all Dutch lands in America—if he could conquer them.

James promptly organized a small invasion fleet to take the colony. When the English arrived, they sent Stuyvesant a letter demanding his surrender. Stuyvesant tore up the note and refused to consider giving up until New Amsterdam's chief gunner reported that the city's sup-ply of gunpowder was damp and useless. Without firing a shot, the English took over New Netherland and renamed the colony New York.

In this chapter, you read about the first European settlements in the Americas.

Discovery and Competition Explorers like Christopher Columbus were looking for a westward route to Asia when they stumbled onto the American continents. European nations competed to claim these new lands and the riches they might contain.

Spain Spain claimed vast territories, including Mexico and the southwestern portion of the future United States. In their search for gold and other treasures, Spanish conquistadors conquered the Aztecs of Mexico and the Incas of Peru. The Spanish also brought enslaved Africans to the Americas to plant and harvest crops. In the American Southwest, Spanish missionaries worked to convert American Indians to Christianity.

France The French staked a claim to much of present-day Canada, as well as Louisiana, the territory west of the Mississippi River. Most French settlers were more interested in trapping and trading furs than in farming or establishing large settlements.

England The English based their claim to North America on John Cabot's 1497 voyage. After several attempts, the English established their first permanent colony at Jamestown in Virginia.

The Netherlands The Dutch established a foothold in North America by founding the colony of New Netherland. The English, however, drove the Dutch out and renamed the colony New York.

Effects on American Indians For American Indians, the arrival of Europeans brought many changes, including new technology and new ideas. But they also brought deadly diseases that killed great numbers of the first Americans.

The exploration and settlement of the American continents brought amazing changes both to Europe and to the Americas.

The Granger Collection, New York

No one knows exactly what Columbus looked like. This is the earliest known portrait of him, painted 13 years after his death.

Who Was the Real Columbus?

Few historical figures are more famous than Christopher Columbus. Yet history has given us many different views of this man. To some people, Columbus was a great hero, the brave explorer who introduced the Americas to Europe. To others, he was a greedy conqueror responsible for the deaths of millions of American Indians. Why do we have such different views of Columbus?

At dawn on a small Caribbean island, a group of Taino people watched from a distance as strange men began to come ashore. The strangers had arrived on three large ships with cloth sails. These ships were very different from the canoes used by the Taino. The men looked very different from the Taino, too. They had white skin, and hair on their faces. They wore clothes and spoke a strange language. The men gathered on the beach and planted flags in the sand.

The date was October 12, 1492. Columbus and his men had just taken their first steps on North American soil. What did the Taino think when they saw these strangers? Were they amazed, or excited, or afraid? We will never know. The Taino had no written language, so they could not record their thoughts. Their views have been lost to history.

Columbus did leave a record of this first encounter, though. He kept a ship's log, or diary, of his travels. Of this first meeting with American Indians, he wrote,

> *No sooner had we concluded the formalities of taking possession of the island than people began to come to the beach . . . They are very well-built people, with handsome bodies and very fine faces . . .*
>
> *I want the natives to develop a friendly attitude toward us . . . I therefore gave red caps to some and glass beads to others. They hung the beads around their necks, along with some other things of slight value that I gave them. And they took great pleasure in this and became so friendly that it was a marvel. They traded and gave everything they had with good will, but it seems to me that they have very little and are poor in everything. I warned my men to take nothing from the people without giving something in exchange.*

What the Sources Say

Most of what we know about Columbus is based on a few primary sources from the time. His log is one of those sources. It tells about Columbus's first voyage, from Spain to the Americas. It describes the islands he visited and the people he found there. It also explains his purpose for making the voyage. He wanted to find a new route to the East Indies that would give Spain access to the spice trade with Asia. Along the way, he also hoped to claim new lands for Spain and to spread the Catholic faith.

In his log, Columbus portrays himself as a thoughtful man who cared about the native peoples he met. But the log also shows that he was driven by the search for gold and other riches. Moving from one island to the next, he wrote, "I do not wish to delay, but to discover and go to many islands to find gold." Finding gold would help justify his voyage and bring wealth and glory to Spain.

The quest for riches had disastrous effects on the native population, however. The Spanish colonists enslaved native peoples and made them work in mines and on farms. As the first governor of the West Indies, Columbus began this policy. In the years that followed, millions of American Indians died from overwork, violence, and disease.

This dark history is the subject of another primary source, *The Devastation of the Indies: A Brief Account*. The author was Bartolomé de Las Casas (bahr-taw-law-MEY day las KA-sas), who came to the West Indies as a colonist in 1502. Like most colonists, he hoped to make his fortune in the Indies. But what he saw there changed his mind. He became a priest instead and spoke out against the cruelty of Spanish rule. He accused the colonists of acting like "wild beasts" who took pleasure in "killing . . . , torturing, and destroying the native peoples." The reason for the Spaniards' actions, he wrote, was their "greed and ambition, the greatest ever seen in the world." Las Casas admired Columbus in many ways and did not blame him for all the harm done to the Indians. But he recognized that Columbus had helped set these events in motion.

How Historians Use the Sources

Historians rely on primary sources like Columbus's log and the writings of Las Casas. They use these sources and other evidence to write a story of the past. But the stories they tell depend on how they interpret this evidence.

For many years, the story of Columbus was mostly positive. He was seen as a man of vision who discovered new lands and expanded European knowledge of the world. In recent years, however, views of Columbus have grown more negative.

One of the first accounts of Columbus as a hero was by Washington Irving. In the early 1800s, Irving went to Spain to research the explorer's life. In 1828, he wrote *The Life and Voyages of Christopher Columbus*.

Las Casas (top) copied Columbus's log, preserving it for history. His own book told a very different story of the encounter between Spanish and Indians. As this 16th-century drawing (bottom) shows, the Spanish burned or hung Indians who resisted them.

Many paintings, like this one, portray Columbus and his crew as noble heroes. This 19th-century painting has hung in the U.S. Capitol building since 1847.

In this book, Irving described Columbus as a man of "great and inventive genius" whose ambition was "lofty and noble." Irving admitted that Columbus took actions that brought harm to native peoples. But he excused those actions as "errors of the times."

Over a century later, the historian Samuel Eliot Morison offered a more balanced view of Columbus. He portrayed Columbus as a real person with strengths and weaknesses. But he argued that his strengths outweighed his flaws. Above all, Morison pointed to Columbus's skill as a sea captain: "There was no flaw, no dark side to the most outstanding . . . of all his qualities—his seamanship. As a master mariner and navigator, Columbus was supreme in his generation." In Morison's view, "the whole history of the Americas" began with Columbus's voyages.

More recently, some historians have offered more critical views of Columbus. One of these writers is Howard Zinn. In his 2003 book *A People's History of the United States,* he focused on the harsh treatment of native peoples by the Spanish. Columbus's trip to the Americas was not a "heroic adventure," Zinn wrote, but the start of a "European invasion." It began a history of "conquest, slavery, and death." Zinn did not deny the importance of Columbus and his achievement. But he emphasized the negative impact.

Why History Varies

Why do historians present such different views of Columbus? The answer has to do with the writing of history. Historians look at the past from different perspectives. In addition, historians must use their judgment in analyzing sources and selecting information. In the process, they are also influenced by their own views and the attitudes of their time.

Irving, for example, wrote his biography of Columbus when the United States was still a young nation. The country was growing and expanding. Irving wanted to inspire his readers with a story of a hero who had great adventures and overcame great obstacles. In Irving's account, Columbus could be seen as an ideal role model for Americans building a new nation.

Morison, on the other hand, wanted to present a more realistic view of Columbus. He portrayed him not as a mythic hero, but as a man with both good and bad qualities. His main goal was to show that Columbus was a brilliant sea captain who changed the course of history.

Zinn had a different idea. He wanted to show the history of Columbus and the Spanish conquest from the point of view of native peoples. He believed that the fate of the Indians had been ignored in the making of the Columbus legend. He wanted people to understand that there was another side to the story.

In fact, the story of the past is always changing, as each new generation adds a new perspective. "Perceptions change, and so does our understanding of the past," notes writer John Noble Wilford. "Accordingly, the image of Columbus has changed through the years, sometimes as a result of new information but most often because of changes in the lenses through which we view him." In other words, the stories we tell about the past always reflect what we, in the present, bring to them.

Both pride and protest continue to surround the history of Columbus. He is honored at celebrations like this Columbus Day parade in New York (left). In Denver (right), protesters blocked marchers at a Columbus Day parade.

Chapter 3

The English Colonies in North America

What were the similarities and differences among the colonies in North America?

go to Page 210

3.1 Introduction

In the mid-1700s, a German schoolteacher named Gottlieb Mittelberger boarded a ship bound for the colony of Pennsylvania, in far-off North America. Mittelberger had borrowed the cost of his passage by signing on as an indentured servant. He would have to settle his debt by working for several years for the master who bought his services.

The voyage across the Atlantic was horrible. Most passengers suffered from illness and hunger. "The people are packed densely," Mittelberger wrote, "like herrings so to say, in the large sea vessels. One person receives a place of scarcely 2 feet width and 6 feet length . . . There is on board these ships terrible misery, stench, fumes, horror, vomiting, many kinds of seasickness, fever, dysentery, headache, heat, constipation, boils, scurvy, cancer, mouth-rot, and the like, all of which come from old and sharply salted food and meat, also from very bad and foul water."

When the nightmarish voyage ended, Mittelberger had to stay on board until his service was bought. Most indentured servants had to work for their masters for three to six years, but commitments varied according to the servants' age and strength. As Mittelberger noted, "young people, from 10 to 15 years, must serve till they are 21 years old."

Why were people willing to go through such hardships to come to the colonies? Many colonists came to North America for the chance to own land and start a new life. Others were seeking freedom to practice their religion. There were also some who did not have a choice. A number of convicts (people in jail) were forced to go to North America to work off their debts as indentured servants. Millions of Africans were kidnapped from their homelands and brought to the colonies as slaves.

In this chapter, you will learn about the people who settled the English colonies. You will read in detail about 8 of the 13 colonies. As you do, pay attention to similarities and differences among the colonies in such areas as geography, **economy,** religion, and government.

Pilgrims from England landed at present-day Plymouth, Massachusetts, on December 22, 1620.

◀ This illustration from 1731 shows the harbor of Boston, a city in the English colony of Massachusetts.

mercantilism an economic policy in which nations tried to gain wealth by controlling trade and establishing colonies

3.2 The New England, Middle, and Southern Colonies

English settlers established colonies in North America for many reasons. Some colonies were set up by groups of businesspeople who hoped to profit from resources found in the Americas. Several colonies were settled by people looking for a place to practice their religion freely. One colony was established as a refuge for debtors (people who owe money), who would otherwise have been tossed into prison.

The English government supported all these efforts in part because it was competing for land in the Americas with such nations as France and Spain. England had another reason for establishing colonies: it was also competing for wealth. Like most western European nations in the late 1600s, England followed an economic policy that is called **mercantilism**. Under this policy, nations tried to gain wealth by controlling trade and establishing colonies. The colonies made money for England by supplying raw materials for its industries. England turned the raw materials into goods that it could sell to other nations and to its own colonies.

By 1733, there were 13 British colonies strung along the Atlantic coastline. They can be grouped into three distinct regions: the New England, Middle, and Southern Colonies. These regions had different climates and resources that encouraged settlers to develop different ways of life.

The New England Colonies The New England region included the colonies of Massachusetts, Rhode Island, Connecticut, and New Hampshire. As you will read, the first settlers of these colonies came to America seeking religious freedom.

In New England, farming was difficult because of the long, cold winters and the region's rocky, hilly wilderness. But the forests and the sea provided useful resources and ways to make a living. New Englanders built their economy on small farms, lumbering, fishing, shipbuilding, and trade.

The Middle Colonies The four Middle Colonies were New York, Pennsylvania, New Jersey, and Delaware. The landscape of this region ranged from the rich soil of coastal New Jersey and Delaware to the valleys and wooded mountains of New York and Pennsylvania. Farmers in the Middle Colonies raised a variety of crops and livestock. Lumbering, shipbuilding, and other occupations added to the many opportunities here.

The people who settled the Middle Colonies represented many cultures and religions.

In New England, the church was at the center of both religious and political life. This church's pews could be removed to make room for tables used in town meetings.

Colonial America, 1770

By 1770, the 13 American colonies had developed a distinctive way of life that would affect the development of America for years to come.

QUEBEC

Maine (part of Massachusetts)

New Hampshire

Massachusetts

New York

Connecticut

Rhode Island

Cape Cod

Long Island

Lake Huron

Lake Ontario

Lake Erie

St. Lawrence River

Lake Champlain

Mohawk R.

Hudson River

Connecticut River

Delaware River

Susquehanna River

Pennsylvania

New Jersey

Maryland

Delaware

Potomac R.

Ohio River

Kanawha River

Chesapeake Bay

Virginia

James River

Roanoke River

ATLANTIC OCEAN

40°N

70°W

35°N

Cape Hatteras

Pamlico Sound

North Carolina

Cape Fear River

Catawba River

Savannah River

South Carolina

Georgia

APPALACHIAN MOUNTAINS

30°N

80°W

0   100   200 miles
0   100   200 kilometers
Albers Conic Equal-Area Projection

Legend

— New England Colonies
— Middle Colonies
— Southern Colonies

Fishing
Furs
I Ironworks
Lumber
Shipbuilding
Whaling
Cattle and grain
Rice and indigo
Tobacco

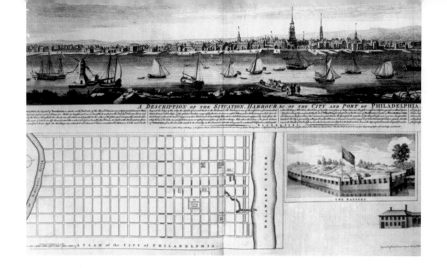

One important group, the Quakers, started the colony of Pennsylvania. Like the early settlers of New England, the Quakers were looking for freedom to practice their religion. Others seeking religious freedom soon followed. Settlements of French, Dutch, Germans, Swedes, Danes, Finns, Scots, Irish, and English spread throughout the Middle Colonies.

By the 1700s, Philadelphia, in the Middle Colony of Pennsylvania, had become a bustling trading center and one of the most important cities in the English colonies. It was the first city in America to use a grid to set up its streets.

The Southern Colonies The five Southern Colonies were Maryland, Virginia, North Carolina, South Carolina, and Georgia. This region featured broad rivers and vast wetlands that gradually merged with the sea. The soil and the hot, wet climate were ideal for growing tobacco, rice, and other **cash crops**.

Wealthy colonists took advantage of these conditions by establishing large farms called plantations. Plantation owners relied on indentured servants and enslaved Africans to sow and harvest their fields. After being harvested, the crops could be brought by river to the coast and loaded on ships for transport to other colonies and to Europe.

Government in the Colonies All the colonies were settled with the permission of the king of England. For each colony, the king issued a **charter**, a formal document that outlined the colony's geographic boundaries and specified how it would be governed. Because the colonies were so far from England, however, they needed to be able to make their own laws and keep peace and order.

The colonies developed different forms of government, depending on the settlement's purpose. Most of the colonies were self-governing. Colonists elected members of their community to a general assembly, which made their laws.

Many colonies also had a governor appointed by the king. As the king's representative, the governor could overrule the elected assembly. Some colonies also had councils, groups of men who represented the English businessmen involved in starting the colony.

In Massachusetts, religious colonists established a theocracy, a government whose leaders ruled in the name of God. In time, however, a system of town meetings evolved in which colonists voted for representatives to govern them.

In many ways, the colonies were more **democratic** than England. Still, not all colonists had a voice in the government. Usually, only free, white, landowning men were allowed to vote. In some colonies, voters also had to belong to the preferred church. Other colonists—including women, servants, slaves, and skilled tradesmen who were not landowners—had no voting rights.

cash crop a crop, such as tobacco, sugar, and cotton, raised in large quantities and sold for profit

charter a formal document issued by the king that outlined a colony's geographic boundaries and specified how it would be governed

democratic ruled by the people. In a democracy, the power to govern belongs to the people.

3.3 Massachusetts: A New England Colony

In the early 1600s, religion was very important in England. The king ruled the official Church of England, also called the Anglican Church. However, not everyone agreed with the church practices.

One group, who came to be called Puritans, wanted to "purify" the Anglican Church by making services simpler and doing away with ranks of authority. Another group, called Separatists, wanted to separate from the English church and form their own congregations. When the king began jailing Separatists for not attending Anglican services, some of them moved to Holland, where they could practice their religion freely.

But Holland wasn't home, and the Separatists wanted their children to grow up in an English culture. In 1620, about 102 Separatists set sail for America aboard the Mayflower. The Separatists were called Pilgrims because they traveled for religious reasons. The Pilgrims hoped to build their idea of a perfect society in America. During their voyage, they signed an agreement called the **Mayflower Compact** that described the way they would govern themselves in the Americas.

After a long, uncomfortable journey across the Atlantic, the Pilgrims landed at Plymouth, near Cape Cod. Luckily for them, the local Indians welcomed them. Without the help of these American Indians, the Pilgrims might not have survived their first winter. The Indians taught them how to plant crops, trap animals, and catch fish. In 1621, the Pilgrims invited the Indians to share their first harvest in a three-day feast of thanksgiving. Americans still celebrate this holiday.

Ten years later, a large group of Puritans decided to follow the Pilgrims to America. The king was relieved to see them go and sent them off with a charter for the colony of Massachusetts Bay. The charter said that the Massachusetts colonists would govern themselves. The Puritans were pleased with the charter because they wanted to build a community governed by the rules of the Bible. They hoped to set an example for the rest of the world. Their governor, John Winthrop, said, "We must consider that we shall be as a city upon a hill. The eyes of all people are upon us."

> **Mayflower Compact** an agreement that Pilgrims wrote and signed describing how they would govern themselves in the Americas

---

Massachusetts New England Colony

- **Founders** Pilgrims led by William Bradford (1620) and Puritans led by John Winthrop (1630)
- **Settlers** Puritans escaping religious persecution
- **Climate** Harsh winters, warm summers
- **Geography** Sandy coast with good ports, rich pastures, forests
- **Economy/Occupations** Crop and livestock farming, lumbering, shops, shipping
- **Religion** Puritan
- **Government** Self-governing, with strong religious influence

John Winthrop was a founder and, later, governor of Massachusetts. Here he is giving a blessing to soldiers in the colony.

Rhode Island New England Colony

- **Founders** Roger Williams and Anne Hutchinson
- **Settlers** People seeking religious freedom
- **Climate** Hot, humid summers; cold, snowy winters
- **Geography** Coastal lowlands; flat, rocky woodlands
- **Economy/Occupations** Farming (large cattle and dairy farms, small independent farms), lumbering, shipbuilding, fishing, whaling, trade
- **Religion** Various faiths
- **Government** Self-governing

This woodcut shows Roger Williams building a crude cabin after he fled Massachusetts in the bitter winter.

3.4 Rhode Island: A New England Colony

The Puritans of Massachusetts gained the freedom to practice their religion the way they wanted to. But instead of granting similar freedom to others, they set up a government that required everyone in the colony to worship as they did.

When a young minister named Roger Williams began preaching different ideas, the Puritans put him on trial. Williams believed that all people should be able to worship in any way they chose. "Forced worship," he declared, "stinks in God's nostrils."

The Puritans ordered Williams sent back to England. Instead, on a cold winter day in 1636, he left his wife and children and fled south. After trudging through snow for days, he met a group of Indians near Narragansett Bay. The Indians cared for him until spring. When his family and a few followers joined him, Williams bought land from the Indians for a settlement. He called it Providence, a word meaning "the guidance and care of God."

Williams welcomed people with different religious beliefs. Two years after he and his followers settled Providence, a colonist named Anne Hutchinson was also forced to leave Massachusetts for preaching against the Puritans. She and her family followed Williams and established a settlement called Portsmouth. In 1647, these and other settlements joined together to become the colony of Rhode Island. In 1663, Rhode Island elected an assembly to govern the colony.

The ideal of freedom in Rhode Island did not extend to enslaved Africans. Sea merchants soon discovered the riches that could be made in the **slave trade**. As a result, Rhode Island became one of the largest slave-trading centers in the world. Slave trading helped make the fortunes of some of the wealthiest families in New England. At the same time, the **isolated** coves along the Rhode Island coast provided perfect hiding places for pirates and smugglers.

Puritans in other colonies were disgusted by these activities. Reverend Cotton Mather of Boston called Rhode Island "the sewer of New England." To these Puritans, the actions of slave traders in Rhode Island justified having rejected these people and ideas from their own communities. Using a word that implied "criminals," they invented their own name for the colony: "Rogues' Island."

3.5 Connecticut: A New England Colony

Even in Massachusetts, not all Puritans shared exactly the same ideas. Thomas Hooker was a Puritan clergyman who lived in New Towne, a fast-growing community next to Boston. Hooker didn't always agree with the laws and leadership in Massachusetts. When he heard about a fertile valley along a river to the west, he convinced his family and about 100 other people to move there with him.

It took Hooker and his followers two weeks to travel to the Connecticut Valley with their animals and belongings. There they established a settlement on the site of an old Dutch fort, where an earlier group of English colonists had settled. They called their new community Hartford. In 1639, Hartford joined with two other settlements to form the colony of Connecticut.

Hooker believed that government should be based on "the free consent of the people," to whom belongs "the choice of public [officials] by God's own allowance." He helped draw up the first written plan of government for any of the colonies. This document was called the Fundamental Orders. The Fundamental Orders guaranteed the right to vote to all men who were members of the Puritan church.

Meanwhile, other Puritans formed a separate colony nearby called New Haven. The Puritans of New Haven agreed to live by the "word of God." Their laws were stricter than those in Hooker's Connecticut colony.

Neither of these colonies, however, was legally **authorized** by the king. Then, in 1662, King Charles II granted a charter for a new Connecticut colony that included New Haven. The charter gave Connecticut colonists more rights than those enjoyed by any other colonists except Rhode Island's. Legend says that when King James II sent Governor Andros to Hartford 15 years later to take back the colonists' charter, someone stole it and hid it in the trunk of a huge white oak tree. The "Charter Oak" became a symbol of Connecticut's freedom.

Thomas Hooker and about a hundred others established the community of Hartford in the fertile Connecticut Valley. It later became a part of the colony of Connecticut.

Connecticut New England Colony

- **Founder** Thomas Hooker
- **Settlers** Puritans seeking a new settlement
- **Climate** Cold winters, mild summers
- **Geography** Forested hills, seacoast
- **Economy/Occupations** Farming (crops and livestock), shipbuilding, fishing, whaling
- **Religion** Puritan
- **Government** written constitution (Fundamental Orders), self-governing

New York Middle Colony

- **Founders** Dutch West India Company (1624); James Duke of York (1664)
- **Settlers** Dutch and English seeking new lives
- **Climate** Cold, snowy winters; hot, humid summers
- **Geography** Wetlands along the coast and Hudson River, forested mountains to the North
- **Economy/Occupations** Fur-trapping, lumbering, shipping, slave trade, merchants and tradesmen, farming, iron mining
- **Religion** Various faiths
- **Government** British-appointed governor and council alternating with elected assembly

3.6 New York: A Middle Colony

The English took control of the settlement of New Netherland in 1664. The English renamed the colony New York in honor of its new **proprietor** (owner), James, the Duke of York. The duke gave huge chunks of his colony to two friends, Sir George Carteret and Lord John Berkeley. These men then established the colony of New Jersey to the south of New York.

The duke also awarded large estates along the Hudson River to wealthy Englishmen. The new landowners charged high rents to farmers working their land. This practice created a great difference in wealth between the landowners and their poor tenants. It also discouraged people from settling in New York.

The duke of York expected his colony to be a moneymaking business. As its owner, he appointed people to run the colony. He also issued his own laws and decided what New Yorkers should pay in taxes.

New York's rich landlords approved of the duke's approach to governing his colony. But farmers, fishers, and tradespeople did not. They demanded the right to elect an assembly to make laws for New York. The duke refused, saying that elected assemblies had a habit of disturbing the "peace of the government."

After years of protest, the duke finally allowed New Yorkers to elect an assembly in 1683. This first assembly passed 15 laws. The most important was a charter listing a number of rights that most colonists thought they should have as English citizens. Among them were the right to elect their own lawmakers, the right to trial by jury, and the right to worship as they pleased.

When the duke saw what the assembly had done, he abolished it. New Yorkers did not get a new assembly until, under the leadership of Jacob Leisler (LIES-ler), they rebelled in 1689. Leisler was elected commander in chief of a democratic council that governed until 1691. That year, New York was finally granted the right to elect an assembly with the power to pass laws and set taxes for the colony.

Ships navigate the harbor of New Amsterdam in the 1660s. The city was later renamed New York and became one of the busiest and most important ports in the world.

3.7 Pennsylvania: A Middle Colony

When William Penn asked King Charles II to let him establish a colony in America, the king had two very good reasons for granting Penn's request. First, he could repay a large debt that he owed to Penn's father, Admiral Penn. Second, he could get rid of William. The younger Penn had been a thorn in the king's side for a long time.

William Penn was a member of the Society of Friends, or Quakers. The Quakers believed in a simple lifestyle and in treating all people equally. They refused to bow before the king, fight in wars, or pay taxes to the Church of England.

In 1668, the king had thrown Penn in jail, hoping to stop him from preaching the Quakers' ideas. To the king's dismay, Penn continued preaching after his release.

With the Quakers unwelcome in England, Penn wanted to establish a colony in America where they would be safe. In 1681, the king granted Penn a huge area of land between the Puritan colonies of New England and the Anglican colonies of the South. In honor of Penn's father, the colony was called Pennsylvania.

Penn advertised his colony all over Europe. In his Great Law of 1682, he promised that people of all faiths would be treated equally.

Penn's appeal attracted settlers from several countries. An early colonist in Pennsylvania marveled at the prosperity and peace in the colony. He wrote, "Poor people (both Men and Women) of all kinds, can here get three times the Wages for their Labour they can in England or Wales . . . Here are no Beggars to be seen . . . Jealousie among Men is here very rare . . . nor are old Maids to be met with; for all commonly Marry before they are Twenty Years of Age."

Penn named his capital city Philadelphia, which is Greek for "City of Brotherly Love." From there, he wrote great documents of government that made Pennsylvania the first democracy in America.

William Penn made a treaty with Indians in about 1683. Penn insisted that the Delaware Indians be treated fairly and paid for their land.

Pennsylvania Middle Colony

- **Founder** William Penn
- **Settlers** English Quakers and other Europeans seeking freedom and equality
- **Climate** Cold winters; hot, humid summers
- **Geography** Rolling hills, trees, and fertile soil
- **Economy/Occupations** Farming (crops and dairy) merchants and tradesman, lumbering, shipbuilding
- **Religion** Various faiths
- **Government** Self-governing

3.8 Maryland: A Southern Colony

The founding of Maryland was a family enterprise. Sir George Calvert, named Lord Baltimore by King James I, was an English gentleman who became a Roman Catholic. In England, with its official Anglican Church, Catholics were treated harshly. Calvert wanted to start a colony "founded on religious freedom where there would not only be a good life, but also a prosperous one for those bold enough to take the risk." As a businessman, he also hoped the colony would make his own family more **prosperous,** or wealthy.

Unfortunately, Calvert died while he was still bargaining with the king. The new king, King Charles I, granted a charter for the colony to Calvert's son Cecil, the new Lord Baltimore. The charter gave the Calverts complete control of the colony, which was called Maryland.

Armed with these powers, Cecil named his brother Leonard to be governor. To make money from the colony, Cecil needed to attract both Protestant and Catholic settlers. He told Leonard to be "very careful to preserve unity and peace . . . and treat the Protestants with as much mildness and favor as justice will permit."

Leonard's expedition arrived in Maryland in 1634. There he and his followers built St. Mary's City on a high, dry bluff they purchased from American Indians. The following year, Leonard agreed to let Maryland elect an assembly to govern the colony.

As more and more settlers arrived, Leonard could see that Catholics would always be outnumbered in the colony. To protect their rights, in 1649 he helped pass America's first law guaranteeing religious liberty, the Act Concerning Religion. This law, however, applied only to Christians. Atheists (people who do not believe in the existence of God) and Jews were not included.

Despite the Calverts' efforts, Protestants and Catholics remained suspicious of one another and waged a tug-of-war in Maryland for more than a century. During this time, the colony's founding family lost and regained power several times. Still, George Calvert's dream was fulfilled. Catholics in Maryland worshiped freely and took part in the colony's government alongside Protestants.

ANNO Dni 1657
Ætatis 79

Sir Cecil Calvert, or Second Lord Baltimore, was the founder of Maryland. Calvert established laws to protect Catholics from persecution in the colony.

The Granger Collection, New York

3.9 Virginia: A Southern Colony

Jamestown, Virginia, was the first successful English settlement in America. After a shaky start, Virginia began to grow and prosper. By 1700, the descendants of those early settlers were wealthy landowners and the most important people in Virginia.

The economy of Virginia was based on tobacco. Tobacco planters needed vast areas of land to be successful. They also needed a large number of workers to grow their crops.

At first, planters tried putting Indians to work. But Indians in this area were not used to farming. Worse, many of them died of diseases they caught from the colonists. The others faded into the forests and disappeared.

Next, tobacco planters tried bringing poor people from England to work their land. In exchange for free passage to Virginia, the workers agreed to become indentured servants for a period of five to seven years. Many men, women, and children came to Virginia as indentured servants. After completing their service, they were given their freedom along with a small plot of land, some clothing, tools, and seeds.

The first Africans brought to Virginia were also treated as indentured servants. At first, they had the same rights and freedoms as white servants. Once their service ended, they could buy land and servants of their own.

Gradually, however, planters turned to slaves to solve their labor problem. Slaves brought from Africa cost twice as much as servants, but they did not leave after a few years.

For the planters, enslaving Africans had other advantages as well. Most Africans were hard workers who were used to farming. And because of their dark skin, it was hard for them to escape from their owners and blend into the rest of the population.

Virginia elected an assembly, called the House of Burgesses, in 1619. In 1661, the House of Burgesses passed a law that made African workers slaves for life. By 1700, Virginia had more than 16,000 enslaved Africans—more than one-fourth of the colony's population. For Virginia, slavery had become a way of life.

Virginia Southern Colony
■ **Founders** Sir Walter Raleigh and the Virginia Company
■ **Settlers** English landowners, skilled laborers (shoemakers, bricklayers, tailors), people seeking profit
■ **Climate** Mild winters; hot, humid summers
■ **Geography** Coastal lowlands, wooded mountains
■ **Economy/Occupations** Farming (plantations and small independent farms)
■ **Religion** Church of England
■ **Government** Self-governing, with elected assembly (House of Burgesses)

The first Africans were brought to Jamestown, Virginia, in 1619, the year before the Pilgrims landed at Plymouth Rock.

The Granger Collection, New York

James Oglethorpe founded the colony of Georgia. He is shown here wearing Scottish clothing and greeting colonists.

3.10 Georgia: A Southern Colony

Georgia, the 13th and last colony, was founded by a group of Englishmen whose business plan was based on a grand and noble idea. They wanted to help poor people in England stay out of debtors' prison. In England, at this time, people who couldn't pay their bills went to jail. James Oglethorpe inspired wealthy Englishmen to give money to help establish a colony where the poor could build better lives instead of going to jail.

King George II and his government liked this plan because the Georgia colony would help keep the Spanish from moving north out of Florida. Georgia would stand between Spanish Florida and the rest of the British colonies to the north.

The Englishmen's plan depended on getting the cooperation of settlers. But there weren't many poor debtors who wanted to start new lives in the wilderness of North America. Some thought prison would be a safer place.

Instead of an army of poor people, the colonists who went with Oglethorpe to Georgia in 1732 were adventurers much like the settlers in the other colonies. In addition, many Protestants, Catholics, and Jews came to Georgia in search of religious freedom.

As many had feared, life was not easy in Georgia. The Spaniards in Florida wanted to control Georgia, and they continually attacked the new settlements. The Georgians fought them off without any help from the other British colonies. To make matters worse, Oglethorpe had specific ideas about how the colonists should live. He established laws against drinking alcohol and owning slaves. He thought the settlers should live on small farms and learn to farm their land themselves.

Georgia Southern Colony

- **Founders** George II and James Edward Oglethorpe
- **Settlers** Debtors from English prisons, Europeans seeking religious freedom and cheap land
- **Climate** Short, mild winters; long, hot, humid summers
- **Geography** Wetlands and red-clay plains; forested mountains
- **Economy/Occupations** Farming (plantations and independent farms), trade, skilled labor
- **Religion** Various faiths
- **Government** Self-governing

The settlers weren't about to go along. They wanted to farm large plantations and own slaves like the wealthy planters in neighboring colonies. They disliked some of Oglethorpe's other rules as well.

After 12 years of governing the colony, Oglethorpe returned to England. In 1752, the people of Georgia elected an assembly.

Chapter Summary

In this chapter, you read about the settlement of the 13 English colonies in the future United States.

Settlers and Slaves Settlers had many reasons to come to America in the 1600s and 1700s. Two important reasons were freedom of religion and the chance to start a new life. However, even though colonists treasured freedom for themselves, they had Africans brought to America by force to work as slaves.

Regional Development The New England, Middle, and Southern Colonies had distinctive geographies and natural resources. As a result, different ways of life developed in each region. Colonies also varied in their form of government, but all were democratic to some degree.

New England Colonies Religion and geography were key influences in these colonies. Although Puritans sometimes disagreed, they hoped to establish model communities based on their religious faith. New England's forests and coastline made lumbering, shipbuilding, and trade very important to the region's economy.

Middle Colonies These colonies were geographically, culturally, and religiously diverse. Catholics, Quakers, Anglicans, and members of other Protestant faiths all found homes in this region.

Southern Colonies In these colonies, climate and geography encouraged the planting of cash crops and the development of large plantations. In time, slave labor would become a major part of this region's economy.

Handbills like this one lured colonists from Europe to the American colonies.

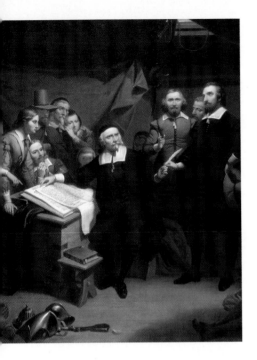

In this painting, William Bradford and other passengers sign the Mayflower Compact. The colonists agreed to unite and form a government based on common interests.

A Colonial Cast of Characters

Many kinds of people settled the English colonies of North America. There were Pilgrims and planters, merchants and craft workers, enslaved Africans and indentured servants. Some came seeking freedom and opportunity. Others came because they had no choice. All of them contributed to life in the colonies. Here are four of their stories.

William Bradford was worried. It was November 1620, and he had just arrived in America on the *Mayflower*. He and his fellow passengers had survived a long and difficult voyage. But they had not reached their intended destination, and trouble was brewing.

Bradford was one of the leaders of a group of Separatists on the *Mayflower*. The Separatists had broken away from the Church of England and were seeking religious freedom in America. They called themselves Pilgrims. They had been granted a patent—a royal permit—to settle in Virginia. But violent storms had blown their ship off course. Now, they sat off the coast of what would become Massachusetts, hundreds of miles from Virginia.

Winter was coming, so the Pilgrims decided to found their colony there. They would call it Plymouth, after a coastal city in England. But another group of people on board had different ideas. They had not come to America for religious reasons, but to own land. Since they had not reached Virginia, they argued that they were not bound by the terms of the patent. They said that no one had the "power to command them."

Facing a possible rebellion, Bradford and the other Pilgrim leaders came up with a plan to unite the colony. They drew up an agreement we call the Mayflower Compact. By signing this document, the members of the new colony agreed to form a "civil body politic," or a form of representative government. They agreed to obey "just and equall laws" created "for the generall good of the Colonie." This was the first written framework for self-government in the English colonies.

Bradford would later become governor of Plymouth Colony. He had never lived under any form of self-government. He had always been ruled by kings. But he did have a strong belief in his rights as an Englishman. This idea of the "rights of Englishmen" would be a foundation for self-rule in the colonies. The idea was rooted in Magna Carta (a 13th-century document limiting royal power) and the English Bill of Rights.

Margaret Hardenbroeck: Dutch Trader

William Bradford came to America to practice his religion. He wanted to build a new society based on religious principles. Margaret Hardenbroeck came for a very different reason. She moved to the colonies to do business, and she became very successful.

Hardenbroeck was born in the Netherlands. In 1659, she moved to New Amsterdam, the Dutch colonial city that later became New York. Unlike most colonists, she had a job when she arrived. She worked as an agent for her cousin, a merchant in Holland. Hardenbroeck sold goods like cooking oil and vinegar and bought furs to send back to Holland. She quickly established a reputation as a skilled trader.

New Amsterdam was a growing trade center at the time. It reflected the commercial spirit of Holland, a country that thrived on trade. The city had an open, tolerant feel. It was a place where people of different religious and national backgrounds could live and do business.

Hardenbroeck benefited from this commercial spirit. She also benefited from the more relaxed Dutch attitude toward women's rights. In Holland, women could get an education and own property. They could conduct business on their own. Women did not enjoy such rights in England at the time.

Not long after Hardenbroeck arrived, she married a wealthy merchant. When he died soon after, she inherited his land and business. In a short time, she had become one of the wealthiest citizens in the colony.

A year later, Hardenbroeck married another trader. Together, they continued to expand their business. They owned a fleet of ships and moved goods from the colonies to Europe and the West Indies and back. They also owned a lot of land, including a plantation in Barbados.

After England took control of New Amsterdam in 1664, Hardenbroeck maintained good relations with her English rulers. English law allowed her less freedom to manage her own affairs, but her business continued to thrive. She remained one of the colony's leading citizens until her death in 1691.

Margaret Hardenbroeck took part in New Amsterdam's growing trade in the 1660s. Merchants in this port city bought and sold goods from around the world.

Olaudah Equiano

Olaudah Equiano: African Slave

Most people came to the colonies of their own free will. For one group, however, coming to America was not a choice. Many black Africans were captured in their homelands and sold to slave traders. Packed onto ships, they were transported to the American colonies. This journey, known as the Middle Passage, was horrific for the enslaved Africans.

One man who made this journey was Olaudah Equiano (oh-LAU-duh ek-wee-AHN-oh). In 1789, he wrote a book about his life, *The Interesting Narrative of the Life of Olaudah Equiano, or Gustavus Vassa, the African, Written by Himself.* He described his early life in Africa, his enslavement, and his eventual freedom.

Equiano was born in the kingdom of Benin, in West Africa. His father was a village chief, and Olaudah was expected to follow in his footsteps. When he was 11, however, he was kidnapped and taken to the coast, where he was loaded onto a slave ship. There he was beaten and chained to the deck, along with other slaves. "I inquired of these what was to be done with us," he wrote. "They gave me to understand we were to be carried to these white people's country to work for them." Equiano was relieved, since he had believed that the white men meant to kill him. But his trials were not over.

When the ship was about to set sail, the Africans were put into cramped quarters below deck. Equiano recalled,

> *The closeness of the place and the heat of the climate, added to the number in the ship, which was so crowded that each had scarcely room to turn himself, almost suffocated us . . . The shrieks of the women and the groans of the dying rendered the whole a scene of horror almost inconceivable.*

Olaudah Equiano was taken to America on a slave ship like this one. Ship captains tried to pack as many people on board as possible. Many people died from overcrowding and disease.

Equiano spent several weeks at sea. He was first taken to Barbados, and then to a plantation in Virginia. There, after less than a month, he was sold to an English naval officer. Equiano traveled the world as this man's servant, and after seven years he was able to buy his freedom. He was relatively fortunate. Hundreds of thousands of Africans were brought to America and never knew freedom again. Most of their children were born into slavery, too.

Matthew Lyon: Indentured Servant

Another large group of people came to the colonies as indentured servants. In fact, around half of all European colonists arrived as indentured workers. As with enslaved Africans, some of these people were brought against their will. Some were kidnapped, while others were convicts who were transported in chains. Most indentured servants agreed to come voluntarily, however, and to work for several years to pay off their ship passage. One of these people was a young Irishman named Matthew Lyon.

Lyon was just 14 when he came to the colonies in 1765. Under the terms of indenture, young people were supposed to work until age 21. But Lyon bribed the ship captain to say that he was 18. So when Lyon was auctioned to a buyer in New York, he was sold for a three-year term of service.

Lyon was too clever to remain a servant for even that length of time, however. A year into his service, he arranged to buy two bulls from a local farmer, promising to pay the farmer when he was free. He then sold the bulls to his master in exchange for his freedom. At that point, Lyon went to work for the farmer to pay back his debt.

Lyon next got a job at an ironworks in Connecticut. He married the owner's niece, and they eventually settled on land to the north that would later become part of Vermont. There, Lyon joined the Green Mountain Boys, a volunteer fighting force set up to protect settlers' rights. In 1775, at the start of the American Revolution, this force captured Fort Ticonderoga, a British fort in upstate New York. Lyon became an officer and led troops in two more important battles of the revolution.

After the war for independence was won, Lyon served as a legislator in the new state of Vermont. He would go on to have a long career in politics and government.

From his early days as an indentured servant, Lyon had worked hard to build a new life in America. Like others who came to the colonies, his spirit and determination helped form the new American nation.

Owners of small businesses, such as this colonial plumber, bought the indentures of workers like Matthew Lyon. The growth of the colonies depended on the labor of indentured servants.

Chapter 4

Life in the Colonies

go to page 208

What was life really like in the colonies?

4.1 Introduction

In 1723, a tired teenager stepped off a boat onto a wharf in Philadelphia. He was an odd-looking sight. Not having luggage, he had stuffed his pockets with extra clothes. The young man followed a group of "clean dressed people" into a Quaker meetinghouse, where he soon fell asleep.

The sleeping teenager with the lumpy clothes was Benjamin Franklin. He had recently run away from his brother James's print shop in Boston. When he was 12, Franklin had signed a **contract** to work for his brother for nine years. But after enduring James's nasty temper for five years, Franklin packed his pockets and left.

In Philadelphia, Franklin quickly found work as a printer's assistant. Within a few years, he had saved enough money to open his own print shop. His first success was a newspaper called the *Pennsylvania Gazette*.

In 1732, readers of the *Gazette* saw an advertisement for *Poor Richard's Almanac*. An almanac is a book, published annually, that contains weather predictions, planting advice for farmers, and information on other useful subjects. According to the ad, *Poor Richard's Almanac* was written by "Richard Saunders" and printed by B. Franklin. Nobody knew then that author and printer were the same person.

Franklin also printed proverbs, or wise sayings, in his almanacs. Some, like these, are still remembered today:

> *A penny saved is a penny earned.*
>
> *Early to bed, early to rise, makes a man healthy, wealthy, and wise.*
>
> *Fish and visitors smell in three days.*

Poor Richard's Almanac sold so well that Franklin was able to retire at age 42. A man of many talents, he spent the rest of his long life as a scientist, inventor, political leader, diplomat, and national postmaster.

Franklin's rise from penniless runaway to wealthy printer was one of many colonial success stories. In this chapter, you will learn what life was like for people throughout the colonies in the 1700s.

Philadelphia was a thriving colonial city in the 18th century.

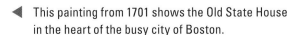

◄ This painting from 1701 shows the Old State House in the heart of the busy city of Boston.

Although most farmers lived in one-room farmhouses, they held out hope that they would achieve wealth like that pictured above.

4.2 Life on a Farm

The colonists developed an economy based on farming, commerce (buying and selling goods), and handcrafts. Nine out of ten people lived on small family farms. Most farm families raised or made nearly everything they needed. One farmer wrote with pride about a typical year, "Nothing to wear, eat, or drink was purchased, as my farm provided all."

The first and hardest task facing farm families was to clear the land of trees. The colonists had only simple, basic tools. They cut down trees with axes and saws. Then they used the same tools to cut square timbers and flat planks for building houses, barns, and fences.

Imagine living on a colonial farm. Your home is a single large room with a fireplace at one end. In this room, your family cooks, eats, and sleeps. Your parents sleep in a large bed built into one corner. Your younger brothers and sisters sleep in a smaller trundle bed, a bed that can slide under the big bed during the day. At bedtime, you climb a ladder next to the chimney to sleep in an attic or a loft. As your family grows, you help to build another room on the other side of the chimney.

The fireplace is the only source of heat for warmth and cooking, so keeping a supply of firewood is important. The fire is kept burning all the time because, without matches, it is very difficult to light a new one.

Cooking is one of the most dangerous jobs on your farm. Food is cooked in heavy iron pots hung over an open fire. While lifting or stirring these pots, your mother might burn her hands, scorch her clothes, or strain her back.

Your day on the farm starts before sunrise. Everyone wakes up early to share the work. Chores include cutting wood, feeding animals, clearing land, tending crops, building fences, making furniture and tools, gathering eggs, spinning thread, weaving cloth, sewing clothes, making candles and soap, cooking, cleaning, and caring for babies.

4.3 Life in Cities

In 1750, one colonist out of 20 lived in a city. Compared to the quiet farm life, cities were exciting places.

The heart of the city was the waterfront. There, ships brought news from England as well as eagerly awaited items such as paint, carpets, furniture, and books.

Just beyond the docks, a marketplace bustled with fishers selling their catch and farmers selling fresh eggs, milk, and cheese. Close by were taverns, where food and drink were served. People gathered there to exchange gossip and news from other colonies.

The nearby streets were lined with shops. Sparks flew from the blacksmith's block as he hammered iron into tools. Shoemakers, clockmakers, silversmiths, tailors, and other craftspeople turned out goods based on the latest designs from England. There were barbers to cut colonists' hair and wigmakers to make it look long again.

Cities were noisy, smelly places. Church bells rang out several times a day. Carts clattered loudly over streets paved with round cobblestones. The air was filled with the stench of rotting garbage and open sewers, but the colonists were used to it. Animals ran loose in the street. During hot weather, clouds of flies and mosquitoes swarmed about.

City homes were close together on winding streets. Most were built of wood with thatched roofs, like the houses the colonists had left behind in Europe. Their windows were small, because glass was costly.

For lighting, colonists used torches made of pine that burned brightly when they were wedged between hearthstones in the fireplace. Colonists also burned grease in metal containers called "betty lamps" and made candles scented with bayberries.

With torches and candles lighting homes, fire was a constant danger. Colonists kept fire buckets hanging by their front doors. When a fire broke out, the whole town helped to put it out. Grabbing their buckets, colonists formed a double line from the fire to a river, pond, or well. They passed the buckets full of water from hand to hand up one line to the fire. Then the empty buckets went back down the opposite line to be refilled.

Colonial cities were very small by today's standards. Philadelphia (pictured below) and Boston, the two largest cities, had fewer than 20,000 people in 1700.

rights powers or privileges that belong to people as citizens and that cannot or should not be taken away by the government

Magna Carta an agreement made in 1215 listing the rights granted by King John to all free men of the kingdom

Parliament the lawmaking body of England, consisting of representatives from throughout the kingdom

English Bill of Rights an act passed by Parliament in 1689 that limited the monarch's power by giving certain powers to Parliament and listing specific rights of the citizens

4.4 Rights of Colonists

Colonists in America saw themselves as English citizens. They expected the same **rights** that citizens enjoyed in England. The most important of these was the right to have a voice in their government.

Magna Carta The English people had won the right to participate in their government only after a long struggle. A key victory in this struggle came in 1215, when King John agreed to sign **Magna Carta,** or "Great Charter." This agreement established the idea that the power of the monarch, or ruler, was limited. Not even the king was above the law.

The next major victory was the founding of **Parliament** in 1265. Parliament was made up of representatives from across England. Over time, it became a lawmaking body with the power to approve laws and taxes proposed by the king or queen.

In 1685, James, the Duke of York, became King James II. The king did not want to share power with an elected assembly in New York. Nor did he want to share power with an elected Parliament in England. When he tried to rule without Parliament, James was forced off his throne. This change in power, which took place without bloodshed, is known as the Glorious Revolution.

The English Bill of Rights In 1689, Parliament offered the crown to Prince William of Orange and his wife, Mary. In exchange, they had to agree to an act, or law, known as the **English Bill of Rights**. This act said that the power to make laws and impose taxes belonged to the people's elected representatives in Parliament and to no one else. It also included a bill, or list, of rights that belonged to the people. Among these were the right to petition the king (request him to change something) and the right to trial by jury.

English colonists saw the Glorious Revolution as a victory not only for Parliament, but for their colonial assemblies as well. They wanted to choose the people who made their laws and set their taxes. After all, this was a cherished right of all English citizens.

The Granger Collection, New York

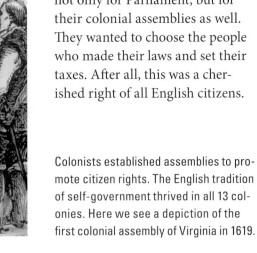

Colonists established assemblies to promote citizen rights. The English tradition of self-government thrived in all 13 colonies. Here we see a depiction of the first colonial assembly of Virginia in 1619.

Crime and Punishment Each colonial assembly passed its own laws defining crimes and punishments. However, most crimes were treated similarly in all the colonies.

Certain very serious crimes could be punished by death. These included murder, treason (acts of disloyalty toward the government), and piracy (robbery at sea). Puritans in New England added other crimes to this list based on their understanding of God's law in the Bible. In New England, colonists could be put to death for "denying the true God" or for striking or cursing their parents.

Crimes such as theft, forgery, and highway robbery carried harsh punishments in every colony. For these crimes, people might be jailed, whipped, or branded with hot irons.

Lesser crimes, such as drunkenness and breaking the Sabbath (working or traveling on Sunday), were punished with fines, short jail terms, or public humiliation. A colonist caught breaking the Sabbath, for example, might be locked in the town stocks. The stocks were a heavy wooden frame with holes for a person's neck, wrists, and ankles. Lawbreakers were locked for hours in this device in a public place where others could ridicule them.

No group had firmer ideas about right and wrong than New England's Puritans. The Puritans required everyone to attend church on Sundays. They also forbade anyone to work or play on that day. The Puritans wrote their Sunday laws in books with blue paper bindings. For this reason, these rules came to be known as blue laws. Some blue laws persist to this day. In Connecticut, for example, it is still illegal for stores to sell alcohol on Sundays.

The Puritans were constantly on the watch for signs of Satan (believed to be an evil angel who rebelled against God). Satan was thought to work through witches. In 1692, fear of witchcraft overtook residents of Salem, Massachusetts, when several girls were seen acting strangely in church. The girls accused their neighbors of being witches and putting spells on them. Nineteen accused witches were put to death during the Salem witch trials before calm was **restored** and the townspeople realized that the girls' accusations were untrue.

Courts, like the one pictured here, were important to social life in the colonies. This painting depicts a woman being tried for witchcraft in Salem, Massachusetts, in 1692.

4.5 Life for African Americans

Slavery in the colonies began in Virginia, with tobacco planters. From there, it spread both north and south. By the early 1700s, enslaved Africans were living in every colony. Even Benjamin Franklin owned slaves for a time. But like most people in the New England and Middle Colonies, Franklin found that hiring workers when he needed them cost less than owning slaves.

In the Southern Colonies, however, slavery expanded rapidly. From Virginia to Georgia, slaves helped raise tobacco, rice, indigo, and other cash crops.

The Atlantic Slave Trade Most of the slaves who were brought to the colonies came from West Africa. Year after year, slave ships filled with cloth, guns, and rum sailed from the colonies to the coast of West Africa. There, these goods were traded for Africans. The ships then returned to the Americas carrying their human cargo.

For the Africans packed onto slave ships, the ocean crossing—known as the Middle Passage—was a nightmare. According to his autobiography, Olaudah Equiano (oh-LAU-duh ek-wee-AH-noh) was just ten years old when he was put onto a slave ship. He never forgot "the closeness of the place . . . which was so crowded that each had scarcely room to turn himself." Nor did he forget "the shrieks of the women, and groans of the dying." The terrified boy refused to eat, hoping "for the last friend, Death, to relieve me."

Although Equiano survived the voyage, many Africans died of sickness or despair. Even so, the Atlantic slave trade was very profitable. Many colonial merchants built fortunes trading in human beings.

The first slaves were brought to the United States in 1619 to help raise tobacco in the Virginia colony. Here, slaves tend tobacco while their owner relaxes, feet up, smoking his pipe.

Work Without Hope The slaves' masters in America demanded that the Africans work hard. Most enslaved Africans were put to work in the fields raising crops. Others worked as nurses, carpenters, blacksmiths, drivers, servants, gardeners, and midwives (people who assist women giving birth). Unlike other colonists, slaves had little hope of making a better life. Their position was fixed at the bottom of colonial society.

Some slaves **rebelled** by refusing to work or running away. But most adapted to their unhappy condition as best they could. Slowly and painfully, they began to create a new African American way of life.

4.6 Religion

Religion was an important part of colonial life. Most colonists tried to lead good lives based on their faith. Children grew up reading the Bible from cover to cover several times over.

Puritan Church Services
In New England, the sound of a drum or horn called Puritans to worship on Sunday morning. "Captains of the watch" made sure everyone was a "Sabbath-keeper." Sometimes houses were searched to ensure that everyone was at church.

Colonial society had a strong religious flavor. Here, colonial citizens gather around a church on Sunday.

Church services were held in the town meetinghouse. This was the most important building in the community and was used for all public meetings. Inside were rows of wooden benches, called pews, and a pulpit (a platform where the preacher stood). A "seating committee" carefully assigned seats, with the best ones going to older, wealthy people.

Services could last as long as five hours. At midday, villagers would go to "noon-houses" near the church to warm themselves by a fire, eat, and socialize. Then they returned to church for the long afternoon sermon.

The Great Awakening Beginning in the 1730s, a religious movement known as the **Great Awakening** swept through the colonies. This movement was spurred by a feeling that people had lost their religious faith. "The forms of religion were kept up," a Puritan observed, but there was "little of the power" of God in it.

To revive people's religious spirit, preachers traveled from town to town holding outdoor "revival" meetings. There, they delivered fiery sermons to huge crowds. Their words touched the hearts and souls of many colonists. Benjamin Franklin wrote about the change he observed in Philadelphia: "It seemed as if all the world were growing religious, so that one could not walk through the town in an evening without hearing psalms [Bible songs] sung in different families of every street."

The Great Awakening had a powerful effect on the colonies. It helped spread the idea that all people are equal in the eyes of God. Ordinary people could understand God's will if they had an open heart and a desire to know God's truth. By encouraging ideas of liberty, equality, and self-reliance, the Great Awakening helped pave the way for the American Revolution.

Great Awakening a revival of religious feeling and belief in the American colonies that began in the 1730s

Children gather with their teacher in a colonial school. These children were among a minority of children who received formal education. Most children did not go to school beyond the elementary level.

4.7 Education

Except in New England, most children in the colonies received little formal education. Neither the Middle nor the Southern Colonies had public schools.

In the Southern Colonies, most families were spread out along rivers. A few neighbors might get together to hire a teacher for their children. Wealthy planters often hired tutors to educate younger children at home. Older children were sent to schools in distant cities, or even England, to complete their education.

In the Middle Colonies, religious differences among Quakers, Catholics, Jews, Baptists, and other religious groups slowed the growth of public education. Each religious group or family had to decide for itself how to educate its children. Some groups built church schools. Others were content to have parents teach their children at home.

Only in New England were towns required to provide public schools. The Puritans' support for education was inspired by their religious faith. They wanted their children to be able to read the Bible.

To encourage education, Massachusetts passed a law in 1647 that required every town with 50 families or more to hire an instructor to teach their children to read and write. Towns with more than 100 families were required to build a school. Similar laws were passed in other New England colonies.

Parents were asked to contribute whatever they could to the village school. Contributions might be money, vegetables, firewood, or anything else the school needed. Often, land was set aside as "school meadows" or "school fields." This land was then rented out to raise money for teachers' salaries.

Schools were one-room buildings with a chimney and fireplace in the center. There were no boards to write on or maps. Pencils and paper were scarce. Students shouted out spelling words and wrote sums in ink on pieces of bark. There was usually one book, the *New England Primer,* which was used to teach the alphabet, syllables, and prayers.

Most colonists believed that boys needed more education than girls. "Female education, in the best families," wrote First Lady Abigail Adams, "went no further than writing and arithmetic; in some few and rare instances, music, and dancing."

4.8 Colonial Families

The concept of family has changed often throughout history. Today, most people think of a family as being made up of parents and their children. In colonial times, however, families might include grandparents, aunts and uncles, cousins, and stepchildren.

Marriage Colonial men and women generally married in their early to mid-20s. Those who arrived in America as indentured servants were not allowed to marry until they had gained their freedom.

Men outnumbered women throughout the colonies. As a result, almost every woman was assured of receiving a marriage proposal. "Maid servants of good honest stock [family]," wrote a colonist, could "choose their husbands out of the better sort of people." For a young woman, though, life as a wife and mother often proved to be even harder than life as an indentured servant.

Large Families Colonial families were generally large. Most families had between seven and ten children. (Benjamin Franklin had 16 brothers and sisters.) Farm families, in particular, needed all the hands they could get to help with chores.

Religious and cultural backgrounds influenced colonists' ideas about raising children. But almost everywhere in the colonies, children were expected to be productive members of the family.

Married women gave birth many times, but nearly half of all children died before they reached adulthood. Childhood deaths were especially high in the Middle and Southern Colonies, where the deadly disease of malaria raged. Adults often died young as well. After the death of a wife or husband, men and women usually remarried quickly. Thus, households often swelled with stepchildren as well as adopted orphans (children whose parents had died).

Whether colonists lived in cities, in villages, or on isolated farms, their lives focused on their families. Family members took care of one another because there was no one else to do so. Young families often welcomed elderly grandparents, aunts, uncles, and cousins into their homes when they could no longer care for themselves. It didn't matter if there was barely enough room for everyone. No one would turn away a needy relative.

Family life was at the center of colonial society. This family is gathered around a fire on a wintry evening. A mother and grandmother work while the father relaxes and the children play.

4.9 Leisure

While most colonists worked hard, they enjoyed their periods of **leisure** (time away from work). They also took advantage of gatherings, such as town meetings and Sunday services, to talk with neighbors and make friends.

Bees and Frolics When possible, colonists combined work and play by organizing "bees" and "frolics." New settlers might hold a "chopping bee" in which all the neighbors helped clear the trees off their land. Other frolics included corn-husking bees for men and quilting bees for women. Sharing the work made it faster and more fun.

The Germans introduced house and barn raisings to the colonies. At these events, neighbors joined together to build the frame of a house or barn in one day. The men assembled the four walls flat on the ground and then raised them into place. Meanwhile, the women prepared a huge feast. At the end of the day, everyone danced on the barn's new floor.

Here, Dutch settlers play a spirited game of bowls in New Amsterdam. Below, colonists enjoy a form of billiards called trock.

The Granger Collection, New York

Toys and Sports Colonial children had a few simple toys, such as dolls, marbles, and tops. They played tag, blindman's bluff, and stoolball, which was related to the English game of cricket (a game like baseball). Children in New England also enjoyed coasting down snowy hills on sleds. Adults must have thought coasting was dangerous, because several communities forbade it.

Adults enjoyed several sports. Almost every village had a bowling green. Here, men rolled egg-shaped balls down a lane of grass toward a white ball called a jack. Colonists also played a game similar to backgammon called tick-tack and a form of billiards (pool) called trock.

In the Southern Colonies, fox hunting with horses and hounds was a popular sport. Card playing was another favorite pastime, one that New England Puritans disapproved of strongly. Horse racing, cockfighting, and bull baiting were also popular in the South.

Fairs were held throughout the colonies. At these events, colonists competed in contests of skill and artistry. There were footraces, wrestling matches, dance contests, and wild scrambles to see who could win a prize by catching a greased pig or climbing a greased pole.

In this chapter, you read about various aspects of life in the American colonies during the early 1700s.

Farms and Cities The colonists developed an economy based on farming, commerce, and crafts. Farm families produced most of what they needed for themselves. In the villages and cities, many trades and crafts developed.

Rights of Colonists American colonists expected to enjoy all the rights of English citizens, especially the right to have a voice in their own government. Colonial assemblies defined crimes and punishments. Punishments were often harsh, but for most of the 1700s, the colonists were content to be ruled by English laws.

Life for African Americans Enslaved African Americans had almost no rights or even hope for liberty. After being brought to America in chains, they faced a life of forced obedience and toil.

Religion Religion was very important to the colonists. The Great Awakening revived religious feeling and helped spread the idea that all people are equal.

Education Most colonial children received little education, except in New England. Instead, they were expected to contribute to the work of the farm or home.

Family and Leisure Most colonial families were large. They often included many relatives in addition to parents and their children. Much of colonial life was hard work, but colonists also found time to enjoy sports and games.

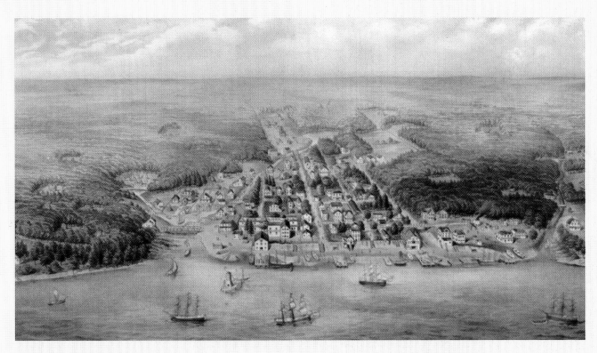

This panorama of Philadelphia in 1702 reveals a number of aspects of colonial life. Government buildings, colonial homes, roads, and ships are all evident in the painting.

Churches, often in the center of town, were central to colonial life. Here, churchgoers sing as they wait to enter their church.

A Great Awakening

In the 1730s and 1740s, the Great Awakening shook up the English colonies. This religious movement caused an outpouring of Christian faith. It also prompted new ways of thinking about the church and society. As a result, it helped lay the foundations for political changes to come.

Nathan Cole was working on his farm on the morning of October 23, 1740, when he heard the news. George Whitefield was coming.

A famous preacher, Whitefield was known for his powerful sermons. He had traveled all over the colonies, drawing huge crowds wherever he went. Now he was in Connecticut. In fact, he was preaching in nearby Middletown that very morning. Cole knew he had to move fast.

> *I dropped my tool . . . and ran to my pasture for my horse with all my might fearing that I should be too late to hear him. I brought my horse home and soon mounted and took my wife up and went forward as fast as I thought the horse could bear . . .*
>
> *And when we came within about half a mile [from the main road] . . . I saw before me a Cloud or fog rising. I first thought it came from the great river, but as I came nearer . . . I heard a noise something like a low, rumbling thunder and presently found it was the noise of horses' feet coming down the road and this Cloud was a Cloud of dust . . . As I drew nearer it seemed like a steady stream of horses and their riders . . . Every horse seemed to go with all his might to carry his rider to hear news from heaven for the saving of Souls.*
>
> —Nathan Cole, in George Leon Walker, *Some Aspects of Religious Life in New England*, 1897

Thousands of people were rushing to Middletown to hear Whitefield speak. "I saw no man at work in his field," Cole wrote, "but all seemed to be gone." When Cole and his wife reached the town, they found a large crowd gathered there. The mood was electric as they waited for Whitefield to appear.

What was behind all this excitement? Why would a preacher's arrival cause a commotion like that of a rock star or a Hollywood celebrity today?

In fact, Whitefield *was* a superstar of his time. He was the most famous figure in a religious revival that was sweeping the colonies. People were seeking a deep spiritual experience and a direct connection to God. They found that connection in preachers like Whitefield.

Origins of the Awakening

Religion played a major role in the lives of colonists in the early 1700s. Most people attended church regularly. There were a number of different churches, but most provided a similar experience. They emphasized traditional religious teachings. Their ministers were educated men who valued reason over emotion. The atmosphere in church was calm and orderly.

Some ministers, however, believed that the church had lost its way. They feared that religion had become a collection of formal, empty rituals. They wanted to wake people up and renew their faith. In their sermons, they offered an emotional message of sin and salvation that was aimed at the heart, not the head.

By the 1730s, a split was developing between old-line ministers and those favoring a new way. These two groups became known as the Old Lights and the New Lights. The Old Lights stressed tradition and respect for authority. The New Lights called for a more individual, personal form of worship. They wanted people to feel the spirit of God for themselves.

George Whitefield was the best-known personality of the revival movement. His powerful sermons "awakened" religious belief in his listeners.

Whitefield and other New Light ministers often preached at open-air revivals. They depicted the glories of heaven and the miseries of hell. Hearing these highly charged sermons, many people were seized by feelings of great joy or despair. They would weep, moan, and fall to the ground. As news of the revivals spread, the movement gained strength.

Leading Lights: Whitefield and Edwards

A number of ministers played key roles in the Great Awakening. The leading figures, however, were George Whitefield and Jonathan Edwards. If Whitefield was the star of the movement, Edwards was its most important thinker.

Whitefield was a young Anglican minister in England when he joined the revival movement. In 1739, he defied church authorities by holding revival meetings across the country.

That same year, he traveled to the colonies, where he caused a sensation. Whitefield was a magnificent speaker with a beautiful voice and the skills of an accomplished actor. His words and gestures could lift audiences into an emotional frenzy. He toured from Maine to Georgia, appearing in towns and cities along the way. In Boston, some 20,000 people gathered to hear him speak. He was the most celebrated man in America.

Jonathan Edwards was one of the first revival preachers. Though he was not as dramatic as Whitefield, his words still carried great weight.

Whitefield was pleased with his success. But he was also troubled by the wealth and vanity he saw in the colonies. Noting the fine clothing worn by wealthy citizens, he argued that Christians should dress simply and plainly. In Boston, he was disturbed to see young children dressed in fancy clothes:

> The little infants who were brought to baptism were wrapped up in such fine things . . . that one would think they were brought thither [there] to be initiated into, rather than to renounce, the pomps and vanities of this wicked world.

While in Massachusetts, Whitefield visited Jonathan Edwards at his home in Northampton. Edwards had helped start the revival movement and had been a great influence on Whitefield. Edwards, in turn, recognized that Whitefield had given new life to the movement. He decided to increase his own efforts to win converts. In this way, he said, he hoped to "make New England a kind of heaven upon earth."

Edwards began to preach in neighboring towns. In 1741, he gave his most famous sermon in Enfield, Connecticut. Called "Sinners in the Hands of an Angry God," this sermon was directed at a congregation that had resisted the revival message. Edwards told them that they had angered God with their sinful ways. God held them in his hand, he said, and could cast them into hell at any moment.

The God that holds you over the pit of hell, much as one holds a spider . . . is dreadfully provoked; his wrath towards you burns like fire . . . 'Tis nothing but his hand that holds you from falling into the fire . . . Oh sinner! Consider the fearful danger you are in . . .

And now you have an extraordinary opportunity, a day wherein Christ has flung the door of mercy wide open, and stands in the door calling and crying with a loud voice to poor sinners; . . . many that were very lately in the same miserable condition you are in, are in now a happy state, . . . rejoicing in the hope of the glory of God. How awful is it to be left behind at such a day!

These words had a devastating effect. The congregation began to wail and beg for mercy. The "shrieks and cries were piercing," wrote one witness. The uproar was so great that Edwards could not even finish his sermon.

The Impact of the Awakening

Over the next few years, such incidents became more common. At the same time, the split between Old Light and New Light ministers grew wider. Churches were breaking apart. For the sake of unity, both sides agreed to make peace and heal their divisions. By the late 1740s, the Great Awakening was over.

The impact of the movement was deep and ongoing, however. New Light preachers had encouraged people to think for themselves and to make their own choices about religious faith. As a result, the church no longer had absolute authority in religious matters. Preachers also taught that everyone was equal in the eyes of God. As one preacher said, "The common people . . . claim as good a right to judge and act for themselves . . . as civil rulers or the learned clergy." By encouraging people to act independently and defy authority, the Great Awakening helped lay the groundwork for rebellion against British rule.

SINNERS

IN THE HANDS OF AN

ANGRY GOD.

A

SERMON

Preached at ENFIELD, July 8th, 1741.

At a Time of great Awakenings; and attended with remarkable Impressions on many of the Hearers.

By JONATHAN EDWARDS, A. M.
Pastor of the Church of CHRIST, in NORTHAMPTON.

Amos ix. 2, 3. *Though they dig into Hell, thence shall mine Hand take them; though they climb up to Heaven, thence will I bring them down. And though they hide themselves in the Top of Carmel, I will search and take them out thence; and though they be hid from my Sight in the Bottom of the Sea, thence I will command the Serpent, and he shall bite them.*

Re-printed by particular Desire.

BOSTON, Printed:
NEW-YORK, Re-printed, and Sold by JOHN HOLT, at the EXCHANGE, 1769.

In "Sinners in the Hands of an Angry God," Edwards spoke of hell as a real place that awaited those who sinned against God. This was a common theme in revival sermons.

Our Colonial Heritage

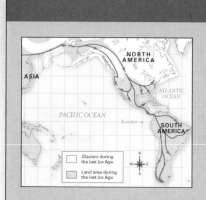

10,000 or more years ago
Humans Reach North America
The first humans, likely Siberian hunter families, reach the Americas by crossing a wide bridge of land between Asia and North America called Beringia.

1492
Columbus Sails to the Americas
Christopher Columbus sails to the Americas and explores the islands in what is now called the Caribbean Sea.

10,000 or more years ago to year 1

| 1000 | 1100 | 1200 | 1300 |

1215
Magna Carta
King John of England signs Magna Carta, limiting his power and giving more rights to the English people.

1400s
American Indian Culture Flourishes
One to two million American Indians live in North America, north of Mexico. American Indian groups have distinct beliefs, customs, foods, dwellings, and clothing.

1500s
Slave Trade
As part of the Atlantic slave trade, Africans are brought to the Americas and sold into slavery. Slavery becomes a way of life in many American colonies.

1636
Providence Founded
Roger Williams breaks from the Puritans and establishes the settlement of Providence, which eventually becomes part of the colony of Rhode Island.

1607
Jamestown Founded
Jamestown becomes the first permanent English colony in North America. Despite initial hardships, the colony survives and flourishes.

1689
English Bill of Rights
Prince William and his wife Mary sign the English Bill of Rights, strengthening the rights of the English people and the power of colonial assemblies.

1400   1500   1600   1700   1800

1620
Mayflower Compact
Pilgrims from England sail to the Americas seeking to establish "a perfect society." During their voyage, they sign the Mayflower Compact, which describes how they will govern themselves.

1681
Pennsylvania Founded
Seeking religious freedom for the Quakers, William Penn establishes the colony of Pennsylvania and promises that people of all faiths will be treated equally.

1692
Salem Witch Trials
Fear of witchcraft erupts among the Puritans in Salem, Massachusetts. Nineteen young women are put on trial and executed.

1730s and 1740s
Great Awakening
The Great Awakening revives religion in the colonies and spreads the ideas of liberty and equality.

Revolution in the Colonies

Dressed like colonists who fought in the American Revolution, these colonial reenactors stand ready for action in Lexington, Massachusetts.

Maine
(part of
Massachusetts)

Lake Huron

St. Lawrence River

Lake Champlain

Lake Ontario

New Hampshire

New York

Albany

Boston

Massachusetts

65°W

40°N

Connecticut

Rhode Island

Lake Erie

M O U N T A I N S

Hudson River

New York

Long Island

Pennsylvania

Delaware River

Princeton

Trenton

Philadelphia

New Jersey

Ohio River

A P P A L A C H I A N

Maryland

Delaware

Delaware Bay

Virginia

Chesapeake Bay

ATLANTIC
OCEAN

James River

Williamsburg

York River

35°N

North Carolina

Wilmington

South
Carolina

N

W   E

S

Georgia

Charleston

Savannah

30°N

0   100   200 miles

0   100   200 kilometers

Albers Conic Equal-Area Projection

80°W

75°W

70°W

Revolution in the Colonies

In this unit, you will learn why some colonists wanted to replace British rule with an independent government. You will also learn about the long, difficult struggle to gain that independence.

In the 1760s, Great Britain began passing new trade and tax laws for the colonies and enforcing old laws passed years before. Picture a southern rice farmer who is required by law to sell his crop only to England, even if he might get a higher price elsewhere. Or think of a northern merchant having to pay a new tax on paper—a tax imposed by a distant government in which he had no representation. How do you think they felt about such laws and taxes?

Colonists who supported Great Britain's policies and British rule were known as Loyalists. Those who resisted called themselves Patriots. When the colonies declared independence, Patriots were opposed by many Loyalists as well as British troops.

The map on the opposite page shows the physical geography of the 13 colonies. Knowing the land was one advantage Patriot forces had over British troops in the American Revolution.

The maps below show (left) where colonists lived in 1775 and (right) where Loyalist support was strong. These settlement patterns, along with the colonies' physical geography and regions of Loyalist strength, helped to shape the military strategies of the revolution.

Population Density of the Thirteen Colonies

New England Colonies

Boston

Middle Colonies

New York

Philadelphia

Southern Colonies

Charleston

0   100   200 miles
0   100   200 kilometers
Albers Conic Equal-Area Projection

Population Density

Per sq. mi.	Per sq. km
Over 40	Over 16
15–40	6–16
2–15	1–6

• Largest cities in 1775

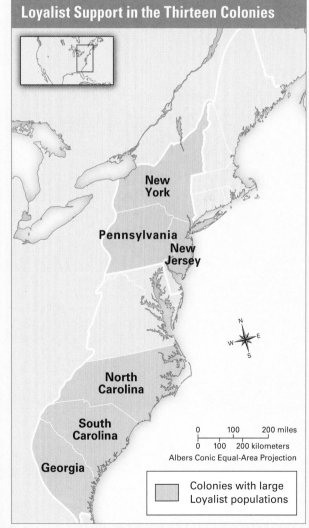

Loyalist Support in the Thirteen Colonies

New York

Pennsylvania

New Jersey

North Carolina

South Carolina

Georgia

0   100   200 miles
0   100   200 kilometers
Albers Conic Equal-Area Projection

Colonies with large Loyalist populations

Chapter 5

Toward Independence

When is it necessary for citizens to rebel against their government?

5.1 Introduction

An almost full moon cast a pale light over Boston on April 18, 1775. But the night was anything but quiet. Mounted on Brown Beauty, one of the fastest horses in Massachusetts, Paul Revere woke up the countryside with alarming news. British troops stationed in Boston were on the move! They had orders to march to the nearby town of Concord and seize weapons the colonists had stored there.

This was news Patriots had been waiting for. Patriots (also called Whigs) were Americans who believed the colonies had the right to govern themselves. On hearing Revere's warning, Patriots around Concord grabbed their muskets and prepared to meet the British troops.

The same news filled Loyalists (also called Tories) with dread. Loyalists were colonists who felt a deep loyalty to Great Britain. They saw themselves as faithful subjects of the king. They were horrified by the idea of taking up arms against British troops. How did colonists come to be so divided in their feelings about the British? Most Americans were content with British rule in the early 1700s. In this chapter, you will learn what happened to change the relationship between Great Britain and the colonies.

The story begins in the 1750s, when Great Britain and the colonies fought a war against the French and their Indian allies. The French and Indian War left Great Britain with huge debts and a vast new empire to protect. To solve its problems, the British government passed new laws that tightened its control of the colonies. Some of these laws also placed new taxes on the colonists.

Colonists were stunned. For the most part, they had been able to make their own laws and determine their own taxes. Suddenly, Great Britain was changing the rules. It wasn't right, the colonists protested. In this chapter, you will see how these feelings led many colonists to consider rebelling against their government.

Why would some colonists have celebrated the dismantling of a statue of the British king?

◀ By the 1770s, the colonists had become deeply divided in their loyalty to Great Britain. Here, some colonists tear down a statue of King George.

Before 1763, Great Britain had relatively little to do with the day-to-day lives of most colonists.

5.2 Before 1763

By 1750, the American colonies were bursting with growth. In just a century, the population of the colonies had grown from 50,000 to more than a million people. What brought about this rapid growth? Cheap land? Religious tolerance? Economic opportunity? All of these were important in attracting people to the colonies. But there was another reason.

For more than a century, the British government had, for the most part, left the colonies alone to solve their own problems. During this time, Americans had learned to govern themselves. Each colony elected its own assembly. Like the British Parliament, the assemblies had the power to pass laws and to create and collect taxes. Each assembly also decided how the colony's tax money should be spent. Americans had more freedom to run their own affairs than ordinary people in any country in Europe. Self-government also made the colonies attractive to settlers.

Conflict in the Ohio Valley As the colonies grew, settlers began to dream of moving across the Appalachian Mountains and into the Ohio Valley—the region between the Ohio and Mississippi rivers. Both Great Britain and France claimed this area. In 1754, the French made good on their claim by building a fort where the city of Pittsburgh stands today. They called it Fort Duquesne (du-KANE).

News of the fort alarmed the governor of Virginia. He ordered a small force of Virginia **militia** to drive the French out of the Ohio Valley. Militias are small armies of citizens who are trained to fight in an emergency. To head the militia, the governor chose a 22-year-old volunteer named George Washington.

Today, Americans remember George Washington as a great Patriot, a military hero, and the first president of the United States. In 1754, however, he was just an ambitious young man with no land or money. Washington believed that his best chance of getting ahead was to become an officer in the British army. There was only one problem with his plan. Most British officers believed that colonists made terrible soldiers.

The expedition into the Ohio Valley gave Washington a chance to prove them wrong. Near Fort Duquesne, he came across a French scouting party that was camped in the woods. Washington ordered his men to open fire. It was an easy victory. "I heard the bullets whistle," he wrote afterward. "And, believe me, there is something charming in the sound."

militia a small army made up of ordinary citizens who are trained to fight in an emergency

The French and Indian War Washington's whistling bullets were the first shots in a conflict known as the French and Indian War. This war was part of a long struggle between France and Great Britain for territory and power. Because many American Indians fought with France in this latest conflict, the colonists called it the French and Indian War.

In 1755, Great Britain sent 1,400 British soldiers to Virginia to finish the job that Washington had begun. They were led by a general named Edward Braddock. The soldiers' job was to clear the French out of the Ohio Valley. Washington joined the army as a volunteer, hoping to make a good impression on General Braddock.

Braddock's march into the Ohio Valley was a disaster. The troops' bright red uniforms made them perfect targets for French sharp-shooters and their Indian allies. Two-thirds of the soldiers were killed.

Washington himself narrowly escaped death. "I had four bullets through my Coat and two horses shot under me," he wrote in a letter. Showing great courage, Washington led the survivors back to Virginia. There, he was greeted as a hero.

The French and Indian War raged for seven long years. The turning point came in 1759, when British troops captured Canada. In 1763, Great Britain and France signed a peace treaty, or agreement, ending the war. In this treaty, France ceded, or gave, Canada to Great Britain.

Americans were thrilled with this victory. Great Britain now controlled a vastly expanded American empire. Never before had the colonists felt so proud of being British. And never before had the future of the colonies looked so bright.

Here George Washington tips his hat to the British flag at Fort Duquesne. The British captured the fort from the French in 1758 during the French and Indian War. It was rebuilt and called Fort Pitt. The city of Pittsburgh was later built here.

The Granger Collection, New York

tyranny the unjust use of government power. A ruler who uses power in this way is called a tyrant.

The Proclamation of 1763 prohibited settlers from moving west of the Appalachians. King George III hoped this would prevent conflict between colonists and American Indians.

5.3 Early British Actions in the Colonies

Changes that were taking place in Great Britain soon clouded the colonists' bright future. A new king, George III, had been crowned in 1760. He was not regarded as a bright man. One historian wrote that "he was very stupid, really stupid." He was also known for being proud and stubborn. He was determined to be a take-charge kind of ruler, especially in the colonies. The people George III chose to help him knew very little about conditions in North America. Before long, they were taking actions that enraged the colonists.

The Proclamation of 1763 The British government faced a number of problems after the French and Indian War. One was how to keep colonists and American Indians from killing each other as settlers pushed westward. Simply draw a line down the crest of the Appalachian Mountains, said George III. Tell settlers to stay east of that line and Indians to stay west of it.

This was what the king ordered in his Proclamation of 1763. To Americans, the king's order suggested **tyranny,** or the unjust use of government power. They argued that the lands east of the Appalachians were already mostly settled. The only place that farmers could find available land was west of the mountains. Besides, the proclamation was too late. Settlers were already crossing the mountains.

The British government ignored these arguments. To keep peace on the frontier, it decided to expand the British army in America to 7,500 men.

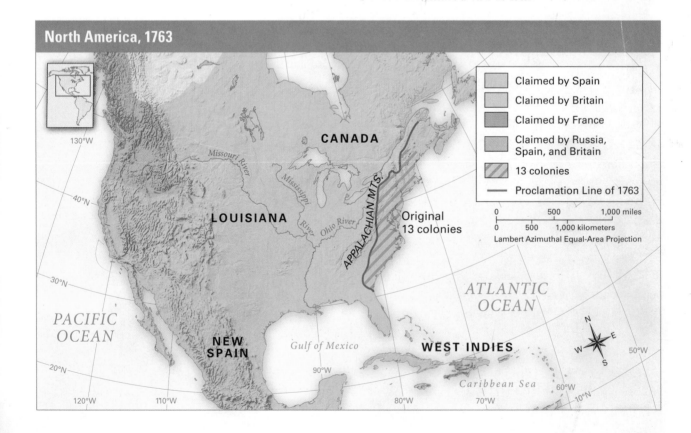

North America, 1763

Legend:
- Claimed by Spain
- Claimed by Britain
- Claimed by France
- Claimed by Russia, Spain, and Britain
- 13 colonies
- Proclamation Line of 1763

0 500 1,000 miles
0 500 1,000 kilometers
Lambert Azimuthal Equal-Area Projection

CANADA

Missouri River

Mississippi River

LOUISIANA

Ohio River

APPALACHIAN MTS.

Original 13 colonies

ATLANTIC OCEAN

PACIFIC OCEAN

NEW SPAIN

Gulf of Mexico

WEST INDIES

Caribbean Sea

The Stamp Act The British government had other problems besides keeping colonists and American Indians from fighting each other. One problem was how to pay off the large debt from the French and Indian War.

The solution seemed obvious to Prime Minister George Grenville, the leader of the British government. People in Great Britain were already paying taxes on everything from windows to salt. In contrast, Americans were probably the most lightly taxed people in the British Empire. It was time, said Grenville, for the colonists to pay their fair share of the cost of protecting them from Indians.

In 1765, Grenville proposed a new act, or law, called the Stamp Act. This law required colonists to buy a stamp for every piece of paper they used. Newspapers had to be printed on stamped paper. Wills, licenses, and even playing cards had to have stamps.

Once again, the colonists sensed tyranny. One newspaper, *The Pennsylvania Journal,* said that as soon as "this shocking Act was known, it filled all British America from one End to the other, with Astonishment and Grief."

It wasn't just the idea of higher taxes that upset the colonists. They were willing to pay taxes passed by their own assemblies, where their representatives could vote on them. But the colonists had no representatives in Parliament. For this reason, they argued, Parliament had no right to tax them. They saw the Stamp Act as a **violation** of their rights as British subjects. "No taxation without representation!" they declared.

Some colonists protested the Stamp Act by sending messages to Parliament. Loyalists simply refused to buy stamps. Patriots, however, took more violent action. Mobs calling themselves Sons of Liberty attacked tax collectors' homes. Protesters in Connecticut even started to bury one tax collector alive. Only when he heard dirt being shoveled onto his coffin did the terrified tax collector agree to resign from his post.

After months of protest, Parliament **repealed,** or canceled, the Stamp Act. Americans greeted the news with great celebration. Church bells rang, bands played, and everyone hoped the troubles with Great Britain were over.

The Stamp Act required colonists to buy stamps like this one for all paper products. The colonists reacted angrily to the act. This illustration shows them hanging effigies, or dummies, of British officials. The colonists' protests forced Parliament to repeal the act.

repeal to take back, or to cancel, a law

The Quartering Act As anger over the Stamp Act began to fade, Americans noticed another law passed by Parliament in 1765. Called the Quartering Act, this law ordered colonial assemblies to provide British troops with quarters, or housing. The colonists were also told to furnish the soldiers with "candles, firing, bedding, cooking utensils, salt, vinegar, and . . . beer or cider."

Of course, providing for the soldiers cost money. New Jersey protested that the new law was "as much an Act for laying taxes" on the colonists as the Stamp Act. New Yorkers asked why they should pay to keep troops in their colony. After all, they said, the soldiers just took up space and did nothing.

In 1767, the New York assembly decided not to approve any funds for "salt, vinegar and liquor" for the troops. The British government reacted by refusing to let the assembly meet until it agreed to obey the Quartering Act. Once again, tempers began to rise on both sides of the Atlantic.

5.4   The Townshend Acts

The next British leader to face the challenge of taxing the colonies was Charles Townshend. He was known as "Champagne Charlie" because of his habit of making speeches in Parliament after drinking champagne. Townshend believed that the colonists' bad behavior made it even more important to **retain** an army in the British colonies. Once he was asked in Parliament whether he would dare to make the colonists pay for that army. Stamping his foot, Townshend shouted, "I will, I will!"

Townshend kept his promise. In 1767, he persuaded Parliament to pass the Townshend Acts. The new laws placed a duty, or tax, on certain goods the colonies imported from Great Britain. These goods included such popular items as glass, paint, paper, and tea.

A Boycott of British Goods To many colonists, the Townshend duties were unacceptable. Once again, colonists were determined not to pay taxes that their assemblies had not voted on.

A Boston Patriot named Samuel Adams led the opposition to the Townshend Acts. Adams was not an attractive man, and he was a failure at business. But he was gifted at stirring up protests through his speeches and writing. The governor of Massachusetts once complained, "Every dip of his pen stung like a horned snake."

Adams wrote a letter protesting the Townshend Acts that was sent to every colony. The letter argued that the new duties violated the colonists' rights as British citizens. To protect those rights, the colonies decided to **boycott** British goods. This was a peaceful form of protest that even Loyalists could support. One by one, all of the colonies agreed to support the boycott.

Women were very important in making the boycott work, since they did most of the shopping. The *Virginia Gazette* wrote that one woman could "do more for the good of her country than five hundred

boycott to refuse to buy one or more goods from a certain source. An organized refusal by many people is also called a boycott.

A VIEW OF PART OF THE TOWN OF BOSTON IN NEW ENGLAND AND BRITISH SHIPS OF WAR LANDING THEIR TROOPS! 1768

noisy sons of liberty, with all their mobs and riots." Women found many ways to avoid buying British imports. They sewed dresses out of homespun cloth, brewed tea from pine needles, and bought only American-made goods.

Repeal of the Townshend Acts Meanwhile, a new leader named Lord North became head of the British government. Described by Townshend as a "great, heavy, booby-looking man," Lord North embarrassed his supporters by taking naps in Parliament. But he was good with numbers, and he could see that the Townshend duties were a big money-loser. The duties didn't begin to make up for all the money British merchants were losing because of the boycott.

Early in 1770, North persuaded Parliament to repeal all of the Townshend duties, except for one—the tax on tea. Some members of Parliament argued that keeping the duty on tea was asking for more trouble. But King George wasn't ready to give up on the idea of taxing Americans. "I am clear that there must always be one tax to keep up the right," the king said. "And, as such, I approve the Tea Duty."

5.5 The Boston Massacre

On the same day that Parliament repealed most of the Townshend duties, a fight broke out between soldiers and colonists in Boston. When the dust cleared, five Bostonians were dead and ten were injured.

Patriots called this incident the Boston Massacre. A massacre is the killing of defenseless people. What really happened was a small riot.

In 1768, the British government sent soldiers to Boston to enforce the Townshend Acts. This engraving made by Paul Revere shows the troops landing.

Trouble had been brewing in Boston for months before the riot. To the British, Boston Patriots were the worst troublemakers in the colonies. In 1768, the British government had sent four regiments of troops to keep order in Boston.

Bostonians resented the British soldiers. They made fun of their red uniforms by calling them "lobsterbacks." Samuel Adams even taught his dog to nip at soldiers' heels.

Despite such insults, the troops were forbidden to fire on citizens. Knowing this only made Bostonians bolder in their attacks. General Thomas Gage, the commander of the British army in America, wrote that "the people were as Lawless . . . after the Troops arrived, as they were before."

Mob Violence Breaks Out On March 5, 1770, a noisy mob began throwing rocks and ice balls at troops guarding the Boston Customs House. "Come on you Rascals, you bloody-backs," they shouted. "Fire if you dare." Some Patriot leaders tried to persuade the crowd to go home. So did Captain Thomas Preston, the commander of the soldiers. But their pleas had no effect.

As the mob pressed forward, someone knocked a soldier to the ground. The troops panicked and opened fire. Two bullets struck Crispus Attucks, a black man at the front of the crowd. He was the first to die, but not the last. The enraged crowd went home only after receiving a promise that the troops would be tried for murder.

Massacre or Self-Defense? Samuel Adams saw this event as a perfect opportunity to whip up anti-British feeling. He called the riot a "horrid massacre" and had Paul Revere, a local silversmith, engrave a picture of it. Revere's engraving shows soldiers firing at peaceful, unarmed citizens.

Prints of Revere's engraving were distributed throughout the colonies. Patriots saw the Boston Massacre as proof that the British should remove all of their troops

Paul Revere's famous engraving of the Boston Massacre stirred up deep colonial resentment against Great Britain.

from the colonies. Loyalists saw the tragedy as proof that troops were needed more than ever, if only to control Patriot hotheads.

One hero came out of this sad event. He was a Boston lawyer named John Adams. Like his cousin Samuel, John Adams was a Patriot. But he also believed that every person, even the British soldiers, had the right to a fair trial. Adams agreed to defend the soldiers, even though he knew that his action would cost him friends and clients.

At the murder trial, Adams argued that the troops had acted in self-defense. The jury found six of the soldiers not guilty. Two of them were found guilty only of manslaughter, or causing death without meaning to.

Throughout his long life, John Adams remained proud of his defense of the British soldiers. He said that upholding the law in this case was "one of the best pieces of service I ever rendered to my country."

5.6 The Boston Tea Party

Despite the hopes of Patriots like Sam Adams, the Boston Massacre did not spark new protests against British rule. Instead, the repeal of the Townshend duties led to a period of calm. True, there was still a small duty on tea. But the tax didn't seem to bother Loyalists very much. Patriots knew they could always drink Dutch tea that had been smuggled into the colonies without paying duties.

Things did not stay peaceful, however. In 1773, a new law called the Tea Act prompted more protests. One of them was the incident that became known as the Boston Tea Party.

The Tea Act The Tea Act was Lord North's attempt to rescue the British East India Company. This large trading company controlled all the trade between Great Britain and Asia. For years, it had been a moneymaker for Great Britain. But the American boycott of British tea hurt the company badly. By 1773, the tea company was in danger of going broke unless it could sell off the 17 million pounds of tea that were sitting in its London warehouses.

The Tea Act lowered the cost of tea that was sold by the British East India Company in the colonies. As a result, even taxed British tea became cheaper than smuggled Dutch tea. The Tea Act also gave the British East India Company a monopoly, or complete control, over tea sales in the colonies. From now on, the only merchants who could sell the bargain-priced tea were those chosen by the company.

Lord North may have thought he could persuade Americans to buy taxed tea by making it so cheap, but colonists weren't fooled. They saw the Tea Act as still another attempt to tax them without their consent.

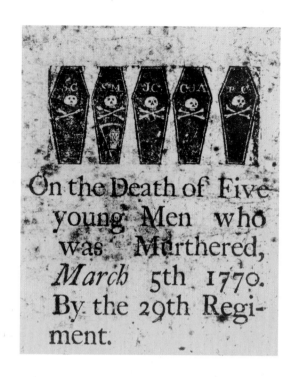

Paul Revere's engraving of five coffins showing the victims of the Boston Massacre appeared on flyers to remind colonists of British brutality.

In addition, many merchants were alarmed by the East India Company's monopoly over the tea trade. They wondered what the British government might try to control next. Would there be a monopoly on cloth? On sugar? Nervous merchants wondered what would happen to their businesses if other goods were also **restricted**.

Tea Ships Arrive When the British East India Company's tea ships sailed into American ports, angry protesters kept them from unloading their cargoes. More than one ship turned back for England, still filled with tea. In Boston, however, the royal governor ordered the British navy to block the exit from Boston Harbor. He insisted that three tea ships would not leave until all their tea was unloaded.

On December 16, 1773, the Sons of Liberty decided to unload the tea, but not in the way the governor had in mind. That night, about 50 men dressed as Mohawk Indians boarded the three ships. One of them, George Hewes, described what happened:

We then were ordered by our commander to open the hatches and take out all the chests of tea and throw them overboard . . . and we immediately proceeded to execute his orders, first cutting and splitting the chests with our tomahawks . . . In about three hours from the time we went on board, we had thus broken and thrown overboard every tea chest to be found on the ship . . . We were surrounded by British armed ships, but no attempt was made to resist us.

To protest the tax on tea, Patriots disguised as American Indians threw 342 chests of tea overboard from three British ships. Colonists later called this the Boston Tea Party.

About 90,000 pounds of tea were dumped into the sea that night. Nothing else on the ships was touched.

News of the Boston Tea Party excited Patriots throughout the colonies. "This is the most magnificent moment of all," wrote John Adams in his journal the next day. "This destruction of the tea is so bold, so daring, so firm . . . it must have . . . important consequences." He was right.

5.7 The Intolerable Acts

Lord North was stunned by news of the Boston Tea Party. As he saw it, he had tried to help the colonists by sending them cheap tea. And what did they do? They threw it in the sea! This time they had gone too far.

King George agreed. To him, the issue was no longer about taxes. It was about Great Britain's control over the colonies. "We must master them totally," he declared, "or leave them to themselves." The king wasn't about to leave the colonies to themselves, however.

Great Britain's anger led Parliament to pass a new series of laws in 1774. These laws were so harsh that many colonists called them intolerable, or unacceptable. Throughout the colonies, they became known as the Intolerable Acts.

Parliament Punishes Massachusetts
The Intolerable Acts were designed to punish Massachusetts for the Boston Tea Party. The first law closed Boston Harbor to all shipping until the ruined tea was paid for. The second law placed the government of Massachusetts firmly under British control. Colonists in Massachusetts could not even hold a town meeting without the colonial governor's permission. The third law said that British soldiers who were accused of murder would be tried in England, not in the colonies. Finally, more troops were sent to Boston to enforce the new laws.

A few British leaders worried that the Intolerable Acts might push the colonies into rebellion. But George III was sure they would force the colonists to give in to British **authority**.

The first of the Intolerable Acts punished Massachusetts for the Boston Tea Party. It closed Boston Harbor to all shipping until the destroyed tea was paid for. As a result, sailors and dockworkers lost their jobs, and stores closed for lack of goods to sell.

The Colonies Begin to Unite In fact, the Intolerable Acts did not force the colonists to give in. Boston Patriots declared they would "abandon their city to flames" before paying a penny for the lost tea. Merchants in other cities showed their support by closing their shops. Many colonies sent food and money to Boston so that its citizens would not starve.

In Virginia, lawmakers drafted a resolution in support of Massachusetts. The Virginians said that everyone's rights were at stake. "An attack made on one of our sister colonies," they declared, "is an attack made on all British America."

The Virginians also called for a congress, or meeting, of delegates from all the colonies. The purpose of the congress would be to find a peaceful solution to the conflicts with Great Britain.

Not all Americans agreed with this plan. In every colony, there were Loyalists who thought that Bostonians had gone too far and should pay for the tea. If they were forced to choose, they would side with the king against Sam Adams and his Sons of Liberty. In their view, it was the misguided Patriots who were causing all the trouble.

The First Continental Congress In September 1774, some 50 leaders from 12 colonies met in Philadelphia. The meeting brought together delegates from most of the British colonies on the North American continent, so it was called the First Continental Congress.

The delegates were used to thinking of themselves as citizens of their own colonies. Patrick Henry, a leader from Virginia, urged them to come together as one people. "I am not a Virginian," he declared, "but an American." But only strong Patriots like Sam and John Adams were ready to think of themselves this way. Many delegates were strong Loyalists who still thought of themselves as British. Still others, like George Washington, were somewhere in between. Only one thing united the delegates—their love of liberty and hatred of tyranny.

In spite of their differences, the delegates agreed to send a respectful message to King George. The message urged the king to consider their complaints and to recognize their rights.

The delegates also called for a new boycott of British goods until Parliament repealed the Intolerable Acts. Finally, they agreed to meet again the following May if the boycott didn't work.

The Colonies Form Militias In towns and cities throughout the colonies, Patriots appointed committees to enforce the boycott. In case the boycott didn't work, they also organized local militias. In New England, the volunteers called themselves Minutemen because they could be ready to fight in 60 seconds.

Across the colonies, militias marched and drilled. In New Hampshire, unknown persons stole 100 barrels of gunpowder and 16 cannons from a British fort. Similar thefts occurred in other colonies. Rather than forcing the colonies to give in, the Intolerable Acts had brought the two sides to the brink of war.

Delegates from the colonies met in Philadelphia at the First Continental Congress in 1774. Patrick Henry of Virginia urged the colonists to unite as Americans, not as citizens of separate colonies.

The Granger Collection, New York

5.8 Lexington and Concord

King George had made many mistakes in his decisions about the colonies. The First Continental Congress listed all these mistakes in its message to the king. Now he made another one.

Rather than consider the colonists' complaints, King George refused even to answer their message. "The New England governments are in a state of rebellion," he said. "Blows must decide whether they are to be subject to this country or independent." In Boston, General Gage, the king's commander of British troops in America, got ready to deliver those blows.

The First Blow at Lexington In April 1775, a spy told General Gage that the colonists were hiding a large supply of gunpowder and weapons in the nearby village of Concord. General Gage decided to strike at once.

The general ordered 700 of his best troops to march to Concord and seize the weapons. To keep the colonists from moving the weapons, the attack had to be a surprise. So Gage had his troops march the 20 miles to Concord at night.

The colonists had their own spies. When Gage's troops slipped out of Boston on April 18, 1775, Patriots were watching their every move. Soon Paul Revere and others were galloping through the countryside, warning colonists that the British soldiers were coming.

The news reached Lexington, a town on the road to Concord, in the early hours of April 19. Led by Captain John Parker, a small band of Minutemen gathered nervously in the chilly night air.

This hand-colored engraving by Connecticut engraver Amos Doolittle shows the British firing upon the Minutemen who are gathered at Lexington. This was the first battle in the war for independence from Great Britain.

At the North Bridge in Concord, the Minutemen fired upon British troops who had occupied the town. Surprised by the fury of the colonial attack, the British fled in panic. The Amos Doolittle engraving above shows the bridge at the time of the battle. The photograph shows the bridge today.

At dawn, the British troops reached the town green. "Stand your ground," ordered Parker. "Don't fire unless fired upon, but if they mean to have a war, let it begin here." As the Minuteman faced the British troops, a shot rang out—from where, no one knew for certain. Without orders, the soldiers rushed forward, shooting wildly. A few Minutemen managed to return fire.

When the firing stopped, eight colonists lay dead or dying. Another ten were limping to safety with painful wounds. The British troops gave three cheers for victory and marched on to Concord.

The Second Blow at Concord By breakfast time, the British were in Concord, searching for gunpowder and weapons. But the colonists had hidden them. In frustration, the soldiers piled up a few wooden tools, tents, and gun carriages and set them on fire.

On a ridge outside the city, militiamen from the surrounding countryside watched the smoke rise. "Will you let them burn the town down?" shouted one man. Captain Isaac Davis replied, "I haven't a man that's afraid to go." Davis marched his volunteers down the hill. As they approached Concord's North Bridge, the British troops opened fire. Davis fell dead, a bullet through his heart.

The British expected the Americans to break and run. To their surprise, the Minutemen stood their ground and fired back. Two minutes later, it was the redcoats who were running away in panic.

The retreat back to Boston was a nightmare for the British. More than 4,000 armed and angry Minutemen lined their route, shooting at every redcoat they saw. By the end of the day, 74 British soldiers were dead and another 200 were wounded or missing. The colonists counted their own losses as 49 dead and 41 wounded. A British officer described what it was like to face the colonists' fury that day. "Whoever looks upon them as an irregular mob," the officer said, "will find himself much mistaken."

Indeed, since the French and Indian War, the British had been mistaken about the colonists again and again. Their biggest mistake was in thinking that ordinary people—farmers, merchants, workers, and housewives—would not fight for the rights that they held dear. At Lexington and Concord, Americans proved they were not only willing to fight for their rights. They were even willing to die for them.

Chapter Summary

In this chapter, you read about tensions between the colonies and Great Britain in the mid-1700s.

Before 1763 During the French and Indian War (1754–1763), Great Britain and France fought for territory and power. When the war ended, France gave up Canada to Great Britain. Great Britain now had a much larger American empire to control.

Early British Actions in the Colonies The war left Great Britain with huge debts. To raise money, Parliament passed the Stamp Act in 1765. Colonists protested the Stamp Act because it was passed without colonial representation. Colonists also protested the Quartering Act, which required them to house British troops at the colonies' expense.

The Townshend Acts and the Boston Massacre The Townshend Acts imposed more taxes on the colonies, which divided many colonists into opposing camps. Loyalists urged obedience to Great Britain, but Patriots resisted "taxation without representation" through protests, boycotts, and riots. Tensions in Boston erupted into violence in 1770 when British troops fired into a crowd of colonists in what become known as the Boston Massacre.

The Boston Tea Party and the Intolerable Acts When Patriots protested a new tax on tea by throwing tea into Boston Harbor in 1773, Great Britain responded by passing the Intolerable Acts to force the colonies to give in to British authority. Patriots responded by forming the First Continental Congress and organizing colonial militias.

Lexington and Concord Fighting between Patriots and British troops at Lexington and Concord in 1775 showed that colonists would not only fight for their rights, but were willing to die for them.

This stone marks the line where Minutemen faced British troops at the battle of Lexington. The stone is inscribed with the words of John Parker, captain of the Lexington Minutemen.

"I Love the Story of Paul Revere, Whether He Rode or Not"

So said President Warren G. Harding in 1923. Like most Americans at that time, Harding probably learned about Revere as a schoolboy when he read a poem by Henry Wadsworth Longfellow. Later, when a skeptic claimed the story of Revere's ride never happened, Harding sprang to the poet's defense. But was Revere the hero Longfellow made him out to be?

In 1860, the young nation whose fight for freedom began at Lexington and Concord was in danger of falling apart. War clouds gathered as Americans debated the issues of slavery and states' rights. The South, which had grown prosperous with slave labor, vigorously defended its way of life. The North, which had grown even more prosperous without slave labor, condemned slavery as morally wrong. Americans had never been so divided or so close to civil war.

Henry Wadsworth Longfellow was then the nation's most popular poet. He was also a Northerner who opposed slavery. As he watched the nation move toward war, Longfellow began thinking about a new poem. He wanted it to be a call to arms for all who loved liberty in such a time of peril.

One day in April 1860, Longfellow took a walk with a friend in Boston. His companion told him a story that took place on another April day, some 85 years earlier. It was the tale of a midnight ride made by a silversmith named Paul Revere to alert the countryside to coming danger. Longfellow was inspired. Like Paul Revere's ride, the poem he planned would be a cry of alarm to awaken a sleeping nation.

Longfellow set to work at once. His finished work, titled "Paul Revere's Ride," was published in 1861. Over the next century, generations of schoolchildren would read and memorize its stirring lines. As you read the excerpt that follows, can you see why the poem captured Americans' imaginations?

Poet Henry Wadsworth Longfellow

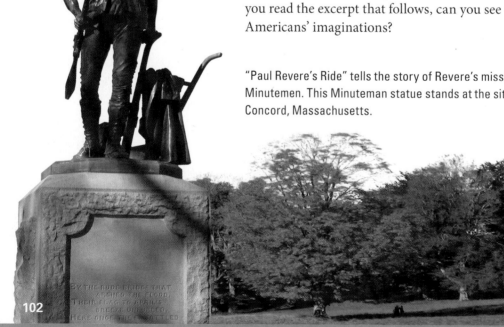

"Paul Revere's Ride" tells the story of Revere's mission to warn the Minutemen. This Minuteman statue stands at the site of the battle in Concord, Massachusetts.

Paul Revere's Ride

Listen, my children, and you shall hear
Of the midnight ride of Paul Revere,
On the eighteenth of April, in Seventy-five;
Hardly a man is now alive
Who remembers that famous day and year.

He said to his friend, "If the British march
By land or sea from the town to-night,
Hang a lantern aloft in the belfry arch
Of the North Church tower as a signal light—
One, if by land, and two, if by sea;
And I on the opposite shore will be,
Ready to ride and spread the alarm
Through every Middlesex village and farm,
For the country folk to be up and to arm."

Then he said, "Good night!" and with muffled oar
Silently rowed to the Charlestown shore . . .

And lo! as he looks, on the belfry's height
A glimmer, and then a gleam of light!
He springs to the saddle, the bridle he turns,
But lingers and gazes, till full on his sight
A second lamp in the belfry burns!

A hurry of hoofs in a village street,
A shape in the moonlight, a bulk in the dark,
And beneath, from the pebbles, in passing, a spark
Struck out by a steed flying fearless and fleet:
That was all! And yet, through the gloom and the light,
The fate of a nation was riding that night;
And the spark struck out by that steed, in his flight,
Kindled the land into flame with its heat . . .

It was one by the village clock,
When he galloped into Lexington.
He saw the gilded weathercock
Swim in the moonlight as he passed,
And the meeting-house windows, blank and bare,
Gaze at him with a spectral glare,
As if they already stood aghast
At the bloody work they would look upon.

It was two by the village clock,
When he came to the bridge in Concord town.
He heard the bleating of the flock . . .
And one was safe and asleep in his bed
Who at the bridge would be first to fall,
Who that day would be lying dead,
Pierced by a British musket-ball.

You know the rest. In the books you have read,
How the British Regulars fired and fled—
How the farmers gave them ball for ball,
From behind each fence and farm-yard wall,
Chasing the red-coats down the lane . . .

So through the night rode Paul Revere;
And so through the night went his cry of alarm
To every Middlesex village and farm—
A cry of defiance and not of fear,
A voice in the darkness, a knock at the door,
And a word that shall echo forevermore!
For borne on the night-wind of the Past,
Through all our history, to the last,
In the hour of darkness and peril and need,
The people will waken and listen to hear
The hurrying hoof-beats of that steed,
And the midnight message of Paul Revere.

This sheet music, for a song inspired by Longfellow's poem, was written in the early 1900s.

Over the years, American artists were drawn to the legend of Paul Revere. Most works, like this 19th-century painting, show Revere as a lone rider.

Longfellow Creates a Legend: The Lone Hero

Longfellow had set out to create a dramatic tale that would make patriotic hearts beat faster. In the process, he transformed Paul Revere from a local folk hero into a national legend. Even today, millions of Americans know the opening lines of Longfellow's poem.

> *Listen, my children, and you shall hear*
> *Of the midnight ride of Paul Revere,*

When we think of the events that launched the American Revolution, we can picture them clearly. Revere asks a friend to send a signal from Boston's Old North Church when the British troops quartered there begin to move out.

> *One, if by land, and two, if by sea;*
> *And I on the opposite shore will be,*

The signal comes and Revere gallops into the night, waking the countryside with the news that the British are coming.

> *So through the night rode Paul Revere;*
> *And so through the night went his cry of alarm*
> *To every Middlesex village and farm—*
> *A cry of defiance and not of fear,*
> *A voice in the darkness, a knock at the door,*
> *And a word that shall echo forevermore!*

Alerted by our lone hero, the colonists rise up to defend their homes and liberties.

> *You know the rest. In the books you have read,*
> *How the British Regulars fired and fled—*
> *How the farmers gave them ball for ball,*
> *From behind each fence and farm-yard wall . . .*

The rest, as they say, is history. Or is it?

Skeptics Raise Doubts: Did Revere Really Ride?

Historians were quick to point out many inaccuracies in Longfellow's telling. For example, the poet omitted the fact that, during his ride, Revere was captured by British troops. Longfellow also left out the names of other messengers who rode that night, such as William Dawes and Samuel Prescott.

As doubts about the poem multiplied, skeptics began to question the entire story. Some said Revere's ride didn't happen at all. Or if it did, Revere was captured before he could warn many Patriots. Such talk annoyed President Harding. "Somebody made the ride and stirred the minutemen in the colonies to fight the battle of Lexington," he said. "I love the story of Paul Revere, whether he rode or not."

As time passed, some doubters threw cold water on the idea that Revere was a hero. One skeptic said that Revere "set out with two other guys for money." When the three were arrested, he "turned stool pigeon and betrayed his two companions." Is this true? Was Revere a traitor to his cause?

The Granger Collection, New York

Paul Revere was well known as a silversmith and a Patriot. When Revere sat for this painting by John Singleton Copley, he chose to hold one of the teapots he had designed. Just five years later, he was one of the Sons of Liberty at the Boston Tea Party.

Historians Weigh In: The Real Meaning of Revere's Ride

Modern historians find no evidence that Revere was paid to ride or that he became an informer when he was captured. But they also remind us that Revere was not the only hero of that momentous night. Within hours of his ride, 122 colonists had lost their lives and many more lay wounded. As one historian writes,

> *Revere's ride was not the major event that day, nor was Revere's warning so critical in triggering the bloodbath. Patriotic farmers had been preparing to oppose the British for the better part of a year . . . His ride to Lexington . . . took on meaning only because numerous other political activists had, like Revere, dedicated themselves to the cause.*
>
> —Ray Raphael, *Founding Myths: Stories that Hide Our Patriotic Past*, 2004

The real meaning of Revere's ride is what it tells us about these unsung heroes. On hearing that the British soldiers were coming, those patriotic farmers had a choice. They could remain safe in their beds or rise up to defend their rights. Looking at their response, historian David Hackett Fischer writes, "The history of a free people is the history of hard choices. In that respect, when Paul Revere alarmed the Massachusetts countryside, he was carrying a message for us."

Chapter 6

The Declaration of Independence

What principles of government are expressed in the Declaration of Independence?

6.1 Introduction

The battles of Lexington and Concord marked the start of the fighting that would lead to independence from Great Britain. The day after the clashes, horseback riders galloped through the colonies with news of the "barbarous murders" of innocent militiamen. Most Americans were deeply shocked. More urgently than ever, they **debated** what the colonies should do about the trouble with Great Britain.

The choices were clear enough. The colonies could declare their independence. Or they could continue with protests and petitions, or formal requests. This second choice would keep the colonies at peace, but at what cost to the colonists' freedom?

No one was more outspoken in his support for independence than Patrick Henry of Virginia. After the passage of the Intolerable Acts, Henry delivered to the Virginia House of Burgesses one of the most famous speeches in American history.

"There is no longer any room for hope," he began. "If we wish to be free . . . we must fight! Our chains are forged! Their clanking may be heard on the plains of Boston. The war is inevitable—and let it come!"

Then Henry spoke to those who treasured peace above freedom:

> *Gentlemen may cry, Peace, peace—but there is no peace. The war is actually begun. The next gale that sweeps from the north will bring to our ears the clash of resounding arms! . . . What is it that gentlemen wish? . . . Is life so dear, or peace so sweet, as to be purchased at the price of chains and slavery? Forbid it, Almighty God! I know not what course others may take; but as for me, give me liberty, or give me death!*

Despite the passionate words of Patriots like Henry, most colonists remained unsure about separating from Great Britain. As you will read, only after the fighting started did they decide to declare independence.

Patrick Henry of Virginia gave a speech in May 1775 that helped lead the colonies closer to independence.

◀ The Declaration of Independence was adopted on July 4, 1776. This painting shows the committee that drafted the Declaration.

The Granger Collection, New York

Orderly rows of British soldiers marched up Breed's Hill and eventually defeated the American forces when the colonists ran out of gunpowder. The fierce fighting proved the British would not easily defeat the colonists.

6.2 The Colonists Organize an Army

On May 10, 1775, the Second Continental Congress met in Philadelphia. By then, New England militia had amassed around Boston. The first question facing Congress was who should command this "New England army." The obvious answer was a New Englander.

George Washington and the Continental Army John Adams of Massachusetts had another idea. He proposed that Congress create a "Continental army" made up of troops from all the colonies. To lead this army, Adams nominated "a Gentleman whose Skill and Experience as an Officer, whose . . . great Talents and excellent universal Character, would [unite] the colonies better than any other person" alive. That man was George Washington of Virginia, who had distinguished himself in the French and Indian War.

The delegates agreed. They unanimously elected Washington to be commander in chief of the new Continental army.

The Battle of Bunker Hill Meanwhile, militiamen near Boston made plans to fortify two hills that overlooked the city: Bunker Hill and Breed's Hill. On the night of June 16, 1775, Israel Putnam led a few hundred men up Breed's Hill. In four hours of furious digging, they erected a crude fort on the top of the hill.

The fort worried British general William Howe, who had just arrived from England with fresh troops. Howe ordered an immediate attack. Under a hot June sun, some 2,000 British troops formed two long lines at the base of Breed's Hill. At Howe's order, the redcoats marched up the slope.

As the lines moved ever closer, Putnam ordered his men, "Don't fire until you see the whites of their eyes." Only when the British were almost on top of them did the militiamen pull their triggers. The red lines broke and fell back in confusion.

The British regrouped and attacked again. Once more the Americans stopped their advance. On their third attack, the redcoats finally took the hill—but only because the Americans had used up all their gunpowder and pulled back.

This clash, which became known as the Battle of Bunker Hill, was short but very bloody. More than 1,000 British troops and nearly half that many Americans were killed or wounded.

General Washington Takes Command

George Washington took command of his new army shortly after the Battle of Bunker Hill. He found "a mixed multitude of people . . . under very little discipline, order, or government." Washington worked hard to **impose** order. One man wrote, "Everyone is made to know his place and keep in it . . . It is surprising how much work has been done."

A month later, however, a dismayed Washington learned that the army had only 36 barrels of gunpowder—enough for each soldier to fire just nine shots. To deceive the British, Washington started a rumor in Boston that he had 1,800 barrels of gunpowder—more than he knew what to do with! Luckily, the British believed the rumor. Meanwhile, Washington sent desperate letters to the colonies begging for gunpowder.

George Washington turned an undisciplined army, composed of troops from all the colonies, into an effective fighting force.

Washington got his powder. But he still did not dare attack the British forces in Boston. To do that he needed artillery—heavy guns, such as cannons—to bombard their defenses. In desperation, Washington sent a Boston bookseller named Henry Knox to Fort Ticonderoga to round up some big guns.

Ticonderoga was an old British fort located at the southern end of Lake Champlain in New York. A few months earlier, militiamen led by Ethan Allen and Benedict Arnold had seized the fort. The Americans had little use for the run-down fort, but its guns would prove priceless.

As winter set in, Knox loaded 59 cannons onto huge sleds and dragged them 300 miles to Boston. Knox's 42 sleds also carried 2,300 pounds of lead for making bullets. Boston was about to be under siege.

The British Abandon Boston

On March 4, 1776, the British soldiers in Boston awoke to a frightening sight. The night before, the ridges of nearby Dorchester Heights had been bare. Now they bristled with cannons, all aimed at the city.

Rather than risk another battle, General Howe abandoned the city. Within days, more than a hundred ships left Boston Harbor for Canada. The ships carried 9,000 British troops as well as 1,100 Loyalists who preferred to leave their homes behind rather than live with rebels.

Some Americans hoped the war was over. Washington, however, knew it was only the beginning.

independence freedom from control by another government or country

petition a formal, written request made to an official person or organization

Common Sense a pamphlet published in 1776 by Thomas Paine that persuaded many American colonists to support independence

Declaration of Independence the document written to declare the American colonies as an independent nation, free from British rule

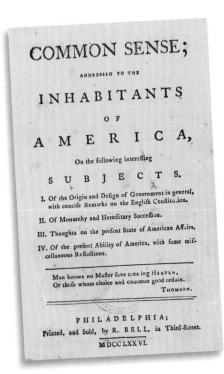

Thomas Paine published the pamphlet *Common Sense* to persuade colonists to support independence from Great Britain.

6.3 On the Eve of Independence

Nearly a year passed between the skirmishes at Lexington and Concord and the British retreat from Boston. During that time, there was little talk of **independence**. Most colonists still considered themselves loyal British subjects. Their quarrel was not with Great Britain itself but with its **policies** toward the colonies.

The Olive Branch Petition Many Americans pinned their hopes for peace on King George. In July 1775, the Second Continental Congress sent a **petition** to George III asking him to end the quarrel. John Adams called the petition an "olive branch." Olive tree branches are an ancient symbol of peace.

By the time the petition reached London, however, the king had declared the colonies to be in "open and avowed Rebellion." He ordered his ministers "to bring the Traitors to Justice."

Being called a traitor was enough to change the mind of one of Washington's generals. The general confessed that he had long "looked with some degree of horror on the scheme of separation." Now he agreed with Patrick Henry that colonists "must be Independent or Slaves."

Common Sense Many colonists, however, still looked with horror at the idea of independence. Then, early in 1776, a Patriot named Thomas Paine published a fiery pamphlet entitled *Common Sense*. Paine scoffed at the idea that Americans owed any loyalty to King George. "Of more worth is one honest man to society," he wrote, "than all the crowned ruffians who ever lived."

Paine also attacked the argument that the colonies' ties to Great Britain had benefited Americans. Just the opposite was true, he said. American trade had suffered under British control. Americans had also been hurt by being dragged into Great Britain's European wars.

Paine ended with a vision of an independent America as a homeland of liberty. "Ye that love mankind!" he urged. "Ye that dare oppose not only the tyranny, but the tyrant, stand forth! . . . The sun never shined on a cause of greater worth."

Within a few months, more than 120,000 copies of *Common Sense* were printed in the colonies. Paine's arguments helped persuade thousands of colonists that independence was not only sensible, but that it was the key to a brighter future.

6.4 Thomas Jefferson Drafts a Declaration

A few weeks after the British left Boston, the Second Continental Congress appointed a committee to write a declaration, or formal statement, of independence. The task of drafting the **Declaration of Independence** went to the committee's youngest member, 33-year-old Thomas Jefferson of Virginia. A shy man, Jefferson said little in Congress, but he stated his ideas brilliantly in writing.

Jefferson's job was to explain to the world why the colonies were choosing to separate from Britain. "When in the Course of human events," he began, if one group of people finds it necessary to break its ties with another, "a decent respect to the opinions of mankind" requires that they explain their actions.

Principles on Which to Base a New Government Jefferson's explanation was simple but revolutionary. Loyalists had argued that colonists had a duty to obey the king, whose authority came from God. Jefferson reasoned quite differently. He based his arguments on the principle of **natural rights**. All people are born equal in God's sight, he reasoned, and all are entitled to the same basic rights. In Jefferson's eloquent words,

> *We hold these truths to be self-evident, that all men are created equal, that they are endowed by their Creator with certain unalienable Rights, that among these are Life, Liberty, and the pursuit of Happiness.*

After Thomas Jefferson wrote the first draft of the Declaration of Independence, Benjamin Franklin and John Adams suggested changes.

Governments are formed, Jefferson said, "to secure these rights." Their power to rule comes from "the consent of the governed." If a government fails to protect people's **fundamental** rights, "it is the right of the people to alter or abolish it." The people can then create a new government that will protect "their Safety and Happiness."

The King's Crimes King George, Jefferson continued, had shown no concern for the rights of colonists. Instead, the king's policies had been aimed at establishing "an absolute Tyranny over these States" (the colonies).

As proof, Jefferson included a long list of the king's abuses. In all these actions, Jefferson claimed, George III had shown he was "unfit to be the ruler of a free people."

The time had come, Jefferson concluded, for the colonies' ties to Great Britain to be broken. "These United Colonies are," he declared, "and of Right ought to be Free and Independent States."

natural rights rights common to everyone, as opposed to those given by law

6.5 The Final Break

On July 1, 1776, the Second Continental Congress met in Philadelphia's State House to debate independence. By noon, the temperature outside had soared into the nineties, and a thunderstorm was gathering. Inside the State House, emotions were equally hot and stormy. By the end of the day, the issue was still undecided.

The next day was cooler and calmer. On July 2, all but one of the 13 colonies voted for independence. New York cast no vote.

No delegate was more excited about the colonies' decision than John Adams. He wrote to his wife Abigail, "The second Day of July . . . will be celebrated, by succeeding Generations, with Pomp and Parade, with Shews (shows), Games, Sports, Guns, Bells, Bonfires and Illuminations, from one End of this Continent to the other from this Time forward forever more."

Debate over Slavery Adams was wrong about the date that would be celebrated as America's birthday, but only because Congress decided to revise Jefferson's declaration. The delegates liked most of what they read, except for a passage on slavery. Jefferson had charged King George with violating the "sacred rights of life and liberty . . . of a distant people [by] carrying them into slavery."

Almost no one liked this passage. Southerners feared that it might lead to demands to free the slaves. Enslaved Africans provided much of the labor used on southern farms. Northerners worried that New England merchants, who benefited from the slave trade, might be offended. Even delegates who opposed slavery felt it was unfair to blame the king for enslaving Africans. The passage was removed.

Any mention of slavery was removed from the Declaration of Independence because the slave trade was important to the economy of many colonies. In the triangular trade shown here, rum and iron were shipped from New England to Africa. In Africa, these products were exchanged for slaves. The slaves were taken to the West Indies, where many were traded for molasses and sugar. Finally, molasses, sugar, and remaining slaves were brought to New England.

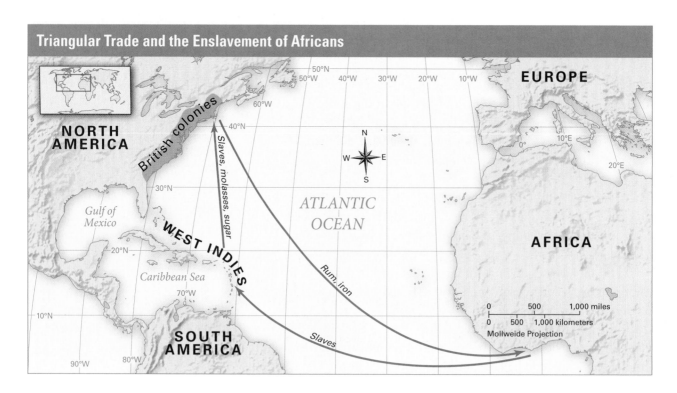

Triangular Trade and the Enslavement of Africans

This poster shows the delegates leaving Independence Hall in Philadelphia to announce the signing of the Declaration of Independence.

Independence Day On July 4, the delegates approved a final version of the Declaration of Independence. When they signed the document, they pledged to support independence with "our Lives, our Fortunes, and our sacred Honor."

This was a serious pledge. Every signer understood that he was committing an act of treason against Great Britain. If the new nation failed to win its freedom, each of them could very well end up swinging from a hangman's rope. Knowing this, Benjamin Franklin told the delegates, "We must all hang together, or assuredly we shall all hang separately."

Chapter Summary

In this chapter, you read how the American colonies took the dramatic step of declaring their independence.

The Colonists Organize an Army George Washington took command of the Continental Army after the Battle of Bunker Hill. The Continental Army used cannons brought from Fort Ticonderoga in New York to force the British to abandon Boston in March 1776.

On the Eve of Independence The failure of the Olive Branch Petition and the success of Thomas Paine's pamphlet *Common Sense* moved the colonies closer to the decision to declare independence from Great Britain.

Thomas Jefferson Drafts a Declaration Thomas Jefferson, a delegate to the Second Continental Congress, was selected to write the Declaration of Independence.

The Final Break On July 4, 1776, the delegates approved the Declaration of Independence. For the first time in history, a government was being established on the principle of people's natural rights and the duty of government to honor those rights.

Little in Thomas Paine's early life gave a hint of his future importance. Yet his pamphlet *Common Sense* would help stir the fires of American independence.

The Power of Common Sense

In January 1776, the pamphlet *Common Sense* was published in Philadelphia. The document caused an immediate sensation. In powerful language, the writer Thomas Paine made a compelling case for separation from Great Britain. Paine had not been in the colonies for long. But his call for an end to British rule would help pave the way for American independence.

On November 30, 1774, the ship *London Packet* arrived in the port of Philadelphia. On board was a 37-year-old Englishman named Thomas Paine. Paine was not even aware that he had landed in America. He was burning up with fever and was barely conscious. He had caught the deadly disease typhus, which had already killed several people on board.

At the time, disease was just one of the perils of travel across the Atlantic. Violent storms, collisions with icebergs, and pirate attacks were other hazards. One ship took so long to cross the ocean that the food ran out and many of the passengers starved to death.

Paine was lucky to be alive, but he was still very ill. Unable to walk, he was carried ashore in a blanket. A local doctor agreed to nurse him back to health.

It was not a promising start to life in America. But then, not very much in Paine's life *had* gone well. He had held—and lost—a number of different jobs. He had been a craftsman, a teacher, a tax collector, and a shopkeeper. In the end, though, he had little to show for his efforts. He had no money and few prospects. But he did have one important asset for his new life: letters of introduction from Benjamin Franklin.

Paine had met Franklin in London and had impressed him with his sharp mind and his interest in science and politics. Franklin encouraged Paine to move to Pennsylvania and gave him letters of reference, calling him "an ingenious, worthy young man." These letters would help Paine start a new life.

Paine Finds His Calling

Paine had arrived in the largest and most prosperous city in colonial America. Philadelphia was a bustling place of around 30,000 people and the third largest port in the British Empire. Set along the banks of the Delaware River, Philadelphia was the financial and cultural capital of the colonies. It was also a center of political activity. In fact, the Continental Congress had held its first meeting there not long before Paine's arrival. The city was buzzing with talk of politics.

With the help of Franklin's introduction, Paine soon landed a job as the editor of a new magazine. He had already done some writing in England. But it was here that he discovered his true calling as a writer. Paine soon made his publication, *Pennsylvania Magazine,* the most widely read magazine in the colonies.

Magazines were fairly new at the time. But along with pamphlets, they were becoming increasingly popular. They were quicker and cheaper to publish than books, and that kept their price low. They also offered the space to cover issues in greater detail than newspapers could. This made them appealing to a public that had a growing appetite for information.

At first, Paine wrote articles mainly about cultural and scientific subjects. But he soon moved on to political topics. Paine's years as a tax collector had left him with no love for the British government. His articles criticized British officials and colonial rule. These stories did not please the Loyalist citizens of Philadelphia, who favored strong ties to Great Britain. On the other hand, they did appeal to readers with Patriot sympathies.

One of these readers was Benjamin Rush, a doctor who would later play a key role in the independence struggle. Rush encouraged Paine to write a pamphlet on independence, though he cautioned him not to use that word. The idea of independence made many colonists uneasy. They might complain about British rule, but the prospect of separating from Great Britain scared them. It did not scare Paine, though. In October 1775, he began working on the essay he would call *Common Sense.*

Philadelphia in the 1770s was a beautiful city with brick streets and fine buildings. Chestnut Street, shown here, was at the center of the city.

An Appeal to Common Sense

By December, Paine had finished his essay. But he had trouble getting it published. The subject of independence was just too hot for many publishers to handle. As Paine noted at the time, colonists were so attached to Great Britain that it was "a kind of treason to speak against it."

Eventually, however, Paine found a publisher who agreed to print a thousand copies as a pamphlet. It was 46 pages long. The pamphlet did not have Paine's name on the cover, but simply said, "written by an Englishman." On January 10, 1776, *Common Sense* appeared in bookstores.

What happened next was astonishing. The first edition sold out in days. Paine had more copies printed, and those sold out, too. Within a few months, readers had bought more than 120,000 copies of *Common Sense*. By the end of the year, 25 editions had been printed. Hundreds of thousands of copies were in circulation throughout the colonies. It is estimated that as many as half of all colonial citizens had either read the pamphlet or had it read to them. *Common Sense* was a runaway success. And Thomas Paine was America's first bestselling author.

What explains this stunning result? Evidently, Paine had touched a nerve. The public was not as resistant to the idea of independence as he and others had feared. Paine's success lay in his ability to present separation as logical and reasonable, as a matter of common sense. He used language that was direct, clear, and powerful. Drawing on the shared experience of colonists, he built a persuasive case for independence. "The sun never shined on a cause of greater worth," he wrote.

> 'Tis not the affair of a city, a country, a province, or a kingdom, but of a continent . . . 'Tis not the concern of a day, a year, or an age . . . Now is the seed-time of continental union, faith, and honor.

One reader in Connecticut wrote, "You have declared the sentiments of millions . . . We were blind, but on reading these enlightening words the scales have fallen from our eyes."

Printers like Robert Bell, who first published *Common Sense,* helped spread the message of independence. Bell and Paine made money on the best seller. But Paine donated all of his profits to the Continental army.

Paine recognized that the main obstacle to independence among colonists was their continued loyalty to the king and crown. So he set out to demolish that loyalty. As one Paine biographer wrote, "*Common Sense* could be considered the first American self-help book, the help being for those who could never imagine life without a monarch."

Paine began by ridiculing the notion that kings had some special, God-given right to rule over their subjects. He called the king the "royal brute of England" and said, "Even brutes do not devour their young, nor savages make war upon their families." He linked the problems of life in the colonies to the evils of British rule and argued that Americans would be much better off on their own. "Everything that is right or natural pleads for separation," he declared. "The blood of the slain, the weeping voice of nature cries, 'tis time to part."

Paine argued that the colonists should unite around a common goal, to create a self-governing nation based on principles of liberty. "We have it in our power to begin the world over again," he wrote. "The birthday of a new world is at hand." And in one stirring passage, he called on America to make itself the refuge of freedom:

> *Every spot of the old world is overrun with oppression. Freedom hath been hunted round the globe. Asia and Africa have long expelled her. Europe regards her like a stranger, and England hath given her warning to depart. O! receive the fugitive, and prepare in time an asylum for mankind.*

The Impact of *Common Sense*

Although Paine's words were powerful, his ideas were not new. Many other colonial leaders, such as Benjamin Franklin, Thomas Jefferson, and John Adams, had expressed similar thoughts. But Paine was able to put those ideas together in a single, compelling argument that spoke to a mass audience. As Benjamin Rush noted, the ideas that Paine put forth in *Common Sense* had previously lain "like stones in a field, useless 'til collected and arranged in a building."

Common Sense did not start the movement for independence. That movement had been building for some time. Nor did it cause colonial leaders to declare independence. Another six months would pass before the Declaration of Independence was issued. But Paine's work opened up the debate on separation from Great Britain. It helped many colonists see independence as a real possibility.

Paine's ideas on rights and liberty also had an influence on other countries, particularly France. In fact, Paine later moved to France to play a role in the French Revolution. He also wrote several books, including *The Rights of Man*. But none of his other works would have quite the impact as *Common Sense,* the pamphlet that helped pave the way for American independence.

Paine believed that his most important message was the attack on King George III. This painting, from 1767, depicts the king in all his royal glory. It shows a formality that had become foreign to his subjects in America.

Chapter 7

The American Revolution

How was the Continental army able to win the war for independence from Great Britain?

7.1 Introduction

When the American war for independence from Great Britain began in 1775, 15-year-old Joseph Martin was too young to join the Continental army. But when recruiters returned to his Connecticut village a year later, he was ready to go.

The recruiters were looking for volunteers to go to New York, where the British were rumored to have 15,000 troops. "I did not care if there had been fifteen times fifteen thousand," Martin said later. "I never spent a thought about numbers. The Americans were invincible, in my opinion."

Just two days after the Declaration of Independence was signed, Martin traded his plow for a musket, an early type of rifle. A week later, he arrived in New York City, where he hoped to "snuff [sniff] a little gunpowder." As he recalled, "I was now, what I had long wished to be, a soldier; I had obtained my heart's desire; it was now my business to prove myself equal to my profession."

If Martin had known what lay ahead, he might not have been so pleased about his new profession. The army in New York was ill trained, ill equipped, and just plain ill. "Almost the whole regiment are sick," reported a Massachusetts officer of his unit.

The British army, in contrast, was well trained, well equipped, and well supported by the British navy. Rather than the 15,000 troops Martin had heard of, the British had assembled a force of 25,000 men in New York. More than 400 British ships floated in the harbor. This was the biggest army and the largest fleet the British had ever sent overseas.

In the face of such overwhelming force, the Americans should have been easily defeated. But they were not. In this chapter, you will read how soldiers like Joseph Martin stood up to mighty Great Britain in a successful revolution that created a new nation.

This painting shows British troops in battle during the American Revolution. Compare this painting to the one on the opposite page. What differences do you see between the soldiers in these two armies?

◀ This painting shows American soldiers at the Battle of Brandywine in 1777 during the war for independence from Great Britain.

At the beginning of the war, American soldiers were poorly trained and poorly equipped. They lacked gunpowder, rifles, food, and clothing. Some men had only spears or axes for weapons.

American Revolution the struggle of the colonies in North America to gain their independence from Great Britain

Continental army the American army during the American Revolution

7.2 American Strengths and Weaknesses

The Patriots were in a weak position when the **American Revolution** began. They had a hastily organized, untrained army and a small navy. Their weaknesses were far more obvious than their strengths.

American Weaknesses The **Continental army** was always short of men. General George Washington never had more than 20,000 troops at one time and place. Many soldiers enlisted for six months or a year. Just when they were learning how to fight, they would pick up their muskets and go home to take care of their farms and families.

Few Americans were trained for battle. Some were hunters and could shoot well enough from behind a tree. But when facing a mass of well-disciplined redcoats, they were likely to turn and run.

The army was plagued by shortages. Guns and gunpowder were so scarce that Benjamin Franklin suggested arming the troops with bows and arrows. Food shortages forced soldiers to beg for handouts. Uniforms were scarce as well. In winter, one could track shoeless soldiers by their bloody footprints in the snow.

Such shortages outraged Washington. But when he complained to the Second Continental Congress, nothing changed. Congress, the new nation's only government, lacked the power to raise money for supplies by taxing the colonies—now the new nation's states.

In desperation, Congress printed paper money to pay for the war. But the value of this money dropped so low that merchants demanded to be paid in gold instead. Like everything else, gold was scarce.

American Strengths Still, the Americans did have strengths. One was the patriotism of people like Joseph Martin, who willingly gave their lives to defend the ideal of a country based on liberty and **democracy**. Without them, the war would have been quickly lost.

The Americans also received help from overseas. Motivated by their old hatred of the English, the French secretly aided the Americans. During the first two years of the war, 90 percent of the Americans' gunpowder came from Europe, mostly from France. In addition, a Polish Jew named Haym Salomon, who immigrated to New York in 1775, helped to finance the war effort.

The Americans' other great strength was their commander. General Washington was more than an experienced military leader. He was also a man who inspired courage and confidence. In the dark days to come, it was Washington who would keep the ragtag Continental army together.

7.3 British Strengths and Weaknesses

In contrast to the American colonies, Great Britain entered the war from a position of strength. Yet, despite both their real and their perceived advantages, the British forces encountered many problems.

British Strengths With a professional army of about 42,000 troops at the beginning of the war, British forces greatly outnumbered the Continental army. In addition, George III hired 30,000 mercenaries from Germany. These hired soldiers were known as Hessians (HEH-shenz) because they came from a part of Germany called Hesse-Cassel. The British were also able to recruit many Loyalists, African Americans, and American Indians to fight on their side.

British and Hessian troops were well trained in European military tactics. They excelled in large battles fought by a mass of troops on open ground. They also had far more experience firing artillery than Americans had.

The British forces were well supplied, as well. Unlike the pitifully equipped Continental army, they seldom lacked for food, uniforms, weapons, or ammunition.

British Weaknesses Even so, the war presented Great Britain with huge problems. One was the distance between Great Britain and America. Sending troops and supplies across the Atlantic was slow and costly. News of battles arrived in England long after they had occurred, making it difficult for British leaders to plan a course of action.

A second problem was that King George and his ministers were never able to convince the British people that defeating the rebels was vital to the future of Great Britain. The longer the war dragged on, the less happy the British taxpayers became about paying its heavy costs.

A third problem was poor leadership. Lord George Germain, the man chosen to direct the British troops, had no real sense of how to defeat the rebels. How could he? He had never set foot in North America. Nor did it occur to him to go see for himself what his army was up against. If he had, Germain might have realized that this was not a war that could be won by conquering a city or two.

To end the revolution, Germain's forces would have to crush the Patriots' will to fight, state by state. Instead, Germain kept changing plans and generals, hoping that some combination of the two would bring him an easy victory.

British soldiers were trained professionals. They were well equipped with plenty of ammunition, good muskets, adequate food, and uniforms.

7.4 Great Britain Almost Wins the War

After the British abandoned Boston in the spring of 1776, Germain came up with his first plan for winning the war. British forces in America, led by General William Howe, were ordered to capture New York City. From that base, British troops would then move north to destroy the **rebellion** at its heart: Massachusetts.

To block the British invasion, Washington hurried with his army from Boston to New York. It was there that he heard the good news: by signing the Declaration of Independence, Congress had finally declared the colonies to be "free and independent states."

Washington had the Declaration of Independence read aloud to his troops. The time had come, he said, to "show our enemies, and the whole world, that free men, contending for their own land, are superior to any mercenaries on Earth." The Declaration made it clear that the troops had the support of all the colonies, who agreed that independence was a prize worth fighting for.

African Americans and the War For African Americans, however, the Declaration of Independence raised both hopes and questions. Did Jefferson's words "all men are created equal" apply to them? Would independence bring an end to slavery? Should they join the revolution?

Even before independence was declared, a number of African Americans had joined the Patriot cause. Black militiamen, both free and slave, fought at Lexington, Concord, and Bunker Hill. Early in the war, however, blacks were banned from the Continental army. Washington did not want the army to become a haven for runaway slaves.

In contrast, the British promised freedom to all slaves who took up arms for the king. As a result, thousands of runaways became Loyalists and fought for Great Britain.

A shortage of volunteers soon forced Washington to change his mind. By 1779, about 15 percent of the soldiers in the Continental army were African Americans. Large numbers of black sailors also served in the Continental navy.

As black Americans joined the war effort, some whites began to question their own beliefs. How could they accept slavery if they truly believed that all people are created equal, with the same rights to life, liberty, and happiness? By the war's end, Vermont, Connecticut, Massachusetts, New Hampshire, Rhode Island, and Pennsylvania had all taken steps to end slavery.

African Americans faced a difficult decision during the revolution. Which country was more likely to give them freedom at the end of the war, America or Great Britain? Many blacks chose to fight with the Americans. With their help, the Continental army defeated the British at the Battle of Cowpens in South Carolina, pictured below.

Defeat in New York On August 27, 1776, the American and British armies met in Brooklyn, New York, for what promised to be a decisive battle. The Americans began their defense of the city in high spirits. But the inexperienced Americans were no match for the British, with their greater numbers and superior training. In two days of fighting, the British lost only 377 men, while the Americans lost 1,407.

Satisfied that the war was nearly won, Howe ordered a halt to the British attack. Washington, he assumed, would do what any self-respecting European general would do in a hopeless situation. He would surrender honorably. And so Howe waited.

Washington had no intention of giving up. But for his army to survive, he would have to retreat. Even though Washington knew this, he could not bring himself to utter the word retreat.

An officer named Thomas Mifflin rescued him from his pride. "What is your strength?" Mifflin asked. "Nine thousand," Washington replied. "It is not sufficient," said Mifflin bluntly. "We must retreat."

Fading Hopes The battle for New York City was the first of many defeats for the Americans. In the weeks that followed, British forces chased the Americans out of New York, through New Jersey, and finally across the Delaware River into Pennsylvania.

For Joseph Martin and his comrades, this was a trying time. There was little food to eat, and the soldiers grew weak from hunger. As the weather turned cold, muddy roads and icy streams added to their misery. With their terms of enlistment nearly up, many soldiers headed for home. Along the way, they spread the word that anyone who volunteered to risk his life in the Continental army had to be crazy.

By the time Washington reached Pennsylvania, only a few thousand men were still under his command. Many of his remaining troops, he reported, were "entirely naked and most so thinly clad [clothed] as to be unfit for service." More troops had to be found, and found quickly, he wrote his brother. Otherwise, "I think the game will be pretty well up."

While chasing the retreating Continental army, British soldiers looted the homes of Americans, both Patriots and Loyalists. Such actions turned many former supporters into enemies.

7.5 A Pep Talk and Surprise Victories

By the end of 1776, the British also thought the war was just about over. General Howe offered to pardon all rebels who signed a statement promising to "remain in peaceful obedience" to the king. Thousands took him up on his offer.

The Crisis Washington knew he had to do something—quickly. Gathering his last troops together, he read to them from Thomas Paine's new pamphlet, *The Crisis.*

> *These are the times that try men's souls. The summer soldier and the sunshine patriot will, in this crisis, shrink from the service of their country; but he that stands it now, deserves the love and thanks of man and woman.*

Next, Washington outlined a daring plan to attack Hessian troops who were camped for the winter in Trenton, New Jersey. Heartened by Thomas Paine's words, his men did not "shrink from the service of their country."

With morale low and his soldiers threatening to return home, George Washington planned a daring attack on the Hessians at Trenton. Crossing the ice-choked Delaware River at night, he surprised the enemy, overwhelming them completely.

Victory in Trenton Late on December 25, 1776, Washington's army crossed the ice-choked Delaware River in small boats. On the New Jersey shore, Washington gave his men the password for the long nighttime march ahead: "Victory or death."

As the American troops made their way toward Trenton, a driving snow chilled them to the bone. Ice and rocks cut through their worn-out shoes. One officer reported to Washington that the troops' guns were too wet to fire. "Use the bayonets," the general replied. "The town must be taken."

When the Americans reached Trenton, they found the Hessians happily sleeping off their Christmas feasts. Caught completely by surprise, the mercenaries surrendered. Washington took 868 prisoners without losing even a single man. A week later, the Americans captured another 300 British troops at Princeton, New Jersey. These defeats convinced Howe that it would take more than capturing New York City and **issuing** pardons to win the war.

News of Washington's victories electrified Patriots. "A few days ago they had given up their cause for lost," wrote an unhappy Loyalist. "Their late successes have turned the scale and they are all liberty mad again." The game was not yet up.

7.6 The Tide Begins to Turn

When the American Revolution began, both sides adopted the same military **strategy,** or overall plan for winning the war. That strategy was to defeat the enemy in one big battle.

After barely escaping from his loss in New York, Washington revised his strategy. In the future, he wrote Congress, he would avoid large battles that might put his army at risk. Instead, the war would be "defensive." Rather than defeating the British, Washington hoped to tire them out.

A New British Strategy Germain revised the British strategy as well. His new plan was to divide the rebels by taking control of New York's Hudson River Valley. Control of this waterway would allow the British to cut New England off from the rest of the states. Without men and supplies from the New England states, the Continental army would surely collapse.

To carry out this plan, General John Burgoyne (ber-GOIN) left Canada in June 1777 with about 8,000 British soldiers and American Indian warriors. He planned to move this army south to Albany, New York. There he would meet up with General Howe, who was supposed to march his army north from New York City.

Problems with Burgoyne's Plan There were two big problems with Burgoyne's plan. The first was that what looked like an easy invasion route on a map was anything but easy. The route Burgoyne chose from Canada to Albany took his army through more than 20 miles of tangled wilderness. His army had to build bridges, chop down countless trees, and lay out miles of log roads through swamps as it crept toward Albany.

To make matters worse, Burgoyne didn't travel light. His army was slowed by more than 600 wagons, 30 of them filled with his personal baggage. Even in the wilderness, "Gentleman Johnny" Burgoyne sipped champagne with his supper.

The second problem with Burgoyne's plan was that General Howe had his own ideas about how to win the war. Instead of marching to Albany, Howe headed for Philadelphia, the rebels' capital. There he hoped to lure Washington into another major battle. Howe hoped it would be the last one.

Washington, however, refused to risk his army in another big battle. He would not fight for Philadelphia. Instead, he played hide-and-seek with Howe, attacking here and there and then disappearing into the countryside.

Catherine Schulyer was the wife of Philip Schulyer, a major general in the Continental army and a member of the Continental Congress. They lived near Albany, in the path of British forces advancing toward Saratoga. To leave nothing useful for the British, Catherine burned the family wheat fields.

strategy an overall plan, such as for winning a war

ally a nation that joins another nation in some common effort, such as fighting a war

A Turning Point By the time the slow-moving Burgoyne finally reached Saratoga Springs on the Hudson River, the area was swarming with militia. Although the rebels outnumbered his army, Burgoyne ordered an attack. Again and again the rebels beat back Burgoyne's troops. On October 17, 1777, Burgoyne accepted defeat.

Burgoyne's surrender marked a turning point in the war. Before the victory at Saratoga, most of the world believed that the American cause was hopeless. Now the Americans had shown they could stand up to a British army and win.

Not long after this victory, France came into the war as an **ally** of the United States. The French government sent money, weapons, troops, and warships to the Americans. Spain also entered the war against Great Britain. The American cause no longer looked quite so hopeless.

Winter at Valley Forge Saratoga was a stunning victory, but the war was far from over. While General Washington's army roamed the countryside, Howe's forces still occupied Philadelphia.

Late in 1777, Congress declared a day of thanksgiving for the army's successes. By this time, Washington and his army were on their way to Valley Forge, Pennsylvania, to make camp for the winter. Joseph Martin described the army's "celebration":

We had nothing to eat for two or three days previous . . . But we must now have what Congress said, a sumptuous [lavish] Thanksgiving . . . It gave each and every man a gill [a few ounces] of rice and a tablespoon of vinegar! The army was now not only starved but naked. The greatest part were not only shirtless and barefoot, but destitute of [without] all other clothing, especially blankets.

George Washington is shown at right with the Marquis de Lafayette at Valley Forge. Lafayette, a Frenchman who aided the Americans, described the American soldiers there as "in want of everything; they had neither coats, nor hats, nor shirts nor shoes; their feet and their legs froze until they grew black."

Washington's troops were hungry because many farmers preferred to sell food to the British. The British paid them in gold, whereas Congress paid them in paper money. As for uniforms and blankets, merchants had raised the prices for these items sky-high. This desire for profits at the army's expense outraged Washington. "No punishment," he fumed, "is too great for the man who can build his greatness upon his country's ruin."

To help lift his men from their misery, Washington put

Baron Friedrich von Steuben (FREE-drik von STU-bin) in charge of training. A military officer from Prussia (in modern-day Germany), von Steuben arrived in December 1777 and set to work turning the Continental army into an organized fighting force. The Prussian's method, wrote Martin, was "continual drill." It worked wonders. "The army grows stronger every day," wrote one officer. "There is a spirit of discipline among the troops that is better than numbers."

Another foreign volunteer, the Marquis de Lafayette (mar-KEE duh la-fey-ET), also helped raise the troops' spirits. Although he was one of the richest men in France, Lafayette chose to share the hardships of Valley Forge. He even used his own money to buy the men warm clothing. "The patient fortitude [courage] of the officers and soldiers," Lafayette wrote, "was a continual miracle."

When at last spring arrived, Washington received news that the British were about to abandon Philadelphia. The time had come to put his newly trained army to the test.

The Battle of Monmouth By this time, Sir Henry Clinton had replaced General Howe as commander of the British forces in North America. In Clinton's view, taking over Philadelphia had gained the British nothing. He ordered his army to retreat to New York City, where the Royal Navy could keep it supplied by sea.

Now it was Washington's turn to chase an army across New Jersey. On June 28, 1778, he caught up with the retreating British near Monmouth, New Jersey. In the battle that followed, Washington seemed to be everywhere, constantly rallying his men to stand and fight. "Cheering them by his voice and example," wrote Lafayette, "never had I beheld [seen] so superb a man."

Late that night, the British slipped across the Hudson River to safety in New York City. Washington camped with his army nearby. It was pleasing, he wrote, "that after two years maneuvering . . . both armies are brought back to the very point they set out from." Neither army knew it yet, but the war in the North was over.

At the Battle of Monmouth in New Jersey, George Washington led his troops in an attack on retreating British forces. Although the Americans won, the British were able to slip away during the night and sail safely to New York.

This engraving shows Francis Marion crossing the Pee Dee River in South Carolina. Marion, known as the "Swamp Fox" because of his tactic of ambushing the British from the marshes of the South, never led a force of more than 70 men.

7.7   The War Moves South

After failing to conquer any state in the North, the British changed strategies yet again. Their new plan was to move the war to the South. There, they believed, thousands of Loyalists were just waiting to join the king's cause.

Clinton began his "southern campaign" with a successful attack on Savannah, Georgia. From Georgia, he moved north to take control of North and South Carolina. At that point, Clinton returned to New York City, leaving Lord Charles Cornwallis to control the war in the South.

Saving the South   Cornwallis soon learned that he did not really control the Carolinas after all. Guerrillas—soldiers who are not part of a regular army—kept the American cause alive. One of them was Francis Marion, who was also known as the "Swamp Fox." Marion's band of rebels harassed the British with hit-and-run raids. They attacked and then faded into the swamps and forests like foxes.

Late in 1780, Washington sent General Nathanael Greene to slow the British advance through the South. Greene's army was too small to meet Cornwallis in a major battle. Instead, Greene led Cornwallis's troops on an exhausting chase through the southern backcountry. He wrote of his strategy, "We fight, get beat, rise, and fight again."

Greene's strategy worked wonderfully. In April 1781, Cornwallis wrote that he was "quite tired of marching about the country." He moved his army to Yorktown, a sleepy tobacco port on Chesapeake Bay in Virginia, for a good rest.

A Trap at Yorktown   By the time Cornwallis was settling into Yorktown, France had sent nearly 5,000 troops to join Washington's army in New York. In August, Washington learned that another 3,000 troops were scheduled to arrive soon in 29 French warships.

Washington used this information to set a trap for Cornwallis. Secretly, he moved his army south to Virginia. When they arrived, they joined the French and surrounded Yorktown on land with more than 16,000 troops.

Meanwhile, the French warships showed up just in time to seal off the entrance to Chesapeake Bay. Their appearance was **crucial** to the American victory. Now Cornwallis was cut off from the British navy and any hope of rescue by sea.

The trap was sprung on October 6, 1781. Joseph Martin watched as a flag was raised to signal that American and French gunners should open fire on Yorktown. "I confess I felt a secret pride swell in my heart," he wrote, "when I saw the 'star-spangled banner' waving majestically." The shelling went on for days, until "most of the guns in the enemy's works were silenced."

Three groups—the British, the Americans, and the French—were involved in the Battle of Yorktown. The Americans, with the aid of the French, were able to surround the British by using forces on both land and sea.

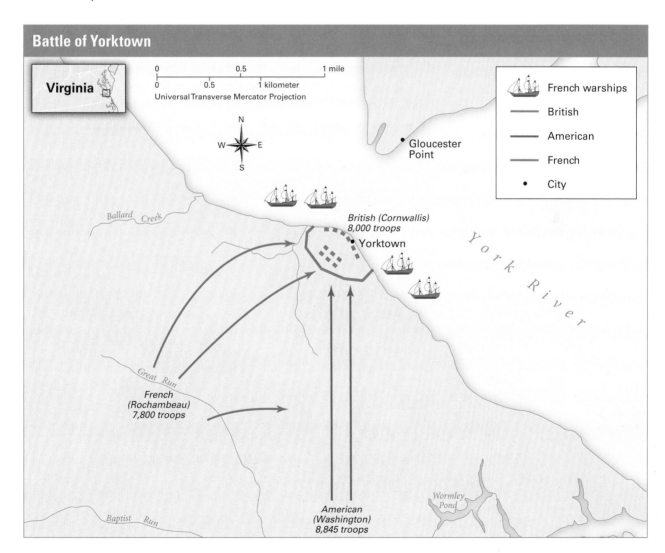

Battle of Yorktown

Virginia

0   0.5   1 mile
0   0.5   1 kilometer
Universal Transverse Mercator Projection

French warships
British
American
French
City

Ballard Creek

Gloucester Point

British (Cornwallis) 8,000 troops

Yorktown

York River

Great Run

French (Rochambeau) 7,800 troops

Baptist Run

American (Washington) 8,845 troops

Wormley Pond

Cornwallis Surrenders At first Cornwallis clung to the hope that the British navy would come to his rescue, even as Yorktown was exploding around him. When no ships arrived, he finally agreed to surrender.

On October 19, 1781, American and French troops formed two long lines that stretched for more than a mile along the road to Yorktown—the French on one side and the Americans on the other. The two lines could not have looked more different. The French were dressed in elegant uniforms that gleamed with gold and silver braid in the afternoon sun. The Americans' uniforms—and not everyone even had uniforms—were patched and faded. Behind the lines stood civilians who had traveled for miles to witness the surrender.

After hours of waiting, the crowd watched as 8,000 British troops left Yorktown to lay down their arms. The defeated troops moved "with slow and solemn step." They were accompanied by a slow tune known as "The World Turned Upside Down." This same sad tune had been played at Saratoga after the British surrender.

Cornwallis did not take part in this ceremony, saying that he was ill. In reality, the British commander could not bear to surrender publicly to an army that he looked down on as "a contemptible and undisciplined rabble [mob]." While Cornwallis sulked in his tent, his men surrendered their arms. Many of them wept bitter tears.

To the watching Americans, there was nothing sad about that day. "It was a noble sight to us," wrote Martin, "and the more so, as it seemed to promise a speedy conclusion to the contest."

This painting by John Trumbull shows the British surrender at Yorktown. At the center is General Benjamin Lincoln leading the British. General Washington is on the right, in front of the American flag. On the left are French, Polish, and Prussian soldiers.

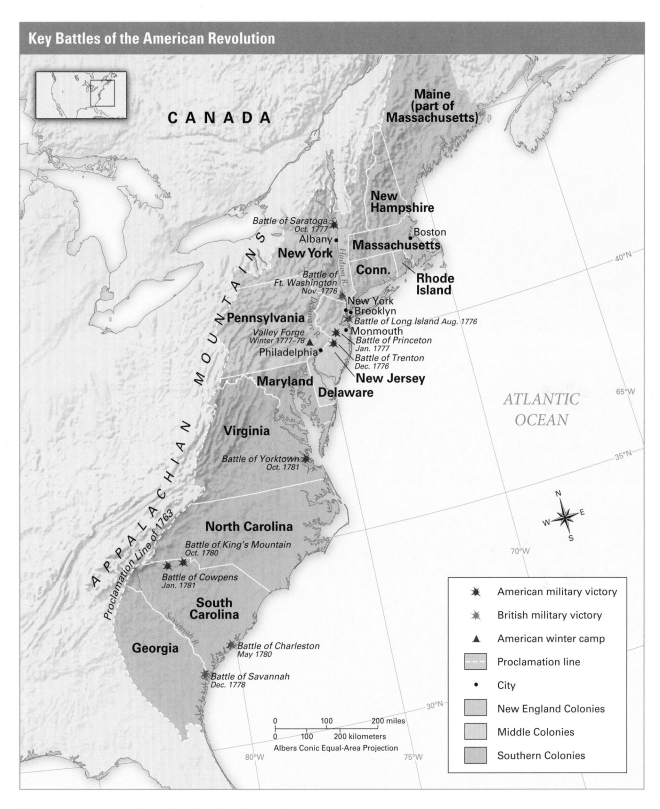

Key Battles of the American Revolution

CANADA

Maine
(part of
Massachusetts)

New
Hampshire

*Battle of Saratoga
Oct. 1777*

Albany •

New York

Massachusetts

• Boston

Conn.

*Battle of
Ft. Washington
Nov. 1776*

Rhode
Island

New York •
• Brooklyn

Pennsylvania

Battle of Long Island Aug. 1776

• Monmouth

*Valley Forge
Winter 1777–78* ▲

*Battle of Princeton
Jan. 1777*

Philadelphia •

*Battle of Trenton
Dec. 1776*

New Jersey

Maryland

Delaware

ATLANTIC
OCEAN

Virginia

*Battle of Yorktown
Oct. 1781*

APPALACHIAN MOUNTAINS

North Carolina

*Battle of King's Mountain
Oct. 1780*

Proclamation Line of 1763

*Battle of Cowpens
Jan. 1781*

South
Carolina

Georgia

*Battle of Charleston
May 1780*

*Battle of Savannah
Dec. 1778*

Hudson R.

Delaware R.

Savannah R.

40°N

65°W

35°N

70°W

30°N

80°W   75°W

N
W   E
S

0   100   200 miles
0   100   200 kilometers
Albers Conic Equal-Area Projection

✸	American military victory
✷	British military victory
▲	American winter camp
----	Proclamation line
•	City
	New England Colonies
	Middle Colonies
	Southern Colonies

This map shows key battles of the American Revolution. In the early
part of the war, major battles took place mostly in the New England
Colonies and the Middle Colonies, in the north. As the war continued,
battles moved southward. In which colony and region did the Battle
of Princeton take place? In which colony and region did the Battle of
Yorktown take place?

The ideals of the American Revolution inspired calls for "Liberty, equality, and fraternity" in France. France's support for the war deepened its national debt and caused suffering among its people. In 1789, France's monarchy was overthrown. This painting shows a violent clash between French commoners and King Louis XVI's troops during the French Revolution.

7.8 The War Ends

The conclusion of the war did not come as quickly as Martin had hoped. When Lord North, the British prime minister, heard about Cornwallis's defeat at Yorktown, he paced up and down the room repeating, "Oh God! It is all over!" When the British people heard about the defeat, most of them accepted it. The loss at Yorktown drained any remaining support for the war. Still, months dragged by before King George was finally forced to accept that the British had been defeated.

For most Americans, the end of the war was a time for joy and celebration. They had gained the freedom to govern themselves and create their own future. But liberty came at a high price. At least 6,200 Americans had been killed in combat. An estimated 10,000 died in camp of diseases, and another 8,500 died while in captivity as British prisoners. As a proportion of the total population, more Americans died fighting in the American Revolution than in any other conflict except the Civil War, in which Americans fought one another.

The Treaty of Paris Early in 1783, representatives of the United States and Great Britain signed a peace treaty in Paris. The Treaty of Paris had three important parts. First, Great Britain agreed to recognize the United States as an independent nation. Second, Great Britain gave up its claims to all lands between the Atlantic Coast and the Mississippi River, from the border of Canada south to Florida. Third, the United States agreed to return all rights and property taken from Loyalists during the war.

Many Loyalists did not trust the treaty's promise of fair treatment —and for good reason. During the war, Loyalists had been treated badly by Patriots. More than 80,000 Loyalists, both black and white, left the United States to settle in British Canada.

The Impact of the American Revolution The American Revolution had a major impact in other parts of the world. In Europe, it thrilled liberals who dreamed of creating their own democracies. The American example was especially influential in France, which soon had its own revolution. As one Frenchman wrote, "They [Americans] are the hope of the human race; they may well become its model." Indeed, in the 1800s, that model would help inspire revolts against European rule in South America.

Chapter Summary

In this chapter, you read how the American colonies won their independence from Great Britain.

American Strengths and Weaknesses The Continental army was short of men, and few men were trained for battle. The Americans also lacked adequate weapons and food. Their strengths included patriotism, support from France, and Washington as their military leader.

British Strengths and Weaknesses British troops greatly outnumbered American troops and were better trained and equipped. Sending troops and supplies to the colonies was slow and costly. The British also had poor leadership and a lack of support from people at home.

Great Britain Almost Wins the War The British won a series of victories early in the war. After the loss of New York City, only Washington's leadership kept the colonists going.

A Pep Talk and Surprising Victories Thomas Paine's *The Crisis* encouraged Americans to keep fighting. Colonial victories at Trenton and Princeton gave new hope for their cause.

The Tide Begins to Turn The colonists' victory in the Battle of Saratoga in 1777 marked a turning point in the war. Shortly afterward, France and Spain joined the colonies as allies.

The War Goes South The British moved south into Georgia and the Carolinas, but American troops slowed their advance. The British surrendered after the Battle of Yorktown.

The War Ends The conflict ended with the signing of the Treaty of Paris in 1783. Under the terms of the treaty, Great Britain recognized the United States as an independent country.

The war officially ended with the signing of the Treaty of Paris in 1783. British troops agreed to leave American soil "with all convenient speed."

George Washington hated to leave his wife, Martha, but he believed in the cause of freedom. So he agreed to lead the colonial war effort.

George Washington: A Warrior Spirit and a Caring Heart

Everyone knows stories about George Washington. From chopping down the cherry tree to helping the nation win independence, the stories make Washington sound larger than life. Washington's writings reveal a more complex person. Behind his strong public presence was a man of many sentiments. He balanced a deep love of his family with a commitment to fighting for his country. He coupled bravery with concern, caution, and compassion.

In 1775, the Continental Congress asked George Washington to lead the colonial army. Washington was living on his estate at Mount Vernon, Virginia, at the time. He had proven his military skills in the French and Indian War. And he had the added benefit of coming from the South. If he were to command the army, Congress thought, he might tie the Southern Colonies more firmly to the cause.

Washington believed deeply in that cause. Still, he had his doubts about taking on the important job Congress offered. Young soldiers like Joseph Plumb Martin, a Connecticut farm boy, looked forward to going to war. But Washington was 43 years old and had fought in wars before. He knew it would be hard to leave his home and family. In a letter to his wife, Martha, he said, "I should enjoy more real happiness in one month with you at home, than I have the most distant prospect of finding abroad [away from home] if my stay were to be seven times seven years."

Eventually, Washington did lead the colonists to victory, but in 1775, he was not sure he would be able to do so. He worried he would not be clever enough to ensure that the colonists would win the war. He thanked Congress for the honor of being asked to lead. He told them about his concerns, but said he would do everything he could to help the colonists reach their goal. In a speech to Congress, he said,

I feel great distress from a consciousness that my abilities and military experience may not be equal to the extensive and important trust. However, as the Congress desire it, I will enter upon the momentous duty, and exert every power I possess in their service and for the support of the glorious cause.

The Man's Compassion

Washington was a general, but he understood the hardships his soldiers faced. At the top of the list was low pay. He felt bad that his men had to do so much hard work for so little money. He also knew that low pay kept some men from enlisting. A soldier "cannot ruin himself and family to serve his country," he told Congress.

Washington witnessed the terrible shortages his soldiers lived with. Joseph Plumb Martin felt the sting of the shortages. He went for days without food and made simple moccasins to keep his feet off the ice. Years later, Martin wrote in his *A Narrative of a Revolutionary Soldier* (1830) that it was ironic that soldiers for a noble cause were so poorly equipped. He described the soldiers marching through Princeton, New Jersey.

> *The young ladies of the town . . . had collected and were sitting in the stoops and at the windows to see the noble exhibition of a thousand half-starved and three-quarters naked soldiers pass in review before them.*

The soldiers' suffering upset Washington. He repeatedly asked for more supplies. During the harsh winter at Valley Forge, he wrote to Congress. In a letter dated December 23, 1777, he accused the congressmen of not understanding what his soldiers went through.

> *I can assure those gentlemen that it is a much easier and less distressing thing to draw remonstrances [listen to protests] in a comfortable room by a good fireside, than to occupy a cold, bleak hill, and sleep under frost and snow, without clothes or blankets. However, although they seem to have little feeling for the naked and distressed soldiers, I feel superabundantly for them, and, from my soul, I pity those miseries, which it is neither in my power to relieve or prevent.*

George Washington cared about his soldiers' suffering. Here he is shown visiting wounded men at Valley Forge during the winter of 1777–78.

Washington expected his soldiers to fight well. But early in the war, he had to lead their retreat from a battle at Long Island, New York.

The General's Concerns

George Washington balanced sympathy for his soldiers with his responsibility as their leader. For example, he knew that soldiers did not want to leave home any more than he did. But his sympathy only went so far. When it came down to it, Washington worried that homesick men made poor soldiers. They threatened his mission. They threatened the colonists' success. "Men just dragged from the tender scenes of domestic life," he wrote, were easily scared by the hard life of a soldier. Such soldiers might desert the army and encourage others to desert, too.

The compassionate Washington wanted his soldiers to get paid more. But he still expected them to fight, and fight hard. He scorned their lack of discipline. He was horrified by what happened at the Battle of New York, in 1776.

> I found the troops . . . retreating [as fast as possible], and those ordered to support them . . . flying in every direction and in the greatest confusion . . . I used every means in my power to rally and get them into some order, but my attempts were . . . ineffectual . . . On the appearance of a small party of the enemy . . . their disorder increased and they ran away in the greatest confusion without firing a single shot.

The general knew that such chaos would never win the war. He did everything he could to see to it that soldiers who neglected their duties were punished.

Similarly, while Washington sympathized with his soldiers being hungry, as general he prohibited them from stealing food. His reason was practical as much as it was moral. Too often, people killed soldiers who tried to steal from them. He wrote to one of his colonels,

> *Every attempt of the men to plunder houses, orchards, gardens, etc., [should] be discouraged, not only for the preservation of property and sake of good order, but for the prevention of those fatal consequences which usually follow such diabolical practices.*

Of course, the general's rules were not always obeyed. During the winter at Valley Forge, an officer ordered Joseph Plumb Martin to steal to help keep the soldiers from starving. The work was "not altogether unpleasant," Martin wrote in *A Narrative of a Revolutionary Soldier*, but it was definitely stealing. He described it this way.

> *I had to travel far and near . . . and at all times to run the risk of abuse, if not injury, from the inhabitants when plundering them of their property, (for I could not, while in the very act of taking their cattle, hay, corn and grain from them against their wills, consider it a whit better than plundering—sheer privateering) [stealing under the authority of a government].*

Worry and Praise, Courage and Kindness

George Washington worried about his reputation. He wanted people to respect him. But if the colonies lost the war, Washington knew that people would think less of him. That worry gave even the great general cause for concern. He once wrote to his cousin that "I never was in such an unhappy, divided state since I was born." To a confidant, he wrote that his army service was "one continued round of annoyance and fatigue."

Nonetheless, Washington kept fighting for the cause of freedom. As the war dragged on, he praised his soldiers for putting up such a good fight against the British, the most powerful army in the world. In a letter, he wrote,

> *Without arrogance . . . it may be said that no history . . . can furnish an instance of an army's suffering such uncommon hardships as ours have done, and bearing them with the same patience and fortitude.*

When the war was over, Washington did everything he could to see that the soldiers received fair pay from the new government.

When he said goodbye to his officers, George Washington again balanced courage and kindness. The commander in chief, one general reported, was "suffused in tears." He could not speak because he had such strong feelings for his men. In the final goodbye, Washington revealed both his warrior spirit and his caring heart.

George Washington bid an emotional farewell to his officers at Fraunces Tavern in New York in 1783. The tavern owner, Samuel Fraunces, was a free black man of French and African descent. He would become chief steward at President Washington's house in Philadelphia.

The Granger Collection, New York

Revolution in the Colonies

1774
Intolerable Acts
British Parliament passes the Intolerable Acts to punish the colonists for their support of the Boston Tea Party.

1754–1763
French and Indian War
This war between France and Great Britain results in a victory for Great Britain and a vastly expanded American empire.

1770
Boston Massacre
Five Bostonians are killed during a brawl between colonists and British soldiers. The incident causes an outcry of injustice throughout the colonies.

1750	1755	1760	1765	1770

1763–1767
Colonial Taxation
British Parliament passes a series of taxes on the colonies, resulting in protests from many colonists.

1774
First Continental Congress
Fifty leaders from the colonies meet to devise peaceful solutions to the conflicts with Great Britain.

1775
Battles of Lexington and Concord
Lexington and Concord become the first sites where the British army and colonial militias battle over control of the colonies. The clashes mark the start of the war for independence from Great Britain.

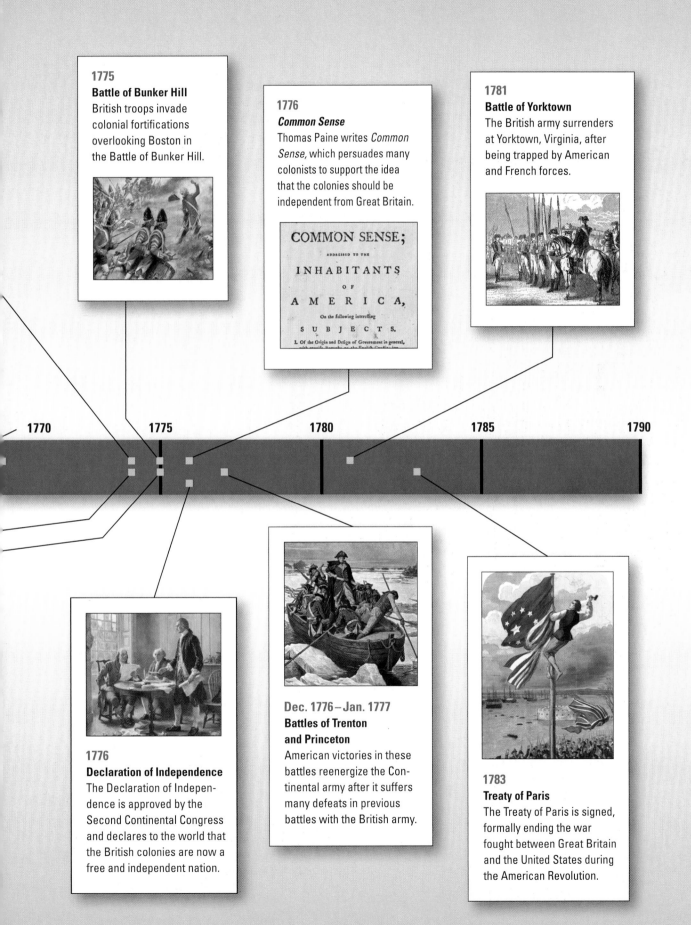

1775
Battle of Bunker Hill
British troops invade colonial fortifications overlooking Boston in the Battle of Bunker Hill.

1776
Common Sense
Thomas Paine writes *Common Sense,* which persuades many colonists to support the idea that the colonies should be independent from Great Britain.

COMMON SENSE;
ADDRESSED TO THE
INHABITANTS
OF
AMERICA,
On the following interesting
SUBJECTS.
I. Of the Origin and Design of Government in general,

1781
Battle of Yorktown
The British army surrenders at Yorktown, Virginia, after being trapped by American and French forces.

1770   1775   1780   1785   1790

1776
Declaration of Independence
The Declaration of Independence is approved by the Second Continental Congress and declares to the world that the British colonies are now a free and independent nation.

Dec. 1776–Jan. 1777
Battles of Trenton and Princeton
American victories in these battles reenergize the Continental army after it suffers many defeats in previous battles with the British army.

1783
Treaty of Paris
The Treaty of Paris is signed, formally ending the war fought between Great Britain and the United States during the American Revolution.

Colonial leaders sat in this room, located in Independence Hall in Philadelphia, Pennsylvania, to adopt the Declaration of Independence and the Constitution of the United States.

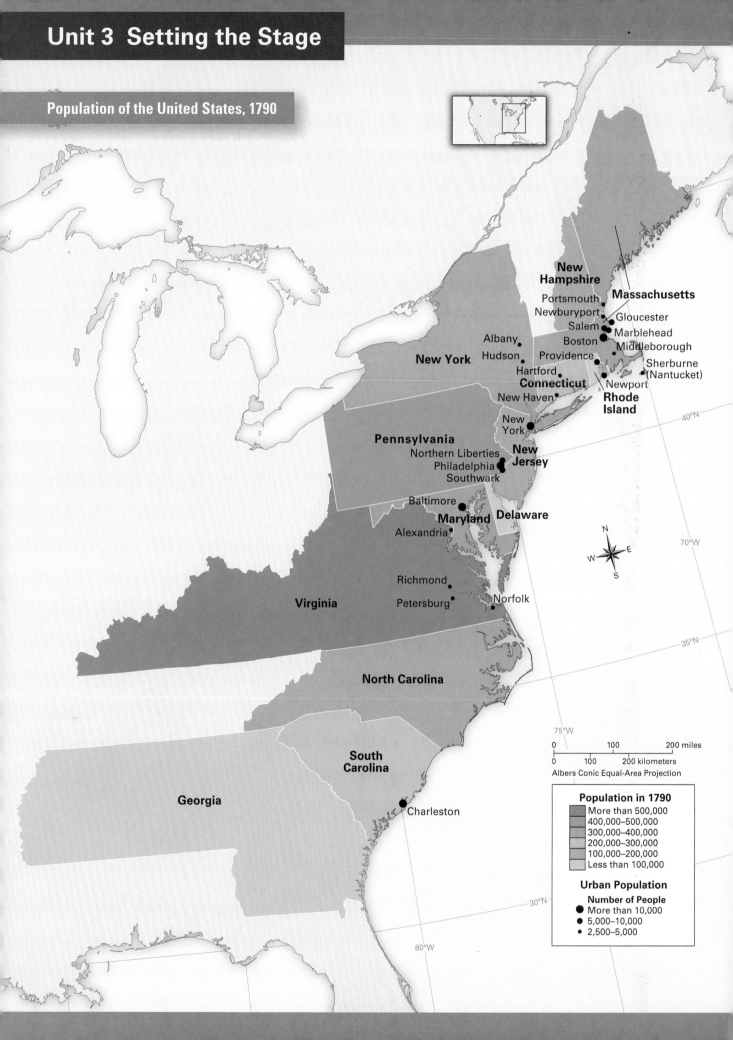

Population of the United States, 1790

New Hampshire

Portsmouth
Newburyport
Massachusetts
Gloucester
Salem
Marblehead
Albany
Boston
Middleborough
New York
Hudson
Providence
Sherburne
(Nantucket)
Hartford
Connecticut
Newport
New Haven
Rhode
Island

New York

Pennsylvania

Northern Liberties
New Jersey
Philadelphia
Southwark

Baltimore
Maryland
Delaware
Alexandria

Richmond
Petersburg
Norfolk

Virginia

40°N
70°W
35°N

North Carolina

75°W

0   100   200 miles
0   100   200 kilometers
Albers Conic Equal-Area Projection

South
Carolina

Georgia

Charleston

30°N

80°W

Population in 1790
More than 500,000
400,000–500,000
300,000–400,000
200,000–300,000
100,000–200,000
Less than 100,000

Urban Population
Number of People
● More than 10,000
● 5,000–10,000
· 2,500–5,000

Forming a New Nation.

The 13 states that independence brought together to form the United States of America had very different physical and human geographic features. Most of the Southern states were larger than most of the Northern states. However, as the map on the opposite page shows, a state's population often had little relation to its size. For example, the populations of tiny Rhode Island and the much larger Georgia were close to the same.

For the colonists, differences between the states' geographic features raised basic questions about what form the nation's government should take. Should a large state like Georgia have the same voice in government as a small state like Connecticut, which had a greater population? Should Connecticut have as much power as New York, which was larger and had more people, too? At first, the answer to both questions was yes. Under the nation's first constitution, called the Articles of Confederation, each state had one vote in Congress.

In time, however, some people began to question the fairness of this system. Yet, basing a state's political power on its population raised other questions. For example, should a state with both slaves and free people have as much power as a state with no slaves and the same total population? The populations of the Southern states contained a high percentage of slaves, as the maps on this page show. The maps also show that counting only free people would drop most of these states in the population rankings, compared to the Northern states.

Such geographic concerns arose in 1787, when representatives of 12 states met to write a new constitution for the United States. In this unit, you will learn how the delegates handled population-related disputes and other issues in framing the form of government we have today.

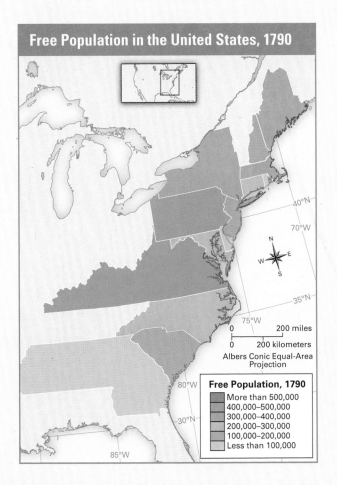

Free Population in the United States, 1790

Albers Conic Equal-Area Projection

0 — 200 miles
0 — 200 kilometers

Free Population, 1790
- More than 500,000
- 400,000–500,000
- 300,000–400,000
- 200,000–300,000
- 100,000–200,000
- Less than 100,000

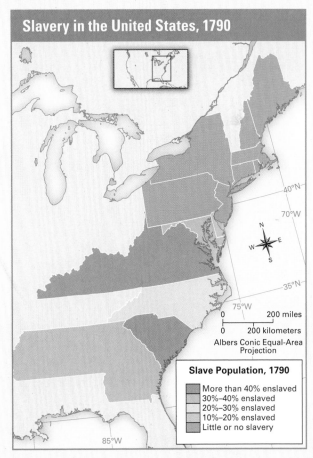

Slavery in the United States, 1790

Albers Conic Equal-Area Projection

0 — 200 miles
0 — 200 kilometers

Slave Population, 1790
- More than 40% enslaved
- 30%–40% enslaved
- 20%–30% enslaved
- 10%–20% enslaved
- Little or no slavery

Chapter 8

Creating the Constitution

What compromises emerged from the Constitutional Convention?

8.1 Introduction

When the American war for independence ended, no one was happier than a serious Virginia Patriot named James Madison. And no one was more worried about the future of the United States. While serving in Congress during the war, Madison had tried and failed to get the states to work easily together. He doubted that things would improve now that the war was over.

After declaring independence in 1776, Congress had tried to unite the states under one national government. This proved to be a difficult task. Most members of Congress were nervous about creating a strong central government. They feared that such a government would trample the very rights they were fighting to preserve.

Their solution was a plan of government known as the Articles of Confederation. The Articles created "a firm league of friendship" in which "each state retains its sovereignty, freedom, and independence." This "league of friendship" was a loose union in which the 13 states cooperated for common purposes. It was run by Congress, in which each state had one vote.

On paper, the Articles of Confederation gave Congress several important powers. It could declare war, raise an army and a navy, print money, and set up a postal system.

In reality, however, these powers were limited by the inability of Congress to impose taxes. Instead, Congress had to ask the states for funds to do anything. All too often, the states ignored Congress's "humble requests." The result, said Madison, was that the Articles were no more effective at binding the states into a nation than "a rope of sand."

In this chapter, you will read about the new nation's shaky start under the Articles of Confederation. You will also learn how Madison and other leaders met in 1787 to revise the Articles and ended up compromising to form "a more perfect Union."

The Granger Collection, New York

Because of his important role in the creation of the document that would give the new nation a plan for government, James Madison is known as the "Father of the Constitution."

◀ The Constitution was signed in Philadelphia on September 17, 1787.

8.2 Early Quarrels and Accomplishments

Even before the American Revolution was over, the states began quarreling among themselves. Many of their quarrels were about taxes on goods that crossed state borders. New York, for example, taxed firewood from Connecticut and cabbages from New Jersey. The states also disagreed over boundaries. The inability of Congress to end such disagreements was one of the key weaknesses of the **Articles of Confederation**.

Developing Western Lands Congress did get the states to agree on one important issue: how to develop the western lands acquired in the Treaty of Paris. At that time, there was no orderly way to divide up and sell these lands. Settlers walked into the wilderness and claimed the land they liked. Disputes over who owned what clogged the courts.

To end this confusion, Congress passed the Land Ordinance of 1785. Under this law, western lands were divided into six-mile squares called townships. Each township was then divided into 36 sections of 640 acres each. One section of each township was set aside to support the township's public schools. The other sections were to be sold to settlers.

Surveyors proceeded to lay out townships in the Ohio Valley, then known as the **Northwest Territory**. By 1787, the government was ready to sell sections to settlers. This raised the question of how these areas should be governed. Were they to be U.S. colonies or new states?

The Northwest Ordinance Congress answered this question in the **Northwest Ordinance** of 1787. This law divided the Northwest Territory into smaller territories, each governed by a territorial governor. As soon as a territory had 5,000 free adult males, it could elect its own legislature, or lawmaking body. When the population reached 60,000, a territory could apply to Congress to become a state.

Articles of Confederation the first written plan of government for the United States. A confederation is an association of states that cooperate for a common purpose.

Northwest Territory a region of the United States bounded by the Ohio and Mississippi rivers and the Great Lakes. The region was given to the United States by the Treaty of Paris in 1783.

Northwest Ordinance a law passed by Congress in 1787 that specified how western lands would be governed

The Land Ordinance of 1785 organized the Northwest Territory into townships. The Northwest Ordinance of 1787 set rules for how western lands would be governed. Within a half-century of its passage, enough people had settled in the Northwest Territory to create five new states.

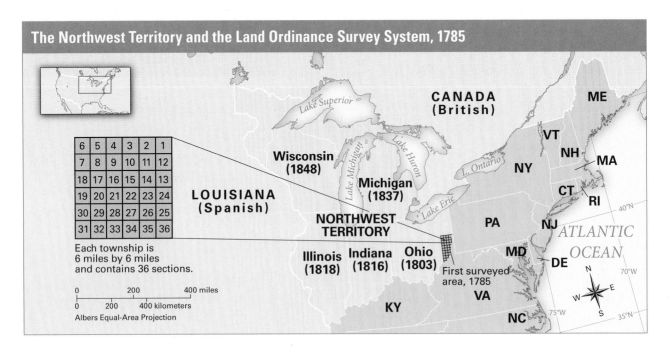

The Northwest Territory and the Land Ordinance Survey System, 1785

Each township is 6 miles by 6 miles and contains 36 sections.

0   200   400 miles
0   200   400 kilometers
Albers Equal-Area Projection

The Northwest Ordinance included a list of rights that gave settlers the same privileges as other citizens, except for one. Slavery was banned in the Northwest Territory.

This system of settlement served the nation well. Over time, the United States would continue to establish territories as it spread to the shores of the Pacific Ocean and beyond.

8.3 Shays's Rebellion and the Need for Change

Under the Articles of Confederation, the new nation had serious money problems. The paper money printed by Congress during the war was worthless. Congress had the power to make coins that would not lose their value. But it lacked gold or silver to mint into coins.

The states reacted to the money shortage by printing their own paper currency. Before long, bills of different sizes and colors were distributed from state to state. No one knew what any of these currencies was worth, but most agreed they were not worth much.

Massachusetts Farmers Rebel The money shortage was particularly hard on farmers who could not earn enough to pay their debts and taxes. In Massachusetts, judges ordered farmers to sell their land and livestock to pay off their debts. Led by Daniel Shays, a hero of the Battle of Bunker Hill, Massachusetts farmers rebelled.

In 1786, Shays and his followers closed down courthouses to keep judges from taking their farms. Then they marched on the national arsenal at Springfield to seize the weapons stored there. Having disbanded the Continental army, Congress was unable to stop them.

The Massachusetts government ended Shays's Rebellion in early 1787 by sending militia troops to Springfield to restore order. To many Americans, however, the uprising was a disturbing sign that the nation they had fought so hard to create was falling apart. "No respect is paid to the federal [national] authority," James Madison wrote to a friend. "It is not possible that a government can last long under these circumstances."

A Call for a Convention Shays's Rebellion shocked Congress into calling for a convention to consider "the situation of the United States." Each state was invited to send delegates to Philadelphia in May 1787 "for the sole and express purpose of revising the Articles of Confederation."

Madison was ready. For the past year, he had devoted himself to the study of governments, both ancient and modern. The lesson of the past was always the same. A nation that was made up of many groups needed a strong central government, or it would soon be torn apart by quarrels. The question was, would Americans heed this lesson?

Daniel Shays, at the top right, and his followers closed down courthouses in Massachusetts to prevent judges from seizing farmers' land when the farmers could not pay their debts.

Constitutional Convention
a meeting held in Philadelphia
in 1787 at which delegates
from the states wrote the
U.S. Constitution

8.4   Opening the Constitutional Convention

Philadelphia was already hot and humid when delegates began drifting into the city. On May 25, 1787, the **Constitutional Convention** met for the first time in the east room of the Pennsylvania State House (now known as Independence Hall). The Declaration of Independence had been debated in this very room just 11 years earlier. The delegates would meet in the east room all summer. On some days, temperatures rose well into the nineties.

The delegates' first action was to elect George Washington president of the convention. No man was more admired and respected than the former commander in chief of the Continental army. When the war ended, Washington could have used his power and popularity to make himself a king. Instead, he went home to Virginia to resume his life as an ordinary citizen. But despite his reluctance to return to public life, Washington would play a key role by presiding over the convention and lending it his prestige.

The Delegates Fifty-five delegates from 12 states attended the Constitutional Convention. Rhode Island, which prided itself as "the home of the otherwise minded" and feared a strong national government, boycotted the meeting.

Some leaders of the revolution were missing. John Adams and Thomas Jefferson were representing the United States in Great Britain and France, respectively. Others who did not attend included Sam Adams, John Hancock, and Patrick Henry. They feared that a strong national government would endanger the rights of states.

The delegates to the Constitutional Convention met on May 25, 1787, in the same hall where the Declaration of Independence was signed. Today, the building is called Independence Hall.

The Granger Collection, New York

As a group, the delegates were, in the words of a modern historian, "the well-bred, the well-fed, the well-read, and the well-wed." Their average age was 42. At 81, Benjamin Franklin of Pennsylvania was the oldest. He arrived at the convention each day in a sedan chair carried by four good-natured prisoners from a nearby jail.

Most of the delegates brought extensive political experience to the meeting. More than two-thirds were lawyers. Most had served in their state legislatures or held a state office. Thomas Jefferson was so impressed by the ability and experience of these men that he called the convention "an assembly of demi-gods."

The Father of the Constitution The best prepared of the delegates was James Madison of Virginia. One delegate wrote of Madison, "In the management of every great question he evidently took the lead in the Convention." Indeed, Madison's influence was so great that later he would be called the "Father of the Constitution."

Madison addressed the convention numerous times. When he was not speaking, he took notes. Sitting near the front of the room so that he could hear everything that was said, Madison wrote down nearly every word. All together, his notes covered more than 600 printed pages. From this remarkable record, we know what went on inside the convention day by day.

Benjamin Franklin, the oldest delegate to the Constitutional Convention, had doubts about the drafting of the Constitution. However, he said, "The older I grow, the more apt I am to doubt my own judgment and pay more respect to the judgment of others."

The Rule of Secrecy At the time, however, no one outside the convention knew what was happening. After choosing a president, the delegates voted on rules for the convention. The most important of these was the rule of secrecy. The delegates wanted to feel free to speak their minds without causing alarm or opposition among the general public. They agreed to keep secret whatever was said in the meeting room until their work was done.

One day, Washington was handed some notes that had been dropped in the hall outside the east room. Washington pocketed the paper until the end of debate the next day. Then, in his sternest voice, he lectured the delegates on the importance of secrecy. "I know not whose paper it is," Washington said as he flung the notes on his desk. "But there it is, let him who owns it take it." The notes were never claimed. Instead, they lay on Washington's desk for days.

Like Washington, the delegates took the rule of secrecy seriously. During that long summer, not a single word about the convention debates appeared in any newspaper.

Shared Beliefs and Clashing Views Once the convention was organized, the delegates got down to business. As a group, the delegates had much in common. But they also had very different views on many issues facing the new nation.

To be sure, all the delegates were **committed** to the ideals of the Declaration of Independence. The basic purpose of government, they believed, was to protect the rights to "life, liberty, and the pursuit of happiness." And they agreed, in the words of the Declaration, that the "just powers" of governments came from "the consent of the governed."

In part, these beliefs reflected the ideas of **Enlightenment** thinkers like England's John Locke. Human institutions, these **liberal** thinkers had argued, should be based on "laws of nature." Among these laws were the rights to liberty and equality. The best way to protect these rights, the delegates agreed, was through some form of **republic**.

From New England's town meetings to lawmaking bodies like the Virginia House of Burgesses, Americans had a long tradition of participating in their own government. After the American Revolution, all the states had adopted **constitutions** that embraced republican ideals. Despite many differences in details, every state had some form of representative government. States had also expanded the rights to vote and to hold office. The state constitutions helped to shape the delegates' thinking.

Despite the delegates' broad agreement on a government "of the people," many questions were left unanswered. For example, who exactly should have a say in a truly "representative" government? Even in liberal Pennsylvania, only free, white males could vote. Some states allowed only wealthier citizens to vote or hold office. Women could not vote in any state except New Jersey. (New Jersey women would lose the right to vote in 1807.)

Perhaps the most troubling question of all was how powerful the national government should be. Many delegates wanted to keep government close to the people by preserving the rights of the states. They feared that a strong national government would threaten individual liberty. Others, including Madison, argued just the opposite. Look at what has happened under the Articles of Confederation, they said, referring to events like Shays's Rebellion. If the central government is too weak, it cannot do its job of protecting liberty and property.

As they met behind closed doors, the delegates wrestled with these and other issues. Tempers often flared. Several times it seemed the convention might collapse in failure. But in the end the delegates found ways to save the convention—and the nation.

Delegates with opposing views were Pennsylvania's James Wilson (left) and New Jersey's William Paterson (right). Wilson, one of the most vocal delegates at the convention, argued for a strong national government. Paterson tried to protect the rights of the states. Many delegates of small states shared his fear of being "swallowed up" by the larger states.

8.5 Issue: How Should States Be Represented in the New Government?

When the convention began, most delegates believed that their task was to revise the Articles of Confederation. To their surprise, the Virginia delegation presented them with a completely new plan of government. After a lengthy debate, the delegates made a bold move. They agreed to throw out the Articles of Confederation and write a new constitution.

While the delegates—later known as the framers—agreed to design a new **framework** of government, they were divided on a key issue. Where should the government's power to rule come from? From the states? Or from the people? Under the Articles of Confederation, the answer was the states. James Madison's answer was that the government's power should come directly from the people.

The Virginia Plan Drafted by James Madison and proposed by Edmund Randolph, the Virginia Plan called for a strong national government with three branches, or parts. A legislative branch would make laws. An executive branch would carry out, or execute, the laws. A judicial branch, or system of courts, would apply and interpret the laws.

Under the Virginia Plan, Congress was to be made up of two houses, the House of Representatives and the Senate. The number of lawmakers that a state could send to Congress depended on the state's population. States with large populations would have more representatives than smaller states would have.

Delegates from Virginia, Pennsylvania, and other large states liked the Virginia Plan. Having the new government represent people, not states, would give them more representatives and more power in both houses of Congress.

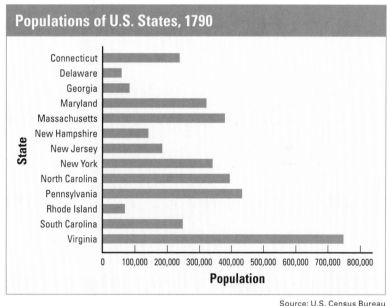

Populations of U.S. States, 1790

Source: U.S. Census Bureau

The New Jersey Plan Not surprisingly, delegates from the small states disliked the Virginia Plan. Just as the convention was about to vote on it, William Paterson of New Jersey introduced a rival proposal.

Like the Virginia Plan, the New Jersey Plan called for a government with three branches. However, the legislative branch would have just one house, not two. Each state would have an equal vote in Congress, no matter how big or small. This plan, Paterson argued, would keep the small states from being "swallowed up" by their more populous neighbors.

A major issue confronting the Constitutional Convention was whether to give each state the same number of representatives or to base representation on population. Based on this graph, which states do you think would want equal representation for each state?

Great Compromise the plan of government adopted at the Constitutional Convention that established a two-house Congress. In the House of Representatives, representation from each state is based on state population. In the Senate, each state is represented by two senators.

8.6 Resolution: The Great Compromise

The New Jersey Plan was warmly received by delegates from small states. The majority of delegates, however, saw William Paterson's plan as offering little improvement over the Articles of Confederation and rejected it. But they could not agree on what should replace it.

Tempers Rise The debate over representation in Congress continued into July, with tempers rising day by day. To most delegates from large states, representation based on population seemed both logical and fair. "Can we forget for whom we are forming a Government?" asked James Wilson of Pennsylvania. "Is it for *men,* or for the imaginary beings called *States*?"

To Wilson, the answer was obvious. But his logic could not overcome the fears of small-state delegates. One hot Saturday afternoon, Gunning Bedford of Delaware tore into the delegates from large states. "They insist," he said, "they will never hurt or injure the lesser states." His reply to his own concern was straightforward. *"I do not, gentlemen, trust you!"* If the large states continued in their efforts to "crush the smaller states," Bedford warned, "the small ones will find some foreign ally of more honor and good faith who will take them by the hand and do them justice."

Rufus King of Massachusetts was shocked at this reference to foreign powers. He said that he was "grieved, that such a thought had entered his heart." Still, every delegate knew that Great Britain, France, and Spain were just waiting for the United States to fall apart so they could pick up the pieces.

A Compromise Is Reached Finally, a compromise was proposed based on a plan put forward earlier by Roger Sherman of Connecticut. The compromise plan kept a two-house Congress. The first house, the House of Representatives, would represent the people. In this house, the number of representatives from each state would be based on the state's population. The second house, the Senate, would represent the states. Each state would have two senators, to be elected by their state legislatures. The vote was very close, but the compromise plan was approved. This plan saved the convention and became known as the **Great Compromise**.

Roger Sherman, a signer of the Declaration of Independence, helped construct the Great Compromise that called for a Congress with two houses.

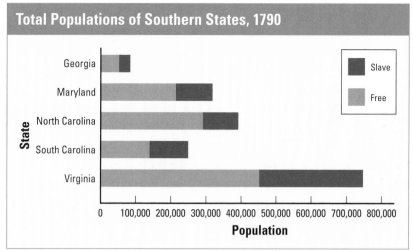

Total Populations of Southern States, 1790

Legend: Slave, Free

States (y-axis): Georgia, Maryland, North Carolina, South Carolina, Virginia

Population (x-axis): 0, 100,000, 200,000, 300,000, 400,000, 500,000, 600,000, 700,000, 800,000

Source: U.S. Census Bureau

How do you think delegates from each of the states shown in this graph would want slaves to be counted? Would they want the slave population to be considered when determining representation in Congress, or would they want slaves to be counted as property that could be taxed?

8.7 Issue: How Should Slaves Be Counted?

The Great Compromise kept the framers working together. But having agreed to base representation in one house of Congress on state population, they faced a new and difficult question. As Gouverneur Morris of Pennsylvania put it, "Upon what principle shall slaves be computed in the representation?"

People or Property? By the time of the convention, nine-tenths of the slaves in the United States lived in the South. Like everyone else, southerners wanted as many representatives in the House as possible. They argued that slaves should be counted the same as any other people in determining representation.

Delegates from the North challenged this idea. Were slaves to be considered people with a right to be represented in Congress? Or were they property? "Blacks are property and are used to the southward as horses and cattle to the northward," argued Elbridge Gerry of Massachusetts. Most northern delegates agreed. Slaves should be counted only as property that could be taxed like any other property. If slaves were to be counted as people in determining representation in Congress, said Morris, "then make them citizens and let them vote."

New Thinking on Slavery This argument signaled a growing division among white Americans. The Declaration of Independence and the American Revolution forced many whites to reexamine their views on slavery. Some became active in trying to end what they now saw as a great evil. Benjamin Franklin, for example, became president of an antislavery society in 1787. In the North, this new thinking led one state after another to pass laws ending slavery.

Although many southerners were uneasy about slavery, they were not yet ready to abolish it. The South's economy was still very dependent on the labor of enslaved African Americans. But some southern states did pass laws making it easier for owners to free their slaves.

Three-Fifths Compromise an agreement made at the Constitutional Convention stating that enslaved persons would be counted as three-fifths of a person when determining a state's population for representation in the House of Representatives

8.8 Resolution: The Three-Fifths Compromise

After a bitter debate, Madison proposed a compromise. Count each slave as three-fifths of a person, he suggested, when determining a state's population for representation in the House of Representatives. The delegates approved this idea, which became known as the **Three-Fifths Compromise,** because it seemed the only way to keep the convention moving forward.

Another Slavery Issue A dispute over trade raised another issue about slavery. To help business in the North, northern delegates favored giving Congress broad power to control trade between the states and other countries. This proposal made southern delegates nervous. They worried that Congress might try to tax southern export crops such as rice and tobacco. Southerners also worried that Congress would use its power over trade to outlaw the slave trade—the importing of slaves from Africa.

This sketch shows a slave auction in Virginia in the 1850s. Southern delegates to the convention were afraid that, if Congress outlawed the slave trade, the South would suffer economically.

Southerners had reason to be fearful. By 1787, several states had outlawed the slave trade within their boundaries. A majority of the convention's delegates favored ending the slave trade completely.

South Carolina and Georgia, however, objected that their economies would collapse without a constant supply of new slaves. Neither state would agree to any constitution that threatened to end the slave trade.

More Compromises on Slavery Again, the delegates settled on a compromise. Congress would have the power to control trade, but with two limitations. First, Congress could not place any tax on exports to other countries. Second, Congress could not interfere with the slave trade for 20 years, or until 1808.

To satisfy southerners, the delegates also agreed to a provision known as the fugitive slave clause. This clause said that escaped slaves had to be returned to their owners, even if they were caught in a free state.

Without such compromises, the states might never have come together in a single union. Still, the compromises only postponed the day when Americans would have to resolve the terrible **contradiction** between slavery and the ideals of liberty and equality. Meanwhile, generations of African Americans would spend their lives in bondage.

8.9 Issue: How Should the Chief Executive Be Elected?

Another major question facing the delegates concerned who would head the new government's executive branch. Early in the convention, Charles Pinckney urged the creation of a "vigorous executive." James Wilson followed with a proposal that a single person serve as the chief executive.

A sudden silence fell over the convention. A single executive? The very idea brought to mind unhappy memories of King George III.

Wilson broke the silence by explaining that good government depends on clear, timely, and responsible leadership. Such leadership, he said, is most likely to be found in a single person.

One Executive or Three? Edmund Randolph of Virginia disliked this proposal. He preferred a three-member executive drawn from different parts of the country. Three people, he argued, could lead the country better than one.

Benjamin Franklin opposed a single executive for different reasons. "The first man put at the helm will be a good one," said Franklin, thinking of George Washington. "Nobody knows what sort may come afterwards." The next chief executive, he warned, might be overly ambitious or too "fond of war."

In spite of these objections, the framers agreed to a single executive, to be called the president. To keep this leader from becoming too king-like, they limited the president's term to four years. A vice president was also to be elected to fill that term if the president died in office.

Choosing the Chief Executive Equally troubling was the issue of how to choose the chief executive. Some delegates wanted Congress to appoint the president. Gouverneur Morris objected. The president "must not be made the flunky of the Congress," he argued. "It must not be able to say to him: 'You owe your appointment to us.'"

Several delegates thought that the people should elect the president. Madison, however, argued that voters would naturally vote for someone from their own state. As a result, this method would not be fair to candidates from small states.

Still others suggested that the president be elected by a specially chosen group of "electors" from each state. Such a group, they felt, would be able to look beyond state interests to make a wise choice for the entire country.

Many delegates felt that ordinary citizens, such as those pictured here, were not suited to elect the president. Roger Sherman stated, "The people should have as little to do as may be about the government. They want information, and are constantly liable to be misled."

Electoral College the group established by the Constitution to elect the president and vice president. Voters in each state choose their electors.

8.10 Resolution: The Electoral College

After some 60 votes on the issue of how to elect the president, the framers reached another compromise. Neither Congress nor the people, they decided, should choose the president and vice president. Instead, a special body called the **Electoral College** would elect the government's leaders.

The Electoral College System The Electoral College is made up of electors who cast votes to elect the president and vice president every four years. Each state has as many electors in the Electoral College as the number of senators and representatives it sends to Congress. The votes cast by electors are called electoral votes.

The delegates left the method of choosing electors up to each state. Before 1820, state legislatures chose electors in most states. Today, the people choose their state's electors when they vote in presidential elections. The electors then cast their ballots for president and vice president on a date chosen by Congress.

Originally, the electors voted for two candidates without saying which one they preferred for president or vice president. The candidate receiving the most votes became president. The runner-up became vice president. This system caused great confusion in the election of 1800 and was later changed.

This is a copy of the Electoral College vote for the election of 1789. At that time, which states had the most electoral votes?

Political Parties and Elections The Electoral College system seems very odd to most Americans today. In our age of instant communication, it is hard to appreciate the framers' concern that voters would not know enough about candidates outside their own state to choose a president wisely.

The delegates could not have predicted how quickly communications would improve in the United States. Nor could they foresee the rise of national political parties. Within a few years of the convention, political parties were nominating candidates for president and educating voters in every state about those candidates.

The Electoral College system still affects presidential elections today. In most states, the candidate who gets the most votes—even if less than a majority—wins all of that state's electoral votes. As a result, a candidate can win a majority in the Electoral College without necessarily winning a majority of the votes cast across the country. In the presidential election of 2000, George W. Bush won the presidency over Al Gore by getting the most Electoral College votes, even though Gore received more votes than Bush in the popular election.

THE FOUNDATION OF AMERICAN GOVERNMENT

Only 39 of the original 55 delegates signed the Constitution on September 17, 1787. Thirteen delegates had returned home before the conclusion of the convention, and three others refused to sign.

8.11 The Convention Ends

By the end of summer, the hard work of designing the Constitution was finished. But the new plan still had to be approved by the states.

Approving the Constitution The first question before the framers was how many states would have to **ratify,** or approve, the Constitution before it could go into effect. Should ratification require approval by all 13 states? By a majority of 7 states? The framers compromised on 9 states.

The second question was who should ratify the Constitution—the people or the state legislatures? Ratification by state legislatures would be faster and easier. James Madison, however, argued strongly that the people were "the fountain of all power" and should decide. The majority of delegates agreed. After the delegates signed the Constitution, the document was later ratified at special conventions by delegates elected by the people in each state. However, ratification did not come without difficulty.

Signing the Constitution On September 17, 1787, the delegates declared the Constitution complete. As this last meeting began, Franklin shared his final thoughts, which would be printed in more than 50 newspapers.

"I confess that I do not entirely approve of this Constitution," Franklin began. Then he pointed out that no convention could produce a perfect plan. "It therefore astonishes me," Franklin continued, "to find this system approaching so near to perfection . . . and I think it will astonish our enemies." Franklin added that he approved the final plan "because I expect no better, and because I am not sure that it is not the best." He urged every member of the convention to "put his name to this instrument."

Not everyone was won over by Franklin's words. Thirteen delegates left the convention before it ended and so did not sign the Constitution.

ratify to formally approve a plan or an agreement. The process of approval is called ratification.

The Federalist Papers a series of essays written by James Madison, Alexander Hamilton, and John Jay in support of the ratification of the Constitution by the states

Three other delegates—Edmund Randolph and George Mason, both of Virginia, and Elbridge Gerry of Massachusetts—also did not sign. Mason believed it gave too much power to the national government. Gerry refused to sign because he believed the new plan did not protect the rights of the people.

When the signing was over, Franklin confessed that he had often looked at the sun carved on the back of George Washington's chair and wondered whether it was about to rise or set. "But now," he said, "I have the happiness to know that it is a rising and not a setting sun." A new day was dawning for the United States.

8.12   The Constitution Goes to the States

Newspapers in every state printed the Constitution as soon as they could get it. What readers found was a plan that would create a "federal" system of government, in which a strong national government shared power with the states. Before long, the entire country was debating the same issues that had kept the convention in session for four long months.

The Federalists   Supporters of the Constitution called themselves Federalists. The Federalists argued that the Constitution would create a national government that was strong enough to unite the quarreling states into a single republic.

James Madison, Alexander Hamilton, and John Jay led the Federalist campaign for ratification. In a series of newspaper essays, they recalled the weaknesses of the government under the Articles of Confederation. They showed how the Constitution would remedy those weaknesses by creating a stronger, more effective union of the states.

The Constitution had to be approved by nine states. This political cartoon shows 11 states, pictured as columns, supporting the Constitution, while two states are hesitating.

The Federalist leaders also addressed the fears of many Americans that a strong government would threaten their freedom or take away their rights. The powers given to the government, they pointed out, were strictly limited. In addition, those powers were divided among three branches so that no one branch could become too powerful. The influential articles written by Madison, Hamilton, and Jay were later collected and published as *The Federalist Papers*.

The CENTINEL.   Vol. IX

REDEUNT SATURNIA REGNA.

On the erection of the Eleventh PILLAR of the great National DOME, we beg leave most sincerely to felicitate "OUR DEAR COUNTRY."

Rise it will.

The foundation good—it may yet be SAVED.

The FEDERAL EDIFICE.
ELEVEN STARS, in quick succession rise—
ELEVEN COLUMNS strike our wond'ring eyes,
Soon o'er the *whole*, shall swell the beauteous DOME,
COLUMBIA's boast—and FREEDOM's hallow'd home.
Here shall the ARTS in glorious splendour shine!
And AGRICULTURE give her stores divine!
COMMERCE refin'd, dispense us more than gold,
And this new world, teach WISDOM to the old—
RELIGION here shall fix her blest abode,
Array'd in *mildness*, like its parent GOD!
JUSTICE and LAW, shall endless PEACE maintain,
And the "SATURNIAN AGE," *return again.*

The Anti-Federalists Opponents of the Constitution were known as Anti-Federalists. They found much to dislike about the new plan. Congress, they feared, would burden the country with taxes. They claimed the president had power enough to rule like a king. The judicial branch, they said, would overpower state courts.

The Anti-Federalists also complained about what was missing from the plan. Their main complaint was that the plan listed the powers of the government but not the rights of the people. Most of all, the Anti-Federalists feared change. The idea of giving up any state power to form a stronger Union made them uneasy.

After listening to the arguments, Madison wrote that the question facing the nation was "whether the Union shall or shall not be continued. There is, in my opinion, no middle ground to be taken."

Chapter Summary

In this chapter, you read about the Constitutional Convention, the historic meeting that replaced the Articles of Confederation with a new plan of government.

Early Quarrels and Accomplishments Under the Articles of Confederation, Congress did not have the power to solve disagreements among states over such issues as taxes. Congress passed laws on how to settle the Northwest Territory.

Shays's Rebellion Shays's Rebellion showed that under the Articles of Confederation, the government was too weak to keep order.

The Great Compromise In 1787, delegates met at the Constitutional Convention and agreed to revise the Articles. The Great Compromise established how states were to be represented in the legislative branch of government.

The Three-Fifths Compromise The Three-Fifths Compromise settled the question of how slaves were to be counted in determining a state's population.

The Electoral College A third compromise created a single chief executive, to be chosen by the Electoral College.

The Constitution Delegates signed the Constitution in September 1787. They agreed that 9 of the 13 states had to ratify the Constitution before it could go into effect.

During the convention, Benjamin Franklin wondered whether the sun decorating George Washington's chair was rising or setting. At the conclusion of the convention, Franklin optimistically concluded it was a rising sun.

The scholarly James Madison finished college in two years, and then studied law. By the time he arrived at the Constitutional Convention, he was experienced in state and national politics.

James Madison and the Long, Hot Summer of 1787

James Madison is often called the "Father of the Constitution." Although many people had a hand in shaping the Constitution, most scholars agree that Madison was the main driving force behind the document's creation. It was a process that took more than 100 days of complex negotiation and compromise. Even so, it did not turn out quite as Madison had wanted.

In the first week of May 1787, James Madison stood alone in the East Room of the Pennsylvania State House. Within a few weeks, many of the nation's political leaders would gather there. Although few of them knew it at the time, their task would be to create a new plan of government for the United States. Madison knew it, though, and he wanted to be ready.

Madison had thought long and hard about the great challenges facing the nation. Under the Articles of Confederation, the United States was floundering. Madison believed that a stronger national government was needed to keep the country on course. Other leaders also agreed on the need for reform. However, many of them had fears of a strong central government. Madison would have to work hard to change those ideas.

Madison had arrived early in Philadelphia to prepare for the convention. He had checked in to one of the city's finest boarding houses, run by Mrs. Mary House. Soon most of his fellow delegates from Virginia would be there also. That would give them a chance to make plans before the convention began.

Unfortunately, it was not a fine time to be in Philadelphia. It had been a wet and rainy spring. Now, as summer neared, it was becoming increasingly hot and humid. To make matters worse, the city was plagued with dense clouds of black flies. Residents had to sleep with their windows closed or be tormented by swarms of buzzing, biting insects. Shutting their windows, however, meant they had to spend their nights sweltering in the heat.

Madison had bigger concerns, though. As he looked around the East Room of the State House, he imagined the events that would soon unfold there. The room was large, with a 20-foot-high ceiling and tall windows. But it would be crowded once all the delegates were seated. Madison decided to sit up front, where he could get a clear view of the proceedings. He planned to take notes and wanted to be able to see and hear everything that took place at the convention.

Madison Leads the Way

Madison was 36 years old at the time of the convention. He was a small man, just five and a half feet tall, with pale skin and thinning hair. He typically dressed in black. He was shy and spoke in a soft voice that was often hard to hear. Nevertheless, he had great energy. He walked with a bounce in his step and could get by on just a few hours of sleep a night. Although he rarely showed personal warmth or charm, he was a brilliant conversationalist who knew how to win others to his side.

Madison was well prepared to play a leading role at the convention. He had spent several years as a member of Congress. He had studied the writings of great political thinkers and understood how political systems worked. He had also helped write the Virginia Constitution of 1776. This document established a state government with separation of powers and a two-house legislature. It was an important model of democratic government. Madison would bring all this past experience to bear at the convention.

Over the next two weeks, the other delegates began to arrive. They were all wealthy, educated white men. Most were lawyers or large landowners. There were no workers or tradesmen. There were also no women, African Americans, or American Indians.

The delegates took rooms at various boarding houses and inns. One of these inns, the Indian Queen, was the largest in the city. Soon it would be filled with leaders from around the nation. Here they would gather to eat, drink, and swap stories. It was a center of social activity during the convention.

By mid-May, most of the Virginia delegation had arrived. This group included three major political figures: George Washington, George Mason, and Edmund Randolph. These men met with Madison late into the night. Together they came up with a plan for a new government, a set of 15 proposals now known as the Virginia Plan. This plan embodied Madison's ideas on the kind of government the nation needed.

With a population of more than 40,000 in 1787, Philadelphia was the nation's largest city. It was filled with inns and taverns like the City Tavern, the unofficial meeting place for the convention.

Now called Independence Hall, this Philadelphia building is the birthplace of our nation's independence. The Declaration of Independence was signed here in 1776. The Articles of Confederation were adopted here in 1781. And the U.S. Constitution was created here in 1787.

The Convention Begins

On May 14, the convention was due to begin, but many delegates had still not arrived. Travel was difficult in those days. The roads were bad and coaches often got stuck in the mud or broke an axle. A trip that normally took a week might take much longer because of problems on the road.

Finally, on May 25, the convention got underway. For the next four months, the delegates would gather in the East Room to debate the issues. To maintain secrecy, they agreed to bolt the doors and shut the windows. As the summer wore on, the heat increased. Many of the men wore wigs and wool suits, and with the doors and windows closed the room was stifling. In this hothouse atmosphere, arguments were often intense.

Through it all, Madison sat at his table near the front, scribbling away at his notes. In the evening, he took these notes back to his room and laboriously copied them out, word for word. It was an ordeal that "almost killed" him, he said. But he was determined to keep a complete and accurate record of the convention.

Debating the Virginia Plan

From the start, the convention focused much of its attention on the Virginia Plan. On May 29, Edmund Randolph presented the various points of the plan. The next day, he summed up its main idea in a bold proposal: "that a national Government ought to be established consisting of a supreme Legislative, Executive & Judiciary." Amazingly, Randolph's proposal was approved with little debate. Madison had achieved his first major goal without a struggle. The convention had agreed to form a new government. But winning support for the plan's details would prove much more difficult.

The toughest issues involved the national legislature. The delegates all agreed that Congress was a key part of government. But they disagreed on how the people and the states should be represented in Congress. Convention leaders like Madison knew that this dispute could derail the convention. So, they focused on what they thought would be a simpler issue—the executive branch. But this turned out to be a tough issue, too. Should there be one executive or three? How long should the executive serve? Should the executive be elected or appointed? For a week, the debate circled around and around these questions. Delegates would vote on a question, discuss it some more, and vote again.

Crafting a Final Document

Frustrated by this seemingly endless debate, on June 9 the delegates decided to tackle the thorny problem of representation in the legislature. The month-long debate was so fierce that, at times, it looked like the convention would fall apart. But the delegates always pulled back from the brink. Finally, on July 16, they approved the Great Compromise, which set different forms of representation for the two houses of Congress. Depressed, Madison realized that he had lost his battle for a legislature based solely on representing the people rather than the states. But with the greatest battle behind them, the framers could work toward a final plan for the new government.

By late August, the delegates formed the Committee on Postponed Matters to take up the few issues that remained to be resolved. A few days later, the committee reported back with its findings. More debate followed. But by early September, a Committee on Style—consisting of Madison and four others—was formed to prepare a final draft to present to the full convention.

Ever mindful of the importance of this plan for the nation, the delegates made a few more changes. Finally, Gouverneur Morris of New Jersey handwrote the final document—4,300 words in all. "On the question to agree to the Constitution, as amended," Madison recorded in his notes, "All the states, ay [yes]." And so at last, on September 17, 1787, most of the delegates signed the Constitution. It was ready to go to the states for ratification.

The exhausted delegates had finally completed their monumental task. The Constitution was not everything James Madison had hoped for. In his view, it left too much power in the hands of the states. But he had done what he could and was prepared to live with the outcome. Now he would turn to the fight for ratification and the task of creating a new government.

Visitors to the National Constitution Center in Philadelphia can make a choice the framers once made: to sign or not to sign a copy of the Constitution. In Signers' Hall, bronze statues of the framers stand together. Visitors are encouraged to consider the choices that each man made in 1787.

Chapter 9

The Constitution: A More Perfect Union

How has the Constitution created "a more perfect Union"?

9.1 Introduction

When the delegates left Independence Hall in September 1787, they each carried a copy of the Constitution. Their task now was to convince their states to approve the document they had worked so hard to write.

Writing the Constitution involved many compromises. Most of all, the framers wanted to create a central government that would be strong and lasting but not so strong that it endangered citizens' freedoms. In this chapter, you will see how the Constitution met these goals.

The delegates wanted ordinary citizens to understand and support the Constitution. For this reason, they organized its contents very clearly. After a short introduction, they divided the Constitution into parts called articles. Then they split each article into numbered sections that present topics in a careful order.

This structure can help you find information in the Constitution. For instance, the first section in the article on the president describes how the president is chosen. The second section lists the president's powers. The third section lists presidential duties, and the fourth explains how the president can be removed from office.

One of the marvels of the Constitution is the way it combines flexibility with a strong framework for the government. In general, the delegates allowed Congress, the president, and the courts to add details to the basic framework. They also included procedures for changing the Constitution.

This combination of strength and flexibility makes the Constitution an enduring document. The Constitution keeps its basic nature, yet the framers created it so it could also change with the times. In this chapter, you will learn more about the enduring quality of this **ingenious** document.

More than 200 years after the Constitution was created for a new nation, a vastly different United States is still governed by this document.

Life-size bronze statues at the National Constitution Center commemorate the drafting of the Constitution.

popular sovereignty the idea that the government's authority comes from the people

9.2 The Preamble Tells the Goals of Government

The delegates who crafted the Constitution chose each word carefully. Some of their best-known words are in the introduction, which is called the Preamble. The Preamble explains the reasons for the new government.

The Constitution begins with the memorable phrase "We the People." With these words, the delegates announced that the Constitution based its authority on the people themselves. The power to form the government did not come from the states or the existing government. It did not come from a sovereign (ruler) appointed by God. Instead, the power came from ordinary Americans. This concept is known as **popular sovereignty**.

The Preamble then lists the goals of the new government. First, the delegates wanted to "form a more perfect Union." What did the delegates mean by this? They wanted the states to cooperate with each other. They also wanted to create a strong relationship between the states and the national government.

The Constitution also aims to "establish Justice." Americans wanted to be ruled by laws, not by the might of soldiers or the decisions of kings. The same laws would apply to all people.

The delegates hoped that the new government would "insure domestic Tranquility." By **domestic,** they meant within the country. By tranquility, they meant peace and order. It was the government's job to keep peace and maintain order within the country.

The new government would "provide for the common defence." In other words, the national government would be responsible for protecting the nation against foreign enemies. This would allow for stronger protection than would be possible if each state had its own army and navy.

The delegates wanted the new government to "promote the general Welfare." This meant that the government could support an economy and a society in which people could prosper.

Finally, the delegates hoped to "secure the Blessings of Liberty to ourselves and our Posterity." By "posterity," the delegates meant the generations that would come after them. They wanted the government to protect the freedoms gained in the American Revolution and preserve them for Americans to enjoy in the future.

The delegates knew that these goals required a national government. However, based on their experience with a king, many people were suspicious of a strong central government. For this reason, the delegates tried to create a balanced framework that people could trust.

Visitors can view the Constitution at the National Archives in Washington, D.C., where it is permanently on display.

9.3 The Legislative Branch Makes Laws

For the framers of the Constitution, the first step in building a trusted government was to create a fair way to make laws. Article I of the Constitution gives the power to make laws to the **legislative branch** of government.

The Structure of Congress The Constitution creates a bicameral, or two-part, national legislature called Congress. The two parts, or houses, of Congress are the House of Representatives and the Senate.

Members of the Senate serve six-year terms so that they can enjoy some independence from the day-to-day opinions of voters. In contrast, members of the House serve two-year terms. As a result, they have to face the voters much more often. In this way, the framers tried to balance the independence and thoughtfulness of the Senate with the House's responsiveness to the changing wishes of the voters.

The framers also designed Congress to balance the rights of large and small states. Thus, while every state gets two senators, representation in the House is based on population. States with more people have more representatives in the House. To determine the number of representatives for each state, the Constitution calls for a census (a count of the population) to be conducted every ten years. In time, the number of representatives in the House was set at 435, divided among the states based on their population.

The framers considered the Senate to be the "upper house" of the legislature. Its members are supposed to be wiser and more experienced than members of the "lower house." Senators must be at least 30 years old, while House members must be 25. Senators must have been citizens for nine years, House members for just seven years.

legislative branch the law-making part of government, called the legislature. To legislate is to make a law.

Originally, the Constitution allowed state legislatures to choose the two senators to represent their state. Today, however, senators are elected by popular vote (direct vote by the people).

How Congress Makes Laws The primary job of Congress is to make laws. Any member of the House or Senate can submit a proposal for a new law, called a bill. However, only the House can propose new taxes. If a majority in one house votes in favor of the bill, it is sent to the other house for debate. If both houses approve the bill, it goes to the president. The bill becomes a law if the president signs it.

The president can veto any proposed law. Congress can override the president's veto, which means passing the bill over the president's objections. But to do so requires a two-thirds majority in both houses.

The Powers of Congress Article I spells out other powers of Congress. For example, only Congress can decide how to spend the money raised through taxes. Other congressional powers include the power to raise an army and navy, to declare war, to pay government debts, and to grant citizenship.

In addition, Congress may "make all Laws which shall be necessary and proper" to carry out its other powers. This power, known as the elastic clause, gives Congress the flexibility needed to do its job. Over the years, the elastic clause has been stretched to allow Congress to do many things that were never listed among its powers in the Constitution.

The Constitution establishes a government of three branches, with separate powers for each branch. By dividing power, the framers hoped to ensure that no single branch would become too powerful.

Powers of the Three Branches of Government

Legislative Branch
- Makes the laws
- Appropriates funds for laws and programs
- Approves treaties and executive appointments
- Establishes federal courts

Executive Branch
- Enforces the laws
- Acts as commander in chief of military
- Negotiates treaties
- Appoints federal judges and other top officials

Judicial Branch
- Interprets the laws
- Reviews lower-court decisions
- Judges whether laws and executive actions are constitutional
- Rules on cases between states

9.4 The Executive Branch Carries Out the Laws

A government needs people to carry out, or execute, the laws passed by the legislature. For instance, when Congress approves a tax, someone must collect the money. When Congress appropriates, or sets aside, money for low-cost housing, someone must build and manage the housing.

Article II of the Constitution describes the branch of government that fills this role, the **executive branch**. The head of the executive branch is the president. The president is often called the chief executive.

Electing the President Delegates at the Constitutional Congress were not prepared to let the people elect the president directly. Instead, they decided that the president would be selected by a group of electors. Each state would have the same number of electors as it had representatives and senators in Congress. To win the presidency, a candidate needs a majority of the electoral vote.

The president serves a four-year term. Under the Twenty-second Amendment, a president may be reelected only once. A new president makes a solemn promise called the oath of office. The Constitution gives the exact words of the oath. The oath calls for the president to "defend the Constitution." These words reinforce the importance of the Constitution as the basic law of the land.

A president must be a natural-born American citizen and at least 35 years old. The Constitution always refers to the president as "he." The delegates to the Constitutional Convention probably assumed that only men would ever vote or hold office. But nothing in the Constitution prevents a woman from being elected president.

Presidents are at the center of the American political stage. Here we see President Obama meeting with his cabinet and other close advisers.

executive branch the part of government that carries out, or executes, the laws

Article II of the Constitution gives the president the responsibility of commanding the nation's armed forces. Here, President Obama speaks to U.S. troops in Iraq.

The Powers of the President In addition to carrying out laws passed by Congress, the president is commander in chief of the nation's military forces. He or she can, with the consent of the Senate, make treaties, or formal agreements, with other nations. The president nominates, or recommends, ambassadors (official representatives to other countries) and Supreme Court justices (judges). Finally, the president can grant pardons to people convicted of violating federal, or national, laws.

The framers expected that the executive branch would need organizations, called departments, to carry out its duties. For example, the State Department handles relations with other nations. The Justice Department is involved in law enforcement as well as court actions. The heads of executive departments are members of the president's cabinet, a formal group of advisers.

Today, the executive branch has over a dozen executive departments. Each executive department contains smaller, specialized agencies. For instance, the Department of Health and Human Services contains the Food and Drug Administration. This agency works to ensure that foods and medicines meet safety standards that have been set by Congress.

Removing the President The Constitution gives Congress the power to remove a president or other officials from office if they commit certain crimes related to their duties. The House of Representatives can vote to impeach the president. To impeach means to formally accuse the president of the crimes specified in the Constitution. These include "Bribery, or other high Crimes and Misdemeanors." If the House votes to impeach, the Senate puts the president on trial, with the senators serving as the jury. If found guilty, the president is removed from office.

9.5 The Judicial Branch Interprets the Law

The framers intended for the Constitution to be the "supreme Law of the Land." That means no other laws or actions by the government or by any state can conflict with the Constitution. Protecting the Constitution is one of the principal responsibilities of the third branch of government, the **judicial branch**. The judicial branch consists of the system of federal courts and judges.

Article III of the Constitution gives the basic framework of the judicial branch. It establishes the country's highest court, the Supreme Court. It also gives Congress the power to create inferior (lower) courts to meet the nation's needs.

Federal courts also have the power to resolve disputes that involve national laws, the federal government, or the states. People accused of breaking national laws can be tried in federal courts.

judicial branch the part of government, consisting of the Supreme Court and lower federal courts, that interprets the laws

Federal Court System Congress has authorized two main sets of inferior federal courts. These lower courts are called district courts and appellate courts.

Most cases involving federal laws are first heard in district court. The United States is divided into large geographic districts. Each district covers several states. Citizens can appeal decisions given in district court, which means asking a higher court to review the case. Courts that review cases are called courts of appeal or appellate courts. An appellate court only considers whether the original trial was fair and legal. A decision by an appellate court can be appealed to the Supreme Court.

The Powers of the Supreme Court The Supreme Court is the last stop in the judicial system. Its decisions are final, and they are binding on all lower courts. The Constitution does not specify the size of the Supreme Court. Congress has set the size at nine members, who are called justices. The Constitution says that all federal judges, including Supreme Court justices, serve for "good Behaviour." Once they are appointed, justices usually serve on the Court for life.

A dispute goes directly to the Supreme Court only if it involves a state or an ambassador from another country. Any other case comes to the Supreme Court after a trial and an appeal in lower courts. Participants in either national or state courts may eventually appeal cases to the Supreme Court.

Every year, lawyers ask the Supreme Court to review thousands of cases, but the Court agrees to consider only about a hundred. The Supreme Court usually reviews a case only if the justices think the decision made by a lower court might conflict with the Constitution or a federal law. After hearing statements from both sides, the justices debate among themselves and vote. Supreme Court decisions are announced and explained in writing. These decisions then guide later decisions in lower courts.

Early in its history, the Supreme Court defined the power of **judicial review**. This is the power to decide whether laws and acts made by the legislative and executive branches conflict with the Constitution. Courts all over the country rely on the Supreme Court for guidance about what is constitutional. Judicial review gives the Supreme Court great power in its role of protecting the "supreme Law of the Land."

> **judicial review** the power of the Supreme Court to decide whether laws and acts made by the legislative and executive branches are unconstitutional

The nine members of the Supreme Court hold important positions in U.S. government. Their legal opinions on such issues as gun control, the death penalty, abortion rights, and prayer in schools are enforced in every state. In 2009, Sonia Sotomayor (second from right) became the first Hispanic justice on the Court.

checks and balances the system that allows each branch of government to limit the powers of the other two branches

9.6 Checks and Balances Between the Branches

The framers of the Constitution were very concerned about achieving a balance between a strong national government and protection for individual freedoms. They hoped that dividing the federal government into three branches was one way to limit the government's power. But what would keep one branch from dominating the others? As one delegate to the Constitutional Convention pointed out, "From the nature of man, we may be sure that those who have power in their hands . . . will always, when they can . . . increase it."

Because of this concern, the framers developed a system that would enable each branch of the government to limit the power of the other two branches. This system is called **checks and balances**.

Checking the Power of Other Branches Checks allow one branch to block the actions of another branch. For instance, Congress has the power to pass laws. But the president can check this power by vetoing a bill before it becomes law. In turn, Congress can check the president's power by overriding the veto by a two-thirds majority vote in each house.

Similarly, the judicial branch can check the actions of the other two branches. Through its power of judicial review, the Supreme Court can declare that a law, a treaty, or an executive action is unconstitutional.

Balancing the Power of Other Branches Balances allow each branch of the government to have some role in the actions and power of the other branches. For instance, judges, ambassadors, and cabinet members are appointed only if the president nominates them and the Senate approves the nomination. Similarly, the president has the power to sign treaties, but they take effect only if the Senate approves them.

The powers of the judicial branch are also balanced against the powers of the other two branches. Even though the Supreme Court can declare laws unconstitutional, it is the president who chooses federal judges—and the Senate must approve these appointments. In addition, Congress can impeach federal judges. In these ways, the legislative and executive branches have some role in the actions of the judicial branch.

These checks and balances keep any one branch of the federal government from being too strong. This balance of powers is one of the most important features of the U.S. system of government.

Checks and balances—one of the most significant features of the Constitution—prevent one branch of government from gaining too much power.

Constitutional Checks and Balances

Approves appointments of Supreme Court justices

Can reject laws that are unconstitutional

Legislative

Can veto bills

Can override vetoes

Can nominate Supreme Court justices

Can reject treaties that are unconstitutional

Judicial

Executive

9.7 The Amendment Process

The framers knew that the Constitution would need to be changed over time. As Thomas Jefferson said, "the earth belongs to the living and not to the dead." At the same time, they wanted the Constitution to provide a lasting and stable framework for the government. To maintain that stability, the framers made changing the Constitution possible but difficult.

Changing the Constitution Article V describes how changes, called amendments, can be made to the Constitution. An amendment may be proposed in one of two ways. Congress may propose an amendment by a vote of at least two-thirds of each house of Congress. Or, a national convention called by Congress at the request of at least two-thirds of the state legislatures may propose an amendment. Thus, either Congress or the states can start the process of amending the Constitution.

Proposing an amendment is only the first step. Before an amendment can become part of the Constitution, it must be ratified. The Constitution gives two ways of ratifying an amendment. An amendment may be approved by the legislatures in at least three-fourths of the states, or it may be ratified by special conventions in at least three-fourths of the states. Once an amendment is approved, it becomes part of the Constitution.

Amending the Constitution

Proposed

Amendment is proposed by a two-thirds vote of each house of Congress. **2/3**

Amendment is proposed by a national convention called by Congress at the request of two-thirds of the state legislatures. NATIONAL CONVENTION **2/3**

Ratified

Amendment is ratified by three-fourths of the state legislatures. **3/4**

Amendment is ratified by three-fourths of the state conventions. STATE CONVENTIONS **3/4**

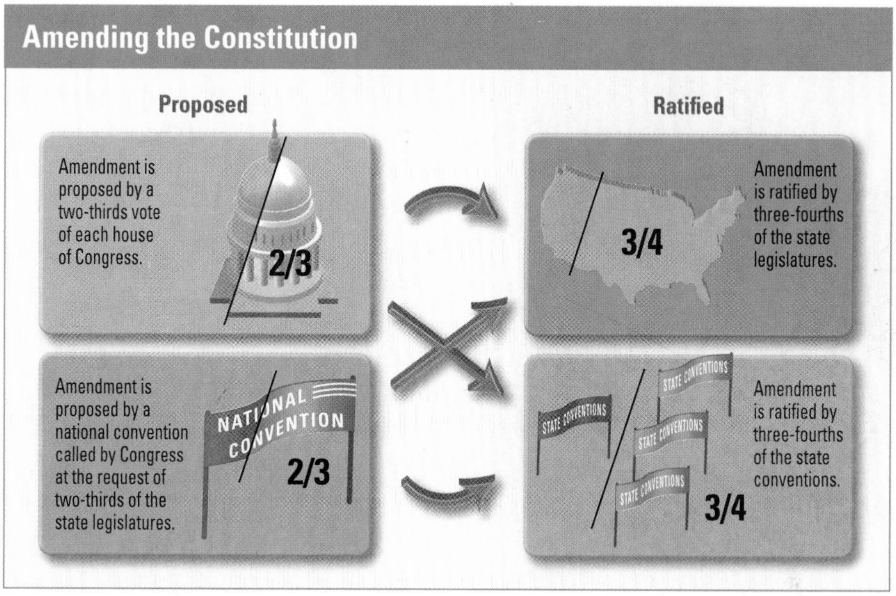

This chart shows the four ways that amendments to the Constitution can be proposed and approved, or ratified. Amendments are proposed in Congress on a regular basis. The vast majority of the proposals fail.

Amendments So Far Over the years, people have suggested more than 10,000 amendments to the Constitution. Only 27 have been approved. The first 10 amendments were added almost immediately after the Constitution was ratified. These amendments were demanded by many Americans in exchange for their support of the Constitution. Called the Bill of Rights, these 10 amendments primarily guarantee specific rights to citizens.

The other 17 amendments became part of the Constitution one at a time. Some of them changed the way certain public officials are elected. Others guaranteed the rights of certain groups of Americans. The Thirteenth Amendment made slavery illegal. The Nineteenth Amendment guaranteed women the right to vote. The Twenty-sixth Amendment gave the right to vote to all citizens over the age of 18.

interstate commerce trade and other business dealings between two or more states

9.8 The Federal System Connects the Nation and the States

The framers of the Constitution wanted a strong national government, but they also wanted the states to keep significant powers. They accomplished both goals by creating a federal system of government in which power is shared between the national and state governments.

Powers Belonging to the National Government The Constitution gives some powers only to the national government. In general, these are powers best exercised by one central authority, such as declaring war and making treaties. The Constitution also says that only the national government can print and coin money. The framers had learned from experience that separate state currencies made no sense.

Similarly, Article I gives Congress the power "to regulate Commerce with foreign Nations, and among the several States, and with the Indian Tribes." Known as the commerce clause, this provision gives the national government the power to regulate **interstate commerce**. For example, a state cannot try to protect its own businesses and industries by taxing goods imported from other states. Under the Articles of Confederation, many states had done just that. As a result, interstate trade threatened to grind to a halt. In effect, the commerce clause made the entire United States a common market, or free-trade zone.

There were several advantages to giving states a common market. First, goods and resources could flow more easily across the country. This is important because different regions do different things well. New Englanders might be very good at making cloth, but their region is not good for growing cotton. Southerners might have lots of cotton but few factories for turning it into cloth. Making interstate trade easier for cloth makers and cotton growers helps both businesses thrive.

Second, the common market made it easier to create large businesses that crossed state lines. This was very important to companies like those that built the nation's railroads in the 19th century.

Third, the common market helped to create a single national economy. Under the Articles of Confederation, it was almost as if the country had 13 small economies. These could never have grown as **diverse** or powerful as the U.S. economy did.

Notice that the commerce clause also gives the national government the right to regulate trade with Indian tribes. In effect, the Constitution treats native tribes as foreign governments. Relations with these "nations within a nation" are the responsibility of Congress, not the states.

Powers Belonging to the States The Constitution does not spell out specific powers of the states. Instead, it says that the states retain, or keep, any powers that are not given to the national government. For instance, the Constitution says nothing about schools, marriage, establishing local governments, owning property, licensing doctors and lawyers, or most crimes. The states make the laws in these areas of life.

Article I of the Constitution gives the national government sole authority to print and coin money.

The Constitution does, however, outline the responsibilities of states to each other. Article IV says that each state must give "full Faith and Credit" to the laws and court decisions of other states. This means accepting other states' laws and court decisions as legal. For example, a driver's license issued in one state is legal in every state. Similarly, states must obey legal contracts that people have made in other states. Like the commerce clause, the full faith and credit provision brings stability to business dealings. States are also required to help each other track down fleeing criminals. Criminals cannot escape justice by fleeing to another state.

The Federal System

Powers of the National Government	Shared Powers	Powers of State Governments
Coin money	Guarantee civil rights and liberties	Conduct elections
Set up a postal system	Levy and collect taxes	Establish local governments
Maintain military forces	Provide for public safety	Establish schools
Declare war	Protect public health	Regulate marriage, divorce, and adoption
Regulate interstate and foreign commerce	Establish courts	Regulate intrastate commerce
Regulate immigration	Punish lawbreakers	Provide fire and police protection
Negotiate treaties with foreign countries	Borrow money	Enact license requirements
	Construct and maintain roads	

The Constitution divides power between the federal and state governments. The idea behind the separation of powers is to create a unified nation while balancing power between the national and the state governments.

Finally, the Constitution does not allow one state to **discriminate** unreasonably against a citizen of another state. A state may not, for example, refuse to let a child who was born in another state attend its public schools.

Shared Powers Federal and state governments also share some powers. For example, both levels of government can collect taxes, build roads, borrow money, and regulate education.

If you think **federalism,** or the sharing of power, sounds complicated, you are right. Consider presidential elections. Congress sets the date for national elections, while the states register voters and run the elections. States count the ballots, while the national government organizes the Electoral College vote, which determines who will be president.

Federalism is also complicated because the Constitution provides only a general framework for the sharing of powers. There was no way for the framers to spell out rules for every possible situation. The federal system continues to evolve through new laws, court decisions, and constitutional amendments.

The Law of the Land Americans may disagree about how to interpret the Constitution, but they may not ignore it. Article VI states that the Constitution and the laws flowing from it are the "supreme Law of the Land." This means that a state's constitution, laws, and judicial decisions must agree with the Constitution. They also must not conflict with any other federal laws or treaties. In addition, everyone who holds a state or federal office must promise to support the Constitution.

federalism the constitutional system that shares power between the national and state governments

Political parties are not mentioned in the Constitution, but they have become a central part of the U.S. political system.

9.9 Popular Participation in Government

The framers of the Constitution designed a government based on the will of the people. They expected people to take part in their own government and to hold leaders responsible for their actions.

For government to reflect the popular will, it makes sense for its decisions to be based on what most people want. The Constitution therefore establishes the principle of **majority rule**. Laws are passed in Congress by majority vote. Elections are decided by a majority of voters.

It is through elections that most people have a say in what the government does. Leaders must listen to the voters, or they will not be elected (or reelected). Elections serve the vital **function** of expressing the will of the people.

But who exactly are "the people"? The framers did not specify who would have the right to vote. Over the years, states established various requirements for voting. It took many years of struggle to establish the principle that all citizens should have the right to vote. Women, for example, were not guaranteed this right until the Nineteenth Amendment was ratified in 1920.

Popular participation in government has evolved in other ways that are not part of the Constitution. For example, the Constitution makes no mention of political parties. Today, parties select most candidates for political office. Becoming active in party affairs is another way that voters can help choose their leaders and influence the positions they take on issues.

People also take part in government indirectly through **interest groups**. There are interest groups for almost any issue that people might care about. Some interest groups represent businesses, industries, and workers. Some represent groups of people, such as churchgoers, women, or minorities. Some are organized around issues, such as the environment or health care.

majority rule a basic principle of democracy that says laws are passed by majority vote and elections are decided by a majority of the voters

interest group an organization that actively promotes the view of some part of the public on specific issues in order to influence government policy

Interest groups influence government in several ways. They rally public opinion, work to elect candidates who promise to listen to them, and try to persuade lawmakers and government officials to take actions they favor.

If the framers were alive today, they might be surprised to see the changes in the system they created. Yet the remarkable thing is how successful they were in building the basic framework of American democracy. As one historian has said, the Constitution "would become the rule of life for a country larger than any of the founders imagined, and would last longer than most of them dared hope."

Chapter Summary

In this chapter, you learned how the Constitution met the delegates' goal of creating "a more perfect Union."

The Preamble As the first words of the Preamble tell us, the Constitution's authority comes directly from the people, not the states. This concept is known as popular sovereignty. The Preamble goes on to list the goals of the new government.

The Legislative Branch Article I of the Constitution creates a bicameral Congress with a House of Representatives and a Senate. Every state is represented by two senators. Representation in the House is based on a state's population. Congress's primary job is to make laws.

The Executive Branch Article II creates the executive branch. The head of the executive branch is the president. The president serves a four-year term and may be reelected once. The president carries out laws passed by Congress. Other powers of the president include making treaties and appointing Supreme Court justices.

The Judicial Branch Article III establishes the Supreme Court and gives Congress the power to create lower courts. Supreme Court decisions are binding on all lower courts. The power of judicial review allows the Supreme Court to decide whether laws and actions by the legislative and executive branches are unconstitutional.

Checks and Balances The framers developed a system of checks and balances that enables each branch of government to limit, or check, the power of the other two branches. The Constitution provides checks and balances in the powers of each branch.

The Amendment Process Article V outlines the process by which amendments can be made to the Constitution. Twenty-seven amendments have been added. The first ten amendments form the Bill of Rights.

The Federal System The Constitution creates a federal system of government in which power is shared between the national government and the states.

Popular Participation in Government Elections serve the vital function of expressing the will of the people. People also participate in government by joining political parties and taking part in interest groups.

Mum Bett was a slave who went to court to gain her freedom. In 1781, a Massachusetts court ruled that she was, in fact, free. But when the U.S. Constitution was written a few years later, it excluded both women and African Americans.

Who Are "We the People"?

The Constitution begins with the words "We the People." But just who were these people who wanted to "secure the Blessings of Liberty"? In 1787, "We the People" excluded more than half the population, including African Americans and women. What were the framers thinking?

Mum Bett had had enough. Born into slavery, she had served in the home of John Ashley of Sheffield, Massachusetts, for more than 30 years. When Mrs. Ashley hit her with a hot kitchen shovel one day in 1781, Mum Bett fled and refused to return.

Instead, Mum Bett asked a lawyer, Theodore Sedgwick, to represent her in court. Mum Bett wanted to be free, and she believed the courts would recognize that she had the right to freedom. Sedgwick took her case.

Mum Bett, who later changed her name to Elizabeth Freeman, knew about the Massachusetts state constitution. It had been ratified in 1780. Mum Bett had heard that it said that "all people were born free and equal." She believed that "all people" included her and that she had a legal right to her freedom. The court agreed, and Mum Bett became a free woman. John Ashley, her former master, had to pay her 30 shillings in damages.

Though the court ruled in favor of Mum Bett, the problem of just who would be included in "We the People" did not go away. It surfaced again just a few years later. In 1787, the leaders of the United States met in Philadelphia. They wrote a constitution for their new country. But they did not pay attention to the Massachusetts court's decision that Mum Bett was free. Initially, the U.S. Constitution excluded women and African Americans from enjoying the full benefits of liberty.

The colonies had fought the revolution to gain their freedom. They created a democracy, but many people were disallowed from participating in it. Neither African Americans nor women could vote or hold office. These groups had to fight for many years to gain the right to take part in these democratic processes. But the question arises: why were they excluded in the first place?

The Responsibilities of Freedom

The 55 white men who wrote the U.S. Constitution were a privileged group. More than half of them had been to college, 34 had studied law, almost half had been in Congress, and at least 20 owned slaves. The delegates were hardly typical of the larger American population at the time. But, in many ways, they reflected the general beliefs of 18th-century American society.

The framers of the Constitution believed that only certain people could handle the responsibilities of freedom. The way they viewed it, only people who controlled their own lives should have a say in the government. Dependent people—those who didn't own property or who worked for someone else—could not exercise their own free will, the framers reasoned. If they voted, they would cast their ballots as they were told to. The framers believed that the votes of such people would damage the entire country.

To the framers, as to many Americans in those days, only a property owner could be an independent thinker. That excluded more than half of the population. "We the People" were white, male, and propertied.

Some of the excluded could eventually join fully in civic life. For example, indentured servants completed their service after a number of years. They might eventually own property. Some women might inherit property from their husbands. But few women were likely ever to enjoy all the rights the Constitution promised.

And many people were completely locked out of economic opportunity. Slaves could never own property. They could never be independent and free. The American system made it impossible for them to share as citizens in the new United States.

Neither women nor African Americans simply accepted their exclusion, however. For many years, until they were successful, both women and African Americans would argue that they should be able to participate fully in American democracy.

The framers of the Constitution had specific ideas about who "We the People" were. In their view, only people who owned property could manage the responsibilities of freedom. In a mural at Antioch College in Ohio, artist Gilbert Wilson painted a different view of American society. In this panel, titled "Order," a diverse group of women and men come together around a common table.

Abigail Adams was an independent thinker who had strong ideas about women's rights. In 1787, she was in Great Britain, where John Adams was serving as the representative of the new United States.

Margaret Brent requested voting rights more than 100 years before the colonies declared independence. In 1648, she asked the Maryland Assembly to grant her two votes—one for owning land and one for being Lord Baltimore's legal representative. The governor refused her request.

The Rights of Women

Perhaps the most famous woman to speak out for women's rights at the time was Abigail Adams. Her husband, John Adams, would become the second president of the United States. In the spring of 1776, when John was a delegate to the Continental Congress, Abigail wrote to him, saying,

> *In the new code of laws which I suppose it will be necessary for you to make, I desire you would remember the ladies . . . Do not put such unlimited power into the hands of husbands. Remember, all men would be tyrants if they could.*

Abigail Adams knew that in the 18th century, women had legal status only through their husbands. A married woman was called a *feme covert,* a legal term that comes from the French words for "covered woman." Women were "covered"—invisible as far as the law was concerned—by their husbands. Abigail warned her husband that women would not follow any laws that did not guarantee their rights. They would not be "bound by any laws in which we have no voice or representation."

John Adams, however, feared that expanding freedom would lead to chaos. He told Abigail that women had more power over their husbands than they realized. That being true, he believed that men would be better off excluding women from the new country's laws. "Depend upon it," he wrote, "we know better than to repeal our masculine systems."

Nonetheless, some women did vote during the republic's early years. A New Jersey law, passed in 1790, identified voters as "he or she." Historians disagree about why. Some point out that New Jersey was home to many Quakers, who believed in equality. Others call attention to the fact that only some counties granted women the vote and say it was more about political power. These counties, they say, hoped

women's votes would affect election outcomes in their favor. Whatever the reasons, women voted in New Jersey until the law was repealed in 1807. It would take more than 100 years—and a hard fight—to pass an amendment to the Constitution that granted women the right to vote.

The Rights of African Americans

When the war ended, many African Americans left the United States. They feared that the new democracy would not include them. Some went to England. Others went to Canada or the West Indies. Most of those who left were fugitive slaves. By some accounts, 30,000 African Americans left Virginia. Another 25,000 left South Carolina.

The majority of the African Americans who stayed were slaves. But some were not. The 1790 census reported that there were about 59,000 free blacks living in the United States. Among them was Benjamin Banneker. Banneker was a Maryland tobacco farmer, a scientist, and a surveyor. He wrote a well-known almanac. He also wrote a letter to Thomas Jefferson. In it, he explained why African Americans should have the same rights as whites.

Banneker wrote the letter in 1791, the year in which he surveyed the land for the new national capital. At the time, Jefferson was secretary of state. Banneker explained that both blacks and whites were created by God. "However variable we may be in society or religion," he wrote, "however diversified in situation or color, we are all of the same family." He went on to quote the Declaration of Independence— to the man who wrote it.

> *"We hold these truths to be self-evident, that all men are created equal; that they are endowed by their Creator with certain unalienable rights, and that among these are life, liberty, and the pursuit of happiness."*

Banneker explained that African Americans deserved those rights, just as whites did. He even went so far as to accuse Jefferson of using "fraud and violence" to keep blacks enslaved.

Although a slaveholder himself, Jefferson wrote back that "No body wishes more than I do, to see such proofs as you exhibit, that nature has given to our black brethren talents equal to those of the other colors of men." But slavery continued in the South until the Civil War.

The freedoms guaranteed by the Constitution would not be extended to African Americans for many years. African American men gained the right to vote in 1870. It would take another 50 years before all women, including African Americans, were granted voting rights. And not until the 1960s were laws passed giving all African Americans the legal protection to exercise their right to vote.

The words "We the People" still begin our Constitution. More than 200 years later, their meaning has changed in ways that Mum Bett, Abigail Adams, and Benjamin Banneker would approve.

Benjamin Banneker published six almanacs between 1792 and 1797. A self-educated scientist, he included information on tides, astronomy, and eclipses that he calculated himself.

Chapter 10

The Bill of Rights

What freedoms does the Bill of Rights protect and why are they important?

10.1 Introduction

To James Madison, the creation of the Constitution seemed nothing less than "a miracle." By 1788, however, it seemed that it would take another miracle to get it adopted.

The adoption of the Constitution depended on ratification, or approval, by 9 of the 13 states. Ratification started off smoothly, with Delaware, Pennsylvania, New Jersey, Georgia, and Connecticut all saying yes. Then came Massachusetts, where opposition ran strong.

When the Massachusetts ratification convention met early in 1788, defeat seemed certain. Opponents objected that the Constitution did not list the rights of the people. Many delegates said they would not vote in favor of ratification unless such a list were added.

In desperation, the Constitution's supporters, the Federalists, looked to John Hancock, the governor of Massachusetts. Hancock had stayed away from the convention, pleading a painful attack of gout (a form of arthritis) in his feet. In fact, he was waiting to make an appearance until he could be sure he would be on the winning side.

The Federalists tried to take advantage of Hancock's vanity. Virginia, they hinted, might not ratify the Constitution. If it did not, then George Washington, a Virginian, could not run for president. And if Washington didn't run, who was the best choice for the honor? Why, none other than the great governor of Massachusetts.

Hancock swallowed the bait. The governor was carried into the convention, his feet wrapped in bandages. In a dramatic speech, he urged the delegates to approve the Constitution as written. At the same time, he promised that the first task of the new Congress would be to amend the Constitution by adding a bill of rights.

The vote was close, but Massachusetts chose to ratify. The Federalists' strategy, "Ratify now, amend later," also worked well in other states. By the end of 1788, the Constitution was the law of the land.

In this chapter, you will learn how Federalists kept their promise to add a list of rights to the Constitution. You will also learn about the freedoms protected by the Bill of Rights and why they are important.

John Hancock helped win approval for the Constitution and pushed for the inclusion of the Bill of Rights.

◀ This illustration represents the Bill of Rights at the time it was approved in 1791.

10.2 Creating the Bill of Rights

For all his hopes, John Hancock never got to be president. By a narrow vote, Virginia did ratify the Constitution. In the first presidential election, held in 1789, George Washington became the nation's first president. John Adams of Massachusetts became vice president.

When the first Congress met that year, no one seemed in much of a hurry to amend the Constitution. Representative James Madison, however, did not forget the promises made during the ratification debate. Originally, he had opposed adding a bill of rights to the Constitution. Such a listing seemed unnecessary to him. Thomas Jefferson helped change his mind. In a letter to Madison, Jefferson argued that "a bill of rights is what the people are entitled to against every government on Earth . . . and what no just government should refuse."

Debate and Approval in Congress While Congress debated other issues, Madison sifted through nearly 100 proposed amendments. He chose those that seemed least **controversial,** or least likely to cause conflict, and presented them to Congress on June 8, 1789.

Critics jumped on Madison's proposals as meaningless "milk-and-water" cures for imaginary problems. The debate that followed was, in Madison's words, "extremely difficult." As months dragged on with no agreement, he wrote to a friend that the task had become a "nauseous project." Still, he persevered until Congress finally approved 12 amendments.

Ratification by the States Under the Constitution, three-quarters of the states must ratify an amendment before it can become law. The states rejected the first two amendments, which dealt with the size of congressional districts and congressional pay raises. Both amendments were considered unnecessary. By 1791, the required number of states (nine) had approved the other ten amendments. Together, these ten amendments form the **Bill of Rights**.

When Madison first proposed the Bill of Rights, some people saw his amendments as useless "paper barriers" against abuses of government power. For more than 200 years, however, his "paper barriers" have proven far stronger than even Madison might have hoped.

10.3 First Amendment Rights

James Madison combined five basic freedoms into the First Amendment. These are the freedoms of religion, speech, the press, and assembly and the right to petition the government. Many people consider these basic freedoms to be the most important part of the Bill of Rights.

These First Amendment rights would have been meaningless, however, without some way to protect them. When a person believes that the government has violated these rights, he or she may challenge the government's action in court. The same is true of all other rights protected in the Constitution.

James Madison, who is often called the "Father of the Constitution," also crafted the Bill of Rights. This listing of the first ten amendments to the Constitution was ratified in 1791.

Bill of Rights a formal listing of the basic rights of U.S. citizens

If the case reaches the Supreme Court, the nine Supreme Court justices decide how the Constitution applies to the situation. After hearing both sides, the justices vote on the case. One of the justices from the majority side then writes a majority opinion. This document explains how the Court interpreted the Constitution to reach its decision. Any justices who disagree with the majority decision may write minority opinions explaining their reasoning. As you read about First Amendment rights, you will see how the Supreme Court has applied these rights to real-life situations.

The Right to Worship Freely The First Amendment has two **guarantees** of religious freedom. The first says, "Congress shall make no law respecting an establishment of religion." This means that Congress cannot make any faith the official religion of the United States. Nor can it make laws that favor any religion over another. As Thomas Jefferson explained in a letter to a friend, the amendment builds "a wall of separation between church and state."

How high should that wall be? The founders of the American republic disagreed about the answer to this question. For example, lawmakers in Virginia proposed using state taxes to help pay for teachers of religion. George Washington was among those who supported this idea as long as no particular church was favored. Opponents of the proposal, like Madison, argued that government and religion should be completely separate.

In a 1971 case known as *Lemon v. Kurtzman,* the Supreme Court sided with Madison's view. This case challenged a Pennsylvania law that used public tax money to pay for books and teachers' salaries at private religious schools. The Court held that the law was unconstitutional because it allowed too close a connection between government and religion.

The second religious guarantee in the First Amendment says, "Congress shall make no law . . . prohibiting the free exercise" of religion. This means that people can hold any religious beliefs, without fear of punishment. However, they cannot necessarily do whatever they want in the name of religious freedom. For instance, the Supreme Court has held that parents are not free to deny their children medical treatment or vaccinations because of their religious beliefs.

The beliefs of minority religious groups, like the Hare Krishna pictured here, are protected by the Bill of Rights.

In the 1960s, students at the University of California, Berkeley, protested limits imposed by the school administration on their freedom of speech. These protests became known as the Free Speech Movement and spread to students at campuses across the country.

The Right to Free Speech and Press The First Amendment protects freedom of speech and freedom of the press. The Supreme Court often treats these rights together as the right of free expression.

Freedom of the press is important because of the vital roles that the press plays in a democratic society. Newspapers, magazines, and other media such as books and television act as watchdogs on the government. They also allow for the free flow of ideas, which citizens need to stay informed and to make up their own minds about important issues. Without a free press, democratic self-government would be impossible.

Americans had learned in colonial days that a free press was their best protection against abuse of government power. In 1735, John Peter Zenger was arrested for printing reports that the governor of New York had taken bribes. The prosecutors said that it was illegal to damage the governor's good name, even if Zenger had published the truth. Zenger's lawyer argued that no one should be jailed for "exposing and opposing arbitrary power by speaking and writing truth." The jury agreed, and Zenger was freed.

Freedom of the press also brings responsibilities, such as taking care not to spread false accusations or publish information that would be helpful to an enemy in wartime. Freedom of speech brings responsibilities as well. Although the First Amendment protects the right to speak freely in public places, like streets and parks, that right is not unlimited. The Supreme Court has allowed limits on some kinds of speech, such as speech that endangers public safety. As one justice said, "The most stringent [strongest] protection of free speech would not protect a man in falsely shouting fire in a theater and causing a panic."

The Supreme Court has held that speech means more than just words. Free expression includes symbolic speech, or actions people take to express their opinions.

Protection of symbolic speech was an issue in the case of *Texas v. Johnson* (1989). This case involved a man who had been convicted in Texas of burning an American flag as a form of protest. When he appealed his case to the Supreme Court, the justices overturned his conviction. No form of expression can be banned, the Court held, just because "society finds the idea itself offensive or disagreeable."

The Right to Assemble and Petition The final two rights protected in the First Amendment are the right to peaceably assemble (meet together with others) and to petition (appeal to) the government. The right to assembly means that citizens can use public property for meetings and demonstrations. Parades, protest marches, and political rallies are all forms of peaceful assembly protected by the First Amendment.

While the First Amendment protects peaceful meetings, it does not give people the right to close streets or buildings or to protest violently. Police can arrest a speaker who urges listeners to riot or to break the law.

What if an assembly is peaceful, but the people watching it are not? This question came up in the case of *Gregory v. Chicago* (1969). The case began when comedian Dick Gregory led a protest march to the home of Chicago's mayor. Residents in the neighborhood began throwing eggs and shouting insults at the marchers. Fearful of a riot, police asked the marchers to leave. When the marchers refused, the police arrested them.

The marchers challenged their arrests in court, claiming that their protest was protected under the First Amendment's right of assembly. The Supreme Court agreed that the marchers had assembled peacefully. If anyone should have been arrested, it was the mayor's neighbors.

This Earth Day demonstration on the Mall in Washington, D.C., illustrates the right of assembly protected under the First Amendment.

10.4 Citizen Protections

The next three amendments protect citizens from various kinds of government abuse. All three reflect the experience of American colonists under British rule.

Second Amendment: The Right to Bear Arms During colonial times, Great Britain had used a standing, or permanent, army to keep order in the colonies. After winning their independence, Americans were suspicious of standing armies. They preferred to rely on volunteer state militias to protect the new nation. The Second Amendment states that "A well-regulated militia, being necessary to the security of a free state, the right of the people to keep and bear arms, shall not be infringed [limited]."

The meaning of this amendment has been much debated. Some people argue that it protects the right of people to own guns only if they are part of an organized militia. An example of such a militia is today's National Guard. Others believe that the Second Amendment protects the right of individuals to own weapons for their own self-defense. In 2008, the Supreme Court supported this view in the case of *District of Columbia v. Heller*. The Court held that the Second Amendment protects an individual's right to own a gun for personal use, including self-defense inside the home.

Third Amendment: Quartering Troops in Homes Before the American Revolution, Great Britain had forced colonists to house British soldiers. The Third Amendment gave Americans the right to refuse such requests.

Today, soldiers are not quartered in homes. The Third Amendment remains important, however, as a warning to the government to respect the privacy of people's homes. As Supreme Court justice Joseph Story said, "A man's house shall be his own castle, privileged against all civil and military intrusion."

In colonial America, guns were an important part of everyday life. They were used for hunting and for protection in a time when police were often far away. Militias also protected colonists against outside invasion and Indian attacks.

The Granger Collection, New York

Fourth Amendment: Searches and Seizures The Fourth Amendment protects people and their belongings from "unreasonable searches and seizures." A seizure is the act of forcibly taking control of a person or property. Before arresting a person or searching someone's home, police must show a judge that there is good reason for such action. The judge then issues a **warrant** that says exactly who will be arrested or what will be searched.

Nowhere in the Fourth Amendment, however, does it say that a warrant is required for every government search. Many Supreme Court cases have held that warrants are not always necessary. But there must be probable cause, or a strong reason for the search.

The Fourth Amendment also does not define "unreasonable search." The Supreme Court provided a definition in 1967 when it held that the search must respect an individual's right to privacy.

Police must follow careful guidelines in searches and seizures of private property.

10.5 Legal Rights and Protections

The next four amendments lay out the rights and protections that apply to people who are accused of crimes or are involved in other legal disputes.

Fifth Amendment: Legal Rights The Fifth Amendment is the longest amendment in the Bill of Rights. It lists five important rights of citizens involved with the justice system.

First, this amendment gives people who are accused of serious crimes the right to a grand jury hearing. A grand jury is a group of citizens who hear the government's evidence and decide whether a trial is justified. If so, the grand jury issues an indictment, or formal charge. If not, the accused person is released.

Second, the amendment protects citizens from **double jeopardy**. Jeopardy means risk. This protection ensures that a person who is tried for a crime and found not guilty cannot be tried again for that same crime.

Third, the amendment prohibits **self-incrimination**. This means that police cannot force people to say things that might be used against them in a trial.

Today, police are required to remind people of their right to remain silent before they start to question them. They must also warn people that anything they do say can be used against them at a trial. This reminder is known as the "Miranda warning," after the case in which the Supreme Court defined this requirement.

warrant an order from a judge that authorizes police or other officials to take a certain action, such as searching someone's property

double jeopardy putting a person on trial more than once for the same crime

self-incrimination giving testimony that can be used against oneself

due process the concept that the government must follow clear rules and act reasonably as it carries out the law

defendant a person who is required to defend himself or herself in a legal action. An example is an accused person who is put on trial for a crime.

The protection against self-incrimination also applies to a defendant testifying in court. Defendants may refuse to answer questions that might damage their case. This refusal is called "taking the Fifth."

Next, the Fifth Amendment says that a person cannot be **deprived** of "life, liberty, or property, without due process of law." The government must follow clear rules and act reasonably as it carries out the law. This concept is known as **due process**. For example, the Supreme Court has held that every person should be presumed innocent until proven guilty. In addition, the government must prove its case against a **defendant** "beyond a reasonable doubt."

Finally, the Fifth Amendment says that the government cannot take someone's private property for public use "without just compensation." Just **compensation** means that the government must pay a fair price when it takes over a person's property for purposes such as building roads or parks.

Sixth Amendment: Criminal Trial Rights The Sixth Amendment lists a number of rights that are designed to provide accused persons with fair trials. It begins with the right to "a speedy and public trial, by an impartial jury."

The right to a speedy trial means that people cannot be kept in jail for long periods before being judged at a trial. Speedy trials also ensure that witnesses testify while their memories of events are still fresh.

"Public" means that trials may not be held in secret. Citizens have a right to attend trials to make sure that justice is being done.

An accused person also has the right to be judged by a jury of people who live in his or her area. The jury must be impartial, which means that jurors are not prejudiced (influenced) against the defendant. Courts have also said that prosecutors cannot exclude potential jurors based on their race or gender.

Monica Goodling was an official in the administration of President George W. Bush. In 2007, she took the Fifth Amendment to avoid testifying before Congress about the dismissal of several U.S. attorneys until she was granted immunity.

Before a trial, the prosecutor must tell the accused person not only the charge, but also the time and place of the supposed crime. This information is essential to the accused person's preparation of his or her defense.

A defendant also has the right to hear and question all witnesses who testify at the trial. In addition, the defendant can ask the court to order reluctant (unwilling) witnesses to testify against their wishes.

Lastly, a defendant has the right to an attorney to assist in his or her defense. The Supreme Court has called this the most important of all the rights of accused persons. Without legal help, an innocent person may all too easily be convicted of a crime. In the past, only people with money to hire lawyers enjoyed this important right. Today, people accused of crimes are provided with a lawyer if they cannot afford to pay for one.

A lawyer's job is to convince the jury to decide in his or her client's favor during a trial. The right to a jury trial is one of a number of citizen protections found in the Sixth Amendment.

Seventh Amendment: Civil Trial Rights Not all trials involve criminal actions. Some trials decide civil cases, or disputes between people or businesses. Civil cases typically involve money, property, or family matters, such as divorce. The Seventh Amendment says that, in all but the most minor cases, people involved in a civil case have a right to a jury trial.

The Seventh Amendment also says that "no fact tried by a jury shall be otherwise reexamined." This means that after a jury decides the facts of a case, no judge can overrule the jury's decision.

Eighth Amendment: Bail and Punishments The Eighth Amendment protects an accused person's rights both before and after trial. Before a trial, it forbids a judge from demanding "excessive" bail. Bail is money or property given to the court to hold until an accused person shows up at trial. If a defendant cannot pay bail, he or she stays in jail until trial. The Eighth Amendment prevents judges from using unreasonably high bail to keep someone in jail before his or her day in court.

After a trial, if the person is found guilty, the Eighth Amendment forbids "excessive fines" and "cruel and unusual punishments." It does not say what such punishments are. In 1791, physical punishments like whipping and branding were common. Today, they are considered cruel. As Supreme Court justice Thurgood Marshall has written, "A penalty that was permissible at one time in our Nation's history is not necessarily permissible today."

Calvin and Hobbes   by Bill Watterson

This cartoon illustrates how passionate Americans are about their rights—even those that don't exist.

The Supreme Court has interpreted this amendment to mean that punishments must be "proportionate" to the crime. Judges cannot, for example, impose long prison terms on people convicted of minor crimes. The Court has also held that this amendment prohibits inhumane prison conditions, such as depriving prisoners of food.

Today, Americans continue to debate whether the death penalty should be banned under the Eighth Amendment. Opponents of the death penalty have argued that executing anyone is a cruel and unusual punishment, no matter how horrible the crime. The Supreme Court has disagreed. In the 1976 case of *Gregg v. Georgia,* the Court's decision stated that "the punishment of death for the crime of murder does not, under all circumstances, violate the Eighth" Amendment.

10.6   Other Rights and Powers

The last two amendments were included to help keep a proper balance of rights and power among the federal government, the people, and the states.

Ninth Amendment: Rights Retained by the People   One argument raised against putting a bill of rights in the Constitution was that no such list could be complete. If some rights were listed and others were not, did this mean that people had only the listed rights?

The Ninth Amendment provides the answer. It says that even though "certain rights" are listed in the Constitution, other rights and liberties not listed there are also "retained [kept] by the people." The rights protected under the Constitution are not the only rights people have. An example of this is the right to privacy.

Tenth Amendment: Powers Reserved to the States   The Tenth Amendment was included to protect the states from excessive federal power. It says that powers not given to the national government by the Constitution are "reserved to the states . . . or to the people."

This amendment is known as the reserved powers clause. Reserved powers are those that the Constitution does not specifically give to the national government or specifically prohibit the states from having.

So what are reserved powers? The examples are numerous, and they affect many areas of everyday life. States use their reserved powers to pass laws regulating speed limits for drivers. Reserved powers allow the states to determine how many days students attend public schools. States have the power to run elections, to regulate businesses inside their borders, and to set up local governments. Do you get your hair cut in a salon or barber shop? Do you visit the doctor when you are sick? The Tenth Amendment gives your state the power to issue business licenses to hair salons and the power to make sure your doctor is licensed to practice medicine in your state.

Chapter Summary

In this chapter, you read about the Bill of Rights—the first ten amendments to the Constitution—and the important freedoms it protects.

Creating the Bill of Rights By 1791, nine of the 13 states had ratified ten amendments drafted by James Madison and approved by Congress. These ten amendment form the Bill of Rights.

First Amendment Rights The First Amendment protects five basic freedoms: the right to worship freely, freedom of speech, freedom of the press, and the rights of assembly and petition.

Citizen Protections The Second, Third, and Fourth Amendments protect people against the abuse of government power.

Legal Rights and Protections The Fifth through the Eighth Amendments are intended to guarantee fair treatment for people involved in legal actions.

Other Rights and Powers The Ninth and Tenth Amendments concern the relationships among the federal government, the states, and the people. The Ninth Amendment protects rights that are not expressly listed in the Constitution. The Tenth Amendment says that powers that are neither given to the national government nor forbidden to the states belong to the states and the people.

The Bill of Rights contains many of the rights that we think of as American freedoms.

Marian Ward (right) was a senior in high school when she legally challenged a federal court's ruling against public prayer at her school.

What Is Religious Freedom?

Freedom of religion is the first right listed in the Bill of Rights. The founders of our nation took this freedom very seriously. Yet, despite its prominent place in the First Amendment, religious freedom is a hotly debated issue. The struggle to define and protect this right continues even today.

September 3, 1999, was a big day in Santa Fe, Texas, a small town just south of Houston. It was the first day of the high school football season. But there was more happening that day than just a football game.

Marian Ward, a student at the school, was going to read a prayer over the loudspeaker before the game. This was a common custom in towns across Texas. But a U.S. district court had recently said that public prayer on school grounds violated religious freedom under the First Amendment. This decision angered many people in Santa Fe, who believed they had a right to hear prayers at football games.

Marian, the daughter of a Baptist minister, defied the court that night and delivered her prayer anyway. "God, thank you for this evening," she began. "Thank you for all the prayers that were lifted up this week for me. I pray that you'll bless each and every person here tonight." When she was done, the crowd erupted in applause.

Not everyone applauded, though. Amanda Bruce, another student, objected that the prayer could be offensive to "every other faith that does not pray to Jesus or God. People need to think about the person sitting next to them who may not be a Christian."

Amanda, who is Catholic, helped to organize a protest before the homecoming game a month later. She and other students carried signs that read, "Prayer is Private." The football game prayers continued through that season, though. The following year, the Supreme Court declared the practice unconstitutional throughout the nation.

The dispute over public prayer at football games highlights a deeper question: What is religious freedom? In theory, it is the right to worship as one pleases, or not to worship at all, without interference from others. But it is not quite that simple. In fact, religious freedom means different things to different people. Most Americans believe strongly in the principle of religious freedom. But they don't always agree on how this right should be defined and protected.

Religious Liberty in the Colonies

The issue of religious freedom has been debated since the earliest days of the American colonies. Many colonists came to America seeking religious freedom. But that does not mean they extended that liberty to people who held different beliefs. For the most part, their attitude seemed to be "religious freedom for me but not for you." Most colonies set up a government-sponsored church and insisted that people attend services. People who practiced a different faith could be punished. They might be fined, jailed, or even whipped.

Gradually, however, things began to change. As more colonists arrived, the variety of religious faiths increased. This made it more difficult to impose any one faith on a colony. Another factor was the growing influence of Enlightenment beliefs. Leading thinkers, such as Thomas Jefferson and James Madison, believed that people had a natural right to equality. This meant that no religion or church should be favored over any other. To do so, they argued, would deny equal rights to all.

Jefferson's Law

In Jefferson's view, in fact, government should not support or oppose any church or religion. All religious matters should be left to the individual. In other words, there should be a clear separation between church and state. In 1776, Jefferson began to promote religious reform in the Virginia Assembly. Three years later, as governor, he proposed a bill to make religious freedom the law in Virginia.

Jefferson's bill aroused great opposition. Some members of the assembly thought it was too radical. They wanted the state to support the Christian religion. While Jefferson was away in France, Madison fought for the bill's passage. Finally, in 1786, it became law.

Jefferson's law, the Virginia Statute for Religious Freedom, said that no one could be forced to attend or support "any religious worship, place, or ministry." It also said that no one should be made to suffer for "his religious opinions or belief." All people, it said, should be free to express "their opinions in matters of religion." Jefferson considered this law one the most important achievements of his life. It laid the foundation for religious freedom in the First Amendment.

Americans have disputed the meaning of religious freedom since colonial times. These football players pray before a game in Odessa, Texas, even though a Supreme Court decision bans public prayer at school events.

The Religion Clause of the First Amendment

Like Jefferson, James Madison was committed to religious liberty. In his proposal for the Bill of Rights, he made sure it contained a clause on religious freedom. In fact, that clause is the first right listed in the First Amendment.

During the months that Congress debated the Bill of Rights, the religion clause was revised several times. Finally, Congress approved the final version, which reads,

> *Congress shall make no law respecting an establishment of religion, or prohibiting the free exercise thereof.*

This sentence may have seemed clear at the time. But it has led to some confusion over the years. First, it mentions Congress but says nothing about the states. Madison tried to include words that would prevent states from limiting religious freedom, but the Senate blocked his efforts.

A second source of confusion is the phrase "an establishment of religion." To some people, this simply means that the government cannot create an official religion or support a particular church. Others argue that the phrase means more than that. They say it forbids all government involvement in religion. To support this view, they cite a letter Jefferson wrote in 1802. In it, he said that the First Amendment builds "a wall of separation between church and state."

From the 1940s on, the Supreme Court has issued decisions on arguments about religious freedom. Even on the Court, the nine justices disagree on interpretation of the First Amendment.

The Issue Moves to the Courts

For 150 years after the Bill of Rights was written, there was little debate over religious freedom. The courts—and most Americans— seemed to agree on what it meant.

In the 1940s, however, that sense of agreement came to an end. The Supreme Court began to hear cases that involved possible violations of religious freedom at the state level. The Court based its actions on the Fourteenth Amendment, which was ratified in 1868. This amendment guarantees equal protection of the laws to all citizens, wherever they live. This means that First Amendment rights, including religious freedom, apply to the states.

One of the Court's first important cases was *Everson v. Board of Education of the Township of Ewing* (1947). This case involved the use of tax money in New Jersey to fund bus transport for students at Catholic schools. A man named Arch Everson claimed that this use of public money represented government support for religion. In its decision, the Court agreed that the First Amendment does not allow public funds to be used for religious activities, including religious education. It said that government must remain "neutral" in religious matters. It cannot promote or oppose any church or religion.

In this case, however, the Court did not agree that the use of tax money violated the First Amendment. It said that providing basic services, such as bus transport, does not qualify as support for religion. It said that students have a right to basic services no matter where they went to school. The Court's decision affirmed the separation of church and state. But it also showed that the details of a case matter. The issue is not always clear-cut.

Since that time, the Court has heard many cases involving religious freedom. School prayer has been a key issue. In *Engel v. Vitale* (1962), the Court struck down the use of an official prayer in New York public schools. In *Lee v. Weisman,* the Court banned school-sponsored prayer at graduation ceremonies. And in *Santa Fe Independent School District v. Doe* (2000)—the football-prayer case—the Court said that schools cannot sponsor a prayer before football games.

These decisions sparked angry protests. Some people claimed that religion belongs in public schools. They said the Court was violating their religious freedom by prohibiting prayer and other religious activities in schools. Some justices on the Court disagreed with the majority decisions. They argued that the Court was opposing religion. For most justices, however, the decisions reflected a neutral position, neither for nor against religion.

Clearly, the issue of religious freedom arouses strong feelings. What seems like a right to some people may not seem like a right to others. These disputes are not resolved easily. In fact, they may never be settled completely. The effort to ensure religious freedom for all remains an ongoing challenge.

In Mississippi, opponents of school prayer made the statement that separation of church and state was pro-Constitution, not anti-religion.

Forming a New Nation

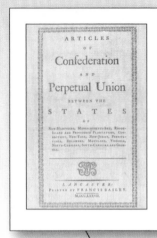

1781
**Articles of
Confederation Adopted**
The states adopt the Articles
of Confederation as the first
plan of government for the
United States. The plan is
too weak to be effective.

Aug. 1786–Feb. 1787
Shays's Rebellion
In Massachusetts, a
rebellion of farmers
shows the weakness
of the new U.S. govern-
ment under the Articles
of Confederation.

1780	1781	1782	1783	1784	1785	1786

NORTHWEST
TERRITORY

1787
Northwest Ordinance
Congress passes the Northwest
Ordinance as the plan under
which the Northwest Territory
will be governed. The law
also establishes the process
for admitting new states to
the Union.

May 1787
Constitutional Convention Opens
Delegates from 12 states meet in Philadelphia, Pennsylvania, and create a new plan of government that becomes the U.S. Constitution. George Washington leads the convention.

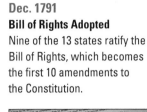

Oct. 1787
The Federalist Papers
Leaders who support ratification of the Constitution, including James Madison, begin publishing a series of essays explaining how the Constitution would create a stronger union of states.

Dec. 1791
Bill of Rights Adopted
Nine of the 13 states ratify the Bill of Rights, which becomes the first 10 amendments to the Constitution.

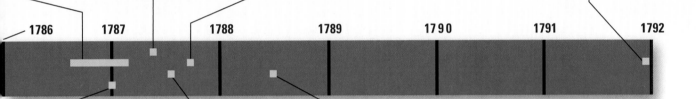

| 1786 | 1787 | 1788 | 1789 | 1790 | 1791 | 1792 |

July 1787
The Great Compromise
Proposed by Roger Sherman, the Great Compromise is accepted by the Constitutional Convention. Under this plan, representation in the House of Representatives is based on each state's population. In the Senate, each state has equal representation.

June 1788
U.S. Constitution Adopted
The U.S. Constitution is adopted after having been ratified by 9 of the 13 states. It becomes the supreme law of the United States and provides the framework for the organization of government.

Unit 4

Launching the New Republic

A statue of George Washington stands before
the columns of Federal Hall in New York City.
Washington was inaugurated as the nation's first
president at this site in 1789.

Launching the New Republic

The 50 years following the drafting of the Constitution were a time of great change for the United States. By 1838, a total of 13 new states had joined the original 13, as shown on the map below. New territory had been added to the republic as well. The nation's first 50 years also saw the birth of the first political parties, another war fought with Great Britain, and the election of the nation's first western president. In addition, transportation links had been built, and many of the nation's American Indians had been relocated west of the Mississippi River.

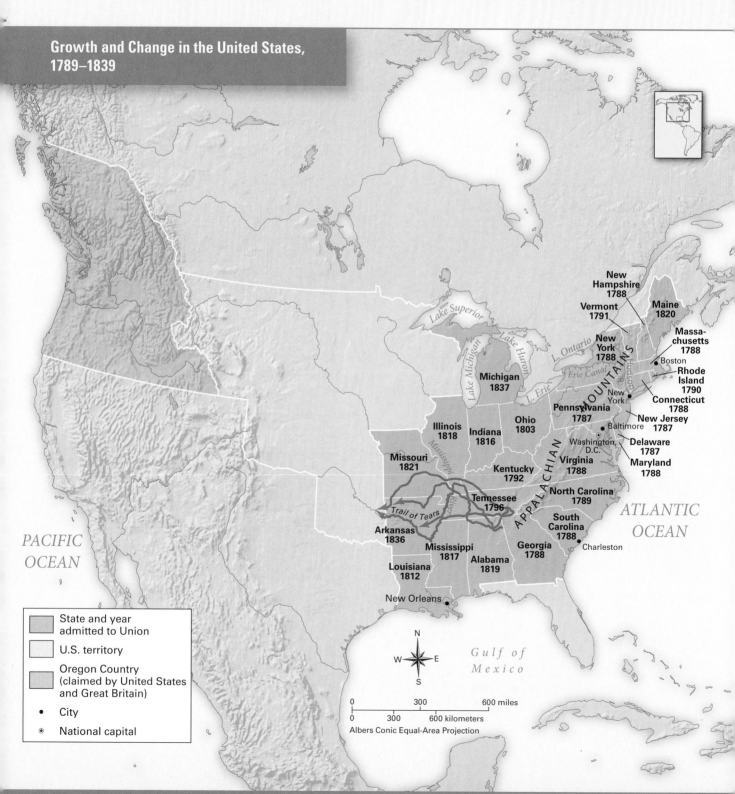

Growth and Change in the United States, 1789–1839

New Hampshire 1788

Vermont 1791

Maine 1820

New York 1788

Massachusetts 1788

Boston

Michigan 1837

Rhode Island 1790

Connecticut 1788

Lake Superior

Lake Michigan

Lake Huron

L. Ontario

Erie Canal

L. Erie

Pennsylvania 1787

New Jersey 1787

New York

Illinois 1818

Indiana 1816

Ohio 1803

Baltimore

Washington, D.C.

Delaware 1787

Missouri 1821

Kentucky 1792

Virginia 1788

Maryland 1788

Trail of Tears

Tennessee 1796

North Carolina 1789

ATLANTIC OCEAN

Arkansas 1836

South Carolina 1788

Charleston

Mississippi 1817

Alabama 1819

Georgia 1788

Louisiana 1812

PACIFIC OCEAN

New Orleans

APPALACHIAN MOUNTAINS

Hudson R.

Gulf of Mexico

N
W   E
S

0   300   600 miles
0   300   600 kilometers
Albers Conic Equal-Area Projection

Legend:
- State and year admitted to Union
- U.S. territory
- Oregon Country (claimed by United States and Great Britain)
- City
- National capital

Along with new states and territories came a steady increase in population, as the graph below shows. Seven presidents served in office from 1789 to 1837, beginning with George Washington and ending with Andrew Jackson. Both men came to the presidency as military heroes—Washington from the American Revolution and Jackson from the War of 1812.

In this unit, you will learn about key events that took place during the administrations of Washington through Jackson. Some of those events are listed below.

1789: George Washington takes the oath of office as the first president of the United States in New York City, the nation's capital at the time.

1794: An army led by President Washington crushes the Whiskey Rebellion, an uprising by some frontier farmers who resisted paying certain taxes.

1800: John Adams, the nation's second president, is the first president to live in Washington, D.C., the new capital city, in the still-unfinished White House.

1814: In a conflict between the United States and Great Britain known as the War of 1812, British forces capture Washington, D.C. The British burn the White House, the Capitol building, and other government buildings.

During the War of 1812, U.S. forces turn back a British attack on Baltimore, Maryland. The Americans' defense of Fort McHenry inspires Francis Scott Key to write "The Star-Spangled Banner," which later becomes the country's national anthem.

1815: An American army led by General Andrew Jackson defeats the British in the Battle of New Orleans. It is the final battle of the War of 1812. It is also the greatest U.S. victory of the war and it makes Jackson a national hero.

1825: The Erie Canal opens. Begun in 1817, the canal creates a water route connecting Lake Erie and the Hudson River. Its success sets off a canal-building boom in the United States. You can locate the Erie Canal on the map on the opposite page. It is located in the state of New York.

1828: Andrew Jackson of Tennessee is elected the nation's seventh president. He is the first president to come from a state other than Virginia or Massachusetts.

1838–1839: Troops round up the remaining Cherokee in the East and move them west along a route that becomes known as the Trail of Tears. The Trail of Tears is shown on the map on the opposite page. It is located in the southern United States.

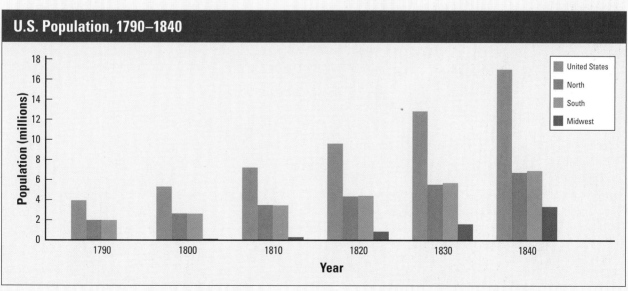

U.S. Population, 1790–1840

Source: U.S. Census Bureau

Chapter 11

Political Developments in the Early Republic

How did the Federalist and Republican visions for the United States differ?

11.1 Introduction

The illustration to the left shows four leaders in the first government formed under the Constitution. On the far right stands former Continental army general George Washington, who had been lured out of retirement to serve as the nation's first president. Seldom has a leader seemed more **reluctant** to take power. "My movements to the chair of government," he wrote on leaving home, "will be accompanied by feelings not unlike those of a culprit [criminal] who is going to the place of his execution."

Henry Knox sits opposite Washington. During the American Revolution, this Boston bookseller became a general and Washington's close friend and adviser. When Washington became president in 1789, he made Knox his secretary of war.

Take a close look at the other two men portrayed here. Alexander Hamilton, who stands beside the president, served as Washington's secretary of the treasury. Thomas Jefferson, who stands behind Knox, served as secretary of state. It was his job to manage relations between the United States and other countries.

Washington chose Hamilton and Jefferson for these positions because of all they had in common. Both were strong patriots. Both had served their country during the war—Hamilton in the Continental army and Jefferson in the Continental Congress. Both had brilliant minds.

But for all they had in common, the two men were opposites in many ways. Hamilton dressed with great care. Jefferson was sloppy with clothes. Hamilton moved with precision. Jefferson slouched. Hamilton was a doer who moved briskly from task to task. Jefferson was a thinker who took time to explore ideas.

As you will discover, Hamilton and Jefferson soon became political rivals. Their rivalry eventually gave rise to the nation's first political parties, which had different visions for the new nation.

Thomas Jefferson (above) and Alexander Hamilton (below) led the first political parties of the new nation.

◀ George Washington, at the far right, meets with his close advisers.

11.2 Launching the New Government

On April 30, 1789, George Washington took the oath of office as the first president of the United States. After his inauguration, Washington addressed both houses of Congress. He asked Congress to work with him to put into place "the wise measures on which the success of this government must depend." At times, his hands shook so much that he had trouble reading his speech.

The Debate over Washington's Title Washington had reason to be nervous. The first Congress was deeply divided. Some members were eager to build a strong national government. Others were just as eager to limit the power of the new government. These differences showed up immediately in a debate over what title to use when addressing the president.

Vice President John Adams pointed out that European heads of government had titles like "Your Excellency" that showed respect for their office. The president, he argued, should have a similar title. Supporters of a strong national government agreed.

Others argued that such titles smelled of royalty and had no place in a democracy. A few members of Congress joked that the rather plump Adams should be given the title "His Rotundity" (His Roundness). The debate finally ended when Washington let it be known that he preferred the simple title "Mr. President."

Setting Up the Executive Branch Next, Congress turned to the task of creating executive departments. As Washington had feared, arguments broke out at once over what those departments should be and what powers they should have.

Congress eventually approved three departments. The Department of State was set up to handle relations with other countries. The Department of War was established to defend the nation. The Treasury Department was set up to oversee the nation's **finances**. Congress also created an attorney general to serve as the president's legal adviser and a postmaster general to head the postal system.

Washington chose men he trusted —such as Thomas Jefferson, Alexander Hamilton, and Henry Knox—to fill these positions. He often met with them to ask for their ideas and advice. The heads of the executive departments came to be known as the president's cabinet.

Martha Washington, on the left, held tea parties on Friday evenings at the presidential mansion in New York City. At these parties, people could discuss important issues with President Washington, shown near the center.

11.3 Washington as President

The most critical problem facing the new government was a lack of funds. The national treasury was empty. Congress had the power to raise funds through taxes. But its members argued endlessly about what to tax and by how much. In 1791, Congress finally agreed to place an excise tax on whiskey and other luxury goods, such as carriages. An excise tax is a tax on the production or sale of a product.

The Whiskey Rebellion

Settlers living west of the Appalachian Mountains reacted angrily to the tax. Western farmers found it too costly to transport their grain across the mountains to sell in eastern cities. Instead, they distilled their bulky wheat into whiskey, which could be shipped more cheaply. Many farmers complained that the tax made their whiskey too expensive, and they refused to pay it.

The Granger Collection, New York

To end these protests, Congress lowered the excise tax in 1793. Most farmers began to pay up, but not the tax rebels of western Pennsylvania. In 1794, these "Whiskey Boys" tarred and feathered tax collectors who tried to enforce the law.

Alexander Hamilton and George Washington saw the **Whiskey Rebellion** as a threat to the authority of the national government. At Hamilton's urging, Washington led 13,000 state militia troops across the mountains to crush the rebels. Faced with overwhelming force, the rebellion ended.

Thomas Jefferson thought that the idea of sending an army to catch a few tax rebels was foolish. Even worse, he believed, was that Hamilton was prepared to violate people's liberties by using armed force to put down opposition to government policies.

The Whiskey Rebellion challenged the new nation's ability to enforce its laws. When several hundred farmers refused to pay a federal whiskey tax, President Washington personally led 13,000 state militia troops to put down the rebellion.

The French Revolution Meanwhile, the nation was caught up in a debate over events in France. In 1789, the French people rebelled against their king. The leaders of the French Revolution dreamed of building a nation based on "liberty, equality, and fraternity [brotherhood]." Three years later, France became a republic and declared "a war of all peoples against all kings."

Many Americans were thrilled by the French Revolution. This was especially true of Jefferson and his followers, who began calling themselves Democratic-Republicans, or simply Republicans. The Republicans saw the French Revolution as part of a great crusade for democracy.

When the French Revolution turned violent and thousands of nobles were beheaded on the guillotine, many Americans withdrew their support for the revolution.

go to page 47

Washington's Farewell Address George Washington's parting message to the nation, given in 1796, in which he warned of threats to the nation's future

In time, news from France caused supporters of the revolution to change their opinion. Cheered on by angry mobs, France's revolutionary government began beheading wealthy nobles. Some 20,000 men, women, and children were killed.

Hamilton and his followers, who called themselves Federalists, were appalled by the bloodshed. Many Federalists were themselves wealthy. After hearing about the fate of wealthy families in France, they began to fear for their own safety, wondering whether such terrors could happen in the United States. "Behold France," warned one Federalist, "an open hell . . . in which we see . . . perhaps our own future."

Washington's Farewell Address The growing division between Republicans and Federalists so disturbed Washington that he agreed to run for a second term as president in 1792. He was the only person, Hamilton and Jefferson told him, who could keep the nation together.

Near the end of his second term, Washington announced that he would not run again. Before leaving office, the president prepared a message that became known as **Washington's Farewell Address**. In it, he reminded Americans of all that bound them together as a people. "With slight shades of difference," he said, "you have the same religion, manners, habits, and political principles. You have in a common cause fought and triumphed together."

Next, Washington warned of two threats to the nation's future. One of those threats was problems the nation was having with other countries. The other threat was the "spirit of party." It was natural for people to hold different opinions, Washington said. But he warned against the dangers of passionate loyalty to parties. If fighting between parties was not controlled, it could tear the young nation apart.

Despite his worries for the future, Washington had much to be proud of as he left office. The new government was up and running. The nation was growing so fast that it had added three new states: Kentucky, Tennessee, and Vermont. Most of all, Washington had steered his government safely through quarrelsome times. He left the nation united and at peace.

11.4 Alexander Hamilton and the Federalist Party

George Washington's warnings did not stop the rise of political parties in the young nation. The Federalist Party appeared first during the debates over the ratification of the Constitution. Its most influential leader was Washington's energetic treasury secretary, Alexander Hamilton.

Personal Background Hamilton was born in the West Indies and raised on the Caribbean island of St. Croix. When Hamilton was 13, a devastating hurricane struck the island. Hamilton wrote a vivid description of the storm that impressed all who read it. A few St. Croix leaders arranged to send the talented teenager to New York, where he could get the education he deserved. Once in America, Hamilton never looked back.

Hamilton's blue eyes were said to turn black when he was angry. But most of the time they sparkled with intelligence and energy. With no money or family connections to help him rise in the world, he made his way on ability, ambition, and charm.

George Washington spotted Hamilton's talents early in the American Revolution. Washington made the young man his aide-de-camp, or personal assistant. Near the end of the war, Hamilton improved his fortunes by marrying Elizabeth Schuyler, who came from one of New York's richest and most powerful families. With her family's political backing, Hamilton was elected to represent New York in Congress after the war. Later, he served as a delegate from New York to the Constitutional Convention.

View of Human Nature Hamilton's view of human nature was shaped by his wartime experiences. All too often, he had seen people put their own interests and desire for personal profit above the cause of patriotism and the needs of the country. "*Every man* ought to be supposed a *knave* [scoundrel]," he concluded, "and to have no other end [goal] in all his actions, but *private interest.*"

Most Federalists shared Hamilton's view that people were basically selfish and out for themselves. For this reason, they distrusted any system of government that gave too much power to "the mob," or the common people. Such a system, said Hamilton, could only lead to "error, confusion, and instability."

American artist John Trumbull painted this portrait of Alexander Hamilton. Hamilton rose from poverty to lead the Federalist Party. His brilliant career was cut short when he was killed in a duel with Vice President Aaron Burr, whom he had accused of being a traitor.

Views on Government Federalists believed that "the best people"—educated, wealthy, public-spirited men like themselves—should run the country. Such people, they believed, had the time, education, and background to run the country wisely. They could also be trusted to make decisions for the general good, not just for themselves. "Those who own the country," said Federalist John Jay bluntly, "ought to govern it."

Federalists favored a strong national government. They hoped to use the new government's powers under the Constitution to unite the quarreling states and keep order among the people. In their view, the rights of states were not nearly as important as national power and unity.

Hamilton agreed. Having grown up in the Caribbean, Hamilton had no deep loyalty to any state. His country was not New York, but the United States of America. He hoped to see his adopted country become a great and powerful nation.

Views on the Economy Hamilton's dream of national greatness depended on the United States developing a strong economy. In 1790, the nation's economy was still based mainly on agriculture. Hamilton wanted to expand the economy and increase the nation's wealth by using the power of the federal government to promote business, manufacturing, and trade.

Before this could happen, the new nation needed to begin paying off the huge debts that Congress and the states had **accumulated** during the American Revolution. In 1790, Hamilton presented Congress with a plan to pay off all war debts as quickly as possible. If the debts were not promptly paid, he warned, the government would lose respect both at home and abroad.

go to page 244

Alexander Hamilton believed that to become strong, the United States needed to develop businesses such as this foundry in Connecticut. A foundry is a factory for melting and shaping metal.

Hamilton's plan for repaying the debts was opposed by many Americans, especially in the South. Most southern states had already paid their war debts. They saw little reason to help states in the North pay off what they still owed.

To save his plan, Hamilton linked it to another issue: the location of the nation's permanent capital. Both northerners and southerners wanted the capital to be located in their section of the country. Hamilton promised to support a location in the South if southerners would support his debt plan. The debt plan was passed, and the nation's new capital—called the District of Columbia—was located in the South, on the Potomac River between Maryland and Virginia.

Hamilton asked Congress to establish the first national bank. The bank collected taxes, printed money, and made loans to businesses.

Next, Hamilton asked Congress to establish a national bank. Such a bank, Hamilton said, would help the government by collecting taxes and keeping those funds safe. It would print paper money backed by the government, giving the nation a stable currency. Most important, the bank would make loans to businesspeople to build new factories and ships. As business and trade expanded, Hamilton argued, all Americans would be better off.

Once again, Hamilton's proposal ran into heavy opposition. Where in the Constitution, his opponents asked, was Congress given the power to establish a bank? In their view, Congress could exercise only those powers specifically listed in the Constitution.

Hamilton, in contrast, supported a **loose construction,** or broad interpretation, of the Constitution. He pointed out that the elastic clause allowed Congress to "make all laws which shall be necessary and proper" for carrying out its listed powers. Since collecting taxes was one of those powers, Congress could set up a bank to help the government with tax collection.

loose construction a broad interpretation of the Constitution, meaning that Congress has powers beyond those specifically given in the Constitution

After much debate, Hamilton was able get his bank approved by Congress. Once established, in 1791, the Bank of the United States helped the nation's economy grow and prosper.

Views on Great Britain and France When the French Revolution began, Hamilton hoped that it would lead to the "establishment of free and good government." But as he watched it lead instead to chaos and bloodshed, his enthusiasm for the revolution cooled.

When war broke out between France and England in 1793, most Federalists sided with Great Britain. Some were merchants and shippers whose business depended on trade with America's former enemy. Others simply felt more comfortable supporting orderly Great Britain against revolutionary France.

Hamilton favored Great Britain for yet another reason. Great Britain was all that he hoped the United States would become one day: a powerful and respected nation that could defend itself against any enemy.

11.5 Thomas Jefferson and the Republican Party

Alexander Hamilton's success in getting his plans through Congress alarmed Thomas Jefferson and his fellow Republicans. In Jefferson's view, almost everything Hamilton did in the name of putting the United States on the path to greatness was instead a step down the road to ruin. The two men held very different views on almost everything.

Personal Background Jefferson was born in Virginia to an old and respected family. One of ten children, he was gifted with many talents. As a boy, he learned to ride, hunt, sing, dance, and play the violin. Later, he carried a violin with him in all his travels.

Jefferson was also a gifted student. When he entered college at age 16, he already knew Greek and Latin. He seemed to know something about almost everything. He once wrote that "not a sprig of grass [is] uninteresting to me." This curiosity would remain with him all his life.

With land inherited from his father, Jefferson set himself up as a Virginia tobacco planter. Like other planters, he used slaves to work his land.

Once he was established as a planter, Jefferson entered Virginia politics. As a politician, he lacked the ability to make stirring speeches. Instead, Jefferson wrote **eloquently** with a pen. His words in the Declaration of Independence and other writings are still read and admired today.

View of Human Nature Jefferson's view of human nature was much more hopeful than Hamilton's. He assumed that informed citizens could make good decisions for themselves and their country. "I have so much confidence in the good sense of man," Jefferson wrote when revolution broke out in France, "that I am never afraid of the issue [outcome] where reason is left free to exert her force."

Jefferson had great faith in the goodness and wisdom of people who worked the soil—farmers and planters like himself. "State a [problem] to a ploughman [farmer] and a professor," he said, and "the former will decide it often better than the latter."

Thomas Jefferson was one of America's greatest patriots. His strongest support came from the middle class: farmers, laborers, artisans, and shopkeepers.

The Granger Collection, New York

Views on Government

Republicans favored democracy over any other form of government. They had no patience with the Federalists' view that only the "best people" should rule. To Republicans, this view came dangerously close to monarchy, or rule by a king.

Republicans believed that the best government was the one that governed the least. A small government with limited powers was most likely to leave the people alone to enjoy the blessings of liberty. To keep the national government small, they insisted on a **strict construction**, or interpretation, of the Constitution. The Constitution, they insisted, meant exactly what it said, no more and no less. Any addition to the powers listed in the document, such as the creation of a national bank, was unconstitutional and dangerous.

Along with advocating for a weak national government, Republicans favored strong state governments. State governments, they argued, were closer to the people, and the people could control them more easily. Strong state governments could also keep the national government from growing too powerful.

Views on the Economy

Like most Americans in the 1790s, Jefferson was a country man. He believed that the nation's future lay not with Federalist bankers and merchants in big cities, but with plain, Republican farmers. "Those who labor in the earth," he wrote, "are the chosen people of God, if ever He had a chosen people."

Republicans favored an economy based on agriculture. They opposed any measures, such as the national bank, designed to encourage the growth of business and manufacturing. In their view, the national bank was not only unconstitutional, but against farmers. While the bank was happy to loan money to businesspeople to build factories and ships, it did not make loans to farmers to buy land.

Agriculture, according to Thomas Jefferson, was the most important part of the economy. He believed farming was the best occupation because it kept people out of corrupt cities.

strict construction a narrow interpretation of the Constitution, meaning that Congress has only those powers specifically given in the Constitution

Views on Great Britain and France

Another topic over which Republicans and Federalists had heated arguments was the French Revolution. Most Americans favored the revolution until it turned violent and led to war. As you have read, most Federalists then turned against the new French republic and sided with Great Britain. For this change of heart, a Republican newspaper called the Federalists "British bootlickers," implying that they were weak and eager to please the British.

Despite the violence of the revolution, most Republicans continued to support France. While regretting the bloodshed, they argued that the loss of a few thousand aristocrats was a small price to pay for freedom. For their loyalty to France, Republicans were scorned in a Federalist newspaper as "man-eating, blood-drinking cannibals."

In 1793, the French government sent Edmond Genêt (zhuh-NAY) to the United States as its new official representative. Genêt preferred to be called "Citizen Genêt." French revolutionaries adopted this title to emphasize the equality of all people. His mission was to convince Americans that they should join France in its war against Great Britain.

Edmond Genêt, the French representative to the United States, attempted to convince Americans to join the French in their war with Britain. After Genêt insulted President Washington, he was ordered to leave the country. Here, Secretary of State Jefferson presents Genêt to the president in 1793.

Republicans welcomed Citizen Genêt as a conquering hero. Large crowds cheered him as he traveled about the country. In Philadelphia, the nation's temporary capital, a great banquet was held in his honor.

When Genêt formally presented himself to President George Washington, he expected another warm and enthusiastic reception. Washington, however, did not want to be drawn into war with Great Britain. His response to Genêt was cool and dignified.

Genêt began making speeches against the president. These attacks on Washington brought thousands of Genêt's supporters into Philadelphia's streets. "Day after day," recalled Vice President John Adams, the protesters "threatened to drag Washington out of his house, and . . . compel [the government] to declare war in favor of the French revolution."

This was too much, even for Jefferson. Calling Genêt "hotheaded . . . disrespectful, and even indecent toward the President," Secretary of State Jefferson asked the French government to recall its troublesome representative.

11.6 The Presidency of John Adams

When the framers of the Constitution created the Electoral College, they imagined that the electors would simply choose the two best leaders for president and vice president. That was how the nation's first two presidential elections worked. By the third election in 1796, however, it was clear that political parties had become part of the election process.

sedition the crime of encouraging rebellion against the government

The Republicans supported Thomas Jefferson for president that year. His support came mainly from farmers in the South and West. The Federalists supported John Adams, who appealed to lawyers, merchants, ship owners, and businesspeople in the North. When the electoral votes were counted, John Adams was elected president by just three votes. Jefferson came in second, making him vice president. The nation's new top two leaders were political leaders from opposing parties.

The Alien and Sedition Acts At first, President Adams tried to work closely with Jefferson. "Party violence," Adams found, made such efforts "useless." Meanwhile, Federalists in Congress passed four controversial laws known as the Alien and Sedition Acts. They argued that these laws were needed as protection against foreigners who might threaten the nation. In fact, the real purpose of the Alien and Sedition Acts was to make life difficult for the Federalists' rivals, the Republicans.

Three of the laws, the Alien Acts, were aimed at aliens, or noncitizens. The first law lengthened the time it took for an immigrant to become a citizen with the right to vote—from 5 to 14 years. Since most immigrants voted Republican, Jefferson saw this law as an attack on his party. The other two Alien Acts allowed the president to either jail or deport aliens who were suspected of activities that threatened the government. Although these laws were never enforced, they did frighten a number of French spies and troublemakers, who then left the country.

The fourth law, known as the Sedition Act, made **sedition**—encouraging rebellion against the government—a crime. Its definition of sedition included "printing, uttering, or publishing any false, scandalous and malicious [hateful] writing" against the government, Congress, or the president. Alexander Hamilton approved of this law, believing that it would punish only those who published lies intended to destroy the government.

Instead, the Sedition Act was used to punish Republican newspaper editors who insulted President Adams in print. One, for example, called him "old, querulous [whiny], bald, blind, crippled, toothless Adams." Twenty-five people were arrested under the new law. Ten of them were convicted of printing seditious opinions.

John Adams, a Federalist, was elected the second president of the United States by only 3 votes in the Electoral College. Thomas Jefferson, a Democratic-Republican who had 68 votes to Adams's 71, became vice president.

nullify to refuse to recognize a federal law. This action by a state is called nullification.

states' rights theory the theory that rights not specifically given to the federal government by the Constitution remain with the states

The Virginia and Kentucky Resolutions Republicans viewed the Sedition Act as an attack on the rights of free speech and free press. Since the federal government was enforcing the act, Republicans looked to the states to protect these freedoms.

Thomas Jefferson and James Madison drew up a set of **resolutions,** or statements, opposing the Alien and Sedition Acts and sent them to state legislatures for approval. They argued that Congress had gone beyond the Constitution in passing these acts. States, therefore, had a duty to **nullify** the laws—that is, to declare them to be without legal force.

Only two states, Virginia and Kentucky, adopted the resolutions. The arguments put forward in the Virginia and Kentucky Resolutions were based on the **states' rights theory** of the Constitution. This theory holds that rights not specifically given to the federal government remain with the states. Of these, one of the most important is the right to judge whether the federal government is using its powers properly.

When no other states approved the Virginia and Kentucky Resolutions, the protest died. The states' rights theory, however, was not forgotten. It would be raised and tested again in the years ahead.

The New National Capital In 1800, the federal government moved to the city of Washington in the District of Columbia. Most of the government's buildings were still under construction. President Adams's wife, Abigail, described the new "President's House" as a "castle" in which "not one room or chamber is finished." She used the large East Room for hanging laundry, as it was not fit for anything else.

In this political cartoon, a devil and a lion, symbolizing Great Britain, encourage a Federalist editor, represented by a hedgehog, to cross out important phrases from America's great documents. Liberty weeps at Benjamin Franklin's tomb.

The Granger Collection, New York

11.7   The Election of 1800

The move to Washington, D.C., came in the middle of the 1800 presidential election. Once again, Republican leaders supported Thomas Jefferson for president. Hoping to avoid the strange outcome of the last election, they chose a New York politician named Aaron Burr to run as his vice president.

The Federalists chose John Adams to run for reelection as president. Charles Pinckney of South Carolina was selected to run for vice president. Some Federalists would have preferred Alexander Hamilton as their presidential candidate. Although he did not run, Hamilton's influence would shape the results of the election.

The Granger Collection, New York

This Republican presidential campaign banner is from 1800. The banner reads, "T. Jefferson President of the United States of America. John Adams no MORE."

The Campaign The candidates outlined their campaign issues early. Jefferson supported the Constitution and states' rights. He promised to run a "frugal and simple" government. Adams ran on his record of peace and prosperity.

The campaign, however, centered more on insults than on issues. Republican newspapers attacked Adams as a tyrant. They even accused him of wanting to turn the nation into a monarchy so that his children could follow him on the presidential throne.

Some Federalist newspapers called Jefferson an atheist. An atheist is someone who denies the existence of God. Jefferson, these newspapers charged, would "destroy religion, introduce immorality, and loosen all the bonds of society." Frightened by these charges, some elderly Federalists buried their Bibles to keep them safe from the "godless" Republicans.

The Divided Federalists Hamilton and his followers refused to support Adams because of disagreements over the president's foreign policy. "We shall never find ourselves in the straight road of Federalism while Mr. Adams is President," stated Oliver Wolcott, one of Hamilton's close allies.

As the campaign heated up, Hamilton worked feverishly behind the scenes to convince the men chosen for the Electoral College to cast their presidential ballots for Pinckney over Adams. Pinckney seemed more likely than Adams to value Hamilton's advice and his firm Federalist principles. With Pinckney as president, Hamilton believed that he would be able to personally guide the United States into the new century.

Here, Republican women help Thomas Jefferson win the election in New Jersey in 1800. Women were allowed to vote in New Jersey until 1808.

11.8 A Deadlock and a New Amendment

When the Electoral College voted early in 1801, it was clear that John Adams had lost the election. But to whom? Under the Constitution, each elector cast two votes, with the idea that the candidate finishing second would be vice president. All of the Republican electors voted for Thomas Jefferson and Aaron Burr. The result was a tie between them.

Breaking the Tie In the case of a tie, the Constitution sends the election to the House of Representatives. There, each state has one vote. Burr could have told his supporters in the House to elect Jefferson president, as his party wanted. Instead, he remained silent, hoping

In the presidential election of 1800, Thomas Jefferson and Aaron Burr received the same number of electoral votes. After almost a week of deadlock in the House of Representatives, Jefferson was elected president. The Twelfth Amendment was ratified in 1804 to prevent such ties in the future.

The Election of 1800			
Presidential Candidate	Party	State	Electoral Votes
Thomas Jefferson	Republican	Virginia	73
Aaron Burr	Republican	New York	73
John Adams	Federalist	Massachusetts	65
Charles Pinckney	Federalist	South Carolina	64
John Jay	Federalist	New York	1

the election might go his way. When the House voted, the result was another tie.

After 6 days and 35 ballots, it was Federalist Alexander Hamilton who broke the deadlock. He asked his supporters in the House to vote for Jefferson. Of the two Republicans, he said, "Jefferson is to be preferred. He is by far not so dangerous a man." The tie was broken, and Jefferson was elected president.

In 1804, the Twelfth Amendment was added to the Constitution to prevent such ties. The amendment calls for the Electoral College to cast separate ballots for president and vice president. If no presidential candidate receives a majority of electoral votes, the House of Representatives chooses a president from the top three candidates. If no candidate for vice president receives a majority, the Senate chooses the vice president.

A Peaceful Revolution The election of 1800 was a victory for Jefferson and his Republican Party. But it was also a victory for the new system of government established by the Constitution. In other countries, power changed hands by means of war or revolution. In the United States, power had passed from one group to another without a single shot being fired.

Chapter Summary

In this chapter, you read about the beginnings of political parties in the United States.

The New Government Under Washington George Washington took office as president in 1789. In 1794, he ended the Whiskey Rebellion, a farmers' protest against taxes.

Alexander Hamilton and the Federalists Hamilton and the Federalists favored a strong national government. They supported a loose construction of the Constitution. They also favored using the government's power to support business, manufacturing, and trade. Alarmed by the violence of the French Revolution, the Federalists favored Great Britain in its war with France.

Thomas Jefferson and the Republicans Jefferson and the Republicans championed states' rights and an economy based on agriculture. They supported a strict construction of the Constitution. Republicans saw the French Revolution as a step toward democracy and attacked the Federalists' support for Great Britain.

The Presidency of John Adams During Adams's presidency, Federalists used the Alien and Sedition Acts to attack Republicans. In response, Republicans urged states to nullify these laws.

The Election of 1800 and the Twelfth Amendment Adams lost the election of 1800 to Thomas Jefferson after the Federalists broke a tie vote between Jefferson and Aaron Burr. In 1804, the Twelfth Amendment was added to the Constitution to prevent such ties.

When John and Abigail Adams arrived, Washington was more an idea than a city. After the site was selected, the District of Columbia had to be built. This view is of the District of Columbia in 1801.

The President's House

What kind of home should the president of a brand new country live in? The early leaders had to decide this question. Congress gave George Washington the freedom to make this decision, and his ideas led to the building we know today as the White House. But it would be the second president, John Adams, who first lived in the house.

John Adams reached Washington on Saturday afternoon, November 1, 1800. Because travel at that time was difficult, no one had known ahead of time exactly when the president would arrive. As it turned out, he was earlier than expected. The only people there to greet him were a few workers and two commissioners who were overseeing work on the nation's capital.

A welcoming committee was not the only thing missing when the president arrived. The building that the president would call home was little more than a shell on that November day. When Adams moved in, only 6 of the 36 rooms in the president's house were fit to live in. Only 18 rooms had finished plaster walls. Fires burned in 13 fireplaces every day to keep the house warm and dry enough to live in. The fires also helped dry the plaster in the rooms that had it.

From the unfinished house, President Adams wrote to his wife, Abigail, who was still at their home in Massachusetts. He told her that "the Building is in a State to be habitable. And now we wish for your Company." Abigail arrived two weeks later.

The First Lady was not happy about the condition of her new home. "Shiver, shiver," she wrote to her daughter. "Surrounded with forests, can you believe that wood [for fires] is not to be had because people cannot be found to cut and cart it." Water, too, was hard to come by. Servants had to haul it nearly half a mile to the president's house.

But Abigail made the best of it. She and John improvised. Abigail used what was to become the formal East Room for hanging laundry. The Adamses even managed to entertain guests in their unfinished home.

The Adamses knew that the building would be beautiful one day. They also hoped that it would last for a very long time—like the nation whose leaders it would house.

A Palace for the President

George Washington had turned down the chance to be king of the United States. But Washington, a Federalist, believed in a strong central government, with the president playing a central role. He wanted the leader of the new republic to live in a house that reflected the president's importance.

Those who disagreed with the Federalist idea of a strong executive wanted a more modest home for the president. Secretary of State Thomas Jefferson, a Republican, favored a small central government. He wanted the president's house to reflect that belief. So he proposed a plain house built of brick. To him, a big house built of stone, like those of European leaders, suggested royalty, and he wanted no part of that.

In 1792, Jefferson announced that he would hold a contest to choose an architect to design the president's house. His advertisement for the contest required applicants to include "an estimate of the Cubic feet of brickwork composing the whole mass of the wall."

But George Washington had other ideas. He wanted a presidential palace that was large and made of stone. He saw pictures of buildings designed by James Hoban, an architect who had trained in Ireland. He liked the buildings, and he wanted Hoban to design the president's house. Hoban entered the contest and, not surprisingly, won.

Hoban's design was for a grand house. It was to have three stories and to be built of stone. But a lack of money limited his elaborate plans. The presidential home would still look like a palace, but it would be only two stories tall, with only the first story made of solid stone. The second story would be made of brick and covered with a layer of stone.

In the end, then, the president's house was something of a compromise. The fact that the new nation had limited time and money meant that Jefferson's republican ideals were present, though Washington's influence is reflected even more.

Building the President's House

George Washington laid the cornerstone for the president's house on October 13, 1792. The outside structure looked finished by 1800, but it took another two years to complete the basic structure inside. In part, that is because builders stopped working on the house in 1799. They reasoned that it would be easy for one man to find a place to sleep—even if that man was the president. Finding a place for the legislature to meet, on the other hand, would be difficult. So they shifted their energy to building the capitol.

These plans from 1793 (top) show the final design for the president's house. In 1800, when John Adams moved in, the building was unfinished. He and his wife Abigail lived there for the last four months of his term before Thomas Jefferson moved in in March 1801. In 1792, James Hoban submitted a plan (bottom) for the second floor of the White House. It looks very close to this today.

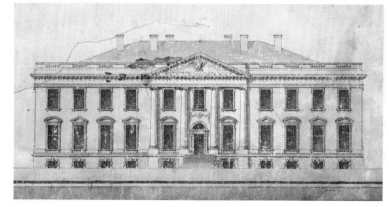

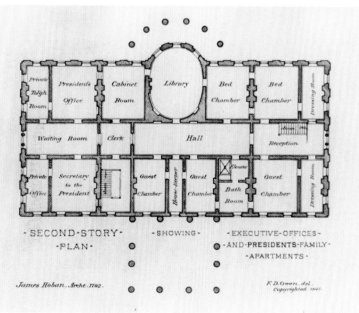

Records show that slaves worked as carpenters on the president's house in May 1795. The men—Tom, Peter, Ben, Harry, and Daniel—"belonged" to architect James Hoban.

Many people were involved in building the president's house. Some were immigrants. Scottish masons built the stone walls and covered the second-story brick with stone. The commissioners who oversaw the process had hoped to bring in other immigrant workers. But they had very little success, so they turned to local laborers.

Many of those laborers were African Americans. Some were free, but many were slaves. The government leased the slaves from their masters. Slaves dug the stone from the quarries in Virginia. They also made bricks, which they used to build the huts they lived in at the work site. In addition, much of the lumber for the building came from a slave-managed mill.

The regal-looking sandstone that George Washington wanted created a problem for the stone masons. Sandstone is porous (absorbent), so the masons made a whitewash to keep moisture out. They applied the whitewash like paint over the brick, but it sealed like glue. That is why the president's house is white—although it was not until 1901 that President Theodore Roosevelt officially called the building the White House.

This 20th-century painting shows how artist N. C. Wyeth imagined the building of the White House. In the painting, President George Washington confers with architect James Hoban.

Continuity and Change

The White House today looks enough like the White House of the past that a viewer can tell it is the same building. But it has gone through many changes over the years.

Wear and tear took their toll on the building, even in the early years. By 1803, so much water had leaked through the roof that the ceiling of the East Room collapsed. Many of the changes to the White House have simply kept the building up to date, outfitting it with modern conveniences. Pipes installed in 1833 brought running water into the house. Heated water piped to the second floor allowed the first family to take hot showers. Starting in 1837, a central furnace took off the chill. Gas lights were installed in 1848 and electric lights in 1891.

Several major renovations have also ensured that the president's house has remained the building for the ages that Abigail Adams envisioned. In 1814, British forces burned the president's house, and only the external structure survived. The entire interior was rebuilt. During Theodore Roosevelt's administration, a 1902 renovation added the West Wing for the president and his staff. In doing so, it doubled the size of the family's living space.

But the 1902 renovation, plus the addition of the third story in the 1920s, put a huge strain on the structure. A 1948 engineer's report concluded that the White House "was standing up purely from habit." A 1952 renovation gutted the building, strengthened the structure, and rebuilt it. Since 1952, no major overhauls have been necessary. However, repairs are ongoing, and in recent years efforts have been made to make the White House more energy efficient.

Although it has changed over time, the White House remains the home of the president, just as it was when John Adams arrived. Carved in the mantle of the State Dining Room today is the blessing that Adams made for his new home in that long-ago November of 1800:

> *I pray Heaven to bestow the best of blessings on this House and all that shall hereafter inhabit it. May none but honest and wise men ever rule under this roof.*

Beginning in 1848, the chandeliers in the East Room were lit by gas rather than candles. Ceiling decorations were added to the room in 1853. In 2009, First Lady Michelle Obama welcomed musician Stevie Wonder as he performed in the East Room.

Chapter 12

Foreign Affairs in the Young Nation

To what extent should the United States have become involved in world affairs in the early 1800s?

12.1 Introduction

Did you know that you are carrying a history lesson in your pocket or purse? You will find it on any $1 bill. Look at a dollar and see for yourself.

On one side, you will see two circles showing the Great Seal of the United States. For thousands of years, governments have used seals like this one to mark their approval of important documents. Our nation's founders thought that a national seal was so important that they began work on it the same day they declared independence: July 4, 1776. In 1782, Congress approved the design we see on our currency today.

The Great Seal symbolizes the nation's principles. For example, the unfinished pyramid on one side of the seal **signifies** strength and endurance. The bald eagle on the other side is a symbol of the United States. In one claw, the eagle holds an olive branch, a symbol of peace. In the other, the eagle holds arrows to symbolize war. The olive branch and arrows of war show that the United States will **pursue** peace but will also protect itself. Notice that the eagle faces peace.

Now turn the dollar bill over. You will see a portrait of George Washington. Americans still honor Washington as the nation's first president. But few remember that Washington defined U.S. foreign policy in the early years of the nation's history.

During his presidency, Washington established policies that would guide the United States in its future dealings with other nations. The United States could be actively involved in world affairs, risking war. Or it could avoid involvement in other nations' conflicts in the hope of staying at peace. Which choice would you have made for the new nation? In this chapter, you will read about four dilemmas that faced early U.S. presidents. Their decisions would shape the foreign policy pursued by later presidents.

George Washington was considered a hero even in his own time. Here we see Lady Liberty crowning a statue of Washington. The inscription on the bust reads, "First in War, First in Peace, First in the Hearts of His Countrymen."

◀ The Great Seal of the United States

George Washington's Farewell Address was published in newspapers in 1796. As part of his advice to the nation, he urged neutrality in foreign relations.

12.2 President Washington Creates a Foreign Policy

When George Washington took office as the nation's first president in 1789, the United States appeared to be weak militarily. The army that Washington had commanded during the American Revolution had disbanded. It had not been replaced for two reasons. First, the government did not have the money to keep its army active. Second, Americans had learned that a standing national army could be used to take away their liberty. State militia troops, they believed, could handle any threats the country might face.

And there were indeed threats. The new nation was surrounded by unfriendly powers. To the north, Great Britain still controlled Canada. The British also refused to abandon their forts in the Ohio Valley, even though this region now belonged to the United States. To the south and west, Spain controlled Florida and Louisiana.

Events in Europe also threatened the new nation. In 1789, the French people rose up against their king and declared France a republic. Most Americans were thrilled by the French Revolution. In 1793, however, France declared war against Great Britain. The war between France and Great Britain presented President Washington with the difficult problem of deciding which side to take.

During its own revolution, the United States had signed a treaty of alliance with France in 1778. Alliances are agreements made with other nations to aid and support each other. In that treaty, the United States had promised to aid France in time of war. Many Americans were eager to honor that pledge, even if it meant going to war with Great Britain.

Washington knew that the United States was not prepared for war. Instead, he announced a policy of **neutrality**. Under this policy, the United States would do nothing to aid either France or Great Britain in their war.

Before leaving office, Washington summed up his foreign policy in a farewell address to the nation. The United States, he said, could gain nothing by becoming involved in other nations' affairs. "It is our true policy," he declared, "to steer clear of permanent alliances with any portion of the foreign world." Washington's policy of avoiding alliances with other countries became known as **isolationism**. For the next century, isolationism would be the foundation of U.S. foreign policy.

neutrality a policy of not choosing sides in a dispute or war between other countries

isolationism a policy of avoiding political or military agreements with other countries

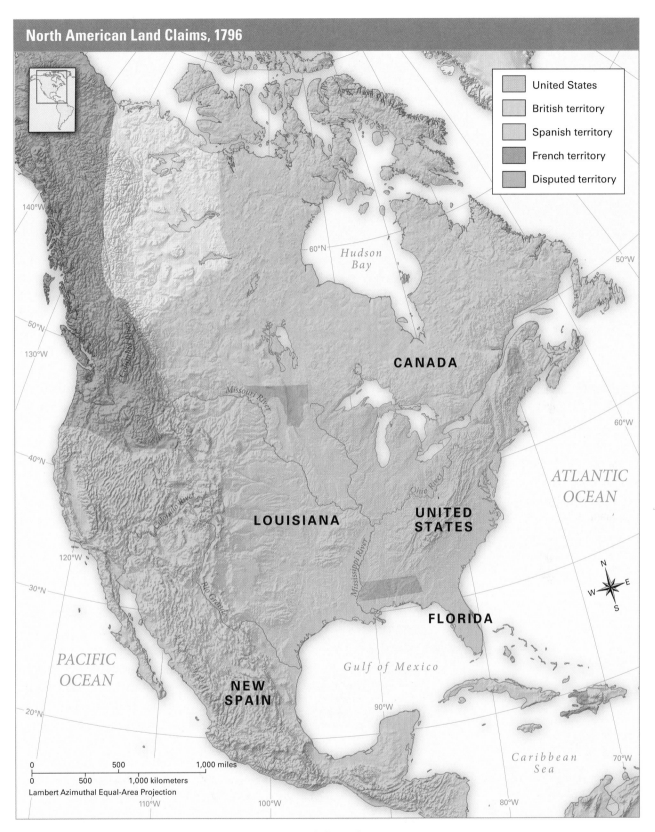

United States
British territory
Spanish territory
French territory
Disputed territory

In 1796, the United States was surrounded by colonies that belonged to the European countries of Great Britain, France, and Spain. What problems do you think this fact might have caused for the newly independent United States?

12.3 President Adams's Dilemma: Protecting U.S. Ships

Isolationism sounded good in theory. But it is often hard to stay out of other countries' conflicts. No one knew this better than John Adams, the nation's second president. Adams tried to follow George Washington's policy of neutrality. With France, however, staying neutral proved to be difficult.

The Jay Treaty French leaders hoped that Great Britain's refusal to leave the Ohio Valley would lead to war between Great Britain and the United States. Those hopes were dashed when Washington sent John Jay, chief justice of the Supreme Court, to London to settle things with the British. In the treaty signed in 1794, known as the Jay Treaty, the British finally agreed to pull their troops from the Ohio Valley. France, still at war with Great Britain, viewed the Jay Treaty as a violation of its own treaty with the United States, made back in 1778. In July 1796, the French navy began attacking U.S. merchant ships bound for Great Britain. Over the next year, French warships seized 316 American ships.

The XYZ Affair President Adams sent three envoys, or representatives, to France to ask the French to end the attacks. French foreign minister Talleyrand refused to speak to the Americans. Instead, they were met by secret agents, later identified only as X, Y, and Z. The agents said that no peace talks would be held unless Talleyrand received a large sum of money as a tribute. A tribute is money given to someone in exchange for that person's protection. Shocked by the request, the American envoys refused.

The XYZ Affair, as it became known, outraged Americans when the story reached home. At President Adams's request, Congress voted to recruit an army of 10,000 men. It also voted to build 12 new ships for the nation's tiny navy. The slogan "Millions for defense, but not one cent for tribute!" was heard everywhere as Americans prepared for war.

Meanwhile, Congress authorized U.S. warships and privately owned ships, called privateers, to launch a "half war" on the seas. During this undeclared war, American ships captured more than 80 armed French vessels.

As war fever mounted, President Adams, never a well-loved leader, found himself unexpectedly popular. His Federalist Party gained support in all parts of the country. The question facing Adams was whether the popular thing—waging an undeclared war on France—was also the best thing for the country.

In this cartoon, American envoys meet with a French diplomat, depicted as a multiheaded monster holding a dagger. The cartoonist shared the negative view of French diplomacy held by most Americans in the 1790s.

The Granger Collection, New York

President John Adams believed that the United States needed a strong navy. Congress approved the construction of 12 warships, including the *Philadelphia*, shown here under construction in 1800.

The Granger Collection, New York

12.4 What Happened: Adams Pursues Peace

President John Adams knew that no matter how good war might be for the Federalist Party, it would not be good for the country. In February 1799, he announced that he was sending a group of men to France to work for peace. Federalist leaders were furious. They pleaded with the president to change his mind, but Adams would not budge.

By the time the peace mission reached France, a French military leader named Napoleon Bonaparte had taken over the French government. Napoleon was eager to make peace with both Great Britain and the United States. He had already ordered the navy to stop seizing American ships and to release captured American sailors.

In a treaty made between France and the United States in 1800, Napoleon agreed to end France's 1778 alliance with the United States. In exchange, the Americans agreed not to ask France to pay for all the ships it had seized. This meant that the U.S. government would have to pay American ship owners for their lost property. To Adams, this seemed a small price to pay for peace with France.

Choosing the olive branch cost Adams political popularity. His pursuit of peace with France created strong disagreements within the Federalist Party. These disagreements lost Adams and the Federalists votes when he ran for reelection in 1800. Jefferson defeated Adams in the election, and the Federalist Party lost much of its support. Over the next few years, Adams would watch his Federalist Party slowly fade away.

Still, Adams had no regrets. He wrote,

I will defend my missions to France, as long as I have an eye to direct my hand, or a finger to hold my pen . . . I desire no other inscription over my gravestone than: "Here lies John Adams, who took upon himself the responsibility of the peace with France in the year 1800."

12.5 President Jefferson's Dilemma: Dealing with Pirates

The peace that John Adams achieved with France did not last long. In 1803, France and Great Britain were again at war. As the conflict heated up, both nations began seizing American ships that were trading with their enemy. President Thomas Jefferson, who took office in 1801, complained bitterly that "England has become a den of pirates and France has become a den of thieves." Still, like Washington and Adams before him, Jefferson tried to follow a policy of neutrality.

Impressment Remaining neutral when ships were being seized was hard enough. It became even harder when Great Britain began impressing American sailors—kidnapping them and forcing them to serve in the British navy. The British claimed that the men they impressed were British deserters. This may have been true in some cases, as some sailors may well have fled the terrible conditions on British ships. Yet thousands of unlucky Americans were also impressed.

American anger over impressment peaked in 1807 after a British warship, the *Leopard,* stopped a U.S. warship, the *Chesapeake,* to search for deserters. When the *Chesapeake*'s captain refused to allow a search, the *Leopard* opened fire. Twenty-one American sailors were killed or wounded. This attack triggered another case of war fever, this time against Great Britain.

Piracy American ships faced a different threat from the Barbary States of North Africa: piracy, or robbery at sea. For years, pirates from Morocco, Algiers, Tunis, and Tripoli had preyed on merchant ships entering the Mediterranean Sea. The pirates seized the ships and held their crews for ransom.

Presidents Washington and Adams both paid tribute to Barbary State rulers in exchange for the safety of American ships. While Americans were shouting "millions for defense, but not one cent for tribute" during the XYZ Affair, the United States was quietly sending money to the Barbary States.

By the time Jefferson became president, the United States had paid the Barbary States almost $2 million. The ruler of Tripoli, however, demanded still more tribute. To show that he was serious, he declared war on the United States. Jefferson hated war. But he also hated paying tribute. The question was, which was worse?

In the late 1700s and early 1800s, the Mediterranean Sea was filled with pirates who attacked U.S. merchant ships. The United States paid tribute to leaders of the Barbary States to prevent these attacks.

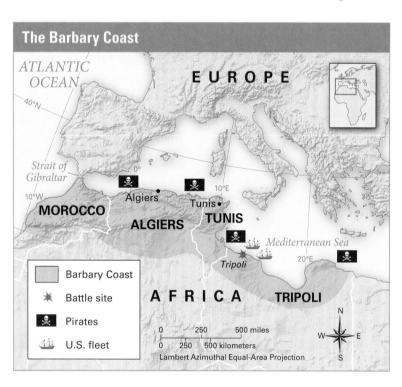

The Barbary Coast

ATLANTIC OCEAN

EUROPE

40°N

Strait of Gibraltar

10°W

0°

10°E

Algiers

Tunis

MOROCCO

ALGIERS

TUNIS

Mediterranean Sea

20°E

Tripoli

AFRICA

TRIPOLI

Legend:
- Barbary Coast
- ✴ Battle site
- ☠ Pirates
- ⛵ U.S. fleet

0   250   500 miles
0   250   500 kilometers
Lambert Azimuthal Equal-Area Projection

N W E S

12.6 What Happened: Jefferson Solves the Problem

As much as Thomas Jefferson hated war, he hated paying tribute more. In 1802, he sent a small fleet of warships to the Mediterranean to protect American shipping interests. The war with Tripoli plodded along until 1804, when American ships began bombarding Tripoli with their cannons.

Then one of the ships, the *Philadelphia,* ran aground on a hidden reef in the harbor. The captain and crew were captured and held for ransom. Rather than let pirates have the *Philadelphia,* a young naval officer named Stephen Decatur led a raiding party into the heavily guarded Tripoli harbor and set the ship afire.

After a year of U.S. attacks and a blockade, Tripoli signed a peace treaty with the United States in 1805. Tripoli agreed to stop demanding tribute payments. In return, the United States paid a $60,000 ransom for the crew of the *Philadelphia.* This was a bargain compared to the $3 million first demanded.

Pirates from other Barbary States continued to raid ships in the Mediterranean. In 1815, U.S. and European naval forces finally destroyed the pirate bases.

Meanwhile, Jefferson tried desperately to convince both France and Great Britain to leave American ships alone. All of his diplomatic efforts failed. Between 1803 and 1807, Great Britain seized at least a thousand American ships. France captured about half that many.

When diplomacy failed, Jefferson proposed an **embargo**—a complete halt in trade with other nations. Under the Embargo Act passed by Congress in 1807, no foreign ships could enter U.S. ports and no American ships could leave, except to trade at other U.S. ports. Jefferson hoped that stopping trade would prove so painful to France and Great Britain that they would agree to leave American ships alone.

The embargo, however, proved far more painful to Americans than to anyone in Europe. Some 55,000 sailors lost their jobs. In New England, newspapers pointed out that *embargo* spelled backward reads "O grab me," which made sense to all who were feeling its pinch.

Congress repealed the unpopular Embargo Act in 1809. American ships returned to the seas, and French and British warships continued to attack them.

President Thomas Jefferson ordered an embargo to force Great Britain and France to leave American ships alone. This political cartoon pictures the embargo as a snapping turtle preventing American merchants from selling their goods overseas.

embargo a government order that forbids trade with another country

12.7 President Madison's Dilemma: Protecting Sailors and Settlers

President James Madison took office in 1809. He tried a new approach to protecting Americans at sea. He offered France and Great Britain a deal: if you agree to **cease** your attacks on American ships, the United States will stop trading with your enemy.

Napoleon promptly agreed to Madison's offer. At the same time, Napoleon gave his navy secret orders to continue seizing American ships headed for British ports. Madison, who desperately wanted to believe Napoleon's false promise, cut off all trade with Great Britain.

Meanwhile, the British continued seizing ships and impressing American sailors. Madison saw only one way to force Great Britain to respect American rights. He began to think about abandoning George Washington's policy of isolationism and going to war with Great Britain.

New Englanders and Federalists generally opposed going to war. Merchants in New England knew that war would mean a **blockade** of their ports by the British navy. They preferred to take their chances with the troubles at sea.

Many people in the South and to the west, however, supported going to war. Like all Americans, they resented Great Britain's policy of impressing U.S. sailors. They also accused the British of stirring up trouble among Indians in the states and territories to the northwest.

Trouble with the Indians was growing as settlers moved into the Ohio and Mississippi valleys and pushed Indians off their lands. Two Shawnee Indians—a chief named Tecumseh and his brother, the Prophet—tried to fight back by uniting Indians along the Mississippi River into one great Indian nation. On November 7, 1811, Shawnee

Indiana governor William Henry Harrison, on the far left, is shown encouraging his troops during the Battle of Tippecanoe Creek. After the battle, Harrison's men discovered that the Indians were armed with British guns, which added to Americans' anger at the British.

warriors fought against a militia force led by Indiana governor William Henry Harrison in the Battle of Tippecanoe Creek. Harrison defeated the Indian forces. After the battle, however, Harrison's men discovered that the Indians were armed with British guns.

Americans were outraged. Several young congressmen from the South and West, including Henry Clay of Kentucky and John C. Calhoun of South Carolina, were so eager for war with Great Britain that they were nicknamed "War Hawks." They argued that to make the northwestern frontier safe for settlers, the United States needed to drive the British out of Canada. Once that was done, Canada could be added to the United States.

Losses at sea, national pride, and a desire to make the frontier safe for settlement all contributed to the reasons for war. Still, Madison hesitated. Was the nation strong enough to launch the arrows of war? Or should he hold tightly to the olive branch of peace?

12.8 What Happened: The War of 1812

James Madison chose to abandon isolationism. At his request, Congress declared war on Great Britain on July 17, 1812. This was a bold step for a nation with an army of 7,000 poorly trained men and a navy of only 16 ships.

Battles on Land and Sea War Hawks were overjoyed when the War of 1812 began. They thought that conquering Canada was "a mere matter of marching." They were wrong. In 1812, 1813, and again in 1814 U.S. forces crossed into Canada, but each time British forces turned them back.

The British, too, found the going much rougher than expected. On September 10, 1813, a U.S. naval force under the command of Oliver Hazard Perry captured a British fleet of six ships on Lake Erie. Perry's victory enabled William Henry Harrison to push into upper Canada, where he defeated the British in a major battle. Chief Tecumseh, who was fighting on the side of the British, was killed. But in December, the British drove the Americans back across the border.

By 1814, Napoleon had been defeated in Europe, and Great Britain was able to send 15,000 troops to Canada. American plans to conquer Canada came to an end.

Meanwhile, in August 1814, another British army invaded Washington, D.C. The British burned several public buildings, including the Capitol and the White House. President Madison had to flee for his life.

Next the British attacked the port city of Baltimore, Maryland. On September 13, an American lawyer named Francis Scott Key watched as the British bombarded Fort McHenry, which guarded the city's harbor. The bombardment went on all night. When dawn broke, Key was thrilled to see that the American flag still waved over the fort, proving that the fort had not been captured. He expressed his feelings in a poem that was later put to music as "The Star-Spangled Banner."

The Shawnee leader Tecumseh united American Indians in an attempt to halt the advance of white settlers onto Indian lands.

The Battle of New Orleans A British fleet had surrendered to U.S. forces after the Battle of Lake Champlain in New York just two days before the unsuccessful attack on Baltimore. In Great Britain, news of this defeat would greatly weaken the desire to continue the war. But the news took time to travel, and in the meantime British commanders in the United States launched another invasion. This time, their target was New Orleans.

New Orleans was defended by General Andrew Jackson and a ragtag army of 7,000 militia, free African Americans, Indians, and pirates. On January 8, 1815, more than 7,500 British troops marched confidently into battle. Jackson's troops met them with deadly fire. Some 2,000 British soldiers were killed or wounded, compared with only about 20 Americans.

This map shows American and British offensives, or attacks, during the War of 1812. Despite victories on both sides, neither country really won the war. Still, the war had important effects in the United States.

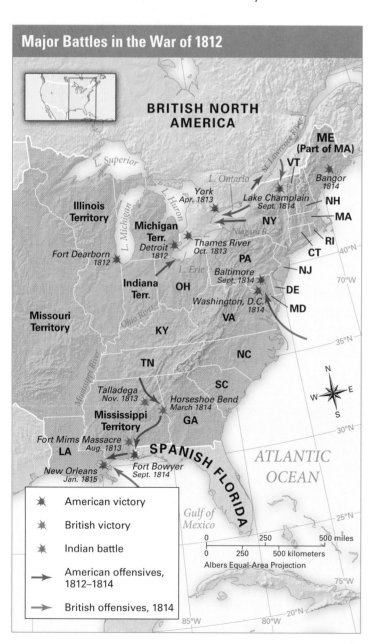

Major Battles in the War of 1812

BRITISH NORTH AMERICA

L. Superior

ME (Part of MA)

VT

L. Ontario

Bangor 1814

York Apr. 1813

Lake Champlain Sept. 1814

NH

Illinois Territory

L. Huron

L. Michigan

Michigan Terr.

Detroit 1812

Thames River Oct. 1813

Niagara R.

NY

MA

RI

CT

40°N

Fort Dearborn 1812

L. Erie

PA

NJ

70°W

Indiana Terr.

OH

Baltimore Sept. 1814

DE

Missouri Territory

Ohio River

Washington, D.C. 1814

VA

MD

35°N

KY

TN

NC

N E S W

Talladega Nov. 1813

Horseshoe Bend March 1814

SC

Mississippi River

Mississippi Territory

GA

30°N

Fort Mims Massacre Aug. 1813

LA

SPANISH FLORIDA

ATLANTIC OCEAN

New Orleans Jan. 1815

Fort Bowyer Sept. 1814

Gulf of Mexico

25°N

- ✳ American victory
- ✳ British victory
- ✳ Indian battle
- → American offensives, 1812–1814
- → British offensives, 1814

0   250   500 miles
0   250   500 kilometers
Albers Equal-Area Projection

75°W

20°N

85°W   80°W

The Battle of New Orleans was the greatest U.S. victory of the War of 1812. It was also totally unnecessary. Two weeks earlier, American and British diplomats meeting in Ghent (GHENT), Belgium, had signed a peace treaty ending the war. The news did not reach New Orleans until after the battle was fought.

Results of the War Although both sides claimed victory, neither Great Britain nor the United States really won the War of 1812. The Treaty of Ghent settled none of the issues that had led to the fighting. Instead, the problems of impressment and ship seizures faded away as peace settled over Europe. Still, the war had important effects.

First, Indian resistance in the Northwest Territory weakened after Tecumseh's death. Over time, most of the American Indians who fought with Tecumseh would be driven out of the Ohio Valley.

Second, national pride in the United States surged. Many Americans considered the War of 1812 "the second war of independence." They felt that by standing up to the British, the United States had truly become a sovereign nation.

Third, the war had political effects. The Federalists were badly damaged by their opposition to the war, and their party never recovered. Two of the war's heroes —William Henry Harrison and Andrew Jackson—would later be elected president.

12.9 President Monroe's Dilemma: A New Foreign Policy Challenge

James Monroe became president in 1817. After the excitement of the War of 1812, he was relieved to return the nation to its policy of isolationism. Americans began to turn their attention away from Europe, however, and direct it to events happening in Latin America. From Mexico to the tip of South America, Latin Americans were rising up in revolt against Spain.

Latin America's Revolutions In Mexico, the revolt against Spanish rule was inspired by a Catholic priest named Miguel Hidalgo (me-GHELL heh-DAHL-goh). On September 16, 1810, Hidalgo spoke to a crowd of poor Indians in the town of Dolores. "My children," Hidalgo said, "will you make an effort to recover from the hated Spaniards the lands stolen from your fore-fathers three hundred years ago? Death to bad government!" Hidalgo's speech, remembered today as the "Cry of Dolores," inspired a revolution that lasted ten years. In 1821, Mexico finally won its independence from Spain.

Two other leaders **liberated** South America. In 1810, a Venezuelan named Simón Bolívar (see-MOHN buh-LEE-var) launched a revolution in the north with this cry: "Spaniards, you will receive death at our hands! Americans, you will receive life!" José de San Martín (ho-ZAY de SAN mar-TEEN), a revolutionary from Argentina, led the struggle for independence in the south. By the end of 1825, the last Spanish troops had been driven out of South America.

A Catholic priest, Miguel Hidalgo (lower center), inspired an independence movement in Mexico. In his upraised hand, Hidalgo holds the flames of revolution that spread throughout Latin America in the early 1800s.

New Latin American Nations Many Americans were excited by independence movements in Latin America. The British also supported the revolutions—for their own reasons. Spain had not allowed other nations to trade with its colonies. Once freed from Spanish rule, the new Latin American nations were able to open their doors to foreign trade, including trade with Great Britain.

Other European leaders were not so pleased. Some even began to talk of helping Spain recover its lost colonies. In 1823, Great Britain asked the United States to join it in sending a message to these leaders, telling them to leave Latin America alone.

President James Monroe asked former presidents Thomas Jefferson and James Madison for advice. Should the United States do something to support the new Latin American nations? If so, what?

With the Monroe Doctrine by his side, Uncle Sam warns foreign powers to keep their "hands off" the Americas. Even though the Monroe Doctrine is more than 180 years old, it still guides U.S. presidents as they make foreign policy decisions.

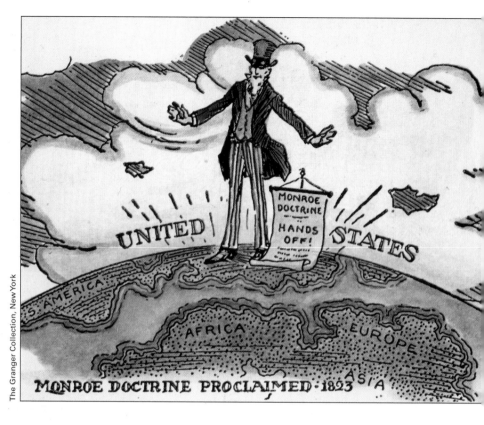

The Granger Collection, New York

MONROE DOCTRINE PROCLAIMED · 1823

12.10 What Happened: The Monroe Doctrine

Both Thomas Jefferson and James Madison liked the idea of joining with Great Britain to send a warning to the nations of Europe. Jefferson wrote to James Monroe, "Our first and fundamental maxim [principle] should be, never entangle ourselves in the broils [fights] of Europe. Our second, never to suffer Europe to intermeddle [interfere] with . . . America, North and South."

President Monroe's secretary of state, John Quincy Adams, agreed with Jefferson. But Adams insisted that "it would be more candid [honest], as well as more dignified," for the United States to speak boldly for itself. President Monroe agreed.

In 1823, Monroe made a speech to Congress announcing a policy that became known as the **Monroe Doctrine**. Monroe stated that the nations of North and South America were "free and independent" and were "not to be considered as subjects for future colonization by any European powers." The United States, he said, would view efforts by Europeans to take over "any portion of this hemisphere as dangerous to our peace and safety."

Europeans denounced Monroe's message as arrogant. By what right, asked a French newspaper, did the United States presume to tell the other nations of the world what they could do in North and South America?

Americans, however, cheered Monroe's message. It made them proud to see the United States stand up for the freedom-loving people of Latin America.

Monroe Doctrine President James Monroe's declaration in 1823 that the Western Hemisphere was no longer open to European colonization

In the years ahead, the Monroe Doctrine joined isolationism as a basic principle of U.S. foreign policy. The doctrine asserted that the United States would not accept European interference in American affairs. It also contained another, hidden message. By its very boldness, the Monroe Doctrine told the world that the United States was no longer a weak collection of quarreling states. It had become a strong and confident nation—a nation to be respected by the world.

Chapter Summary

In this chapter, you learned about the development of foreign policy in the United States under the nation's first five presidents.

President Washington Creates a Foreign Policy The first U.S. president knew that the young nation was unprepared for war. George Washington established a policy of isolationism to avoid alliances with other countries, which could draw the country into wars abroad.

President Adams's Dilemma During the presidency of John Adams, France attacked U.S. ships. Adams followed Washington's policy of isolationism and kept the United States at peace by securing a treaty with France.

President Jefferson's Dilemma President Thomas Jefferson also faced threats at sea. When peace talks failed, he passed the Embargo Act of 1807. It, too, was unsuccessful.

President Madison's Dilemma President James Madison offered a trade deal to both France and Great Britain, but the attacks at sea continued. He finally abandoned isolationism and declared war on Great Britain. The War of 1812 ended in a peace treaty with Great Britain.

President Monroe's Dilemma President James Monroe, in support of the new Latin American states, issued a policy called the Monroe Doctrine. In it, he warned European nations to respect the newly independent colonies. The Monroe Doctrine established the United States as a strong nation, willing to stand up for its own freedom and that of its neighbors.

In this artwork, the American eagle holds the olive branch of peace in one talon and the arrows of war in the other. Both are necessary to protect the liberty (at the top) that Americans hold so dear.

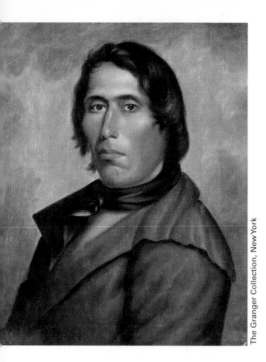

The Granger Collection, New York

Tecumseh was one of the greatest American Indian leaders. By all accounts, he was an imposing figure. This portrait was based on a sketch made during Tecumseh's lifetime.

Tecumseh, the Shooting Star

In the early 1800s, American Indians in Ohio and other parts of the Northwest Territory faced a critical choice. White settlers were moving in and taking their land. The Indians could give up their land peacefully and try to live among the settlers. Or, they could stand and fight for their way of life. For one visionary American Indian leader, the choice was never in doubt.

The Shawnee canoes slid swiftly down the Wabash River. They were painted in bright colors, the colors of war. The Shawnee were headed for the town of Vincennes, the capital of the Indiana Territory.

The date was August 12, 1810. The Shawnee—about 75 of them—had come to meet with the governor, William Henry Harrison. They camped a mile outside of town. Several days later, the meeting began at the governor's mansion. The governor had set up tables and chairs on the mansion's large porch, but the Shawnee chief, Tecumseh, said he wanted to sit on the lawn. As he put it, "The earth was the most proper place for the Indians, as they liked to repose [rest] on the bosom of their mother."

As everyone took a seat, Tecumseh remained standing. He was a tall, handsome man, with long hair and an athletic body. Everyone would later agree that he had a commanding presence and a gift for words. In Shawnee, his name meant "Shooting Star."

Tecumseh faced Governor Harrison and began to speak. He described the injustices his people had suffered at the hands of the U.S. government. He spoke of unfair treaties and broken promises that had stripped them of their land. He said the government had persuaded Indians to sell land that did not belong to them. The land, he said, "was never divided, but belongs to all." And he continued,

No tribe has the right to sell, even to each other, much less to strangers. Sell a country? Why not sell the air, the great sea, as well as the earth? Did not the Great Spirit make them all for the use of his children?

Tecumseh claimed to speak for all American Indians. He said his people wanted to live in peace, but they would fight if necessary. Harrison was unmoved by Tecumseh's words, but he knew he could not ignore the Shawnee leader. He later called him "one of those uncommon geniuses which spring up occasionally to produce revolutions and overturn the established order of things." He wanted to make sure Tecumseh did not stand in the way of U.S. expansion.

Who was Tecumseh, and how did he become such a powerful figure?

The meeting at Vincennes was a confrontation between two strong, powerful men. This drawing was made just 30 years after the encounter.

The Making of a Warrior

Tecumseh was born in the Ohio Territory around 1768. Ohio was a beautiful land of rivers and forests, rich in wildlife. It was a sacred place to the Shawnee. They called it the "center of the world."

Tecumseh grew up in troubled times, however. White settlers were crossing the Appalachians and taking Indian lands. During the American Revolution, most Indians fought on the British side, hoping to halt western settlement. After the war, however, westward expansion continued. And so did the conflict between Indians and white Americans.

Indians called the Americans "Long Knives" because of the army swords some of them carried. Tecumseh lost his father in fighting with the Long Knives. He and his family also had to move many times, as the Americans raided and burned their villages.

These experiences led Tecumseh to become a warrior. As a boy, he saw Shawnee war parties prepare for battle. He watched them paint their faces and put on their war feathers. As a young man, he learned the arts of warfare. By his early twenties, he had become a brave and skillful warrior.

At first, the Indians enjoyed great success in their battles with the Long Knives. But, in 1794, they suffered a crushing defeat at the Battle of Fallen Timbers. The following year, they were forced to sign the Treaty of Greenville. Under this treaty, they gave up most of the Ohio Territory to white settlement. In exchange, they received money and the promise of lands in western Ohio and Indiana.

Tecumseh refused to sign the treaty. He knew that the government had failed to honor previous treaties. He also believed that Ohio was the land of his people. Many older Indian leaders had grown tired of fighting. They did not believe they could defeat the Long Knives. But Tecumseh would not give up.

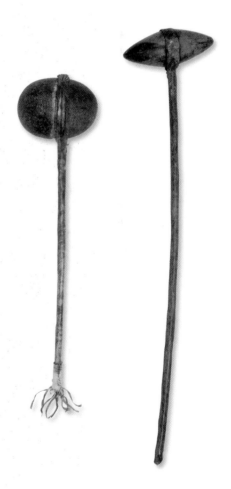

Historians believe that these war clubs belonged to Tecumseh.

Tecumseh's brother was known as "the Prophet." He helped Tecumseh launch a movement for Indian unity. His Indian name was Lalawethika. He later changed it to Tenskwatawa, meaning "open door."

The Quest for Indian Unity

After the Treaty of Greenville, Tecumseh and his followers moved west into the Indiana Territory. But the white settlers continued to move closer. They cleared the land and killed the wild game. Soon there would be nothing left to sustain the Indian way of life.

By the early 1800s, Tecumseh knew that he had to do something to save his people. The only solution, he believed, was to form a single Indian nation.

This was not a new idea. Indians had formed tribal confederacies in the past. But Tecumseh's plan was much bigger. He imagined a grand confederation of Indian peoples, stretching from the Great Lakes to the Gulf of Mexico. This confederation would unite dozens of tribes around the common goal of defending their land. To these various tribes, he declared, "Brothers, we all belong to one family."

It was an enormous challenge, perhaps too big even for an inspired leader like Tecumseh. But he got crucial help from his younger brother, Lalawethika.

In 1805, Lalawethika fell into a fire and nearly died. But in his suffering he had a mystical vision that told him how his people could be saved. They had to embrace Indian customs and reject the ways of the white world. If they did this, the white people would be driven from their land. This message had a powerful effect on other Indians, who began calling Lalawethika "the Prophet." Tecumseh realized that he could combine the Prophet's message with his own call for Indian unity to forge a powerful movement.

Together, the two brothers founded a new Indian village, called Prophetstown. Indians began flocking there to join the movement.

These events made Governor Harrison very nervous. But he continued with his plans to settle Indiana. In 1809, he gathered a number of Indian leaders together and persuaded them to sign the Treaty of Fort Wayne. They agreed to sell 3 million acres of land to the government for just pennies an acre.

Tecumseh was furious. In his view, the Indians had no right to sell the land. He went to meet Harrison at Vincennes—the famous meeting of 1810—and told him that the treaty was invalid. But Harrison refused to listen. Tecumseh went away more convinced than ever that only Indian unity—and war—could save his people.

Tecumseh's Defeat

War came sooner than Tecumseh wanted. In the fall of 1811, while Tecumseh was away trying to win new allies, Governor Harrison made his move. He marched his militia to Prophetstown and told the Indians to leave. Tecumseh had warned the Prophet not to get drawn into war while he was gone. But the Prophet ignored this order. He believed his spiritual power would protect the Indians from harm.

Just before dawn on November 7, the Indians crept into the militia camp. They were a much smaller force—several hundred warriors against a thousand soldiers—but they hoped to take the camp by surprise. With a flurry of war cries, they fell on the unsuspecting soldiers. The Battle of Tippecanoe had begun.

At first, it seemed their strategy might work. In the darkness and confusion of battle, the Indians quickly gained the upper hand. But as the day dawned and the fighting wore on, it was clear that they were outnumbered and outgunned. Finally, they were forced to retreat. Harrison and his troops entered Prophetstown and burned it to the ground. The governor returned home in victory.

This defeat struck hard at Tecumseh's plans. But the fighting had just begun. Tecumseh continued to build his confederacy. When the War of 1812 began, he and his Indian allies joined with British forces in Canada to fight the U.S. army.

Once again, Tecumseh showed his bravery and brilliance. The British commanders were awed by his military genius. In 1813, however, Tecumseh and the British were defeated by a much larger U.S. force at the Battle of the Thames. The British quickly fled the battlefield, but Tecumseh refused to retreat. "Our lives are in the hands of the Great Spirit," he said. "We are determined to defend our lands, and if it is his will, we shall leave our bones upon them." He was killed in the battle.

In the end, Tecumseh failed to realize his vision of a great American Indian nation. Indians continued to lose their lands and their lives to U.S. expansion. But he set an example in his dedication to his ideals and his commitment to his people. For a brief time, his star burned bright. Today, Tecumseh is regarded as an American hero.

Tecumseh was killed on October 5, 1813, at the Battle of the Thames. The battle was a decisive victory for the Americans in the War of 1812.

241

Chapter 13

A Growing Sense of Nationhood

What did it mean to be an American in the early 1800s?

13.1 Introduction

If you had been there on that rainy night in Maryland during the War of 1812, you might have mistaken the bombardment for thunder. But Maryland lawyer Francis Scott Key knew better. He huddled in a boat in Baltimore harbor and watched as British warships fired on Fort McHenry.

Fort McHenry had a flag so big "that the British would have no trouble seeing it from a distance," boasted the fort's commander. It was 30 feet high and 42 feet long. You can see a photograph of that very flag on the opposite page. Key knew that if the flag came down, it meant that both the fort and Baltimore had been defeated. But when the sun rose, the flag was still there and the British were retreating.

Key celebrated by writing a poem, "The Defence of Fort McHenry." Six days later, it was published in a newspaper. Before long, it had been reprinted across the country. It was set to music in 1814 and sung as "The Star-Spangled Banner." In 1931, it was **proclaimed** the national anthem.

Moments like these during the War of 1812 helped give Americans a feeling of national identity. But what did being American mean? How was it different from being European? Alexis de Tocqueville, a French nobleman who toured the United States in 1831 and 1832, had one answer. "I do not know a country where the love of money holds a larger place in the heart of man," he wrote in his book *Democracy in America*. The pursuit of wealth was an important element of the **emerging** American identity. But there were also other elements that united Americans of different backgrounds and experiences. In this chapter, you will learn how a growing sense of nationhood developed during the early 1800s in spite of significant differences between various regions of the country.

This painting depicts Francis Scott Key watching the flag flying over Fort McHenry during the Battle of Baltimore in 1814.

◀ The flag that inspired the writing of "The Star-Spangled Banner" is displayed at the Smithsonian's National Museum of American History.

13.2 Developing a Nation in a Land of Differences

In the early 1800s, the United States was a very young country. Older adults at that time could still remember when they were British subjects. Even after the American Revolution, the United States seemed less like a single nation than a collection of states.

A surge of patriotism following the War of 1812 helped forge a new national identity. Because many Federalists had been opposed to the war—a stance their opponents described as disloyal—the Federalist Party struggled to survive in the face of this growing patriotism. Leaders like James Monroe hoped that partisan strife, or fighting between political parties, was a thing of the past. Most Americans looked with pride on a rapidly growing country whose brightest days, they believed, lay ahead.

frontier unexplored wilderness at the edge of the country

The United States in the Early 1800s The nation in 1800 was very different from what it is today. Two out of every three Americans still lived within 50 miles of the Atlantic Coast. Fewer than one in ten lived west of the Appalachians. These round-topped, forested mountains extended like a bumpy spine from Maine through Georgia. They made travel between east and west very difficult.

Beyond the mountains, the land flattened out and was covered by dense woods. More and more settlers crossed the Appalachians in the early 1800s, clearing trees and starting farms and mills. For Americans of the day, this land between the eastern mountains and the Mississippi River was known as "the West." Across the Mississippi lay the **frontier,** a vast, unexplored wilderness.

In 1820, most Americans lived east of the Mississippi River. To the west of the river lay the great frontier.

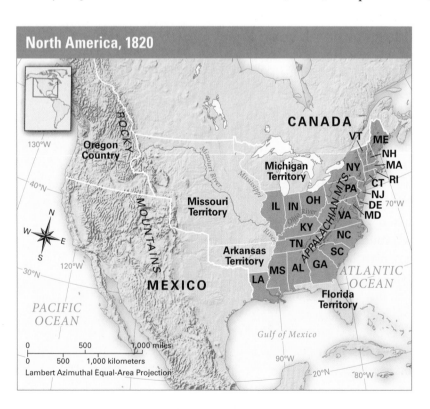

North America, 1820

Everywhere, travel was difficult and slow. Nothing moved faster than a horse could run—not people, not goods, not messages. News could take weeks to travel from one city to another, as the post office labored to deliver letters and newspapers over rutted, muddy roads.

In part because of geographical differences, **distinct** regional lifestyles developed. This led to **stereotypes,** or exaggerated images, of different groups. The "Yankees" of the Northeast, with its growing cities and bustling trade, were seen as enterprising, thrifty, and—in the eyes of southerners—quick to chase a dollar. The rich plantation owners of the South were seen as gracious,

cultured, and—in the eyes of northerners—lazy. The frontier settlers who sought their fortunes in the West were seen as rugged, hardy, and—in the eyes of people on the East Coast—crude.

Many of the country's leaders knew they would have to overcome geographical obstacles and stereotypes to truly unite the country. One idea they favored was an ambitious program of building roads and canals to make transportation easier and faster.

The U.S. Capitol, shown here in an 1824 painting after the structure was rebuilt following the War of 1812, is a powerful symbol of national unity.

Symbols and Values Uniting the nation required more than building roads and waterways. Citizens needed to *feel* American. One way to accomplish this was to build on Americans' pride in their government. After the British burned Washington, D.C., during the War of 1812, Congress hired architects to rebuild the White House and the Capitol in a style that would equal the grand, stately buildings of Europe. Congress complained about the cost, but not about the result. These magnificent buildings are admired to this day as national symbols.

Another national symbol was born during this period: Uncle Sam. Legend has it that the name came from Sam Wilson, a New York butcher. "Uncle Sam," it was said, had provided the army with meat during the War of 1812. More likely the name was made up to match the initials *U.S.* for United States. After the war, "Uncle Sam" became a popular nickname for the federal government.

A national identity requires more than symbols. Citizens need to share values as well. White American men saw themselves as devoted to individualism and equality. Their commitment to these values may not have extended to enslaved African Americans, American Indians, or women. Still, they were united in the belief that they were different —and better—than Europeans.

Alexis de Tocqueville sensed this feeling just four days into his visit. "The Americans carry national pride to an altogether excessive length," he noted. By the end of his trip, however, he had come to admire this distinctly American spirit. That spirit was reflected in every aspect of life, from politics to art, music, and literature.

James Monroe was the last president to have fought in the American Revolution. When he ran for reelection, no one opposed him. He won the Electoral College vote, 231 to 1.

go to Page 300

capitalism an economic system based on the private ownership of farms and businesses

American System a proposal to the government that called for taxes on imports, federally funded transportation projects, and a new national bank

13.3 Politics: The Era of Good Feelings

After being elected president in 1816, James Monroe went on a good-will tour. Huge crowds greeted him so warmly that a newspaper proclaimed an "Era of Good Feelings." Monroe's eight years as president are still known by this name today. To many Americans at the time, it seemed that a new period of national unity had dawned.

Economic Nationalism The swelling of nationalist spirit was reflected in proposals that the federal government take a more active role in building the national economy. One of the leading supporters of such measures in Congress was Henry Clay of Kentucky.

Clay was a persuasive speaker, full of charm and intelligence. Driven by ambition, Clay wanted to be president. He campaigned for the office five times, but was never elected.

Clay believed that America's future lay in **capitalism,** an economic system in which individuals and companies produce and distribute goods for profit. Most supporters of capitalism agreed that government should have a limited role in the economy. But Clay believed that the national government had a role to play in encouraging economic growth. Clay supported an economic plan called the **American System.** This plan called for taxes on imported goods to protect industry as well as federal spending on transportation projects like roads and canals.

A third part of Clay's plan was a new national bank to standardize currency and provide credit. Congress adopted this idea in 1816 when it created the second Bank of the United States. (The first national bank had lapsed in 1811.) The bank was a private business, but the government owned one-fifth of it and deposited government funds there.

Another early champion of economic nationalism was South Carolina's John C. Calhoun. In Congress, Calhoun supported the national bank, a permanent road system, and a tax on imports. Yet in other ways he resisted federal power. By the 1830s, he would become the leading spokesman for states' rights, largely to protect slavery in the South. His career illustrates the tensions between nationalism and the pull of regional differences.

A third proponent of nationalism was Daniel Webster of Massachusetts. Webster served several terms in both the House and Senate. Unlike Clay, who was a War Hawk, Webster bitterly opposed the War of 1812. After the war, however, he voiced strong support for Clay's American System. "Let us act under a settled conviction, and an habitual feeling, that these twenty-four states are one country," Webster urged in 1825. Later, he would strongly challenge Calhoun's claim that states had the right to defy the federal government.

Judicial Nationalism Both nationalism and commerce had a friend in the Supreme Court's chief justice, John Marshall. Appointed by John Adams in 1801, Marshall wrote some of the most important court decisions in U.S. history.

Marshall's decisions had two major effects. First, they strengthened the role of the Supreme Court itself and the federal government's power over the states. Second, they encouraged the growth of capitalism, as a few specific cases show. In *McCulloch v. Maryland* (1819), the Court confirmed Congress's authority to create a national bank that was free from state interference. This strengthened the federal government's position. In another case, the Marshall Court held that business contracts could not be broken, even by state legislatures. This decision gave contracts a fundamental place in constitutional law. In *Gibbons v. Ogden* (1824), the Court further reduced state powers. This case ended a monopoly that New York State had granted to a steamboat company operating between New York and New Jersey. Only Congress, the Court said, had the authority to regulate interstate commerce. Besides strengthening the power of the federal government, this decision promoted business growth by limiting the ability of states to regulate transportation.

The End of the Era of Good Feelings In 1824, four candidates, including Clay, competed to succeed Monroe as president. None of the candidates won a majority in the Electoral College. As a result, the election had to be decided by the House of Representatives. The House elected John Quincy Adams, the son of John Adams.

The House's action enraged the candidate who had received the most votes on Election Day. That candidate was Andrew Jackson of Tennessee, one of the heroes of the War of 1812. Jackson vowed to run again in the next election. The voters who rallied around him in 1828 would become the heart of a new political party, the Democrats. The Era of Good Feelings was over. Partisan strife was here to stay.

Americans were on the move in the 1800s, with many bound for the frontier. Henry Clay envisioned a government-built system of roads and canals that would link regions of the frontier with the nation's cities.

folk art art made by ordinary people (as opposed to trained artists) using traditional methods

13.4 Early American Art

Americans had brought European art traditions with them to the colonies, but by the 1800s they were expressing their national identity by developing styles all their own. Not all artists were professionals. Ordinary people produced many kinds of **folk art**. Men carved weather vanes and hunting decoys. Women sewed spare bits of cloth into quilts. Untrained artists created signs, murals, and images of national symbols like the American flag. Such folk art was simple, direct, and often very colorful.

Most professional artists made a living doing portraits. Portrait artists of the period tried to capture the personalities and emotions of their subjects. The best-known portrait artist was Gilbert Stuart. The image of George Washington on a dollar bill is adapted from a Stuart painting. The painting was so treasured that when the British attacked Washington, D.C., during the War of 1812, President Madison's wife, Dolly, saved Stuart's painting of Washington from the burning White House.

Strangely enough, it was an Englishman whose work led to a uniquely American brand of fine art. When Thomas Cole arrived from England in 1818, he fell in love with the immense and varied American landscape. His most famous works feature both storm clouds and sunny skies over broad stretches of land. The glowing light made a striking contrast to the stormy darkness. Fellow artists followed Cole's example and started what became known as the Hudson River School of painting. These painters focused on nature rather than people, often choosing to paint broad, scenic vistas.

In *The Subsiding of the Waters of the Deluge* (1829), Thomas Cole bathed his scene in a soft, glowing light. Like other painters of the Hudson River School, Cole favored grand vistas that celebrated the nation's natural beauty.

Other artists portrayed more particular aspects of nature. John James Audubon painted finely detailed portraits of birds. In some respects, Audubon was more a naturalist than an artist. He made accurate, realistic studies of the species he observed in the fields and woods. No one in the United States would print his four-volume book, so he found a publisher in England. *The Birds of America* made him the country's first internationally famous artist.

Philadelphia's George Catlin turned his eye on the natives of the American West. He saw that American Indians' traditional ways were disappearing. For years, Catlin crisscrossed the West, drawing the native people and capturing in rich colors their villages, hunts, and rituals.

By choosing as their subject the wondrous features of their new country, Americans gave their art a distinct identity. At times, they presented dangerous landscapes in deceptively positive tones. Still, the vividness and optimism of their work accurately reflected the national outlook.

13.5 Early American Music

Americans' national identity was also expressed through music. Until the 1800s, music in the United States was performed and heard mostly in church. Songs were performed outside church, too, but they were usually old tunes with new lyrics. The music for "The Star-Spangled Banner," for instance, came from an English tune.

With growing prosperity came an outburst of musical activity. In the North, orchestras played classical music from Europe. They also provided the music for the cotillion, in which groups of four couples danced together with elegantly coordinated movements. Dancers swirled through ballrooms, performing lively minuets, gavottes, mazurkas, and waltzes. Sometimes, female dancers lifted their floor-length petticoats to show off their footwork. Displaying their ankles was considered quite daring.

Some Americans relaxed with folk songs and fiddle tunes, while others listened to classical orchestras and performed formal dances. From the North to the South, music was a popular form of entertainment.

In the South, slaves combined the hymns of white churchgoers with African musical styles to create **spirituals**. They also entertained themselves—and sometimes slave owners—with folk songs accompanied by violin, drum, and banjo (an African American invention).

In the South and West, square dances became common. These were less formal versions of the popular cotillion. As fiddles played, a "caller" told dancers which steps to perform.

As demand for popular songs grew, composers answered with a stream of patriotic anthems. The best known is "America," written in 1832 by Samuel Francis Smith. It begins "My country, 'tis of Thee" and is sung to the tune of England's "God Save the King."

White composers from the South, inspired by the music of African Americans, created a type of music known as minstrel songs. These songs honored black music by mimicking it. But at the same time, the performers mocked African Americans by blackening their own white faces, wearing shabby clothes, and singing in exaggerated African American dialects. One white composer, Thomas Dartmouth Rice, caused a national sensation in 1828 with his song "Jump Jim Crow":

Weel about and turn about and do jis so
Ebery time I weel about I jump Jim Crow.

spiritual a religious folk song of African American origin

The racist phrase "Jim Crow," which came from Rice's black minstrel show character, had a long life. Many years later, laws that discriminated against African Americans would be known as "Jim Crow laws."

Minstrel shows became the most popular form of entertainment in the country. They inspired composer Stephen Foster to write such famous songs as "Old Folks at Home," "Camptown Races," and "Oh! Susanna." Foster earned nationwide fame, proof that a truly American musical tradition had arrived.

13.6 Early American Literature

In 1820, a British writer sneered, "Who reads an American book? or goes to an American play? or looks at an American picture or statue?" In the eyes of Europeans, the United States was a culturally backward nation. Yet America was finding its cultural voice, especially in literature.

Like the painters of the Hudson River School, writers began to use uniquely American subjects and settings. One of the first to achieve literary fame was Washington Irving. He drew on German folklore for his colorful tales of "Rip Van Winkle" and "The Legend of Sleepy Hollow," but he set them in the wilds of upstate New York. Irving's enchanted stories were an immediate hit.

One of the nation's first novelists was James Fenimore Cooper. In books such as *The Pioneers* and *The Last of the Mohicans*, Cooper wrote about the adventures of settlers in the wilderness. His descriptions of frontier life and American Indians attracted worldwide interest. In France, 18 publishers competed to publish *The Pioneers*.

Davy Crockett was a real-life frontiersman who spun tall tales about his life as a hunter, scout, soldier, and explorer. His election to Congress from Tennessee horrified Alexis de Tocqueville. The Frenchman described Crockett as a man "who has no education, can read with difficulty, has no property, no fixed residence, but passes his life hunting, selling his game to live, and dwelling continuously in the woods." But that very image captivated Americans, who saw Crockett as the fictional frontier hero come to life. Crockett's autobiography, which was full of his plain backwoods speech and rough humor, helped give popular literature a new, distinctly American accent.

New England's Henry Wadsworth Longfellow was one of the first serious American poets. He wrote America's first epic poem, *The Song of Hiawatha*, based on stories of American Indians. Other poems, like his famous "Paul Revere's Ride," touched on patriotic themes. In "The Building of the Ship," Longfellow celebrated the growing importance of the United States to the world:

> *Sail on, O Ship of State!*
> *Sail on, O Union, strong and great!*
> *Humanity with all its fears,*
> *With all the hopes of future years,*
> *Is hanging breathless on thy fate!*

In a typical humorous boast, frontiersman Davy Crockett described himself as "half-horse, half-alligator." Crockett became a national celebrity, and books bearing his name were best sellers in the 1830s.

In both subject matter and style, writers like these encouraged the growth of a national identity. In particular, they promoted the myth of rugged individualism that for many people—at home and abroad—best characterized the United States.

Chapter Summary

In this chapter, you read about the growing sense of nationhood in the United States after the War of 1812.

Developing a Nation in a Land of Differences A spirit of patriotism after the War of 1812 helped the United States form a national identity, even though distinct lifestyles developed in different regions of the country. This national identity was shown in Americans' pride in symbols, such as the White House, the Capitol, and Uncle Sam, and in shared values, such as equality.

Politics: The Era of Good Feelings James Monroe became president in 1816. His presidency is known as the Era of Good Feelings because of the national unity the country experienced between 1816 and 1824. During these years, leaders like Henry Clay, John C. Calhoun, and Daniel Webster supported proposals that called for the federal government to take a more active role in developing the nation's economy. Also during this period, the chief justice of the Supreme Court, John Marshall, helped strengthen federal power over the states and encourage the growth of capitalism.

Early American Art, Music, and Literature American art forms also helped the nation develop a unique identity. Painters of the Hudson River School created artworks that highlighted the landscape's natural beauty, and George Catlin painted scenes of American Indian life. New forms of music included spirituals and patriotic anthems. Writers used uniquely American settings and subjects to create such stories as "Rip Van Winkle" and "The Legend of Sleepy Hollow" and popular novels like *The Pioneers* and *The Last of the Mohicans*.

Capturing the spirit of national pride, painter George Caleb Bingham showed democracy at work on the frontier. *The Verdict of the People* (1855) shows a lively crowd of voters, eager to hear the results of a local election.

A New Literature Celebrates a New Nation

As the country grew, American writers began to develop a uniquely American literature. Stories and novels took place in beautiful American settings. They also focused on distinctly American topics, both celebrating the new nation and pondering its future.

An elderly Rip Van Winkle returned home after sleeping for 20 years. This 1836 painting shows Rip, still pleased to be a subject of King George III, confronted by angry Patriots who were proud of their newly won independence.

Rip Van Winkle, the title character of an 1819 short story by Washington Irving, was a happy man. He lived in New York's lush Hudson Valley and spent his days hanging out with his friends, shooting squirrels, and avoiding his domineering wife.

One afternoon, as he rested in the hills after hunting with his dog, Rip heard someone call his name. He saw a strange-looking, elflike man who wanted his help. Rip helped the little man carry a heavy keg to a green valley. There he saw more small, oddly dressed men, who were bowling on a lawn.

Rip wondered if there was something magical about the scene. How had the little man known his name? And why, every time a ball hit some pins, did thunder roar? Soon Rip's curiosity about what was in the keg—and his desire to avoid his wife—overcame him, and he had a drink. He had a few more drinks, and then he fell asleep.

When Rip woke the next morning, everything had changed. The little men were gone, and when he made his way home, he saw that his "village seemed altered; it was larger and more populous" than it had been when he had left. He felt that the "character of the people seemed changed." A "busy, bustling" tone had replaced the "drowsy tranquility" that Rip had known. In fact, Rip Van Winkle had slept for 20 years, although it felt like just one night to him.

Rip soon discovered that he had become an old man. "He found himself stiff in the joints," and he looked different. When he passed the local villagers,

> *They all stared at him with equal marks of surprise, and whenever they cast eyes upon him, invariably stroked their chins. The constant recurrence of this gesture, induced Rip, involuntarily, to do the same, when, to his astonishment, he found his beard had grown a foot long!*
> —Washington Irving, "Rip Van Winkle," from *The Sketch Book of Geoffrey Crayon, Gent*, 1819

More than Rip's appearance had changed during his long night. While he slept, the American colonies had fought and won a war for independence. Imagine Rip's confusion on visiting the local tavern, where the political changes were visible.

He recognized on the sign . . . the ruby face of King George, under which he had smoked so many a peaceful pipe, but even this was singularly metamorphosed [transformed]. The red coat was changed for one of blue and buff, a sword was stuck in the hand instead of a sceptre, the head was decorated with a cocked hat, and underneath was painted in large characters, GENERAL WASHINGTON.

Talking with the townsfolk, Rip discovered what had happened. "Instead of being a subject of his Majesty George the Third," he found out, "he was now a free citizen of the United States."

In the story "Rip Van Winkle," 20 years seemed to pass overnight. A man fell asleep, and the colony where he lived had become part of a new country. Many people consider "Rip Van Winkle" to be the United States' first short story. Written not long after independence, it expressed wonder and shock at how quickly a revolution had happened and how much it had changed the lives of the people of the new nation.

At the same time that American writers were setting stories in the American landscape, painters were painting it. Thomas Cole was one of those painters. *View on the Catskill, Early Autumn* shows the beauty of the area where the story of Rip Van Winkle took place.

This drawing appeared in an 1893 version of *The Pioneers*. It shows Natty Bumppo at the grave of his friend Chingachgook. White settlement dramatically altered the ways of life of both the American Indian and the frontier scout.

Washington Irving was not the only writer to choose American topics for his work. At the same time Irving was writing, James Fenimore Cooper penned the first American novels. Set in the fictional town of Templeton, New York, *The Leatherstocking Tales* told about the settlement and rapid disappearance of the frontier.

The Pioneers was the first of the series, written in 1823. It introduced readers to Natty Bumppo. This fictional character, a former wilderness scout, was probably modeled after Daniel Boone. He was called Leatherstocking because he wore leather chaps to cover his legs. In Cooper's novels, Natty Bumppo tried to protect both nature and his own way of life from the onslaught of civilization.

In one scene, Cooper described the clash between the pioneers, who represented civilization, and a flock of birds, which represented nature. The excitement began early one morning. "The gulls are hovering over the lake already," one Templeton resident exclaimed, "and the heavens are alive with pigeons. You may look an hour before you can find a hole through which to get a peep at the sun."

The excited townspeople gathered. Cooper wrote, "If the heavens were alive with pigeons, the whole village seemed equally in motion with men, women, and children." They brought their guns—all kinds of guns—and started to shoot at the pigeons. There were so many birds that the hunters didn't even need to aim. They simply shot into the air and the pigeons fell. At one point, the hunters grew so enthusiastic that two of them brought out a cannon to shoot even more pigeons. That was too much for Natty Bumppo. He harshly criticized the settlers for recklessly spoiling nature.

> *"This comes of settling a country!" he said. "Here have I known the pigeon to fly for forty long years, and, till you made your clearings, there was nobody to skear [scare] or to hurt them. I loved to see them come into the woods, for they were company to a body, hurting nothing—being, as it was, as harmless as a garter-snake."*
>
> —James Fenimore Cooper, *The Pioneers*, 1823

In describing the hunters as not even bothering to see whether the birds were dead or to pick them up off the ground, Cooper seemed to agree with Natty that the settlers threatened the natural world.

On the other hand, the settlers did have some valid reasons for their actions. Cooper sympathized with them, too. One hunter, Billy Kirby, heard Natty's outrage and replied,

> *"What! old Leather-Stocking," he cried, "grumbling at the loss of a few pigeons! If you had to sow your wheat twice, and three times, as I have done, you wouldn't be so massyfully [mercifully] feeling toward the divils. Hurrah, boys! scatter the feathers!"*

The settlers were farmers, and the birds threatened the crops they needed to survive. In Cooper's eyes, the settlers' motive was as valid as Leatherstocking's anger. But the needs of nature and the needs of the pioneers clashed—and would continue to clash—until the settlers finally won out.

A Disappearing World

Washington Irving and James Fenimore Cooper were two of the first truly American writers. Both had lived overseas and wanted Europeans to respect the budding American culture. Both saw themselves as voices for the new nation.

The content of their writing was distinctly American. Irving and Cooper set their stories in the beautiful American landscape. They also addressed American issues. They were proud of their new country. But they also knew that, along with the nation's growth, there would be unforeseen changes.

Actor Daniel Day-Lewis played Natty Bumppo in a film version of *The Last of the Mohicans*. The novel, one of *The Leatherstocking Tales,* takes place during the French and Indian War.

Chapter 14

Andrew Jackson and the Growth of American Democracy

How well did President Andrew Jackson promote democracy?

14.1 Introduction

The presidential campaign of 1828 was one of the dirtiest in U.S. history. The two candidates were John Quincy Adams, running for reelection, and Andrew Jackson, the popular hero of the War of 1812's Battle of New Orleans.

During the campaign, both sides hurled accusations at each other, a practice called mudslinging. Adams, for example, was called a "Sabbath-breaker" for traveling on Sunday. He was accused of using public money to purchase "gambling furniture" for the White House. In reality, he had used his own money to buy a billiard table.

The Granger Collection, New York

Jackson, at the upper left, greets his supporters after winning the presidency in the election of 1828.

The president's supporters lashed back. They called Jackson a crude and **ignorant** man who was unfit to be president. They also brought up old scandals about his wife. Jackson was called "Old Hickory" by his troops because he was as tough as "the hardest wood in all creation." But when he read such lies, he broke down and cried.

When the votes were counted, Jackson was the clear winner. But his supporters came from among the general population, not the rich and upper class. In this chapter, you will discover how his presidency was viewed by different groups of people. You will also learn how Jackson's government affected the growth of democracy in the nation.

◀ Men line up to vote in the presidential election of 1828.

Andrew Jackson was born on the South Carolina frontier. In the early 1800s, he moved to Tennessee and bought a plantation called the Hermitage. His first home there was a log cabin similar to this one.

14.2 From the Frontier to the White House

Andrew Jackson was born in 1767, on the South Carolina frontier. His father died before he was born, leaving the family in poverty. Young Jackson loved sports more than schoolwork. He also had a hot temper. A friend recalled that he would pick a fight at the drop of a hat, and "he'd drop the hat himself."

The American Revolution ended Jackson's childhood. When he was just 13, Jackson joined the local militia and was captured by the British. One day, a British officer ordered Jackson to polish his boots. "Sir," he replied boldly, "I am a prisoner of war, and claim [demand] to be treated as such." The outraged officer lashed out with his sword, slicing the boy's head and hand. Jackson carried these scars for the rest of his life.

Frontier Lawyer After the war, Jackson decided to become a lawyer. He went to work in a law office in North Carolina. He quickly became known as "the most roaring, rollicking, game-cocking, horse-racing, card-playing, mischievous fellow" in town.

In 1788, Jackson headed west to Nashville, Tennessee, to practice law. At that time, Nashville was a tiny frontier settlement of rough cabins and tents. But the town grew quickly, and Jackson's practice grew with it. He soon earned enough money to buy land and slaves and set himself up as a gentleman farmer.

Despite his success, Jackson never outgrew his hot temper. A slave trader named Charles Dickinson found this out when he called Jackson "a worthless scoundrel." Enraged, Jackson challenged Dickinson to a duel with pistols. At that time, duels were accepted as a way of settling **disputes** between gentlemen. Jackson killed Dickinson with a single shot, even though Dickinson shot first and wounded him.

The People's Choice Jackson entered politics in Tennessee, serving in both the House and Senate. But he did not become widely known until the Battle of New Orleans during the War of 1812. His defense of the city made "Old Hickory" a national hero.

In 1824, Jackson ran for president against three other candidates: Henry Clay, William Crawford, and John Quincy Adams. Jackson won the most popular votes as well as the most electoral votes. But he did not have enough electoral votes for a majority. When no candidate has an electoral majority, the House of Representatives chooses a president from among the three leading candidates.

Clay, who had come in fourth, urged his supporters in the House to vote for Adams. That support gave Adams enough votes to become president. Adams then chose Clay to be his secretary of state.

It made sense for Adams to bring Clay into his cabinet, because the two men shared many of the same goals. Jackson's supporters, however, accused Adams and Clay of making a "corrupt bargain" to rob their hero of his rightful election. They promised revenge in 1828.

Jackson's supporters used the time between elections to build a new political organization that came to be called the Democratic Party, the name it still uses today. This new party, they promised, would represent ordinary farmers, workers, and the poor, not the rich and upper class who controlled the Republican Party.

Jacksonian Democracy the idea that the common people should control the government

In the election of 1828, Jackson's supporters worked hard to reach the nation's voters. Besides hurling insults at Adams, they organized parades, picnics, and rallies. At these events, supporters sang "The Hunters of Kentucky"—the nation's first campaign song—and cheered for Old Hickory. They wore Jackson badges, carried hickory sticks, and chanted catchy campaign slogans like "Adams can write, but Jackson can fight."

The result was a great victory for Jackson. But it was also a victory for the idea that the common people should control their government. This idea eventually became known as **Jacksonian Democracy**.

This campaign poster shows the theme of Jackson's presidential campaign. His supporters said that if Jackson were elected, the government would finally be in the hands of ordinary people, not just the rich and upper class.

Jackson Forever!
The Hero of Two Wars and of Orleans!
The Man of the People!
HE WHO COULD NOT BARTER NOR BARGAIN FOR THE
PRESIDENCY!

Who, although "*A Military Chieftain*," valued the purity of Elections and of the Electors, MORE than the Office of **PRESIDENT** itself! Although the greatest in the gift of his countrymen, and the highest in point of dignity of any in the world,

BECAUSE
It should be derived from the
PEOPLE!

No Gag Laws! No Black Cockades! No Reign of Terror! No Standing Army or Navy Officers, when under the pay of Government, to browbeat, or
KNOCK DOWN
Old Revolutionary Characters, or our Representatives while in the discharge of their duty. To the Polls then, and vote for those who will support
OLD HICKORY
AND THE ELECTORAL LAW.

14.3 The Inauguration of Andrew Jackson

On March 4, 1829, more than 10,000 people, who came from every state, crowded into Washington, D.C., to witness Andrew Jackson's inauguration. The visitors overwhelmed local hotels, sleeping five to a bed. "I never saw such a crowd here before," observed Senator Daniel Webster. "Persons have come five hundred miles to see General Jackson, and they really seem to think that the country is rescued from some dreadful disaster!"

Many of the people flocking into the capital were first-time voters. Until the 1820s, the right to vote had been limited to the rich and upper class. Until then, only white men with property were thought to have the education and experience to vote wisely.

The new states forming west of the Appalachians challenged this argument. Along the frontier, all men—rich or poor, educated or not—shared the same opportunities and dangers. They believed they should also share the same rights, including the right to vote.

With the western states leading the way, voting laws were changed to give the "common man" the right to vote. This expansion of democracy did not yet include African Americans, American Indians, or women. Still, over one million Americans voted in 1828, more than three times the number who voted in 1824.

Many of these new voters did believe they had rescued the country from disaster. In their view, the national government had been taken over by corrupt "monied interests"—that is, the rich. Jackson had promised to throw the rich out and return the government to "the people." His election reflected a shift in power to the West and to the farmers, shopkeepers, and small-business owners who supported him.

After Jackson was sworn in as president, a huge crowd followed him to the White House. As the crowd surged in, the celebration turned into a near riot. "Ladies fainted, men were seen with bloody noses, and such a scene of confusion took place as is impossible to describe," wrote an eyewitness, Margaret Bayard Smith. Jackson was nearly "pressed to death" before escaping out a back door. "But it was the People's day, and the People's President," Smith concluded. "And the people would rule."

People of every color, age, and class mobbed the White House to attend a public reception after Andrew Jackson took the oath of office. One observer claimed that the scene was like the invasion of barbarians into Rome.

In this political cartoon, titled "Office Hunters for the Year 1834," Andrew Jackson is shown as a winged demon dangling government jobs over a crowd of people reaching out to grab them. What is the cartoonist's opinion of Jackson and his practice of rewarding political supporters with government jobs?

The Granger Collection, New York

14.4 Jackson's Approach to Governing

Andrew Jackson approached governing much as he had leading an army. He listened to others, but then did what he thought was right.

The Kitchen Cabinet Jackson did not rely only on his cabinet for advice. He made most of his decisions with the help of trusted friends and political supporters. Because these advisers were said to meet with him in the White House kitchen, they were called the "kitchen cabinet."

The rich men who had been used to influencing the government viewed the "kitchen cabinet" with deep suspicion. In their eyes, the men around the president were not the proper sort to be running the country. One congressman accused Amos Kendall, Jackson's closest adviser, of being "the President's . . . lying machine." Jackson ignored such charges and continued to turn to men he trusted for advice.

The Spoils System Jackson's critics were even more upset by his decision to replace many Republican officeholders with loyal Democrats. Most of these **civil servants** viewed their posts as lifetime jobs. Jackson disagreed. Rotating people in office was more democratic than lifetime service, he said, because it gave more people a chance to serve their government. Jackson believed that after a few years in office, civil servants should go back to making a living as other people do.

Jackson's opponents called the practice of rewarding political supporters with government jobs the **spoils system**. This term came from the saying "to the victor belong the spoils [prizes] of war."

Jackson's opponents also exaggerated the number of Republicans removed from office. Only about 10 percent of civil servants were replaced—and many deserved to be. One official had stolen $10,000 from the Treasury. When he begged Jackson to let him stay, the president said, "I would turn out my own father under the same circumstances."

civil servant an employee of the government

spoils system the practice of rewarding political supporters with government jobs

tariff a tax imposed by the government on goods imported from another country

secede to withdraw from an organization or alliance

14.5 The Nullification Crisis

Andrew Jackson's approach to governing met its test in an issue that threatened to break up the United States. In 1828, Congress passed a law raising **tariffs,** or taxes on imported goods such as cloth and glass. The idea was to encourage the growth of manufacturing in the United States. Higher tariffs meant higher prices for imported factory goods. American manufacturers could then outsell their foreign competitors.

Northern states, humming with new factories, favored the new tariff law. But southerners opposed tariffs for several reasons. Tariffs raised the prices they paid for factory goods. High tariffs also discouraged trade among nations, and planters in the South worried that tariffs would hurt cotton sales to other countries. In addition, many southerners believed that a law favoring one region—in this case, the North—was unconstitutional. Based on this belief, John C. Calhoun, Jackson's vice president, called on southern states to declare the tariff "null and void," or illegal and not to be honored.

In this cartoon, John C. Calhoun, who believed states have the right to nullify federal laws, is reaching toward a crown. The crown symbolizes his desire for power. Andrew Jackson is pulling on the coat of a Calhoun supporter. He wants to prevent Calhoun from trampling on the Constitution and destroying the Union.

Jackson understood southerners' concerns. In 1832, he signed a new law that lowered tariffs—but not enough to satisfy the most extreme supporters of states' rights in South Carolina. Led by Calhoun, they proclaimed South Carolina's right to nullify, or reject, both the 1828 and 1832 tariff laws. Such an action was called nullification.

South Carolina took the idea of states' rights even further. The state threatened to **secede** if the national government tried to enforce the tariff laws.

Even though he was from South Carolina, Jackson was outraged. "If one drop of blood be shed there in defiance of the laws of the United States," he raged, "I will hang the first man of them I can get my hands on to the first tree I can find." He called on Congress to pass the Force Bill, which would allow him to use the federal army to collect tariffs if needed. At the same time, Congress passed a compromise bill that lowered tariffs still further.

Faced with such firm opposition, South Carolina backed down and the nullification crisis ended. However, the tensions between the North and the South would increase in the years ahead.

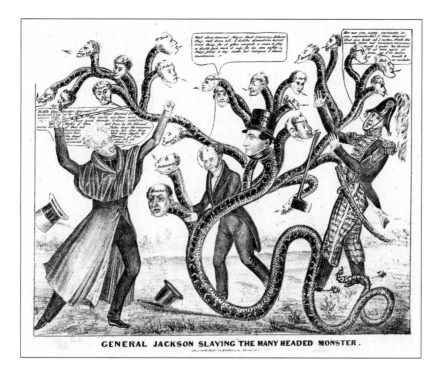

GENERAL JACKSON SLAYING THE MANY HEADED MONSTER.

Andrew Jackson, on the left, attacks the many-headed Bank of the United States with a veto stick. Bank president Nicholas Biddle, in the center, wears a top hat. The many heads represent the 24 state directors of the bank. Vice President Martin Van Buren, in the center, chokes Massachusetts and Delaware.

14.6 Jackson Battles the Bank of the United States

Andrew Jackson saw himself as the champion of the people, and never more so than in his war with the Bank of the United States. The bank was partly owned by the federal government, and it had a monopoly on federal deposits.

Jackson thought that the bank benefited rich eastern depositors at the expense of farmers and workers, as well as smaller state banks. He felt that the bank stood in the way of opportunity for capitalists in the West and other regions. He also distrusted the bank's president, Nicholas Biddle, who was everything Jackson was not: wealthy, upper class, well educated, and widely traveled.

The bank's charter, or contract, was due to come up for renewal in 1836. Jackson might have waited until after his reelection to "slay the monster." But Henry Clay, who planned to run for president against Jackson in 1832, decided to force the issue. Clay pushed a bill through Congress that renewed the bank's charter four years early. He thought that if Jackson signed the bill, the farmers who shared his dislike of banks would not reelect him. If Jackson vetoed the bill, he would lose votes from businesspeople who depended on the bank for loans. What Clay had forgotten was that there were many more poor farmers to cast votes than there were rich bankers and businesspeople.

Jackson vetoed the recharter bill. Even though the Supreme Court had held that the bank was constitutional, Jackson called the bank an unconstitutional monopoly that existed mainly to make the rich richer. The voters seemed to agree. In 1832, a large majority elected Jackson to a second term.

Rather than wait for the bank to die when its charter ran out, Jackson decided to starve it to death. In 1833, he ordered the secretary of the treasury to remove all federal deposits from the bank and put the money in state banks. Jackson's enemies called these banks "pet banks" because the president's supporters ran them.

Delegations of business owners begged Jackson not to kill the bank. Jackson refused. Abolishing the bank, he believed, was a victory for economic democracy.

Sequoyah (sih-KWOI-uh) developed an 86-letter alphabet for the Cherokee language. The alphabet contained both Roman letters and symbols Sequoyah created. Even though these Indians developed what many whites considered an advanced civilization, wealthy planters and poor settlers were determined to force them out and seize their lands.

14.7 Jackson's Indian Policy

As a frontier settler, Andrew Jackson had little sympathy for American Indians. During his presidency, it became national policy to remove Indians who remained in the East by force.

White settlers had come into conflict with Indians ever since colonial days. After independence, the new national government tried to settle these conflicts through treaties. Typically, the treaties drew boundaries between areas claimed for settlers and areas that the government promised to let the Indians have forever. In exchange for giving up their old lands, Indians were promised food, supplies, and money.

Despite the treaties, American Indians continued to be pushed off their land. By the time Jackson became president, only 125,000 Indians still lived east of the Mississippi River. War and disease had greatly reduced the number of Indians in the East. Other Indians had sold their lands for pennies an acre and moved west of the Mississippi. Jackson was determined to remove the remaining Indians to a new Indian Territory in the West.

Most of the eastern Indians lived in the South. They belonged to five groups, called tribes by whites: the Creek, Cherokee, Chickasaw, Choctaw, and Seminole. Hoping to remain in their homelands, these Indians had adopted many white ways. Most had given up hunting to become farmers. Many had learned to read and write. The Cherokee had their own written language, a newspaper, and a constitution modeled on the U.S. Constitution. Whites called these Indians the "Five Civilized Tribes."

While the Five Civilized Tribes may have hoped to live in peace with their neighbors, many whites did not share this goal. As cotton growing spread westward, wealthy planters and poor settlers alike looked greedily at Indian homelands. The Indians, they decided, had to go.

The Indian Removal Act In 1830, urged on by President Jackson, Congress passed the Indian Removal Act. This law allowed the president to make treaties in which American Indians in the East traded their lands for new territory on the Great Plains. The law did not say that the Indians should be removed by force, and in 1831 the Supreme Court held that Indians had a right to keep their lands. An angry Jackson disagreed. Groups that refused to move west **voluntarily** were met with military force, usually with tragic results.

This was true of the Sac and Fox Indians of Illinois. Led by a chief named Black Hawk, the Sac and Fox fought removal for two years. Black Hawk's War ended in 1832 with the slaughter of most of his warriors. As he was taken off in chains, the chief told his captors,

> *Black Hawk is an Indian. He has done nothing for which an Indian ought to be ashamed. He has fought for his countrymen, the squaws [women] and papooses [young children], against white men who came, year after year, to cheat them of and take away their land. You know the cause of our making war. It is known to all white men. They ought to be ashamed of it.*

The Trail of Tears Many whites were ashamed over the treatment of Indians and sent protests to Washington, D.C. Still, the work of removal continued. In 1836, thousands of Creek Indians who refused to leave Alabama were rounded up and marched west in handcuffs. Two years later, under President Martin Van Buren, more than 17,000 Cherokees were forced from their homes in Georgia and herded west by federal troops. Four thousand of these Indians died during the long walk to Indian Territory, which took place in the winter. Those who survived remembered that terrible journey as the **Trail of Tears**. A soldier who took part in the Cherokee removal called it "the cruelest work I ever knew."

Trail of Tears the removal of Cherokee Indians from Georgia to Indian Territory in 1838 and 1839

This artist painted an unrealistic picture of the Trail of Tears. Most of the Cherokees had no horses or warm blankets. They were dragged from their homes and allowed to take only the clothes they had on. Many died as they walked barefoot for hundreds of miles.

Led by a young chief named Osceola (ah-see-OH-luh), the Seminoles of Florida resisted removal for ten years. Their long struggle was the most costly Indian war ever fought in the United States. A number of Seminoles were finally sent to Indian Territory. But others found safety in the Florida swamps. Their descendants still live in Florida today.

When Andrew Jackson left office, he was proud of having "solved" the American Indian problem for good. In reality, Jackson had simply moved the conflict between American Indians and whites across the Mississippi River.

In the 1830s, American Indians were removed from their homelands and sent to a government-created territory in the West. Many Indians became ill or died during this forced removal.

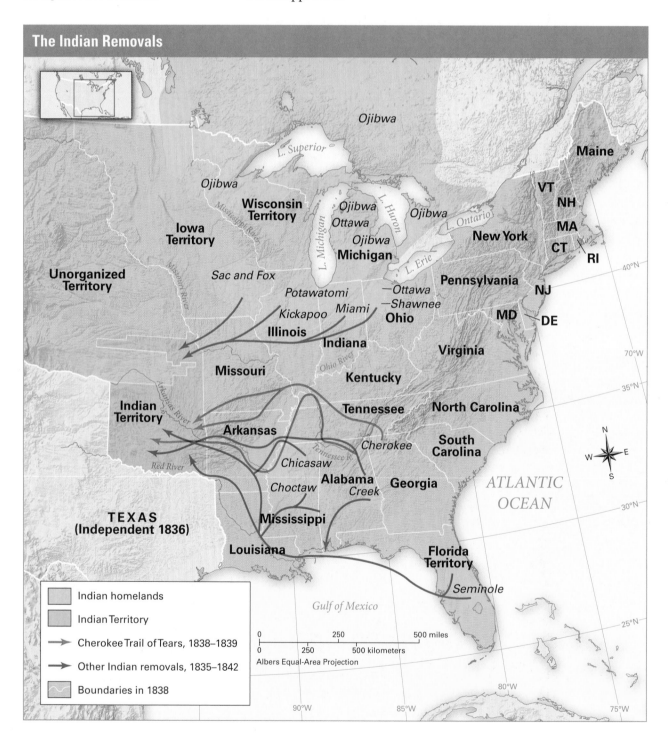

The Indian Removals

Legend:
- Indian homelands
- Indian Territory
- Cherokee Trail of Tears, 1838–1839
- Other Indian removals, 1835–1842
- Boundaries in 1838

Albers Equal-Area Projection

In this chapter, you read about the presidency of Andrew Jackson and evaluated how well he promoted democracy from the perspectives of various groups.

From the Frontier to the White House Andrew Jackson was a self-made man who rose from poverty to become president of the United States. First-time voters, many of them farmers and frontier settlers, helped elect Jackson in 1828. His supporters celebrated his election as a victory for the "common man" over the rich and powerful.

Jackson's Approach to Governing As president, Jackson relied on his "kitchen cabinet" rather than the official cabinet. He replaced a number of Republican civil servants with Democrats in a practice that became known as the spoils system.

The Nullification Crisis A controversy over higher tariffs led to the nullification crisis, in which South Carolinians threatened to secede from the United States. Although Jackson forced them to back down, the crisis was another sign of developing tensions between North and South.

The Battle Against the Bank Jackson thought the Bank of the United States benefited rich eastern depositors at the expense of farmers, workers, and smaller state banks. He also thought it stood in the way of opportunity for capitalists in the West and other regions. Jackson vetoed the bank's renewal charter.

Jackson's Indian Policy Jackson's Indian policy was simple: move the eastern Indians across the Mississippi to make room for whites. The Indian Removal Act caused great suffering for tens of thousands of American Indians.

Andrew Jackson was the nation's first president from the frontier. He came to office with great popular support. His supporters viewed him as a president of the people. His critics did not believe he was the sort of man who should be running the government.

Images cannot convey the realities of the Cherokee experience. In paintings like this, *Left in the Care of the Grandmothers,* however, artists try to show the desolation of the journey.

The Trail Where They Cried

In the 1830s, thousands of Cherokees were forcibly removed from their homeland in the Appalachian Mountains. They had tried valiantly to hold on to their land, but their efforts were in vain. Like other eastern Indians, they were driven west on the Trail of Tears.

In 1890, John G. Burnett, a former soldier, wrote a story to his family on the occasion of his 80th birthday. He wanted to tell them about his experiences with the Cherokees. "The removal of the Cherokee Indians . . . in the year of 1838," he recalled, took place when he was "a young man in the prime of life."

Burnett had grown up in eastern Tennessee, on the edge of Cherokee Territory. As a young man, he had roamed the hills and valleys of the Appalachians. He had fished for trout and hunted for deer and wild boar. He had also gotten to know many Cherokees. He spent time "hunting with them by day and sleeping around their campfires by night," he wrote. "I learned to speak their language, and they taught me the arts of trailing and building traps and snares." Through his experiences, Burnett learned to respect the Cherokees' way of life.

When the removal began, Burnett was a private in the U.S. Army. Because he spoke Cherokee, he was brought in as an interpreter. In that role, he witnessed what he called "the most brutal order in the history of American Warfare." He recalled,

> I saw the helpless Cherokees arrested and dragged from their homes, and driven at the bayonet point into the stockades [fenced-in enclosures]. And in the chill of a drizzling rain on an October morning I saw them loaded like cattle or sheep into six hundred and forty-five wagons and started toward the west . . .
> On the morning of November the 17th we encountered a terrific sleet and snow storm with freezing temperatures and from that day until we reached the end of the fateful journey on March the 26th, 1839, the sufferings of the Cherokees were awful. The trail of the exiles was a trail of death.

Burnett called the Cherokee removal a form of murder. Why was this tragedy inflicted on the Cherokees?

The Cherokee Nation

For centuries, the Cherokees had lived in the southern Appalachians. This was their ancient home and the center of their world. Like other southeastern Indians, they had lost land to white settlers during the colonial period. By the end of the American Revolution, their homeland was much reduced in size. But they were determined to hold on to it.

Unlike some American Indians who continued to fight white settlement, the Cherokees tried to work with the U.S. government to keep their land. They accepted the terms of treaties that limited their territory. They also agreed to the government's efforts to "civilize" them. They took up farming as their main activity. They dressed in European clothing. They went to school and learned to read and write. They even created a republican form of government with a written constitution. They embraced the values of American democracy. They were, in the eyes of many Americans, a "model" Indian people.

The Cherokees were not willing to do everything the government wanted, though. They were not willing to sell their land and blend in with other Americans. They wanted to maintain their own identity as a separate Cherokee nation. This meant they were still an obstacle to white settlement and expansion in the South.

The state of Georgia, in particular, found the Cherokee position unacceptable. Georgia settlers felt they had a right to Cherokee land, and they had strong supporters to back up their claim. One of these supporters was Andrew Jackson.

The Cherokees had been faithful allies of the United States during the War of 1812. They had even fought under Jackson's command against other Indians. But Jackson did not believe that Indians could live alongside white Americans. He wanted them moved out of the way, to lands in the West.

As president, Jackson allowed Georgia to put pressure on the Indians. This pressure increased after gold was discovered on Cherokee land in 1829. The following year, Congress passed the Indian Removal Act with Jackson's support. But the president still could not force the Cherokees to move. Their land rights were based on a treaty with the government. They would have to sign another treaty giving up their land.

To the Cherokees, their homeland was the spiritual as well as the geographical center of their world. The thought of abandoning it was devastating.

Cherokee chief John Ross led his people for more than 30 years. After losing the battle to preserve their homelands, Ross helped the Cherokees move west.

American Indian artist Brummet Echohawk depicted the hardships of the removal in his painting *Trail of Tears*. As the soldier moves the marchers along, one who did not survive is buried by the roadside.

The Removal

The Cherokee government, under Chief John Ross, had worked hard to prevent removal. It had appealed to the American people to win sympathy for its cause. It had also taken its case to court, asking the justice system to support the Cherokees' right to their land.

But not all Cherokees supported these efforts. A number of Cherokee leaders believed that removal was inevitable. In 1835, these men signed the Treaty of New Echota, agreeing to give up the land and move west to Indian Territory. Chief Ross and the majority of Cherokees were outraged. They called the treaty illegal and asked Congress to cancel it. But their appeals failed. Everyone would have to go, they were told.

Some Cherokees—mainly those who supported the treaty—left voluntarily. But most waited until the deadline of May 1838. At that point, an army of 7,000 U.S. soldiers surrounded Cherokee Territory. They forced the Cherokees out of their homes and into temporary camps or stockades. "The soldiers came and took us from home," one Cherokee woman recalled. "They drove us out of doors and did not permit us to take anything with us, not even a . . . change of clothes."

Many Cherokees were held in the camps for months. Conditions were harsh. One missionary reported that the Indians "were obliged at night to lie down on the naked ground, in the open air, exposed to wind and rain, and herd[ed] together . . . like droves of hogs." Some Cherokees escaped and fled into the mountains, only to be captured by soldiers and returned to the camps.

The march west began in the summer of 1838. It took place in several phases and along several routes. The first parties set out in June, traveling by land and river. But summer heat and drought conditions caused great suffering. The government decided to postpone further actions until fall.

In October, the removals began again. The 850-mile journey west took several months. Although some Cherokees traveled in wagons or on horseback, most went on foot. One witness wrote, "Even aged females, apparently nearly ready to drop into the grave, were traveling with heavy burdens attached to the back—on the sometimes frozen ground . . . with no covering for the feet except what nature had given them." As winter took hold, conditions worsened. One wagon driver reported,

> *There is the coldest weather in Illinois I ever experienced any-where. The streams are all frozen over something like eight or twelve inches thick. We are compelled to cut through the ice to get water for ourselves and [the] animals.*
> —Martin Davis, in a letter of December 1838

Several parties were held up by winter weather, unable to go forward for weeks on end. They suffered from exposure, disease, and starvation. These conditions were especially hard on children and the elderly. One woman recalled that "there was much sickness and a great many little children died of whooping cough." Many Cherokees were buried along the trail.

Finally, in the spring of 1839, the last of the groups arrived in Indian Territory. By that time, some 4,000 Cherokees—around a fourth of all those removed—had died. The survivors would call this journey Nu-No-Du-Na-Tlo-Hi-Lu, or "The Trail Where They Cried."

The Aftermath

At first, life in Indian Territory was hard. The Cherokees had no homes and few possessions. In addition, many of the later arrivals had bitter feelings toward the treaty supporters who had moved west before them. They considered these people traitors. Violence sometimes flared between the newer and older groups of settlers.

Gradually, however, the Cherokee people got back on their feet. They formed a new government and set up farms and businesses. They also established a good public school system. John Ross continued to lead the Cherokees until his death in 1866.

Today, the Cherokee Nation in Oklahoma has around 240,000 citizens. Smaller, separate bands of Cherokees live in Oklahoma and North Carolina. Many other Americans also have Cherokee ancestry. For all Cherokees, the Trail of Tears represents a great tragedy in their history. But they also take pride in what they have achieved. As Chad Smith, the current leader of the Cherokee Nation, put it, "We are not a people of the past. We are a people of the present, and for many centuries, we will be a people of the future."

The Cherokee heritage is preserved in the lives of modern Cherokee people, as well as in museums. In this Alabama museum, on the site of ancient burial mounds, a Cherokee guide (right) explains traditional uses of furs to visitors.

Launching the New Republic

1789
Washington Becomes President
George Washington is inaugurated as the nation's first president.

1791
Bank of the United States
Congress forms the Bank of the United States, the idea of Treasury Secretary Alexander Hamilton, a Federalist who wanted a strong national government.

1796
Washington's Farewell Address
Before leaving office in 1797, George Washington calls for a foreign policy of isolationism, stressing that the United States should not entangle itself in other nations' affairs.

1780   1785   1790   1795   1800   1805   1810

1794
Whiskey Rebellion
President Washington successfully ends the Whiskey Rebellion, a domestic revolt against a tax on whiskey.

1797
Adams Becomes President
John Adams, a Federalist, defeats Thomas Jefferson, a Republican, to become the nation's second president.

1798
Alien and Sedition Acts
The controversial Alien and Sedition Acts, which target immigrants and traitors, are signed into law by President Adams. Republicans are outraged by the acts.

1801
Jefferson
Becomes President
Thomas Jefferson becomes the nation's third president. Jefferson believed in a limited national government.

1812–1815
War of 1812
At Madison's request, Congress declares war against Great Britain to protect U.S. sailors at sea and to drive the British out of the northwest.

1829
Jackson
Becomes President
Andrew Jackson becomes president, ushering in a new era of government known as Jacksonian Democracy and extending democratic rights to the common people.

1810   1815   1820   1825   1830   1835   1840

1809
Madison
Becomes President
James Madison takes office. His presidency is characterized by a feeling of national unity.

1823
Monroe Doctrine
President James Monroe declares that the Western Hemisphere is no longer open to European colonization.

1838–1839
Trail of Tears
Under the Indian Removal Act, thousands of Cherokee Indians die when they are forced to leave their home-lands and journey to Indian Territory.

By the 1850s, the United States stretched from the Atlantic to the Pacific. Explorers like Lewis and Clark, who traveled on this river in Idaho in 1805, helped the nation expand.

U.S. Territorial Acquisitions, 1803–1853

BRITISH CANADA

ROCKY MOUNTAINS

CASCADE RANGE

OREGON
COUNTRY,
1846

Portland

Claimed by
U.S. and Britain,
to U.S. 1818

Missouri River

Lake Superior

Lake Michigan

Lake Huron

Ontario

L. Erie

APPALACHIAN MOUNTAINS

Boston

New York

Fort Hall
South
Pass

Snake River

LOUISIANA
TERRITORY,
1803

GREAT PLAINS

SIERRA NEVADA

Sacramento

San
Francisco

MEXICAN
CESSION,
1848

Great
Salt Lake

Platte R.

UNITED STATES,
1800

Independence

St. Louis

Ohio River

Los Angeles

Colorado River

Santa Fe

Arkansas River

Red River

Mississippi River

ATLANTIC
OCEAN

GADSDEN
PURCHASE,
1853

TEXAS,
1845

FLORIDA,
1819

New
Orleans

Claimed by
U.S. and Spain,
to U.S. 1819

PACIFIC
OCEAN

MEXICO

Gulf of Mexico

Legend	
Formed by independence from Great Britain in 1783	
Purchased from France	
Annexed by treaty with Spain	
Annexed by treaty with Texas	
Gained by treaty with Great Britain	
Annexed by treaty after war with Mexico	
Purchased from Mexico	

Santa Fe Trail
Oregon Trail
Mormon Trail
California Trail
Old Spanish Trail
Present-day boundary

N W E S

100°W   90°W   80°W

0   400   800 miles

0   400   800 kilometers

Lambert Azimuthal Equal-Area Projection

130°W

50°N

40°N

30°N

120°W

20°N

10°N

An Expanding Nation

In this unit, you will learn about the growth of the United States from about 1800 to the early 1850s. In 1800, the United States was bordered by the Atlantic Ocean to the east and the Mississippi River to the west. Farther west lay regions claimed by Great Britain, Russia, France, and Spain. By the 1850s, the United States had acquired these lands, more than doubling its size, and extended its western border to the Pacific Ocean. The map on opposite page shows the steps by which the nation's growth took place.

Picture yourself moving west along a trail pioneers used—the Oregon Trail or the Santa Fe Trail. The first half of your journey will cross a vast, treeless plain. On a good day, your wagon train might travel 20 miles. Rivers slow you down, though, as crossing them is dangerous.

Several weeks on the trail will bring you to an even greater obstacle—the ranges of the rugged Rocky Mountains. Here your progress will slow from 20 miles per day to 20 or so miles per week. Timing is everything on this part of your journey. The high mountain passes are open for only a short time each year. If you reach the mountains too late in the year, you may end up trapped by snow—which will likely mean your death.

Despite such challenges, thousands of settlers made this journey in the 1840s and 1850s. The map on the opposite page shows the nation's pattern of settlement in 1860. As the map below shows, the plains and mountains the pioneers crossed remained largely unpopulated by U.S. citizens, although American Indians had lived on those lands for thousands of years. Before long, however, that situation would change.

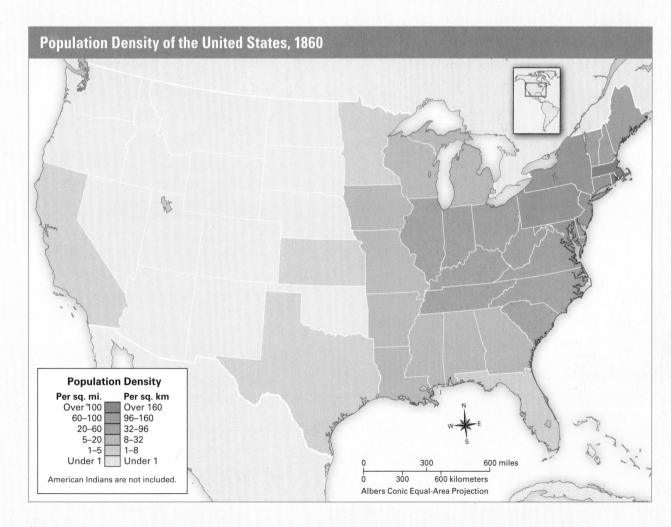

Population Density of the United States, 1860

Population Density

Per sq. mi.	Per sq. km
Over 100	Over 160
60–100	96–160
20–60	32–96
5–20	8–32
1–5	1–8
Under 1	Under 1

American Indians are not included.

0   300   600 miles
0   300   600 kilometers
Albers Conic Equal-Area Projection

Chapter 15

Manifest Destiny and the Growing Nation

How justifiable was U.S. expansion in the 1800s?

15.1 Introduction

More than 150 years ago, the phrase *manifest destiny* inspired great hopes and dreams among many Americans. It led to a war with Mexico. And it changed the map of the United States.

Manifest destiny means "obvious fate." John O'Sullivan, a New York newspaper editor, first used the phrase in 1845. O'Sullivan wrote that it was the United States' "manifest destiny to overspread and to possess the whole of the continent." Looking at the land beyond the Rocky Mountains, he argued that Americans had a **divine** right to settle this area and make it their own.

The fact that Great Britain claimed part of this land—a huge area known as Oregon—made no difference to O'Sullivan. After all, the United States had stood up to Great Britain in the War of 1812.

Nor was O'Sullivan impressed by Mexico's claims to much of the West. Like many Americans of the time, he believed that the United States had a duty to extend the blessings of democracy to new lands and peoples. It was God's plan, he wrote, for Americans to expand their "great experiment of liberty."

When Americans began their "great experiment" in 1776, the idea that the United States might one day spread across the continent seemed like a dream. By 1848, however, the dream was a reality. In this chapter, you will learn how the United States tripled its size in a little more than a single lifetime.

Manifest destiny took many forms. The United States expanded through treaties, settlement, and war. As you read, think about how each new area was acquired and whether the decisions that led to U.S. expansion across North America were **justifiable**.

◀ *American Progress,* painted in 1872 by John Gast

The spirit of manifest destiny helped the continental United States more than double in size between 1803 and 1853.

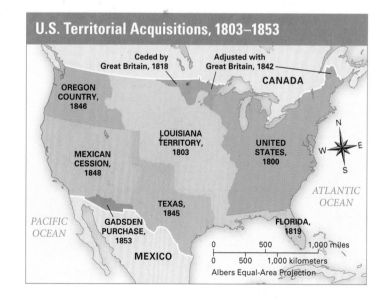

U.S. Territorial Acquisitions, 1803–1853

15.2 The Louisiana Territory

The nation's first opportunity for expansion during the early 1800s involved the vast **territory** to the west of the Mississippi River, then known as Louisiana. The United States wanted possession of the port city of New Orleans, near the mouth of the Mississippi River. By 1800, thousands of farmers were settling land to the west of the Appalachian Mountains. To get their crops to market, they floated them down the Mississippi to New Orleans. There the crops were shipped to Europe or to cities on the East Coast.

The farmers depended on being able to move their crops freely along the Mississippi. "The Mississippi," wrote James Madison, "is to them everything. It is the Hudson, the Delaware, the Potomac, and all the navigable rivers of the Atlantic States formed into one stream."

Louisiana Across the Mississippi River lay the unexplored territory of Louisiana. This immense region stretched from Canada in the north to Texas in the south. From the Mississippi, it reached west all the way to the Rocky Mountains. First claimed by France, it was given to Spain after the French and Indian War. In 1800, the French ruler Napoleon Bonaparte convinced Spain to return Louisiana to France.

Napoleon had plans for Louisiana. He hoped to settle the territory with thousands of French farmers. These farmers would raise food for the slaves who worked on France's sugar plantations in the Caribbean.

Napoleon's plans alarmed frontier farmers. New Orleans was part of Louisiana. If Napoleon closed the port to American goods, farmers would have no way to get their crops to market.

"A Noble Bargain" President Thomas Jefferson understood the concerns of American farmers. In 1803, he sent James Monroe to France with an offer to buy New Orleans for $7.5 million. By the time

American diplomats (standing) work out the final details of the Louisiana Purchase with Talleyrand, the French foreign minister.

THE LOUISIANA PURCHASE.
MESSRS. MONROE AND LIVINGSTONE COMPLETING NEGOTIATIONS WITH TALLYRAND, APRIL 30, 1803

Monroe reached France, Napoleon had changed his plans. A few years earlier, a slave named Toussaint L'Ouverture [too-SAN loo-ver-TEER] had led a slave revolt in the French Caribbean colony known today as Haiti. The former slaves defeated the French troops who tried to take back the colony. As a result, Napoleon no longer needed Louisiana.

In addition, France and Great Britain were on the brink of war. Napoleon knew that he might lose Louisiana to the British. Rather than lose Louisiana, it made sense to sell it to the United States.

Napoleon's offer to sell all of Louisiana stunned James Monroe. Instead of a city, suddenly the United States had the opportunity to buy an area as big as itself.

It didn't take long for Monroe to agree. On April 30, 1803, he signed a treaty giving Louisiana to the United States in exchange for $15 million. Said the French foreign minister, "You have made a noble bargain for yourselves, and I suppose you will make the most of it."

The Purchase Debate To most Americans, the Louisiana Purchase looked like the greatest land deal in history. The new territory would double the country's size at a bargain price of just 2 to 3 cents an acre.

Still, not everyone approved. Some people worried that such a large country would be impossible to govern. Politicians in the East fretted that they would lose power. Sooner or later, they warned, Louisiana would be carved into enough new states to outvote the eastern states in Congress.

Others objected to the $15 million price tag. "We are to give money of which we have too little," wrote a Boston critic, "for land of which we already have too much."

Opponents also accused Jefferson of "tearing the Constitution to tatters." They said that the Constitution made no provision for purchasing foreign territory.

Jefferson was troubled by the argument that the Louisiana Purchase was unconstitutional. Still, he believed it was better to stretch the limits of the Constitution than to lose a historic opportunity.

Late in 1803, the Senate voted to ratify the Louisiana Purchase treaty. Frontier farmers welcomed the news. "You have secured to us the free navigation of the Mississippi," a grateful westerner wrote Jefferson. "You have procured an immense and fertile country: and all these great blessings are obtained without war and bloodshed."

In this painting, the American flag is raised in New Orleans as the French flag is taken down. The ceremony marked the official transfer of the Louisiana Territory in 1803.

Escaped slaves were accepted into Seminole Indian communities. Here we see Chief Abraham, a Seminole leader of both African and Seminole heritage.

diplomacy the art of conducting negotiations with other countries

15.3 Florida

Having acquired Louisiana through **diplomacy**, President Jefferson turned next to Florida. Spain had colonized Florida in the late 1500s. By the 1800s, Florida had a diverse population of Seminole Indians, Spanish colonists, English traders, and runaway slaves. In 1804, Jefferson sent two diplomats to Spain to buy Florida. Spain's answer was "no deal."

Many white Americans in the Southeast wanted the United States to take over Florida. Slave owners in Georgia were angry because slaves sometimes ran away to Florida. (Seminole Indians welcomed some of the escaped slaves.) In addition, white landowners in Georgia were upset by Seminole raids on their lands.

Over the next few years, Spain's control of Florida weakened. The Spanish government could do nothing to stop the raids on farms in Georgia by Seminoles and ex-slaves.

Andrew Jackson Invades Florida In 1818, President James Monroe sent Andrew Jackson—the hero of the Battle of New Orleans—to Georgia with orders to end the raids. Jackson was told that he could chase raiding Seminoles into Florida. But he did not have the authority to invade the Spanish colony.

Despite his orders, Jackson marched into Florida with a force of 1,700 troops. Over the next few weeks, he captured Spanish military posts and arrested, tried, and executed two British subjects for stirring up Indian attacks. He also replaced the Spanish governor with an American. Spain demanded that Jackson be called back to Washington and punished for his illegal invasion.

"Govern or Get Out" Fearing war, President Monroe asked his cabinet for advice. All but one of his cabinet members advised him to remove Jackson and apologize to Spain. The exception was Secretary of State John Quincy Adams. Rather than apologize, Adams convinced Monroe to send a blunt message to Spain. The message was this: govern Florida properly or get out.

Equally fearful of war, Spain decided to get out. In 1819, the Spanish government agreed to yield Florida to the United States. In exchange, the United States agreed to pay off $5 million in settlers' claims against Spain. The United States also agreed to honor Spain's longtime claim to Texas.

Not all Americans were happy about leaving Spain in charge of Texas. One newspaper declared Texas was "worth ten Floridas." Even so, the Senate ratified the Florida treaty two days after it was signed.

15.4 Texas

There was a reason many Americans felt that Texas was so valuable. Much of this region was well suited for growing cotton, the South's most valuable cash crop. Many southerners hoped that one day Texas would become part of the United States.

Americans Come to Texas The story of Texas begins with Moses Austin, a banker and business owner who dreamed of starting a U.S. colony in Spanish Texas. In 1821, Spanish officials granted Austin a huge piece of land. After Moses Austin died that same year, his son Stephen took over his father's dream.

Stephen F. Austin arrived in Texas just as Mexico declared its independence from Spain. Now Texas was a part of Mexico. Mexican officials agreed to let Austin start his colony—under certain conditions. Austin had to choose only moral and hardworking settlers. The settlers had to promise to become Mexican citizens and to join the Catholic church.

Austin agreed to Mexico's terms. By 1827, he had attracted 297 families—soon known as the "Old Three Hundred"— to Texas.

Rising Tensions The success of Austin's colony started a rush of settlers to Texas. By 1830, there were about 25,000 Americans in Texas, compared to 4,000 Tejanos (tay-HA-nos), or Texans of Mexican descent. Soon tensions between the two groups began to rise.

The Americans had several complaints. They were used to governing themselves, and they resented taking orders from Mexican officials. They were unhappy that all official documents had to be in Spanish, a language most of them were unwilling to learn. In addition, many were slaveholders who were upset when Mexico outlawed slavery in 1829.

The Tejanos had their own complaints. They were unhappy that many American settlers had come to Texas without Mexico's permission. Worse, most of these new immigrants showed little respect for Mexican culture and had no intention of becoming citizens.

The Mexican government responded by closing Texas to further U.S. immigration. The government sent troops to Texas to enforce the immigration laws.

The Texans Rebel Americans in Texas resented these actions. A group led by a lawyer named William Travis began calling for revolution. Another group led by Stephen F. Austin asked the Mexican government to reopen Texas to immigration and to make it a separate Mexican state. That way, Texans could run their own affairs.

Stephen F. Austin made his father's dream a reality when he founded a colony in Texas in 1822. Here we see Austin talking with a group of Anglo American settlers about the rules that Mexico required them to live by.

In 1833, Austin traveled to Mexico and presented the Texans' demands to the new head of the Mexican government, General Antonio López de Santa Anna. The general was a power-hungry **dictator** who once boasted, "If I were God, I would wish to be more." Rather than bargain with Austin, Santa Anna tossed him in jail for promoting rebellion.

Soon after Austin was released in 1835, Texans rose up in revolt. Determined to crush the rebels, Santa Anna marched north with some 6,000 troops.

The Alamo In late February 1836, a large part of Santa Anna's army reached San Antonio, Texas. About 180 Texan volunteers, including eight Tejanos, defended the town. The Texans had taken over an old mission known as the Alamo. Among them was Davy Crockett, the famous frontiersman and former congressman from Tennessee. Sharing command with William Travis was James Bowie, a well-known Texas "freedom fighter."

The Alamo's defenders watched as General Santa Anna raised a black flag that meant "Expect no mercy." The general demanded that the Texans surrender. Travis answered with a cannon shot.

Slowly, Santa Anna's troops began surrounding the Alamo. The Texans were vastly outnumbered, but only one man fled.

Meanwhile, Travis sent messengers to other towns in Texas, pleading for reinforcements and vowing not to abandon the Alamo. "Victory or death!" he proclaimed. But reinforcements never came.

Fewer than 200 Texans fought 4,000 Mexican troops at the Alamo. When the battle was over, they were all dead—including James Bowie and Davy Crockett.

For 12 days, the Mexicans pounded the Alamo with cannonballs. Then, at the first light of dawn on March 6, Santa Anna gave the order to storm the fort. Desperately, the Texans tried to fight off the attackers with rifle fire.

For 90 minutes, the battle raged. Then it was all over. By day's end, every one of the Alamo's defenders was dead. By Santa Anna's order, those who had survived the battle were executed on the spot.

Santa Anna described the fight for the Alamo as "but a small affair." But his decision to kill every man at the Alamo filled Texans with rage.

Texas Wins Its Independence Sam Houston, the commander of the Texas revolutionary army, understood Texans' rage. But as Santa Anna pushed on, Houston's only hope was to retreat eastward. By luring Santa Anna deeper into Texas, he hoped to make it harder for the general to supply his army and keep it battle-ready.

Houston's strategy wasn't popular, but it worked brilliantly. In April, Santa Anna caught up with Houston near the San Jacinto (san ha-SIN-to) River. Expecting the Texans to attack at dawn, the general kept his troops awake all night. When no attack came, the weary Mexicans relaxed. Santa Anna went to his tent to take a nap.

Late that afternoon, Houston's troops staged a surprise attack. Yelling, "Remember the Alamo!" the Texans overran the Mexican camp. Santa Anna fled, but he was captured the next day. In exchange for his freedom, he ordered all his remaining troops out of Texas. The **Texas War for Independence** had been won, but Mexico did not fully accept the loss of its territory.

To Annex Texas or Not? Now independent, the Republic of Texas earned the nickname Lone Star Republic because of the single star on its flag. But most Texans were Americans who wanted Texas to become part of the United States.

Despite their wishes, Texas remained independent for ten years. People in the United States were divided over whether to **annex** Texas. Southerners were eager to add another slave state. Northerners who opposed slavery wanted to keep Texas out. Others feared that annexation would lead to war with Mexico.

The 1844 presidential campaign was influenced by the question of whether to expand U.S. territory. One of the candidates, Henry Clay, warned, "Annexation and war with Mexico are identical." His opponent, James K. Polk, however, was a strong believer in **manifest destiny**. He was eager to acquire Texas. After Polk was elected, Congress voted to annex Texas. In 1845, Texas was admitted as the 28th state.

Texas War for Independence the 1836 rebellion of Texans against Mexican rule that resulted in Texas becoming an independent nation

annex to add a territory to a country. Such an addition is called an annexation.

manifest destiny the belief that it was America's right and duty to spread the nation across the North American continent

Collection of the Star of the Republic Museum, Washington, Texas

Sam Houston was elected the first president of the independent country of Texas in 1836. In 1845, Texas was admitted to the United States. This is the only known official Lone Star flag of the Republic of Texas.

15.5 Oregon Country

Far to the northwest of Texas lay Oregon Country. This enormous, tree-covered wilderness stretched from the Rocky Mountains to the Pacific Ocean. To the north, Oregon was bounded by Alaska, which belonged to Russia. To the south, it was bordered by Spanish California and New Mexico.

In 1819, Oregon was claimed by four nations: Russia, Spain, Great Britain, and the United States. Spain was the first to drop out of the scramble. As part of the treaty to purchase Florida, Spain gave up its claim to Oregon. A few years later, Russia also dropped out. By 1825, Russia agreed to limit its claim to the territory that lay north of the 54°40′ parallel of latitude. Today that line marks the southern border of Alaska.

That left Great Britain and the United States. For the time being, the two nations agreed to a peaceful "joint occupation" of Oregon.

Discovering Oregon The United States' claim to Oregon was based on the Lewis and Clark expedition. Between 1804 and 1806, Meriwether Lewis and William Clark had led a small band of explorers to the Oregon coast.

Lewis thought that many more Americans would follow the path blazed by the expedition. "In the course of 10 or 12 Years," he predicted in 1806, "a tour across the Continent by this rout [route] will be undertaken with as little concern as a voyage across the Atlantic."

That was wishful thinking. The route that Lewis and Clark had followed was far too rugged for ordinary travelers. There had to be a better way.

In 1824, a young fur trapper named Jedediah Smith found that better way. Smith discovered a passage through the Rocky Mountains called South Pass. Unlike the high, steep passes used by Lewis and

In the 1800s, wagon trains transported thousands of families from established eastern settlements to the rugged West. This wagon train is winding its way across Nebraska toward Oregon Country.

Clark, South Pass was low and flat enough for wagons to use in crossing the Rockies. Now the way was open for settlers to seek their fortunes in Oregon.

Oregon Fever The first American settlers to travel through South Pass to Oregon were missionaries. These missionaries made few converts among Oregon's Indians. But their glowing reports of Oregon's fertile soil and towering forests soon attracted more settlers.

These early settlers wrote letters home describing Oregon as a "pioneer's paradise." The weather was always sunny, they claimed. Disease was unknown. Trees grew as thick as hairs on a dog's back. And farms were free for the taking. One man even joked that "pigs are running about under the great acorn trees, round and fat, and already cooked, with knives and forks sticking in them so you can cut off a slice whenever you are hungry."

Reports like these inspired other settlers who were looking for a fresh start. In 1843, about 1,000 pioneers packed their belongings into covered wagons and headed for Oregon. A year later, nearly twice as many people made the long journey across the plains and mountains. "The Oregon Fever has broke out," reported one observer, "and is now raging."

Settlers who braved the 2,000-mile trek from Independence, Missouri, to Oregon Country were rewarded with fertile land in the Willamette Valley.

All of Oregon or Half? Along with Texas, "Oregon fever" also played a role in the 1844 presidential campaign. Polk won the election with such stirring slogans as "All of Oregon or none!" and "Fifty-four forty or fight!" Polk promised he would not rest until the United States had annexed all of Oregon Country.

But Polk didn't want Oregon enough to risk starting a war with Great Britain. Instead, he agreed to a compromise treaty that divided Oregon roughly in half at the 49th parallel. That line now marks the western border between the United States and Canada.

The Senate debate over the Oregon treaty was fierce. Senators from the South and the East strongly favored the treaty. They saw no reason to go to war over "worse than useless territory on the coast of the Pacific." Senators from the West opposed the treaty. They wanted to hold out for all of Oregon. On June 18, 1846, the Senate ratified the compromise treaty by a vote of 41 to 14.

Polk got neither "fifty-four forty" nor a fight. What he got was a diplomatic settlement that both the United States and Great Britain could accept without spilling a drop of blood.

Volunteers from Exeter, New Hampshire, line up as they leave New England to fight in the war against Mexico.

Mexican-American War the war with Mexico from 1846 to 1847 that resulted in Mexico ceding to the United States a huge region from Texas to California

15.6 The Mexican-American War

You might think that Texas and Oregon were quite enough new territory for any president. But not for Polk. This humorless, hardworking president had one great goal. He wanted to expand the United States as far as he could.

Polk's gaze fell next on the huge areas known as California and New Mexico. He was determined to have them both—by purchase if possible, by force if necessary.

These areas were first colonized by Spain but became Mexican territories when Mexico won its independence in 1821. Both were thinly settled, and the Mexican government had long neglected them. That was reason enough for Polk to hope they might be for sale. He sent a representative to Mexico to try to buy the territories. But Mexican officials refused even to see Polk's representative.

War Breaks Out in Texas When Congress voted to annex Texas, relations between the United States and Mexico turned sour. To Mexico, the annexation of Texas was an act of war. To make matters worse, Texas and Mexico could not agree on a border. Texas claimed the Rio Grande as its border on the south and west. Mexico wanted the border to be the Nueces (new-AY-sis) River, about 150 miles northeast of the Rio Grande.

On April 25, 1846, Mexican soldiers fired on U.S. troops who were patrolling along the Rio Grande. Sixteen Americans were killed or wounded. This was just the excuse for war that Polk had been waiting for. Mexico, he charged, "has invaded our territory and shed American blood upon American soil." Two days after Polk's speech, Congress declared war on Mexico. The **Mexican-American War** had begun.

The Fall of New Mexico and California A few months later, General Stephen Kearny led the Army of the West out of Kansas. His orders were to occupy New Mexico and then continue west to California.

Mexican opposition melted away in front of Kearny's army. The Americans took control of New Mexico without firing a shot. "Gen'l Kearny," a pleased Polk wrote in his diary, "has thus far performed his duty well."

Meanwhile, a group of Americans launched a rebellion against Mexican rule in California. The explorer John C. Frémont heard about the uprising and gave his support to the Americans. The Americans arrested and jailed General Mariano Guadalupe Vallejo (vuh-YAY-oh), the Mexican commander of northern California. Then they raised a crude flag showing a grizzly bear sketched in blackberry juice. California, they declared, was now the Bear Flag Republic.

When Kearny reached California, he joined forces with the rebels. Within weeks, all of California was under U.S. control.

The United States Invades Mexico The conquest of Mexico itself was far more difficult. U.S. troops under General Zachary Taylor battled their way south from Texas. Taylor was a no-nonsense general who was known fondly as "Old Rough and Ready" because of his backwoods clothes. After 6,000 U.S. troops took the Mexican city of Monterrey, an old enemy stopped them. General Santa Anna had marched north to meet Taylor with an army of 20,000 Mexican troops.

In February 1847, the two forces met near a ranch called Buena Vista (BWEY-nuh VIS-tuh). After two days of hard fighting, Santa Anna reported that "both armies have been cut to pieces." Rather than lose his remaining forces, Santa Anna retreated south. The war in northern Mexico was over.

A month later, U.S. forces led by General Winfield Scott landed at Veracruz (ver-uh-CROOZ) in southern Mexico. Scott was a stickler for discipline and loved fancy uniforms. These traits earned him the nickname "Old Fuss and Feathers." For the next six months, his troops fought their way to Mexico City, Mexico's capital.

Outside the capital, the Americans met fierce resistance at the castle of Chapultepec (chuh-PUHL-tuh-PEK). About 1,000 Mexican soldiers and 100 young military cadets fought bravely to defend the fortress. Six of the cadets chose to die fighting rather than surrender. To this day, the boys who died that day are honored in Mexico as the *Niños Héroes* (NEEN-yos EHR-oh-ace), the boy heroes.

Despite such determined resistance, Scott's army captured Mexico City in September 1847. Watching from a distance, a Mexican officer muttered darkly, "God is a Yankee."

In this painting, the U.S. cavalry overwhelms the enemy in the Battle of Resaca de la Palma, Texas, in May 1846.

289

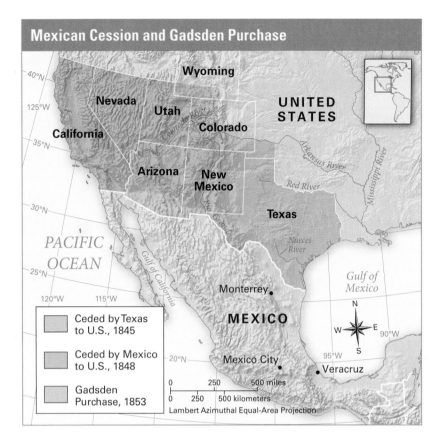

Mexican Cession and Gadsden Purchase

Ceded by Texas to U.S., 1845

Ceded by Mexico to U.S., 1848

Gadsden Purchase, 1853

Lambert Azimuthal Equal-Area Projection

The Mexican Cession added California, Nevada, Utah, Arizona, and New Mexico to the United States, as well as parts of Colorado and Wyoming. The Gadsden Purchase was a region of land purchased from Mexico that was added to Arizona and New Mexico.

The Treaty of Guadalupe Hidalgo Early in 1848, Mexico and the United States signed the Treaty of Guadalupe Hidalgo (gwa-duh-LOO-pay hih-DAHL-go). Mexico agreed to give up Texas and a vast region known as the Mexican Cession. (A cession is something that is given up.) This area included the present-day states of California, Nevada, Utah, Arizona, and New Mexico, as well as parts of Colorado and Wyoming.

Under this agreement, Mexico gave up half of all its territory. In return, the United States agreed to pay Mexico $15 million. It also promised to protect the 80,000 to 100,000 Mexicans living in Texas and in the Mexican Cession. Most of these promises, however, were not kept.

In Washington, a few senators spoke up to oppose the treaty. Some of them argued that the United States had no right to any Mexican territory other than Texas. They believed that the Mexican-American War had been unjust and that the treaty was even more so. New Mexico and California together, they said, were "not worth a dollar" and should be returned to Mexico.

Other senators opposed the treaty because they wanted even more land. They wanted the Mexican Cession to include a large part of northern Mexico as well. To most senators, however, the Mexican Cession was a manifest destiny dream come true. The Senate ratified the treaty by a vote of 38 to 14.

The Gadsden Purchase A few years later, the United States acquired still more land from Mexico. In 1853, James Gadsden arranged the purchase of a strip of land just south of the Mexican Cession for $10 million. Railroad builders wanted this land because it was relatively flat and could serve as a good railroad route. The acquisition of this land, known as the Gadsden Purchase, created the present-day border of the southwestern United States with Mexico.

Most Americans were pleased with the new outlines of their country. Still, not everyone rejoiced in this expansion. Until the Mexican-American War, many people had believed that the United States was too good a nation to bully or invade its weaker neighbors. Now they knew that such behavior was the dark side of manifest destiny.

In this chapter, you read about how Americans extended their nation to the west and the south. The idea of manifest destiny fueled many of the events that led to expansion.

The Louisiana Purchase In 1803, the United States added the vast territory known as Louisiana. The Louisiana Purchase doubled the nation's land area.

Florida A treaty with Spain added Florida to the United States in 1819.

Texas In 1836, Americans in Texas rebelled against the Mexican government there and created the Lone Star Republic. In 1845, Congress admitted Texas into the union. The Lone Star Republic was formally dissolved in 1846.

Oregon Country A treaty with Great Britain added Oregon Country in 1846.

War with Mexico In 1846, the United States went to war with Mexico in the Mexican-American War. In an 1848 treaty with Mexico, the United States acquired the present-day states of California, Nevada, Utah, Arizona, and New Mexico, as well as parts of Colorado and Wyoming. Five years later, the Gadsden Purchase completed the outline of the continental United States.

As the 1800s progressed, more and more settlers were lured to the West by hopes of free land and an independent and prosperous life.

Born into a wealthy family, Susan Shelby Magoffin was raised in Kentucky. She was one of only a few women to travel the Santa Fe Trail.

Westward on the Santa Fe Trail

"Calling all adventurers!" the signs might have said. "It's 1821, and the Santa Fe Trail is open for business." And business it was. Traders loaded their wagons in Missouri and crossed plains, deserts, and mountains to sell their goods in Mexico. The action lasted about 60 years before the railroads came. But in its brief history, the Santa Fe Trail became the stuff of legend.

On June 11, 1846, newlywed Susan Shelby Magoffin left Independence, Missouri. She was headed for Santa Fe, then part of Mexico. Just 18 years old, Susan Magoffin was very excited about her upcoming honeymoon adventure. "My journal tells a story tonight different from what it has ever done before. The curtain rises now with a new scene," she wrote as she and her husband set out on their journey, part of a wagon train on the Santa Fe Trail.

Susan's husband Samuel was 27 years older than his bride. He had been traveling and trading on the Santa Fe Trail for nearly 20 years. The couple's honeymoon trip was also a business trip: Samuel was overseeing 14 wagonloads of American goods. He planned to sell his cargo in Mexico, at the towns of Santa Fe and Chihuahua.

Over the years, Samuel Magoffin had made a fortune on the Santa Fe Trail. Like other businessmen of his day, he had seen possibility in trading with Mexico. In search of profit, these entrepreneurs had charted a course from the western edges of what was then the United States to the lands beyond. And when Santa Fe became part of the United States in 1848, after the Mexican War, the booming business did not stop.

The trips were risky. Dust storms, illness, possible attacks by hostile Indians, and lack of water all threatened their efforts. But for nearly 60 years, men like Samuel Magoffin took those risks. In the process, they helped expand the United States' southwestern border. Fortunately for historians, people like Susan Magoffin kept detailed journals of their experiences. Their accounts bring to life a time of adventure on the American frontier.

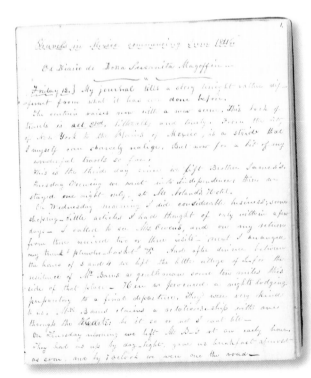

Almost 100 years after she wrote it, Susan Magoffin's diary was found in the attic of one of her descendants. As a daily record of the Magoffins' journey west, the 206-page diary is an invaluable historical document.

The Path West

In the 1800s, several trails left the United States heading west. Settlers, farmers, ranchers, and miners took the Oregon Trail toward new lives in the Pacific Northwest. Families traveled along what became known as the Mormon Trail, looking for religious freedom in the desert. And across the California Trail, prospectors and others marched toward what they hoped would be great wealth.

The Santa Fe Trail was different. Its main purpose was trade. Political events made that trade possible. In 1821, Mexico won its independence from Spain. Spain had prohibited trade with the United States, but Mexico welcomed it. With the door open, American businessmen like Samuel Magoffin and his brother James headed west.

The Santa Fe Trail began in Missouri and spanned 900 miles across North America. Traders braved bad weather, hostile Indians, dangerous animals, and lack of water. They were in search of profits, and they found them. In 1822, trade on the trail totaled $15,000. By 1860, it had reached $3.5 million. When the railroad ended trade on the Santa Fe Trail in 1880, as many as 6,000 wagons were using the trail every year.

If money was important to Santa Fe traders, so was adventure. Many traders and other travelers loved the excitement of life on the trail. Some simply loved the beautiful outdoors. One wrote, "The air . . . is many times clearer and incomparably drier than in the eastern part of the United States, and the heavens burn nightly with millions of magnified stars which the people of the East never dreamed of."

This painting, *Traders on the Santa Fe Trail,* appeared in Josiah Gregg's book *Commerce of the Prairies* in 1844. In his classic account of the Santa Fe Trail, Gregg reported on the enthusiasm of the traders and said "even the mules prick up their ears."

On the trail, Susan Magoffin appreciated being free from the strict rules of society. In her diary, she wrote,

There is such independence, so much free uncontaminated air, which [fills] the mind, the feelings, nay every thought, with purity. I breathe free without that oppression and uneasiness felt in the gossiping groups of a settled home.

Joy and Hardship on the Trail

When Samuel Magoffin set off to Santa Fe with his young wife, he was determined that she travel in comfort. So, he hired servants and outfitted carriages to make his first home with Susan as nice as possible. The Magoffins slept in a tent, but not in sleeping bags on the ground. No, they slept in a bed that the servants put up every night. There were sheets on the mattress, plus blankets, pillows, and mosquito netting. Tables, cabinets, and carpets added to the luxury.

Their meals were often equally elegant. Susan and Samuel brought chickens with them so that they could have fresh eggs. They also ate ham, fresh buffalo, and sometimes even one of the chickens. They might top off a good meal with gooseberry tarts. "It is the life of a wandering princess, mine," Susan wrote in her journal.

During the days, Susan wrote, sewed, studied Spanish, and knit. When she wanted flowers but didn't want to climb out of her carriage, "servants riding on mules pick them for me." Her devoted greyhound, Ring, kept her company. Ring also helped her feel protected by barking at the wolves and coyotes. "I felt safe with this trusty soldier near me," she wrote.

Susan Magoffin stayed at Bent's Fort in 1846 after an accident on the trail. Her room had a dirt floor, but she had her own furniture. The fort, in Colorado, has been re-created based on extensive historical descriptions and is part of a National Historic Site.

But life on the trail wasn't all luxury, even for wealthy travelers like Susan and Samuel Magoffin. Difficulties abounded. Dust storms and prairie fires plagued travelers. Rattlesnakes frightened them. And then, there were the mosquitoes. "Millions upon millions are swarming upon me," Susan wrote, "and their knocking against the carriage reminded me of a hard rain."

Fear of hostile Indians also troubled the travelers. At Pawnee Rock, Susan stopped to carve her name on the sandstone, as others had done. Samuel and Susan's servant, Jane, kept watch because the rock was the site of Pawnee attacks. From the rock, the hostile Indians could "dash down upon the Santa Fe traders like hawks, to carry off their plunder and their scalps," wrote one traveler.

Susan didn't encounter any Indians at Pawnee Rock, but she did have a terrible accident as the caravan moved on. The wagon she was riding in went over the edge of a river bank. She described what happened.

We were whirled completely over with a perfect crash. One to see the wreck of that carriage now with the top and sides entirely broken to pieces, could never believe that people had come out of it alive. But strange, wonderful to say, we are almost entirely unhurt!

That wasn't quite true. Susan was knocked unconscious during the crash. Pregnant at the time, she lost the baby due to the accident.

It took 11 weeks for the Magoffins to reach Santa Fe, partly because travel was difficult and partly because Susan's ill health required them to spend nearly two weeks at Bent's Fort, an important stopping point along the trail. When they arrived in Santa Fe, they met up with Samuel's brother James and joined in the high society life of the village, such as it was. Susan attended a nearby church, practiced her Spanish, and spent time with the local people.

Over the next 10 years, Susan and Samuel Magoffin had three children. Eventually, the family settled in St. Louis, where Susan Magoffin died in 1855. She was only 29 years old.

Spanish colonists founded Santa Fe in 1608 on a site where Pueblo people had lived for hundreds of years. Far from the cities of Mexico or the United States, it was still a tiny town when the Magoffins arrived.

Chapter 16

Life in the West

What were the motives, hardships, and legacies of the groups that moved west in the 1800s?

16.1 Introduction

The vast region that stretches from the Mississippi River to the Pacific Ocean is one of the most extraordinary landscapes on Earth. Tourists come from all over to see its mountains, canyons, deserts, and plains.

To American settlers east of the Mississippi River, this great expanse of grasslands, mountains, and deserts was the West. For all its beauty, the West was a challenging environment. Look at the names that settlers gave to its features. Where else in the United States can you find a mountain range called the Crazies, a scorching desert named Death Valley, a blood-red canyon called Flaming Gorge, or a raging river known as the River of No Return?

Despite its geographic challenges, the West was never empty. Perhaps as many as 3 million American Indians lived there before Europeans arrived. These first westerners were far more diverse in language and culture than the Europeans who claimed their land.

For most Americans in the early 1800s, however, the West was mostly a blank map. By 1850, it had become the land of opportunity. The West boasted wide-open spaces and great wealth in timber, gold, silver, and other natural resources. It became a magnet for immigrants and for easterners looking for a new start in life. As Americans began their westward trek, they created new markets for eastern merchants. In time, the West changed the nation's economy and politics. It also created folklore of "rugged individualism" that has become a lasting part of American culture.

Newspaperman Horace Greeley captured the growing enthusiasm for "going west" when he wrote, "If you have no family or friends to aid you, and no prospect [opportunity] opened to you . . . turn your face to the Great West, and there build up a home and fortune." In this chapter, you will learn about eight groups of people who turned their faces to the West in the first half of the 1800s. You will learn about their **motives** for heading West, the hardships they faced, and the legacies they left behind.

Westward-bound settlers had to cross mountains, deserts, and wide-open spaces in their quest for new opportunities.

◀ *Westward the Course of Empire Takes Its Way,* painted in 1861 by Emanuel Gottlieb Leutze

This painting shows members of the Lewis and Clark expedition at Three Forks, Montana. The woman is Sacagawea. To her right are Meriwether Lewis, William Clark, and Clark's slave, York.

16.2 The Explorers

In the early 1800s, a number of expeditions set out from the United States to explore the West. The most famous was the **Lewis and Clark expedition,** which was ordered by President Thomas Jefferson.

The major motive behind the expedition was to make friendly contact with Indian groups that might be interested in trade. A second motive was to find the Northwest Passage, a water route across North America that explorers had been seeking ever since Columbus reached the Americas. With the purchase of Louisiana from France in 1803, the expedition gained a third motive—finding out just what the United States had bought.

Lewis and Clark expedition
a journey made from 1804 to 1806 by Meriwether Lewis and William Clark to explore the territory gained in the Louisiana Purchase

Up the Missouri River In May 1804, the 45-member expedition left St. Louis, Missouri, in three boats. Jefferson's private secretary, Meriwether Lewis, and his friend William Clark led the expedition. Its members included soldiers, frontiersmen, and an African American slave named York, who worked for Clark.

It was hard going from the first day. Rowing upstream against the Missouri River's strong current left the explorers' hands blistered and their muscles sore. Mosquitoes feasted on their sunburned faces.

By summer, the explorers had reached Indian country. Most American Indians welcomed the strangers, and York fascinated the Indians. They had never seen a black man before. Again and again, wrote Clark in his journal, York allowed his skin to be rubbed with a wet finger to prove "that he was not a painted white man."

The explorers made camp for the winter near a Mandan village in what is now North Dakota. There, a French fur trapper joined them along with his 16-year-old wife, a Shoshone (shuh-SHOW-nee) woman named Sacagawea (sah-kuh-juh-WEE-uh), and their infant son. As a girl, Sacagawea had been kidnapped from her people by another Indian group. Lewis and Clark hoped she would translate for them when they reached Shoshone country.

To the Pacific and Back In the spring of 1805, the explorers set out once more. As they moved up the Missouri River, rapids and waterfalls slowed their progress. When they hauled their boats by land around these obstacles, the thorns of the prickly-pear cactus pierced their feet. Meanwhile, grizzly bears raided their camps. Game became scarce.

By late summer, the explorers could see the Rocky Mountains looming ahead. To cross the mountains before the first snows of winter closed the high passes, they would have to find horses—and soon.

Fortunately, the expedition had reached the land of Sacagawea's childhood. One day, a group of Indians approached. To Sacagawea's great joy, they proved to be Shoshone. Learning that her brother was now a Shoshone chief, Sacagawea persuaded him to provide the explorers with the horses they desperately needed.

The explorers made it over the Rockies, but they were more dead than alive. The Nez Perce (nehz pers), an Indian people living in the Pacific Northwest, saved them from starvation. A grateful Lewis wrote in his journal that the Nez Perce "are the most hospitable, honest, and sincere people that we have met with in our voyage."

As winter closed in, the explorers reached their final destination, the Pacific Ocean. Clark marked the event by carving on a tree, "William Clark December 3rd 1805 By Land from the U. States."

The Explorers' Legacy After a wet and hungry winter in Oregon, the explorers headed home. In September 1806, two years and four months after setting out, they returned to St. Louis. Lewis proudly wrote to Jefferson, "In obedience to our orders, we have penetrated the Continent of North America to the Pacific Ocean."

Lewis and Clark had good reason to be proud. They had not found the Northwest Passage, for it did not exist. But they had traveled some 8,000 miles. They had mapped a route to the Pacific. They had established good relations with western Indians. Most of all, they had brought back priceless information about the West and its peoples.

Other explorers added to this **legacy** and helped prepare the way for the settlement of the West. In 1806, the same year Lewis and Clark returned to St. Louis, 26-year-old army lieutenant Zebulon Pike set out to explore the southern part of the new Louisiana Territory. Pike and his party traveled up the valley of the Arkansas River into present-day Colorado. There, Pike saw the mountain that today is called Pikes Peak.

Pike went on to explore Spanish territory along the Rio Grande and the Red River. His reports of the wealth of Spanish towns brought many American traders to the Southwest. But Pike was not impressed with the landscape. He called the West the "Great American Desert."

Another famed explorer, John C. Frémont, helped to correct this image. Nicknamed "the Pathfinder," Frémont mapped much of the territory between the Mississippi Valley and the Pacific Ocean in the 1840s. His glowing descriptions of a "land of plenty" inspired many families to try their luck in the West.

legacy a person's or a group's impact on future generations

Zebulon Pike's published reports of his expedition spurred American interest in the Southwest. Part of his route would become the Santa Fe Trail, which was used by thousands of pioneers.

The prosperity and pride of the Californios is evident in this painting of a Spanish landowner with his workers.

16.3 The Californios

If Lewis and Clark had turned south from Oregon after reaching the Pacific, they would have found Spain's best-kept secret: a sun-drenched land called California.

The California Missions In 1769, a Spanish missionary named Junipero Serra (who-NEE-peh-ro SEHR-ra) led soldiers and priests north from Mexico to California. Serra's goal was to convert the California Indians to Christianity. To do this, he established a chain of missions that eventually stretched from San Diego to just north of San Francisco. Each mission controlled a huge area of land, as well as the Indians who worked it.

Although the missionaries meant well, the missions were deadly to native Californians. Indians were sometimes treated harshly, and thousands died of diseases brought to California by the newcomers.

Settlers followed the missionaries to California. "We were the pioneers of the Pacific coast," wrote Guadalupe Vallejo, "building pueblos [towns] and missions while George Washington was carrying on the war of the Revolution." To reward soldiers and attract settlers, the Spanish began the practice of making large grants of land.

When Mexico won its independence in 1821, California came under Mexican rule. In 1833, the Mexican government closed the missions. Half of the mission land was supposed to go to Indians. Mexico, however, established its own system of land grants in the Southwest and gave most of California's mission lands to soldiers and settlers. The typical Spanish-speaking Californian, or *Californio,* was granted a **rancho** of 50,000 acres or more.

rancho a land grant made by the Mexican government, used mostly for raising cattle and crops

Life on the Ranchos Life on the ranchos combined hard work and the occasional *fiesta*, or social gathering. Most families lived in simple adobe houses with dirt floors. The Californios produced almost everything they needed at home. Indian servants did much of the work.

The ranchos were so huge that neighbors lived at least a day's journey apart. As a result, strangers were always welcome for the news they brought of the outside world. During weddings and fiestas, Californios celebrated with singing, dancing, and brilliant displays of horsemanship.

In the 1830s, cattle ranching became California's most important industry. Cattle provided hides and tallow (beef fat) that could be traded for imported goods brought by ship. Among the goods that an American sailor named Richard Henry Dana carried to California in his trading ship were teas, coffee, sugars, spices, raisins, molasses, hardware, dishes, tinware, cutlery, clothing, jewelry, and furniture.

Because California was so far from the capital in Mexico City, the Mexican government neglected the territory. Soldiers were not paid, and they took what they needed to survive from the people they were supposed to protect. Officials sent to govern California were often unskilled and sometimes dishonest.

The Californios' Legacy In 1846, the United States captured California as part of the war with Mexico. Before long, Californios were a minority in California.

Still, the Californios left a lasting mark. California is full of Spanish place names such as San Diego, Los Angeles, and San Francisco. The Californios also introduced many of California's famous crops, such as grapes, olives, and citrus fruits. Most of all, they opened California to the world—and the world soon rushed in.

16.4 The Mountain Men

The Lewis and Clark expedition **stimulated** new interest in an old industry: the fur trade. Inspired by the explorers' reports of finding beaver in the Rockies, a Spanish trader named Manuel Lisa followed their route west. In 1807, Lisa led 42 trappers up the Missouri River. The next year, he took 350 trappers into the Rockies. For the next 30 years, trappers crisscrossed the West in search of valuable furs.

The Trapper's Life The trappers, who were also called mountain men, lived hard and usually died young. During the spring and fall, they set their traps in icy streams. In July, they traveled to trading posts to swap furs for supplies or gathered for an annual rendezvous, or get-together.

Mountain men, like the one pictured here, were rugged individualists. They often wore shirts and trousers made from animal hides and had hair that hung to their shoulders.

The Granger Collection, New York

In their search for furs, mountain men established new routes to Oregon and California.

The rendezvous may have been fun, but the trappers' lives were filled with hazards. Fur thieves, Indians, wolves, and bears attacked them. Mountain man Hugh Glass was mauled by a mother bear that threw chunks of his flesh to her hungry cubs before friends rescued him.

Accidents were common, too. A single misplaced step on a mountain, or a misjudged river rapid, often meant sudden death. Disease also took a heavy toll. When one man asked for news about a party of trappers, he learned that "some had died by lingering diseases, and others by the fatal [rifle] ball or arrow." Out of 116 men, he wrote, "there were not more than sixteen alive."

Freedom and Adventure Trappers braved this dangerous way of life because of the freedom and adventure it offered. A good example is Jim Beckwourth, an African American from Virginia who became a fur trapper and explorer. While hunting beaver in the Rockies, Beckwourth was captured by Crow Indians. According to Beckwourth, an old woman identified him as her long-lost son, and he was adopted into the tribe. "What could I do?" he wrote later. "Even if I should deny my Crow origin, they would not believe me."

Beckwourth lived with the Crow for six years and became a chief. By the time he left the tribe in the 1830s, the fur trade was in decline. Like other mountain men, however, Beckwourth continued his adventurous life as an explorer, army scout, and trader. In 1850, he discovered the lowest pass across the Sierra Nevada range, known today as Beckwourth Pass.

The Mountain Men's Legacy In their search for furs, the mountain men explored most of the West. The routes they pioneered across mountains and deserts became the Oregon and California Trails. Their trading posts turned into supply stations for settlers moving west along those trails.

A surprising number of mountain men left another kind of legacy: personal journals. Their stories still have the power to make us laugh and cry—and to wonder how they lived long enough to tell their tales.

16.5 The Missionaries

Ever since Lewis and Clark appeared among them, the Nez Perce had been friendly toward Americans. In 1831, three Nez Perce traveled to St. Louis to learn more about the white man's ways. There, the Nez Perce asked if someone would come west to teach their people the secrets of the "Black Book," or Bible.

Several missionaries answered that call. The best known were Marcus and Narcissa Whitman and Henry and Eliza Spalding. In 1836, the two couples traveled west from St. Louis along the **Oregon Trail**.

It was a difficult journey. Narcissa described the Rockies as "the most terrible mountains for steepness." Still, the missionaries arrived safely in Oregon, proving that women could endure the journey west.

A Difficult Start On reaching Oregon, the group split up. The Spaldings went to work with the Nez Perce. The Whitmans worked among a neighboring group, the Cayuse. Neither couple knew very much about the people they hoped to convert. The result was a difficult start.

After three years, the Spaldings finally made their first converts. In 1839, Henry baptized two Nez Perce chiefs. A year later, one of the chiefs had his infant son baptized as well. The child would grow up to be the leader best known as Chief Joseph.

The Whitmans were less successful. The Cayuse were far more interested in the whites' weapons and tools than in their religion. The couple also offended the Cayuse. They refused to pay for the land they took for their mission or to offer visitors gifts, as was the Indians' custom. Not a single Cayuse converted to the new faith.

A Pioneer's Paradise Marcus Whitman was far more successful at converting Americans over to the belief that Oregon was a pioneer's paradise. "It does not concern me so much what is to become of any particular set of Indians," he wrote. "Our greatest work is . . . to aid the white settlement of this country and help to found its religious institutions."

In 1842, Marcus traveled east on horseback. Along the way, he urged Americans to settle in Oregon. On his return, he guided a large group of settlers along the Oregon Trail. More settlers soon followed. "The poor Indians are amazed at the overwhelming number of Americans coming into the country," observed Narcissa. "They seem not to know what to make of it."

In 1847, measles came west with settlers and swept through the Whitman mission. Marcus treated the sick as best he could. The Cayuse noticed that whites usually recovered, while their own people were dying. Rumors spread that Whitman was giving deadly pills to Indians. Cayuse Indians attacked the mission, killing both Marcus and Narcissa.

Oregon Trail an overland route that stretched about 2,000 miles from Independence, Missouri, to the Columbia River in Oregon

In 1836, Marcus and Narcissa Whitman married and set out for Oregon to establish a mission. Here, they are offering prayers for a safe journey.

The Missionaries' Legacy Like the Spanish priests in California, American preachers in Oregon hoped their legacy would be large numbers of Christian Indians. In fact, relatively few Indians became Christians. Many, however, died of the diseases that came west with the missionaries.

The missionaries' true legacy was to open the West to settlement. In California, Oregon, and other territories, settlers followed in the footsteps of the missionaries.

16.6 The Pioneer Women

Women pioneers shared in the danger and the work of settling the West. Most of these women were wives and mothers, but some were single women with motives of seeking homesteads, husbands, or other new opportunities. Pioneer women not only helped to shape the future of the West, but also earned new **status** for themselves and for women throughout the United States.

On the Trail Between 1840 and 1869, about 350,000 people traveled west in covered wagons. Most westward-bound pioneers gathered each spring near Independence, Missouri. There they formed columns of wagons called wagon trains.

The journey west lasted four to six months and covered about 2,000 miles. Wagon space was so limited that pioneers were forced to leave most of the comforts of home behind. When the way became steep, they often had to toss out the few treasures they managed to bring. The Oregon Trail was littered with furniture, china, books, and other cherished objects.

Women were expected to do the work they had done back home, but while traveling 15 to 20 miles a day. They cooked, washed clothes, and took care of the children. Meals on wheels were simple. "About the only change we have from bread and bacon," wrote Helen Carpenter, "is to bacon and bread."

The daily drudgery wore many women down. Lavinia Porter recalled, "I would make a brave effort to be cheerful and patient until the camp work was done. Then starting out ahead of the team and my men folks, when I thought I had gone beyond hearing distance, I would throw myself down on the unfriendly desert and give way like a child to sobs and tears."

Trail Hazards The death toll on the trail was high. Disease was the worst killer. Accidents were also common. People drowned crossing rivers. Indian attacks were rare, but the **prospect** of them added to the sense of danger.

Although pioneer women had to travel 15 to 20 miles a day, they were still expected to take care of household chores when the wagon train stopped for the night.

By the end of the journey, each woman had a story to tell. Some had seen buffalo stampedes and prairie fires on the Great Plains. Some had almost frozen to death in the mountains or died of thirst in the deserts. But most survived to build new lives in the West.

One group of pioneer women—African Americans who had escaped from slave states or who were brought west by their owners—faced a unique danger. Even though slavery was outlawed in most of the West, bounty hunters were often able to track down fugitive slaves. But for some African American women, the move west brought freedom. For example, when Biddy Mason's owner tried to take her from California (a free state) to Texas, Mason sued for her freedom and won. She moved to Los Angeles, where she became a well-known pioneer and community leader.

The Pioneer Women's Legacy The journey west changed pioneer women. The hardships of the trail brought out strengths and abilities they did not know they possessed. "I felt a secret joy," declared one Oregon pioneer, "in being able to have the power that sets things going."

Women did set things going. Wherever they settled, schools, churches, libraries, literary societies, and charitable groups soon blossomed. Annie Bidwell, for example, left behind a remarkable legacy. When Annie married John Bidwell, she moved to his ranch in what is now the town of Chico, California. There she taught sewing to local Indian women and helped their children learn to read and write English. Annie convinced John to give up drinking—he closed the tavern that had been part of his home—and encouraged the building of Chico's first church.

Before setting out on the trail, pioneers who were headed west met in the spring to form groups called wagon trains.

Annie was active in other causes as well, including the movement to give women a right that had long been denied them in the East: the right to vote. Wyoming Territory led the way by granting women the right to vote in 1869. By 1900, a full 20 years before women across the nation would win the right to vote, women were voting in four western states. The freedom and sense of equality enjoyed by women in the West helped pave the way for more equal treatment of women throughout the United States. This was perhaps the greatest legacy of the women pioneers.

16.7 The Mormons

In 1846, a wagon train of pioneers headed west in search of a new home. Looking down on the shining surface of Great Salt Lake in what is now Utah, their leader, Brigham Young, declared, "This is the place!"

It was not a promising spot. One pioneer described the valley as a "broad and barren plain . . . blistering in the rays of the midsummer sun." A woman wrote, "Weak and weary as I am, I would rather go a thousand miles further than remain." But that was one of the valley's attractions. No one else wanted the place that Brigham Young claimed for his followers, the **Mormons**.

A Persecuted Group The Mormons were members of the Church of Jesus Christ of Latter-Day Saints. Joseph Smith had founded this church in New York in 1830. Smith taught that he had received a sacred book, *The Book of Mormon,* from an angel. He believed it was his task to create a community of believers who would serve God faithfully.

Smith's followers lived in close communities, working hard and sharing their goods. Yet, wherever they settled—first New York, then Ohio, Missouri, and Illinois—their neighbors **persecuted** them.

Many people were offended by the Mormons' teachings, especially their acceptance of polygamy—the practice of having more than one wife. Others resented the Mormons' rapidly growing power and wealth. In 1844, resentment turned to violence when a mob in Illinois killed Joseph Smith.

After Smith's death, Brigham Young took over as leader of the Mormons. Young decided to move his community to Utah. There, the Mormons might be left alone to follow their faith in peace.

West to Utah Young turned out to be a practical as well as a religious leader. "Prayer is good," he said, "but when baked potatoes and pudding and milk are needed, prayer will not supply their place."

Young carefully planned every detail of the trek to Utah. The pioneers he led west stopped along the way to build shelters and plant crops for those who would follow.

Even with all this planning, the journey was difficult. "We soon thought it unusual," wrote one Mormon, "to leave a campground without burying one or more persons."

Mormons members of the Church of Jesus Christ of Latter-Day Saints, founded by Joseph Smith in 1830

When he arrived at Great Salt Lake, Young laid out his first settlement, Salt Lake City. By the time he died in 1877, Utah had 125,000 Mormons living in 500 settlements.

To survive in this dry country, Mormons had to learn new ways to farm. They built dams, canals, and irrigation ditches to carry precious water from mountain streams to their farms in the valley. With this water, they made the desert bloom.

The Mormons' Legacy The Mormons were the first Americans to settle the Great Basin. They pioneered the farming methods adopted by later settlers of this dry region. They also helped settlers make their way west. Salt Lake City quickly became an important stop for travelers in need of food and supplies.

To the Mormons, however, their greatest legacy was the faith they planted so firmly in the Utah desert. From its center in Salt Lake City, the Mormon church has grown into a worldwide religion with more than 11 million members.

When Mormons were unable to purchase wagons or oxen for the journey to Utah, they pulled their belongings in handcarts.

16.8 The Forty-Niners

In 1848, a carpenter named James Marshall was building a sawmill on
the American River in northern California. Suddenly, he spotted something shining in the water. "I reached my hand down and picked it up,"
he wrote later. "It made my heart thump, for I felt certain it was gold."

When word of Marshall's discovery leaked out, people across California dropped everything to race to the goldfields. "All were off to the
mines," wrote a minister, "some on horses, some on carts, and some
on crutches."

The World Rushes In By 1849, tens of thousands of gold seekers
from around the world had joined the California gold rush. About two-
thirds of these forty-niners were Americans. The motive of fortune
also brought settlers from Mexico, South America, Europe, Australia,
and even China.

The forty-niners' first challenge was simply getting to California.
From China and Australia, they had to brave the rough crossing of
the Pacific Ocean. From the East, many traveled by ship to Panama
in Central America, crossed through dangerous jungles to the Pacific
side, and boarded ships north to San Francisco. Others made the
difficult journey overland.

Most forty-niners were young, and almost all were men. When
Luzena Wilson arrived in Sacramento with her family, a miner offered
her $5 for her biscuits just to have "bread made by a woman." When she

The search for gold was difficult.
Miners spent long days searching
through the mud and stones of freezing
streams for this precious metal.

hesitated, he doubled his offer. "Women were scarce in those days," she wrote. "I lived six months in Sacramento and saw only two."

Life in the Mining Camps Wherever gold was spotted, mining camps with names like Mad Mule Gulch and You Bet popped up overnight. At Coyote Diggings, Luzena found "a row of canvas tents." A few months later, "there were two thousand men . . . and the streets were lined with drinking saloons and gambling tables." Merchants made fortunes selling eggs for $6 a dozen and flour for $400 a barrel.

With no police to keep order, the camps were rough places. Miners frequently fought over the boundaries of their claims, and they took it on themselves to punish crimes. "In the short space of twenty-four hours," wrote Louise Clappe, "we have had murders, fearful accidents, bloody deaths, a mob, whippings, a hanging, an attempt at suicide, and a fatal duel."

Digging for gold was hard and tedious work. The miners spent long days digging up mud, dirt, and stones while standing knee-deep in icy streams. All too soon, the easy-to-find gold was gone. "The day for quick fortune-making is over," wrote a miner in 1851. "There are thousands of men now in California who would gladly go home if they had the money."

Miners shoveled gravel into a narrow box called a sluice. The water running through washed away the lighter particles, and the gold remained.

The Forty-Niners' Legacy By 1852, the gold rush was over. While it lasted, about 250,000 people flooded into California. For California's Indians, the legacy of this invasion was dreadful. Between 1848 and 1870, warfare and disease reduced their number from about 150,000 to just 30,000. In addition, many Californios lost their land to the newcomers.

The forty-niners also left a prosperous legacy. By 1850, California had enough people to become the first state in the far west. These new Californians helped to transform the Golden State into a diverse land of economic opportunity.

16.9 The Chinese

Gam Saan, or "Gold Mountain," was what people in China called California in 1848. To poor and hungry Chinese peasants, Gam Saan sounded like a paradise. There, they were told, "You will have great pay, large houses, and food and clothing of the finest description . . . Money is in great plenty."

By 1852, more than 20,000 Chinese had ventured across the Pacific to California. That year, one of every ten Californians was Chinese.

Thousands of Chinese left their homeland and flocked to the California goldfields. Most failed to strike it rich. However, many settled in California's Central Valley, where their knowledge of farming helped the area develop.

An Uncertain Welcome At first, the Chinese were welcomed. Lai Chun-Chuen, an early immigrant, observed that they "were received like guests" and "greeted with favor." In 1852, the governor of California praised Chinese immigrants as "one of the most worthy classes of our newly adopted citizens."

As gold mining became more difficult, however, attitudes toward immigrants began to change. A miner from Chile complained, "The Yankee regarded every man but . . . an American as an interloper [intruder] who had no right to come to California and pick up the gold." The Chinese, too, came under attack.

American miners called on the government to drive foreigners out of the goldfields. In 1852, the state legislature passed a law requiring foreign miners to pay a monthly fee for a license to mine. As the tax collectors arrived in the camps, most of the foreigners left. One traveler saw them "scattered along the roads in every direction," like refugees fleeing an invading army.

The Chinese Stay The Chinese, however, paid the tax and stayed on. When the miners' tax failed to drive off the Chinese, Americans tried to force them into leaving. Whites hacked off the long *queues* (kyus), or braids, worn by Chinese men. They burned the shacks of Chinese miners. Beatings followed burnings.

Discouraged Chinese immigrants left the mines to open restaurants, laundries, and stores in California's growing cities. "The best eating houses in San Francisco," one miner wrote, were those opened by the Chinese. So many Chinese settled in San Francisco that local newspapers called their neighborhood Chinatown. Today, San Francisco's Chinatown remains the oldest and largest Chinese community in the United States.

Other Chinese put their farming skills to work in California's fertile Central Valley. They drained swamps and dug irrigation ditches to water arid fields. In time, they would help transform California into America's fruit basket and salad bowl.

The Legacy of the Chinese Immigrants Most of the Chinese who came to California in search of gold hoped to return to China as rich men. A few did just that. Most, however, stayed on in the United States. Despite continued prejudice against them, their hard work, energy, and skills greatly benefited California and other western states. "In mining, farming, in factories and in the labor generally of California," observed a writer in 1876, "the employment of the Chinese has been found most desirable."

The Chinese not only helped to build the West, but they also made it a more interesting place to live. Wherever they settled, Chinese immigrants brought with them the arts, tastes, scents, and sounds of one of the world's oldest and richest cultures.

Chapter Summary

In this chapter, you learned about the people who settled the West in the 1800s.

The Explorers Explorers Meriwether Lewis and William Clark went west to find the Northwest Passage and to establish friendly relations with native people. The expedition helped prepare the way for future settlement.

The Californios In California, Spanish-speaking settlers followed in the footsteps of missionaries. The Californios' way of life centered on the rancho and the raising of cattle.

The Mountain Men Valuable beaver furs—and a life of freedom and adventure—attracted fur trappers to the West. Many of these hardy mountain men stayed on as scouts, guides, and traders.

The Missionaries People traveled to Oregon and other western territories in hopes of converting Indians to Christianity. Although they made few converts, the missionaries attracted other settlers to the West.

The Pioneer Women Many women pioneers sought new opportunities in the West. Besides working to establish homes and farms, women often brought education and culture to new settlements.

The Mormons Mormon pioneers traveled to Utah in search of religious freedom. They built cities and towns and introduced new methods of farming to the dry plains.

The Forty-Niners Gold seekers from all over the world rushed to California in 1849. Few became rich, but many stayed to help build the new state's economy.

The Chinese The gold rush attracted thousands of Chinese immigrants to California. Although they often had to fight prejudice, most of them remained in the United States, working as laborers and starting new businesses and farms.

Much of California's gold was mined from streams and rivers. But the mining was not easy or pleasant work, as this painting seems to show, and miners were not all white men.

Gold Rush Pioneers

During the gold rush of 1849, thousands of fortune seekers flocked to California. Most of them were white American men, but not all. Women, African Americans, Californios, and people from around the world also caught "gold fever." They all dreamed of riches and a better life. What they found in California rarely lived up to their dreams. But through hard work, they helped build a new state.

Luzena Wilson and her husband, Mason, were living on a farm in Missouri when they heard about the discovery of gold in California. "The gold excitement spread like wildfire, even out to our log cabin in the prairie," she later recalled.

> *As we had almost nothing to lose, and we might gain a fortune, we early caught the fever. My husband grew enthusiastic and wanted to start immediately, but I would not be left behind. I thought where he could go I could, and where I went I could take my two little toddling babies . . . I little realized then the task I had undertaken. If I had, I think I should still be in my log cabin in Missouri. But . . . it sounded like such a small task to go out to California, and once there fortune, of course, would come to us.*

The Wilsons packed up their wagon and traveled overland to Sacramento, California, arriving in September 1849. There, they sold their oxen and bought a share in a hotel business. With Luzena as cook and manager, they soon prospered. But over the next few years, their fortunes would rise and fall and rise again.

After a few months, a severe flood swamped Sacramento and wiped out the Wilsons's business. They decided to move to the mining town of Nevada City and start again. The town was rich from gold strikes. "Everybody had money, and everybody spent it," Luzena recalled. "Money ran through one's fingers like water through a sieve." She started cooking meals for miners and they soon opened another hotel, the El Dorado. Before long, their business was booming.

In March 1851, disaster struck. A fire raged through Nevada City and burned much of the town, including the El Dorado. Once again, the Wilsons lost nearly everything. They were still determined to succeed, however. They moved to a valley west of Sacramento. There, they farmed hay for livestock and started another hotel.

They prospered again, and this time their fortune lasted. Their business was on the road from Sacramento to San Francisco. Other settlers came and put down roots. Before long, the town of Vacaville was born. Luzena Wilson and her husband remained there for the rest of their lives. They had not struck it rich, but they had built a life in California.

An Irish Immigrant's Story

Thomas Kerr also found life in California a challenge. Unlike the Wilsons, he never enjoyed much success. In fact, he never even made it to the gold country.

Kerr left his native Ireland during the great famine of 1845–1850. A disease had destroyed the Irish potato crop, causing hunger, hardship, and death. Along with many other Irish, Kerr decided to try his luck in America. He said goodbye to his wife and child and sailed to San Francisco, arriving in March 1850.

Kerr tried to earn money to pay his passage to the goldfields. But work was hard to find in San Francisco, and costs were high. He eventually got a job building a house near Sacramento. That was as close as he would get to the gold country.

The job paid very little. In addition, the work was hard and the conditions were tough. Kerr wrote in his journal, "God knows any money a man earns in Calafornia, its dearly won, for he deprives himself of all the comforts . . . in addition to being burned up with a scurching sun . . . and eaten alive by Muskeatoes [mosquitoes]."

Kerr returned to San Francisco, where his wife and child joined him in 1852. He continued to get odd jobs, ending up in the grocery business. But he never made the fortune he imagined. "People may talk . . . about the Gold of Calafornia," he wrote, "but its very difficult to obtain it."

Women were rare in gold rush towns—and even rarer in the goldfields. Some cooked meals and washed clothes for miners. In return, the miners paid them well and treated them with respect.

A Chilean Migrant's Tale

Many other foreigners also came to California hoping to strike it rich. Among these immigrants were approximately 7,000 Chileans. Many had already worked as miners in Chile. One of these men was Vicente Pérez Rosales.

Pérez came from a wealthy, landowning family that had lost its fortune in the 1820s. He had tried his hand at various jobs since then, including gold mining and cattle ranching, with little success. Then he learned of the gold strikes in California. Late in 1848, he left Chile with several partners on a ship bound for San Francisco.

Pérez was not confident that his group would find gold, but he did believe they could profit from the gold rush. "We felt sure only a lazy man could fail to make money," he wrote in his journal, "and we were willing to work hard. But little did we know what we faced."

Pérez and his party soon headed for the gold country. They worked at various gold diggings and had some success, but not enough to justify their efforts. "There was plenty of gold," Pérez wrote, "but not enough for all the men in California looking for it." Competition for gold claims was fierce, and violence often broke out. Much of this violence was directed at foreign miners, particularly Mexicans, Chileans, and Chinese. Eventually, Pérez and his party fled the goldfields.

Seeking another way to earn a living, they set up a stand on a street in Sacramento and sold such goods as cheese, peaches, and beef jerky. But an epidemic of disease struck the city, and once again they had to flee. Pérez recalled,

We had been miners and had failed at that . . . Then we had become merchants, and . . . that too, as they say, came tumbling down. We had begun to think that, with our luck, if we started a hat factory we could expect men would be born without heads!
—Vicente Pérez Rosales, *Diary of a Journey to California,* 1848–1849

Almost overnight, the gold rush changed San Francisco from a sleepy village into a bustling city. Money flowed freely to those who were skilled at running businesses. Banking, trade, and investment flourished.

314

After that, Pérez started a restaurant in San Francisco. But after initial success, that failed too. He and his partners had already decided to return to Chile in late 1850 when a fire broke out in San Francisco and burned down their building. They barely escaped with their lives. Two months later, they were back in Chile.

A Black Forty-Niner's Success

Although the gold rush did not pan out for many forty-niners, some did find gold and achieve their dreams. This was the case for hundreds of enslaved African Americans who came west to work in the goldfields and managed to win their freedom.

Among these black miners, Alvin Coffey stands out as a particular success. In April 1849, he set out from Missouri with his owner, Dr. Bassett, who put him to work digging for gold. In his memoirs, Coffey recalled, "We dug and dug to the first of November. At night it commenced raining, and rained and snowed pretty much all the winter. We had a tent but it barely kept us all dry."

By the next year, Coffey had dug up $5,000 in gold. Bassett kept the money and took Coffey back to Missouri, where he sold him to another man. The new owner was kinder, however. He agreed to let Coffey buy his way to freedom. In 1854, Coffey returned to California and earned $7,000 in the goldfields, enough to free himself and his family.

Coffey settled down in northern California and became a prosperous farmer. His children and grandchildren prospered, too. For Alvin Coffey, the gold rush had lived up to its promise.

The Results for California

The gold rush also brought statehood to California. Vicente Pérez Rosales was there to witness the election of the new California legislature. He saw parades, campaign speeches, and even fistfights between rival candidates. Overall, though, he was impressed by the peaceful nature of the election. "There was no pistol shooting," he recalled. "Arms on that day were silent." And he went on,

> *How different it all was from the way these things are handled in other countries. Not only that, but once the election was over all the voters accepted the man elected . . . They dropped the private preferences to hail the majority's choice, and showed as much enthusiasm . . . as if they had contributed to his triumph themselves.*

The gold rush had helped lay the foundation for California's political and economic future. And it appeared, in 1850, that that future would be very bright indeed.

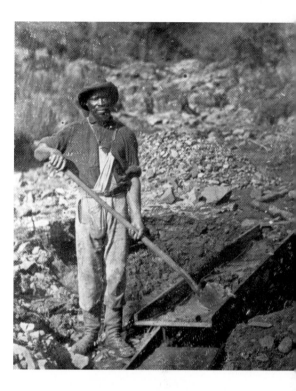

By 1852, when this photograph was taken, more than 2,000 African Americans were living in California. Most lived and worked in the goldfields.

Even today, California's gold rush history is an important part of the state's image. The state's motto, "Eureka"— a Greek word meaning "I have found it" —reflects the excitement of the successful miners.

Chapter 17

Mexicano Contributions to the Southwest

How have Mexicano contributions influenced life in the United States?

17.1 Introduction

The Texas War for Independence and the Mexican-American War in the 1840s had a lasting effect on the people of the Southwest. Spanish-speaking people had made their homes in the region since the days of the conquistadors in the 1500s. By 1848, from 80,000 to 100,000 Mexicanos, or Mexican citizens, lived in the territories given up by Mexico in the Treaty of Guadalupe Hidalgo. Most of these people remained in the Southwest and became U.S. citizens.

The treaty with Mexico promised Mexican Americans full citizenship rights, the right to keep their property, and the right to use their language. These promises were not kept. Armed with the belief that they were a superior people, white settlers pushed Mexicanos off their land. Whites also made it illegal for Mexicano children to speak Spanish in schools. They found ways to keep Mexicanos from exercising their right to vote.

Mexicanos protested each of these assaults on their rights. But the government did little to protect them. Before long, Mexican Americans found themselves, in the words of one historian, "foreigners in their native land."

The problems of prejudice, poverty, and lack of political power persisted well into the 20th century. Despite much progress, many of these problems are still with us today.

Yet, Mexican Americans also had a deep influence on their new country. Even though most white settlers had little respect for Mexican Americans, they freely borrowed much that was useful from them. Spanish words and Mexican foods, laws, technology, and architecture all became a lasting part of the Southwest culture. In this chapter, you will learn about many contributions Mexicanos made to American life.

This Mexicano family is shown in front of their adobe home in 1887.

◀ The del Valles, one of California's leading Mexican American families, posed for this portrait in the late 1880s.

This is an arrastra, or grinding mill. A horse moved a round stone to crush gold-bearing rocks, from which miners could then remove the precious metal.

17.2 Mining

Mining in the West developed in three waves—gold, silver, and copper. Each wave depended on the contribution of Mexican miners. **Mexicanos** came to the Southwest with a rich mining **tradition**. They knew where to look for precious metals and how to get them out of the ground.

Gold Mining The Americans who rushed to California in 1849 had many skills. But they knew nothing about mining. Mexicanos introduced them to the *batea* (bah-TAY-ah), or gold pan. Miners scooped up mud from streambeds with the batea. Then they swished it around to wash away the lightweight sand. The heavier flakes of gold sank to the bottom of the pan.

Mexicanos also brought the riffle box to the goldfields. The bottom of this long box was crossed with pieces of wood called riffles. As mud washed through the box, the heavy gold sank and was trapped behind the riffles. The riffle box was used extensively by both American and Chinese miners.

Before long, miners discovered that the gold they were picking up in streams came from veins of quartz rock in the Sierra Nevada. Quartz mining was a mystery to Americans, but it was familiar to Mexicanos. Mexicanos taught other miners how to dig the quartz out of mountains. They also showed miners how to use a simple *arrastra* (ar-RAS-trah), or grinding mill, to crush the rock so they could easily remove the gold.

Silver and Copper Mining A Mexicano miner sparked the West's first big silver strike. In 1859, a prospector named Henry Comstock was looking for gold in Nevada. Much to his annoyance, his gold was mixed with a lot of worthless "blue stuff." One day, a Mexicano miner looked at the blue stuff and started shouting, *"Mucha plata! Mucha plata!"* ("Much silver!") In its first 20 years, the Comstock Lode yielded over $300 million in silver and gold.

Mexicanos discovered copper in the Southwest in the early 1800s. When Americans began to mine copper in Arizona, they turned to Mexican miners for help. By 1940, Arizona mines had produced $3 billion worth of copper—copper that carried electricity and telephone calls to millions of homes across America.

Mexicanos Spanish-speaking people who, in the 1800s, lived in parts of the United States that previously belonged to Mexico

17.3 Cattle Ranching

Cattle ranching in the West was built on traditions brought north from Mexico. Spanish colonists imported the first cattle to the Americas. The animals adapted well to the dry conditions of Mexico and the American Southwest. In time, millions of Spanish cattle ran wild in Texas and California.

Spanish cattle were thin, wiry creatures with long, wide-spreading horns. They moved quickly and were dangerous. *Californios* (Mexicanos in California) often found themselves dodging behind trees or diving into ditches to escape the charge of an angry longhorn.

With cattle so abundant, Californios and Tejanos found ranching to be a good business. So did the Americans who learned the cattle business from Mexican *rancheros,* or ranchers.

The Rancho Western cattle ranching was nothing like dairy farming in the East. Eastern dairy farms were small family businesses that produced mostly milk, butter, and cheese. By comparison, western ranchos were huge. In the arid Southwest, large grants of land were needed to provide enough food and water for cattle herds. Instead of dairy products, the main products of ranchos were meat, hides, and tallow (fat).

Ranch life followed traditions that had been developed in Spain and perfected in Mexico. Rancheros spent most of their day on horseback, overseeing their land and herds. Caring for the cattle was the work of hired *vaqueros* (vah-KAIR-ohs), or cowboys.

The Roundup Among the vaqueros' most important jobs were the *rodeo,* or roundup, and branding. Branding, or using a hot iron to burn a mark into the hide of cattle, was essential because herds belonging to different owners mixed together on unfenced grasslands. To avoid conflicts, every owner had to mark his cattle with a distinctive brand.

During the rodeo, vaqueros drove unbranded calves to a roundup area. There, the calves were branded with the brand their mothers bore.

As Americans took up ranching, they adopted the rancheros' practice of branding cattle. Along with cowboys and the roundup, cattle brands are still part of ranch life in the West.

During the rodeo, vaqueros drove unmarked cattle to special roundup areas. There the animals were branded with a rancho's distinctive identification mark. Branding was necessary because cattle belonging to different owners grazed on the same land.

17.4 The Cowboy

Hollywood movies make it seem that nothing is more American than the western cowboy. Cowboys, however, learned their job from the Mexican vaquero. Across the Southwest, vaqueros were admired for their skill at riding, roping, and handling cattle. American cowboys adopted the vaqueros' clothes and gear, as well as much of their language.

Cowboy Clothes and Gear From head to toe, cowboys dressed in clothing borrowed from the vaqueros. For example, the cowboys' "ten-gallon hats," which shaded their eyes and sometimes served as a water pail or a pillow, came from the vaqueros' wide-brimmed *sombreros* (sohm-BRER-ohs). The leather chaps that protected the cowboys' legs from cacti and sagebrush were modeled on the vaqueros' *chaparreras* (chap-ar-REHR-ahs). The high-heeled, pointed-toe boots that slipped so easily into the cowboys' stirrups were based on the vaqueros' *botas* (BO-tas). Even the *poncho* that protected cowboys from cold and rain was borrowed from the vaqueros.

Mexicanos also invented the western, or cowboy, saddle, with its useful horn. The saddles brought to America from Europe did not have horns. When a vaquero on a European saddle roped a steer, he had to tie his rope to the horse's tail to keep it anchored. This method was hard on both the horse and the rider. By adding a horn to the saddle, vaqueros made their job easier—and their horses' job as well.

Cowboys borrowed another essential piece of gear from the vaqueros: *la riata* (la ree-AH-tah), or the lariat. Vaqueros were masters of the art of throwing a 60-foot rope great distances with amazing accuracy. This skill was especially useful for roping calves during a roundup. In a remarkable display of roping skill, a vaquero named José Romero once roped a full-grown eagle right out of the sky.

The vaquero's sombrero shaded him from the sun. His neckerchief, when worn over his mouth, protected him from dust. His high-heeled, pointed boots kept him secure in the stirrups of his saddle.

Cowboy Lingo American cowboys borrowed or adapted many ranching words from the vaqueros as well. The terms *bronco, stampede, corral, lasso, burro, buckaroo,* and *vamoose* all come from Spanish-Mexican words. So do *mesa, canyon, mesquite, chaparral,* and other terms used to describe the southwestern landscape. The cowboy slang word for jail, *hoosegow,* came from the Spanish *juzgado* (hooz-GA-doh). And of course, the terms ranch and rancher came from *rancho* and *ranchero.*

17.5 Sheep Raising

In New Mexico, the most important industry was sheep raising. From the founding of the territory up to the Mexican Cession, sheep fed, clothed, and supported Spanish and Mexican settlers.

The Spanish brought a long tradition of sheep raising to the Americas. Two kinds of sheep were raised in Spain: the *merinos* (meh-REE-nohs) with their fine wool and the *churros* (CHUR-rohs) with their coarse wool. The Spanish brought the scrawny churro to New Mexico, and for good reason. This tough little sheep knew how to survive in a dry environment like that of the Southwest.

Sheep raising was the most important industry in New Mexico when the territory belonged to Mexico. An owner of a sheep ranch might have over a million sheep.

The Spanish Sheep-Raising System When Americans came to New Mexico, they did not think of sheep raising as a business. In the East, a farmer might raise a few sheep as a sideline, but not large herds. Once they saw the Spanish sheep-raising system in New Mexico, however, some Americans changed their minds.

Under the Spanish system, sheep raising was a large and well-organized business. The Spanish governor of New Mexico, for example, once owned 2 million sheep and employed 2,700 workers.

At the top of this business stood the *patron* (pah-TROHN), or owner of the herds. Below him were several layers of managers. These supervisors and range bosses spent their days on horseback, checking range conditions and the health of the sheep.

The lowest-level worker was the *pastor* (pahs-TOHR), or herder. Each pastor was responsible for 1,500 to 2,000 sheep. A pastor stayed with his flock night and day, slowly guiding it from place to place so that the sheep could graze as they moved. During spring lambing season, the pastor assisted with difficult births, cared for orphaned lambs, and helped the newborns survive. One pastor described this busy time as a "month-long hell of worry and toil."

Americans Adopt the Spanish System Americans soon adopted the Spanish system as their own. Large-scale sheep raising spread from New Mexico across the Southwest. In California, the churro was crossed with the merino to produce a sheep with far better wool. As a result, between 1862 and 1880, U.S. wool production soared from 5 million to 22 million pounds a year.

The Mexicanos introduced a system of irrigation that allowed settlers in the Southwest to turn deserts into productive, fertile fields.

17.6 Irrigated Farming

Americans coming to the Southwest knew as little about irrigated farming as they did about mining, cattle ranching, and sheep raising. In the East, enough rain fell year-round to water a farmer's crops. **Irrigation** was unnecessary and unknown. But in the Southwest, where six months could go by with no rain, irrigation was essential.

Mexicano settlers in the Southwest brought with them irrigation techniques that had been developed centuries earlier in Spain and North Africa. They borrowed other techniques from the Pueblo Indians of New Mexico. When the settlers first arrived, the Pueblos were irrigating from 15,000 to 25,000 acres of cropland in the arid Rio Grande Valley.

The Mexican System of Irrigation Bringing water to fields involved an enormous amount of work. First, farmers had to redirect water from local streams to their fields. They began by building a dam of rocks, earth, and brush across the stream. The water that backed up behind the dam was brought to the fields by irrigation ditches.

To keep from wasting this precious water, Mexicanos carefully leveled their fields. Then they divided the fields into squares. Each square was marked off by a wall of earth high enough to hold in water. When one square had been soaked with water, farmers made a hole in its wall. The water then flowed to the next square. The farmers continued in this way until the entire field was soaked. This method of irrigation was known as the Mexican system.

America's Fruit Basket Using crops introduced by Mexicanos and the Mexican system of irrigation, American settlers turned the Southwest into America's "fruit basket." Among the many fruits brought by Mexicanos to the Southwest were grapes, dates, olives, apples, walnuts, pears, plums, peaches, apricots, and quinces. Mexicano settlers also brought the first citrus fruits—lemons, limes, and oranges—to the region. Many of these fruits were unknown in the East, where the climate was too cold for them to grow. But they thrived in sunny Arizona and California. With the help of Mexicano farmworkers, American farmers transformed dry deserts into irrigated fruit orchards and citrus groves.

irrigation a system for bringing water to farmland by artificial means, such as using a dam to trap water and ditches to channel it to fields

17.7 Food

In 1835, William Heath Davis became one of the first Americans to settle in California. There he got his first taste of Mexican food. Davis later wrote of the Californios,

> *Their tables were frugally [simply] furnished, the food clean and inviting, consisting mainly of good beef broiled on an iron rod, or steaks with onions, also mutton [sheep], chicken, eggs . . . The bread was tortillas; sometimes made with yeast. Beans were a staple dish . . . Their meat stews were excellent when not too highly seasoned with red pepper.*

Davis may not have known it, but the food he was enjoying in California brought together the best of two worlds.

A Food Revolution The Spanish conquest of Mexico in 1521 began one of the great food revolutions in history. The Spanish came to Mexico in search of gold, but the greatest treasures they found were Indian foods unknown in Europe. These foods included corn, tomatoes, chocolate, peanuts, vanilla, beans, squash, avocados, coconuts, sunflower seeds, and chili peppers.

The Spanish shipped these new foods back to Spain. From there, they spread throughout Europe, greatly expanding people's food choices.

In turn, the Spanish brought the foods of Europe to Mexico. They introduced meats such as pork, beef, lamb, chicken, and goat. They brought nuts and grains such as almonds, walnuts, rice, wheat, and barley. They planted fruits and vegetables such as apples, oranges, grapes, olives, lettuce, carrots, sugarcane, and potatoes (which they discovered in Peru). And they introduced herbs and spices such as cinnamon, parsley, coriander, oregano, and black pepper.

Corn, a food of the native Indians, was a staple in the Mexicano diet. Here, a Mexicano woman is grinding corn that she will use to make a flat corn bread called *tortillas*.

A New Style of Cooking Mexican cooks combined these foods of diverse origins to create a rich and flavorful style of cooking that was neither Indian nor Spanish. It was distinctly Mexican.

As Americans settled the Southwest, they were introduced to Mexican food. Many of them liked the new tastes, and they borrowed recipes from Mexicano cooks. In Texas, the mingling of Mexican and American dishes resulted in a style of cooking known as Tex-Mex. Across America, a spicy stew of beef and beans known simply as chili became as American as apple pie.

17.8 Architecture

Throughout the Southwest, the Mexicano contribution to architecture is easy to see. Many buildings can be found with the thick walls, red-tile roofs, rounded arches, and courtyards that are typical of Spanish architecture.

Spanish-style architecture took root in Mexico during the colonial period. Mexican settlers brought their knowledge of this tradition to the Southwest. Their missions, homes, and other structures were simple and attractive. They were ideally suited to the hot, dry climate of the Southwest.

Rounded arches, thick walls, and red-tile roofs are characteristics of Spanish-style architecture.

Adobe Buildings Since wood was scarce in the Southwest, Mexicanos used adobe (ah-DOH-beh) bricks as their main building material. Adobe is a mixture of earth, grass, and water that is shaped into bricks and baked in the sun. Mexicanos covered their adobe homes with colorful red clay tiles. Besides being attractive and fireproof, a tile roof kept the adobe walls from being washed away during heavy rains.

Many adobe buildings featured patios and verandas. A *patio* is a roofless inner courtyard, often located at the center of a home. A *veranda* is a roofed porch or balcony extending along the outside of a building. Patios and verandas allowed Mexicanos to spend much of their time outdoors while still protected from the hot sun and dry desert winds.

Newcomers Adopt the Spanish Style Americans moving to the Southwest quickly saw the advantages of building with adobe. Because of their thick walls, adobe structures stayed cooler in summer and warmer in winter than the wood buildings that Americans from the East were used to. Adobe structures could also be easily constructed from locally available materials.

American settlers used adobe to build not only homes, but also courthouses, trading posts, post offices, and other buildings. Later, builders adapted Spanish architecture to new materials such as concrete and stucco. By the 1930s, nearly a million Spanish-style homes had been built in California. "Who would live in a structure of wood and brick if they could get a palace of mud?" wrote an admiring easterner. "The adobes [make] the most picturesque and comfortable [homes] . . . and harmonize . . . with the whole nature of the landscape."

17.9 Laws

The Mexicanos of the Southwest were used to being governed by Mexican laws. These laws often differed from American laws. For example, Mexico had outlawed slavery in 1829. Slaves from the American South sometimes ran away to find freedom in Mexican settlements. (Recall that Mexico's abolition of slavery was one of the issues that led Texans to fight for their independence from Mexico.)

In time, both Mexican and American legal traditions would shape laws in the West. Particularly important were Mexicano laws governing mining, water, and community property.

Mining Law Before the discovery of gold in California, there was so little mining in the United States that Americans had no mining law. Once in the goldfields, the forty-niners desperately needed rules to keep order.

With the help of Mexicano miners, Americans developed a "law of the mines" based on Mexican mining law. California miners later carried this law of the mines to other parts of the Southwest.

Water Law The water law brought west by Americans worked well enough in the East, where rainfall was abundant. Under American law, water flowing across a field or farm belonged to the owner of that land. Landowners could use their water in whatever ways they wanted.

This principle did not work well in the West, where water was scarce and precious. Disputes over who controlled streams led to endless legal conflicts and even water wars.

To end these conflicts, settlers wrote new laws based on Mexican "pueblo law." Pueblo law said that water was too valuable to be owned or controlled by any one person. Instead, water belonged to an entire community and should be used for the benefit of all.

Community Property Law For women, the most important legal principle borrowed from Mexican law was the idea of community property. In eastern states, married women had few property rights. Any property acquired by a married couple—such as a home, farm, or business—belonged solely to the husband.

In contrast, Mexican law said that all property acquired during a marriage was "community property." If a couple separated, half of that property belonged to the wife, half to the husband.

American settlers liked the idea of sharing the gains of marriage between husband and wife. Today, Texas, California, New Mexico, Arizona, Idaho, Nevada, Washington, Wisconsin, and Louisiana are all community property states.

The Mexicano legal principle of community property gave women property rights they did not have under British law. According to the Mexican principle, women were entitled to half of all property acquired during a marriage.

This couple is performing the fandango. During this popular Mexican dance, the man and woman play castanets, which are small pieces of wood held in the palm of the hand and clicked together.

17.10 Entertainment

The Californios, observed William Heath Davis, "were about the happiest and most contented people I ever saw." Californios worked hard. But they also knew how to entertain themselves with music, dance, and *fiestas* (celebrations). Americans settling the Southwest shared in these entertainments.

Music and Dancing Mexicano music greatly influenced country and western music in the Southwest. The most important contribution was the *corrido* (kor-REE-doh), or folk ballad. A corrido is a dramatic story sung to the **accompaniment** of guitars. The subjects of corridos ranged from exciting tales of heroes and bandits to sad songs of love and betrayal.

American settlers admired the color and energy of traditional Mexicano dance. Dancing was an important part of any Mexicano fiesta. Favorite dances included the *jota* (HOH-tah), the *fandango,* and *la bamba*. The last of these, the bamba, was danced by a young woman balancing a full glass of water on her head. Generations of schoolchildren learned another popular dance, the *jarabe tapatío* (hah-RAH-beh tah-pah-TEE-oh), or "Mexican hat dance," as part of their southwestern cultural heritage.

Fiestas and Rodeos Throughout the year, Mexicanos held a variety of religious fiestas. One of the most important honored Our Lady of Guadalupe, the patron saint of Mexico. In San Antonio, Texas, Tejanos marked this day (December 12) with an elaborate **procession** to the cathedral. After attending church services, the Tejanos danced all night long in their homes.

Today, the most widely celebrated Mexicano holiday is *El Cinco de Mayo* (el SEEN-koh day MY-oh), which means the Fifth of May. This holiday commemorates an important victory in Mexico's fight for independence from French rule in 1862. Cinco de Mayo fiestas bring together Mexican and non-Mexican Americans to enjoy Mexicano music, dance, and food.

For millions of Americans, rodeo is an exciting professional sport. Rodeo's roots go back to cattle roundups on Mexicano ranchos. During these get-togethers, Mexicano cowboys competed with each other in events such as calf roping, bull riding, and bronco busting. American cowboys joined in these contests, and soon rodeos became annual events in western cities. To its many fans, the rodeo, with its mixed Mexicano and American heritage, represents the best of the West.

Mexicano contributions played a central role in turning the southwestern United States into a unique, prosperous section of the country.

Chapter Summary

In this chapter, you learned about Mexicano contributions to the Southwest and how they have influenced life in the United States.

Mining Mexicano knowledge, skills, and techniques advanced the development of mining in the Southwest. These contributions helped build the gold, silver, and copper mining industries.

Cattle, Cowboys, and Sheep American settlers learned about cattle ranching, cowboy life, and sheep raising from Mexicanos. They adopted Mexicano traditions for raising cattle and sheep. The American cowboy's language was enriched by Spanish-Mexican words like burro, rodeo, and lasso.

Farming and Food White settlers in the Southwest adopted irrigation techniques that had been pioneered by Mexicanos and Pueblo Indians. They also learned to appreciate Mexicano food.

Architecture, Laws, and Entertainment Today, Mexicano culture survives in such American adaptations as Spanish-style homes and buildings as well as legal traditions regarding mining, water, and community property. Millions of Americans enjoy music, dances, festivals, and rodeos that come from Mexicano traditions.

Mexicano Culture Today

Just as Mexicanos influenced life in the United States in the 1800s, they influence American life today. In the arts, Mexicanos create beauty as they tell their stories. Through performances and festivals, they share their cultural heritage.

The mural called *The Great Wall of Los Angeles* is half a mile long. It is painted on a concrete wall. In lively pictures, it tells California's history. Images at one end show people who lived in the area long, long ago. Images at the other end show Los Angeles life in the 1950s.

Judith Baca, a Mexican American artist, designed the wall. Neighborhood kids and teenagers painted it. Baca, the director of the Social and Public Art Resource Center in Venice, California, said,

> *When I first saw the [blank] wall I envisioned a long narrative of another history of California; one which included ethnic peoples, women and minorities . . . The discovery of the history of California's multi-cultured peoples was a revelation to me as well as to the members of my teams.*

One panel, for example, shows a scene from the Chavez Ravine neighborhood of Los Angeles. In the late 1950s, the city evicted the area's residents. The city government wanted to use the space to build Dodger Stadium. But at least one resident refused to leave. The mural shows a police officer taking away Aurora Archega. She wears a red dress and clenches her fist. Dodger Stadium looms behind her. This story and others reveal a past that many people do not know about. It is a past that means a lot to the local residents.

The process of making the *Great Wall* has been as important to the local Mexicano community as the wall's content. Between 1974 and

These murals in El Paso, Texas, show pride in the mixing of cultures in this city, which is on the border between the United States and Mexico.

Murals tell stories of Mexican American lives. This panel, from *The Great Wall of Los Angeles,* shows a woman protesting being evicted from her neighborhood to make way for a new stadium.

1983, more than 400 young people have contributed to the wall. They were joined by many artists and historians. The wall has truly been a community effort.

Murals Showcase Community

Mural making became important in Mexico about 100 years ago. Murals there taught history to people who could not read. As Mexicans immigrated to the United States, they brought the mural-making tradition with them.

Murals by Mexican Americans now adorn walls in cities beyond Los Angeles and states beyond California. They are part of American culture, and they are different from the art seen in museums.

The images in South Tucson's "tattoo mural" reflect what is important to the neighborhood's residents. Using tattoo images is part of the community connection. "Tattoos . . . go back generations," explained Alex Garza, one of the project's leaders.

For one thing, they are in public places where everyone can view them without paying an entry fee—or even entering a building. For another, it is not just where they are shown that makes them unique. It is how they are made. Many are made by teams of people, rather than by individual artists.

While each Mexicano mural is unique, many express a neighborhood's identity. Take the "tattoo mural," for example. This mosaic is on a wall on 29th Street in South Tucson, Arizona. It is called the tattoo mural because Mexican American body art inspired many of its images.

"This mural was meant to honor everything that happens in South Tucson," said Alex Garza, one of the lead muralists for the project. That is why the mural overflows with imagery that is meaningful to the people of South Tucson.

Community members themselves produce many murals. As with *The Great Wall of Los Angeles,* young neighborhood residents made the tattoo mural. Garza and Lupe Ruiz oversaw the mural's production. The project was part of Las Artes, a youth development program. The muralists finished high school while they worked at Las Artes.

Murals serve many purposes. They beautify urban neighborhoods. They tell stories that have not been told. They express community pride, and they provide meaningful work for young people who need it. Any way you look at it, the murals are a success story.

Mexicano Theater

The time: 1965. The place: the back of a flatbed truck in the bean fields of California's Central Valley. On this day, the back of the truck serves as a stage. Amateur actors perform plays for Mexicano farmworkers. Based on the farmworkers' lives, the plays tell stories that are familiar to the audience. In fact, the actors are farmworkers themselves.

EL TEATRO CAMPESINO

PRESENTED BY:
CAC
MIDWEST COUNCIL OF LA RAZA
CENTRO DE ESTUDIOS CHICANOS E INVESTIGACIONES
SOCIALES
CHICANO STUDIES PROGRAM
MECHA
SATURDAY MARCH 31 at 8 p.m.
WASHINGTON HALL, Notre DAME
ADMISSION BY DONATION
CAC DANCE + DRAMA PATRONS - FREE

Luis Valdez, founder of El Teatro Campesino, believes that art enables people to understand each other. "Ultimately it is artistry that . . . cuts across the barriers to understanding," he said. From the plays of the 1960s (above) to performances on college campuses today (below), ETC brings Valdez's philosophy to life.

For years, farmworkers had labored in California's fields for long hours and low pay. In 1965, they formed a union, the United Farm Workers (UFW), to organize for their rights.

The theater in the bean fields was a way to tell the workers' stories. The *actos,* or plays, helped articulate the workers' concerns. The plays became an important part of the political work the UFW was doing.

The theater in the fields was called El Teatro Campesino—The Farmworkers' Theater—and it still exists today. Its performances do not take place in the bean fields any more. Now, El Teatro Campesino (ETC) has its own theater in a former packing plant in San Juan Bautista, California. And it is no longer part of the union. Now it is an independent theater company. But it still tells the stories of the lives of Mexicanos. It still gives voice to their concerns.

El Teatro Campesino has always had a two-part mission. Luis Valdez, the group's founder and artistic director, explained it this way:

> Until we had the artists who could express what the people [farmworkers] were feeling and saying, we wouldn't really register politically. Art gives us the tools of that expression.

Today, ETC has spread far beyond the bean fields. The group has performed around the United States, Latin America, and Europe. Luis Valdez has also brought stories about Mexicanos to much larger audiences. *Zoot Suit,* his historically based play about a fight for justice in 1940s Los Angeles, became a Broadway show in 1979. It was made into a movie in 1982.

El Teatro Campesino sparked a Mexicano theater movement. Theater companies formed across the Southwest and in other parts of the country. Like ETC, they showcase Mexicano talent and tell Mexicano stories.

Charro Days and Ballet Folklórico

Mexicano culture is murals and theater, but it is a lot more, too. You can see the influence of Mexicano culture in many parts of American life today.

Once a year, for example, people gather on both sides of the border that separates the United States and Mexico to celebrate Charro Days. Street parties abound. There is food, music and dancing, costumes, and of course the *charros* (CHAR-rohs).

Charros are gentleman cowboys who are known for

Ballet folklórico draws on the traditions of the many ethnic groups that make up Mexico. The Ballet Folklórico de México performs traditional dances around the world.

their brightly colored clothes and wide sombreros. They came from Spain to Mexico hundreds of years ago. Over time, they moved into the southwestern United States. Today, although there are few working cowboys left, people on both sides of the border celebrate the charros.

Brownsville, Texas, and Matamoros, Mexico—two cities connected by international bridges—hold joint Charro Day celebrations every year. "I believe this is the only parade that starts in one country and ends in another," says Charro Days president John Patriarca.

You can also see Mexicano influence in the traditional dances called *ballet folklórico* (bahl-LAY fohk-LOHR-ee-koh). The women wear flowing skirts in splashy colors with ruffled blouses. The men wear black pants, waist-length jackets, and wide-brimmed hats.

Ballet folklórico is not one specific dance or even one specific kind of dance. Rather, the term refers to a lot of different dances. Some came from native people. Others came from the Spanish who ruled Mexico for hundreds of years. Still others celebrate Mexican independence. What the dances have in common is that they express the diversity of Mexican life—and Mexican American life.

Ballet folklórico troupes have sprung up across the United States, with many in areas where there is a large Mexicano population. The dance companies help audiences appreciate the heritage that Mexican immigrants brought with them to the United States.

Through the arts, Mexicanos have celebrated their culture and told their stories. Their efforts have inspired pride among Mexicanos and encouraged greater understanding of Mexicanos among other Americans. Their art has also made Mexicano culture a vibrant part of American culture.

An Expanding Nation

1819
Acquisition of Florida
Spain avoids war with the United States by ceding Florida to the United States.

1803
Louisiana Purchase
In a diplomatic treaty made during Thomas Jefferson's administration, the United States buys the Louisiana Territory from France. The Louisiana Purchase doubles the size of the nation.

1836–1845
Lone Star Republic Founded
Following the Battle of San Jacinto in 1836, Texas wins its freedom from Mexico and remains an independent nation for 10 years.

1800   1810   1820   1830   1840

1804–1806
Lewis and Clark Expedition
Meriwether Lewis and William Clark lead an expedition to explore the Louisiana Territory, the nation's newly acquired region west of the Mississippi River.

1840–1870
Settlers Move West
Several hundred thousand settlers move west across the Oregon, California, and Mormon trails.

1846
Compromise in Oregon Country
The United States chooses diplomacy over war with Great Britain in order to acquire the lower half of Oregon Country.

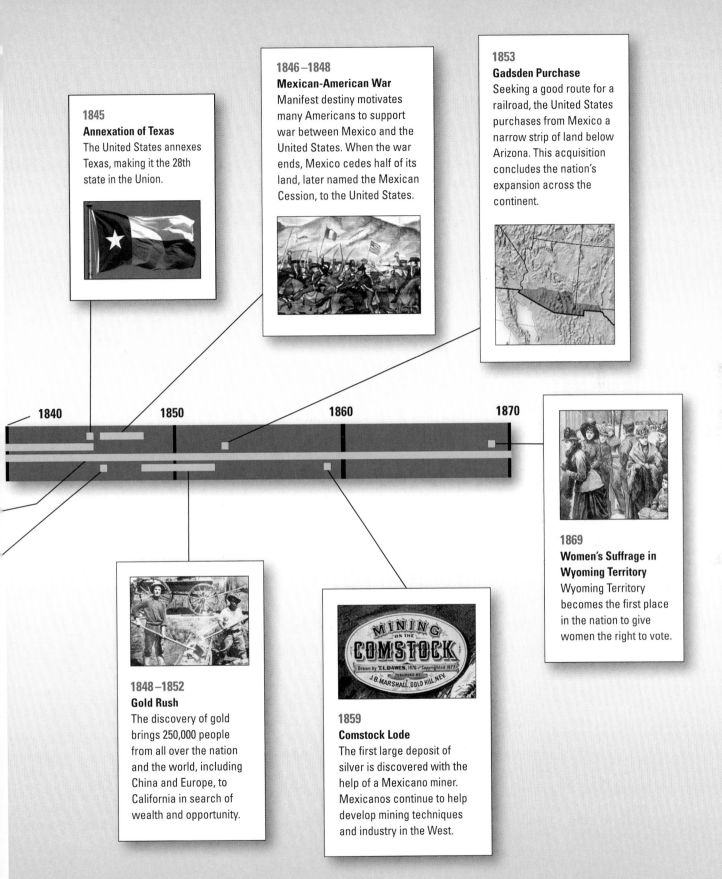

1845
Annexation of Texas
The United States annexes Texas, making it the 28th state in the Union.

1846–1848
Mexican-American War
Manifest destiny motivates many Americans to support war between Mexico and the United States. When the war ends, Mexico cedes half of its land, later named the Mexican Cession, to the United States.

1853
Gadsden Purchase
Seeking a good route for a railroad, the United States purchases from Mexico a narrow strip of land below Arizona. This acquisition concludes the nation's expansion across the continent.

1840   1850   1860   1870

1869
Women's Suffrage in Wyoming Territory
Wyoming Territory becomes the first place in the nation to give women the right to vote.

1848–1852
Gold Rush
The discovery of gold brings 250,000 people from all over the nation and the world, including China and Europe, to California in search of wealth and opportunity.

1859
Comstock Lode
The first large deposit of silver is discovered with the help of a Mexicano miner. Mexicanos continue to help develop mining techniques and industry in the West.

Most Americans in the mid-1800s lived in the eastern half of the country. This view of New York was painted around 1850.

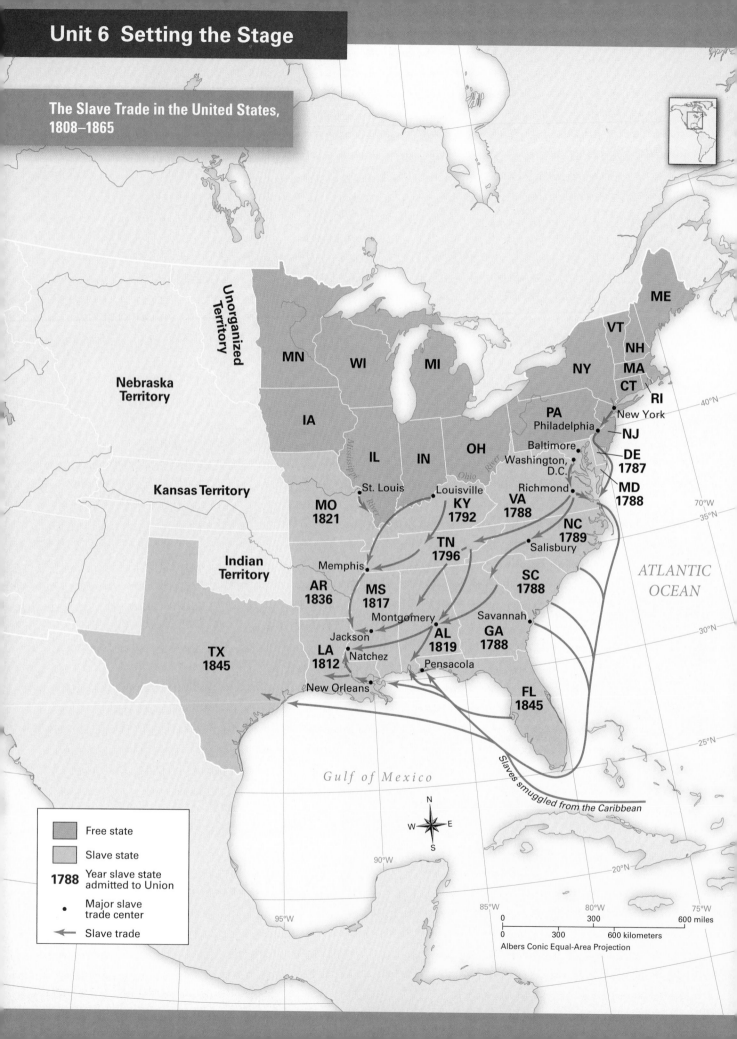

Unit 6 Setting the Stage

The Slave Trade in the United States,
1808–1865

Unorganized Territory

Nebraska Territory

Kansas Territory

Indian Territory

ME

VT

NH

NY

MA

CT

RI

New York

MN

WI

MI

PA

Philadelphia

NJ

Baltimore

DE
1787

Washington, D.C.

MD
1788

IA

IL

IN

OH

Mississippi River

Ohio River

St. Louis

Louisville

Richmond

MO
1821

KY
1792

VA
1788

NC
1789

Salisbury

TN
1796

SC
1788

ATLANTIC
OCEAN

Memphis

AR
1836

MS
1817

Montgomery

Savannah

GA
1788

Jackson

AL
1819

TX
1845

LA
1812

Natchez

Pensacola

New Orleans

FL
1845

Gulf of Mexico

Slaves smuggled from the Caribbean

N
W   E
S

90°W

95°W

85°W

80°W

75°W

40°N

70°W

35°N

30°N

25°N

20°N

0   300   600 miles

0   300   600 kilometers

Albers Conic Equal-Area Projection

Legend

Free state

Slave state

1788 Year slave state admitted to Union

• Major slave trade center

→ Slave trade

Americans in the Mid-1800s

In 1787, "in Order to form a more perfect Union," a group of political leaders wrote the Constitution of the United States. Some 50 years later, however, some people believed that the Union was still far from perfect. Most of them were not political leaders. Instead, they were everyday Americans—men and women, black and white, ministers and teachers.

From the 1830s through the 1850s, these reformers tried to improve American society in many ways. Some of their efforts met with great resistance. One of the most controversial issues was the struggle to end slavery. Many Northerners, as well as many white Southerners, thought slavery was morally wrong. However, the South's economy depended on slave labor. Over time, that dependence grew.

The Constitution banned the importation of slaves starting in 1808. Yet, as white Southerners moved westward, the demand for slave labor increased. This demand was met by the natural growth of slave populations in older parts of the South. Slaveholders in these areas sold slaves to buyers from other regions. The map on the opposite page shows the cities where much of this slave trade took place. It also shows how slavery spread west. The map below shows the distribution of the slave population in 1860.

In this unit, you will learn about the movement to end slavery and about other attempts at reform. You will also learn about Northern and Southern society, including differences in the lives of free African Americans and slaves. Finally, you will learn about the economies of the North and South and why they made the end of slavery so difficult to achieve.

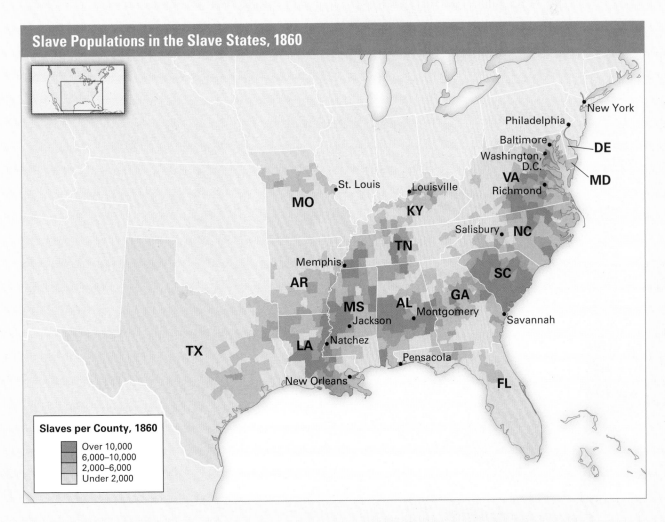

Slave Populations in the Slave States, 1860

Slaves per County, 1860
- Over 10,000
- 6,000–10,000
- 2,000–6,000
- Under 2,000

LUCRETIA MOTT.

ELIZABETH CADY STANTON.

LUCY STONE.

JULIA WARD HOWE.

SUSAN B. ANTHONY.

MRS. MARTHA C. WRIGHT.
First President N. Y. State Suffrage Association. Elected 1860.

MRS. JEAN BROOKS GREENLEAF.
Fourth President N. Y. State Suffrage Assn. Served 6 years, 1890-96.

REV. ANNA H. SHAW,

MRS. ELIZABETH BOYNTON HARBERT.

Rev. Anna H. Shaw

DOROTHEA LYNDE DIX.

A. D R.
C 1887
AC 6294/ADD 3

Chapter 18

An Era of Reform

To what extent did the reform movements of the mid-1800s improve life for Americans?

18.1 Introduction

In 1851, a group of people gathered in a church in Ohio to discuss the rights of women. A tall African American woman made her way through the crowd and sat down. Her name was Sojourner Truth. A former slave, she had learned to pay careful attention to white people. Now she listened as whites discussed whether women should have the same rights as men.

Truth heard one speaker after another explain that women didn't need more rights because they weren't smart or strong enough to do much besides raise children. Women, they argued, needed help from men. One man summed it up by saying, "Women are weak."

Truth had heard enough. She rose slowly to her feet and walked to the pulpit. The room grew quiet as everyone waited for her to speak.

"That man over there says that women need to be helped into carriages, and lifted over ditches, and have the best place everywhere," she began. "Nobody ever helps me into carriages, or over mudpuddles, or gives me any best place!"

Her voice rose to a thunderous pitch. "And ain't I a woman? Look at me! Look at my arm! I have plowed and planted, and gathered into barns, and no man could head [outdo] me. And ain't I a woman? I could work as much and eat as much as a man—when I could get it—and bear the lash as well! And ain't I a woman? I have borne thirteen children, and seen them most all sold into slavery, and when I cried out with my mother's grief, none but Jesus heard me. And ain't I a woman?"

When she finished, people applauded. Some cried. One witness said, "She had taken us up in her strong arms and carried us safely."

Sojourner Truth represented two of the great reform movements in America in the 1800s: the movement for women's equality and the movement to end slavery. Between about 1820 and 1850, many Americans devoted themselves to such causes as ending slavery, promoting women's rights, and improving education. In this chapter, you will learn to what extent these reform movements improved life for Americans.

Sojourner Truth, a former slave, gave speeches throughout the North against slavery and, later, in support of women's rights.

◀ This scrapbook page from the late 1800s contains pictures of women who led various reform movements.

reform to make changes in order to bring about improvement, end abuses, or correct injustices

Second Great Awakening a revival of religious feeling and belief from the 1800s to the 1840s

Preachers at religious meetings like this one proclaimed that people could help earn their salvation by doing good works. This message encouraged many people to work to improve society.

18.2 The Spirit of Reform

It was fitting that the meeting attended by Sojourner Truth took place in a church. New religious movements played a key role in inspiring thousands of Americans to try to **reform** society.

The Second Great Awakening A revival of religious feeling swept across the nation from the 1800s to the 1840s. Church leaders called this period the **Second Great Awakening**. Day after day, people gathered in churches and big white tents to hear messages of hope. Preachers like Charles G. Finney, a leader of the movement, urged Christians to let themselves be "filled with the Spirit of God." Their listeners prayed, shouted, and sang hymns. Sometimes they cried for hours or fell down in frenzies.

Like the Great Awakening during the 1730s and 1740s, this religious revival appealed to people's emotions. But the Second Great Awakening offered something new. In the past, most Christian ministers had said that God had already decided who would be saved. Now many preachers said everyone could gain forgiveness for their sins. Many of them taught that doing good works could help them to be saved.

This optimistic message attracted enthusiastic followers throughout the West and North. It gave men and women alike a reason to work for the improvement of society. Charles Finney's preaching, for example, inspired many people to oppose slavery.

Optimistic Ideas Other optimistic ideas also inspired Americans during this time. In New England, Ralph Waldo Emerson, a former minister, was the central figure in a movement called **transcendentalism**. Emerson believed that every human being has unlimited potential. But to realize their godlike nature, people have to transcend, or go beyond, purely logical thinking. They can find the answers to life's mysteries only by learning to trust their emotions and **intuition**.

Transcendentalists added to the spirit of reform by urging people to question society's rules and institutions. Do not **conform** to others' expectations, they said. If you want to find God—and your own true self—look to nature and the "God within."

Emerson's friend Henry David Thoreau captured this new **individualism** in a famous essay. "If a man does not keep pace with his companions," wrote Thoreau, "perhaps it is because he hears a different drummer. Let him step to the music which he hears."

Thoreau practiced what he preached. In 1845, he went into the woods near Concord, Massachusetts, to live alone and as close to nature as possible. Thoreau spent more than two years in solitude, recording his thoughts in a 6,000-page journal. In 1846, he was jailed overnight for refusing to pay taxes because of his opposition to the government's involvement in the Mexican-American War.

Model Communities While Thoreau tried to find the ideal life in solitude, other transcendentalists tried to create ideal communities. In 1841, George Ripley started a community called Brook Farm near Boston. Residents at Brook Farm tried to live in "brotherly cooperation" instead of competing with each other, as people in the larger society did. They shared the labor of supporting themselves by farming, teaching, and making clothes.

Brook Farm was only one of hundreds of model communities started by reformers in the first half of the 1800s. Most of these experiments lasted only a few years. But they were a powerful expression of the belief that people of good will could create an ideal society.

18.3 Prison Reform

One day in 1841, a Boston woman named Dorothea Dix agreed to teach Sunday school at a jail. What she witnessed that day changed her life forever.

Dix was horrified to see that many prisoners were bound in chains and locked in cages. Children accused of minor thefts were jailed with adult criminals. Were conditions this bad everywhere?

Dix **devoted** herself to finding out the answer to her question. She visited hundreds of jails and prisons throughout Massachusetts. She also visited debtors' prisons, or jails for people who owed money. Most of the thousands of Americans in debtors' prisons owed less than 20 dollars. While they were locked up, they could not earn money to repay their debts. As a result, they remained imprisoned for years.

transcendentalism a philosophy emphasizing that people should transcend, or go beyond, logical thinking to reach true understanding, with the help of emotions and intuition

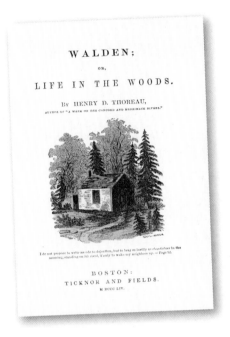

In 1854, Henry David Thoreau published *Walden; or, Life in the Woods,* an account of his experience living in a cabin he built near Concord, Massachusetts. There he meditated on the meaning of his life, society, nature, and the human spirit.

Dorothea Dix worked tirelessly to improve conditions for prisoners and the mentally ill.

Treatment of the Mentally Ill What shocked Dix most of all was the way mentally ill people were treated. Most were locked in dirty, crowded prison cells. If they misbehaved, they were whipped.

Dix and other reformers believed that the mentally ill needed treatment and care, not punishment. Massachusetts had one private asylum, or hospital for the mentally ill. Only the wealthy could afford to send a family member there. Even so, the asylum was filled to overflowing.

Campaigning for Better Conditions For two years, Dix gathered information about the horrors she had seen. Then she prepared a detailed report for the Massachusetts state legislature. "I come as the advocate of helpless, forgotten, insane . . . men and women," she said. "I proceed . . . to call your attention to the present state of insane persons, confined . . . in cages, closets, cellars, stalls, pens! Chained, naked, beaten with rods, and lashed into obedience!" Shocked by Dix's report, the lawmakers voted to create public asylums for the mentally ill.

Dix visited prisons in other states as well. After she prepared reports demanding humane treatment for the mentally ill, those states also created special mental hospitals.

Dix continued campaigning for prison reform for the rest of her life. By the time she died in 1887, state governments no longer put debtors in prison. Most states had created special justice systems for children in trouble. Many had outlawed cruel punishments, such as branding people with hot irons. Dix had shown that reformers could lead society to make significant changes.

18.4 Education Reform

A second reform movement that won support in the 1800s was the effort to make education available to more children. The man who would become known as "the father of American public schools," Horace Mann, led this movement.

The Need for Public Schools As a boy in Massachusetts in the early 1800s, Horace Mann attended school only ten weeks a year. The rest of the time, he had to work on his family's farm.

Mann was lucky to have even this limited time in school. In Massachusetts, Puritans had established town schools, but few other areas had public schools, or schools paid for by taxes. Wealthy parents sent their children to private schools or hired tutors. On the frontier, 60 children might attend a part-time, one-room school. Their teachers had limited education and received little pay. Most children simply did not go to school at all.

In the cities, some poor children stole, destroyed property, and set fires. Reformers believed that education would help these children escape poverty and become good citizens. Influenced by the need for education in its big cities, New York set up public elementary schools in every town as early as the 1820s.

Meanwhile, in Massachusetts, Mann became the state's supervisor of education. In towns and villages, he spoke out on the need for public schools. "Our means of education," he stated, "are the grand machinery by which the 'raw material' of human nature can be worked up into inventors and discoverers, into skilled artisans and scientific farmers."

Citizens in Massachusetts responded to Mann's message. They voted to pay taxes to build better schools, to provide teachers with higher salaries, and to establish special training schools for teachers.

An Unfinished Reform By 1850, many states in the North and West used Mann's ideas. Soon most white children, especially boys, attended free public schools.

But states still did not offer public education to everyone. Most high schools and colleges did not admit girls. States as far north as Illinois passed laws to keep African Americans out of public schools. When towns did allow blacks to attend school, most made them go to separate schools that received less money. In the South, few girls and no African Americans could attend public schools.

Education for girls and women did make some progress. In 1837, Oberlin College in Ohio became the first college to admit women as well as men. When states opened the first public universities in the 1860s, most accepted female students.

Prior to the reforms in public education led by Horace Mann, most children did not attend school. Those who did usually had to suffer overcrowded classrooms, like this one, and poorly trained teachers.

African Americans, however, had few options. When Prudence Crandall admitted a black student to her girls' school in Connecticut in 1833, white parents took their children out of the school. Crandall responded by opening a school for African American girls. Angry white people threw stones at the school and had Crandall jailed. In 1834, she was forced to close her school.

Horace Mann realized that much more needed to be done to increase educational opportunities for women and African Americans. In 1853, he became the first president of a new college for men and women, Antioch College in Ohio. There, he urged his students to become involved in improving society. "Be ashamed to die," he told them, "until you have won some victory for humanity."

18.5 The Movement to End Slavery

abolitionist a person who supported abolition, or the ending of slavery

In 1835, a poster appeared on walls throughout Washington, D.C. The poster showed two drawings. One drawing, labeled "The Land of the Free," showed the founding fathers reading the Declaration of Independence. The other, labeled "The Home of the Oppressed," showed slaves trudging past the U.S. Capitol building, the home of Congress. The poster posed a challenging question: How could America, the "land of the free," still allow slavery? By the 1830s, growing numbers of people were asking this question. These people were called **abolitionists**.

The Struggle Begins Some Americans had opposed slavery even before the American Revolution began. Quakers stopped owning slaves in 1776. By 1792, every state as far south as Virginia had antislavery societies.

Congress passed a law that ended the Atlantic slave trade in 1808. Once it became illegal to import slaves, Northern shipping communities had no more interest in slavery. Northern textile mills, however, wanted the cheap cotton that slave labor in the South provided. Although slavery ended in the North by the early 1800s, many Northerners still accepted slavery.

Abolitionists wanted to end slavery, but they did not always agree about how to do it. Some abolitionists tried to inspire slaves to rise up in revolt. Others wanted to find a peaceful way to end slavery immediately. Still others wanted to give slaveholders time to develop farming methods that didn't rely on slave labor.

From its earliest days, both blacks and whites worked in the abolition movement, sometimes together, sometimes separately. Black activists often kept their distance from their white counterparts. One African American journalist remarked, "As long as we let them think and act for us . . . they will outwardly treat us as men, while in their hearts they still hold us as slaves."

In 1831, a deeply religious white man, William Lloyd Garrison, started a fiery abolitionist newspaper, *The Liberator.*

William Lloyd Garrison (above left) published a newspaper called *The Liberator* in the 1830s. His newspaper called for not only an end to slavery but full equality for African Americans. The abolition movement gained public attention through Garrison's articles.

Braving the disapproval of many Northerners, Garrison demanded the immediate freeing of all slaves. "I will be as harsh as truth," he wrote. "I will not retreat a single inch—and I will be heard!" Angry proslavery groups destroyed Garrison's printing press and burned his house.

Frederick Douglass Speaks Out One day, Garrison heard an escaped slave, Frederick Douglass, speaking at a meeting of abolitionists. Over six feet tall, Douglass spoke with a voice like thunder. When he described the cruel treatment of enslaved children, people cried. When he made fun of ministers who told slaves to love slavery, people laughed. When he finished, Garrison jumped up and cried, "Shall such a man be held a slave in a Christian land?" The crowd called out, "No! No! No!"

Douglass quickly became a leader in the abolitionist movement. His autobiography, published in 1845, was an instant best seller. A brilliant and independent thinker, Douglass eventually started his own newspaper, *North Star*. Its motto read, "Right is of no Sex—Truth is of no Color—God is the Father of us all, and we are all Brethren [brothers]."

Women Get Involved Many women were inspired by religious reform movements to become involved in the fight against slavery. Like other abolitionists, they sometimes faced violence. When a young woman named Angelina Grimke spoke against slavery, an anti-abolition mob threw stones at her. When she kept speaking, they burned the building she was speaking in.

Angelina and her sister Sarah had been raised in a South Carolina slaveholding family. After traveling North and becoming Quakers, they saw slavery in a new way. In the 1830s, the two sisters began speaking out about the poverty and pain of slavery. At first, they spoke only to other women, but soon they were addressing large groups of men and women throughout the North. The Grimkes led the way for other women to speak in public.

Some abolitionists, like Sojourner Truth, were former slaves. Truth had always been strongly spiritual and had preached throughout the North at religious meetings and on street corners. When she met Douglass and Garrison, their enthusiasm inspired her to speak out loudly about slavery. An outstanding speaker, Truth argued that God would end slavery peacefully.

Abolitionists were a minority, even in the North. But their efforts, and the violence directed at them, helped change Northerners' attitudes toward slavery. In addition, the antislavery fight helped pave the way for the next great reform movement: the struggle for women's rights.

Frederick Douglass, a former slave, was an important leader in the abolitionist movement. Through his writings and speeches, he waged a fierce campaign against slavery.

In this painting from about 1850, women are represented in traditional ways—shy, in the background, or serving men. During the mid-1800s, many women began to work to change the way women were viewed.

18.6 Equal Rights for Women

Women abolitionists were in a strange position. They were trying to convince lawmakers to make slavery illegal, yet they themselves could not vote or hold office. They worked to raise money for the movement, yet their fathers and husbands controlled their money and property. They spoke out against slave beatings, yet their husbands could discipline them however they wanted.

Even wealthy women like the Grimke sisters started to see that women and slaves had much in common. "What *then* can woman do for the slave," asked Angelina Grimke, "when she is herself under the feet of man and shamed into silence?"

The Movement Begins The organized movement for women's rights was sparked by the friendship between Lucretia Mott and Elizabeth Cady Stanton. The two women met in 1840 at the World Anti-Slavery Convention in London. When they arrived, they were outraged to discover that women were not allowed to speak at the meeting. The men who ran the convention made women sit in the balcony, behind a curtain.

The men's decision may have backfired, because it was in the balcony that Mott and Stanton met. At first glance, the two women seemed quite different. Mott was 47 years old, the mother of four children, and an active reformer. Inspired by the Grimke sisters and her Quaker faith, Mott had preached against slavery in both white and black churches. She had also helped Prudence Crandall try to find students for her school for black girls.

Stanton was 25 years old and newly married. She had never spoken in public. As a young girl, she had overheard women beg her father, a judge, to protect them from husbands who had beaten them. He had to tell them that there was no law against it. Later, she attended Troy Female Seminary, the nation's first high school for girls. She knew from her history studies that the United States did not treat women fairly. When she met Mott in London, she readily agreed that something had to be done about the injustices suffered by women.

Unequal Treatment of Women Even a fine education like Stanton's did not mean women would receive equal treatment. When Lucy Stone graduated from Oberlin College in 1847, the faculty invited her to write a speech. But a man would have to give the speech, since the school did not allow women to speak in public. Stone refused. After graduation, she spoke out for women's rights. Because women could not vote, she refused to pay property taxes. "Women suffer taxation," she said, "and yet have no representation."

Stone's sister-in-law, Elizabeth Blackwell, wanted to be a doctor. She had studied mathematics, science, and history. Yet she was rejected by 29 medical schools before one finally accepted her. In 1849, she graduated at the top of her class, becoming the country's first female doctor. Still, no hospitals or doctors would agree to work with her.

To overcome such barriers, women would have to work together. By the time Stanton and Mott left London, they had decided "to hold a convention . . . and form a society to advocate the rights of women."

Lucretia Mott (on the left) and Elizabeth Cady Stanton (on the right) met at an anti-slavery convention in 1840. Their friendship helped spark the organized movement for women's rights.

Seneca Falls Convention
the gathering of supporters of women's rights in July 1848 that launched the movement for women's right to vote

Declaration of Sentiments a formal statement of injustices suffered by women, written by the organizers of the Seneca Falls Convention. Sentiments means "beliefs" or "convictions."

The Seneca Falls Convention Eight years passed before Stanton and Mott met again. Over afternoon tea at the home of Mott's sister, they decided to send a notice to the local newspaper announcing a women's convention in Seneca Falls, New York. The organized movement for women's rights was about to begin.

On July 19, 1848, nearly 300 people, including 40 men, arrived for the **Seneca Falls Convention**. Many were abolitionists, Quakers, or other reformers. Some were local housewives, farmers, and factory workers.

The convention organizers modeled their proposal for women's rights, the **Declaration of Sentiments,** on the Declaration of Independence. "We hold these truths to be self-evident," the document began, "that all men and women are created equal."

Just as the Declaration of Independence listed King George's acts of tyranny over the colonists, the new declaration listed acts of tyranny by men over women. Man did not let woman vote. He did not give her the right to own property. He did not allow her to practice professions like medicine and law.

Stanton's presentation of the declaration at the convention was her first speech. A few other women also spoke. One of them, Charlotte Woodward, was a 19-year-old factory worker. "Every fibre of my being," she said, "rebelled [against] all the hours that I sat and sewed gloves for a miserable pittance [small amount of money] which, as it was earned, could never be mine."

Debate About the Right to Vote The convention passed resolutions in favor of correcting the injustices listed in the Declaration of Sentiments. Then Stanton proposed that women demand the right to vote. For many, this step was too much. Even Mott cried, "Thou will make us ridiculous! We must go slowly."

At this point, Stanton received powerful support from another participant at the convention: Frederick Douglass. Everyone who believed that black men should have the right to vote, Douglass argued, must also favor giving black women the right to vote. And that meant all women should have this important right. Inspired by Douglass's speech, the convention voted narrowly to approve this last resolution.

Elizabeth Cady Stanton (on the left) and Susan B. Anthony (on the right) worked together in the campaign for women's rights. Stanton wrote powerful speeches, which Anthony traveled from town to town to deliver.

The Legacy of Seneca Falls The Seneca Falls Convention helped to create an organized campaign for women's rights. Sojourner Truth, who would later mesmerize an audience with her "Ain't I a woman?" speech, became an active campaigner in the movement.

Stanton didn't like speaking at conventions, but she could write powerful speeches. She befriended Susan B. Anthony, a reformer with a flair for public speaking. While Stanton stayed in Seneca Falls to raise her children, Anthony traveled from town to town, speaking for women's rights. Of their lifelong teamwork, Stanton said, "I forged the thunderbolts, she fired them."

Slowly, reformers for women's rights made progress. New York gave women control over their property and wages. Massachusetts and Indiana passed more liberal divorce laws. Elizabeth Blackwell started her own hospital, which included a medical school to train other female doctors.

Other reforms, including the right to vote in all states, would take decades to become reality. Of all the women who signed the declaration at Seneca Falls, just one would live to vote for president legally: Charlotte Woodward.

Chapter Summary

In this chapter, you read about the reform movements in the United States from about 1820 to 1850.

The Spirit of Reform Many Americans were inspired by the Second Great Awakening, which emphasized the role of good works in the lives of Christians. Transcendentalist writers like Ralph Waldo Emerson and Henry David Thoreau, who urged people to question society's rules and institutions, also inspired Americans. Some transcendentalists formed communities that attempted to create an ideal society of cooperation.

Prison Reform Dorothea Dix pioneered the reform of prisons and the treatment of people with mental illness. Her efforts led to improvements in state prison systems and the creation of public institutions and hospitals for the mentally ill.

Education Reform Horace Mann led the movement to make education freely available to all. His ideas led many Northern states to establish public schools. Education reform did not improve opportunities for most girls, women, and African Americans, however.

The Movement to End Slavery Inspired in part by religious revivalism, abolitionists worked to end the practice of slavery. Key leaders in the movement included William Lloyd Garrison, Frederick Douglass, Angelina and Sarah Grimke, and Sojourner Truth.

Equal Rights for Women The women's rights movement began with the Seneca Falls Convention and its Declaration of Sentiments. Elizabeth Cady Stanton and Lucretia Mott organized the convention. Susan B. Anthony was another key leader in the movement.

To its founders, Brook Farm was the ideal place for an ideal community. Their goal was to create a rural haven in an increasingly industrialized world.

Brook Farm and the Utopian Dream

In the early 1800s, social reformers were seeking ways to improve American life. Some were inspired by dreams of a perfect society. They formed model, or utopian, communities based on principles they believed would lead to a better world. One of the best known of these social experiments was Brook Farm in Massachusetts.

In April 1841, the writer Nathaniel Hawthorne became a resident at Brook Farm. He had not yet achieved the fame that would come with the publication of his novel *The Scarlet Letter*. But he was well known in Boston literary circles and had friends in the transcendentalist movement. Seeking a place to live and write, he decided to join the Brook Farm community.

Soon after his arrival, Hawthorne got his first taste of farm life. "I have done wonders," he wrote about his first day of farm labor.

> *Before breakfast, I went out to the barn, and began to chop hay for the cattle . . . Then I brought wood and replenished the fires; and finally sat down to breakfast and ate up a huge mound of buckwheat cakes. After breakfast, Mr. Ripley put a four-pronged instrument into my hands, which he gave me to understand was called a pitch-fork; and he and Mr. Farley being armed with similar weapons, we all three commenced a gallant attack upon a heap of manure.*
> —Nathaniel Hawthorne, from a letter to Sophia Peabody, 1841

Hawthorne was not used to this kind of work, but he took to it with relish. He even referred to the manure pile as the "gold mine," in a joking effort to glorify farmwork. It was "a delectable way of life," he wrote. "We get up at half-past six, dine at half-past twelve, and go to bed at nine."

Brook Farm was one of more than a hundred utopian communities that sprang up across the country in the first half of the 1800s. The word *utopian* comes from the 16th-century book *Utopia*, which describes a perfect society on an imaginary island. These communities were all based on ideals and practices aimed at building a new society, free of social ills like poverty, crime, and injustice. Most of the communities had religious foundations. But even those that did not, like Brook Farm, were meant to create a kind of heaven on Earth.

The Origins of Brook Farm

George Ripley, a former minister, founded Brook Farm with his wife, Sophia, and several partners in March 1841. Ripley was concerned about the social problems he saw in urban, industrial America. He wanted to form a rural community where people could live a healthier life, in harmony with nature. He also wanted to bring different social classes together and help the working poor.

In a letter, Ripley expressed his goals for Brook Farm. It would be a place, he said, to "combine the thinker and the worker . . . in the same individual; to guarantee the highest mental freedom, by providing all with labor, adapted to their tastes and talents." He said that he hoped to "prepare a society of liberal, intelligent, and cultivated persons, whose relations with each other would permit a more simple and wholesome life."

In Ripley's vision, residents at Brook Farm would enjoy the benefits of physical labor. But they would also have time to take walks, create art and music, and converse. It would be the perfect blend of work and play. The community would support itself by selling goods produced on the farm. Everyone would share the profits equally.

These ideas reflected the era's reform spirit. But they also arose from the special features of the transcendentalist movement. Transcendentalists believed that people carried the light of God within them. They could experience that light by opening up to the beauties of nature and a simpler life.

Many young people at the time were also filled with the spirit of change, or what they called the "Newness." Freedom was in the air. Young men grew beards and let their hair grow long. They wore floppy hats and loose-fitting clothes. They embraced new ideas, such as vegetarian diets, and new ways of speaking. This sense of freedom was reflected at Brook Farm.

The farm itself was set in beautiful, rolling country just eight miles west of Boston. Its 170 acres were

Brook Farm was a pretty place that charmed nearly everyone who saw it. A visitor painted this picture of the farm in 1848.

dotted with woods, pastures, and meadows. Running through the property was a little brook that gave the farm its name. A two-story farmhouse became the principal residence. Residents called it the "Hive" because it was the hub of activity. There was also a large barn with stalls for cattle and horses. Brook Farm was an ideal setting for a rural retreat.

Keeping a good balance between work and play was important at Brook Farm. Providing food like milk and cheese for the community was essential, but so was taking time for skating and other recreation.

Life on the Farm

Everyone at Brook Farm was expected to work. But they were free to choose the kind of work they did. Women could plow the fields, if they wanted, and men could do housework. All labor was "sacred, when done for a common interest," wrote one resident. Everyone was paid the same, and no one worked more than ten hours a day or six days a week. At the time, that was considered a short workweek.

Most residents seemed to enjoy work on the farm. One young woman, Marianne Dwight, took special pleasure in what she called "fancy work": sewing caps and other clothing for sale in Boston. She believed that the money and skills gained through this work would help aid the cause of women's rights. "We may start other branches of business," she wrote in a letter, "so that all our proceeds may be applied to the elevation of women forever . . . How the whole aspect of society will be changed!"

Residents at the farm did more than work. They also held dances, attended concerts and lectures, and performed in plays. During the winter, they enjoyed snow sports like skating and sledding.

Children attended a school on the farm. The quality of education was excellent, and the school soon attracted students from the surrounding area. The school became the farm's most profitable activity.

By the summer of 1842, 70 people were living at Brook Farm. Most were not permanent residents, however. Students and other temporary lodgers lived there as well. Many visitors also came to the farm, including such noted figures as the writers Ralph Waldo Emerson and Henry David Thoreau.

Other visitors were less notable, and some were downright odd. There were "dreamers and schemers of all sorts," one resident wrote. For example, one visitor claimed he could survive without sleep, until he was caught snoring in the library. Another claimed to live on a diet of raw wheat. But he was found behind the barn one day, eating table scraps set out for the chickens.

Although visitors paid for their stay on the farm, they did not contribute labor. The farm had to add new buildings to house them. This placed a burden on the farm's finances.

The End of the Dream

In fact, Brook Farm's finances had never been solid. In the beginning, Ripley had asked members to invest in the farm, but few had done so. He had also hoped to sell farm products, but few residents had any farming experience. Furthermore, the farm's soils were not very good for growing crops. As a result, the farm was always short of money.

Residents began to drift away from the farm. Some complained of financial difficulties. Others tired of farmwork. Even Nathaniel Hawthorne lost his enthusiasm for farm life. He left after six months, saying he feared his soul might "perish under a dung-heap."

Concerned about the future, in 1844 Ripley and other residents decided to reorganize the farm. They established a new set of principles to promote small industry and put the farm on a firmer footing. They invited new members to join, including a number of craft workers and laborers. They also began construction of a new, much larger building and bought a steam engine to power new machinery. To pay for these improvements, the farm took out new loans.

Before long, however, tensions developed in the community. Some members insisted on holding religious services, which others opposed. Also, some of the new members complained of poor treatment by the original members. Creditors began to demand repayment of loans.

Difficulties were mounting when disaster struck. On March 3, 1846, a fire broke out in the new building and burned it to the ground. After that, more people chose to leave the community. The Ripleys and a handful of others stayed on until the fall of 1847. Then they, too, abandoned the farm.

Despite its short history, Brook Farm was not a total failure. It changed the lives of many of its members and influenced various reform movements, including the abolition and women's rights movements. It also inspired many people with its ideals of workplace equality and a simpler, more sustainable life. Those ideals live on today.

Unlike Brook Farm, the utopian Oneida community of New York developed various communal industries. At this sewing bee, men and women make traveling bags. From their profits, the community members built a large mansion.

Chapter 19

The Worlds of North and South

How was life in the North different from life in the South?

19.1 Introduction

Eli Whitney, a young man from Massachusetts, listened politely to the Georgia planters' complaints. Tobacco prices were low, and rice and indigo prices weren't much better. Cotton grew well, but cleaning the seeds out of cotton fibers was a big problem. A slave picking out seeds by hand could clean only a few pounds a day. At that rate, even using cheap slave labor, there was little profit in raising cotton.

As the planters talked, a solution to their problem began to take shape in Whitney's mind. While growing up in Massachusetts, Whitney had revealed a gift for invention. As a boy, he had invented a machine to manufacture nails more quickly than making them by hand. From nails, he had gone on to hat pins and men's canes. After graduating from college in 1792, Whitney went to Georgia to work as a tutor. Instead of tutoring, however, he became intrigued by the problem of cotton cleaning and, he wrote, "struck out a plan of a Machine in my mind."

The result, as you will read, was an invention that changed life in both the North and the South—but in very different ways. This probably did not surprise Whitney. As a Northerner living in the South, he had already noticed many differences between the two areas of the country.

As American citizens, Northerners and Southerners shared a fierce pride in their country and a faith in democracy. Yet their outlooks and attitudes about many things were quite different. The two areas also differed in their economies, transportation systems, and societies. Between 1800 and 1850, these differences led to sharply conflicting views on many national issues—so much so that, at times, Northerners and Southerners seemed to be living in two separate worlds.

Inventor Eli Whitney's cotton gin would greatly affect life in both the North and the South.

◀ Geography, economy, transportation, and society made life in the North very different from life in the South.

19.2 Geography of the North

From the rocky shores of Maine to the gently rolling plains of Iowa, the North had a variety of climates and natural features. Northerners adapted to these geographical differences by creating different industries and ways of making a living.

Climate All the Northern states experienced four distinct seasons, from freezing winters to hot, humid summers. But the most northerly states, such as Maine and Minnesota, had colder winters and shorter summer growing seasons than states farther south, such as Pennsylvania and Ohio.

Natural Features Different areas of the North had distinctive natural features. The jagged New England coast, for example, had hundreds of bays and inlets that were perfect for use as harbors. Shipbuilding, fishing, and commerce flourished in this area, while towns such as Boston became busy seaports.

Inland from the sea lay a narrow, flat plain with a thin covering of rocky soil. Farming was not easy here. Instead, many people turned to trade and crafts. Others moved west in search of better farmland.

New England's hills rose sharply above V-shaped valleys carved by steep streams. The hillsides offered barely enough land for small farms, but they were covered with thick forests of spruce and fir. New Englanders found that they could make money by harvesting timber. The wood was used for shipbuilding and in trade with other countries.

Farther south in New York, Pennsylvania, and New Jersey, broad rivers like the Hudson and the Delaware had deposited rich soil over the plains. People living in these areas supported themselves by farming.

Across the Appalachian Mountains lay the Central Plains, a large, forested region drained by the Ohio and Mississippi rivers. The Central Plains boast some of the best agricultural soil in the world. From Ohio to Illinois, settlers cleared the forests to make way for farms.

Industrious Northerners were thus changing the landscape. One result was **deforestation,** or the clearing of forests. By 1850, Americans had cleared about 177,000 square miles of dense forest. And with the growth of industry, the demand for coal and other minerals led to a big increase in mining after about 1820, especially in Pennsylvania.

deforestation the clearing away of forests

This photograph shows a section of New England coastline. What geographic features can you identify?

19.3 Geography of the South

The South extended from Maryland south to Florida and from the Atlantic Coast west to Louisiana and Texas. Climate and natural features encouraged Southerners to base their way of life on agriculture.

This photograph shows a Southern waterway. What geographic features can you identify?

Climate Compared to the North, the Southern states enjoyed mild winters and long, hot, humid summers. Plentiful rainfall and long growing seasons made this a perfect place for raising warm-weather crops that would have withered and died farther north.

Natural Features Wide coastal plains edged the southern shoreline from Chesapeake Bay to the Gulf of Mexico. These fertile lowlands stretched inland for as much as 300 miles in parts of the South.

Along the coast, the plains were dotted with swamps and marshes. These damp lowlands were ideal for growing rice and sugarcane, which thrived in warm, soggy soil. Indigo was grown on the dry land above the swamps, and tobacco and corn were farmed farther inland. A visitor to this area noted that "the Planters by the richness of the Soil, live [in] the most easie and pleasant Manner of any People I have ever met with."

Above the plains rose the Appalachians. Settlers who ventured into this rugged backcountry carved farms and orchards out of rolling hills and mountain hollows. Some backcountry farmers worked on land so steep that it was joked that they kept falling out of their cornfields.

Although most people in the South were farmers, Southerners used natural resources in other ways as well. In North Carolina, they harvested thick pine forests for lumber. From Chesapeake Bay in Virginia and Maryland, they gathered fish, oysters, and crabs.

An especially important feature of the South was its broad, flat rivers. Many of the South's earliest towns were built at the mouths of rivers. As people moved away from the coast, they followed the rivers inland, building their homes and farms alongside these water highways. Oceangoing ships could even sail up Southern rivers to conduct business right at a planter's private dock. Here, the ships were loaded with tobacco or other cash crops for sale in the Caribbean or Europe.

agrarian a person who favors an agricultural way of life and government policies that support agricultural interests

plantation a large area of privately owned land where crops were grown through the labor of workers who lived on the land

cotton gin a hand-operated machine that cleans seeds and other unwanted material from cotton

19.4 Economy of the South

The South's economy was based on agriculture. Most white Southerners were **agrarians** who favored a way of life based on farming. This was especially true of rich **plantation** owners, who did not have to do the hard work of growing crops themselves.

Although most white Southerners worked their own small farms, plantation owners used slaves to grow such cash crops as tobacco, rice, sugarcane, and indigo. By the early 1790s, however, the use of slaves had begun to decline. Europeans were unwilling to pay high prices for tobacco and rice, which they could purchase more cheaply from other British colonies. Cotton was a promising crop, but growers who experimented with it had a hard time making a profit. Until some way was found to clean the seeds out of its fiber easily, cotton was of little value. Discouraged planters were buying fewer slaves, and even letting some go free.

In 1793, a young Yale graduate named Eli Whitney took a job tutoring children on a Georgia plantation. There, he saw his first cotton boll. Observing the way cotton was cleaned by hand, Whitney had an idea. "If a machine could be invented which would clean the Cotton with expedition [speed]," he wrote his father, "it would be a great thing . . . to the Country."

Whitney set to work. Six months later, he had a working machine that would change agriculture in the South.

The Impact of the Cotton Gin

Whitney's "cotton engine," called the **cotton gin** for short, was a simple machine that used rotating combs to separate cotton fiber from its seeds. Using a cotton gin, a single worker could clean as much cotton as 50 laborers working **manually,** or by hand.

Across the South, planters began growing cotton. Within ten years, cotton was the South's most important crop. By 1860, sales of cotton overseas earned more than all other U.S. exports combined.

The cotton gin, invented in 1793, made the process of separating cotton fiber from the seeds quicker and easier. As a result, cotton quickly became the most important crop in the South.

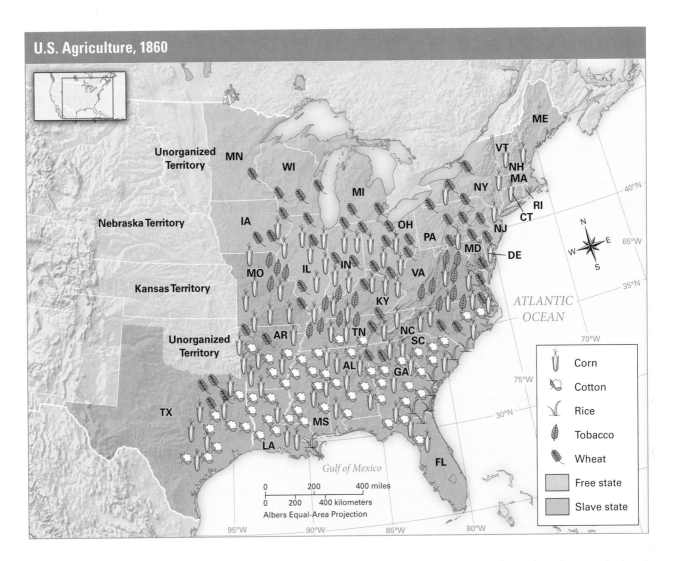

U.S. Agriculture, 1860

Legend:
- Corn
- Cotton
- Rice
- Tobacco
- Wheat
- Free state
- Slave state

Expanding Demand for Land and Slaves Raising cotton in the same fields year after year soon wore out the soil. In search of fresh, fertile soil, cotton planters pushed west. By 1850, cotton plantations stretched from the Atlantic Coast to Texas.

Whitney had hoped his invention would lighten the work of slaves. Instead, it made slavery more important to the South than ever. As cotton spread westward, slavery followed. Between 1790 and 1850, the number of slaves in the South rose from 500,000 to more than 3 million.

With many white Southerners putting money into land and slaves, the South had little interest in building factories. As a result, wrote an Alabama newspaper, "We purchase all our luxuries and necessities from the North . . . the slaveholder dresses in Northern goods, rides in a Northern saddle, sports his Northern carriage, reads Northern books. In Northern vessels his products are carried to market."

One successful Southern factory was the Tredegar Iron Works in Richmond, Virginia. Using mostly slave labor, the factory made ammunition and weapons for the U.S. army, as well as steam engines, rails, and locomotives. But the vast majority of white Southerners made their living off the land.

This map shows the primary agricultural products of the United States in 1860. Which crops were primarily grown in the North? Which crops were primarily grown in the South?

Industrial Revolution the dramatic change in economies and cultures brought about by the use of machines to do work formerly done by hand

industrialist a person whose wealth comes from the ownership of industrial businesses and who favors government policies that support industry

The fast-flowing rivers of the North provided the power source for textile mills, like the one pictured here.

19.5 Economy of the North

While the cotton gin made cotton the South's dominant crop, other types of machines were causing changes in the North. The people and the ideas behind these machines were part of the **Industrial Revolution**, which began in England in the late 1700s and spread to the United States and the rest of the world by the early 1800s. During the Industrial Revolution, people shifted from making things and doing work by hand to making things and doing work with machines. It created a new class of workers as well as a new class of **industrialists**, owners of large factories and other businesses based on manufacturing.

The Growth of Industry in the North One of the people who helped bring the Industrial Revolution to the United States was Francis Cabot Lowell, a Boston business owner. In 1810, Lowell visited England. There he saw how textile mill owners were using machines to spin cotton into thread and weave the thread into cloth. To power these devices, they used fast-moving streams to turn a wheel, which in turn supplied energy to the machinery.

Lowell memorized the design of the British machines. When he returned to Massachusetts, he built even better ones. By 1815, he and his partners had built one of the first American textile factories, along the Merrimack River outside Boston. This factory combined spinning and weaving machinery in the same building. One observer marveled that Lowell's mill "took your bale of cotton in at one end and gave out yards of cloth at the other, after goodness knows what digestive process."

To run his machinery, Lowell hired young women, who jumped at the chance to earn cash wages. The "Lowell girls" toiled 12 to 15 hours each day, with only Sundays off. Soon textile mills were springing up all along other Northern rivers.

By the 1830s, inventors in both the United States and Europe had learned to use steam engines to power machinery. With steam engines, businesspeople could build factories anywhere, not just along rivers. Meanwhile, the inventive Eli Whitney showed manufacturers how they could assemble products even more cheaply by making them from identical, interchangeable parts.

New inventions and manufacturing methods made goods cheaper and more plentiful. But these **innovations** also shifted work from skilled craftspeople to less-skilled laborers. When Elias Howe developed the sewing machine in 1846, for example, skilled seamstresses could not compete. Some took jobs in garment factories, but they earned much less money working the sewing machines than they had sewing by hand.

For Northern industrialists, the new machines and production methods were a source of great wealth. Factory owners tended to favor a strong national government that could promote improvements in manufacturing, trade, and transportation. Southern agrarians, however, looked down on the newly rich industrialists and the laborers who worked for them. Proud Southerners called factory workers "wage slaves." But they also worried that Northern interests might grow too powerful and threaten the South's way of life.

Factories such as this one produced more goods and made them more affordable. However, they also put many skilled craftspeople out of work.

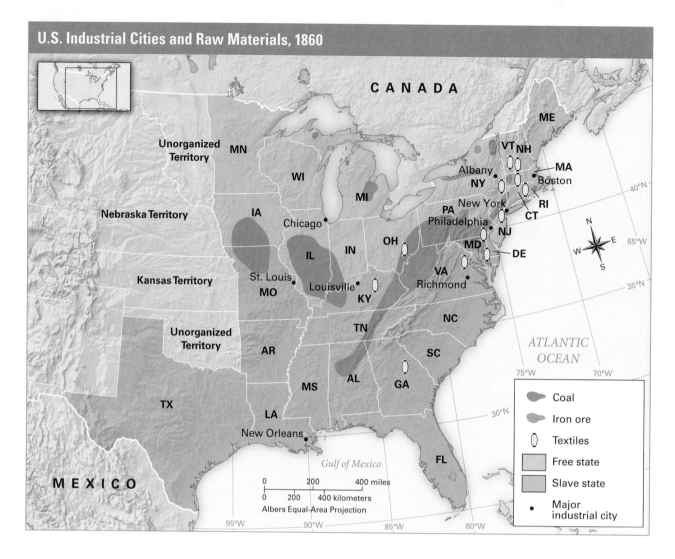

U.S. Industrial Cities and Raw Materials, 1860

Coal
Iron ore
Textiles
Free state
Slave state
Major industrial city

This map shows industries and raw materials in the United States in 1860. What relationship do you see between where coal and iron ore are found and where industries are primarily located?

Machines Make Agriculture More Efficient The Industrial Revolution had effects on farming as well. New machines increased the rate at which agricultural goods could be produced. In 1831, Virginia farmer Cyrus McCormick built a working model of "a right smart" machine called a reaper. A reaper could cut 28 times more grain than a single man using a scythe, which is a hand tool with a long, curved blade.

In 1847, McCormick built a reaper factory in Chicago, Illinois. Using interchangeable parts, his factory was soon producing several thousand reapers a year.

Around the same time, John Deere invented the steel-tipped plow. This innovation **drastically** reduced the amount of labor needed to plow a field. By making it easier to plant and harvest large quantities of wheat, inventions like the steel-tipped plow and the reaper helped transform the Central Plains into America's "bread basket."

Thanks to the Industrial Revolution, the Northern economy grew rapidly after 1800. By 1860, the value of manufacturing in the North was ten times greater than in the South.

19.6 Transportation in the North

Factory owners needed fast, inexpensive ways to deliver their goods to distant customers. South Carolina congressman John C. Calhoun had a solution. "Let us bind the republic together," he said, "with a perfect system of roads and canals." Calhoun called such projects **internal** improvements.

Building Better Roads In the early 1800s, most American roads were rutted boneshakers. In 1806, Congress funded the construction of a National Road across the Appalachian Mountains. The purpose of this highway was to connect the new western states with the East. With its smooth gravel surface, the National Road was a joy to travel.

As popular as the National Road was, in 1816 President James Monroe vetoed a bill that would have given states money to build more roads. Monroe argued that spending federal money for a state's internal improvements was unconstitutional.

Fast Ships and Canals Even with better roads, river travel was still faster and cheaper than travel by land. But moving upstream against a river's current was hard work. To solve this problem, inventors in both the United States and Europe experimented with boats powered by steam engines.

In 1807, Robert Fulton showed that steamboats were practical by racing the steamboat *Clermont* upstream on New York's Hudson River. Said Fulton, "I overtook many boats and passed them as if they had been at anchor." A Dutchman watching the strange craft from the shore shouted, "The devil is on his way up-river with a sawmill on a boat!" By the 1820s, smoke-belching steamboats were chugging up and down major rivers and across the Great Lakes.

Many new and faster forms of transportation were put to use in the North. How many of them can you identify in this painting?

Museum of Art, Rhode Island School of Design/Mary B. Jackson Fund

Of course, rivers weren't always located where people needed them. In 1817, the state of New York hired engineers and workers to build a 363-mile canal from the Hudson River to Lake Erie. The Erie Canal provided the first all-water link between farms on the Central Plains and East Coast cities. It was so successful that other states built canals as well.

Overseas traders also needed faster ways to travel. Sailing ships sometimes took so long to cross the Pacific Ocean that the goods they carried spoiled. In the 1840s, sleek clipper ships were introduced that cut ocean travel time in half. The clipper ships led to increased Northern trade with foreign ports around the world.

Traveling by Rail The future of transportation, however, lay not on water, but on rails. Inspired by the success of steamboats, inventors developed steam-powered locomotives. These trains traveled faster than steamboats and could go wherever tracks could be laid—even across mountains.

So many railroad companies were laying tracks that, by the 1840s, railroads were the North's biggest business. By 1860, more than 20,000 miles of rail linked Northern factories to cities hundreds of miles away.

This map shows the locations of railroads in 1860. Notice that the railroad lines in the North connect to one another more than those in the South. How might this difference have affected the growth of trade and industry in the two areas?

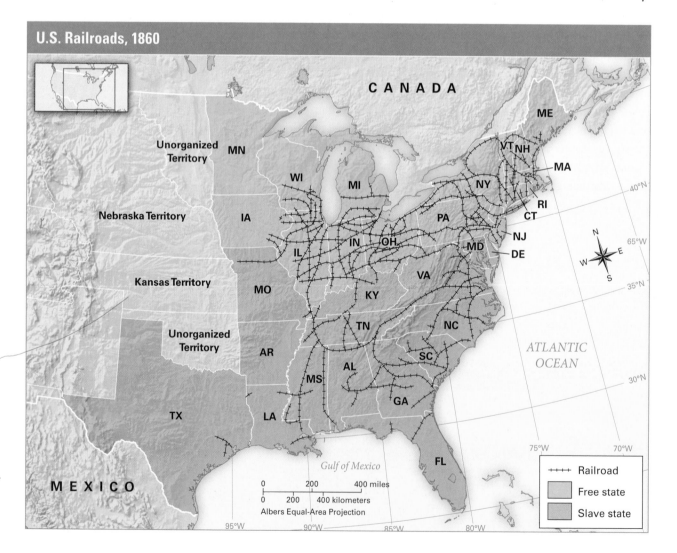

U.S. Railroads, 1860

19.7 Transportation in the South

Most of the rail lines in the United States were in the North. In the South, people and goods continued to move on rivers. The slow current and broad channels of Southern rivers made water travel easy and relatively cheap.

Cotton was the most important Southern product shipped by water. On plantation docks, slaves loaded cotton bales directly onto steam-powered riverboats. The riverboats then traveled hundreds of miles downstream to such port cities as Savannah, Georgia, or Mobile, Alabama. West of the Appalachians, most cotton moved down the Mississippi River, the largest of all the Southern waterways. The cotton boom made New Orleans, the port at the mouth of the Mississippi, one of the South's few big cities. Once the cotton reached the sea, it was loaded onto sailing ships headed for ports in England or the North.

Because river travel was the South's main form of transportation, most Southern towns and cities sprang up along waterways. With little need for roads or canals to connect these settlements, Southerners opposed bills in Congress that would use federal funds for internal improvements. Such projects, they believed, would benefit the North far more than the South.

Some railroads were built in the South, including lines that helped Southern farmers ship their products to the North. Southerners were proud of the fact that the iron rails for many of the area's railroads came from Virginia's Tredegar Iron Works. Still, in 1860 the South had just 10,000 miles of rail, compared with over 20,000 miles in the North.

This photograph shows products being loaded onto steam-powered riverboats. What geographic feature of the South made riverboats the most practical way to transport goods?

The Granger Collection, New York

Wealthy Southern planters modeled their homes and lives on European nobility. Their large mansions had tall columns and fancy gardens. Most Southern whites, however, owned or worked on small farms, with few of the luxuries enjoyed by the rich.

19.8 Society in the South

For the most part, the South was not greatly affected by the Jacksonian spirit of equality and opportunity or the reform movements of the mid-1800s. Many Southerners in 1860 still measured wealth in terms of land and slaves. The result was a rigid social structure with a few rich plantation owners at the top, white farmers and workers in the middle, and African Americans—mostly enslaved—at the bottom.

Slavery deeply affected the lives of all Southerners, black and white. As long as the slave economy could be preserved, the South had little incentive to make progress economically or culturally. Even religion was affected. Southern church leaders defended the practice—taking a position that divided them from many churches in the North, whose leaders taught that slavery was un-Christian. In the words of one historian, "The South grew, but it did not develop."

White Southerners A small group of wealthy plantation owners dominated the economy and politics of the South. They enjoyed a leisurely way of life, filled with parties and social visits. While their sons often went to colleges and universities, their daughters received little education. Instead, girls were brought up to be wives and hostesses.

Most white families owned some land, but only about one in four owned even one slave. The majority of white families worked their own fields and made most of what they needed themselves. About 10 percent of whites were too poor to own any land. They rented rugged mountain or forest land and paid the rent with the crops they raised. Since public schools were few and often inferior to those in the North, many white children were illiterate.

African Americans in the South A small minority of the African Americans in the South were free blacks. Free blacks were often forced to wear special badges, pay extra taxes, and live separately from whites. Most lived in towns and cities, where they found jobs as skilled craftspeople, servants, or laborers.

The great majority of African Americans in the South were slaves. Some worked as cooks, carpenters, blacksmiths, house servants, or nursemaids. But most were field hands who labored from dawn until past dusk.

19.9 Society in the North

As in the South, most people in the North were neither wealthy nor powerful. By 1860, about seven in ten Northerners still lived on farms. But more and more Northerners were moving to towns and cities. Between 1800 and 1850, the number of cities with populations of at least 2,500 had increased from 33 to 237. Except for a few cities around the Great Lakes, such as Chicago and Detroit, nearly all of the 50 largest urban areas were in the Northeast. Only 12 were in the slave states of the South. And Northern cities were growing rapidly. Between 1840 and 1860, the populations of New York, Philadelphia, and Boston nearly tripled. By 1860, more than a million people lived in New York.

New or old, Northern cities often lacked sewers and paved streets. In dirty and crowded neighborhoods, diseases spread rapidly. "The streets are filthy," wrote one observer about New York City, "and the stranger is not a little surprised to meet the hogs walking about in them, for the purpose of devouring the vegetables and offal [trash] thrown into the gutter."

African Americans in the North After the American Revolution, all of the Northern states had taken steps to end slavery. Although blacks in the North were free, they were not treated as equal to whites. In most states, they could not vote, hold office, serve on juries, or attend white churches and schools.

In 1860, most Northerners still lived on farms, but more and more people were moving to towns and cities like this one. These cities often sprang up near factories and railroad hubs.

The Granger Collection, New York

The Granger Collection, New York

This engraving shows Irish immigrants aboard a ship bound for the United States in 1850. Most Irish immigrants settled in northeastern cities.

African Americans responded by forming their own churches and starting their own businesses. Because few employers would give them skilled jobs, African Americans often worked as laborers or servants.

Immigrants Arrive in the North Between 1845 and 1860, four million **immigrants**—most of them from Ireland and Germany— swelled the North's growing population. In Ireland, a potato famine from 1845 to 1849 drove hundreds of thousands of families to the United States. In the German states, failed revolutions sent people fleeing overseas. Some immigrants had enough money to buy land and farm. But most settled in cities, where they found jobs in mills and factories.

Some Americans resented the newcomers, especially the Irish. Irish immigrants faced **hostility** because they were Roman Catholic. The United States at the time was mostly Protestant. In addition, many Irish immigrants were poor. Because they would accept very low wages, they were thought to take jobs away from native-born workers. German immigrants did not experience the same hostility that Irish immigrants endured. Most German immigrants were Protestant and middle class.

Between 1820 and 1860, more than one-third of all U.S. immigrants came from Ireland. More than 1 million Irish immigrants came to the United States between 1846 and 1855. Too poor to travel, most of them settled in northeastern cities, including New York, Boston, and Philadelphia.

immigrant a person who moves from one country to another. Such a movement is called immigration.

In this chapter, you learned how the North and the South developed differently from each other in the first half of the 1800s.

Geography Geography was one reason why Northerners and Southerners developed different ways of life. In the North, physical features such as harbors encouraged the growth of shipbuilding, fishing, and commerce. The land and climate supported the harvesting of timber and such crops as corn and wheat. In the South, the climate and land was ideal for warm-weather crops like cotton, rice, and sugarcane.

Economy In contrast to the variety of trades and businesses in the North, the South depended primarily on agriculture. Although only a minority of white Southerners owned slaves, much of the South's economy depended on slave labor. In the North, the new inventions of the Industrial Revolution led to the development of mills and factories. Increasing numbers of people went to work as wage earners.

Transportation Steamboats and railroads improved transportation for Northerners, making it easier for them to travel and to ship goods over long distances. In the South, however, people continued to travel by river, and rail lines were fewer.

Society In the South, the wealthy few enjoyed great influence and power. But even the poorest whites ranked above African Americans, whether free or slave. The North, too, had its wealthy class. But farmers and laborers alike believed they could create comfortable lives for their families through hard work.

The Granger Collection, New York

Look at these images of the North (left) and the South (right). How many features of geography, economy, transportation, and society can you identify?

The Mill Girls of Lowell

In the first half of the 1800s, factory work gave girls and young women a taste of city life. Many of these young women came from farms to work in New England's textile mills. They wanted to earn money. They also wanted to find adventure in the cities that were growing up around the factories.

Row after row of looms line the huge wooden floor of a red-brick factory building. Long pulleys connect the looms to the ceiling and their power source. During a workday, hundreds of machines are running at one time. The racket is deafening. Clouds of cotton dust foul the air. The factory has huge glass windows, but they are kept closed so the air stays humid. That keeps the threads from breaking as machines turn them into cloth.

It is 1850. Over a mile of five- and six-story red-brick buildings line the banks of the Merrimack River in Lowell, Massachusetts. Six miles of canals run waterwheels for the 40 mill buildings. In the buildings, the waterwheels power 10,000 looms and 320,000 spindles. More than 10,000 people work in the factories of the young city. Every week, Lowell's mills produce nearly a million yards—or 568 miles—of cloth.

The cloth is made of cotton. The cotton has traveled hundreds of miles by ship or rail from the South. Northern textile manufacturers, including those who own the factories in Lowell, get virtually all their cotton from the South, where African American slaves have planted, tended, harvested, and cleaned it.

On the factory floor, workers dart quickly back and forth between machines, so they can tend more than one at a time. Most of the workers are girls and women. Many have left family farms across New England to make a new life in Lowell and other cities that had sprouted up along New England's rivers.

Factory work was difficult, but great rewards waited for the women who worked in the mills. Money, culture, and independence changed the lives of countless farm girls who, for a while at least, became factory workers.

The Mill-Girl Workforce

In big, bold letters, the recruiting notice announced jobs for 75 young women in the cotton mills in Lowell and Chicopee, Massachusetts. The women would commit to work for a year. In exchange, they would earn a dollar a week, paid in cash every month.

Today, the promise of a factory job might not seem so inviting, but it was quite appealing in the 1830s. The factories had an almost magnetic pull for many young women, especially those who had been raised on

Water from rivers like the Merrimack powered the machinery of the textile mills. At the mills, machines and workers turned cotton from the South into thread and wove the thread into cloth.

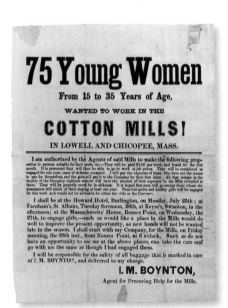

One Lowell mill girl explained why young women responded to recruiting posters: "Girls come here from the country of their own free will, because they can earn more money, and because they wish to see and know more of the world."

New England farms. If they stayed on the farms, most of them could count on marrying, having children, and working on the farm their whole lives. And farming in New England challenged even the hardiest workers. The population was growing, making land scarce. The soil was rocky, and the growing season was short. More and more people were looking elsewhere for work—to crafts, to the West, or to the cities.

Answering the call of the factory recruiter promised something new, different, and profitable. One young woman, Sally Rice, left her family in Vermont, eventually to work in a factory in Connecticut. In a letter written in 1839, she explained her reasons for leaving home.

I can never be happy there in among so many mountains . . . I am [al]most 19 years old. I must of course have something of my own before many years have passed over my head. And where is that something coming from if I go home and earn nothing . . . You may think me unkind but how can you blame me for wanting to stay here. I have but one life to live and I want to enjoy myself as well as I can while I live.

Many other women shared Sally Rice's feelings, and like her, they went to work in the factories.

While most of the women who first staffed the factories came from farms, some girls came for other reasons. Harriet Hanson's mother moved to Lowell from Boston with her four small children after her husband died. Harriet started working at the mills when she was ten years old. After Lucy Larcom's mother was widowed, she moved the family to Lowell from a nearby town. Lucy started working in a factory when she was 11.

At the very least, life in the mills offered girls and women survival. At the most, it promised a chance to have something of their own, including adventure, before they settled down and married.

This Lowell mill girl was photographed at her loom in 1850. On 10,000 looms like this one, mill workers produced more than 500 miles of cloth every week.

A Mill Girl's Life

In the 1830s, it would not have been considered proper for a young woman to move to a city alone, without an adult chaperone. The mill owners had to find a way to make the move to factory life feel safe for their workers and to reassure the workers' parents. They also wanted to make sure the workers were well disciplined so that they would be efficient.

For those reasons, the manufacturing companies built boarding houses. The young women lived there under the protective watch of an older woman. They ate their meals at the boarding house, slept there, and often became friends with other boarders. One Lowell mill worker wrote to her father in New Hampshire that "I have a very good boarding place . . . The girls are all kind and obliging. The girls that I room with are all from Vermont and good girls too."

The mill girls had opportunities in Lowell that they would never have had on the farm. They could attend lectures and plays, and join literary discussion groups and libraries. And their wages allowed them to shop. One woman whose sister worked in Lowell described how the women who went to the factories came home changed: "They went in their plain, country-made clothes, and after working several months, would come home for a visit, or perhaps to be married, in their tasteful city dresses and with more money in their pockets than they had ever owned before."

Young women in Lowell even started their own magazine, *The Lowell Offering*. From 1840 to 1845, the girls wrote essays, stories, and poems. Some of their writing told about how much they liked their lives in Lowell. Other pieces told stories about women coming to work in the mills so they could help their families out of financial problems. But when historians looked at other sources—like bank accounts—they discovered that most of the mill girls were not helping their families at all. Instead, they were saving money to use later for school, clothes, or a dowry (money they would bring to a marriage).

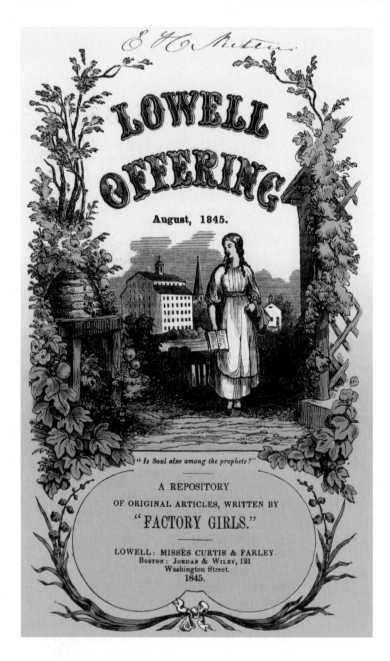

A monthly magazine, *The Lowell Offering,* published the writings of the "factory girls." The writers told of their lives and the working conditions in Lowell.

" Is Saul also among the prophets ?"

A REPOSITORY
OF ORIGINAL ARTICLES, WRITTEN BY
"FACTORY GIRLS."

LOWELL: MISSES CURTIS & FARLEY.
BOSTON: JORDAN & WILEY, 121
Washington Street.
1845.

Hard Work at the Mills

The mill girls enjoyed the opportunities they had in Lowell and other mill towns. But they had to work very hard in the factories to support themselves.

Workdays were long and ruled by the bell. In the summer, the wake-up bell rang at 4:30 A.M. Twenty minutes later, the girls reported to work. They had a half-hour break for breakfast and another for dinner. (Dinner was the afternoon meal). They did not finish their workday until 7 P.M.

Not only were the workdays long, but the work was hard. Harriet Hanson described her work as a doffer. Doffers were the youngest girls. Their job was to take bobbins that had filled with yarn off the machines and replace them with empty ones. She remembered her job many years later:

> *I can see myself now, racing down the alley, between the spinning-frames, carrying in front of me a bobbin-box bigger than I was. [Doffers] had to be very swift in their movements, so as not to keep the spinning-frames stopped long.*
>
> —Harriet H. Robinson, *Loom & Spindle or Life Among the Early Mill Girls,* 1898

Lucy Larcom described being overwhelmed by a machine she was supposed to tend: "It had to be watched in a dozen directions every minute," she wrote. "I felt as if the half-live creature with its great, groaning joints, and whizzing fan, was aware of my incapacity to manage it."

The mill work got more demanding for women over time. Company owners wanted to make more money, so they increased the amount of work the women had to do and lowered their wages.

The mill girls did not simply accept such changes. Several times, they went out on strike to protest pay cuts and increases in the fees they paid to live in the boarding houses. The women described themselves as "daughters of freemen." Their ancestors had fought to be free from English rule, they said. They believed that the factory owners' actions interfered with their freedom, and so they rebelled.

Over time, mill girls began to leave the factories, finding better opportunities elsewhere. By the 1850s, as immigrants began filling the mill jobs, the era of the mill girls was coming to a close.

Proud of their work, mill girls often posed for photographs with the tools of their trade. These women are holding the bobbins they use to weave cloth.

Shown here is a work schedule from 1853. The mill girls sang a song to protest pay cuts and long hours: "Oh! Isn't it a pity, such a pretty girl as I / Should be sent to the factory to pine away and die? / Oh! I cannot be a slave, I will not be a slave / For I'm so fond of liberty / That I cannot be a slave."

Chapter 20

African Americans in the Mid-1800s

How did African Americans face slavery and discrimination in the mid-1800s?

20.1 Introduction

By 1850, the population of the United States had grown to just over 23 million. This figure included 3.6 million African Americans. The great majority of African Americans lived in slavery. Harriet Powers, the woman who created the quilt on the opposite page, was one of them.

Powers was born into slavery in Georgia in 1837. Like many slaves, she grew up hearing Bible stories. In her quilts, she used animals and figures from Africa and the United States to illustrate those stories, along with scenes from her life. Hidden in her images were messages of hope and freedom for slaves.

Not all African Americans were slaves. By mid-century, there were about half a million free blacks as well. Many were former slaves who had escaped to freedom.

Whether African Americans lived in slavery or freedom, discrimination (unequal treatment) shaped their lives. Throughout the country, whites looked down on blacks. Whites ignored the contributions blacks made to American life. They thought of the United States as "their country." Such racist thinking later prompted African American scholar and **reformer** W. E. B. Du Bois to ask,

> *Your country? How came it to be yours? Before the Pilgrims landed we were here. Here we brought you our three gifts and mingled them with yours; a gift of story and song, soft, stirring melody in an . . . unmelodious land; the gift of sweat and brawn [physical strength] to beat back the wilderness . . . and lay the foundations of this vast economic empire . . . the third, a gift of the Spirit.*

In this chapter, you will explore how African Americans faced and endured discrimination and slavery in the mid-1800s. You will also learn more about the gifts that African Americans brought to America.

Harriet Powers's quilts are considered the best examples of 1800s Southern quilting. Two of her quilts survive. They are preserved in museums in Washington, D.C., and Boston, Massachusetts. Above is a detail from the quilt at left.

◀ Quilt created by Harriet Powers (top); slaves and their overseer in a Mississippi cotton field (bottom)

Free African Americans usually held low-paying jobs. The barber pictured here is one example.

racism the belief that one race is superior to another

20.2 North and South, Slave and Free

The experiences of African Americans in the mid-1800s depended on where they lived and whether they lived in slavery or freedom. Former slave Frederick Douglass toured the North talking to white audiences about slavery. To him, the biggest difference between slaves and free blacks was their legal status. Free blacks had some rights by law. Slaves did not. Whether free or slave, however, the lives of African Americans were shaped by **racism,** the belief that one race is superior to another.

Slaves' Legal Status The law defined slaves as property. Legally, slaveholders could do almost anything with their slaves. They could buy and sell slaves. They could leave slaves to their children or heirs. They could give slaves away to settle a bet. But in many states, they could not set slaves free.

As property, slaves had none of the rights that free people took for granted. "In law, the slave has no wife, no children, no country, no home," Douglass said. "He can own nothing, possess nothing, acquire nothing."

Rural and Urban Slaves Most slaves worked on farms and plantations across the South. By 1860, there were also about 70,000 slaves living in towns and cities. Most were hired out, or sent to work in factories, mills, or workshops. The wages they earned belonged to their owners. Often, urban slaves were allowed to "live out" on their own, rather than under the watchful eyes of their owners. Because of such freedom, observed Douglass, "A city slave is almost a freeman, compared with a slave on the plantation."

Free Blacks in the South About half of all free African Americans lived in the South. Most worked as laborers, craftspeople, or household servants in towns and cities.

Many white Southerners viewed free blacks as a dangerous group that had to be controlled so that, in the words of South Carolina slaveholders, they would not create "discontent among our slaves." Free blacks were forbidden to own guns. They could not travel freely from town to town or state to state. Blacks were not allowed to work at certain jobs. Such restrictions led Douglass to conclude, "No colored man is really free in a slaveholding state."

Free Blacks in the North African Americans in the North lived freer lives. But blacks experienced **discrimination,** or unequal treatment, everywhere they turned. In many states, African Americans were denied the right to vote. They had trouble finding good jobs. In the 1850s, some 87 percent of free blacks in New York held low-paying jobs. "Why should I strive hard?" asked one young African American. "What are my prospects? . . . No one will employ me; white boys won't work with me."

In addition to unequal treatment, policies of **segregation** separated blacks from whites in nearly all public places. Black children were often denied entry into public schools. Those states that did educate black children set up separate schools for that purpose. A New Yorker observed around 1860,

> *Even the noblest black is denied that which is free to the vilest [worst] white. The omnibus, the [railroad] car, the ballot-box, the jury box, the halls of legislation, the army, the public lands, the school, the church, the lecture room, the social circle, the [restaurant] table, are all either absolutely or virtually denied to him.*

Douglass discovered how deeply rooted this racism was when he tried to join a church in New Bedford, Massachusetts, and was turned away. "I tried all the other churches in New Bedford with the same result," he wrote.

African Americans responded to discrimination by organizing to help themselves. In 1816, Richard Allen, a former slave, became the first bishop of the African Methodist Episcopal Church. The AME, which still exists today, quickly became a center of African American life. Allen also created organizations to improve the lives of blacks, such as the African Society for the Education of Youth.

Other Northern blacks started their own schools, churches, and self-help organizations. In 1853, free blacks formed the National Council of Colored People to protest the unequal treatment they received. Such treatment, the council declared, "would humble the proudest, crush the energies of the strongest, and retard the progress of the swiftest." That blacks were neither humbled nor crushed by prejudice and discrimination was evidence of their courage and spirit.

discrimination unequal treatment based on a person's race, gender, religion, place of birth, or other arbitrary characteristic

segregation the social separation of groups of people, especially by race

Lemuel Haynes, shown here preaching from a pulpit, fought at Lexington during the Revolutionary War. He was the first black minister of a white congregation.

The Granger Collection, New York

20.3 The Economics of Slavery

Only wealthier planters could afford to buy slaves. The great majority of white Southerners did not own slaves. Why, then, did the South remain so loyal to slavery? Part of the answer to that question lies in the growth of the Southern economy after the invention of the cotton gin in 1793.

The cotton gin made cotton a hugely profitable cash crop in the South. In 1790, the South produced just 3,000 bales of cotton. By the 1850s, production had soared to more than 4 million bales a year. Cotton brought new wealth to the South. Robert Fogel, a historian who has studied the economics of slavery, wrote,

> If we treat the North and South as separate nations . . . the South would stand as the fourth most prosperous nation of the world in 1860 . . . more prosperous than France, Germany, Denmark, or any of the countries in Europe except England.

Whether they owned slaves or not, white Southerners understood that their economy depended on cotton. They also knew that cotton planters depended on slave labor to grow their profitable crop. For planters with few or no slaves, however, the prospect of owning slaves became less likely as the demand for, and the price of, slaves rose.

The South's economy depended upon slave labor to grow and harvest cotton, the South's most valuable export.

High prices were both good and bad for the men and women trapped in slavery. As prices went up, slaves became more valuable to their owners. This may have encouraged slaveholders to take better care of their workers. At the same time, the rising value of their slaves made slaveholders less willing to listen to talk of ending slavery. In their eyes, freeing their slaves could only mean one thing: utter financial ruin.

The map shows the increase in cotton production from the early to the mid-1800s. The graph shows that by 1860, the nation's slave population was concentrated in the South. Northern states had outlawed slavery by this time.

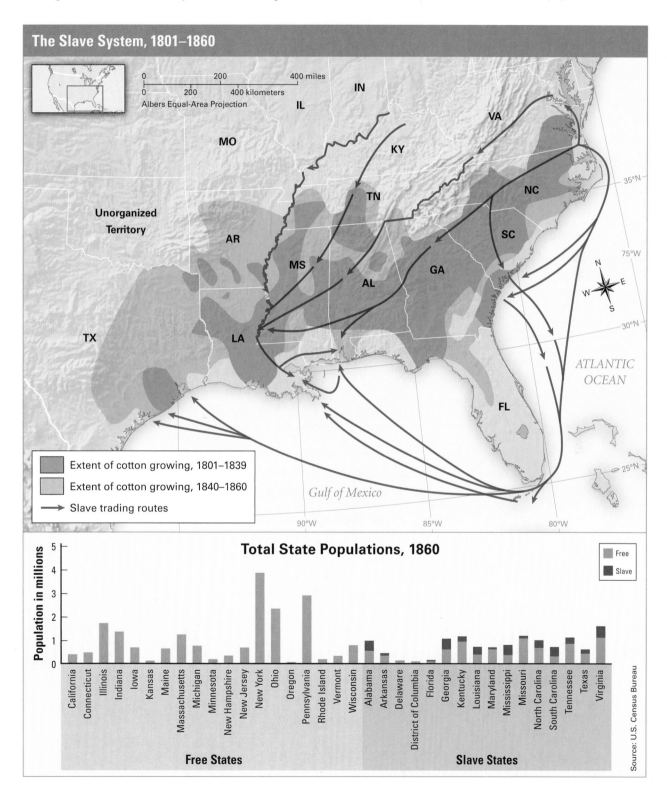

The Slave System, 1801–1860

200 miles / 400 miles
200 kilometers / 400 kilometers
Albers Equal-Area Projection

IN
IL
MO
VA
KY
35°N
TN
NC
Unorganized Territory
SC
AR
75°W
MS
GA
AL
TX
30°N
LA
ATLANTIC OCEAN
25°N
FL
Gulf of Mexico

Extent of cotton growing, 1801–1839
Extent of cotton growing, 1840–1860
Slave trading routes

90°W   85°W   80°W

Total State Populations, 1860

Population in millions

Free
Slave

Free States
California, Connecticut, Illinois, Indiana, Iowa, Kansas, Maine, Massachusetts, Michigan, Minnesota, New Hampshire, New Jersey, New York, Ohio, Oregon, Pennsylvania, Rhode Island, Vermont, Wisconsin

Slave States
Alabama, Arkansas, Delaware, District of Columbia, Florida, Georgia, Kentucky, Louisiana, Maryland, Mississippi, Missouri, North Carolina, South Carolina, Tennessee, Texas, Virginia

Source: U.S. Census Bureau

Slaves who worked as field hands labored from dawn until well into the night. They might be beaten if they failed to pick their usual amount.

20.4 Working Conditions of Slaves

Slaves worked on farms of various sizes. On small farms, owners and slaves worked side by side in the fields. On large plantations, planters hired overseers to supervise their slaves. Overseers were paid to "care for nothing but to make a large crop." To do this, they tried to get the most work possible out of the slaves who worked in the fields.

About three-quarters of rural slaves were field hands who toiled from dawn to dark tending crops. An English visitor described a field hand's day:

He is called up in the morning at day break, and is seldom allowed time enough to swallow three mouthfuls of hominy [boiled corn], or hoecake [cornbread], but is driven out immediately to the field to hard labor . . . About noon . . . he eats his dinner, and he is seldom allowed an hour for that purpose . . . Then they return to severe labor, which continues until dusk.

Even then, a slave's workday was not finished. After dark, there was still water to carry, wood to split, pigs to feed, corn to shuck, cotton to clean, and other chores to be done. One slave recalled,

I never know what it was to rest. I just work all the time from morning till late at night. I had to do everything there was to do on the outside. Work in the field, chop wood, hoe corn, till sometime I feels like my back surely break.

Not all slaves worked in the fields. Some were skilled seamstresses, carpenters, or blacksmiths. Others worked in the master's house as cooks or servants. When asked about her work, a house slave replied,

What kind of work I did? . . . I cooked, [then] I was house maid, an' I raised I don't know how many [children] . . . I was always good when it come to [the] sick, so [that] was mostly my job.

No matter how hard they worked, slaves could never look forward to an easier life. Most began work at the age of six and continued until they died. As one man put it, "Slave young, slave long."

20.5 Living Conditions of Slaves

Most masters viewed their slaves as they did their land—things to be "worn out, not improved." They provided only what was needed to keep their slaves healthy enough to work. Slaves lived crowded together in rough cabins. One recalled,

> We lodged in log huts, and on bare ground. Wooden floors were an unknown luxury. In a single room were huddled, like cattle, ten or a dozen persons, men, women, and children . . . We had neither bedsteads, nor furniture of any description. Our beds were collections of straw and old rags, thrown down in the corners.

Slaves seldom went hungry. "Not to give a slave enough to eat," reported Frederick Douglass, "is regarded as . . . meanness [stinginess] even among slaveholders." Slaves received rations of cornmeal, bacon, and molasses. Many kept gardens or hunted and fished to vary their diets. The owner described below fed his slaves well:

> Marse [master] Alec had plenty for his slaves to eat. There was meat, bread, collard greens, snap beans, 'taters, peas, all sorts of dried fruit, and just lots of milk and butter.

Slaves wore clothing made of coarse homespun linen or rough "Negro cloth." Northern textile mills made this cloth especially for slave clothes. Douglass reported that a field hand received a yearly allowance of "two coarse linen shirts, one pair of linen trousers . . . one jacket, one pair of trousers for winter, made of coarse Negro cloth, one pair of stockings, and one pair of shoes." Children too young to work received "two coarse linen shirts per year. When these failed them, they went naked" until the next year.

While slaves were poorly housed and clothed compared to most white Southerners, they were more likely to receive medical care. Slaveholders often hired doctors to treat sick or injured slaves. Given doctors' limited medical knowledge, this care probably did little to improve slaves' health.

Most slave cabins consisted of a single room where the entire family lived. They had a fireplace for cooking and heat. The windows usually had no glass.

Some slave owners beat or whipped slaves as a way of controlling them. However, most slave owners avoided savage beatings because injured slaves could not work and lash marks reduced their resale value.

20.6 Controlling Slaves

Slavery was a system of forced labor. To make this system work, slaveholders had to keep slaves firmly under control. Some slaveholders used harsh punishments—beating, whipping, branding, and other forms of torture—to maintain that control. But punishments often backfired on slaveholders. A slave who had been badly whipped might not be able to work for some time. Harsh punishments were also likely to make slaves feel more resentful and rebellious.

Slaveholders preferred to control their workforce by making slaves feel totally dependent on their masters. Owners encouraged such dependence by treating their slaves like grown-up children. They also kept their workers as ignorant as possible about the world beyond the plantation. Frederick Douglass's master said that a slave "should know nothing but to obey his master—to do as it is told to do."

Slaves who failed to learn this lesson were sometimes sent to slave-breakers. Such men were experts at turning independent, spirited African Americans into humble, obedient slaves. When he was 16, Douglass was sent to a slave breaker named Edward Covey.

Covey's method consisted of equal parts violence, fear, and over-work. Soon after Douglass arrived on Covey's farm, he received his first whipping. After that, he was beaten so often that "aching bones and a sore back were my constant companions."

Covey's ability to instill fear in his slaves was as effective as his whippings. Slaves never knew when he might be watching them. "He would creep and crawl in ditches and gullies," Douglass recalled, to spy on his workers.

Finally, Covey worked his slaves beyond endurance. Wrote Douglass,

We worked in all weathers. It was never too hot or too cold; it could never rain, blow, hail, or snow too hard for us to work in the field . . . The longest days were too short for him, and the shortest nights too long for him. I was somewhat unmanageable when I first got there, but a few months of this discipline tamed me . . . I was broken in body, soul, and spirit . . . The dark night of slavery closed in upon me.

20.7 Resistance to Slavery

Despite the efforts of slaveholders to crush their spirits, slaves found countless ways to resist slavery. As former slave Harriet Jacobs wrote after escaping to freedom, "My master had power and law on his side. I had a determined will. There is might [power] in each."

Day-to-Day Resistance For most slaves, resistance took the form of quiet, or **passive,** acts of rebellion. Field hands pulled down fences, broke tools, and worked so sloppily that they damaged crops. House slaves sneaked food out of the master's kitchen.

Slaves pretended to be dumb, clumsy, sick, or insane to get out of work. One slave avoided working for years by claiming to be nearly blind, only to regain his sight once freed.

In some instances, resistance turned deadly when house servants put poison into slave owners' food. So many slaves set fire to their owners' homes and barns that the American Fire Insurance Company refused to insure property in the South.

Open Defiance Quiet resistance sometimes flared into open defiance. When pushed too hard, slaves refused to work, rejected orders, or struck back violently. Owners often described slaves who reacted in this way as "insolent" (disrespectful) or "unmanageable."

Frederick Douglass reached his breaking point one day when the slave breaker Covey began to beat him for no particular reason. Rather than take the blows, as he had so many times before, Douglass fought back. He wrestled Covey to the ground, holding him "so firmly by the throat that his blood followed my nails." For Douglass, this moment was "the turning point in my career as a slave."

> *My long-crushed spirit rose, cowardice departed, bold defiance took its place; and I now resolved that, however long I might remain a slave in form, the day had passed when I could be a slave in fact. I did not hesitate to let it be known of me, that the white man who expected to succeed in whipping, must also succeed in killing me.*

Covey knew this and never laid a hand on Douglass again.

Running Away Some slaves tried to escape by running away to freedom in the North. The risks were enormous. Slaveholders hired professional slave catchers and their packs of bloodhounds to hunt down runaway slaves. If caught, a runaway risked being mauled by dogs, brutally whipped, or even killed. Still, Douglass and countless other slaves took the risk.

This 1872 engraving shows escaping slaves resisting slave catchers. At the upper right is a notice of a reward being offered for escaped slaves.

Harriet Tubman

Slaves found many ways to escape bondage. Some walked to freedom in the North, hiding by day and traveling at night when they could follow the North Star. Others traveled north by boat or train, using forged identity cards and clever disguises to get past watchful slave patrols. A few runaways mailed themselves to freedom in boxes or coffins.

Thousands of runaways escaped to free states and to Canada with the help of the **Underground Railroad,** a secret network of free blacks and **sympathetic** whites. The members of the Underground Railroad provided transportation and "safe houses" where runaways could hide. A number of guides, or "conductors," risked their lives to help escaping slaves travel the "freedom train." One of the most successful was Harriet Tubman. Having escaped slavery herself, Tubman courageously returned to the South approximately 20 times between 1850 and 1860, guiding more than 300 men, women, and children to freedom.

Rebellion At times, resistance erupted into violent rebellion. Slave revolts occurred in cities, on plantations, and even on ships at sea. Fear of slave uprisings haunted slaveholders. Planters, wrote one visitor to the South, "never lie down to sleep without . . . loaded pistols at their sides."

In 1822, authorities in Charleston, South Carolina, learned that Denmark Vesey, a free black, was preparing to lead a sizable revolt of slaves. Vesey, along with more than 30 slaves, was arrested and hanged.

Nine years later, in 1831, a slave named Nat Turner led a bloody uprising in Virginia. In what became known as **Nat Turner's Rebellion,** Turner and his followers set out to kill every white person they could find. Armed with axes and guns, they killed at least 57 people over a period of two days.

Vesey's and Turner's rebellions panicked white Southerners. In response, Southern states passed strict slave codes that tightened owners' control of their slaves and provided for harsher punishment of slaves by authorities. As one frightened Virginian remarked, "A Nat Turner might be in any family."

Underground Railroad a secret network of free blacks and whites who helped thousands of slaves escape to free states and to Canada

Nat Turner's Rebellion a slave rebellion led by Nat Turner that took place in Virginia in 1831

The bloodiest slave uprising in the South was organized in 1831 by Nat Turner, a black preacher. This wood engraving, entitled *Nat Turner and His Confederates in Conference,* shows Turner leaning on a pole and speaking to his companions.

This photograph shows five generations of a slave family on a South Carolina plantation. Slaves often found it difficult to keep their families together. Southern laws did not recognize slave marriages or families, and owners could split up families as they wished.

20.8 Slave Families and Communities

Slavery made community and family life difficult. Legally, slave families did not exist. No Southern state recognized slave marriages. Legal control of slave children rested not with their parents, but with their masters. Owners could break up slave families at any time by selling a father, a mother, or a child to someone else. Of all the things they endured, slaves most feared being sold away from their loved ones.

Most slaves grew up in families headed by a father and mother. Unable to marry legally, slaves created their own weddings, which often involved the tradition of jumping over a broomstick. One slave recalled,

> The preacher would say to the man, "Do you take this woman to be your wife?" He says, "Yes." "Well, jump the broom." After he jumped, the preacher would say the same to the woman. When she jumped, the preacher said, "I pronounce you man and wife."

Caring for children was never easy. Booker T. Washington's mother "snatched a few moments for our care in the early morning before her work began, and at night after the day's work was done." Still, parents found time to teach the lessons children would need to survive.

Silence around whites was one such lesson. Elijah Marrs recalled that "Mothers were necessarily compelled to be severe on their children to keep them from talking too much." Obedience was another lesson. William Webb's mother taught him "not to rebel against the men that were treating me like some dumb brute, making me work and refusing to let me learn."

Parents also taught their children other essential lessons about caring, kindness, pride, and hope. They taught them to respect themselves and other members of the slave community, especially older slaves. "There is not to be found, among any people," wrote Douglass, "a more rigid enforcement of the law of respect to elders."

These were the lessons that helped slaves, under the most difficult conditions, to create loving families and close communities. In doing so, they met the most basic of human needs—the need for a place to feel loved, respected, and safe.

20.9 Leisure Time Activities

These simple words capture the constant weariness that slaves endured:

Come day,
Go day,
God send Sunday.

Slaves toiled all week in fields that seemed to stretch "from one end of the earth to the other." But, on Saturday night and Sunday, their time was their own.

Saturday nights were a time for social events, like corn-husking or pea-shelling parties. These social events combined work and fun. One slave recalled,

I've seen many a corn huskin' at ole Major's farm when the corn would be piled as high as the house. Two sets of men would start huskin' from opposite sides of the heap. It would keep one man busy just getting the husks out of the way, and the corn would be thrown over the husker's head and filling the air like birds. The women usually had a quilting at those times, so they were pert and happy.

A quilting bee was one of the rare times when slave women could gather to work and talk. In those few precious hours, they were free to express themselves with needle and cloth. The quilts they created were not only beautiful, but also very much needed as bedding for their families.

After the sewing, men joined the party for a "quilting feast" and dancing. Slaves made music out of almost anything. "Stretch cowhides over cheese-boxes and you had tambourines," one former slave recalled. "Saw bones from off a cow, knock them together, and call it a drum. Or use broomstraws, on fiddle-strings, and you had your entire orchestra."

Sunday was a day for religion and recreation. Slaves spent their Sundays going to church, eating, hunting, fishing, dancing, singing, telling tales, naming babies, playing games, and visiting with friends. In New Orleans, hundreds of slaves gathered on Sunday afternoons in public spaces to dance, sing, and talk. All of these activities helped African Americans forget the sorrows of slavery.

In this painting, black house servants are shown celebrating a wedding party in the kitchen. Dancing, singing, and telling tales allowed slaves to temporarily forget their harsh conditions.

Kitchen Ball at the White Sulfur Springs, Virginia, 1838 by Christian Mayr, North Carolina Museum of Art, Raleigh. Purchased with funds from the State of North Carolina.

20.10 Slave Churches

Many slaveholders encouraged their slaves to attend church on Sunday. Some read the Bible to their workers and prayed with them. Owners and white ministers preached the same message: "If you disobey your earthly master, you offend your heavenly Master."

Not surprisingly, this was not a popular lesson among slaves. "Dat ole white preacher [just] was telling us slaves to be good to our marsters," recalled Cornelius Garner. "We ain't kerr'd a bit 'bout dat stuff he was telling us 'cause we wanted to sing, pray, and serve God in our own way."

Instead, slaves created their own "invisible church" that brought together African roots and American needs. This invisible church met in slave quarters or secret forest clearings known as "hush arbors." One slave reported that,

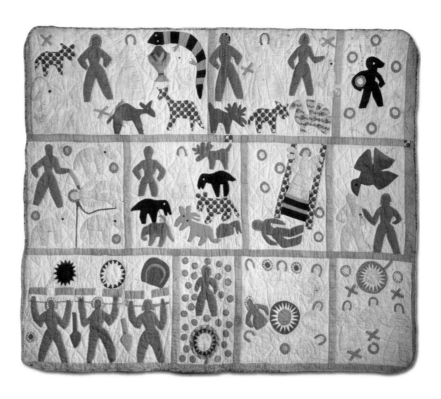

Biblical stories were frequently illustrated on quilts made by slaves. This is one of the two surviving quilts created by Harriet Powers.

> When [slaves] go round singing, "Steal Away to Jesus" that mean there going to be a religious meeting that night. The masters . . . didn't like them religious meetings, so us naturally slips off at night, down in the bottoms or somewheres. Sometimes us sing and pray all night.

Rather than teach about obedience, black preachers told the story of Moses leading his people out of slavery in Egypt. Black worshipers sang spirituals that expressed their desire for freedom and faith in a better world to come. One black preacher wrote,

> The singing was accompanied by a certain ecstasy of motion, clapping of hands, tossing of heads, which would continue without cessation [stopping] about half an hour . . . The old house partook of their ecstasy; it rang with their jubilant shouts, and shook in all its joints.

Whites sometimes criticized the enthusiasm of black worshipers, saying they lacked true religious feeling. Many slaves, however, believed it was their masters who lacked such feeling. "You see," explained one man, "religion needs a little motion—specially if you gwine [going to] feel de spirit."

Religion helped slaves bear their suffering and still find joy in life. In their prayers and spirituals, they gave voice to their deepest longings, their greatest sorrows, and their highest hopes.

This watercolor, entitled *The Old Plantation,* shows one aspect of the rich culture slaves developed in spite of their bondage. Dances, songs, quilts, and folk stories all reflected African traditions as well as the new life slaves faced in America.

The Granger Collection, New York

20.11 African American Culture

Africans arrived in the United States speaking many languages and following many cultural traditions. To survive, they had to learn a new language—English—and adopt a new way of life. Yet they did not forget their African roots. Across the South, slaves combined their old traditions and new realities to create a distinctive African American culture.

This combining of cultures is **evident** in Harriet Powers's story quilt. In square after square, Powers used animals from Africa and America to illustrate Bible stories that she learned as a slave on a Georgia plantation. The doves in her quilt are symbols of a slave's yearning for freedom. As one spiritual expressed, "Had I the wings of a dove, I'd fly away and be at rest."

You can also hear this combining of cultures in the songs and spirituals sung by slaves. These songs throb with the rhythms and harmonies of Africa, but speak about the realities of slavery. Slaves sang about faith, love, work, and the kindness and cruelty of masters. They also expressed their **oppression,** as in this song recorded by Frederick Douglass:

> We raise the wheat, dey gib [they give] us the corn;
> We bake the bread, dey gib us the cruss;
> We sif the meal, dey gib us the huss;
> We peel the meat, dey gib us the skin;
> And dat's the way dey takes us in.

Slave dances were based on African traditions as well. Dancing helped slaves to put aside their cares, express their feelings, and refresh their spirits. According to one former slave, good dancers "could play a tune with their feet, dancing largely to an inward music, a music that was felt, but not heard."

oppression the feeling of being weighed down or held back by severe and unfair force

African legends and folktales survived in the stories and jokes told by slaves. For example, Br'er Rabbit, the sly hero of many slave tales, was based on the African trickster Shulo the Hare. In these stories, the small but clever brother rabbit always managed to outwit larger, but duller, brother bear or brother fox—just as slaves hoped to outwit their more powerful masters.

Chapter Summary

In this chapter, you learned what life was like for African Americans during the 1800s.

North and South, Slave and Free African Americans had a great impact on the development of American life. The South's economy was built on slave labor. Some blacks lived in freedom in the North and South, but nowhere could they escape racism and discrimination.

The Economics of Slavery Most white Southerners did not own slaves. Whether they owned slaves or not, whites understood that the South's economy depended on cotton and the slave labor needed to grow it.

Working and Living Conditions of Slaves All slaves worked constantly —in the fields, as house servants, or at skilled trades. Most slaves lived in simple, dirt-floor cabins.

IN THE COTTON FIELD.

Controlling Slaves and Resistance to Slavery Some slave owners used harsh punishments to control slaves. Most slaves resisted slavery using quiet acts of rebellion, while some fought back openly. At great risk, many tried to run away. Some slaveholders would rather kill runaways than allow them to escape.

Slave Families, Leisure, and Churches Enslaved African Americans created families and communities under the most difficult conditions. Slaves spent Saturday nights at social events and worshiped in their own churches on Sundays. They prayed and sang spirituals to help themselves find joy and hope in their hard lives.

African American Culture Africans brought many languages and cultural traditions to the United States. The combination of old and new cultural traditions was expressed through their quilts, songs, dances, and folktales.

THE SALE.

These cards show scenes of slavery in the United States.

FREE!

THE PARTING "Buy us too."

Before the Civil War, Harriet Tubman helped hundreds of people escape slavery in the South. Because of her wits and bravery, she is a symbol of the Underground Railroad.

Harriet Tubman, Moses of the Underground Railroad

No one did more to help enslaved African Americans escape slavery than Harriet Tubman. People began to call her Moses for her role in guiding people to freedom in the North. But first, she had to get there herself.

In the fall of 1849, Harriet Tubman decided to escape her life as a slave. She had been born into slavery in eastern Maryland, sometime around 1820. When she heard that she would be sold to a new owner farther south, she decided to flee.

It was not an easy decision. She would have to leave her family behind, including her husband, who refused to go. She also knew that women rarely managed to escape on their own. If she were caught, she would be severely punished and perhaps killed. But she felt she had no choice. "I had reasoned this out in my mind," she later recalled. "There was one of two things I had a right to, liberty or death; if I could not have one, I would have the other."

Like most slaves, Tubman had led a hard life. She had been whipped repeatedly and forced to labor in the fields. She once suffered a near-fatal injury when an overseer struck her in the head with a lead weight. For the rest of her life, she would periodically and unexpectedly fall into a deep sleep. But her experiences also gave her strength and taught her how to survive. She would need that strength on her flight north.

Tubman left at night, under cover of darkness. She had no idea where to go, but fortunately there were people to help her. They were part of the Underground Railroad, the name people gave to a network of safe houses and escape routes leading to the North. The safe houses were known as "stations" and the people who ran them as "stationmasters." These men and women—and sometimes children—put their lives at risk to help slaves escape to freedom.

Not wanting to endanger those who helped her, Tubman never revealed the details of her escape. But she probably took a route heading northeast to Delaware and then to Pennsylvania. It was a journey she would take many times later, when she had become the most famous "conductor" on the Underground Railroad.

Crossing to Freedom

Tubman's first stop was the home of a sympathetic white woman who lived nearby. This woman told her how to find the nearest safe house. Tubman walked through the night to get there. When she arrived, a woman opened the door, handed her a broom, and told her to sweep the yard. This puzzled Tubman until she realized that playing the part of a black servant would help avoid suspicion.

When the woman's husband came home that evening, he hid Tubman in his wagon, drove her out of town, and dropped her off with directions to the next safe house. For the rest of her journey, Tubman went from one "station" to the next at night and hid during the day.

Most of the time she traveled on foot, staying out of sight. Slave catchers were a real danger, so she avoided roads and listened for the sound of bloodhounds on her trail. She knew that one careless mistake could lead to her capture.

She left Maryland and crossed into Delaware. But she was still not safe. Although Delaware was a free state, slave catchers worked there, and many people would turn over a fugitive for the reward money.

Finally, after two or three weeks on the run, Tubman crossed the Pennsylvania border, a dividing line between North and South. Now she was truly free. Years later she recalled that moment:

> I looked at my hands to see if I was the same person. There was such a glory over everything. The sun came like gold through the trees and over the fields, and I felt like I was in heaven.

Refuge in Philadelphia

Tubman went to Philadelphia, which was then home to thousands of African Americans, including many escaped slaves. The city had a strong abolitionist community and was a center of the Underground Railroad. Tubman soon found work and settled into her new life.

But she would not remain at rest for long. She missed her family in Maryland and could not bear the idea that they were still living in slavery. "I was free," she said, "and they should be free."

Escaping slaves fled slavery any way they could. In this painting, "conductors" help men, women, and children from boats and into wagons that would take them farther north.

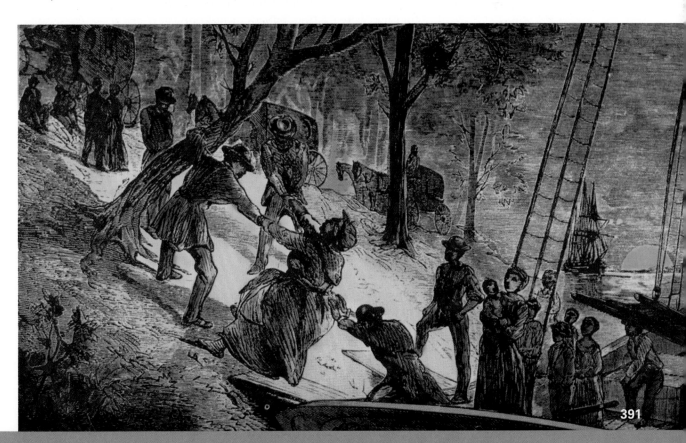

The Granger Collection, New York

Born free in New Jersey, abolitionist William Still played a central role in the Underground Railroad. He interviewed every escaping slave he met. The detailed records he kept are an invaluable source of information today.

Riding the Liberty Lines

By the fall of 1850, Tubman decided to act. She had learned that one of her sister's daughters, a niece named Kizzy, was going to be sold south. Kizzy had two children, and Tubman was determined to rescue all three of them. No one knows exactly how she did it, but Harriet managed to slip into Maryland and bring all of them north.

The following spring, she made another trip, this time to get one of her brothers. A few months later, she brought back a second brother, along with ten other people. Eventually she would rescue most of her family, including her elderly parents. She took most of them to Canada, where they could not be seized by slave catchers and returned to their owners.

Tubman could not have made these trips without the help of the Underground Railroad. She followed routes, known as "liberty lines," and made use of Underground Railroad safe houses. Some of these houses had tunnels and secret closets where fugitives could hide.

She also relied on "agents" such as Thomas Garrett and William Still. Garrett was a white stationmaster in Wilmington, Delaware, who helped more than 2,500 slaves escape from the South. Still, an African American, was an important leader of the antislavery movement in Philadelphia. These and other members of the Underground Railroad were critical to Tubman's success over the years.

Another secret to her success was her methods. She usually made her trips in the fall and winter, when the nights were long and people tended to stay indoors. She always set out on a Saturday night. Sunday was usually a slave's only day off, so slave owners might not miss absent slaves until Monday morning. When nearing a hiding place where fugitives were waiting, Tubman would sing a special song. These songs were a kind of code to signal her presence or to provide instructions.

Sometimes she wore disguises, such as men's clothing. Once, when she ran into a former owner, she pulled her hat over her face and pretended to read a newspaper. The man, who assumed his former slave could not read, never realized who she was.

One admirer recalled, "She could elude patrols and pursuers with as much ease and unconcern as an eagle would soar through the heavens." She was also fearless. When she developed a bad toothache during one escape, she used a pistol to knock her teeth out and ease the pain.

The Granger Collection, New York

$150 REWARD

RANAWAY from the subscriber, on the night of the 2d instant, a negro man, who calls himself *Henry May*, about 22 years old, 5 feet 6 or 8 inches high, ordinary color, rather chunky built, bushy head, and has it divided mostly on one side, and keeps it very nicely combed; has been raised in the house, and is a first rate dining-room servant, and was in a tavern in Louisville for 18 months. I expect he is now in Louisville trying to make his escape to a free state, (in all probability to Cincinnati, Ohio.) Perhaps he may try to get employment on a steamboat. He is a good cook, and is handy in any capacity as a house servant. Had on when he left, a dark cassinett coatee, and dark striped cassinett pantaloons, new—he had other clothing. I will give $50 reward if taken in Louisvill; 100 dollars if taken one hundred miles from Louisville in this State, and 150 dollars if taken out of this State, and delivered to me, or secured in any jail so that I can get him again. WILLIAM BURKE.

Bardstown, Ky., September 3d, 1838.

Slave owners put up wanted posters for the return of runaway slaves. Agents for the Underground Railroad sometimes tore the posters down to help slaves escape.

The Rescue of Joe Bailey

Between 1852 and 1860, Tubman made one or more trips a year into the South. Blacks soon began calling her Moses, the leader who guided her people to freedom. As Moses's reputation grew, slave owners demanded the capture of this mysterious person who was leading their slaves away. But they did not know who Moses was or even that she was a woman.

On one trip in November 1856, Tubman brought five people north, including a man named Joe Bailey. Bailey was highly valued by his owner, who offered $1,500 for his return. A $12,000 bounty was also placed on the head of "Moses."

After a risky escape from Maryland, Tubman and her party reached the outskirts of Wilmington. There, Thomas Garrett hid them under a wagonload of hay and helped them get through the city. From there, they went to Philadelphia and New York, on their way to Canada.

Bailey got a shock in New York, however. There, a man identified him from a poster advertising a reward for his capture. Fortunately, the man was an abolitionist. Nonetheless, Bailey was plunged into gloom, fearing he would never make it out of the country without getting caught. He failed to cheer up for the rest of the journey, even refusing to look as he passed by Niagara Falls and crossed into Canada.

At that point, Tubman shook him, saying, "Joe, you're free!" Bailey looked up, saw where he was, and burst into tears. Then he began to sing:

Glory to God and Jesus too;
One more soul is safe!
Oh, go and carry the news;
One more soul got safe!

Tubman's Legacy

It is said that Harriet Tubman made almost 20 trips on the Underground Railroad and freed more than 300 people. In all of her journeys, she said, "I never ran my train off the track, and I never lost a passenger." She made her last trip shortly before the outbreak of the Civil War, in 1861.

During the war, she joined the Union cause as a nurse and a spy. On one raid into South Carolina, she helped free several hundred slaves from captivity.

After the war, Tubman became a strong voice in the fight for women's rights and racial justice. But it was her daring work with the Underground Railroad that made her a great hero and liberator of her people.

In 1978, the U.S. Postal Service honored Harriet Tubman with a stamp. To former slaves like the men and women in the photograph below, Tubman (far left) was a hero in her own time.

The Granger Collection, New York

Harriet Tubman

Black Heritage USA 13c

Americans in the Mid-1800s

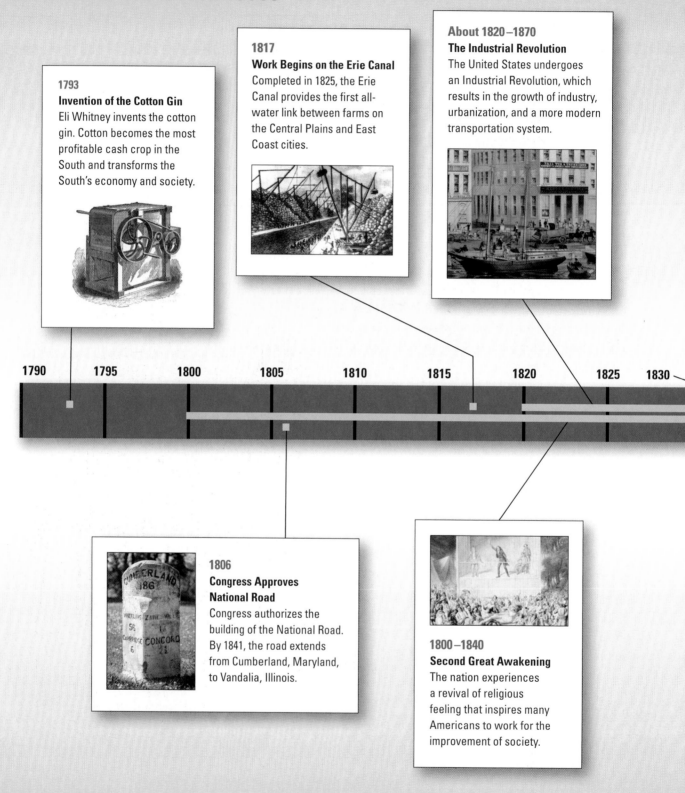

1793
Invention of the Cotton Gin
Eli Whitney invents the cotton gin. Cotton becomes the most profitable cash crop in the South and transforms the South's economy and society.

1817
Work Begins on the Erie Canal
Completed in 1825, the Erie Canal provides the first all-water link between farms on the Central Plains and East Coast cities.

About 1820–1870
The Industrial Revolution
The United States undergoes an Industrial Revolution, which results in the growth of industry, urbanization, and a more modern transportation system.

1790   1795   1800   1805   1810   1815   1820   1825   1830

1806
Congress Approves National Road
Congress authorizes the building of the National Road. By 1841, the road extends from Cumberland, Maryland, to Vandalia, Illinois.

1800–1840
Second Great Awakening
The nation experiences a revival of religious feeling that inspires many Americans to work for the improvement of society.

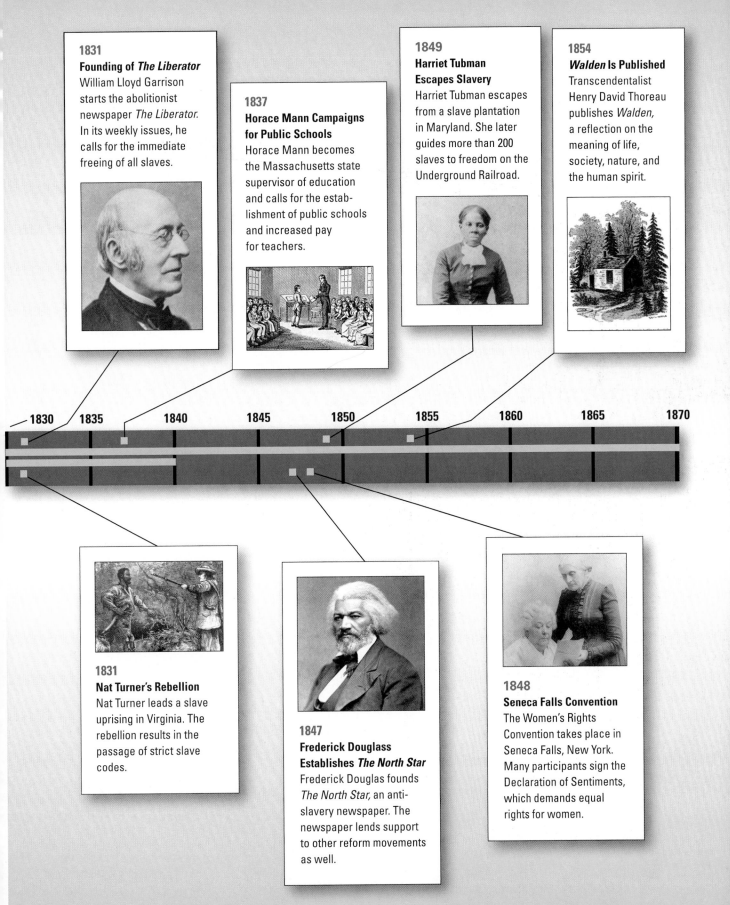

1831
Founding of *The Liberator*
William Lloyd Garrison starts the abolitionist newspaper *The Liberator*. In its weekly issues, he calls for the immediate freeing of all slaves.

1837
Horace Mann Campaigns for Public Schools
Horace Mann becomes the Massachusetts state supervisor of education and calls for the establishment of public schools and increased pay for teachers.

1849
Harriet Tubman Escapes Slavery
Harriet Tubman escapes from a slave plantation in Maryland. She later guides more than 200 slaves to freedom on the Underground Railroad.

1854
***Walden* Is Published**
Transcendentalist Henry David Thoreau publishes *Walden*, a reflection on the meaning of life, society, nature, and the human spirit.

1830   1835   1840   1845   1850   1855   1860   1865   1870

1831
Nat Turner's Rebellion
Nat Turner leads a slave uprising in Virginia. The rebellion results in the passage of strict slave codes.

1847
Frederick Douglass Establishes *The North Star*
Frederick Douglas founds *The North Star,* an anti-slavery newspaper. The newspaper lends support to other reform movements as well.

1848
Seneca Falls Convention
The Women's Rights Convention takes place in Seneca Falls, New York. Many participants sign the Declaration of Sentiments, which demands equal rights for women.

The Civil War divided the nation for four years between 1861 and 1865. Shown here is the site of the Battle of Gettysburg, which took place in Pennsylvania.

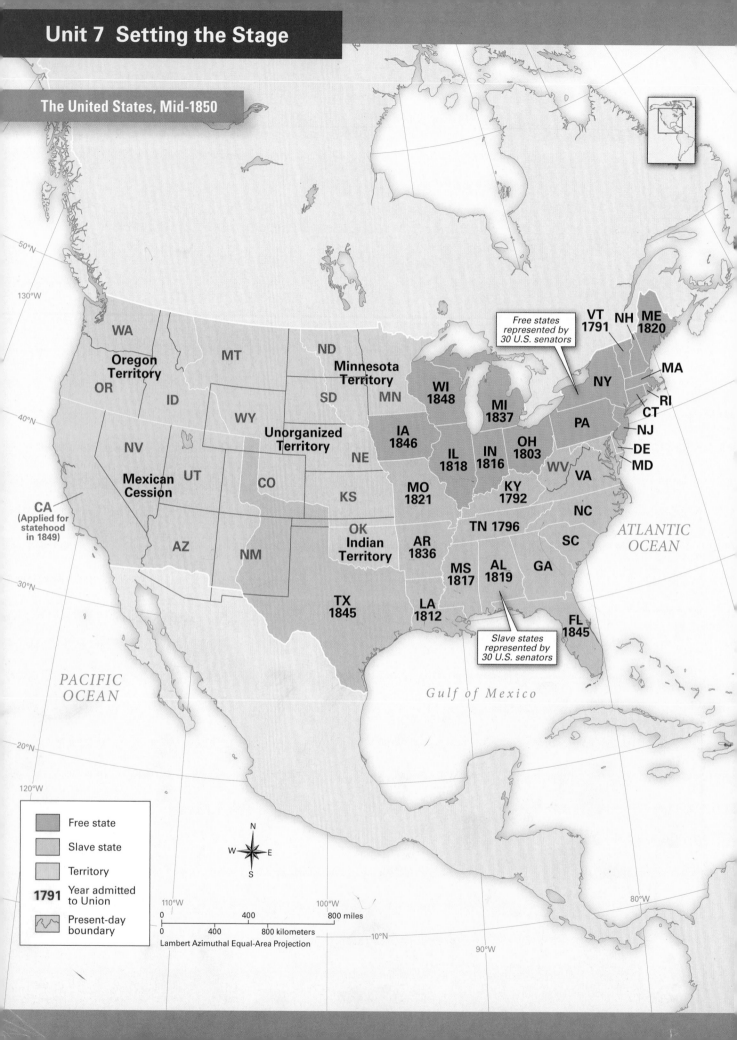

The United States, Mid-1850

WA

Oregon
Territory

OR

ID

MT

ND

Minnesota
Territory

SD

MN

WI
1848

MI
1837

Free states
represented by
30 U.S. senators

VT
1791

NH

ME
1820

NY

MA

RI

CT

NJ

DE

MD

NV

Mexican
Cession

UT

WY

Unorganized
Territory

NE

IA
1846

IL
1818

IN
1816

OH
1803

PA

CA
(Applied for
statehood
in 1849)

AZ

CO

KS

MO
1821

WV

VA

KY
1792

NC

NM

OK
Indian
Territory

AR
1836

TN 1796

SC

TX
1845

MS
1817

AL
1819

GA

ATLANTIC
OCEAN

LA
1812

FL
1845

Slave states
represented by
30 U.S. senators

PACIFIC
OCEAN

Gulf of Mexico

50°N

130°W

40°N

30°N

120°W

20°N

110°W

100°W

90°W

80°W

10°N

Legend

■	Free state
■	Slave state
■	Territory
1791	Year admitted to Union
	Present-day boundary

N
W E
S

0   400   800 miles
0   400   800 kilometers
Lambert Azimuthal Equal-Area Projection

The Union Challenged

The maps on these two pages show the United States in mid-1850, the year tensions over slavery reached a breaking point. In this unit, you will learn why this crisis developed and how Congress handled it. You will also learn about events after 1850 that further divided the North and South and turned the dispute over slavery into war.

As the map on the opposite page shows, some states allowed slavery. Notice, however, that the same number of states banned it. This balance gave the slave states and the free states an equal number of votes in the U.S. Senate. However, as the map on this page shows, that equality did not exist in the House of Representatives, where each state's votes are based on its population.

The Constitution requires that the House and Senate agree on new laws. Southerners believed that as long as the Senate remained balanced, Congress could not pass laws to affect slavery. Then, in 1849, California asked to become a state. California's new constitution, however, banned slavery. Admitting California as a free state, many Southerners warned, would upset the equal balance between slave states and free states—making the slave states a minority.

The 1850s were one of the most troubled decades in U.S. history. Yet, they were mild compared to the 1860s, a time of war, bitterness, and the repair of a broken nation. As you explore the topics in this unit, picture what it must have been like to live during such difficult times. The era's events drew the American people into a deadly struggle over slavery, freedom, and the very survival of the nation.

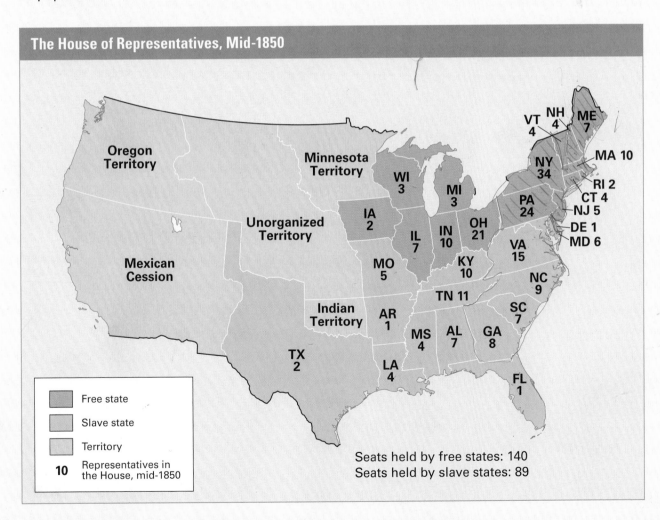

The House of Representatives, Mid-1850

Oregon Territory

Minnesota Territory

Mexican Cession

Unorganized Territory

Indian Territory

VT 4
NH 4
ME 7
NY 34
MA 10
RI 2
CT 4
NJ 5
DE 1
MD 6
PA 24
WI 3
MI 3
IA 2
IL 7
IN 10
OH 21
VA 15
MO 5
KY 10
NC 9
TN 11
AR 1
SC 7
MS 4
AL 7
GA 8
TX 2
LA 4
FL 1

Free state
Slave state
Territory
10 Representatives in the House, mid-1850

Seats held by free states: 140
Seats held by slave states: 89

Chapter 21

A Dividing Nation

Which events of the mid-1800s kept the nation together and which events pulled it apart?

21.1 Introduction

In 1860, after one of the strangest elections in the nation's history, a tall, plainspoken Illinois lawyer named Abraham Lincoln was elected president. On learning of his victory, Lincoln said to the reporters covering the campaign, "Well, boys, your troubles are over; mine have just begun."

Within a few weeks, it became clear just how heavy those troubles would be. By the time Lincoln took office, the nation had split apart over the issue of states' rights regarding slavery and was preparing for civil war. The survival of the United States of America, and the fate of 4 million slaves, rested in Lincoln's hands.

The troubles Lincoln faced were not new. The issues dividing the nation could be traced back to 1619, when the first slave ship arrived in Virginia. Since that time, slavery had ended in half of the United States. The question was, could the nation continue half-slave and half-free?

For decades, Americans tried to avoid that question. Many hoped slavery would simply die out on its own. Instead, slavery began to expand into new territories, and the question could no longer be ignored.

Between 1820 and 1860, Americans tried to fashion several compromises on the issue of slavery. Each compromise, however, created new problems and new divisions.

Lincoln understood why. Slavery was not simply a political issue to be worked out through compromise. It was a deeply moral issue. As Lincoln wrote in a letter to a friend, "If slavery is not wrong, nothing is wrong."

In this chapter, you will learn how Americans tried to keep the United States united despite their deep divisions over slavery. Some events during this period kept the nation together, while others pulled it apart. You will also find out how Americans finally answered the question of whether a nation founded on the idea of freedom could endure half-slave and half-free.

This portrait of Abraham Lincoln was taken before he won the presidential election of 1860. By the time he took office just a few months later, the nation had divided over the issue of slavery.

◀ In 1850, U.S. senators debated the issue of whether California should enter the Union as a free state or a slave state.

21.2 Confronting the Issue of Slavery

A traveler heading west across the Appalachians after the War of 1812 wrote, "Old America seems to be breaking up and moving westward." It was true. By 1819, settlers had formed seven new states west of the Appalachians.

In the Northwest Ordinance of 1787, Congress had established a process for forming new states. Besides outlining the steps leading to statehood, this law also banned slavery north of the Ohio River. As a result, the three western states that were formed north of the river—Ohio, Indiana, and Illinois—were free states. The four states that were formed south of the Ohio River—Kentucky, Tennessee, Louisiana, and Mississippi—permitted slavery.

In 1819, Alabama and Missouri applied to Congress for statehood as slave states. No one in Congress questioned admitting Alabama as a slave state. Alabama was located far south of the Ohio River and was surrounded by other slave states.

Congress had another reason for admitting Alabama with no debate. For years, there had been an unspoken agreement in Congress to keep the number of slave states and free states equal. The admission of Illinois as a free state in 1818 had upset this balance. By accepting Alabama with slavery, Congress was able to restore the balance between slave and free states. Missouri, however, was another matter.

In 1819, the number of slave and free states stood at 11 each. This balance was threatened when Missouri applied for statehood as a slave state.

The United States in 1819

Slave States	Free States
Delaware	Pennsylvania
Maryland	New Jersey
Virginia	Connecticut
North Carolina	Massachusetts
South Carolina	New Hampshire
Georgia	New York
Kentucky (1792)	Rhode Island
Tennessee (1796)	Vermont (1791)
Louisiana (1812)	Ohio (1803)
Mississippi (1817)	Indiana (1816)
Alabama (1819)	Illinois (1818)

Original 13 states
States admitted to the Union, 1791–1819

Questions About Missouri Some Northerners in Congress questioned whether Missouri should be admitted as a slave state. Most of Missouri, they observed, lay north of the point where the Ohio River flows into the Mississippi. On the eastern side of the Mississippi, slavery was banned north of that point. Should this ban not also be applied west of the Mississippi?

This question led to another one. If Missouri were allowed to enter the Union as a slave state, some asked, what would keep slavery from spreading across all of the Louisiana Territory? The vision of a block of new slave states stretching from the Mississippi to the Rocky Mountains was enough to give some Northerners nightmares.

The Tallmadge Amendment When the bill to make Missouri a state came before Congress, Representative James Tallmadge of New York proposed an amendment to the bill. The amendment said that Missouri could join the Union, but only as a free state.

Southerners in Congress protested Tallmadge's amendment. What right, they asked, did Congress have to decide whether a new state should be slave or free? According to the theory of states' rights favored by many Southerners, Congress had no power to impose its will on a state, old or new.

This illustration shows African Americans being sold at a slave auction in the South in 1861. Scenes like this added to the moral outrage many people felt toward slavery.

Instead, the people of each state should decide whether to permit slavery. The fight over slavery thus involved a basic question about the powers of the federal and state governments under the Constitution.

A Deadlocked Congress Southerners' protests were based on their view that if Congress were allowed to end slavery in Missouri, it might try to end slavery elsewhere. The North already had more votes in the House of Representatives than the South. Only in the Senate did the two sections have equal voting power. As long as the number of free states and slave states remained equal, Southern senators could defeat any attempt to interfere with slavery. But if Missouri entered the Union as a free state, the South would lose its power to block anti-slavery bills in the Senate. If that happened, Southerners warned, it would mean disaster for the South.

In the North, the Tallmadge Amendment awakened strong feelings against slavery. Many towns sent petitions to Congress, condemning slavery as immoral and unconstitutional. Arguing in favor of the amendment, New Hampshire representative Arthur Livermore spoke for many Northerners when he said,

An opportunity is now presented . . . to prevent the growth of a sin which sits heavy on the soul of every one of us. By embracing this opportunity, we may retrieve the national character, and, in some degree, our own.

The House voted to approve the Tallmadge Amendment. In the Senate, however, Southerners were able to defeat it. The two houses were now deadlocked over the issue of slavery in Missouri. They would remain so as the 1819 session of Congress drew to a close.

Missouri Compromise an agreement made by Congress in 1820 under which Missouri was admitted to the Union as a slave state and Maine was admitted as a free state

21.3 The Missouri Compromise

When Congress returned to Washington in 1820, it took up the question of Missouri statehood once again. By then, the situation had changed, for Maine was now asking to enter the Union as a free state.

For weeks, Congress struggled to find a way out of its deadlock over Missouri. As the debate dragged on and tempers wore thin, Southerners began using such dreaded words as secession and civil war.

"If you persist," Thomas Cobb of Georgia warned supporters of the Tallmadge Amendment, "the Union will be dissolved. You have kindled a fire which a sea of blood can only extinguish."

"If disunion must take place, let it be so!" thundered Tallmadge in reply. "If civil war must come, I can only say, let it come!"

A Compromise Is Reached Rather than risk the breakup of the Union, Congress finally agreed to a compromise crafted by Representative Henry Clay of Kentucky. The **Missouri Compromise** of 1820 admitted Missouri to the Union as a slave state and Maine as a free state. In this way, it maintained the balance of power between slave and free states.

At the same time, Congress drew an imaginary line across the Louisiana Purchase at latitude 36°30′. North of this line, slavery was to be banned forever, except in Missouri. South of the line, slaveholding was permitted.

Reactions to the Compromise The Missouri Compromise kept the Union together, but it pleased few people. In the North, congressmen who voted to accept Missouri as a slave state were called traitors. In the South, slaveholders deeply resented the ban on slavery in territories that might later become states.

Under the Missouri Compromise, Missouri entered the Union as a slave state, while Maine entered as a free state. North of the 36°30′ parallel, slavery was prohibited, except for in Missouri. South of this parallel, slavery would be allowed.

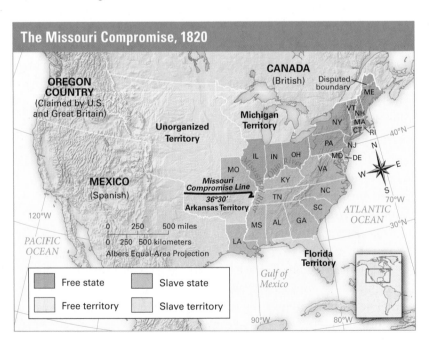

The Missouri Compromise, 1820

Meanwhile, as Secretary of State John Quincy Adams recognized, the compromise had not settled the future of slavery in the United States as a whole. "I have favored this Missouri compromise, believing it to be all that could be effected [accomplished] under the present Constitution, and from extreme unwillingness to put the Union at hazard [risk]," wrote Adams in his diary. "If the Union must be dissolved, slavery is precisely the question on which it ought to break. For the present, however, the contest is laid asleep."

21.4 The Missouri Compromise Unravels

As John Quincy Adams predicted, for a time the "contest" over slavery was settled. But a powerful force was building that soon pushed the issue into the open again: the Second Great Awakening. Leaders of the religious revival of the 1820s and 1830s promised that God would bless those who did the Lord's work. For some Americans, the Lord's work was the abolition of slavery.

The "Gag Rule" During the 1830s, abolitionists flooded Congress with antislavery petitions. Congress, they were told, had no power to interfere with slavery in the states. Then what about the District of Columbia? asked the abolitionists. Surely Congress had the power to ban slavery in the nation's capital.

Rather than **confront** that question, Congress voted in 1836 to table—or set aside indefinitely—all antislavery petitions. Outraged abolitionists called this action the "gag rule," because it gagged, or silenced, all congressional debate over slavery.

In 1839, the gag rule prevented consideration of an antislavery proposal by John Quincy Adams, who was now a member of Congress. Knowing that the country would not agree on abolishing slavery altogether, Adams proposed a constitutional amendment saying that no one could be born into slavery after 1845. Congress, however, refused to consider his proposal.

Many Northern periodicals and newspapers detailed the horrors of slavery.

Southern Fears Abolitionists were far from silenced by the refusal of Congress to debate slavery. They continued to attack slavery in books, in newspapers, and at public meetings.

White Southerners deeply resented the abolitionists' attacks as an assault on their way of life. After Nat Turner's slave rebellion in 1831, resentment turned to fear. Southern states adopted strict new laws to control the movement of slaves. Many states tried to keep abolitionist writings from reaching slaves. Mississippi even offered a reward of $5,000 for the arrest and conviction of any person "who shall utter, publish, or circulate" abolitionist ideas.

Fugitive Slaves Nat Turner's rebellion was the last large-scale slave revolt. But individual slaves continued to rebel by running away to freedom in the North. These **fugitives** from slavery were often helped in their escape by sympathetic people in the North.

To slaveholders, these Northerners were no better than bank robbers. They saw a slave as a valuable piece of property. Every time a slave escaped, it was like seeing their land vanish into thin air. Slaveholders demanded that Congress pass a fugitive slave law to help them recapture their property.

In this painting, Northerners help a group of fugitive slaves make their escape. The assistance Northerners gave to escaped slaves angered many Southern slaveholders.

Slavery in the Territories The gag rule kept the slavery issue out of Congress for ten years. Then, in 1846, President James Polk sent a bill to Congress asking for funds for the war with Mexico. Pennsylvania representative David Wilmot added an amendment to the bill known as the **Wilmot Proviso**. (A proviso is a condition added to an agreement.) The Wilmot Proviso stated that "neither slavery nor involuntary servitude shall ever exist" in any part of the territory that might be acquired from Mexico as a result of the Mexican-American War.

Southerners in Congress strongly opposed Wilmot's amendment. They maintained that Congress had no right to decide where slaveholders could take their property. The Wilmot Proviso passed the House, but it was rejected by the Senate.

Statehood for California For the next three years, Congress debated what to do about slavery in the territory gained from Mexico. Southerners wanted all of the Mexican Cession open to slavery. Northerners wanted all of it closed.

As a compromise, Southerners proposed a bill that would extend the Missouri Compromise line all the way to the Pacific. Slavery would be banned north of that line and allowed south of it. Northerners in Congress rejected this proposal.

Then, late in 1849, California applied for admission to the Union as a free state. Northerners in Congress welcomed California with open arms. Southerners, however, rejected California's request. Making California a free state, they warned, would upset the balance between slave and free states. The result would be unequal representation of slave states and free states in Congress.

The year ended with Congress deadlocked over California's request for statehood. Once again, Southerners spoke openly of withdrawing from the Union. And once again, angry Northerners denounced slavery as a crime against humanity.

fugitive a person who flees or tries to escape (for example, from slavery)

Wilmot Proviso a proposal made in 1846 to prohibit slavery in the territory added to the United States as a result of the Mexican-American War

21.5 The Compromise of 1850

On January 21, 1850, Henry Clay, now a senator from Kentucky, trudged through a Washington snowstorm to pay an unexpected call on Senator Daniel Webster of Massachusetts. Clay, the creator of the Missouri Compromise, had come up with a plan to end the deadlock over California. But to get his plan through Congress, he needed Webster's support.

Something for Everyone Clay's new compromise had something to please just about everyone. It began by admitting California to the Union as a free state. That would please the North. Meanwhile, it allowed the New Mexico and Utah territories to decide whether to allow slavery, which would please the South.

In addition, Clay's plan ended the slave trade in Washington, D.C. Although slaveholders in Washington would be able to keep their slaves, human beings would no longer be bought and sold in the nation's capital. Clay and Webster agreed that this compromise would win support from abolitionists without threatening the rights of slaveholders.

Finally, Clay's plan called for passage of a strong fugitive slave law. Slaveholders had long wanted such a law, which would make it easier to find and reclaim runaway slaves.

The Compromise Is Accepted Hoping that Clay's compromise would end the crisis, Webster agreed to help it get passed in Congress. But despite Webster's support, Congress debated the **Compromise of 1850** for nine frustrating months. As tempers frayed, Southerners talked of simply leaving the Union peacefully.

Webster dismissed such talk as foolish. "Peaceable secession!" he exclaimed. "Your eyes and mine are never destined to see that miracle . . . I see it as plainly as I see the sun in heaven—I see that [secession] must produce such a war as I will not describe."

A war over slavery was something few Americans wanted to face. In September 1850, Congress finally adopted Clay's plan. Most Americans were happy to see the crisis end. Some Southerners, however, remained wary of the compromise.

> **Compromise of 1850** the agreements made in order to admit California into the Union as a free state. These agreements included allowing the New Mexico and Utah territories to decide whether to allow slavery, outlawing the slave trade in Washington, D.C., and creating a stronger fugitive slave law.

The Compromise of 1850 admitted California as a free state and allowed the southwestern territories to be set up without restriction on slavery.

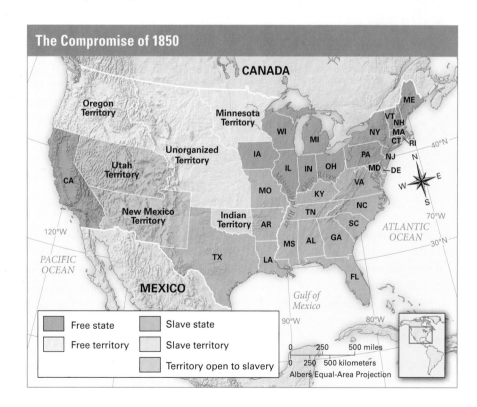

The Compromise of 1850

Legend:
- Free state
- Free territory
- Slave state
- Slave territory
- Territory open to slavery

21.6 The Compromise of 1850 Fails

Henry Clay and Daniel Webster hoped the Compromise of 1850 would quiet the slavery controversy for years to come. In fact, it satisfied almost no one—and the debate grew louder each year.

The Fugitive Slave Act People in the North and the South were unhappy with the Fugitive Slave Act, though for different reasons. Northerners did not want to enforce the act. Southerners felt the act did not do enough to **ensure** the return of their escaped property.

Under the Fugitive Slave Act, a person arrested as a runaway slave had almost no legal rights. Many runaways fled all the way to Canada rather than risk being caught and sent back to their owners. Others decided to stand and fight. Reverend Jarmain Loguen, a former slave living in New York, said boldly, "I don't respect this law—I don't fear it—I won't obey it . . . I will not live as a slave, and if force is employed to re-enslave me, I shall make preparations to meet the crisis as becomes a man."

The Fugitive Slave Act also said that any person who helped a slave escape, or even refused to aid slave catchers, could be jailed. This provision, complained New England poet Ralph Waldo Emerson, made "slave catchers of us all."

Opposition to the act was widespread in the North. When slave catchers came to Boston, they were hounded by crowds of angry citizens shouting, "Slave hunters—there go the slave hunters." After a few days of this treatment, most slave catchers decided to leave.

Northerners' refusal to support the act infuriated slaveholders. It also made enforcement of the act almost impossible. Of the tens of thousands of fugitives living in the North during the 1850s, only 299 were captured and returned to their owners during this time.

The Fugitive Slave Act was passed as part of the Compromise of 1850. This 1851 poster warned free African Americans in Boston to watch out for slave catchers looking for escaped slaves. Even people who helped escaped slaves could be jailed.

Uncle Tom's Cabin Nothing brought the horrors of slavery home to Northerners more than *Uncle Tom's Cabin,* a novel by Harriet Beecher Stowe. The novel grew out of a vision Stowe had while sitting in church on a wintry Sunday morning in 1851. The vision began with a saintly slave, known as Uncle Tom, and his cruel master. In a furious rage, the master, Simon Legree, had the old slave whipped to death. Just before Uncle Tom's soul slipped out of his body, he opened his eyes and whispered to Legree, "Ye poor miserable critter! There ain't no more ye can do. I forgive ye, with all my soul!"

Racing home, Stowe scribbled down what she had imagined. Her vision of Uncle Tom's death became part of a much longer story that was first published in installments in an abolitionist newspaper. In one issue, readers held their breath as the slave Eliza chose to risk death rather than be sold away from her young son. Chased by slave hunters and their dogs, Eliza dashed to freedom across the ice-choked Ohio River, clutching her child in her arms. In a later issue, Stowe's readers wept as they read her account of how the character of Uncle Tom died at the hands of Simon Legree.

In 1852, *Uncle Tom's Cabin* was published as a novel. Plays based on the book toured the country, thrilling audiences with Eliza's dramatic escape to freedom. No other work had ever aroused such powerful emotions about slavery. In the South, the novel and its author were scorned and cursed. In the North, *Uncle Tom's Cabin* made millions of people even more angry about the cruelties of slavery.

The Ostend Manifesto and the Kansas-Nebraska Act Northerners who were already horrified by slavery were roused to fury by two events in 1854: the publication of the so-called Ostend Manifesto and the Kansas-Nebraska Act.

The document known as the Ostend Manifesto was a message sent to the secretary of state by three American diplomats who were meeting in Ostend, Belgium. President Franklin Pierce, who had taken office in 1853, had been trying to purchase the island of Cuba from Spain, but Spain had refused the offer. The message from the diplomats urged the U.S. government to seize Cuba by force if Spain continued to refuse to sell the island. When the message was leaked to the public, angry Northerners charged that Pierce's administration wanted to buy Cuba in order to add another slave state to the Union.

Early that same year, Senator Stephen A. Douglas of Illinois introduced a bill in Congress that aroused an uproar. Douglas wanted to get a railroad built to California. He thought the project was more likely to happen if Congress organized the Great Plains into the Nebraska Territory and opened the region to settlers. This territory lay north of the Missouri Compromise, and Douglas's bill said nothing about slavery. But Southerners in Congress agreed to support the bill only if Douglas made a few changes—and those changes had far-reaching consequences.

Few other novels in American history have had the political impact of *Uncle Tom's Cabin*. Written by Harriet Beecher Stowe and published in 1852, the novel helped fuel the antislavery movement.

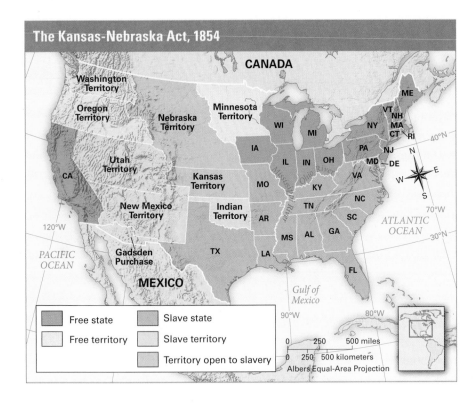

The Kansas-Nebraska Act, 1854

CANADA

Washington Territory
Oregon Territory
Nebraska Territory
Minnesota Territory
Utah Territory
Kansas Territory
New Mexico Territory
Indian Territory
Gadsden Purchase
MEXICO

ME
VT NH MA CT RI
NY
PA
NJ
MD DE
VA
OH
IN
IL
WI
MI
IA
MO
KY
TN
NC
SC
AR
MS AL GA
LA
TX
FL

CA

PACIFIC OCEAN

ATLANTIC OCEAN

Gulf of Mexico

120°W
90°W
80°W
70°W
40°N
30°N

Free state
Free territory
Slave state
Slave territory
Territory open to slavery

0   250   500 miles
0   250   500 kilometers
Albers Equal-Area Projection

The Kansas-Nebraska Act outraged Northerners because it abolished the Missouri Compromise. Under the terms of the act, the question of slavery would be decided by settlers in the newly organized territories of Kansas and Nebraska.

Douglas's final version of the bill, known as the **Kansas-Nebraska Act,** created two new territories, Kansas and Nebraska. It also abolished the Missouri Compromise by leaving it up to the settlers themselves to vote on whether to permit slavery in the two territories. Douglas called this policy popular sovereignty, or rule by the people. The Kansas-Nebraska Act was passed in 1854.

The Kansas-Nebraska Act hit the North like a thunderbolt. Once again, Northerners were haunted by visions of slavery marching across the plains. Douglas tried to calm their fears by saying that the climates of Kansas and Nebraska were not suited to slave labor. But when Northerners studied maps, they were not so sure. Newspaper editor Horace Greeley charged in the *New York Tribune,*

> *The pretense of Douglas & Co. that not even Kansas is to be made a slave state by his bill is a gag [joke]. Ask any Missourian what he thinks about it. The Kansas Territory . . . is bounded in its entire length by Missouri, with a whole tier of slave counties leaning against it. Won't be a slave state! . . . Gentlemen! Don't lie any more!*

Bloodshed in Kansas After the Kansas-Nebraska Act was passed in 1854, settlers poured into Kansas. Most were peaceful farmers looking for good farmland. Some settlers, however, moved to Kansas either to support or to oppose slavery. In the South, towns took up collections to send their young men to Kansas. In the North, abolitionists raised money to send weapons to antislavery settlers. Before long, Kansas had two competing governments in the territory, one for slavery and one against it.

The struggle over slavery soon turned violent. On May 21, 1856, proslavery settlers and so-called "border ruffians" from Missouri invaded Lawrence, Kansas, the home of the antislavery government. Armed invaders burned a hotel, looted several homes, and tossed the printing presses of two abolitionist newspapers into the Kaw River. As the invaders left Lawrence, one of them boasted, "Gentlemen, this is the happiest day of my life."

Kansas-Nebraska Act an act passed in 1854 that created the Kansas and Nebraska territories and abolished the Missouri Compromise by allowing settlers to determine whether slavery would be allowed in the new territories

The raid on Lawrence provoked a wave of outrage in the North. People raised money to replace the destroyed presses. And more "Free-Soilers," as antislavery settlers were called, prepared to move to Kansas.

Meanwhile, a fiery abolitionist named John Brown plotted his own revenge. Two days after the Lawrence raid, Brown and seven followers, including four of Brown's sons and his son-in-law, invaded the pro-slavery town of Pottawatomie, Kansas. There, they dragged five men they suspected of supporting slavery from their homes and hacked them to death with swords.

Violence in Congress The violence in Kansas greatly disturbed Senator Charles Sumner of Massachusetts. To Sumner, it was proof of what he had long suspected—that Senator Stephen Douglas had plotted with Southerners to make Kansas a slave state.

In 1856, Sumner voiced his suspicions in a passionate speech called "The Crime Against Kansas." In harsh, shocking language, Sumner described the "crime against Kansas" as a violent assault on an innocent territory, "compelling it to the hateful embrace of slavery." He dismissed Douglas as "a noisome [offensive], squat, and nameless animal." Sumner also heaped abuse on many Southerners, including Senator Andrew P. Butler of South Carolina.

Just what Sumner hoped to accomplish was not clear. However, copies of his speech were quickly printed up for distribution in the North. After reading it, New England poet Henry Wadsworth Longfellow congratulated Sumner on the "brave and noble speech you made, never to die out in the memories of men."

Certainly, it was not about to die out in the memories of enraged Southerners. Two days after the speech, Senator Butler's nephew, South Carolina representative Preston Brooks, attacked Sumner in the Senate, beating him with his metal-tipped cane until it broke in half. By the time other senators could pull Brooks away, Sumner had collapsed, bloody and unconscious.

Reactions to the attack on Sumner showed how divided the country had become. Many Southerners applauded Brooks for defending the honor of his family and the South. From across the South, supporters sent Brooks new canes to replace the one he had broken on Sumner's head.

Preston Brooks savagely beat Charles Sumner on the Senate floor in retaliation for Sumner's speech against the raid on Lawrence, Kansas. It took Sumner over three years to recover.

The Granger Collection, New York

Most Northerners viewed the beating as another example of Southern brutality. In their eyes, Brooks was no better than the proslavery bullies who had attacked the people of Lawrence. One Connecticut student was so upset that she wrote to Sumner about going to war. "I don't think it is of very much use to stay any longer in the high school," she wrote. "The boys would be better learning to hold muskets, and the girls to make bullets."

21.7 The Dred Scott Decision

In 1857, the slavery controversy shifted from Congress to the Supreme Court. The Court was about to decide a case concerning a Missouri slave named Dred Scott. Years earlier, Scott had traveled with his owner to Wisconsin, where slavery was banned by the Missouri Compromise. When he returned to Missouri, Scott went to court to win his freedom. He argued that his stay in Wisconsin had made him a free man.

Dred Scott sued for his freedom in the Supreme Court. The Court ruled that African Americans had no right to sue in federal courts. The Court also struck down the Missouri Compromise, making slavery legal in all the territories.

Questions of the Case There were nine justices on the Supreme Court in 1857. Five, including Chief Justice Roger Taney, were from the South. Four were from the North. The justices had two key questions to decide. First, as a slave, was Dred Scott a citizen who had the right to bring a case before a federal court? Second, did his time in Wisconsin make him a free man?

Chief Justice Taney hoped to use the Scott case to settle the slavery controversy once and for all. So he asked the Court to consider two more questions: Did Congress have the power to make any laws at all concerning slavery in the territories? And, if so, was the Missouri Compromise a constitutional use of that power?

Nearly 80 years old, Taney had long been opposed to slavery. As a young Maryland lawyer, he had publicly declared that "slavery is a blot upon our national character and every lover of freedom confidently hopes that it will be . . . wiped away." Taney had gone on to free his own slaves. Many observers wondered whether he and his fellow justices would now free Dred Scott as well.

Dred Scott decision

a Supreme Court decision in 1857 that held that African Americans could never be citizens of the United States and that the Missouri Compromise was unconstitutional

Two Judicial Bombshells On March 6, 1857, Chief Justice Taney delivered the Dred Scott decision. The chief justice began by reviewing the facts of Dred Scott's case. Then he dropped the first of two judicial bombshells. By a vote of five to four, the Court had decided that Scott could not sue for his freedom in a federal court because he was not a citizen. Nor, said Taney, could Scott become a citizen. No African American, whether slave or free, was an American citizen—or could ever become one.

Second, Taney declared that the Court had rejected Scott's argument that his stay in Wisconsin had made him a free man. The reason was simple. The Missouri Compromise was unconstitutional.

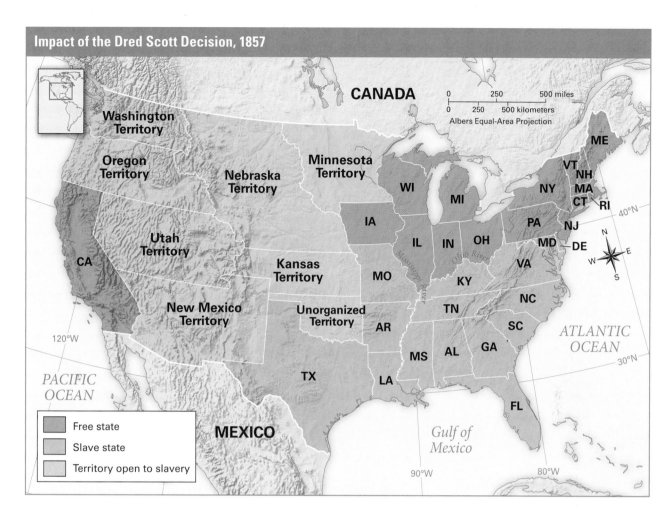

Impact of the Dred Scott Decision, 1857

As a result of the Dred Scott decision, slavery was allowed in all territories.

Taney's argument went something like this. Slaves are property. The Fifth Amendment to the Constitution says that property cannot be taken from people without due process of law—that is, a proper court hearing. Taney reasoned that banning slavery in a territory is the same as taking property from slaveholders who would like to bring their slaves into that territory. And that is unconstitutional. Rather than banning slavery, he said, Congress has a constitutional responsibility to protect the property rights of slaveholders in a territory.

The Dred Scott decision delighted slaveholders. They hoped that, at long last, the issue of slavery in the territories had been settled—and in their favor.

Many Northerners, however, were stunned and enraged by the Court's ruling. *The New York Tribune* called the decision a "wicked and false judgment." The *New York Independent* expressed outrage in a bold headline:

The Decision of the Supreme Court
Is the Moral Assassination of a Race and Cannot Be Obeyed!

21.8 From Compromise to Crisis

During the controversy over the Kansas-Nebraska Act, antislavery activists formed a new political organization, the Republican Party. The Republicans were united by their beliefs that "no man can own another man . . . That slavery must be prohibited in the territories . . . That all new States must be Free States . . . That the rights of our colored citizen . . . must be protected."

In 1858, Republicans in Illinois nominated Abraham Lincoln to run for the Senate. In his acceptance speech, Lincoln pointed out that all attempts to reach compromise on the slavery issue had failed. Quoting from the Bible, he warned, "A house divided against itself cannot stand." Lincoln went on: "I believe this government cannot endure, permanently half-slave and half-free. I do not expect the Union to be dissolved—I do not expect the house to fall—but I do expect it will cease to be divided. It will become all one thing, or all the other."

Abraham Lincoln addresses an audience during one of the Lincoln-Douglas debates. Stephen Douglas is directly behind Lincoln on the platform.

The Granger Collection, New York

The Lincoln-Douglas Debates Lincoln's opponent in the Senate race was Senator Stephen Douglas. The Illinois senator saw no reason why the nation could not go on half-slave and half-free. When Lincoln challenged him to debate the slavery issue, Douglas agreed.

During the **Lincoln-Douglas debates,** Douglas argued that the Dred Scott decision had put the slavery issue to rest. Lincoln disagreed. In his eyes, slavery was a moral, not a legal, issue. He declared, "The real issue in this controversy . . . is the sentiment of one class [group] that looks upon the institution of slavery as a wrong, and of another class that does not look upon it as a wrong."

Lincoln lost the election. But the debates were widely reported, and they helped make him a national figure. His argument with Douglas also brought the moral issue of slavery into sharp focus. Compromises over slavery were becoming impossible.

John Brown's Raid While Lincoln fought to stop the spread of slavery through politics, abolitionist John Brown adopted a more extreme approach. Rather than wait for Congress to act, Brown planned to seize the federal arsenal at Harpers Ferry, Virginia. An arsenal is a place where weapons and ammunition are stored. Brown wanted to use the weapons to arm slaves for a rebellion that would end slavery.

Lincoln-Douglas debates
a series of political debates between Abraham Lincoln and Stephen Douglas, who were candidates in the Illinois race for U.S. senator, in which slavery was the main issue

Brown launched his raid in 1859. It was an insane scheme. All of Brown's men were killed or captured during the raid. Brown himself was convicted of treason and sentenced to die. On the day of his hanging, he left a note that read, "I John Brown am now quite certain that the crimes of this guilty land will never be purged away but with Blood."

Such words filled white Southerners with fear. If a slave rebellion did begin, it was Southern blood that would be spilled. The fact that many Northerners viewed Brown as a hero also left white Southerners uneasy.

In this eyewitness drawing, U.S. marines are shown storming the arsenal at Harpers Ferry that was raided by John Brown and his men. Brown was charged with treason, convicted, and then executed by hanging.

21.9 The Election of 1860 and Secession

The 1860 presidential race showed just how divided the nation had become. The Republicans were united behind Lincoln. The Democrats, however, had split between Northern and Southern **factions**. Northern Democrats nominated Stephen Douglas for president. Southern Democrats supported John C. Breckinridge of Kentucky. The election became even more confusing when a group called the Constitutional Union Party nominated John Bell of Tennessee.

Abraham Lincoln Is Elected President With his opposition divided three ways, Lincoln sailed to victory. But it was an odd victory. Lincoln won the presidential election with just 40 percent of the votes, all of them cast in the North. In ten Southern states, he was not even on the ballot.

For white Southerners, the election of 1860 delivered an unmistakable message. The South was now in the minority. It no longer had the power to shape national events or policies. Sooner or later, Southerners feared, Congress would try to abolish slavery. And that, wrote a South Carolina newspaper, would mean "the loss of liberty, property, home, country—everything that makes life worth living."

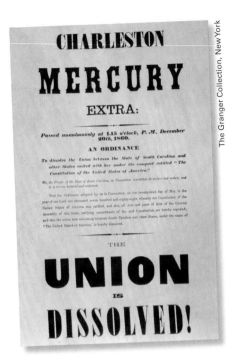

This broadside, printed in December 1860, boldly announces the secession of South Carolina from the Union.

The opening shots of the Civil War were fired at Fort Sumter on April 12, 1861. No one was killed in the 33-hour bombardment. It was a bloodless opening to the bloodiest war in U.S. history.

The South Secedes from the Union In the weeks following the election, talk of secession filled the air. Alarmed senators formed a committee to search for yet another compromise that might hold the nation together. They knew that finding one would not be easy. Still, they had to do something to stop the rush toward disunion and disaster.

The Senate committee held its first meeting on December 20, 1860. Just as the senators began their work, events in two distant cities dashed their hopes for a settlement.

In Springfield, Illinois, a reporter called on President-Elect Abraham Lincoln. When asked whether he could support a compromise on slavery, Lincoln's answer was clear. He would not interfere with slavery in the South. And he would support enforcement of the Fugitive Slave Act. But Lincoln drew the line at letting slavery extend into the territories. On this question, he declared, "Let there be no compromise."

Meanwhile, in Charleston, South Carolina, delegates attending a state convention voted that same day—December 20, 1860—to leave the Union. The city went wild. Church bells rang. Crowds filled the streets, roaring their approval. A South Carolina newspaper boldly proclaimed, "The Union Is Dissolved!" Six more states soon followed South Carolina's lead. In February 1861, those states joined together as the Confederate States of America.

The Civil War Begins On March 4, 1861, Lincoln became president of the not-so-united United States. In his inaugural address, Lincoln stated his belief that secession was both wrong and unconstitutional. He then appealed to the rebellious states to return in peace. "In your hands, my dissatisfied fellow countrymen, and not in mine," he said, "is the momentous issue of civil war."

A month later, Confederates in Charleston, South Carolina, forced the issue. On April 12, 1861, they opened fire on Fort Sumter, a federal fort in Charleston Harbor. After 33 hours of heavy shelling, the defenders of the fort hauled down the Stars and Stripes and replaced it with the white flag of surrender.

The news that the Confederates had fired on the American flag unleashed a wave of patriotic fury in the North. All the doubts that people had about using force to save the Union vanished. A New York newspaper reported excitedly, "There is no more thought of bribing or coaxing the traitors who have dared to aim their cannon balls at the flag of the Union . . . Fort Sumter is temporarily lost, but the country is saved."

The time for compromise was over. The issues that had divided the nation for so many years would now be decided by a civil war.

Chapter Summary

In this chapter, you learned how a series of compromises failed to keep the United States from splitting in two over the issue of slavery.

Confronting the Issue of Slavery The issue of granting Missouri statehood threatened to upset the balance of free and slave states. Northerners were concerned that if Missouri entered the Union as a slave state, other territories would also be admitted as slave states. Southerners worried that if Congress banned slavery in Missouri, it would try to end slavery elsewhere.

The Missouri Compromise In 1820, the Missouri Compromise resolved the issue by admitting Missouri as a slave state and Maine as a free state. It also drew a line across the Louisiana Territory. In the future, slavery would be permitted only south of that line.

The Compromise of 1850 The furor over slavery in new territories erupted again after the Mexican-American War. The Compromise of 1850 admitted California as a free state and allowed the New Mexico and Utah territories to decide whether to allow slavery. It also ended the slave trade in Washington, D.C., and included a stronger fugitive slave law. Attitudes on both sides were hardened by Harriet Beecher Stowe's novel *Uncle Tom's Cabin* and the Kansas-Nebraska Act.

The Dred Scott Decision In 1857, the Supreme Court issued a decision in the Dred Scott case: African Americans were not citizens and the Missouri Compromise was unconstitutional.

From Compromise to Crisis Antislavery activists formed a new political party: the Republican Party. The party nominated Abraham Lincoln for the Illinois Senate. Slavery was the focus of debates between Lincoln and opponent Stephen Douglas. Lincoln lost the election, but the debates brought slavery into sharp focus. A raid launched by abolitionist John Brown raised fears of a slave rebellion.

The Election of 1860 and Secession Lincoln won the presidency in 1860. Soon afterward, South Carolina and six other Southern states seceded from the Union and formed the Confederate States of America. In early 1861, Confederate troops fired on Fort Sumter in Charleston, South Carolina, marking the beginning of the Civil War.

Anthony Burns was 19 years old when he fled slavery in Virginia. Living as a free man in Boston, Burns was arrested, tried, and sent back to slavery under the Fugitive Slave Act.

Slavery Divides Boston

Boston was a magnet for people who opposed slavery. The American Anti-Slavery Society was based in Boston, as was the abolitionist newspaper *The Liberator*. But the issue of slavery divided even the people of Boston. Tensions in Boston increased, as they did in other places. Boston, like the nation, was splitting apart.

On June 2, 1854, about 50,000 people lined the streets of Boston. Hundreds more gathered on rooftops. Businesses closed. People looked out of the windows and doorways of the buildings where they usually worked.

Women dangled black shawls out of second- and third-story windows. By the city's harbor, black fabric covered the Commonwealth Building. From its upper windows hung six American flags, all draped in black. Samuel May, who was born during the American Revolution, hung two U.S. flags upside down from his hardware store as a protest. At ground level, a black coffin displayed the word *Liberty*.

Then, Anthony Burns emerged from the courthouse. Surrounded by federal marshals, he was walking to the docks where he would board a ship to Virginia. Burns, an escaped slave, was being returned to his owner.

Burns had escaped from slavery in Virginia by hiding in the cargo hold of a ship. He had settled in Boston just a few months earlier, believing that people in the free state of Massachusetts would welcome him. They did.

Now, many Bostonians were outraged that Burns was being forced back into slavery. Massachusetts had outlawed the institution decades earlier. Many escaped slaves lived as free people in the state.

Burns's three-block walk to the pier was dramatic. Boston's mayor had called on the military to keep order, fearing that angry crowds would use force to free Burns. Each guard who walked with Burns held a pistol in one hand and a sword in the other.

One woman described watching the procession from an upstairs office along the route from the courthouse to the pier. She reported that she and her companions "called out, Shame and Shame . . . in our most expressive and scornful voices" at the men who escorted Burns.

What was going on in Boston? Why was Anthony Burns being sent back to slavery?

A MAN KIDNAPPED!

A PUBLIC MEETING AT

FANEUIL HALL!

WILL BE HELD

THIS FRIDAY EVEN'G,

May 26th, at 7 o'clock,

To secure justice for A MAN CLAIMED AS A SLAVE by a

VIRGINIA KIDNAPPER!

And NOW IMPRISONED IN BOSTON COURT HOUSE, in defiance of the Laws of Massachusetts. Shall he be plunged into the Hell of Virginia Slavery by a Massachusetts Judge of Probate!

BOSTON, May 26th, 1854.

Posters and handbills advertised a public meeting to protest the arrest of Anthony Burns. Thousands of Burns's supporters gathered on May 26, saying that Burns had been kidnapped by his former owner.

The Fugitive Slave Act

According to Massachusetts law, Anthony Burns had been a free man for the months he lived in Boston. Nonetheless, because of the federal Fugitive Slave Act, he was still a fugitive from slavery. Passed by the U.S. Congress in 1850, the Fugitive Slave Act said that slave owners could retrieve their runaway slaves. Burns's master had come to Boston to reclaim his "property." He did so with the full power of the law behind him. The outrage that greeted him in Boston was a symptom of the divisions tearing apart the country.

Burns was not the only one affected. Many slaves had fled to Northern states, where they lived in freedom. The new law meant that they were no longer safe in their Northern homes. They could be captured and returned to their owners at any time.

With the new law in place, many former slaves saw that their only chance for real safety was to get out of the country entirely. William and Ellen Craft escaped slavery in Macon, Georgia, in 1848. They went first to Philadelphia, and then farther north to Boston. Even there, they weren't safe. Under the Fugitive Slave Act, slave catchers pursued them. William locked himself in his clothing store, while abolitionist friends hid Ellen somewhere else. When the immediate danger had passed, Boston's activists arranged for the couple to go to Liverpool, England. There, they could live in freedom, unthreatened by slave catchers or their status as fugitive slaves.

The Fugitive Slave Act affected Northern abolitionists as well as escaped slaves. The law now involved Northerners in the slave system that many of them hated. No matter how much the people of Boston opposed slavery, federal law overruled them. Meant to ease tensions between North and South, the Fugitive Slave Act only heightened them.

And so crowds of sad and angry Bostonians watched helplessly as Anthony Burns left their haven in the North. Outraged by the injustice they watched unfolding before them, they vowed to keep up the fight to end slavery.

Boston abolitionists were outraged by the fate of Anthony Burns. Boston officials feared violence as Burns was marched to the ship that would take him back to Virginia.

The Granger Collection, New York

The Cradle of Liberty Meets the Evil of Slavery

Boston had long been a symbol of freedom, sometimes called "the cradle of liberty." It was in Boston, after all, that the colonists first rebelled against British rule. And Massachusetts was one of the first states to outlaw slavery. Bostonians in particular had a long commitment to abolition. How had that commitment led to the terrible day in 1854 when Anthony Burns boarded the boat to return to Virginia and become, once again, a slave?

No one could have foreseen that day back in 1829 when David Walker, an African American living in Boston, published a pamphlet called *Walker's Appeal to the Coloured Citizens of the World.* In the pamphlet, Walker urged black Americans to resist slavery. He even suggested that violence might be necessary. Walker also warned white Americans that God would punish them for the crime of slavery.

Many others spoke out against the evils of slavery. William Lloyd Garrison was one of them. In his newspaper, *The Liberator,* he made some radical claims. He said that slaves must be freed immediately. Many abolitionists at the time said it would be best to end slavery gradually. He said that African Americans should not start colonies in Africa, as some reformers believed. Instead, they should live as free people in the United States. And perhaps most radical of all, he said that blacks should not only be free, but that they should have all the same rights as whites.

Of course, Bostonians who opposed abolition disliked Garrison and his ideas. In 1835, a mob nearly killed him.

Not everyone in Boston was against slavery. In 1835, an angry mob tried to lynch William Lloyd Garrison after one of his antislavery lectures.

Garrison later described how a few men carried him to safety. He hated the hypocrisy of accepting slavery in the land of the free.

I was thus conducted [carried] . . . over the ground that was stained with the blood of the first martyrs in the cause of LIBERTY and INDEPENDENCE . . . What a scandalous and revolting contrast! My offence was in pleading for LIBERTY—liberty for my enslaved countrymen.

Like Garrison, others in Boston suffered for their efforts to end slavery. One of them described what she and others had gone through.

It has occasioned our brothers to be dismissed from [their jobs as ministers]—our sons to be expelled from colleges and theological seminaries—our friends from professorships—ourselves from literary and social privileges.
—Maria Weston Warren, Boston Female Anti-Slavery Society

It took courage to oppose slavery. Some sources estimate that only about 1 percent of Northerners were active abolitionists.

Their numbers may have been small, but Boston abolitionists fought on. They took strong steps to protect the free blacks who lived in the city. In 1842, a fugitive slave named George Lattimer went to jail in Boston. He had to wait there while his owner traveled to Virginia to get the papers that would prove that Lattimer was a slave. Angry abolitionists filed legal claims on Lattimer's behalf. Their efforts failed. Lattimer did not become free until black Bostonians paid his owner $400.

Free blacks realized how shaky their freedom was. Slave catchers could return them south. So they took the lead in distributing a petition calling for a state law to protect Massachusetts citizens. Those who signed the petition did so "desiring to free this commonwealth and themselves from all connection with domestic slavery and to secure the citizens of this state from the danger of enslavement."

As a result of their efforts, the state passed the Personal Liberty Law in 1843. The law said that state officials and facilities could not be used to capture and return fugitive slaves.

But the Fugitive Slave Act overruled the state's Personal Liberty Law. It put federal, not state, officials in charge of returning fugitive slaves.

And so, Anthony Burns had to return to Virginia as a slave. Eventually, Boston's activists bought his freedom. But the experience highlighted the fact that the North and South were bound to clash again until slavery was abolished.

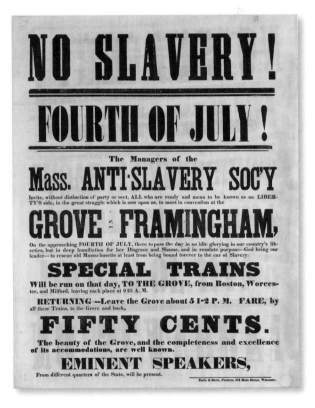

William Lloyd Garrison called the Constitution a proslavery document. In a dramatic flourish, he burned a copy of it at a public speech shortly after the Anthony Burns incident.

Chapter 22

The Civil War

What factors and events influenced the outcome of the Civil War?

22.1 Introduction

The Confederate bombardment of Fort Sumter in Charleston, South Carolina, ended months of confusion. The nation was at war. The time had come to choose sides. For most whites in the South, the choice was clear. Early in 1861, representatives from six of the seven states that had seceded from the Union met to form a new nation called the Confederate States of America. Southerners believed that just as the states had once voluntarily joined the Union, they could voluntarily leave it now. The men who fought for the South were proud defenders of Southern independence.

For many Northerners, the choice was just as clear. "There can be no neutrals in this war," declared Senator Stephen Douglas after the attack of Fort Sumter, "*only patriots—or traitors.*" Most Northerners viewed the secession of Southern states as a traitorous act of rebellion against the United States. They marched off to war eager to defend what they saw as their union, their constitution, and their flag.

Choosing sides was harder for the eight slave states located between the Confederacy and the free states. Four of these so-called border states—Virginia, Arkansas, Tennessee, and North Carolina—joined the Confederacy. The western counties of Virginia, however, remained loyal to the Union. Rather than fight for the South, they broke away to form a new state called West Virginia. The other four border states—Delaware, Maryland, Kentucky, and Missouri—remained in the Union, although many of their citizens fought for the South.

As Americans took sides, they began to see why a civil war—a conflict between two groups of citizens in one country—is the most painful kind of war. This conflict divided not only states, but also families and friends. In this chapter, you will learn how this "brothers' war" turned into the most destructive of all American wars. As you read, put yourself in the shoes of the soldiers and civilians who were part of this long and tragic struggle.

More soldiers died during the Civil War than in all other U.S. wars combined. Here, some of the dead lay where they fell on the battlefield. The Civil War claimed the lives of more than 620,000 Union and Confederate soldiers.

◄ The Civil War divided Americans into two opposing nations. Union soldiers (left) fought fellow Americans and Confederate soldiers (right).

The North and the South had different strengths at the beginning of the war. The North had far more factories and railroad lines (left). The South had better military leadership (right).

22.2 North Versus South

President Abraham Lincoln's response to the attack on Fort Sumter was quick and clear. He called for 75,000 volunteers to come forward to preserve the Union. At the same time, Jefferson Davis, the newly elected president of the **Confederacy**, called for volunteers to defend the South. For the first time, Americans were fighting a **civil war**.

Strengths and Weaknesses of the North The North began the war with impressive strengths. Its population was about 22 million, compared to the South's 9 million. The North was both richer and more **technologically** advanced than the South. About 90 percent of the nation's manufacturing, and most of its banks, were in the North.

The North had geographic advantages, too. It had more farms than the South to provide food for troops. Its land contained most of the country's iron, coal, copper, and gold. The North controlled the seas, and its 21,000 miles of railroad track allowed troops and supplies to be transported wherever they were needed.

The North's greatest weakness was its military leadership. At the start of the war, about one-third of the nation's military officers resigned and returned to their homes in the South. During much of the war, Lincoln searched for effective generals who could lead the Union to victory.

Strengths and Weaknesses of the South In contrast to the North, the South's great strength was its military leadership. Most of America's best military officers were Southerners who chose to fight for the Confederacy. This was not an easy decision for many of them. Colonel Robert E. Lee, for example, was not a supporter of either slavery or secession. But he decided that he could not fight against his native Virginia. Lee resigned from the U.S. Army to become commander in chief of the Confederate forces.

Confederacy another name for the Confederate States of America, made up of the 11 states that seceded from the Union

civil war a war between opposing groups of citizens from the same country

The South had geographic advantages as well. To win the war, the North would have to invade and conquer the South. The sheer size of the South made this a daunting task. The South, in contrast, could win simply by defending its territory until Northerners grew tired of fighting.

The South did have an important geographic disadvantage. If the Union could control the Mississippi River, it could split the Confederacy in two.

The South's main weaknesses were its economy and its transportation systems. The region's agriculturally based economy could not support a long war. It had few factories to produce guns and other military supplies. The Confederacy also faced serious transportation problems. The South lacked the railroads needed to haul troops or supplies over long distances.

Abraham Lincoln versus Jefferson Davis The North's greatest advantage was its newly elected president, Abraham Lincoln. Through even the darkest days of the war, Lincoln never wavered from his belief that the Union was **perpetual**—never to be broken. Throughout his presidency, Lincoln related the preservation of the Union to the ideals of the American Revolution. In his first inaugural address, he said that the Union was begun by the American Revolution, "matured and continued" by the Declaration of Independence, and affirmed by the Constitution.

At the time of the secession **crisis,** Jefferson Davis was a U.S. senator from Mississippi. A firm believer in states' rights, he resigned his seat in the Senate when Mississippi left the Union. Like Lincoln, Davis often spoke of the American Revolution. When Southerners formed their own government, Davis said in his inaugural address, they "merely **asserted** a right which the Declaration of Independence of 1776 had defined to be inalienable." He believed the South was fighting for the same freedom cherished by the nation's founders.

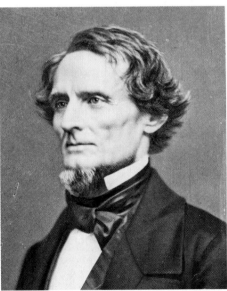

Abraham Lincoln (left) and Jefferson Davis (right) at the start of the Civil War

22.3 Bull Run: A Great Awakening

In the spring of 1861, President Lincoln and General Winfield Scott planned the Union's war strategy. Step one was to surround the South by sea to cut off its trade. Step two was to divide the Confederacy into sections so that one region could not help another. Step three was to capture Richmond, Virginia, the capital of the Confederacy, and destroy the Confederate government. Journalists called this strategy the Anaconda Plan because it resembled the crushing death grip of an anaconda snake.

Rose Greenhow is pictured here with her daughter. Greenhow collected valuable information about Union plans to attack Richmond and passed it on to Confederate leaders through a coded message like the one shown above.

Rose Greenhow's Dilemma Most Northerners believed that the war could be won with a single Union assault on Richmond. In 1861, thousands of volunteers poured into Washington, D.C., shouting, "On to Richmond!" A young widow and Washington social leader named Rose O'Neal Greenhow watched these eager troops carefully.

Greenhow was a strong supporter of the Southern cause. She used her friendship with government officials to learn just when and how the Union planned to attack Richmond. Her challenge was to find a way to deliver this information to Confederate leaders without being discovered.

The Battle of Bull Run On a hot July morning, long lines of Union soldiers marched out of Washington heading for Richmond. Their voices could be heard singing and cheering across the countryside. Parties of civilians followed the army, adding to the excitement. They had come along to see the end of the rebellion.

The troops would not have been so cheerful had they known what was waiting for them at Manassas, a small town on the way to Richmond. Greenhow had managed to warn Southern military leaders of Union plans. She had smuggled a coded note to them in a young girl's curls. Southern troops were waiting for the Union forces as they approached Manassas. The two armies met at a creek known as Bull Run.

At first, a Union victory looked certain. But Confederate general Thomas Jackson and his regiment of Virginians refused to give up. "Look," shouted South Carolina general Bernard Bee to his men, "there is Jackson with his Virginians, standing like a stone wall." Thus inspired by "Stonewall" Jackson's example, the Confederate lines held firm until **reinforcements** arrived. Late that afternoon, Jackson urged his men to "yell like furies" as they charged the Union forces. The charge overwhelmed the inexperienced Union troops, who fled in panic back to Washington.

The Battle of Bull Run was a smashing victory for the South. For the North, it was a shocking blow. Lincoln and his generals now realized that ending the war would not be easy.

Women Support the War Over the next year, both the North and the South worked to build and train large armies. As men went off to war, women took their places on the home front. Wives and mothers supported their families by running farms and businesses. Many women went to work for the first time in factories. Others found jobs as nurses, teachers, or government workers.

Women also served the military forces on both sides as messengers, guides, scouts, smugglers, soldiers, and spies. Greenhow was arrested for spying shortly after the Battle of Bull Run. Although she was kept under guard in her Washington home, she continued to smuggle military secrets to the Confederates. The following year, Greenhow was allowed to move to the South, where President Jefferson Davis welcomed her as a hero.

Women also volunteered to tend sick and wounded soldiers. Dorothea Dix was already well known for her efforts to improve the treatment of the mentally ill. She was appointed director of the Union army's nursing service. Dix insisted that all female nurses be over 30 years old, plain in appearance, physically strong, and willing to do unpleasant work. Her rules were so strict that she was known as "Dragon Dix."

While most nurses worked in military hospitals, Clara Barton followed Union armies into battle, tending troops where they fell. Later generations would remember Barton as the founder of the American Red Cross. To the soldiers she cared for during the war, she was "the angel of the battlefield."

During the Civil War, many women went to work in factories, such as the munitions plant illustrated here. The women replaced men who were away fighting.

427

For 12 hours, Confederate and Union forces fought at Antietam in what was the bloodiest day of the Civil War. Some of the 2,770 Confederates who died that day are shown here.

22.4 Antietam: A Bloody Affair

The Battle of Bull Run ended Northerners' hopes for a quick victory. In the months that followed that sobering defeat, the Union began to carry out the Anaconda Plan.

The Anaconda Plan in Action Step one of the Anaconda Plan was to blockade the South's ports and cut off its trade. In 1861, the Union navy launched the blockade. By the end of the year, most ports in the South were closed to foreign ships. The South had long exported its cotton to Great Britain and France. The Confederacy looked to Great Britain to send ships to break through the blockade. The British, however, refused this request. As a result, the South could not export cotton to Europe or import needed supplies.

Early in 1862, the Union began to put step two of the Anaconda Plan into action. The strategy was to divide the Confederacy by gaining control of the Mississippi River. In April, Union admiral David Farragut led 46 ships up the Mississippi River to New Orleans. This was the largest American fleet ever assembled. In the face of such overwhelming force, the city surrendered without firing a shot.

Meanwhile, Union forces headed by General Ulysses S. Grant began moving south toward the Mississippi from Illinois. In 1862, Grant won a series of victories that put Kentucky and much of Tennessee under Union control. A general of remarkable determination, Grant refused to accept any battle outcome other than unconditional, or total, surrender. For this reason, U. S. Grant was known to his men as "Unconditional Surrender" Grant.

Later in 1862, Union general George McClellan sent 100,000 men by ship to capture Richmond. Again, a Union victory seemed certain. But despite being outnumbered, Confederate forces stopped the Union attack in a series of well-fought battles. Once more, Richmond was saved.

The Battle of Antietam At this point, General Robert E. Lee, the commander of the Confederate forces, did the unexpected. He sent his troops across the Potomac River into Maryland, a slave state that remained in the Union. Lee hoped this show of strength might persuade Maryland to join the Confederacy. He also hoped that a Confederate victory on Union soil would convince European nations to support the South.

On a crisp September day in 1862, Confederate and Union armies met near the Maryland town of Sharpsburg along Antietam Creek. All day long, McClellan's troops pounded Lee's badly outnumbered forces. The following day, Lee retreated to Virginia.

McClellan claimed Antietam as a Union victory. But many who fought there saw the battle as a defeat for both armies. Of the 75,000 Union troops who fought at Antietam, about 2,100 were killed. About 10,300 were wounded or missing. Of the 52,000 Confederates who fought at Antietam, about 2,770 lost their lives, while 11,000 were wounded or missing. In that single day of fighting, more Americans were killed than in the War of 1812 and the Mexican War combined. The Battle of Antietam was the bloodiest day of the war.

The New Realities of War The horrifying death toll at Antietam reflected the new realities of warfare. In past wars, battles had been fought in hand-to-hand combat using bayonets. During the Civil War, improved weapons made killing from a distance much easier. Rifles, which replaced muskets, were accurate over long distances. Improved cannons and artillery also made it easier for armies to attack forces some distance away. As a result, armies could meet, fight, die, and part without either side winning a clear victory.

Medical care was not as advanced as weaponry. Civil War doctors had no understanding of the causes of infections. Surgeons operated in dirty hospital tents with basic instruments. Few bothered to wash their hands between patients. As a result, infections spread rapidly from patient to patient. The hospital death rate was so high that soldiers often refused medical care. An injured Ohio soldier wrote that he chose to return to battle rather than see a doctor, "thinking that I had better die by rebel bullets than Union quackery [unskilled medical care]."

As staggering as the battle death tolls were, far more soldiers died of diseases than wounds. Unsanitary conditions in army camps were so bad that about three men died of typhoid, pneumonia, and other diseases for every one who died in battle. As one soldier observed, "these big battles [are] not as bad as the fever."

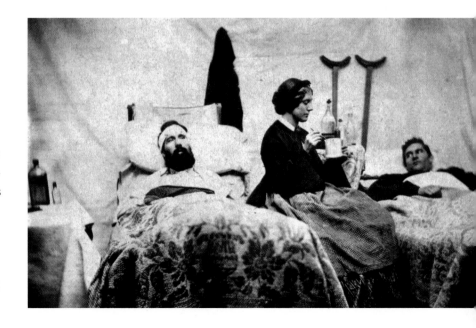

Medical care was shockingly poor during the Civil War. Thousands of soldiers died from infections or diseases. Nevertheless, nurses performed heroically as they cared for the sick and wounded.

22.5 Gettysburg: A Turning Point

While neither side won the battle of Antietam, it was enough of a victory for Lincoln to take his first steps toward ending slavery. When the Civil War began, Lincoln had resisted pleas from abolitionists to make emancipation, or the freeing of slaves, a reason for fighting the Confederacy. He himself opposed slavery. But the purpose of the war, he said, "is to save the Union, and is not either to save or destroy slavery."

The Emancipation Proclamation As the war dragged on, Lincoln changed his mind. He decided to make abolition a goal of the Union. Lincoln realized that European nations that opposed slavery would never support the side that did not want slavery to end. Freeing slaves could also deprive the Confederacy of a large part of its workforce.

On January 1, 1863, President Lincoln issued the **Emancipation Proclamation**. The proclamation, or formal order, declared slaves in all Confederate states to be free. This announcement had little immediate effect on slavery. The Confederate states ignored the document. Slaves living in states loyal to the Union were not affected by the proclamation.

Still, for many in the North, the Emancipation Proclamation changed the war into a crusade for freedom. The Declaration of Independence had said that "all men are created equal." Now the fight was about living up to those words.

In this illustration, slaves wait for the Emancipation Proclamation. While the proclamation had little immediate effect, it meant the Union was now fighting to end slavery.

The Battle of Gettysburg In the summer of 1863, Lee felt confident enough to risk another invasion of the North. He hoped to capture a Northern city and help convince the weary North to seek peace.

Union and Confederate troops met on July 1, 1863, west of Gettysburg, Pennsylvania. The Union troops, about 90,000 strong, were led by newly appointed General George C. Meade. After a brief skirmish, they occupied four miles of high ground along an area known as Cemetery Ridge. About a mile to the west, some 75,000 Confederate troops gathered behind Seminary Ridge.

The following day, the Confederates attempted to find weak spots in the Union position. The Union lines held firm. On the third day, Lee ordered an all-out attack on the center of the Union line. Cannons filled the air with smoke and thunder. George Pickett led 15,000 Confederate soldiers in a charge across the low ground separating the two forces.

Pickett's charge marked the northernmost point reached by Southern troops during the war. But as Confederate troops pressed forward, Union gunners opened great holes in their advancing lines. Those men who managed to make their way to Cemetery Ridge were struck down by Union soldiers in hand-to-hand combat.

Although Gettysburg was a victory for the Union, the losses on both sides were staggering. More than 17,500 Union soldiers and 23,000 Confederate troops were killed or wounded in three days of battle. Lee, who lost about a third of his army, withdrew to Virginia. From this point on, he would only wage a defensive war on Southern soil.

Emancipation Proclamation an order issued by President Lincoln on January 1, 1863, declaring slaves in the Confederate states to be free

Opposition on the Union Home Front Despite the victory at Gettysburg, Lincoln faced a number of problems on the home front. One was opposition to the war itself. A group of Northern Democrats were more interested in restoring peace than in saving the Union or ending slavery. Republicans called these Democrats "Copperheads" after a poisonous snake with that name.

Other Northerners opposed the war because they were sympathetic to the Confederate cause. When a proslavery mob attacked Union soldiers marching through Maryland, Lincoln sent in troops to keep order. He also used his constitutional power to temporarily suspend the right of **habeas corpus**. During the national emergency, citizens no longer had the right to appear before a court to face charges. People who were suspected of disloyalty were jailed without being charged for a crime.

Lincoln's Gettysburg Address In 1863, President Lincoln traveled to Gettysburg. Thousands of the men who died there had been buried in a new cemetery. Lincoln was among those invited to speak at the dedication of this new burial ground. The nation would never forget Lincoln's **Gettysburg Address**.

The president deliberately spoke of the war in words that echoed the Declaration of Independence. The "great civil war," he said, was testing whether a nation "conceived in liberty, and dedicated to the proposition that all men are created equal . . . can long endure." He spoke of the brave men, "living and dead," who had fought to defend that ideal. "The world . . . can never forget what they did here." Finally, he called on Americans to remain

dedicated to the great task remaining before us—that from these honored dead we take increased devotion to that cause for which they gave the last full measure of devotion—that we here highly resolve that these dead shall not have died in vain—that this nation, under God, shall have a new birth of freedom—and that government of the people, by the people, for the people, shall not perish from the earth.

On July 3, 1863, General George Pickett led 15,000 Confederate troops in a charge against the Union lines. Row after row of Confederate soldiers fell under a rain of bullets until they finally retreated.

habeas corpus the right of an accused person to appear in court so a judge can determine whether he or she is being imprisoned lawfully

Gettysburg Address a speech by President Abraham Lincoln in 1863 at the site of the Battle of Gettysburg in memory of the Union soldiers who had died trying to protect the ideals of freedom upon which the nation was founded

22.6 Vicksburg: A Besieged City

The Civil War was a war of many technological firsts. It was the first American war to use railroads to move troops and to keep them supplied. It was the first war in which telegraphs were used to communicate with distant armies. It was the first conflict to be recorded in photographs. It was also the first to see combat between armor-plated steamships.

The *Merrimac* and the *Monitor* Early in the war, Union forces withdrew from the navy yard in Norfolk, Virginia. They left behind a warship named the *Merrimac.* The Confederacy began the war with no navy. They covered the wooden *Merrimac* with iron plates and added a powerful ram to its prow.

In response, the Union navy built its own ironclad ship called the *Monitor.* Completed in less than 100 days, the *Monitor* had a flat deck and two heavy guns in a revolving turret. It was said to resemble a "cheese box on a raft."

In March 1862, the *Merrimac,* which the Confederates had renamed the *Virginia,* steamed into Chesapeake Bay to attack Union ships. With cannonballs harmlessly bouncing off its sides, the iron monster destroyed three wooden ships and threatened the entire Union blockade fleet.

The next morning, the *Virginia* was met by the *Monitor.* The two ironclads exchanged shots for hours before withdrawing. Neither could claim victory, and neither was harmed.

The battle of the *Merrimac* and the *Monitor* showed that iron-clad ships were superior to wooden vessels. After that, both sides added ironclads to their navies. The South, however, was never able to build enough ships to end the Union blockade of Southern harbors.

In 1862, the *Monitor* and the *Merrimac,* two iron-clad ships, fought to a standstill. The battle signaled the end of wooden warships.

Control of the Mississippi Ironclads were part of the Union's campaign to divide the South by taking control of the Mississippi River. After seizing New Orleans in 1862, Admiral David Farragut moved up the Mississippi to capture the cities of Baton Rouge and Natchez. At the same time, other Union ships gained control of Memphis, Tennessee.

The Union now controlled both ends of the Mississippi. The South could no longer move men or supplies up and down the river. But neither could the North, as long as the Confederates continued to control one key location—Vicksburg, Mississippi.

The Siege of Vicksburg The town of Vicksburg was located on a bluff above a hairpin turn in the Mississippi River. The city was easy to defend and difficult to capture. Who-ever held Vicksburg could, with a few well-placed cannons, control move-ment along the Mississippi. But even Farragut had to admit with fellow of-ficer David Porter that ships "cannot crawl up hills 300 feet high." An army would be needed to take Vicksburg.

In May 1863, General Ulysses S. Grant battled his way to Vicksburg with the needed army. For six weeks, Union gunboats shelled the city from the river while Grant's army bom-barded it from land. Slowly but surely, the Union troops burrowed toward the city in trenches and tunnels.

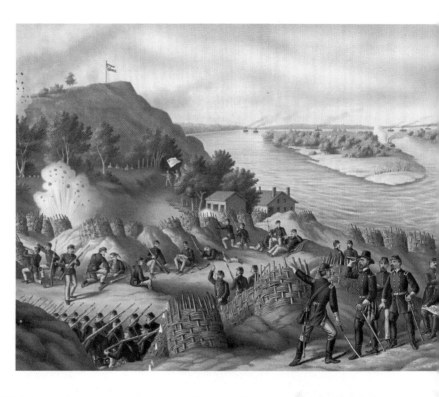

For more than a month, Union forces bom-barded Vicksburg with an average of 2,800 shells a day. Forced to eat horses, mules, dogs, and rats, the Confederates finally surrendered.

As shells pounded the city, people in Vicksburg dug caves into the hillsides for protection. To survive, they ate horses, mules, and bread made of corn and dried peas. "It had the properties of Indian rubber," said one Confederate soldier, "and was worse than leather to digest."

Low on food and supplies, Vicksburg surrendered on July 4, 1863. The Mississippi was now a Union waterway, and the Confederacy was cut in two.

Problems on the Confederate Home Front As the war raged on, life in the South became grim. Because of the blockade, imported goods disappeared from stores. What few items were available were extremely expensive.

Unable to sell their tobacco and cotton to the North or to other countries, farmers planted food crops instead. Still, the South was often hungry. Invading Union armies destroyed crops. They also cut rail lines, making it difficult to move food and supplies to Southern cities and army camps.

As clothing wore out, Southerners made do with patches and homespun cloth. At the beginning of the war, Mary Boykin Chesnut had written in her journal of well-dressed Confederate troops. By 1863, she was writing of soldiers dressed in "rags and tags."

By 1864, Southerners were writing letters like this one to soldiers on the battlefront: "We haven't got nothing in the house to eat but a little bit o' meal. I don't want to you to stop fighten them yankees . . . but try and get off and come home and fix us all up some." Many soldiers found it hard to resist such pleas, even if going home meant deserting their units.

African American soldiers displayed their courage during their attack on Fort Wagner. The 54th Massachusetts Infantry charged across 200 yards of open beach in their effort to reach the fort.

22.7 Fort Wagner: African Americans and the War

Early in the war, abolitionists had urged Congress to recruit African Americans for the army. But at first, most Northerners regarded the conflict as "a white man's war." Congress finally opened the door to black recruits in 1862. About 186,000 African Americans, many of them former slaves, enlisted in the Union army. Another 30,000 African Americans joined the Union navy.

The Massachusetts 54th Regiment Massachusetts was one of the first states to organize black regiments. The most famous was the 54th Massachusetts Infantry, commanded by Colonel Robert Gould Shaw. Two of the 54th Infantry's 1,000 soldiers were sons of Frederick Douglass.

The men of the Massachusetts 54th were paid less than white soldiers. When the black soldiers learned this, they protested the unequal treatment by refusing to accept any pay at all. In a letter to Lincoln, Corporal James Henry Gooding asked, "Are we Soldiers, or are we Laborers? . . . We have done a Soldier's duty. Why can't we have a Soldier's pay?" At Lincoln's urging, Congress finally granted black soldiers equal pay.

After three months of training, the Massachusetts 54th was sent to South Carolina to take part in an attack on Fort Wagner outside of Charleston. As they prepared for battle, the men of the 54th faced the usual worries of untested troops. But they also faced the added fear that if captured, they might be sold into slavery.

African Americans at War The assault on Fort Wagner was an impossible mission. To reach the fort, troops had to cross 200 yards of open, sandy beach. Rifle and cannon fire poured down on them. After losing nearly half of their men, the survivors of the 54th regiment retreated. But their bravery won them widespread respect.

During the war, 166 African American regiments fought in nearly 500 battles. Black soldiers often received little training, poor equipment, and less pay than white soldiers. They also risked death or enslavement if captured. Still, African Americans fought with great courage to save the Union.

22.8 Appomattox: Total War Brings an End

During the first years of the war, Lincoln had searched for a commander who was willing to fight the Confederates. The president finally found the leader he needed in General Grant. He made Grant commander of the Union forces in March 1864. Grant's views on war were quite straightforward: "The art of war is simple enough. Find out where your enemy is. Get at him as soon as you can. Strike at him as hard as you can and as often as you can, and keep moving on."

Using this strategy, Grant mapped out a plan for ending the war. He would lead a large force against Lee to capture Richmond. At the same time, General William Tecumseh Sherman would lead a second army into Georgia to take Atlanta.

In 1864, Lincoln gave command of all Union forces to Ulysses S. Grant. Grant believed in using his larger army to wear down the enemy regardless of the casualties that his own forces suffered.

Grant Invades Virginia In May 1864, General Grant invaded Virginia with a force of more than 100,000 men. They met Lee's army of 60,000 in a dense forest known as the Wilderness. In two days of fierce fighting, Grant lost 18,000 men. Still, Grant would not retreat. "I propose to fight it out along this line," he said, "if it takes all summer." He followed Lee's army to Cold Harbor, Virginia, where he lost 7,000 men in 15 minutes of fighting.

By the time the two forces reached Petersburg, a railroad center 20 miles south of Richmond, Grant's losses almost equaled Lee's entire army. But he was able to reinforce his army with fresh troops. Lee, who had also suffered heavy losses, could not.

Total War Grant believed in total war—war on the enemy's will to fight and its ability to support an army. With his army tied down in northern Virginia, Grant ordered General Philip Sheridan to wage total war in Virginia's grain-rich Shenandoah Valley. "Let that valley be so left that crows flying over it will have to carry their rations along with them," ordered Grant.

General Sherman, a believer in total war, cut a path of destruction through Georgia. This photograph shows the burned ruins of Atlanta.

In May 1864, General Sherman left Tennessee for Georgia with orders to inflict "all the damage you can against their war resources." In September, Sherman reached Atlanta, the South's most important rail and manufacturing center. His army set the city ablaze.

The Reelection of Lincoln Any hope of victory for the South lay in the defeat of President Lincoln in the election of 1864. Northern Democrats nominated General George McClellan to run against Lincoln. Knowing that the North was weary of war, McClellan urged an immediate end to the conflict.

Lincoln doubted he would win reelection. Grant seemed stuck in northern Virginia, and there was no end in sight to the appalling bloodletting. Luckily for the president, Sheridan's destruction of the Shenandoah Valley and Sherman's capture of Atlanta came just in time to rescue his campaign. These victories changed Northern views of Lincoln and his prospects for ending the war. In November, Lincoln was reelected.

Sherman's March Through Georgia After burning Atlanta, Sherman marched his army across the state toward Savannah, promising to "make Georgia howl." His purpose was to destroy the last untouched supply base for the Confederacy.

As they marched through Georgia, Sherman's troops destroyed everything that they found of value. They trampled or burned fields and stripped houses of their valuables. They burned supplies of hay and food. Dead horses, hogs, and cattle that his troops could not eat or carry away lined the roads. The troops destroyed everything useful in a 60-mile-wide path.

In December 1864, Sherman captured Savannah, Georgia. From there, he turned north and destroyed all opposition in the Carolinas. Marching 425 miles in 50 days, he reached Raleigh, North Carolina, by March 1865. There he waited for Grant's final attack on Richmond.

The War Ends For nine months, Grant's forces battered Lee's army at Petersburg, the gateway to Richmond. On April 1, 1865, the Union forces finally broke through Confederate lines to capture the city. Two days later, Union troops marched into Richmond.

Grant's soldiers moved quickly to surround Lee's army. Lee told his officers, "There is nothing left for me to do but go and see General Grant, and I would rather die a thousand deaths."

On April 9, 1865, General Lee, in full dress uniform, arrived at Wilmer McLean's house in the village of **Appomattox Court House**. He was there to surrender his army to General Grant. The Union general met him in a mud-splattered and crumpled uniform.

Appomattox Court House a village in Virginia that was the site of the Confederate surrender to Union forces under the command of General Ulysses S. Grant

Most battles during the Civil War took place in or near border states or in Confederate states.

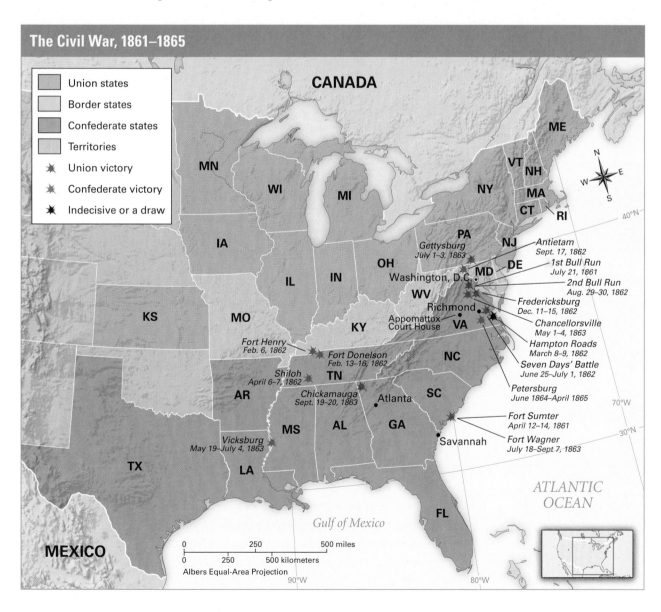

The Civil War, 1861–1865

Union states
Border states
Confederate states
Territories
Union victory
Confederate victory
Indecisive or a draw

CANADA

MEXICO

Gulf of Mexico

ATLANTIC OCEAN

MN
WI
MI
IA
IL
IN
OH
KS
MO
KY
TN
AR
MS
AL
GA
TX
LA
FL
SC
NC
VA
WV
MD
DE
PA
NJ
NY
ME
VT
NH
MA
CT
RI

Washington, D.C.
Richmond
Appomattox Court House
Atlanta
Savannah

Gettysburg
July 1–3, 1863

Antietam
Sept. 17, 1862

1st Bull Run
July 21, 1861

2nd Bull Run
Aug. 29–30, 1862

Fredericksburg
Dec. 11–15, 1862

Chancellorsville
May 1–4, 1863

Hampton Roads
March 8–9, 1862

Seven Days' Battle
June 25–July 1, 1862

Petersburg
June 1864–April 1865

Fort Sumter
April 12–14, 1861

Fort Wagner
July 18–Sept 7, 1863

Fort Henry
Feb. 6, 1862

Fort Donelson
Feb. 13–16, 1862

Shiloh
April 6–7, 1862

Chickamauga
Sept. 19–20, 1863

Vicksburg
May 19–July 4, 1863

0   250   500 miles
0   250   500 kilometers
Albers Equal-Area Projection

40°N
70°W
30°N
90°W
80°W

General Lee, seated at left, surrendered to General Grant at Appomattox Court House, Virginia. Grant was generous to Lee's soldiers, sending food to the troops and allowing them to keep their horses and mules.

Grant's terms of surrender were generous. Confederate soldiers could go home if they promised to fight no longer. They could take with them their own horses and mules, which they would need for spring plowing. Officers could keep their swords and weapons. Grant also ordered that food be sent to Lee's men. Lee accepted the terms.

As Lee returned to his headquarters, Union troops began to shoot their guns and cheer wildly. Grant told them to stop celebrating. "The war is over," he said, "the rebels are our countrymen again."

"Touched by Fire" No one who fought in the Civil War would ever forget the intensity of the experience. "In our youth," wrote Oliver Wendell Holmes Jr., "our hearts were touched by fire."

The nation, too, had been touched by fire. Many compared the Civil War to a great furnace that burned away one country and forged a new one in its place. In this new country, neither slavery nor the right to secession had any place. Just as Lincoln had said, the Union was a single whole, not a collection of sovereign states. Before the war, Americans tended to say "the United States are." After the war, they said "the United States is."

These momentous changes came at a horrifying cost. Billions of dollars had been spent on the conflict. Almost every family had lost a member or a friend. More than 620,000 Union and Confederate soldiers were dead. Thousands more came home missing an arm or a leg. It would take generations for the South to recover from the environmental destruction wrought by the war. Croplands lay in ruins. Two-fifths of the South's livestock had been destroyed.

Many historians have called the Civil War the first truly modern war. It was the first war to reflect the technology of the Industrial Revolution: railroads, the telegraph, armored ships, more accurate and destructive weaponry. It also introduced total war—war between whole societies, not just uniformed armies.

As devastating as it was, the Civil War left many issues unsettled. The old society of the South had been destroyed, but the memory of it lingered. Thousands of white Southerners clung to a romantic picture of the prewar South. Decaying plantation houses became shrines. In the years to come, many in the South would try to re-create their vanished way of life. Secession and slavery were gone, but conflicts over states' rights and the status of African Americans would continue long into the future.

Chapter Summary

In this chapter, you read about the Civil War between the Union and the Confederacy.

The North Versus the South Both sides had strengths and weaknesses going into the war. The North had a larger population and more factories and railroads than the South, but it lacked strong military leadership. The South had serious economic and transportation problems, but it had better military leadership and the advantage of fighting a defensive war.

Bull Run: An Awakening The Battle of Bull Run in 1861 was a victory for the Confederacy and showed the Union that ending the war would not be easy. As the North and South built their armies, women supported their families and the military forces.

Antietam: A Bloody Affair Using a strategy called the Anaconda Plan, Union forces blockaded Southern ports and gained control of the Mississippi River. High death tolls at the Battle of Antietam reflected new methods of warfare that included improved weapons.

Gettysburg: A Turning Point The Battle of Gettysburg ended the South's last attempt to invade the North. From that point on, Confederate forces fought a defensive war in Southern territory.

Vicksburg: A Besieged City In 1863, Confederate forces continued to hold Vicksburg, a key location on the Mississippi River. Capturing Vicksburg would divide the Confederacy in two and allow the Union to control the Mississippi River. After weeks of bombardment, Vicksburg surrendered.

Fort Wagner: African Americans and the War African Americans were able to join Union military forces in 1862. They fought in nearly 500 battles. The most famous black regiment was the 54th Massachusetts Infantry, which fought in the Battle of Fort Wagner.

Appomattox: Total War Brings an End In April 1865, Union forces captured the Confederate capital of Richmond and surrounded General Lee's Confederate army. Lee surrendered at Appomattox Court House.

Benjamin Hardin Helm

|
married

Emilie Todd Helm

sisters

Mary Todd Lincoln   **Abraham Lincoln**

married

Benjamin Hardin Helm's Dilemma
Benjamin Hardin Helm was born in the Southern state of Kentucky and married a Southern woman. But that led to family connections, and even job opportunities, with the most powerful family in the North. Which side would he choose?

Divided House, Divided Families

Before the Civil War, Abraham Lincoln had warned, "A house divided against itself cannot stand." But the nation did divide. People took sides, North or South. For most of them, the choice was clear. But for some, especially in the border states, the decision was difficult and painful. Not only was the country divided, but many families were, too.

Even as the Civil War began, Benjamin Hardin Helm had the prospect of a bright future in front of him. President Lincoln had offered him a good job with the Union army. The position paid well and would not require Helm to fight. It was a job many people wanted. "The position you offer me is beyond what I had expected in my most hopeful dreams," Helm told the president. Still, he could not decide.

Helm was from Kentucky, a border state divided in its loyalties between North and South. He came from a prominent family and had served in the state legislature. He had also been an officer in the U.S. Army. Helm favored the South, and many of his family members and friends did, too. But he also had friends and family who supported the North. Even his father, a former governor, backed the Union.

There was a further complication. Helm was married to Emilie Todd, a sister of Mary Todd Lincoln, President Lincoln's wife. That made Helm the president's brother-in-law. He and Emilie were close to the Lincolns.

Helm struggled with his decision. Lincoln's offer was generous. By accepting it, however, Helm would be turning against much of his family, including members who had joined the Confederate army. By refusing it, he would cut himself off from other members of the family, such as the Lincolns. "I had a bitter struggle with myself," he told a friend.

In the end, Helm turned down the president's offer. It was "the most painful moment of my life," he said, but he felt he could not take up arms against the South. Instead, he joined the Confederate cause and fought against the Union.

Helm's dilemma, though difficult, was not unusual. Many people found themselves torn between competing loyalties during the Civil War. This was especially true in border states like Kentucky, Maryland, Missouri, and Delaware. Although these states remained in the Union, many of their citizens felt sympathy for the South. Families in border states were often deeply divided over the war.

Lee's Decision
Virginia was also a border state, but one that joined the Confederacy. Robert E. Lee was one of its military heroes. Like Hardin Helm, Lee faced a tough decision. He, too, was offered a key position in the Union army. And like Helm, he turned it down, with great misgivings.

Robert E. Lee was a brilliant soldier who left the U.S. Army to fight for his home state. He became the Confederacy's top general and personal military adviser to the Confederate president, Jefferson Davis.

Before the war, Lee was one of the most promising officers in the U.S. Army. A graduate of West Point, he had served with distinction during the Mexican War. As the Civil War began, Lincoln sent word to Lee offering him command of the Union army.

Lee was honored by the president's offer. He supported the Union and thought secession was a mistake. But he was a loyal Virginian above all and would not turn against his home state. "With all my devotion to the Union," he wrote, "I have not been able to . . . raise my hand against my relatives, my children, my home."

Lee resigned his position and became a Confederate general. The man who might have led the Union army eventually became the top commander of the Confederate forces.

Lincoln's Family Troubles

Robert E. Lee's decision probably came as little surprise to Lincoln. He knew that Southern officers had divided loyalties in the same way that states and families did. Lincoln's own family was a case in point.

The president actually had little immediate family of his own. But his wife's family, the Todds, was quite large. Mary Todd Lincoln had 14 brothers and sisters, all from Kentucky. Of these, 6 supported the Union and 8 backed the Confederacy. Several of her brothers fought in the Confederate army.

The Todds were important to Lincoln, and he did everything in his power to help them, even when they turned against him. Just as he tried to hold the nation together, he tried to keep the family together. But this was too much for even the president to accomplish.

As Kentucky Goes, So Goes the Nation

President Lincoln saw Kentucky as a symbol of the nation's divisions. In fact, the Union and Confederate leaders—Lincoln and Jefferson Davis—were both from Kentucky. They were born just 100 miles apart. The state's white soldiers were split almost evenly between North and South. Two-fifths fought for the Confederacy and three-fifths for the Union. No other state was so evenly divided.

Lincoln believed it was essential to keep Kentucky in the Union. "I think to lose Kentucky is nearly the same as to lose the whole game," he said. "Kentucky gone, we cannot hold Missouri, nor, as I think, Maryland." Officially, Kentucky remained neutral in the war, and Lincoln did what he could to keep it from seceding. "I hope to have God on my side," he supposedly said, "but I must have Kentucky."

Fathers and Sons Divided

Among Kentucky families, some of the bitterest divisions arose between fathers and sons. The Crittenden family was one example.

John J. Crittenden was a respected member of Congress who had worked hard to prevent the Civil War. Early in the war, he wrote to his oldest son, George, urging him to remain loyal to the Union. Kentucky "loves the Union," he wrote, "and will cling to it as long as possible. And so, I hope, will you." His words were in vain. George joined the Confederate army and, in turn, Crittenden cut off all contact with his son.

Another case involved the Breckenridge family. Robert J. Breckenridge was a strong Union supporter. But his son Robert Jr. decided to join the Confederacy. He wrote his father, "Be . . . as lenient as possible in your thoughts of me." Breckenridge was stunned. He wrote his other son, Willie, saying, "[Your brother] has hopelessly ruined himself." Then Willie joined the Confederacy, too. Breckenridge was doubly stricken.

One young Kentuckian, Henry Lane Stone, ran away from home to join the rebel forces. He did so in secret because he knew his father and brothers would object. One of his brothers had already joined the Union army. A month later, Stone wrote home to his father. "I can imagine how your feelings are, one son in the Northern and another in the Southern army," he wrote. "But so it is . . . Your rebelling son, Henry."

Henry Lane Stone joined the Ninth Kentucky Cavalry, led by General John H. Morgan. He took part in various battles, including a famous raid into Union territory.

Brother Against Brother

Henry Stone and his brother fought on opposing sides in the war. This was not uncommon. In fact, the Civil War was sometimes called the "brothers' war." One notable case of brother against brother involved the Campbell brothers from Scotland.

James and Alexander Campbell came to America in the 1850s. James settled in Charleston, South Carolina. Alexander chose New York. When the war began, both signed up to fight, though on opposite sides.

In June 1862, Alexander's regiment was part of an invasion force sent to retake Charleston from the Confederates. At the Battle of Secessionville, Union troops attacked Ft. Lamar, one of the forts guarding the city. Although neither brother knew it at the time, they were both involved in the battle. Alexander held the U.S. flag at the base of the fort's walls, while James stood above, firing down on the attackers. James later wrote his brother,

At the end of the Civil War, grateful families welcomed the soldiers home. In divided families, the homecomings were not always easy.

> *I was astonished to hear from the prisoners that you [were] color Bearer of the Regiment that assaulted the Battery . . . I hope you and I will never again meet . . . on the Battlefield but if such should be the case . . . I will strive to discharge my duty to my country and my cause.*

The two brothers fought in other battles of the war, but never again in the same place. After the war, they corresponded with each other and remained on good terms.

Another soldier, Matthew H. Peters, later recounted his own experience of the brothers' war in a poem:

> *Both of us fought for what we thought right,*
> *But of duty each took a different view;*
> *Both of us entered the perilous fight*
> *And did our duty as patriots do—*
> *But he wore the gray and I wore the blue.*
>   —Matthew H. Peters, "My Brother and I," 1893

Unlike these soldiers, Hardin Helm did not survive the war. He was killed at the Battle of Chickamauga in 1863. When Lincoln got the news, he was devastated. "I never saw Mr. Lincoln more moved than when he heard of the death of his young brother-in-law," said a friend. Helm had died fighting for the Confederacy, but he was still family.

For Lincoln, Helm's death was yet another tragedy of the divided nation. Families and communities had been torn apart by the war. It would take years for the wounds to heal.

Chapter 23

The Reconstruction Era

To what extent did Reconstruction bring African Americans closer to full citizenship?

23.1 Introduction

By the end of the Civil War, Americans longed for peace. But what kind of peace? One that punished the South for its rebellion? A peace that helped rebuild the devastated region? A peace that helped the 4 million African Americans freed from slavery become full and equal citizens? In his second inaugural address, delivered in 1865, President Abraham Lincoln spoke of a healing peace:

> *With malice [hatred] toward none, with charity for all, with firmness in the right as God gives us to see the right, let us strive on to finish the work we are in, to bind up the nation's wounds, to care for him who shall have borne the battle and for his widow and orphan, to do all which may achieve and cherish [hold dear] a just and lasting peace.*

The nation would never know how Lincoln planned to achieve such a peace. On April 14, 1865, just five days after the war ended, the president was assassinated while attending a play at Ford's Theater in Washington, D.C. The assassin was an actor named John Wilkes Booth. Booth thought that killing Lincoln would somehow save the Confederacy.

After Lincoln's death, Vice President Andrew Johnson became president. The task of rebuilding the South and bringing the Southern states back into the Union would not be easy for Johnson's administration. For while the nation was united again, Americans remained deeply divided.

As you read this chapter, think about Lincoln's dream of "a just and lasting peace." Did the end of the war and the end of slavery lead to a peace based on liberty and justice for all? Did these events bring African Americans closer to the ideals of liberty and justice, including the rights of citizenship?

Five days after the Civil War ended, President Lincoln was shot dead by an assassin. The task of rebuilding the nation fell to Vice President Andrew Johnson, who became president when Lincoln died. Pictured here is Lincoln's funeral procession from the White House to the Capitol on April 19, 1865.

◄ In the years following the Civil War, African American men were granted the right to vote.

Reconstruction the period of time after the Civil War in which Southern states were rebuilt and brought back into the Union

Thirteenth Amendment a change to the Constitution, ratified in 1865, abolishing slavery in the United States

Freedmen's Bureau an agency established by Congress at the end of the Civil War to help and protect newly freed black Americans

During Reconstruction, former slaves gained the rights to marry and to reunite families divided by slavery. Forms such as this one allowed freedmen to keep family records.

23.2 Presidential Reconstruction

As the Civil War ended, people in the United States had sharply different views about how to rebuild the Southern states and bring them back into the Union. This period of time came to be called **Reconstruction**. For President Andrew Johnson, a Southerner from Tennessee, Reconstruction had two major aims. First, Southern states had to create new governments that were loyal to the Union and that respected federal authority. Second, slavery had to be abolished once and for all.

These aims left many issues to be **resolved**. For example, who would control the new state governments in the South—former Confederates? Would freed slaves have the same rights as other citizens? And what would the relationship be between freed slaves and former slave owners?

Many Republicans in Congress believed that strong measures would be needed to settle these issues. To them, Reconstruction meant nothing less than a complete remaking of the South based on equal rights and a free-labor economy. The stage was set for a battle over the control—and even the meaning—of Reconstruction.

President Johnson's Reconstruction Plan In May 1865, President Johnson announced his Reconstruction plan. A former Confederate state could rejoin the Union once it had written a new state constitution, elected a new state government, repealed its act of secession, and canceled its war debts. There was a final requirement as well. Every Southern state had to ratify the **Thirteenth Amendment**, which abolished slavery throughout the United States.

By the fall of 1865, every Southern state had met the president's requirements. The Thirteenth Amendment became part of the Constitution. Presidential Reconstruction had begun.

The Freedmen's Bureau For former slaves, called freedmen, the freedom guaranteed by the Thirteenth Amendment brought problems as well as opportunities. Frederick Douglass described the freedman as "free from the individual master but a slave of society." Douglass wrote,

> He had neither money, property, nor friends. He was free from the old plantation, but he had nothing but the dusty road under his feet . . . He was turned loose, naked, hungry, and destitute [penniless] to the open sky.

To assist former slaves, Congress established the **Freedmen's Bureau** in March 1865. Over the next four years, the bureau provided food and medical care to both blacks and whites in the South. It helped freedmen arrange for wages and good working conditions. It also distributed some land in 40-acre plots to "loyal refugees and freedmen."

Some whites, however, attacked the bureau as an example of Northern interference in the South. Ultimately, the hope of many freedmen for "forty acres and a mule" died when Congress refused to take land away from Southern whites.

The most lasting benefit of the Freedmen's Bureau was in education. Thousands of former slaves, both young and old, flocked to free schools built by the bureau. Long after the bureau was gone, such institutions as Howard University in Washington, D.C., continued to provide educational opportunities for African Americans.

Black Codes As new state governments took power in the South, many Republicans in Congress were alarmed to see that they were headed by the same people who had led the South before the war—wealthy white planters. Once in office, these leaders began passing laws known as **black codes** to control their former slaves.

The black codes served three purposes. The first was to limit the rights of freedmen. Generally, former slaves received the rights to marry, to own property, to work for wages, and to sue in court. But they did not have other rights of citizenship. Blacks, for example, could not vote or serve on juries in the South.

The second purpose of the black codes was to help planters find workers to replace their slaves. The codes required freedmen to work. Those without jobs could be arrested and hired out to planters. The codes also limited freedmen to farming or jobs requiring few skills. African Americans could not enter most trades or start businesses.

The third purpose of the black codes was to keep freedmen at the bottom of the social order in the South. Most codes called for the segregation of blacks and whites in public places.

The Freedmen's Bureau built more than 1,000 schools for African Americans between 1865 and 1872.

black codes laws passed in 1865 and 1866 in the former Confederate states to limit the rights and freedoms of African Americans

civil rights the rights guaranteed by the Constitution to all people as citizens, especially equal treatment under the law

Fourteenth Amendment a change to the Constitution, ratified in 1868, granting citizenship to anyone born in the United States and guaranteeing all citizens equal protection of the law

Based on the belief that the South had no legal governments, Congress reorganized the South into the five military districts shown here. Tennessee, which met the standards for readmission before the military districts were established in 1867, was not included in one.

23.3 Congressional Reconstruction

As 1865 came to a close, President Johnson announced that Reconstruction was over. The Southern states were ready to rejoin the Union.

A group of Republicans in Congress did not agree with Johnson. Known as the Radical Republicans, these lawmakers had an additional goal for Reconstruction. They believed that the South would not be completely rebuilt until freedmen were granted the full rights of citizenship.

Radical Republicans wanted the federal government to take a more active role in Reconstruction—a role that would involve tougher requirements for restoring Southern governments. In the House of Representatives, Thaddeus Stevens of Pennsylvania led the Radical Republicans. In the Senate, they were led by Charles Sumner of Massachusetts.

Early in 1866, Radical Republicans joined with more moderate lawmakers to enact two bills designed to help freedmen. The first extended the life of the Freedmen's Bureau. The second was the Civil Rights Act of 1866. It struck at the black codes by declaring freedmen to be full citizens with the same **civil rights** as whites. Johnson declared both bills unconstitutional and vetoed them. An angry Congress overrode his vetoes.

The Fourteenth Amendment To further protect the rights of African Americans, Congress approved the **Fourteenth Amendment**. This amendment granted citizenship to "all people born or naturalized in the United States." It also guaranteed all citizens "the equal protection of the laws." This meant that state governments could not treat some citizens as less equal than others.

President Johnson opposed the Fourteenth Amendment and called on voters to throw Republican lawmakers out of office. Instead, Republican candidates won a two-thirds majority in both houses of Congress in the 1866 election. From then on, Congress controlled Reconstruction.

Military Reconstruction Act Early in 1867, Congress passed the Military Reconstruction Act. Once again, it did so over Johnson's veto. This plan divided the South into five military districts, each governed by a general supported by federal troops. The state governments set up under Johnson's Reconstruction plan were declared illegal. New governments were to be formed by Southerners loyal to the United States—both black and white. Southerners who had supported the Confederacy were denied the right to vote.

Military Reconstruction Districts, 1870

1870 Date of readmission to the Union

0   250   500 miles
0   250   500 kilometers
Albers Equal-Area Projection

Congress also passed two acts designed to reduce Johnson's power to interfere with congressional Reconstruction. The Command of the Army Act limited his power over the army. The Tenure of Office Act barred him from firing certain federal officials without the Senate's consent. President Johnson blasted both laws as unconstitutional. Then, to prove his point, he fired one of the officials protected under the Tenure of Office Act.

President Johnson Is Impeached The House of Representatives responded to Johnson's challenge by voting to impeach the president. Besides violating the Tenure of Office Act, the House charged, Johnson had brought "the high office of the President of the United States into contempt, ridicule, and disgrace, to the scandal of all good citizens."

During his trial in the Senate, the president's lawyers argued that Johnson's only "crime" had been to oppose Congress. If he were removed from office for that reason, they warned, "no future President will be safe who happens to differ with a majority of the House and Senate."

Two-thirds of the Senate had to find the president guilty to remove him from office. Despite heavy pressure to convict him, 7 Republicans and 12 Democrats voted "not guilty." Johnson escaped removal from office by one vote, but he had lost his power.

Sharecropping While Congress and the president battled over Reconstruction, African Americans in the South worked to build new lives. Most former slaves desperately wanted land to farm but had no money to buy it. Meanwhile, former slave owners needed workers to farm their land but had no money to pay them. Out of the needs of both groups came a farming system called sharecropping.

Planters who turned to sharecropping divided their land into small plots. They rented these plots to individual tenant farmers—farmers who paid rent for the land they worked. A few tenants paid the rent for their plots in cash. But most paid their rent by giving the landowner a portion of what they raised. This payment of crops was called a share. Usually it was about a third or a half of the tenant's crop.

Sharecropping looked promising to freedmen at first. They liked being independent farmers who worked for themselves. In time, they hoped to earn enough money to buy a farm of their own.

However, most sharecroppers had to borrow money from planters to buy the food, seeds, tools, and supplies they needed to survive until harvest. Few ever earned enough from their crops to pay back what they owed. Rather than leading to independence, share-cropping usually led to a life-time of poverty and debt.

Sharecroppers, such as these cotton growers, rented their land from plantation owners. In exchange, most paid one-third to one-half of their crops back to the landowners.

23.4   Southern Reconstruction

Under the terms of the Military Reconstruction Act, the U.S. Army returned to the South in 1867. The first thing it did was begin to register voters. Because Congress had banned former Confederates from voting, the right to vote in the South was limited to three groups: freedmen, white Southerners who had opposed the war, and Northerners who had moved south after the war.

The South's New Voters   African Americans made up the South's largest group of new voters. Most black voters joined the Republican Party—the party of Lincoln and emancipation.

White Southerners who had not supported secession were the next largest group. Many were poor farmers who had never voted before. In their eyes, the Democratic Party was the party of wealthy planters and secession. As a result, they also supported the Republican Party. Southern Democrats were appalled. They saw any white man who voted Republican as a traitor to the South. Democrats scorned such people as scalawags, or worthless scoundrels.

The last group of new voters were Northerners who had moved south after the war. Southerners called these newcomers "carpetbaggers" after a type of handbag used by many travelers. They saw carpetbaggers as fortune hunters who had come south to "fatten" themselves on Southerners' misfortunes.

The Election of 1868   New voters in the South cast their first ballots in the 1868 presidential election. The Republican candidate was former Union general Ulysses S. Grant. Grant supported Reconstruction and promised to protect the rights of African Americans in the South. His Democratic opponent, Horatio Seymour, promised to end Reconstruction and return the South to its traditional leaders—white Democrats.

Seymour won a majority of white votes. Grant, however, was elected with the help of half a million black votes. The election's lesson to Republicans was that if they wanted to keep control of the White House and Congress, they needed the support of African American voters.

The Fifteenth Amendment   In 1869, at President Grant's urging, Congress passed the **Fifteenth Amendment**. This amendment said that a citizen's right to vote "shall not be denied . . . on account of race, color, or previous condition of servitude." It guaranteed every male citizen the right to vote, regardless of race.

This poster—which pictures students, soldiers, preachers, teachers, and lawmakers—celebrated the passage of the Fifteenth Amendment.

With the passage of this amendment, most abolitionists felt their work was done. The American Anti-Slavery Society declared the Fifteenth Amendment to be "the capstone and completion of our movement; the fulfillment of our pledge to the Negro race; since it secures to them equal political rights with the white race."

New State Constitutions When the army finished registering voters, Southern Reconstruction got underway. Across the South, delegates were elected to constitutional conventions. About a fourth of those elected were African Americans.

The conventions met and wrote new constitutions for their states. These constitutions were the most progressive, or advanced, in the nation. They guaranteed the right to vote to every adult male, regardless of race. They ended imprisonment for debt. They also established the first public schools in the South. The Georgia constitution stated that these schools should be "forever free to all the children of the state." However, under the new state constitutions, these schools were open only to whites.

New State Governments Elections were then held to fill state offices. To the dismay of Southern Democrats, a majority of those elected were Republicans. About a fifth were African Americans.

The South's new state governments quickly ratified the Fourteenth and Fifteenth Amendments. By 1870, every Southern state had finished this final step of Reconstruction and rejoined the Union.

Next, Southern governments turned to the task of rebuilding. Work was begun on damaged roads, bridges, and railroads. Schools and hospitals were built. To pay for these projects, state legislatures raised taxes. Between 1860 and 1870, taxes in the South increased by up to 400 percent.

During Reconstruction, many African Americans were elected to the House of Representatives and the Senate. Robert B. Elliott, a congressman from South Carolina, delivers a speech in support of civil rights.

African Americans in Office About a fifth of the South's new officeholders were African Americans. Blacks served in every Southern legislature and held high offices in three states. Twenty-two African Americans represented their states in Congress—20 in the House and 2 in the Senate. After watching these representatives, many of whom had been born slaves, Pennsylvania congressman James G. Blaine said,

> *The colored men who took their seats in both the Senate and House did not appear ignorant or helpless. They were as a rule studious, earnest, ambitious men, whose public conduct . . . would be honorable to any race.*

Thomas Nast's political cartoon "Is This a Republican Form of Government?" condemns Northern indifference to the violence African Americans endured as Reconstruction ended.

23.5 The End of Reconstruction

Most whites in the South bitterly resented the Southern Reconstruction governments. They hated the fact that these governments had been "forced" on them by Yankees.

Many taxpayers also blamed their soaring tax bills on corruption —the misuse of public office for personal gain—by the South's new leaders. While some Southern officeholders did line their pockets with public funds, most, whether black or white, were honest, capable leaders. Still, when taxes increased, opposition to the new state governments increased as well.

But what bothered many Southerners most about their Reconstruction governments was seeing former slaves voting and holding public office. Across the South, Democrats vowed to regain power and return their states to "white man's rule."

Violence Against African Americans At first, Democrats tried to win black voters away from the Republican Party. When that tactic failed, they attempted to use legal means to keep blacks from voting or from taking office. In Georgia, for example, the legislature refused to seat elected black lawmakers until they were forced to by the state supreme court. When legal methods failed, whites turned to violence.

Throughout the South, whites formed secret societies to drive African Americans out of political life. The most infamous of these groups was the Ku Klux Klan. Dressed in long, hooded robes and armed with guns and swords, Klansmen did their work at night. They started by threatening black voters and officeholders. African Americans who did not heed their threats were beaten, tarred and feathered, and even murdered.

The Enforcement Acts In 1870 and 1871, Congress passed three laws to combat violence against African Americans. Known as the Enforcement Acts, these laws made it illegal to prevent another person from voting by bribery, force, or scare tactics.

President Grant sent troops into the South to enforce these acts. Hundreds of people were arrested for violence against blacks. Those who were brought to trial, however, were seldom convicted. Few witnesses and jurors wanted to risk the Klan's revenge by speaking out against one of its members.

The Amnesty Act of 1872 By this time, most Northerners were losing interest in Reconstruction and the plight of the freedmen. It was time, many people said, to "let the South alone."

One indication of this changing attitude was the passage of the Amnesty Act of 1872. Amnesty means forgiveness for past offenses. The Amnesty Act allowed most former Confederates to vote once again.

The effects of the Amnesty Act were seen almost immediately. By 1876, Democrats had regained control of all but three states in the South. Republicans clung to power in South Carolina, Louisiana, and Florida, but only with the help of federal troops.

The Disputed Election of 1876 In 1876, Americans went to the polls to choose a new president. The Democrats nominated New York governor Samuel J. Tilden as their candidate. Rutherford B. Hayes was the Republican nominee. When the votes were counted, Tilden won a majority of popular votes and 184 electoral votes, just one short of the 185 needed for election. Hayes received 165 electoral votes. Twenty electoral votes from four states were in dispute.

Congress, which was controlled by Republicans, appointed a commission to decide which candidate should get the disputed electoral votes. The commission awarded all 20 to Hayes, giving him exactly the 185 electoral votes he needed to win. The Democrats threatened to block the commission's decision. Inauguration day grew near with no new president in sight.

The Compromise of 1877 After weeks of negotiation, Democratic and Republican leaders in Congress agreed to a compromise. The Democrats accepted the electoral commission's decision, allowing Hayes to become president. In return, Hayes agreed to withdraw the remaining federal troops still occupying Southern states.

Once President Hayes withdrew all remaining federal troops from the South in 1877, Reconstruction was officially over. After that, Democrats quickly took control of the last Southern states. "This is a white man's country," boasted South Carolina senator Ben Tillman, "and white men must govern it."

Most white Southerners celebrated the end of Reconstruction. But for freedmen, the return of the South to "white man's rule" was a giant step backward. "The whole South—every state in the South," observed a Louisiana freedman, "has got into the hands of the very men that held us as slaves."

This cartoon compares the Reconstruction policies of President Grant and President Hayes, who succeeded Grant in office. In the first panel, Grant is shown riding in a carpetbag supported by an oppressed South. Two soldiers symbolize martial law. In the second panel, Hayes is shown plowing under the carpetbag. The label on the plow reads "Let 'Em Alone Policy." Which president do you think the cartoonist favored?

The Reconstruction Era **453**

This painting shows a new South rising from the ashes of the Civil War. Although Southern leaders hoped this would be the future of the South, most whites and blacks continued to live in poverty.

23.6 Reconstruction Reversed

With Reconstruction over, Southern leaders talked of building a "New South" humming with mills, factories, and cities. Between 1880 and 1900, the number of textile mills in the South grew rapidly. Birmingham, Alabama, became a major iron-making center. Still, most Southerners, black and white, remained trapped in an "Old South" of poverty.

Losing Ground in Education During Reconstruction, freedmen had pinned their hopes for a better life on education provided by the South's first public schools. When Southern Democrats regained control of states, however, they cut spending on education. "Free schools are not a necessity," explained the governor of Virginia. Schools, he said, "are a luxury . . . to be paid for, like any other luxury, by the people who wish their benefits."

As public funding dried up, many schools closed. Those that stayed open often charged fees. By the 1880s, only about half of all black children in the South were attending school.

Losing Voting Rights Southern Democrats also reversed political gains made by freedmen after the war. Many Southern states passed laws requiring citizens who wanted to vote to pay a poll tax. The tax was set high enough that voting, like education, became a luxury that many black Southerners could not afford.

Some Southern states also required citizens to pass a literacy test to show they could read before allowing them to vote. These tests were designed so that any African American, regardless of his education, would fail.

In theory, these laws applied equally to blacks and whites and, for that reason, did not violate the Fifteenth Amendment. In practice, however, whites were excused from paying poll taxes or taking literacy tests by a **so-called** "grandfather clause" in the laws. This clause said the taxes and tests did not apply to any man whose father or grandfather could vote on January 1, 1867. Since no blacks could vote on that date, the grandfather clause applied only to whites.

African Americans protested that these laws denied them their constitutional right to vote. The Supreme Court, however, found that the new voting laws did not violate the Fifteenth Amendment because they did not deny anyone the right to vote on the basis of race.

Drawing a "Color Line" During Reconstruction, most Southern states had outlawed segregation in public places. When Democrats returned to power, they reversed these laws and drew a "color line" between blacks and whites in public life. Whites called the new segregation acts **Jim Crow laws**. Jim Crow was a black character in an entertainer's act in the mid-1800s.

Not all white Southerners supported segregation. When a Jim Crow law was proposed in South Carolina, a *Charleston News and Courier* editorial tried to show how unjust it was by taking segregation to ridiculous extremes.

> *If there must be Jim Crow cars on railroads, there should be Jim Crow cars on the street railways. Also on all passenger boats . . . There should be Jim Crow waiting saloons [waiting rooms] at all stations, and Jim Crow eating houses . . . There should be Jim Crow sections of the jury box, and a separate Jim Crow . . . witness stand in every court—and a Jim Crow Bible for colored witnesses to kiss.*

Instead of being a joke, as intended, most of these ridiculous suggestions soon became laws.

Plessy v. Ferguson African Americans argued that segregation laws violated the Fourteenth Amendment's guarantee of equal protection of the laws. Homer Plessy, who was arrested for refusing to obey a Jim Crow law, took his protest all the way to the Supreme Court.

The Supreme Court decided his case, *Plessy v. Ferguson*, in 1896. The majority of the Supreme Court justices found that segregation laws did not violate the Fourteenth Amendment as long as the facilities available to both races were roughly equal. Justice John Marshall Harlan, a former slaveholder, disagreed. In his dissenting opinion, he wrote, "Our Constitution is color blind, and neither knows nor **tolerates** classes among citizens."

After the Supreme Court's decision in *Plessy*, states passed additional Jim Crow laws. Blacks and whites attended separate schools, played in separate parks, and sat in separate sections in theaters. Despite the Court's decision that these separate facilities must be equal, those set aside for African Americans were almost always **inferior** to facilities labeled "whites only."

Jim Crow laws laws enforcing segregation of blacks and whites in the South after the Civil War

For decades, African Americans lived under segregation legalized by the *Plessy* decision. Separate facilities for blacks were rarely equal. This photograph is of a one-room segregated school in Kentucky in 1916.

Two units of African American cavalrymen, the Ninth and Tenth U.S. Cavalry, fought in the Indian wars. Known as "Buffalo Soldiers," the men served loyally but were often mistreated by the white settlers they were protecting. Twenty-three Buffalo Soldiers earned the Medal of Honor for heroism.

23.7 Responding to Segregation

African Americans responded to segregation in many ways. The boldest protested openly. Doing so, however, was dangerous. Blacks who spoke out risked being attacked by white mobs. Some were lynched, or murdered, often by hanging, for speaking out against "white rule." During the 1890s, an African American was lynched somewhere in the United States almost every day.

African American Migration Thousands of African Americans responded to segregation by leaving the South. A few chose to return to Africa. In 1878, some 200 Southern blacks chartered a ship and sailed to Liberia, a nation in West Africa that had been founded in 1821 for the settlement of freed American slaves.

Many more African Americans migrated to other parts of the United States. Not only were they pushed from the South by racism and poverty, but they were pulled by the lure of better opportunities and more equal treatment. Some sought a new life as wage earners by migrating to cities in the North. There, they competed for jobs with recent immigrants from Europe and often faced racism, if not Southern-style segregation. Others headed to the West, where they found work as cowboys and Indian fighters. Two all-black U.S. Cavalry units known as the Buffalo Soldiers fought on the front lines of the Indian wars. Some blacks found new homes with American Indian nations.

Thousands of black families left the South for Kansas in the Exodus of 1879. The "exodusters," as the migrants were known, faced many hardships on their journey west. Bands of armed whites patrolled roads in Kansas in an effort to drive the migrants away. Still, the exodusters pushed on, saying, "We had rather suffer and be free."

Self-Help Most African Americans, however, remained in the South. They worked hard in their families, churches, and communities to improve their lives. While most blacks farmed for a living, a growing number started their own businesses. Between 1865 and 1903, the number of black-owned businesses in the South soared from about 2,000 to 25,000.

Families, churches, and communities also banded together to build schools and colleges for black children. Because of these efforts, literacy among African Americans rose rapidly. When slavery ended in 1865, only 5 percent of African Americans could read. By 1900, more than 50 percent could read and write.

Chapter Summary

In this chapter, you learned about the period of Reconstruction in the South from 1865 to 1877.

Presidential Reconstruction Under President Johnson's Reconstruction plan, every Southern state rejoined the Union after it had written a new constitution, elected a new state government, cancelled its war debts, and ratified the Thirteenth Amendment, which abolished slavery.

Congressional Reconstruction Congressional Reconstruction began in 1866, when Republican leaders in Congress worked to give freedmen the full rights of citizenship. Congress passed, and the states ratified, the Fourteenth Amendment, which gave citizenship to all people born in the United States and equal protection of the law to all citizens.

Southern Reconstruction Under the Military Reconstruction Act, federal troops returned to the South in 1867 and began registering voters. New Southern voters helped former Union general Ulysses S. Grant become president. In 1869, Congress passed the Fifteenth Amendment, which protected the right of African American men to vote. Many blacks were elected to state government offices during this third phase of Reconstruction.

The End of Reconstruction Southern whites used legal means as well as violence to keep blacks from voting or taking office. Reconstruction officially ended in 1877, when President Rutherford B. Hayes withdrew all remaining federal troops from the South once he took office after the disputed election of 1876.

Reconstruction Reversed After Reconstruction, African Americans lost educational and political gains. Many Southern states closed schools that had been opened to freedmen. They also passed laws designed to keep blacks from voting. Jim Crow laws and the Supreme Court's decision in *Plessy v. Ferguson* legalized many forms of discrimination against blacks.

Responding to Segregation Many African Americans responded to segregation by leaving the South. Many migrated to other parts of the United States. Those who remained in the South worked hard to improve their lives.

This Thomas Nast cartoon celebrates the Civil Rights Bill of 1875. This bill and other Reconstruction legislation tried to give full citizenship rights to African Americans.

The Granger Collection, New York

Elizabeth Eckford was one of the nine African American students who integrated Central High School in Little Rock, Arkansas. Like the others, she faced anger and harassment.

The Long Road to Equal Rights

During Reconstruction, Congress added three amendments to the Constitution to guarantee equal rights to African Americans. Still, it took another 100 years and large-scale political action to make those guarantees real.

The station wagon rolled down West 28th Street in Little Rock, Arkansas. It was part of a convoy, with one jeep in front of it and another behind. Each jeep carried soldiers and a machine gun. Each soldier carried a rifle. In the station wagon, nine high school students sat nervously. It was their first day of school at Little Rock's Central High School.

More soldiers waited at the school for the convoy to arrive. One of the students, Ernest Green, recalled that frightening moment.

> *The whole school was ringed with paratroopers and helicopters hovering around. We marched up the steps . . . with this circle of soldiers with bayonets drawn.*

It was 1957. The students, who came to be known as the Little Rock Nine, would be the first African Americans to attend the city's all-white Central High School.

The students had tried to enter the school twice before, just a few weeks earlier, but had met fierce resistance. Many of Little Rock's white citizens were determined to keep them out. Melba Pattillo, one of the students, described what she went through.

> *On the first day, the kinds of things that I endured were parents kicking, parents hitting, parents throwing things. You would get tripped; people would just walk up and hit you in the face. And you couldn't hit back.*

On those first days, police had escorted the Little Rock Nine into a side entrance of the school building. But the principal had sent the nine students home. He said he feared for their safety.

The third time the Little Rock Nine began their school year, they did so with military protection. On national television that night, President Dwight Eisenhower explained why. "I have today issued an executive order directing the use of troops under federal authority to aid in the execution of federal law at Little Rock." The federal law that Eisenhower referred to was the law to integrate public schools. The military would be sure it was obeyed.

The Fourteenth Amendment Comes of Age

Efforts to integrate public schools began long before the Little Rock Nine entered Central High. In a sense, they began in 1868 during Reconstruction. That is when the Fourteenth Amendment was ratified.

It said that no state could limit privileges or deny any American equal protection under the law. The amendment guaranteed freed slaves the same rights that white Americans had.

Unfortunately, that guarantee was soon modified. In 1896, the Supreme Court held that it was legal to segregate public places. As long as facilities for blacks were equal to those for whites, the court said, segregation did not violate the Fourteenth Amendment. So, under this doctrine of "separate but equal," segregation continued. Although the Constitution guaranteed equal rights, African Americans would have to fight to exercise those rights.

Focused efforts to end segregation in schools began in the 1930s. The long haul toward school integration began with a vision. A young African American lawyer named Charles Houston believed that the way to get equal rights was for black lawyers to challenge segregation in court. But there were very few black lawyers at the time. Most law schools were segregated or accepted only a few black students. But Houston had a plan. At the historically black Howard University in Washington, D.C., Houston trained a generation of black lawyers. Among them was his star pupil, Thurgood Marshall.

Those lawyers confronted segregation in one case after another for more than 20 years. They started by arguing against segregated law schools and then segregated graduate schools. It was not until the 1950s that they took on the segregated public schools.

Their efforts culminated in the 1954 Supreme Court case *Brown v. Board of Education of Topeka, Kansas.* In their decision, the Court held that separate schools could never be equal. This meant that public schools would have to integrate. Three years later—nearly 90 years after the Fourteenth Amendment was added to the Constitution—the Little Rock Nine, under armed guard, followed that law and entered Central High School.

The Fifteenth Amendment Comes of Age

The struggle to integrate schools and other public places did not end at Central High. There would be other battles to win for African Americans to have equal rights. In 1963, to mark 100 years since Abraham Lincoln had emancipated the slaves, more than 200,000 people marched to the steps of the Lincoln Memorial in Washington.

Linda Brown (front center) had to cross railroad tracks and catch a bus to attend a segregated school in Topeka, Kansas. After the Supreme Court's decision in *Brown v. Board of Education of Topeka, Kansas,* Linda could attend the formerly all-white school in her neighborhood.

The voting rights movement urged blacks to register so they could vote. "So long as I do not . . . possess the right to vote, I do not possess myself," Martin Luther King Jr. said.

At that historic event, Martin Luther King Jr. spoke of the work that was still unfinished.

Five score [one hundred] years ago, a great American, in whose symbolic shadow we stand today, signed the Emancipation Proclamation . . . But one hundred years later, we must face the tragic fact that the Negro is still not free. One hundred years later, the life of the Negro is still sadly crippled by the manacles of segregation and the chains of discrimination. One hundred years later, the Negro lives on a lonely island of poverty in the midst of a vast ocean of material prosperity [wealth]. One hundred years later, the Negro is still languishing [suffering] in the corners of American society and finds himself in exile in his own land.

Voting rights, like integration, had been promised after the Civil War, but that promise had not been fulfilled when King spoke in 1963. The Fifteenth Amendment, which was ratified in 1870, granted African Americans the right to vote. But in the 1960s, very few black citizens in the South were able to exercise that right.

The reason? Laws in many Southern states made voting impossible for most African Americans. Some places had literacy tests, for example. Anyone who could not read and write was not allowed to register to vote. The tests were often rigged with questions no one could answer, so that even literate blacks could not pass them. Taxes and property requirements were other methods that made it impossible for most African Americans to exercise their right to vote.

That is why, in the 1960s, African Americans were fighting to register to vote in places like Selma, Alabama. In Selma, the registration office was only open two days a month. The workers there often arrived late, left early, and took long breaks. In 1963, only 156 of Selma's 15,000 eligible black voters were registered.

Through 1963 and 1964, black citizens of Selma tried again and again to register to vote. Again and again, the county sheriff and other white leaders tried to stop them. In 1965, the situation in Selma came to a head.

In cities like Selma, Alabama, African Americans lined up to register to vote. Often, white officials intimidated them by asking, "Does your employer know you're here?" The message was clear: If your boss knows you are here, you could lose your job.

On Sunday, March 7, about 600 people gathered in Selma. They planned to march 50 miles to the state capital in Montgomery to insist on their right to vote. When they reached the Edmund Pettus Bridge, Alabama state troopers ordered them to leave. They stayed. The police advanced. They knocked people to the ground and fired tear gas. Riding horses, the police charged at the marchers.

That day, which came to be called Bloody Sunday, marked a turning point in the struggle for voting rights. On television and in newspapers, images of the violence in Selma reached people across America. Many had not known about the extent of segregation or the violent methods used to enforce it. They were horrified. The mayor of Selma, Joe Smitherman, remembered that the tide turned that day.

John Lewis, a leader of the Student Nonviolent Coordinating Committee, later said of the march, "You had to go—it was more than an ordinary march. To me there was never a march like this one before, and there hasn't been one since."

> *When that beating happened at the foot of the bridge, it looked like war. That went all over the country [on the television news]. And the people, the wrath of the nation came down on us.*

The clashes in Selma continued for days. Then, President Lyndon Johnson put voting rights legislation before Congress. "Their cause must be our cause too," Johnson said to the American people. "Because it is not just Negroes, but really it is all of us who must overcome the crippling legacy of bigotry and injustice."

Days later, thousands of people began the march from Selma to Montgomery. Five days after that, 25,000 people gathered at the state capitol in Montgomery. They celebrated their success and braced themselves for the hard work ahead. Later that year, Congress passed the historic Voting Rights Act of 1965. The act supported the rights that the Constitution had promised blacks nearly 100 years earlier.

Some historians say that the civil rights movement of the 1950s and 1960s was a "Second Reconstruction." They point out that the three Reconstruction amendments—the Thirteenth, Fourteenth, and Fifteenth—promised equal rights to African Americans. Yet, it took another century for those rights to be realized.

President Lyndon B. Johnson (left) congratulates Martin Luther King Jr. (right) and other civil rights leaders. He had just signed the Voting Rights Act of 1965.

The Union Challenged

1854
Kansas-Nebraska Act
This acts opens up the Great Plains to settlement and nullifies the Missouri Compromise by allowing the territory to choose whether to allow slavery. Eventually, it results in violence throughout Kansas as antislavery and proslavery settlers battle for control of the territory.

1857
Dred Scott Decision
After Dred Scott, a slave, sues for his freedom, the Supreme Court declares that blacks have no rights as citizens and that Congress cannot make laws concerning slavery in the territories.

1820	1825	1830	1835	1840	1845

1820
Missouri Compromise
Congress defines where slavery is permitted in the territories west of the Mississippi River. By making this compromise, Missouri is admitted to the Union as a slave state.

1850
Compromise of 1850
When California applies for statehood as a free state, some Southerners threaten to secede. Congress resolves the crisis by redefining where slavery is permitted in the territories and enacting a stronger fugitive slave law.

1860
Lincoln Becomes President
Abraham Lincoln is elected president of the United States, prompting 11 states to secede from the Union.

1861–1865

The Civil War

A Southern attack on Fort Sumter ignites the Civil War. Major battles in such places as Antietam and Vicksburg bring the death toll to over 620,000 by the war's end.

1863

Gettysburg

The last Confederate invasion of the North results in a major battle and a Southern defeat near Gettysburg, Pennsylvania. Four months later, President Lincoln travels to the site and gives the Gettysburg Address, encouraging Americans to stay strong in the fight to preserve the Union and the principles of the Declaration of Independence.

1865

The Confederacy Surrenders

General Lee and his Confederate forces surrender to General Grant at Appomattox Court House, Virginia, bringing an end to the Civil War.

| 1845 | 1850 | 1855 | 1860 | 1865 | 1870 |

1863

Emancipation Proclamation

President Lincoln's Emancipation Proclamation frees the slaves in the Confederate states.

1865

Thirteenth Amendment

The Thirteenth Amendment is ratified. It outlaws slavery in the United States.

1868

Fourteenth Amendment

The Fourteenth Amendment is ratified, granting citizenship and equal civil and legal rights to African Americans and former slaves.

1870

Fifteenth Amendment

The ratification of the Fifteenth Amendment ensures that no citizen will be denied the right to vote based on race, color, or previous enslavement.

The motors of industry—like this 6,000-horse-power motor at a steel mill in Indiana—supplied energy for the nation's factories during the 1900s. So did hundreds of thousands of workers.

Population Density of the United States, 1870

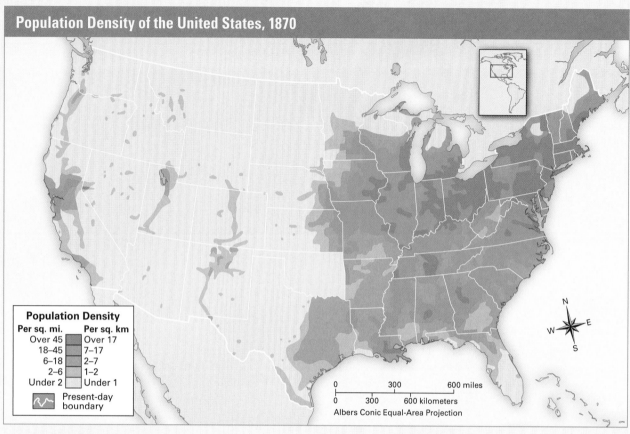

Population Density

Per sq. mi.	Per sq. km
Over 45	Over 17
18–45	7–17
6–18	2–7
2–6	1–2
Under 2	Under 1

Present-day boundary

0   300   600 miles
0   300   600 kilometers
Albers Conic Equal-Area Projection

Population Density of the United States, 1890

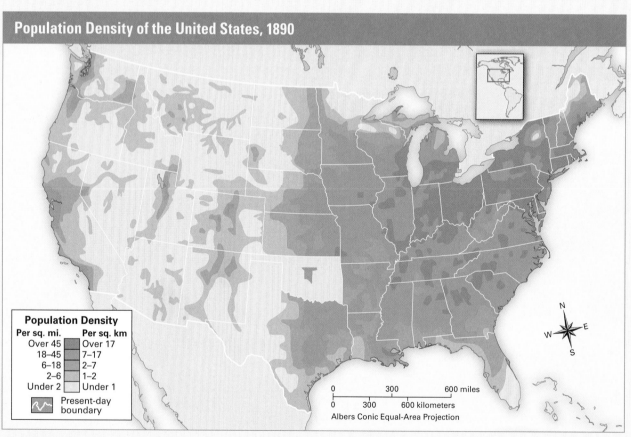

Population Density

Per sq. mi.	Per sq. km
Over 45	Over 17
18–45	7–17
6–18	2–7
2–6	1–2
Under 2	Under 1

Present-day boundary

0   300   600 miles
0   300   600 kilometers
Albers Conic Equal-Area Projection

Migration and Industry

In this unit, you will learn about the growth of industry and agriculture in the decades after the Civil War. Mining, ranching, and farming boomed on the Great Plains and farther west. So did manufacturing in the East. The key to this growth, and the link that connected the nation geographically, was the railroad.

The map on this page shows the nation's main railroad lines for two different years, 1870 and 1890. Compare railroads in the country by 1870 with railroads by 1890. Notice the difference between the amount and location of track. In fact, the total miles of track in the United States more than tripled between 1870 and 1890.

Think about being a farmer on the Great Plains in 1870. It would be a hard life and, for many, a lonely one. Farm machinery and luxuries such as glass for windows would not

be easy to obtain. The cost of transporting such goods from eastern factories by wagon would make them very expensive. But railroads changed that. By 1890, such goods could travel most of the way to the Great Plains by train.

The people, machinery, and other goods that trains carried west spurred the growth of mining, ranching, and farming. The same trains also moved ore, livestock, and farm products east to become raw materials for the nation's industries. The growth of industry created jobs, and people came to the nation's industrial cities to fill those jobs.

The maps on the opposite page show the nation's patterns of settlement in 1870 and 1890. The population changes they show, especially in the West, are almost as dramatic as the changes in the railroad maps. That is because, to a great extent, railroad growth was directly or indirectly responsible for them.

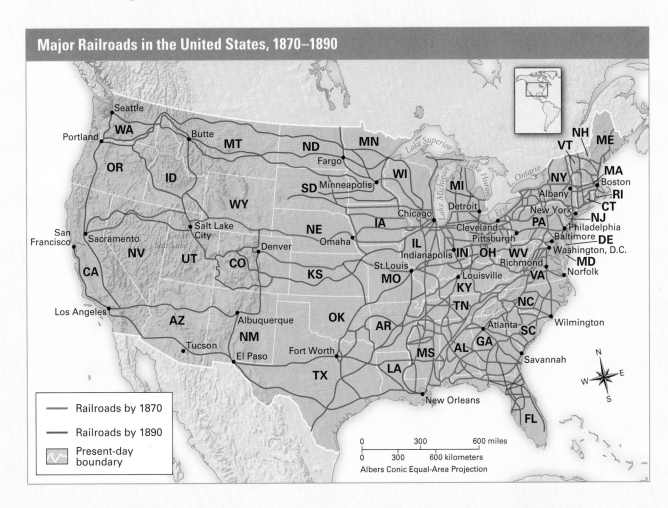

Major Railroads in the United States, 1870–1890

Railroads by 1870
Railroads by 1890
Present-day boundary

0   300   600 miles
0   300   600 kilometers
Albers Conic Equal-Area Projection

CHIEF JOSEPH.
NEZ PERCES.

Chapter 24

Tensions in the West

How did settlers change the West and affect American Indians?

24.1 Introduction

In the spring of 1889, two white women arrived at the Nez Perce lands in Lapwai, Idaho. One of them, Jane Gay, had nursed soldiers during the Civil War. The other, Alice Fletcher, had been a leader in the growing movement for women's rights. Now a new cause had brought these women west. They wanted to improve the lives of American Indians.

Gay and Fletcher were just two of the thousands of Americans who moved west after the Civil War. As you have read, during this period politicians in the East were arguing over Reconstruction. Meanwhile, railroad builders, miners, ranchers, and farmers continued to move westward. In this chapter, you will learn how the settlers' dreams of freedom and opportunity clashed with the dreams of the American Indians who already lived in the West.

The conflict between settlers and Indians was not just a fight over land. It was a conflict between two very different cultures and ways of seeing the world.

Jane Gay and Alice Fletcher discovered these deep differences soon after they arrived at Lapwai. Like other Indians, the Nez Perce had already been forced onto reservations—areas of land set aside by the government—to make way for new settlers. Now Fletcher told the Indians that the government wanted to divide the Lapwai Reservation into farm plots. Each family would receive one plot. Then the Nez Perce could live like other Americans.

The Indians listened in stony silence. Settlers might think of owning a plot of land as a way to be free. But to a Nez Perce, being tied to one spot of earth would be like being in jail.

Finally, one man spoke. "We do not want our land cut up in little pieces," the Indian said. "We have not told you to do it."

This Indian's words show why tensions were bound to develop between settlers and American Indians. As you read about the Nez Perce and other Indian groups, you will discover the great impact that the settlement of the West had on American Indians.

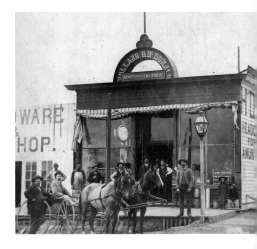

Hardware stores, like this one in Nebraska in 1886, supplied tools for farmers and ranchers settling in the West. The settlement of the West had a devastating effect on the Indians who lived there.

◀ Chief Joseph became the leader of the Nez Perce Indians in 1871. This portrait was made around 1897.

24.2 The Nez Perce

For centuries, the Nez Perce freely roamed the lush mountains and valleys where Oregon, Washington, and Idaho come together today. Their name, which means "pierced nose" in French, was given to them by French explorers. The French had confused the Nez Perce with other Indians who decorated their noses with pieces of shell. In reality, the Nez Perce did not usually pierce their noses or wear nose ornaments.

When horses arrived in the Northwest in the 1700s, the Nez Perce became expert riders and horse breeders. They developed their own special breed, the Appaloosa. These beautiful, spotted horses were fast and strong. The Nez Perce trained them to ride into stampeding buffalo herds and single out one animal for the kill.

The Nez Perce treasured their homeland and way of life. But after the Civil War, more and more settlers came from the East to settle in the Pacific Northwest. The world of the Nez Perce would never be the same.

Friendship with Whites For decades, the Nez Perce were among the friendliest of all western Indians toward whites. In 1805, they saved Lewis and Clark and their expedition from starvation. They were also friendly with the first trappers, traders, and missionaries who came to the Northwest. The Nez Perce had never killed a white person.

Americans' hunger for land and riches finally broke that friendship. In the 1860s, miners swarmed over Nez Perce land, looking for gold. Settlers followed. Some Nez Perce signed treaties in which they agreed to give up their land and move to a **reservation** in Lapwai, Idaho. Other members of the Nez Perce tribe refused to sign any treaty.

One of these "no treaty" groups of Nez Perce lived in the Wallowa Valley of eastern Oregon. It was led by a man whose Indian name meant "Thunder Rolling in the Mountains." The settlers called him Chief Joseph. In 1877, representatives of the U.S. government presented Chief Joseph with a terrible choice. You can give up your land peacefully and move to Lapwai, they told him, or army troops will come and force you to relocate there.

Fearing a war he could not win, Chief Joseph agreed to move. "I would give up everything," he said, "rather than have the blood of white men upon the hands of my people."

Blood Is Shed That summer, 700 Nez Perce left the Wallowa Valley, their hearts filled with bitterness. One night, a group of angry young warriors slipped out of camp and murdered several whites. Chief Joseph knew that the killings would bring soldiers to punish his people. For the first time, the Nez Perce would be at war with whites.

The soldiers came. Still hoping to avoid war, Indians carrying the white flag of peace came forward to talk. The troops opened fire anyway. Minutes later, 34 soldiers lay dead. "I have been in lots of scrapes," reported a survivor, "[but] I never went up against anything like the Nez Perces in all my life."

Nez Percé war chief Looking Glass, shown here, joined Chief Joseph in leading about 700 Nez Percé on their flight to escape relocation to a reservation.

reservation an area of land set aside by the federal government for the use of an American Indian tribe

The Flight to Canada In desperation, the Nez Perce headed for the one place where they might still live free—Canada. For the next three months, Chief Joseph led the U.S. Army on a chase of more than 1,000 miles through rugged mountain country. Although greatly outnumbered, his warriors won several battles.

The chase ended less than 40 miles from the Canadian border. Forced to surrender, Chief Joseph spoke his heart in these words:

> *I am tired of fighting. Our chiefs are killed . . . The old men are all dead . . . It is cold and we have no blankets. The little children are freezing to death. My people, some of them, have run away to the hills, and have no blankets, no food; no one knows where they are . . . Hear me, my chiefs! I am tired; my heart is sick and sad. From where the sun now stands, I will fight no more forever.*

After their surrender in 1877, Chief Joseph and his followers were sent to a barren reservation in Oklahoma. There they began to fall sick and die. Soon they had a cemetery just for babies, with more than a hundred graves.

Chief Joseph begged the government to allow his people to join the rest of the Nez Perce in Lapwai. Although some did go to Lapwai, others, including Chief Joseph, were sent to the Colville Reservation in Washington in 1885. They never went back to their homeland. When Chief Joseph died in 1904, the doctor listed the cause of death as "a broken heart."

When Chief Joseph and his Nez Perce surrendered, they were taken first to Kansas. This drawing shows them boarding a train to be transferred to a reservation in Oklahoma.

As settlers moved west, they seized more and more land from the American Indians who lived and hunted there. Here we see an American Indian village near Fort Laramie, in what is now Wyoming.

homesteader a farmer who is given a plot of public land, or homestead, in return for cultivating it

transcontinental railroad a railroad that crosses a continent

subsidy money or other things of value, such as land, that a government contributes to an enterprise considered to benefit the public

24.3 New Interest in the West

Settlers had been gradually forcing American Indians from their land ever since the first colonists arrived in North America. Still, by the start of the Civil War, the West was populated mostly by Indians and huge herds of buffalo. Then, in 1862, Congress passed two laws that stirred new interest in the West—the Homestead Act and the Pacific Railway Act.

The Homestead Act The Homestead Act offered farmers 160 acres of public land in the West for free. All the farmer, or **homesteader,** had to do was clear the land and farm it for five years. At the end of that time, the homesteader received ownership of the land.

The impact of the new law was enormous. Year after year, the promise of free land drew hopeful homesteaders westward. Between 1860 and 1910, the number of farms in the United States tripled from 2 million to more than 6 million.

The Pacific Railway Act The Pacific Railway Act called for the building of a **transcontinental railroad** to link the Atlantic and Pacific coasts. This huge construction project was given to two railroad companies: the Union Pacific and the Central Pacific.

To help the railroad companies pay for the project, Congress gave them **subsidies** in the form of sections of free land for every mile of track they laid. The railroads could sell this land to settlers later. The government also loaned the two companies more than $60 million.

The Pacific Railway Act kicked off the greatest period of railroad construction in the nation's history. By 1900, the railroads had laid 170,000 miles of track, much of it in the West. "Rail barons" like the Central Pacific's Leland Stanford and Charles Crocker made vast fortunes.

Railroads opened the West to a flood of new settlers. The newcomers included farmers and ranchers, prospectors and preachers, and more than a few crooks. But most were ordinary people who dreamed of a new start. For them, the West was a place where a lot of hard work and a little luck could make their dreams come true.

24.4 Railroad Builders

The plan for building a transcontinental railroad looked simple enough on paper. The Union Pacific would start in Nebraska and build tracks westward across the Great Plains and the Rocky Mountains. Meanwhile, the Central Pacific would start in California and lay tracks eastward across the mountains of the Sierra Nevada and then across the Great Basin. The two lines would meet somewhere in between the starting points. The company that laid the most track would get more land, more loans, and more profits.

Laying track was hard work. First, the surveyors studied the land and chose the route for the tracks. They were followed by the graders, who prepared the land. Armed with picks and shovels, the graders cut through hills and filled up valleys to make the route as level as possible.

Next came the tracklayers. They put down wooden ties and hauled in heavy iron rails. One rail weighed 700 pounds, and there were 400 rails in each mile of track. Last came the spikers. The spikers nailed the rails to the ties with spikes—ten spikes per rail, three hammer blows for every spike.

This group of workers, photographed in 1866, paused to look at the camera as they hauled heavy rails to lay track for the Union Pacific railroad.

The Union Pacific Builds West The Union Pacific Railroad got off to a slow start. Then, in 1866, a former Civil War general named Grenville Dodge took charge of construction. Dodge had built railroads before the war, and, as a military officer, he knew how to lead men. Now he commanded a force of 10,000 workers. Most of them were Irish immigrants who were fleeing the slums of eastern cities. They were joined by other immigrants, ex-soldiers, Mexicans, and freed slaves. All were young men who needed jobs. Most of all, they hoped to start new lives in the open spaces of the West.

By 1867, Dodge's crews were laying as much as seven miles of track a day across the plains. The workers lived in tent cities that followed the tracks west. These portable towns were rough and often dangerous places. A reporter wrote, "Not a day passes but a dead body is found somewhere in the vicinity with pockets rifled of their contents."

For the Plains Indians, the railroad was an invasion of their homeland. They watched as millions of buffalo were slaughtered to feed railroad workers, destroying their main source of food. Some Indian warriors attacked the work crews and derailed supply trains by prying up sections of track. Grenville Dodge demanded military help, and soon he had 5,000 troops guarding his crews as they inched their way west.

American Indians depended on the buffalo for food, shelter, and clothing. As the railroad moved west, hunters shot buffalo out the windows of trains. By 1900, there were fewer than 50 buffalo left in the United States.

The Granger Collection, New York

Chinese laborers were recruited to do the backbreaking work required to lay rails across the Sierra Nevada.

The Central Pacific Builds East In California, the Central Pacific Railroad faced different problems. Soon after the company began laying track, many of the workers dashed off to newly discovered silver mines in Nevada. Construction practically stopped.

In desperation, Charles Crocker, the head of construction, hired 50 Chinese workers. He doubted that the Chinese were big enough to do heavy construction. But the Chinese surprised him. They could do as much work in a day as any other crew, and often more.

Crocker was so impressed that he sent agents to China to hire more workers. The agents were lucky. War and unrest had driven millions of Chinese into poverty and debt. Young men jumped at the chance of going to America to build a railroad. Most of them planned to save their money and return to China as wealthy men.

More than 12,000 Chinese laborers worked for the Central Pacific. They cleared trees, shoveled dirt, blasted tunnels, and laid tracks. At least 1,000 Chinese workers lost their lives in explosions, snow slides, and other accidents. Despite these losses, the workers managed to lay up to ten miles of track in a day.

The Two Lines Meet On May 10, 1869, the two lines came together at Promontory Summit in Utah Territory. A golden spike was driven in to complete the 1,800 miles of track. In time, a network of railroads would bring new settlers, encourage the construction of towns and cities, and allow mail and supplies to be shipped clear across the country.

The Chinese workers, who had contributed so much to building the railroad, were not **acknowledged** at the celebration. Their reward for their years of hard work was to lose their jobs. A few of them fulfilled their dream of returning to China. But most stayed on in America, helping to build new farms and businesses across the West.

The discovery of gold or silver often resulted in instant towns throughout the West. Pictured here is Leadville, Colorado, in the 1870s.

24.5 Miners

A second group of pioneers, the miners, dreamed of striking it rich. The discovery of gold in California in 1848 set off a great treasure hunt in the mountains and deserts of the West. By 1874, gold or silver had been found in what are now the states of California, Oregon, Washington, Nevada, Montana, Colorado, Arizona, and New Mexico. Although some immigrants also came to seek their fortunes, most miners were young, white American males who dreamed of striking it rich.

Boomtowns and Ghost Towns Mining in the West followed a predictable pattern. First came the discovery of gold or silver. Soon, fortune seekers from around the world flocked to the site. Almost overnight, mining camps grew into fast-growing settlements called boomtowns.

Newspaper reporter J. Ross Browne described the birth of one such town, Gila City, in present-day Arizona:

Enterprising men hurried to the spot with barrels of whiskey and billiards tables . . . Traders crowded in with wagons of pork and beans. Gamblers came with cards . . . There was everything in Gila City within a few months but a church and a jail.

Boomtowns had no government, no law, and little order. Robbery and murder were common. Miners fought back by forming "vigilance committees" to control crime. The members of these committees, called vigilantes, handed out quick justice. A suspected murderer might be arrested, tried, convicted, and hanged all in the same day. If asked about their methods, the vigilantes pointed out that there were no courts or jails nearby. No miner had time to waste guarding criminals.

When the easy-to-find gold or silver was gone, most miners moved on. Just seven years after its birth, for example, Gila City was a ghost town. All that remained, wrote Browne, were "three chimneys and a coyote."

Mining Changes the West In many ways, mining was destructive. It damaged the land and displaced many American Indians. But most Americans saw mining as a source of wealth and opportunity. Some boomtowns, like Reno and Denver, survived to become prosperous cities. Mining also opened up the West's mountains and deserts to other settlers. Some were businesspeople who invested in the heavy equipment needed to extract hard-to-find ore from western mountains. Others were farmers and ranchers. These were the people who would turn territories into new western states.

24.6 Ranchers and Cowboys

A third group of western settlers consisted of ranchers and the cowboys who tended their herds of cattle. At the end of the Civil War, millions of longhorn cattle roamed the Texas plains. The cattle earned their name from their impressive horns, which could measure more than seven feet from tip to tip. The market for all this beef was the crowded cities of the East. Cattle worth $3 a head in Texas might be sold for $50 in New York or Chicago. The problem was how to transport the cattle to the cities. This challenge was complicated by the presence of Indians and stampeding buffalo herds.

The Extermination of the Buffalo The railroads made the ranchers' task much easier. As the railroads moved onto the Great Plains, buffalo hunters followed. The hunters killed huge numbers of buffalo for their hides and bones, which were shipped by rail for sale in the East.

The Plains Indians, who depended on the buffalo for food, were horrified by the slaughter. So were some other Americans. In 1874, Congress passed a bill outlawing the killing of more buffalo than could be used for food. But President Grant refused to sign the bill into law. General Philip Sheridan supported Grant's decision. "You ought to give each hunter a medal," he said. "Let them kill, skin and sell until the buffalo are exterminated [wiped out]. Then your prairies can be covered with cattle and the cowboy."

By 1880, the buffalo had all but vanished. With their food gone, the Plains Indians had little choice but to move to reservations. The plains were now open to ranchers and their cattle.

Cowboys like Nat Love moved out west to herd cattle. Many cowboys dreamed of getting their own herd and making their fortune in the rapidly growing cattle empire.

The Long Drive The railroads also solved the ranchers' transportation problem. In 1867, Joseph McCoy built a stockyard next to the railroad in Abilene, Kansas. A stockyard is a large holding pen where cattle are kept temporarily. That summer, cowboys herded a few thousand cattle from Texas to the Abilene stockyard, in what they called the "long drive." There the cattle were loaded into boxcars and shipped east. Over the next 20 years, cowboys drove more than 5 million cattle to Abilene and other "cow towns" beside the rails.

Being a cowboy was dangerous and low-paying work. Still, life on the trail attracted many young adventurers. Most were Texans. About a third were of Mexican or African American heritage. Rarely, however, were black cowboys promoted to trail boss. Jim Perry, for example, was an expert rider, roper, and trail cook. Prejudice against blacks, he believed, was the only reason he was not the boss of his own team.

During the long drive, cowboys worked 17 hours a day, seven days a week, for three to four months. Much of the work was boring—except for moments of terror when a herd stampeded. By the time they reached the end of the trail, most cowboys were ready for rowdy fun, including drinking, gambling, and brawling. That made the cow towns wild, noisy, and often dangerous places.

The most notorious cow town was Dodge City, Kansas. An eastern newspaper described it as "a wicked little town." Between 1872 and 1878, 64 victims of gunfights were buried on the hill above the town. Later, several graves were dug up to make way for a new school. The gravediggers turned up a fine collection of skeletons, most still wearing their cowboy boots. To this day, the Dodge City cemetery is known as Boot Hill.

Dodge City, Kansas, was a wild cow town. When cowboys reached the end of the drive, they were ready for adventure.

The Granger Collection, New York

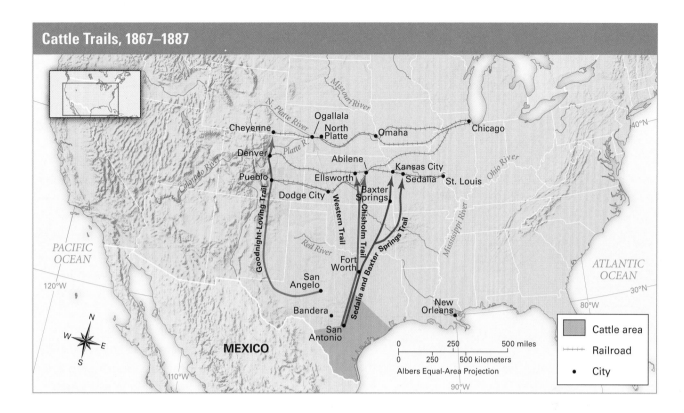

Cattle Trails, 1867–1887

The End of the Long Drive After growing rapidly for 20 years, the cattle industry collapsed in 1887. The winter of 1886–1887 was the worst anyone could remember. Whole herds of cattle froze to death. Ranchers called that terrible winter the "Great Die-Up." Many of them lost everything. The ranchers who were still in business reduced their herds and fenced their grazing lands. They built barns and raised hay so that they could shelter and feed their animals in winter. The days of the long drive were over. Wild cow towns became **civilized** ranching centers. Adventuresome cowboys settled down to work as ranch hands.

The cattlemen's glory years faded into the past. Still, they had left their mark on the West. They had opened the Great Plains to settlement. And they had created an industry that remains an important part of life in the West today.

Cattle trails led from Texas to rail centers in the Midwest. Between 1867 and 1887, cowboys drove millions of cattle to rail centers, where the cattle were shipped to meatpacking centers such as Chicago, St. Louis, Kansas City, and Omaha.

24.7 Homesteaders

Farmers followed the ranchers onto the Great Plains. For half a century, the plains had been viewed as too dry for farming. Mapmakers labeled the area the "Great American Desert." Then, in the 1870s, a few homesteaders plowed and planted the grassland. They were lucky. These were years of plentiful rain, and their fields yielded fine crops.

The western railroads and land dealers made the most of this good luck. Maybe the plains used to be too dry for farming, they said, but not any more. Some even said that rain had followed the rails west. "The increase of railroads," wrote a Colorado journalist, "has the . . . effect of producing more showers." Others gave farming the credit for the wet years, claiming that "rain follows the plow."

The plains greeted newcomers with miles and miles of treeless grassland. Since lumber was expensive or unavailable, farmers built homes out of sod. Sod houses were cool in the summer and warm in the winter.

Homesteaders Arrive Rain might not follow the rails or the plow, but a rush of new settlers did. By 1900, some 500,000 homesteaders had moved onto the Great Plains. Many were farm families from the East who were lured west by the promise of free or cheap land. Some were former slaves looking for a new start in freedom. Tens of thousands of European immigrants also settled the plains. While most of them were seeking land, one group, Russian Mennonites, came looking for religious freedom.

Farming the Dry Plains The homesteaders faced huge challenges as they struggled to turn grasslands into grain fields. Rain was unreliable. Some years their crops withered under the hot prairie sun. Other years, locusts—large grasshoppers that travel in swarms—swept across the plains, eating everything in their path. In addition, the plains had few trees, so there was little wood for homes.

Over time, the homesteaders solved these problems. Instead of using wood, they built houses out of chunks of sod, or soil held together by grassy roots. They used windmills to pump water from deep in the ground. They learned how to plow deeply to reach moist soil. The Mennonites introduced a type of winter wheat that thrived on the plains. With hard work and the right crop, homesteaders made the Great Plains the most productive wheat-growing region in the world.

24.8 War on the Plains

The flow of miners, ranchers, and farmers to the West led to a change in federal policy toward American Indians. Under the Indian Removal Act of 1830, American Indians had been promised lands in the Great Plains in exchange for giving up their homelands in the East. By the mid-1800s, however, whites were pushing deep into this "Indian Territory." A number of small wars raged as Indians resisted the tide of white settlement. More and more, government officials saw Indians as standing in the way of the agricultural and industrial development of the West.

In 1867, Congress tried to separate American Indians and settlers by moving the Indians onto reservations. In exchange for their land, Indians were promised food, farm tools, and schools where their children would learn to "live like whites."

The new policy was backed up by force. The U.S. Army was authorized to round up Indians and keep them on reservations.

Many American Indians fought this effort to take away their land and change their way of life. In the 1870s, the wars on the plains would settle the issue once and for all.

Reservation Life The nomadic Plains peoples hated the idea of being penned up on a reservation. A Sioux chief named Sitting Bull spoke for many Indians when he said,

> *I will remain what I am until I die, a hunter, and when there are no buffalo or other game I will send my children to hunt and live on prairie mice, for when an Indian is shut in one place, his body becomes weak.*

Despite Sitting Bull's words, the buffalo were disappearing, and most Plains Indians had little choice but to move to reservations. Once they did, however, the promised food often failed to arrive. Sometimes dishonest whites, working as federal agents, sold it to settlers instead. Often the food was spoiled by the time it reached the Indians.

Hungry and unhappy with reservation life, many warriors left the reservations to look for game or to attack settlers. When they did, they were hunted down by army troops.

General George Crook sympathized with the Indians. "I do not wonder that when these Indians see their wives and children starving they go to war," he wrote. "And then we are sent out to kill. It is an outrage."

Sioux chief Sitting Bull resisted white settlement with passion and courage. Nevertheless, his leadership was not enough to stop the massive loss of Indian lands to white settlement.

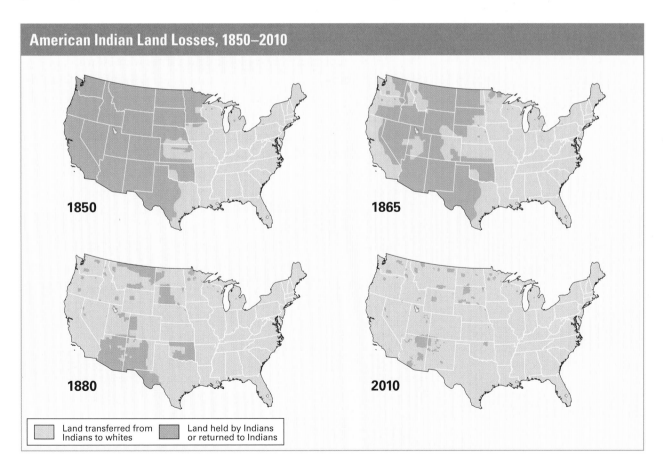

American Indian Land Losses, 1850–2010

1850

1865

1880

2010

Land transferred from Indians to whites

Land held by Indians or returned to Indians

This artist's depiction of the Battle of the Little Big Horn shows Sioux warriors overwhelming Custer's troops. Custer himself was killed by a gunshot to the head. The battle lasted only half an hour.

The Battle of the Little Big Horn The most famous battle in this long struggle was fought near the Little Big Horn River in present-day Montana. The Battle of the Little Big Horn soon came to be known by another name: "Custer's Last Stand."

The conflict began when soldiers led by a former Civil War officer named George Custer found gold in the Black Hills of Dakota Territory. Within months, 15,000 gold-hungry whites were swarming over Sioux land. Rather than remove the miners, the government demanded that the Sioux sell the Black Hills. The Sioux refused. "I never want to leave this country," a leader named Wolf Necklace told the government agents. "All my relatives are lying here in the ground, and when I fall to pieces I am going to fall to pieces here."

The army was ordered to force the Indians out. In June 1876, army scouts reported that several thousand Sioux and Cheyenne were camped beside the Little Big Horn River. Custer was ordered to locate the camp and then wait for reinforcements.

Once Custer spotted the Indian camp, however, he decided to attack at once. The attack ended in disaster. Custer split up his troops, and the group that he led suddenly found itself surrounded by angry warriors.

The battle, one warrior said, lasted no longer than a hungry man needs to eat his dinner. In those few minutes, Custer and all his men—about 260 soldiers—were killed.

Angry whites called the battle a massacre. Over the next few months, the army tracked down the Sioux and Cheyenne and forced them onto reservations. Ignoring earlier treaties, Congress took the Black Hills and another 40 million acres of land away from the Sioux.

By 1887, most American Indians had been moved onto reservations. Never again would Indians roam freely across the West.

In this chapter, you read about tensions that developed between settlers and American Indians in the West after the Civil War.

The Nez Perce For centuries, Nez Perce Indians had roamed the area where Oregon, Washington, and Idaho come together today. The Nez Perce saved the Lewis and Clark expedition from starvation in 1805. As settlers moved west, American Indians were pushed off their lands and onto reservations. In 1877, when the Nez Perce resisted relocation, the U.S. Army chased them and their leader, Chief Joseph, almost to Canada. The Indians surrendered and were sent to a barren reservation, where many died.

The Homestead Act and the Pacific Railway Act During the Civil War, two government acts aroused new interest in the West. The Homestead Act of 1862 gave homesteaders a plot of land to cultivate. The Pacific Railway Act of 1862 resulted in the building of a transcontinental railroad that made it easier for settlers to travel westward.

Railroad Builders, Miners, Ranchers and Cowboys, and Homesteaders The completion of the first transcontinental railroad—built by Chinese and Irish immigrants, ex-soldiers, Mexicans, and freed slaves—in 1869 opened the West to a flood of new settlers. Miners came in search of gold and silver. Ranchers and cowboys introduced large-scale cattle ranching to the Great Plains. Homesteaders turned the Great Plains into the most productive wheat-producing region in the world.

War on the Plains The flow of settlers led to changes in federal policy toward American Indians. Under the Indian Removal Act of 1830, Indians had been promised lands in the Great Plains in exchange for giving up their homelands in the East. In 1867, Congress tried to force American Indians onto reservations, promising them food, farm tools, and schools in exchange for their land. Ongoing wars between settlers, soldiers, and Plains Indians came to a head in the Battle of the Little Big Horn, also known as Custer's Last Stand, in June 1876. The Indians won the battle, but the U.S. Army soon tracked them down and forced them onto reservations. Most American Indians had been moved onto reservations by 1887. They would never again freely roam across the West.

Settlers rush to claim land in the Oklahoma Territory in 1893.

Ho for Kansas!

Brethren, Friends, & Fellow Citizens:

I feel thankful to inform you that the

REAL ESTATE

AND

Homestead Association,

Will Leave Here the

15th of April, 1878,

In pursuit of Homes in the Southwestern Lands of America, at Transportation Rates, cheaper than ever was known before.

For full information inquire of

Benj. Singleton, better known as old Pap,

NO. 5 NORTH FRONT STREET.

Beware of Speculators and Adventurers, as it is a dangerous thing to fall in their hands,

Nashville, Tenn., March 18, 1878.

Promotional fliers urged migration to Kansas in the 1870s. Some of these fliers made exaggerated claims, which helped to promote "Kansas fever."

Black Exodus

In the 1870s, the end of Reconstruction and the return of "white man's rule" caused many African Americans to flee the South. Thousands moved west, hoping to start a new life as homesteaders on the Great Plains. What they found there was not a paradise, but it did give them a taste of freedom.

In 1879, a remarkable event took place across the South. Thousands of African Americans left their homes and set out on a great migration. Some of them traveled on foot, following roads leading west. Others crowded onto the banks of the Mississippi to catch riverboats bound for St. Louis. From there, they moved on to Kansas and other western states. The migrants, called exodusters, were part of a migration known as the "Exodus of 1879."

The exodusters were trying to escape hardship and oppression in the South. After Reconstruction, conditions had worsened for southern blacks. White leaders restricted black voting rights and imposed segregation through Jim Crow laws. They passed black codes, laws that restricted African Americans' freedoms. Some of the laws prevented blacks from buying or leasing land, thus keeping them under the control of white landowners. Whites also used violence to terrorize black communities. Although slavery had ended, most African Americans in the South still did not feel free. As one black Texan, C. P. Hicks, noted in 1879,

> There are no words which can fully express or explain the real condition of my people throughout the South, nor how deeply and keenly they feel the necessity of fleeing from the wrath and long pent-up hatred of their old masters.

The migrants were not only being pushed out of the South by harsh conditions. They were also being pulled out by the prospects of a brighter future elsewhere.

For many, that future seemed to lie in Kansas. Many southern blacks believed that Kansas was the Promised Land, a place where they could own their own land and live as free men and women. This dream did not turn out quite the way they imagined. But despite great challenges, many of the migrants would still find a better life outside the South.

Black Pioneers

The 1879 exodus was not the first time African Americans had gone west. Black explorers, trappers, and missionaries had roamed the West in the early 1800s. Black miners had gone west to seek their fortune during the California gold rush.

Other African Americans moved west to escape slavery. In 1864, for example, Howard Bruce and his future wife fled from bondage in Missouri. They went to Leavenworth, Kansas, where they settled down.

Black families also moved west as pioneer settlers after the Civil War. Nancy Lewis went to Leavenworth as a teenager in 1865. She married a black soldier stationed there. The two of them later joined a wagon train to Colorado, where they made their new home.

Why Kansas?

Kansas appealed to migrants because it had lots of land for homesteading. But it also held a special appeal for many former slaves, who saw it as a symbol of freedom.

This idea stemmed from the antislavery struggles of the 1850s. At the time, some Kansans had fought to prevent Kansas from becoming a slave state. One southern black man later wrote to the governor of Kansas, "I am anxious to reach your state . . . because of the sacredness of her soil washed by the blood of humanitarians for the cause of freedom."

In the early 1870s, black leaders and businessmen began to promote Kansas as a destination for migrants. Two important promoters were Henry Adams and Benjamin "Pap" Singleton. Adams was a former slave and Union soldier. He favored black migration to the African country of Liberia. But he also backed migration to Kansas as a way to get blacks out of the South.

Singleton, also a former slave, was even more involved in the Kansas migration. He gave speeches and printed fliers praising the benefits of Kansas. With partners, he formed several black "colonies" in the state and began to take settlers there. He would later claim, "I am the whole cause of the Kansas migration!" Although this was an exaggeration, Singleton did play a major role in promoting migration. By the late 1870s, he had helped plant the seeds for the great exodus.

For many exodusters, the quickest route to Kansas was up the Mississippi River. Migrants waited for boats to take them to St. Louis, though many could barely afford the passage.

Kansas Fever!

In the spring of 1879, interest in Kansas suddenly exploded in a mass movement. Rumors began to circulate that the government was offering free land, transportation, and supplies to migrants who arrived in Kansas. These rumors were false, but they sparked great excitement. "Kansas fever" quickly spread across the South.

Many people began to pack up their belongings and head west. Six thousand exodusters moved in the first few months of 1879. As many as 20,000 people had migrated by the end of the year. They joined some 30,000 blacks who had already gone west during the 1870s.

This mass migration caused a panic among white southerners. Fearing the loss of black farmworkers, they tried to prevent the exodusters from leaving. They blocked roads and warned riverboat captains not to pick up black migrants. They even threatened to sink boats carrying exodusters.

Many migrants were left stranded along the Mississippi with no way forward. Others got to St. Louis, but then discovered there was no free transport to Kansas. Some of them got stuck there and had to rely on donations of food and clothing to survive. Others returned to the South. Under these circumstances, the exodus quickly lost steam. Within a few years, it was over.

Many of those who did get to Kansas were overjoyed, though. When John Solomon Lewis arrived with his family in 1879, he said it was like a dream come true.

African Americans who made the exodus dreamed of better lives for their children. These children of black pioneers posed for a photograph near their new home in Nebraska.

> When I landed on the soil, I looked on the ground and I says this is free ground. Then I looked on the heavens, and I says them is free and beautiful heavens. Then I looked within my heart, and I says to myself I wonder why I never was free before?

Others had a different reaction. Williana Hickman could hardly believe her eyes when she arrived in Nicodemus, a black settlement on the treeless plains of western Kansas, in 1878.

> I said, "Where is Nicodemus? I don't see it." My husband pointed out various smokes coming out of the ground and said, "That is Nicodemus." The families lived in dugouts [in the ground] . . . The scenery was not at all inviting, and I began to cry.

Life on the Plains

Williana Hickman got over her disappointment. Within a few years, she and her husband had managed to build a new life for themselves. Her husband, Daniel, was a Baptist minister. Together, they founded the First Baptist Church in Nicodemus.

Nicodemus was one of more than a half-dozen black settlements in Kansas and more successful than most. Founded in 1877, it took several years to get on its feet. The first winter was especially hard. The settlers lived in sod dugouts. It was cold, and many settlers went hungry. But when spring came, they planted their first crops and began building houses.

Without trees, settlers were unable to build wooden houses. Like many others, the Speese family cut brick-shaped pieces of sod from the earth to build their house.

By 1880, around 700 people lived in Nicodemus. The town had three churches, a bank, two hotels, several stores, and a newspaper. It continued to grow throughout the 1880s, adding more churches, a second newspaper, and even a baseball team.

The residents of Nicodemus hoped that the Union Pacific Railroad would build a rail line through their town. When it didn't, the town began a slow, steady decline. Today, it has only a handful of residents. But it remains the oldest surviving western town founded by African Americans. In 1996, it was declared a national historic site.

Black migrants also settled in other Plains states, including Nebraska. By 1890, there were nearly 9,000 African Americans living in Nebraska. One descendant of these early settlers, Ava Speese Day, wrote about her experiences growing up in western Nebraska in the early 1900s. She and her family lived in a one-room sod house. They planted corn, beans, and vegetables. They also raised cattle. "We fought tumbleweeds all year round," she wrote. "It was a never ending battle. In spring they came up thick . . . Come fall they dried and tumbled across the land. Some were bigger than we were tall."

Residents of Nicodemus today honor both their community's past and the history of the Exodusters in an annual homecoming celebration.

Poverty remained a problem for many African Americans who moved west. Many also experienced racism and discrimination from white residents.

Overall, though, life for most migrants seemed to improve. Blacks in the West were generally more prosperous than they were in the South. They enjoyed more economic opportunity and more political freedom. The black exodus of the 1870s may not have led to the Promised Land, but it did lead to a better life for most migrants.

Chapter 25

The Rise of Industry

Did the benefits of industrialization outweigh the costs?

25.1 Introduction

The tragedy began late in the afternoon on March 25, 1911. The quitting bell had just sounded at the Triangle Shirtwaist Factory in New York City. Nearly 500 employees, most of them young immigrant women, headed toward the exit. It was Saturday, and they were looking forward to a day off with family and friends.

One woman sniffed the air. Something was burning! Another spotted flames leaping out of a pile of cloth scraps. Before she could react, the wooden table above the fabric was ablaze. From there, the flames jumped to the paper fabric patterns hanging above the table. Flaming bits of paper and fabric whirled around the room, setting other tables on fire.

The room filled with smoke. The air became so hot that it burst the windows. Fresh air poured into the room, sending the flames even higher. The fire started to scorch workers' clothing and hair.

"I heard somebody cry, 'Fire!' I left everything and ran for the door," recalled one woman. "The door was locked and immediately there was a great jam of girls before it." She could see at once that "if we couldn't get out, we would all be roasted alive."

Factories and their dangers were a relatively new part of life in the United States. The Industrial Revolution spread to the United States in the early 1800s. After the Civil War, new inventions and business methods allowed Americans to create industry on a much larger scale than ever before. The nation's new mills and factories produced an amazing assortment of goods that made life better for many. Industrial progress, though, brought not only economic benefits, but also serious social costs. The people who were employed in these new industries often lived and worked in the most miserable, even dangerous, conditions.

In this chapter, you will read the rest of the story of the Triangle Shirtwaist Factory fire. You will also learn about both the benefits and the costs of industrialization.

Firefighters could do little to stop the blaze that claimed 146 lives at the Triangle Shirtwaist Factory fire in 1911. Unsafe working conditions contributed to the high death toll.

◄ This photograph, taken around 1910, shows a typical workroom in a sewing factory.

entrepreneur a person who assembles and organizes the resources necessary to produce goods and services. Entrepreneurs are willing and able to take the risks involved in starting and managing a business.

laissez-faire a theory that economies work best when there is minimal involvement from government

25.2 A Nation Transformed

Industrialization clearly brought benefits to some. On March 26, 1883, Alva Vanderbilt threw a party to show off her family's new home in New York City. It was not just a party, it was a grand ball—the most dazzling social event in the city's history. And it was not just any home. The Vanderbilts had built a mansion in the style of a European castle, complete with medieval furniture, tapestries, and armor.

But then, the Vanderbilts were not just any family. Mrs. Vanderbilt's husband was William Kissam Vanderbilt, a railroad industrialist. He was the grandson of Cornelius Vanderbilt, who had made a fortune in banking and shipping. The Vanderbilt clan was one of the country's wealthiest and most powerful families.

More than 1,200 of New York's social elite flocked to Mrs. Vanderbilt's ball, dressed in glittering costumes. Many of the guests came as kings and queens. But Mrs. Vanderbilt's sister-in-law decided to be more modern. She came dressed as the electric light.

Mrs. Vanderbilt's party reflected the way industrialization was transforming American life in the decades after the Civil War. Cities like New York were booming. **Entrepreneurs** in banking, commerce, and industry were gaining enormous wealth. Technological marvels like the electric light were changing how Americans lived and worked. But as the workers in the Triangle Shirtwaist Factory knew, not everyone benefited from this progress.

Industrialization produced a wide range of affordable consumer goods. Giant catalogs like this one offered American families everything from pots and pans to pianos.

The Growth of Big Business Families like the Vanderbilts made huge profits from the growth of big business after the Civil War. Businesses got bigger in part because of new technology and manufacturing practices. They also grew because there was more money to **invest** in them. Bankers and investors were happy to provide the necessary funds in hopes of earning large returns. Some of the money that fueled industrialization came from the large-scale mining of gold and silver in the West.

Government policies also contributed to the boom in big business. According to the theory of **laissez-faire** (leh-say-FAIR), economies work best with minimal government involvement. (*Laissez-faire* is French for "to let alone.") The idea of laissez-faire was that government should not regulate the price or quality of goods, the working conditions of laborers, or the business practices of bankers and industrialists.

Some types of government involvement protected business and industry. Federal, state, and local governments helped business and industry through favorable laws and subsidies, such as the land grants given to railroads and farmers. Congress passed higher and higher tariffs. These made imported goods more expensive and, therefore, less competitive with those produced in the United States.

The business boom fed the growth of American cities. For 100 years, Americans had been going west to seek their fortunes. In 1890, the Census Bureau said that the frontier line no longer existed. This was the imaginary line on the continent beyond which the country's population density was less than two persons per square mile. The 1890 census marked the closing of the frontier. The new "land of opportunity" was located in the cities of the Northeast and around the Great Lakes, where factories provided thousands of new jobs.

Outside the cities, even farming was getting to be big business. In the Midwest, commercial farmers used new machinery and techniques to grow crops on a larger scale than ever before. "The wildest dream has become reality," marveled one writer in 1887. "Nothing is too large for belief. Twenty and even thirty thousand acre farms, and a hundred bushels to the acre . . . The New West . . . is a veritable 'Wonderland.'"

The Gilded Age As businesses got bigger, so did the fortunes of those who owned or invested in them. Between 1860 and 1892, the number of millionaires in the United States grew from 400 to more than 4,000. The newly rich filled their palace-like homes with elaborate decorations and European art and antiques. In 1873, the great American writer Mark Twain dubbed this time of showy wealth "the Gilded Age." (*Gilded* means overlaid with gold.)

Twain's name stuck, but it did not describe the lives of most Americans. While wealthy capitalists lived like royalty, many workers lived in dismal poverty. Those who were immigrants often faced prejudice and discrimination. During business downturns, many workers lost their jobs. People were angry about the relationships between some business owners and politicians that resulted in widespread corruption. As you will learn, these conditions eventually sparked protests and calls for reform.

The Vanderbilts were one of the wealthiest and most powerful families of the Gilded Age. This is the lavishly decorated dining room of their summer home in Newport, Rhode Island.

25.3 Improved Technology

By the 1860s, many of the factors necessary for the rapid industrialization of the United States were already in place. Machines had taken over much of the work once done by hand. Work had moved from homes to factories. Railroads had begun to connect customers and manufacturers with an efficient transportation system.

After the Civil War, new inventions and improved technology prompted the growth of new industries. Some of these innovations, or new ideas, helped businesses to grow and become more efficient. Others made daily life easier for many Americans.

The Age of Steel Before the Civil War, the nation's railroads ran on iron rails that wore out quickly. Railroad owners knew that rails made of steel—a mixture of iron, carbon, and sometimes other metals—were stronger and would last longer. Steel, however, was difficult and costly to make.

In 1872, a Scottish immigrant named Andrew Carnegie went to England to study a less expensive method of making steel, a method invented by Henry Bessemer. Carnegie owned a company that made iron bridges for railroads. He knew that his bridges would be better if they were made of steel. Carnegie was so impressed by the Bessemer process that he brought it back to the United States. "The day of iron has passed," he announced. "Steel is king!"

Carnegie was right. Within a decade, steel was replacing iron in rails, locomotives, and bridges. Other industries took advantage of steel, which was less expensive than iron. Steel nails, needles, and knives became common household items.

The nation's major steel plants in 1900 were located near or in regions with rich deposits of iron and coal. Railroads shipped ore to mills and finished steel to customers.

Iron and Steel Production, 1900

Many steel companies competed fiercely to supply steel for such products. To remain the leader, Carnegie hired scientists to improve the quality of his company's steel. He employed good managers to make his steel mill run efficiently. His recipe for success was "adopt every improvement, have the best machinery, and know the most."

To keep costs low, Carnegie set out to control every step in the steelmaking process. He purchased iron mines to supply his ore, coalfields to fire his furnaces, and railroads to ship his finished steel to customers.

To reduce his competition, Carnegie also bought up several

rival steel companies. He then combined them all to form the giant Carnegie Steel Company. By 1900, Carnegie Steel produced a quarter of the nation's steel.

Electric Power In 1876, Thomas Edison opened an "invention factory" in New Jersey. With a team of workers, he set out to create a "minor" invention every ten days and a major one "every six months or so."

Edison succeeded brilliantly. More than any other inventor, he helped turn electricity into an everyday source of light and power. His workshop turned out the first practical electric lightbulb, the phonograph (record player), the motion picture projector, and many other inventions.

In 1882, Edison built the first electrical power station and distribution system in New York City. His team invented everything the system required, including generators, regulators, meters, switches, light sockets, fuse boxes, and underground electric cables. When he finally turned the generator on, electricity began to flow to homes, stores, and factories. The age of electricity had begun.

By 1900, some 25 million lightbulbs were glowing across the country. Many factories were replacing waterwheels and steam engines with electric motors. Streetcars powered by electricity carried workers and shoppers along city streets. New electric-powered devices, such as washing machines and vacuum cleaners, were making housework easier.

The Collection of the New-York Historical Society, negative #2946.

Thomas Edison's invention of the light-bulb transformed the nation and gave birth to the age of electricity. In this picture of New York in the late 1880s, electric lines formed a crisscross canopy over the street. At night, these buildings glowed with electric light.

The Telephone The telephone was invented by a Scottish immigrant, Alexander Graham Bell. In 1876, as he was getting ready to test his "talking machine," Bell spilled acid on himself. "Watson—come here—I want to see you," he commanded his assistant. Thomas Watson, who was in another room, heard every word over Bell's telephone.

Bell's invention worked so well that, by 1915, Americans were communicating with one another over 9 million telephones. All these telephones made American industry more efficient and competitive by allowing producers, sellers, and customers to communicate quickly and easily.

New Production Methods New methods of organizing work were also making businesses more efficient. Factory owners adopted Eli Whitney's idea of assembling a wide variety of products from interchangeable parts. They also used the assembly line. In a shoe factory, for example, one worker operated a heel-cutting machine. Another operated a sole-cutting machine. Another made shoelaces. Still other workers assembled, labeled, and packaged the shoes.

Henry Ford was one person who foresaw the great potential in the assembly line. Ford created a moving assembly line to mass-produce automobiles. In Ford plants, workers stood in place all day, while a conveyor brought the work to them. After each worker did one or two tasks, the belt moved the product to the next worker's station.

These techniques of **mass production** enabled workers to produce more goods per day at a lower cost. As prices dropped, more Americans could afford to buy manufactured products. More customers meant more factories. By 1900, almost four times as many Americans worked in factories as had a generation earlier.

The Triangle Factory
Mass Production in New York

The Triangle Shirtwaist Factory was just one of many new businesses that took advantage of improved technology to mass-produce a quality product at a good price. The Triangle Factory specialized in a style of women's blouse known as a shirtwaist. A shirtwaist had puffy sleeves, a neat collar, front buttons, and a snug waist. Women liked shirtwaists so much that by 1909, New York City had more than 500 factories that made only this style of blouses.

Sam Bernstein, the production manager at the Triangle Shirtwaist Factory, loved watching his workers use the newest tools and production methods. Each person at the cutting tables had a special steel knife. This knife could slice through many layers of fabric at a time. This meant that a worker could cut dozens of sleeves, fronts, and backs at one time.

On another floor of the building, Bernstein could hear the whirring of 240 sewing machines. The machines were neatly laid out in 16 tightly packed rows. Flexible belts connected each machine to a rotating axle running down each row just above the floor. This axle, which was spun by an electric motor, delivered power to the machines. The machines clattered loudly as

Lying flat on the lower wing of the 1903 Wright flyer, Orville Wright begins the first successful airplane flight in history as his brother Wilbur runs alongside during takeoff. The Wright brothers designed and built the flyer out of wood and cloth. It was powered by a gasoline engine of the Wrights' own design.

Air Transport While Henry Ford was turning out cars on the assembly line, brothers Orville and Wilbur Wright were experimenting with flying. In 1903, with his brother Wilbur running alongside, Orville successfully piloted the first "flying machine" in Kitty Hawk, North Carolina. Although the flight was only 12 seconds in duration, it sparked worldwide interest in flying.

By the late 1920s, an industry based on air travel had emerged. The U.S. postal service used planes to transport mail across the country while the military used planes for exploration and scouting. At the same time, wealthy Americans took their first commercial flights across the country.

women sewed the pieces of shirtwaists together.

Piles of finished blouses were then lifted to the floor above by electric freight elevators. There, two rows of workers gave the shirtwaists a final pressing. Finally, shipping clerks packed the shirtwaists into boxes for shipment.

Usually, the factory almost ran itself. But if a problem occurred, the company's switchboard operator could reach Bernstein by telephone on any of the factory's three floors.

Sewing machines, seamstresses, bobbins, and piles of cloth crowd this factory. Imagine working here in the heat of summer.

corporation a business that is owned by many investors

trust a group of corporations that unite in order to reduce competition and control prices in a business or an industry

monopoly a company that controls all production and sales of a particular product or service

25.4 The Rise of Big Business

When Andrew Carnegie opened his first factory in 1865, most businesses were still owned by one person or a few partners. Because the owners' funds were limited, businesses were small. Owners knew their employees and often treated them like family.

Growth of Corporations A partnership might work well for a garment, or clothing, factory. But big businesses, such as railroads, needed much more capital (money to start a business) than a few partners could provide. To raise larger sums of money, entrepreneurs set up corporations. A **corporation** is a business that is owned by many investors, or people who help pay the business's **initial** expenses.

A corporation raises funds by selling stock, or shares in a business. Investors who buy the stock are known as stockholders. In return for their investment, stockholders hope to receive dividends, or a share of the corporation's profits.

The money invested by the stockholders is used to build the business. To make sure their money is used properly, stockholders elect a board of directors. The people on the board of directors oversee the running of the corporation.

After the Civil War, corporations attracted large amounts of money from investors. By the 1880s, thousands of corporations were doing business across the United States.

Rockefeller's Oil Trust A giant in the oil business, John D. Rockefeller introduced another form of business organization, the **trust**. A trust is a group of corporations run by a single board of directors.

Rockefeller invested in his first oil refinery in 1862, at the age of 23. At that time, petroleum, or oil found underground, was just becoming a valuable resource. Oil refineries purify petroleum into fuel oil. During the 19th century, oil was used to light homes, cook food, and run engines and generators.

Before long, many small refineries were competing fiercely in the oil business. The amount of oil these firms produced rose and fell wildly, along with prices. Rockefeller saw this as wasteful and inefficient. To reduce competition, he did everything he could to drive his rivals out of business. Companies he could not destroy, he bought.

Like Carnegie, Rockefeller took control of every step of his business. He bought oil fields along with railroads, pipelines, and ships to move his oil. He built his own warehouses and even made his own oil barrels for storing oil products. By 1880, Rockefeller controlled 95 percent of the nation's oil-refining industry.

To manage his many businesses, Rockefeller combined them into the Standard Oil Trust. The trust made the oil industry more efficient than ever before. But, as a **monopoly,** the trust had the power to control oil prices. This worried people who depended on oil in their homes and businesses.

In 1901, J. P. Morgan bought Carnegie's steel company and turned it into U.S. Steel, the nation's first billion-dollar corporation.

The "people's entrance" to the U.S. Senate is "closed" in this 1889 cartoon. According to the cartoonist, the Senate was controlled by business trusts, shown as giant, bloated moneybags.

Following Rockefeller's example, entrepreneurs created trusts in other businesses such as railroads, meatpacking, sugar, whiskey, and tobacco. The business leaders who controlled these huge trusts became fabulously wealthy. Because most had made their fortunes by crushing their competitors, critics called them "robber barons."

The Evils of Trusts The growth of trusts alarmed many Americans. They saw these monopolies as a threat to the free-enterprise system. This system depends on free competition among businesses to provide the public quality products at fair prices. A monopoly, people argued, has little reason to improve its products or to keep prices low because it has no competition.

People also worried about the influence of trusts on the political process. Wealthy entrepreneurs, they complained, were using their enormous wealth to buy elections and corrupt public officials. As the *Chicago Tribune* warned, "liberty and monopoly cannot live together."

The Triangle Factory
The Owners

The Triangle Shirtwaist Factory would never be the size of U.S. Steel or Standard Oil. However, it was the largest shirtwaist factory in the entire country. The two men who owned the factory, Max Blanck and Isaac Harris, were famous in the garment industry and had been nicknamed "the shirtwaist kings."

The owners worked well together. While Blanck entertained buyers from stores to convince them to carry Triangle products, Harris ran the factory. Harris kept up with garment production, machinery maintenance, and work flow. He did not, however, try to keep up with his workforce.

The factory had too many workers for him to get to know them all personally.

The shirtwaist business made Blanck and Harris very wealthy. They drove fancy cars and enjoyed comforts that their workers could only dream about. Both had worked hard in a competitive business and probably felt they had earned their success.

This family is shown in a New York City tenement in the early 1900s. Cramped, dirty, dark, and crowded, tenements spread disease and misery among inhabitants.

25.5 The Growth of Cities

Industrialization brought with it **urbanization,** or city growth. Most of the nation's new industries were located in **urban** areas. Immigrants and **rural** Americans flocked to these industrial centers looking for jobs. Chicago, for example, more than tripled its population between 1880 and 1900.

Urban Tenements As urban populations increased, demand for cheap housing exploded. To meet this demand, developers threw up cheap apartment buildings called tenements. One person described tenements as "great prison-like structures of brick, with narrow doors and windows, cramped passages and steep, rickety stairs." By 1900, about two-thirds of New Yorkers lived in such buildings.

A poor family might occupy just one or two rooms in a tenement, usually with no heat or water. Friends or family often took in newcomers who arrived in cities without money for rent. As a result, tenement neighborhoods were some of the most densely populated areas on Earth.

Tenements were unclean and even dangerous places to live. Only a few rooms had windows to provide light and fresh air. The rest were

The Triangle Factory
The Building and the Workers

Blanck and Harris located their thriving shirtwaist business on the top three floors of the ten-story Asch Building in New York City. They chose this space partly because of the morning sunlight that streamed in through the large windows. Their landlord, Joseph Asch, stated that when construction was completed in 1901, "the architects claimed my building was ahead of any other building of its kind which had previously been constructed."

It may have been ahead of other buildings, but the Asch Building was far from perfect. It had only two staircases, even though the city building code required three. The city had agreed to count the building's fire escape as the third staircase. But the fire escape ended at the second floor. Nor was the Asch Building well de-signed for evacuation during an emergency. Its staircases were narrow. In addition, instead of opening outward to let people escape easily, the building's doors opened inward. Despite previous scares from several small fires in the building, Asch had not addressed any of these problems.

The Triangle Factory's workforce was made up primarily of young immigrant women. Most of these women were Italians and Jews from Eastern Europe. Often their

dark and airless. In some tenements, the only source of water was a single faucet in a courtyard. Many lacked sewer services. In such conditions, diseases such as typhoid and cholera spread quickly, killing infants and young children. Fire was another constant worry.

urbanization the growth of cities

Cities Expand Upward As cities expanded, urban land costs shot up. In New York, land that had sold for $80 in 1804 was selling for $8,000 by 1880. Such prices inspired builders to construct more building space on less land by expanding upward. Using lightweight steel beams to support walls and ceilings, builders constructed skyscrapers that rose ten or more stories into the air. Electric elevators whisked people and freight effortlessly from floor to floor.

Businesspeople rented space in city skyscrapers for their offices and factories. Factory owners preferred the top floors. Rents were cheaper higher up, and the natural light was better, saving owners money on electric lighting. The cost of insurance was low as well because steel buildings were thought to be fireproof. By the early 1900s, more than half of New York City's workers labored above the seventh floor.

City Excitement For all their problems, cities were also exciting places to live. Stores were filled with products never seen by people who had grown up on farms. City dwellers enjoyed all sorts of entertainment, from operas and art museums to dance halls and sporting events. When writer Hamlin Garland came to Chicago with his brother, he found that "Everything interested us . . . Nothing was commonplace; nothing was ugly to us."

jobs provided their family's only source of income. Even if these workers had been aware of the building's safety problems, they would have hesitated to demand improvements for fear of being fired.

Like most factory workers, Triangle employees could afford housing only in crowded slums. "I lived in a two-room tenement with my mother and two sisters and the bedroom had no windows," recalled one employee. "There was nothing to look forward to."

The workers at the Triangle Shirtwaist Factory lived in tenements like this one. They were not paid enough to afford better housing.

This young girl stands between looms in a textile factory. At the turn of the century, millions of children worked long hours in mines, mills, and factories.

25.6 Working Conditions

Working conditions in most industries were appalling. Gone were the days when business owners knew and cared about the people who worked for them. Men like Carnegie and Rockefeller knew little about their workers.

Working Families Gone too were the days when factory workers could expect decent pay. With so many people looking for jobs, business owners could pay low wages. Many wages were so low that men

The Triangle Factory
A Hazardous Workplace

Saturday was payday at the Triangle Shirtwaist Factory. Most workers earned only $9 per week, with the most experienced employees making up to $12. The younger workers, some only 13 years old, earned just $6 per week for sewing on buttons all day. The very youngest earned even less. Worker Pauline Newman recalled, *We were young, eight, nine, ten years old . . . The hours were from 7:30 in the morning to 6:30 at night when it wasn't busy. When the [busy] season was on*

we worked until 9 o'clock. No overtime pay, not even supper money . . . My wages were $1.50 for a seven-day week.

These pay rates were what workers earned before deductions. The company charged its employees for the thread and electricity they used, for the chairs they sat on, and even for using Triangle's coat lockers.

Employees were expected to work at least 59 hours a week. This included every Saturday, plus occasional Sundays. To keep workers from claiming

overtime pay, the managers sometimes set the clock back. To keep workers from being "interrupted," the heavy steel doors to the hall and stairs were locked until closing time.

To make sure workers didn't steal, the factory built a narrow corridor leading to the elevators. Every day at quitting time, employees filed through this corridor one at a time so that a watchman could inspect each woman's handbag.

Working at Triangle was unhealthy, uncomfortable, and unsafe. Managers seldom let workers leave to use the bathroom or to drink from the dirty

could not support their families. To get by, wives and children had to work as well, usually at even lower wages.

Most factory women earned about $1 to $3 per day. If business was slow, wages dropped. A boss might not pay a new worker anything until she had learned her job. Then he would charge her for maintaining the sewing machine she worked on. If a worker complained, she could easily be replaced with a new one, perhaps for less money.

Millions of young children worked in mines, mills, and factories. A newspaper reported that young boys hired by coal miners to separate lumps of coal from rocks "go to work . . . at seven o'clock in the morning and work till it is too dark to see any longer. For this they get $1 to $3 a week." They also got curved spines from bending over piles of coal all day.

Inside the Factories Mills and factories were hot in summer and cold in winter. To keep costs low, owners crowded workers together rather than finding additional space.

Of all workplace dangers, fire claimed the most lives. In New York, tall buildings often lacked fire escapes. New York City's fire chief wanted buildings to have fire escapes and sprinkler systems that could put out fires quickly. But factory owners objected to such expenses.

New York City did require that factory doors "open outwardly" and "shall not be locked" so workers might escape quickly in a fire. The law was not enforced, however. In 1910, about 94 percent of all factory doors in the city opened inward instead of outward.

tap in the hallway. In the sewing room, women could barely squeeze by each other's machines without catching their clothes in the moving parts. The chairs often lacked backs to support the sewers while they worked. With all the machines in use, the noise could be deafening.

Fire hazards abounded. The city prohibited smoking, but the factory rarely enforced that rule. Workers stuffed leftover fabric into wooden bins where it sat for months just waiting for a spark to set it ablaze. The building's only fire protection was a few hundred pails of water scattered throughout its ten floors.

An inspector points to a bolted door in the Triangle Shirtwaist Factory. The inspection came too late for the women who would lose their lives in the fire.

Strikes often pitted police against labor organizers. This painting shows a policeman being shot on Haymarket Square in Chicago during a strike of the Knights of Labor in 1886.

25.7 Labor Unions

As a teenager, Rose Schneiderman found work in a cap factory. After three years, she later wrote, "It began to dawn on me that we girls needed an organization. We were helpless; no one girl dare stand up for anything alone."

Workers like Schneiderman had been forming unions since the 1830s. These early organizations were **labor unions**. They organized workers in the same trade, or job, to fight for better wages and working conditions. Sometimes workers in these unions went out on strike, refusing to work until their employers agreed to meet their demands.

labor union an organization that brings together workers in the same trade, or job, to fight for better wages and working conditions

The Triangle Factory Fire Ends in Tragedy

About 5,000 workers from the Triangle Shirtwaist Factory were part of the strike of 1909. Their demands included unlocked doors during working hours and safer fire escapes in the Asch Building.

Rather than meet those demands, Blanck and Harris responded by locking the strikers out of the factory and advertising for replacements. "If the union had won, we would have been safe," said striker Rose Safran. "But the bosses defeated us and we didn't get the open doors or the better fire escapes." Because of that defeat, 146 workers would die tragically.

The cause of the fire that swept through the Triangle Shirtwaist Factory in 1911 was never known. But one Saturday afternoon, people on the eighth floor began to cry, "Fire!" Within minutes, the entire floor was a "mass of flames." Escaping workers rushed to the stairs or pushed their way into the two small elevators. The stairs, however, were soon ablaze, and the elevators stopped running.

On the tenth floor, Mary Alter was warned of the fire by telephone. Owner Isaac Harris and production manager Sam Bernstein led some people out onto the roof. People from nearby buildings stretched

ladders between the rooftops to help those on the roof escape.

Workers on the ninth floor had no warning. The fire just appeared. Some women died immediately. Firemen later found them as "skeletons bending over sewing machines." Those who had time to escape found themselves trapped by the locked factory door. In desperation, they rushed to the windows and began to jump.

The crowd that gathered outside the Asch Building watched in horror as girls began to fall out of the sky—"fire streaming back from their hair and dresses"—and drop to their deaths on the pavement below.

Firefighters arrived quickly but had trouble bringing their equipment close to the build-

Knights of Labor In 1869, Uriah Stephens organized a new union known as the Knights of Labor. Stephens hoped to unite "men and women of every craft, creed, and color" into "one common brotherhood." The Knights led several successful strikes against telegraph and railroad companies. With such victories, the union grew to over 700,000 members.

In 1886, nearly 200,000 workers went on strike nationwide to demand an eight-hour workday. During a rally at Haymarket Square in Chicago, someone threw a bomb at police. The police shot back, injuring many workers. Four workers were sentenced to death for the bombing, even though no evidence tied them to the bomb.

Fearing more violence, employers fired anyone associated with the Knights. Membership dropped quickly, and the organization faded away.

American Federation of Labor As the number of Knights declined, a group of local trade unions formed the American Federation of Labor. Led by Samuel Gompers, the AFL tried to negotiate agreements with employers on such issues as wages.

Despite the AFL's peaceful approach, many employers made their workers sign pledges not to join unions. They also fired union members and exchanged lists of such "troublemakers" with other employers.

ing because of the bodies on the pavement. There was little the firemen could do, however. Their ladders were not tall enough to reach beyond the sixth floor. Their safety nets were just as useless. The workers fell with such force, said one fireman, that they "went right through the life nets."

It was all over in half an hour.

At the funeral for the victims, garment workers marched under a banner proclaiming, "We demand fire protection." As she marched, Rose Schneiderman glanced up at the buildings lining the funeral procession. "There they were. Girls right at the top of hundreds of buildings, looking down on us," she recalled. "The structures were no different from the Asch Building . . . many were in a far worse condition."

This New York paper ran an eyewitness account of barred doors at the Triangle fire next to a cartoon that demanded "Who Is Responsible?"

Shirtwaist workers display strike leaflets for a newspaper photographer. Strikers wanted shorter hours, higher pay, and safer working conditions.

The Homestead Strike Some business owners used force to defeat unions. When workers struck at a Carnegie steel plant in Homestead, Pennsylvania, Henry Clay Frick, Carnegie's partner, refused to talk about their demands. Instead Frick made plans to reopen his plant with non-union workers. To protect these strikebreakers, he hired 300 armed guards.

When the guards arrived in Homestead, they faced an angry crowd of strikers. A battle broke out in which both guards and strikers died. Still, Frick went ahead with his plan. When the Homestead plant reopened with strikebreakers, the union collapsed in defeat.

Working Women Organize Such tactics kept many women from joining unions, but not Rose Schneiderman. Upset by pay cuts, Schneiderman organized the women in her factory as part of the National Board of United Cloth Hat and Cap Makers. Soon after she joined the union, she wrote,

A strike was declared in five of the biggest factories. There are 30 factories in the city. About 100 girls went out. The result was a victory, which netted us—I mean the girls—$2 increase in our wages on the average . . . But all was not lovely by any means, for the bosses were not at all pleased with their beating and had determined to fight us again.

The largest women's union was the International Ladies' Garment Workers' Union (ILGWU), which represented women in clothing factories. In 1909, thousands of New York City garment workers walked off their jobs to protest poor working conditions and low pay. As the strike grew, so did public sympathy for the young women. The newspapers called this movement "The Uprising of the 20,000."

The strike ended months later when employers agreed to a shorter workweek and better pay. They also ended fees for the use of factory equipment. The employers refused, however, to meet the workers' demands for safety improvements. Most garment factories remained unsafe.

In this chapter, you read about the rapid industrialization of the United States and how this progress influenced the way average people earned their livings.

A Nation Transformed Rapid industrialization transformed American life in the decades following the Civil War. Entrepreneurs in banking, commerce, and industry amassed enormous wealth. Businesses grew larger in part because of new technologies, new investors, and policies such as laissez-faire. According to this theory, economies work best when governments do not interfere.

Improved Technology New inventions and manufacturing methods prompted the growth of new industries. A less expensive method of making steel made it possible for businesses to grow in size and efficiency. Other inventions, such as the electric light and the telephone, made daily life easier for many Americans.

The Rise of Big Business While new innovations allowed more Americans to afford manufactured items, there was a hidden price. With the rise of big business through corporations, trusts (such as Rockefeller's Standard Oil Trust), and monopolies, the wealthy got wealthier and the poor got poorer.

The Growth of Cities As cities grew, factories rose ten or more stories above the ground, and people from all over came looking for jobs. People lived in crowded, unclean, and dangerous tenement buildings.

Working Conditions Men, women, and children worked long hours for low wages in crowded, unsafe factories. Doors were kept locked, and workers could not leave their stations without permission. Workers didn't dare speak up for fear of losing their jobs.

Labor Unions By joining labor unions, workers could fight as a group for better wages and working conditions. When organized workers went on strike, factory owners often responded with violence or by hiring non-union workers. Although labor unions had some successes, many factories remained unsafe.

This political cartoon shows the women of the Triangle Factory desperately trying to open one of the few exit doors. A man dressed in a suit decorated with dollar signs holds the door closed.

Edison suffered a hearing loss as a child. But he turned his disability into an advantage in his career as a telegraph operator. "Unlike other operators," he said "I was not bothered by the [noise of the] other instruments." His efforts to improve the telegraph led eventually to his invention of the phonograph, a machine that played recorded sound.

The Celebrity Inventor

Thomas Alva Edison was a legend in his own time. In part, his fame came from inventing things that changed people's lives—things we take for granted today like recorded music, the lightbulb, and movies. Edison was also a legend because he invented his own image. He knew how to get publicity and make himself a star.

From her home in Norton, Kansas, Mrs. W. G. Lathrop felt moved to write a fan letter. The letter wasn't going to a rock star, a movie star, or a sports hero. It was 1921, and Mrs. Lathrop was writing a fan letter to her favorite inventor, Thomas Edison. "Dear Sir," she began,

> *It is not always the privilege of a woman to thank personally the inventor of articles which make life livable for her sex. I feel that it is my duty as well as privilege to tell you how much we women of the small town are indebted to you . . . Positively as I hear my wash machine chugging along . . . as I write this it does seem as though I am entirely dependent on the fertile brain of one [who is] thousand[s of] miles away for every pleasure and labor saving device I have.*

Lathrop then filled in the specifics. She described how Edison's inventions affected a typical day in her life.

> *The house is lighted by electricity. I cook on a Westinghouse electric range, wash dishes in an electric dishwasher. An electric fan even helps to distribute the heat over part of the house . . . I wash clothes with an electric machine and iron on an electric mangle [pressing machine] and with an electric iron. I clean house with electric cleaners. I rest, take an electric massage and curl my hair on an electric iron . . . Then start the Victrola [record player] and . . . listen to [music], forgetting that I'm living in a tiny town of two thousand where nothing much ever happens.*

It is strange today to think about writing a letter like this one. But Thomas Edison was a celebrity. How did an inventor—someone who worked in a laboratory that was anything but glamorous—become so famous and well loved?

The Invention that Launched the Legend

No one but his mother would have guessed that little Thomas Edison would one day become a famous inventor. He was a poor student, "dreamy" and distracted. He doodled and didn't complete his lessons. He had such a hard time at school that after only three months, his mother decided to teach him at home.

When he was 15, Edison learned how to run a telegraph machine. The telegraph used bursts of electric current to send messages quickly over long distances. Edison was fascinated by the machine.

It was while trying to improve the telegraph that Edison made a momentous discovery. He developed a machine that could record and transmit the sound of a human voice. He called it a phonograph.

It is hard to imagine today just how amazing this was. Until the phonograph, people had only heard the voices of those who were physically near them. But Edison had made a machine that could record a voice. The recording could be played when the speaker was nowhere to be seen. It could, in fact, be played long after the speaker had died. The phonograph seemed magical.

Soon, a promoter was traveling the country, demonstrating how the phonograph worked. Audiences were thrilled.

You should hear me bring down the House by singing in the Phonograph . . . The effect when they hear me is stupendous, but when they hear the Phonograph reproducing my song with all its imperfections they endanger the walls with clamor.

—Edward Johnson, 1878

The New York Sun newspaper ran this headline about Edison and his phonograph on February 22, 1878: "A Man of Thirty One Revolutionizing the Whole World." Thomas Edison became a celebrity.

Once Edison saw the public's enthusiasm, he was more than happy to promote the new machine. By mid-1878, he published a list of ten possible uses for the phonograph. The list included recording books, music, and lectures. Edison also thought the phonograph could be used to teach languages and write letters. Today, we use recordings for all those purposes—and many more that even Edison could never have dreamed up.

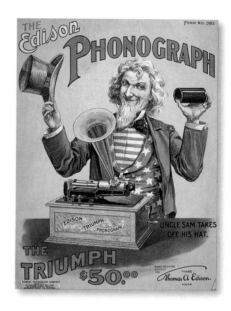

The phonograph amazed people around the world. In this advertisement, a smiling Uncle Sam shows off one of the cylinders used to play recorded sound.

Within about ten years after its invention, the phonograph had become a commercial product. For the first time, people could listen—and dance—to recorded music.

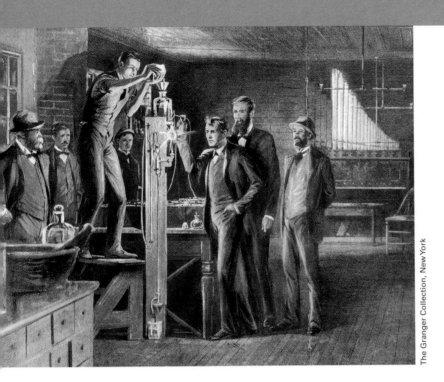

The Granger Collection, New York

"Genius is one percent inspiration and ninety-nine percent perspiration," Edison was fond of saying. His adoring public loved both images: inspired genius and hardworking inventor. In his lab in Menlo Park, New Jersey, Edison worked with assistants for two years to create a successful electric light.

Electricity and the Lightbulb

Edison is most famous today for inventing the electric lightbulb. In fact, other inventors had been working on lightbulbs for 50 years. But it was Edison who solved the problem that had plagued them all: how to make a bulb that would burn for more than just a few minutes.

A lightbulb works by electric current moving through a filament (thread). When the filament gets hot, it gives off light. Other inventors knew this, but they had not been able to figure out what kind of filament to use. After years of trying to use platinum, Edison switched to carbon. A carbon-coated thread did the trick. It would not melt or catch fire, and it could produce light for hours.

In October 1879, the *New York Herald* poetically described the light emitted by Edison's bulb. It was "like the mellow sunset of an Italian autumn . . . a little globe of sunshine, a veritable Aladdin's lamp," reporter Marshall Fox gushed. Better yet, it stayed lit for 13 and a half hours. Previous bulbs had lit up for only a few minutes.

A full year before he so impressed the *New York Herald*, Edison had announced that making a lightbulb was so simple that "everybody will wonder why they have never thought of it." Unfortunately, it was not so simple. When Edison made that statement, he was still struggling to get his electric lightbulb to work. But he was happy to keep the public interested with promises that the light from his bulb would last "almost forever."

At the same time that Edison was working on the lightbulb, he was also working on a way to distribute electricity. He planned to build a power plant on Pearl Street in lower Manhattan. The power plant would light the whole neighborhood.

Before the Pearl Street plant was finished, Edison had a private customer. William Vanderbilt, son of the railroad tycoon, wanted to outfit his house on Fifth Avenue with electricity. So Edison had an electrical power plant built in the basement. On the chosen evening, the lights came on as planned. Everything seemed to be going well—until someone noticed the smell of something burning. It turned out that the wallpaper had metallic thread in it and had almost caught fire. Mrs. Vanderbilt was not at all pleased. She demanded that the entire electrical system be removed.

At last, on September 4, 1882, the Pearl Street generator started up and a small part of Manhattan lit up. But it was not the earth-shattering event that some books describe. It had taken Edison four years to fulfill his promise of centrally generated electricity. The public had become bored. For his part, Edison was eager to start making money from his years of hard work. He was also ready to cement his reputation as an earth-changing inventor, regardless of how long it took him to follow through on his promises.

An Inventor Who Changed the World

Edison kept his inventions coming. As the 1800s came to a close, he applied himself and his staff to making moving pictures. He called his device a kinetoscope, which means "an instrument for viewing movement." He promised that it would do "for the Eye what the phonograph does for the Ear."

As with the phonograph, Edison did not immediately see how much people would like moving pictures. And as with the lightbulb, he was not the only inventor working on the device. Edison faced stiff competition. But in 1897, he starred in his own 30-second moving picture, *Mr. Edison at Work in His Chemical Laboratory*. The public loved it.

Thomas Edison had indeed changed the world. He invented—and helped invent through his competition with others—the phonograph, the electric lightbulb, the centralized distribution of electricity, the movies, and more. It is nearly impossible to imagine life today without any one of these or the later inventions they led to.

Decades before he died, Edison reached heights of celebrity and fame. The "Man Who Defeated Darkness," the "Dean of Inventors," and the "Greatest Citizen of the World" are just some of the titles given to him. He was happy to accept the praise, and people today are happy to accept his inventions.

Thomas Edison was a savvy businessman. When he bought the rights to another successful projector, he took full credit for its invention and called it the Vitascope. The new movie projector could turn these 45 still pictures of a man sneezing (right) into a five-second moving picture.

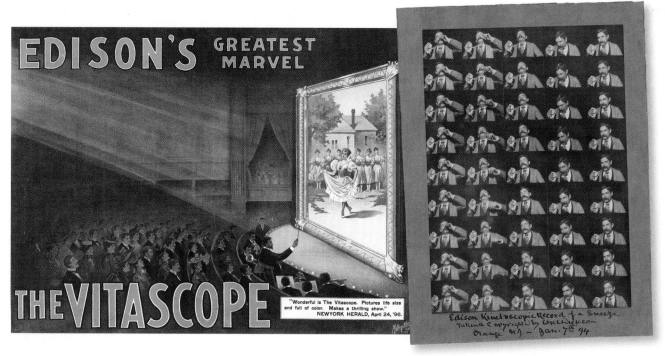

Chapter 26

The Great Wave of Immigration

What was life like for immigrants in the early 1900s?

26.1 Introduction

In the early 1880s, a young American Jew named Emma Lazarus saw a boatload of Jewish immigrants who had just arrived in New York City. The Jews on the boat were fleeing a religious massacre in Russia. Inspired by their suffering, Lazarus wrote a poem in which the Statue of Liberty welcomes immigrants. The poem begins,

> *Give me your tired, your poor,*
> *Your huddled masses yearning to breathe free.*

In 1903, a plaque inscribed with Lazarus's poem was attached to the base of the statue. Her words expressed the hopes of millions of people who made their way to the United States during a great wave of immigration between 1880 and 1920. Over those 40 years, more than 23 million immigrants arrived in the United States. Many were escaping poverty, political violence, and religious persecution. Others came seeking economic opportunity in a land of seemingly boundless promise.

Most of the newcomers flocked to cities, where industry was booming and jobs were plentiful. The sheer number of immigrants changed the face of the nation. The newcomers often clustered in rapidly growing ethnic neighborhoods. In both New York and San Francisco, for example, "Little Italy" districts grew up alongside "Chinatowns."

The new arrivals spurred the growth of the nation's cities and industries. Their languages, customs, music, and food made cities like New York, Chicago, and San Francisco more diverse and exciting places. Yet many native-born Americans responded to the new arrivals with suspicion and prejudice. For immigrants, these attitudes added to the challenge of starting life in a new country.

In this chapter, you will learn about the experiences and contributions of immigrant groups from around the world. You will also discover how Americans' attitudes toward immigration changed by the 1920s.

Immigrants arriving in New York City first landed at Ellis Island, where they went through an examination process to enter the country. This portrait of a young Jewish immigrant was taken at Ellis Island in 1905.

◀ Immigrants arriving by ship to New York City in 1915 gaze at the Statue of Liberty.

refugee a person who flees his or her home or country to escape war, persecution, or other dangers

assimilation the process by which immigrants or other newcomers acquire the attitudes, behaviors, and cultural patterns of the society around them

26.2 Immigration from Around the Globe

Patterns of immigration to the United States changed in the 1880s. Before this time, most immigrants came from northern Europe, particularly Ireland and Germany. By 1890, most were coming from countries in southern and eastern Europe, such as Italy, Greece, Russia, and Poland. Other people came from China, Japan, Korea, and the Philippines. Still others crossed the borders from Canada and Mexico.

Many of these newcomers were **refugees** escaping violence or poverty in their homelands. Compared to earlier arrivals, they tended to be poorer, less well educated, and less likely to speak English. Among these refugees were many Jews and Catholics, as well as Buddhists and Confucianists—a major change for a country that had always been largely Protestant.

The Struggle for Acceptance Americans wondered how the throngs of immigrants would affect the country. Most favored the **assimilation** of foreign-born people into the culture of their new homeland. They expected immigrants to become "Americanized"—to talk, dress, and act like their native-born neighbors. Others believed that the new immigrants, especially nonwhites, were too "different" to be assimilated. Their prejudices were **reinforced** when ethnic groups clustered in their own towns or neighborhoods, in part for **mutual** support and in part because they were not accepted elsewhere.

Many immigrants were eager to adopt American ways. Others had little choice. Public schools taught in English, and most stores sold only American-style clothes, food, and other goods. Many employers demanded that their workers speak English on the job.

Between 1880 and 1920, more than 23 million people came to the United States in search of a better life. The hardships of their journey were only the beginning of the challenges they would face in their new homeland.

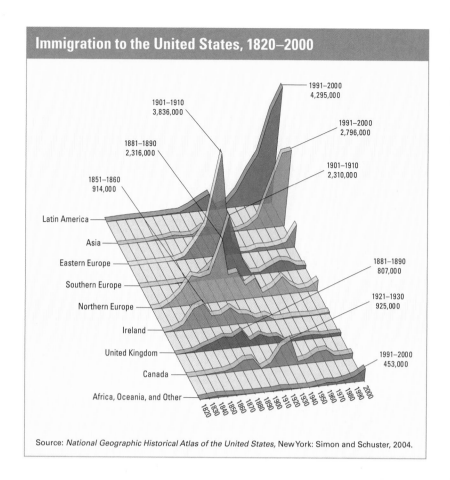

Immigration to the United States, 1820–2000

1901–1910
3,836,000

1991–2000
4,295,000

1991–2000
2,796,000

1881–1890
2,316,000

1901–1910
2,310,000

1851–1860
914,000

Latin America

Asia

Eastern Europe

Southern Europe

1881–1890
807,000

Northern Europe

1921–1930
925,000

Ireland

United Kingdom

Canada

1991–2000
453,000

Africa, Oceania, and Other

1820 1830 1840 1850 1860 1870 1880 1890 1900 1910 1920 1930 1940 1950 1960 1970 1980 1990 2000

Source: *National Geographic Historical Atlas of the United States,* New York: Simon and Schuster, 2004.

This graph shows immigration to the United States from different regions of the world. Each region's period of peak immigration is labeled. For example, between 1901 and 1910 more than 2 million people came to the United States from southern Europe.

Some immigrants did cling to their own languages and ways of life. But even those who tried hardest to assimilate often met with abuse and discrimination. Immigrants also faced resentment from workers who saw them as competing for jobs.

Contributions of Immigrants The new immigrants made **vital** contributions to the nation's rapidly industrializing society. As you know, immigrants helped to build the railroad. They worked in oil-fields; in gold, silver, and coal mines; and in rubber and steel mills. They labored in meat-packing plants, manufacturing plants, and clothing factories. Without the immigrants' skills and labor, the nation's cities and industries would not have grown nearly as fast as they did.

Immigrants also brought a vibrant diversity to their adopted land. The United States became a society **enriched** by the customs, foods, languages, and faiths of people from around the globe.

26.3 Italian Immigrants

When Pascal D'Angelo heard that his father was leaving their poor Italian village to work overseas, he was angry. "America was stealing my father from me," he later said. His mother tried to soothe him, saying that soon Papa would return, "laden with riches." But Pascal begged his father to take him along. His father agreed. The two of them boarded a steamship bound for the United States.

From Italy to America Like millions of other Italians, Pascal and his father came to the United States to escape poverty. In the late 1800s, much of Italy, and especially southern Italy, could not support the country's rapidly growing population. Farmers struggled to make a living on worn-out, eroded land where crops too often failed. There were few factories to provide other jobs.

Poor immigrants like Pascal and his father usually made the ocean passage in "steerage." Steerage was a deck, deep in the ship, that was reserved for the passengers who paid the lowest fares. These passengers were given narrow beds in crowded compartments that smelled of spoiled food, human waste, and sweating people who had nowhere to bathe.

Steerage passengers were allowed on deck only once a day. The rest of the time, they tried to amuse themselves by playing games, singing, and making music with accordions, mandolins, and other instruments.

After almost two weeks, the travelers arrived at the immigration station on Ellis Island in New York Harbor. There they had to pass medical examinations and answer questions about how they planned to support themselves in the United States. People who did not pass these inspections could be sent home, even if other family members were allowed to enter. So many families were forced to separate that Italians started calling Ellis Island "The Island of Tears."

Starting a New Life Judged healthy and ready to work, Pascal and his father arrived in New York City. A fellow Italian, a work agent called a *padrone* (puh-DROH-nee), helped them to find jobs building roads. Padrones helped many Italian immigrants get unskilled work building sewers, subways, and roads; cleaning streets; and laying bricks for new tenement buildings. By 1890, Italians made up 90 percent of New York's public works employees and 99 percent of Chicago's street workers.

Many Italian immigrants were "birds of passage"—young men who came to earn some money and return home. When several co-workers died in a work accident, Pascal's father decided to return to Italy as well. "We are not better off than when we started," he said.

Millions of Italian immigrants traveled by ship to the United States between 1890 and 1900. During the voyage, they endured crowded conditions and poor-quality food.

Pascal, however, decided to stay in his new country. He settled in an Italian neighborhood in New York, one of the many "Little Italys" that sprang up in U.S. cities. These mostly Italian neighborhoods bulged with residents who could afford only the cheapest tenement housing. Crowded together in tiny apartments, most families had no privacy.

Fortunately, Italian neighborhoods also offered opportunities for fun. Most Italians were Catholics who celebrated saints' days as they had in Italy. They strung colored lights, flags, and streamers along the shops and streets. Families strolled among booths that offered food and games. Fireworks, music, and dancing reminded everyone of life back home.

Above everything else, Italians valued family closeness. Some Italian parents didn't send their children to school because they feared that learning English would separate their children from the family. Besides, a child in school wasn't earning money to help the family. As a result, many immigrant children never learned the skills they needed for better jobs.

Because many Italian newcomers were poor and uneducated, Americans tended to look down on them. When a few Italians turned to crime and became notorious gangsters, some people started thinking of all Italians as criminals. As a group, however, Italian immigrants were generally more law-abiding than average Americans.

Some Americans feared that immigrants from Italy would always be poor and illiterate. Pascal D'Angelo was one of many who proved them wrong. After coming to the United States, Pascal bought himself a dictionary and learned to read and write English. In time, he became a well-known poet whose work was published in national magazines.

Italian immigrants often moved to "Little Italys" such as Mulberry Street in New York City, shown in this photograph. Here, rents were cheap and living conditions crowded.

pogrom an organized and violent persecution of a minority group

26.4 Jewish Immigrants from Eastern Europe

Maryusha Antonovksy was no more. In her place stood Mary Antin, the same immigrant Jewish girl but with a new "American" name. Mary had also bought "real American machine-made garments" to replace her "hateful" homemade European-style clothes. "I long to forget," she said. "It is painful to be conscious of two worlds."

Fleeing Persecution Mary Antin's first world had been a Jewish village in Russia. For centuries, Russians had discriminated against Jews, who dressed, worshiped, and ate differently from their Christian neighbors. By the 1800s, Russia had hundreds of anti-Jewish laws. Jews could live only in certain areas. They couldn't live in big cities or own land.

In 1881, assassins killed the Russian monarch Czar Alexander II. Nervous government leaders blamed Jews for his murder, even though the assassin was not Jewish. Angry Russians raged through Jewish villages, burning, looting, and killing. These attacks, called **pogroms,** happened repeatedly for more than 30 years. The word *pogrom* comes from Russian words meaning "like thunder."

Many Jews fled such persecution, hoping to find refuge in America. Between 1881 and 1924, some 2.4 million Jews came to the United States from Russia and other countries in eastern Europe. Mary Antin's father was one of them.

When immigrants arrived at Ellis Island, they faced the dreaded medical inspection. Medical examinations were quick but thorough. Here, a new arrival undergoes an exam to check for eye disease.

Mary's father left for America in 1891, hoping to earn enough money to send for his family. In his first letter home, Mary sensed "an elation [joy], a hint of triumph . . . My father was inspired by a vision. He saw something—he promised us something. It was this 'America.'"

When her father sent a steamship ticket for his family to join him, the people in Mary's village gathered together, filled with longing. "They wanted to handle the ticket," Mary remembered, "and mother must read them what is written on it."

After long rides in overcrowded trains and weeks of delay, her family finally boarded a ship in Hamburg, Germany. Although richer immigrants enjoyed comfortable cabins, the Antins were crowded together with hundreds of other passengers deep down in the ship. Seasick at first, they frequently came up on deck for fresh air, where "sailors and girls had a good many dances."

Like most European immigrants, the Antins entered the United States by way of New York Harbor. Wealthier passengers in first-class and second-class cabins were questioned briefly before being admitted to their new country. But the majority of arrivals were taken on crowded barges to the immigration station on Ellis Island. Often they had to wait for hours while inspectors and doctors examined each person. Fortunately, most new arrivals spent less than a day on the island before proceeding to shore and the beginning of their new life in America.

Jewish Life in America From Ellis Island, Jews headed for New York City's Lower East Side neighborhood. There they established shops, newspapers, religious schools, and synagogues (community centers and places of worship). The Lower East Side became the most densely populated neighborhood in the city. People lived packed into cheap tenements, often sleeping three or four to a room.

Some Jews worked as street vendors, using pushcarts to sell everything from coal to second-hand clothes. Pushcart vendors saved their money to buy horse-drawn carts and then small stores. Although most Jews were poor, they arrived in the United States with a wide range of skills. Jews worked as cobblers, butchers, carpenters, and watchmakers. Almost half found jobs in the city's garment factories.

Immigrants took work into their own homes or labored in different types of factories. Here, garment workers sew clothes in a tenement apartment.

Jewish immigrants did whatever they could to keep their children in school. In Europe, Jews had honored educated people, but schooling had cost money. As a result, many Jews had never learned to read and write. In America, Mary Antin wrote, "Education was free . . . It was the one thing that [my father] was able to promise us when he sent for us: surer, safer than bread or shelter."

Parents who made a little money often sent their sons, and sometimes their daughters, to the city's inexpensive public colleges. By 1910, more Jewish youths over the age of 16 were still in school than were young people of any other ethnic group.

Like other immigrant groups, Jews faced prejudice and discrimination. Most private schools and clubs refused to accept Jews. Hospitals would not hire Jewish doctors. The New York Bar Association would not admit Jews as lawyers. Many ads for jobs stated simply, "Christians only."

Still, eastern European Jews were grateful to be in their new country. One immigrant recalled, "There were markets groaning with food and clothes . . . There was no military on horseback and no whips."

26.5 Chinese Immigrants

The first Chinese immigrants came to the United States to seek gold in California. Later, many helped to build the country's first transcontinental railroad. Some of these immigrants returned to China with money they had earned. Their good fortune inspired 16-year-old Lee Chew to leave his poor village for the United States in 1880.

Chinese immigrants were sometimes detained for several months on Angel Island before they were allowed to enter the United States. Some carved poems on the wooden walls of the crowded barracks.

Traveling to California Lee paid 50 dollars for a bunk on a crowded steamship to make the month-long voyage to San Francisco, California. On the ship, he got his first taste of foreign food and marveled at machinery he had never seen before. "The engines that moved the ship were wonderful monsters," he wrote, "strong enough to lift mountains."

Lee arrived just in time. In the United States, discrimination against the Chinese had been growing ever since whites had pushed Chinese off their mining claims. As the number of Chinese immigrants increased, U.S. labor leaders warned of Chinese workers who would work for less pay than whites and take away their jobs. In 1882, Congress passed the Chinese Exclusion Act, which banned Chinese laborers from immigrating to the United States. The law also denied Chinese immigrants the right to become citizens.

As a result of the Chinese Exclusion Act, Chinese immigration slowed to almost nothing. Then, in 1906, an earthquake and fire destroyed much of San Francisco, including most birth records. Suddenly, many Chinese men could claim to be native-born citizens. As citizens, they were allowed to bring their wives and children to the United States.

Chinese claiming American birth started arranging for people in China to immigrate to the United States as their relatives. On the long ship voyage, the newcomers studied hundreds of pages describing their "families." When they reached San Francisco Bay, they threw the papers overboard.

These "paper relatives" landed at Angel Island in San Francisco Bay. Government immigration officials "locked us up like criminals in compartments like the cages in zoos," said one Chinese immigrant. Chinese usually remained on the island for three to four weeks, but sometimes they spent months or even years there. To pass the time, they carved poems on the wooden walls with silverware smuggled from the dining halls. One wrote,

Why do I have to sit in jail? It is only because my country is weak and my family is poor. My parents wait at the door in vain for news. My wife and child wrap themselves in their quilt, sighing with loneliness.

Before being allowed to leave Angel Island, each immigrant faced detailed questioning by officials. "How many steps are there in your house?" "Where do you sleep in your house?" "Who lives next door?" Then they asked a "family" witness from San Francisco the same questions. If the answers didn't match, officials could deport the newcomer. Nearly one in ten Chinese who came to the United States was sent back to China.

Chinese Life in the United States When Lee Chew arrived in San Francisco, he worked first as a servant and then set up his own laundry. Many Chinese started laundries because, as Lee explained, "It requires little capital and is one of the few opportunities that are open. Men of other nationalities who are jealous of the Chinese . . . have shut him out of working on farms or in factories or building railroads."

Like Lee, most Chinese settled in city neighborhoods like San Francisco's bustling Chinatown. Here, they could find work at Chinese laundries, restaurants, and stores. Chinese newspapers, herbal medicines, foods, and festivals provided familiarity, comfort, and support.

For many years, most Chinese immigrants were men. In 1900, only about 1 in 20 Chinese on the U.S. mainland was female. With so few women and families, the Chinese population began to decline. In 1880, about 105,000 Chinese lived in the United States. By 1920, there were 61,600.

Gradually, more women and children arrived, especially in San Francisco. Housing was closed to Chinese in most areas, so Chinatown became more and more crowded.

Chinese immigrants settled in Chinatowns like this one in San Francisco. There they preserved the culture they had left behind.

passport a document issued
by a citizen's home government
that identifies a person and permits travel to other countries

26.6 Mexican Immigrants

Soldiers were shooting all around. A flying bullet almost hit him. That
was when Pablo Mares (PAH-blow MAHR-ess) decided he had to get
out of Mexico. "I had to come to the United States," he said later, "because it was impossible to live down there with so many revolutions."

Mares had been caught in the middle of a bloody civil war. The
conflict began when Mexico's president allowed wealthy landowners
to take over the lands of 6 million Indians and 8 million poor farmers.
In 1910, landless farmers rebelled, breaking up large landholdings and
giving the land to poor families. In response, soldiers attacked villages,
killing thousands of peasants.

Crossing the Border The Mexican Revolution dragged on for ten
years. Between 1910 and 1920, about 500,000 Mexicans entered the
United States. They entered freely, without **passports** or money.

Many Mexicans walked hundreds of miles to reach the border, carrying all they owned on their backs. In just one day, a Texas reporter
saw "hundreds of Mexicans, all journeying northward on foot, on
burroback and in primitive two-wheel carts." Others traveled north by
rail. By 1900, railroad lines connected American and Mexican cities.
Railroads provided both transportation and jobs for Mexican immigrants. One Mexican newspaper reported, "There is not a day in which
passenger trains do not leave for the border, full of Mexican men who
are going in gangs to work on railroad lines in the United States."

By 1900, railroad lines linked the United States and Mexico. Trains provided convenient transportation for Mexicans, who were free to enter the United States without passports.

Mexicans in America Many American employers welcomed the Mexicans. Expanding railroads and large-scale farms and ranches in the Southwest depended on laborers who were willing to work hard for little pay. After Congress banned Chinese immigration in 1882, these employers looked to Mexico for new workers. "Where I came from," said one Mexican construction worker, "I used to work ten hours for $1.25 . . . Then I came here and they paid $1.25 for eight hours—it was good."

Some Mexican immigrants found jobs with railroads, mines, factories, and canneries. But most found work in agriculture. Mexican farmworkers moved from region to region, harvesting crops as they ripened. They picked oranges in southern California, almonds in central California, and then apples in Oregon. They harvested cotton in Texas and Arizona and then moved on to sugar beets in Colorado.

Farmwork paid very little. One Texas farmer paid "Pancho and his whole family 60 cents a day . . . He worked from sun to sun." Children worked in the fields with their parents to help support their families. Few of them had a chance to attend school.

Farmworkers often lived in camps that they built near the fields. "Shelters were made of almost every conceivable thing—burlap, canvas, palm branches," said one visitor. Some farms and ranches provided housing for their workers. Either way, these temporary homes usually lacked running water and basic sanitation.

After harvest season, farmworkers sometimes moved to nearby towns. *Barrios,* or Mexican neighborhoods, sprang up on the edges of cities near such farming areas as Los Angeles, California, and San Antonio, Texas. Food stands and grocery stores in the barrio offered familiar tastes and smells. Residents helped each other take care of the sick and find jobs. On Mexican religious holidays, Catholic churches held special ceremonies. On those days, the barrio was filled with singing, dancing, and fireworks.

Many Mexican immigrants originally planned to return to Mexico once the revolution was over. Whites who believed that Mexicans were taking their jobs encouraged such returns. One wrote, "I wish the Mexicans could be put back in their country."

Mexicans who remained in the United States often faced strong prejudice. Compared to whites, they earned very low wages, and they had little say in their working conditions. In schools, white children were sometimes taught to "boss" their Mexican classmates, as they were expected to do when they grew up.

Despite these problems, many Mexican immigrants chose to stay. Like Isidro Osorio, a farm and railroad worker, they hoped for a better future in their new homeland. "I have worked very hard to earn my $4.00 a day," reported Osorio. "That is why I want to give a little schooling to my children so that they won't stay like I am."

Some Mexicans, such as those in this photograph, found jobs in mines. Most, however, were employed as agricultural workers.

26.7 Closing the Door on Immigration

In 1920, a mob stormed through the Italian neighborhood of West Frankfort, a small town in Illinois. The crowd was frustrated by a mining strike and angered by bank robberies that Italian criminals were rumored to have committed. For three days, mobs beat up Italian immigrants and burned their homes. This attack reflected a surge of **nativism,** or anti-immigrant feeling, that peaked in the United States around this time.

The Tide Turns Against Immigrants The United States has always been a nation of immigrants, yet time and again nativism has sparked actions and policies directed against newer arrivals. Sometimes nativism is rooted in economic competition. Sometimes it stems from ethnic, religious, and other differences. In the 1830s, for example, Protestant nativists charged that Catholic immigrants were enemies of democracy. They feared that Catholics had more loyalty to the pope in Rome, who was the head of their church, than to the U.S. government.

The surge in immigration that began in the 1880s fueled another rise in nativism. Some native-born Americans blamed immigrants for everything from slums and crime to hard times. Fearing competition for jobs, many labor leaders discriminated against nonwhites. In 1909, for example, the president of the United Mine Workers wrote of Asians that "as a race their standard of living is extremely low, and their assimilation by Americans impossible."

This 1871 cartoon shows Columbia, a symbol of the United States, protecting a Chinese immigrant facing discrimination. In 1882, a federal law banned immigration from China.

nativism an attitude of resentment and superiority toward foreign-born people

quota a limit based on numbers or proportions, such as the proportion of a country's population allowed to immigrate to the United States

Restricting Immigration Politicians responded to the growing prejudice against immigrants. As you have read, in 1882 Congress passed the Chinese Exclusion Act, banning further immigration by Chinese laborers.

In 1907, Japanese immigrants were forbidden entry to the United States. In 1917, Congress required immigrants to prove they could read and write in at least one language before they were allowed into the United States.

To further limit immigration, Congress established a **quota** system in 1921 and refined it in 1924. Under this system, by 1927 only 150,000 immigrants were allowed to enter the United States each year. People from East Asia were completely excluded. In addition, quotas limited immigration from any one country to 2 percent of the number of people from that country who lived in the United States in 1890. Most eastern and southern Europeans had arrived after that year. As a result, most of the quota spaces were reserved for immigrants from England, Ireland, and Germany.

The new laws did not limit Mexican immigration. However, Mexicans now needed passports and visas to enter the United States. Visas allow people from other nations to stay in the United States for a limited period of time. For the first time, the nation was closing its doors.

Chapter Summary

In this chapter, you read about the great wave of immigration to the United States between 1880 and 1920.

Immigrants from Around the Globe The immigrants of this period were far more diverse than earlier arrivals. Many were refugees escaping poverty, wars, or persecution. Others were drawn by the promise of economic opportunity. With their skills and labor, these new immigrants helped build the nation's booming cities and industries. But they also faced many challenges, including the tension between assimilation and preserving their way of life.

Italian Immigrants Millions of Italians came to the United States to escape poverty. Many settled in cities, where they lived in mostly Italian neighborhoods.

Jewish Immigrants from Eastern Europe Between 1881 and 1924, some 2.4 million Jews came to the United States from Russia and other countries. Many came to escape persecution in their home countries.

Chinese Immigrants People from China had come to the United States since the late 1860s. As the number of Chinese immigrants increased, so too did discrimination against them. In 1882, Congress passed the Chinese Exclusion Act.

Mexican Immigrants Many Mexicans came to the United States between 1910 and 1920, during the years of the Mexican Revolution. Most found work in agriculture, although the work paid very little.

Closing the Door on Immigration In the 1920s, nativism led Congress to limit the number of foreigners who would be allowed into the United States. Quotas brought an end to the great wave of immigration. By then, the United States had become a far more diverse country.

The great wave of immigration during the late 19th century created a nation of rich, diverse cultures. People from many backgrounds came together and became Americans. In this photograph, a mix of immigrants are in class together learning English.

More than a million immigrants settle in the United States every year. They come from countries around the world. A large percentage of them are young people like Carmen and Fidinarivo, who proudly hold their newly acquired certificates of U.S. citizenship.

Young Immigrants Today

Throughout its history, the United States has been a nation of immigrants. Immigrants continue to come here for the same reasons they always have. Some are fleeing oppression or war. Others are simply seeking a better life, with more opportunities and greater freedom. Many of these immigrants are young people.

Manyang came to the United States in 2001, at the age of 18. He was a refugee from the African country of Sudan. For Manyang, coming to this country was an escape from the violence of war.

Manyang was just six years old when gunmen raided his village in southern Sudan. Civil war had been raging in Sudan for years. Now, the fighting had come to Manyang's village. Hearing gunshots, he ran out of his house, looking for his parents. In that moment, he saw his father shot dead.

Manyang escaped his village unharmed. He could not find his mother or his brothers and sisters, but he did find his uncle Malic. Together, they joined other refugees on a long trek to neighboring Ethiopia. After two months of walking, starving and exhausted, they arrived at a United Nations refugee camp. There they received food, clothing, and shelter.

Several years later, however, civil war broke out in Ethiopia. Pursued by rebel soldiers, the refugees fled back to Sudan. At one point, Manyang had to cross a river teeming with crocodiles. He pulled himself across the river on a rope, but his uncle was killed by the rebels.

Eventually, Manyang arrived at another UN camp, this time in Kenya. He stayed there for nine years. Life was hard in the camp. Food was scarce, and the refugees got just one meal a day. But Manyang was able to go to school. He began to study English and math. He realized that education could be his route to a better life.

One day, Manyang learned that the United States was allowing some boys like him to immigrate. Americans called them the "Lost Boys" because they had lost their families and their country. Manyang told his story to immigration officials. Finally, his application was accepted. In May 2001, he came to the United States to begin a new life.

Manyang was "adopted" by a church in Connecticut. With the support of church members, he continued his schooling. But it was not easy. Although Manyang had studied hard in Kenya, his schooling there was very different from an American education. Once again, Manyang worked hard to be successful. At the graduation ceremony, after he passed his courses, Manyang spoke about the importance of education in his life.

Since then, Manyang has entered college and become an American citizen. One day, he hopes to become a lawyer and to help his people in Sudan. But he will always appreciate what life in the United States has given him and other Lost Boys. "Lots of people opened their hearts and homes to us," he says. "I will never forget."

Modern Immigration

Manyang is one of millions of immigrants who have come to this country in recent decades. Since 1970, the immigrant population in the United States has more than tripled. By 2008, about 38 million immigrants lived here. That is the largest number in the nation's history.

This new wave of immigration differs from the last great wave in the late 1800s and early 1900s. Then, most immigrants came from Southern and Eastern Europe. Today, most come from Latin America and Asia, with smaller numbers from Africa and the Middle East.

Despite high levels of immigration, immigrants still make up a smaller share of the U.S. population than they did in 1900. At that time, around 15 percent of all U.S. residents were foreign born. Today, that figure is approximately 12 percent.

Many of the new immigrants are young. A survey taken in the 1990s showed that 45 percent were under the age of 30. In general, the immigrant population is younger than the American population as a whole.

After the terrorist attacks of September 11, 2001, the United States tightened immigration controls. More immigrants were detained and deported. Many people felt that discrimination against immigrants was on the rise. In a 2009 survey of immigrants, however, most said they were glad they had come to the United States. They said their lives had improved as a result. Most of them hoped to make this country their permanent home.

When Manyang came to the United States, he said, "From the first, our aim was to get an education." Holding his high school diploma after graduation, he knew he had succeeded in his dream.

Inayet's Story

Inayet is an Afghan Muslim who came to this country in 1991. He tells his story in the book *Kids Like Me: Voices of the Immigrant Experience* by Judith M. Blohm and Terri Lapinsky.

Inayet's parents are from Afghanistan. They fled to Pakistan in the 1980s after the Soviet Union invaded their country. Inayet was born in a refugee camp, where he spent the first eight years of his life before coming to the United States. Although he attended school in the camp, it was a terrible experience. The teachers seemed to care little about education and often beat the students.

The United Nations and other relief agencies operate refugee camps around the world. These camps help millions of people displaced by war. Manyang, Inayet, and Pang Houa all spent years in camps like this one.

When Inayet started school here, he was surprised that his teachers did not hit him. He soon realized that education could help him succeed in life. Like Manyang, he graduated from high school and went on to college.

Everything did not go easily for Inayet, however. Some students were mean to him. They did not understand his culture and customs and told him to go back to his own country. Some also asked him if he was a "terrorist." Despite these difficulties, Inayet grew to appreciate the advantages of life in the United States. Here, he says, people have economic opportunities and freedom of religion. Here, he believes, people have the "freedom to live."

Pang Houa's Story

Pang Houa, a Hmong (MUNG) from Southeast Asia, was also born in a refugee camp. In her case, the camp was in Thailand. Her parents fled there from Laos just after the Vietnam War. She came to the United States in 1984, when she was four years old.

In *Kids Like Me,* Pang Houa described how she and her family settled in Minnesota, where many Hmong immigrants now live. She went to school, first with other Hmong children and then with Americans. She did well in school and was happy. She said she never felt discrimination from her classmates. In fact, when she later went to college, she said that other students found her background fascinating. They wanted to know more about Hmong culture and customs.

She got a surprise when she went to France to study for a while, however. Even though she tried to blend in, she realized that she spoke and acted like any other American. She had arrived in the United States as an immigrant, but she no longer felt like one. She had become an American.

Yulia's Story

Yulia came to the United States from Russia when she was 16 years old. Her parents wanted to give her and her siblings a better future. Two years later, she told her story to author Marina Budhos for the book *Remix: Conversations with Immigrant Teenagers.*

In many ways, Yulia adapted quickly to life in this country. She went to school, made friends, and learned English. In fact, she adapted much faster than her parents. While she was becoming more American, her parents remained tied to their Russian values.

This led to tensions between Yulia and her mother. In Russia, teenage girls have less freedom than they do in the United States. When Yulia began to go out with her friends, her mother did not like it. "She treats me like a child," Yulia said.

Yulia did not blame her mother, though. She understood that problems like this sometimes arise between parents and children. She also respected her mother and wanted to stay close to her family. She tried to find a way to honor her mother's values while also making a new life for herself in America.

Tito's Story

Tito was four when he came to the United States from Mexico. His father was an American citizen, living in California. Tito and his mother and brothers moved north to join him. Ten years later, when Tito was 14, Janet Bode interviewed him for her book *New Kids in Town.*

Tito lived in a rough neighborhood in Los Angeles, where drug dealers and gangs were common. But Tito's parents were strict. With their help, he managed to avoid trouble and stay in school.

Tito's family blended many aspects of Mexican and American culture. They spoke both English and Spanish at home. Tito was proud of his Mexican heritage, but he also knew that he was an American. What matters most, he says, is to know who you are.

Tito believes that Mexican immigrants make an important contribution to American life. He points out that the United States is made up of people from many countries and cultures. In an ideal society, he says, "there's a little bit of every culture and it goes together just right." In his view, immigrants have helped the United States grow and prosper.

At this California polling place, a sign informs voters in seven languages: English, Chinese, Japanese, Korean, Spanish, Tagalog, and Vietnamese.

Migration and Industry

1848
Gold Rush Begins
Gold is discovered in California. Miners from all over the world flock to the West in hopes of becoming rich.

1876
Battle of the Little Big Horn
Sioux and Cheyenne Indians successfully fight off an attack by the U.S. Army in the Battle of the Little Big Horn, also known as Custer's Last Stand. All the soldiers in the battle are killed.

1879
Invention of the Lightbulb
Thomas Edison's workshop invents the first practical electric lightbulb. By the end of the 1880s, small electrical stations provide power to city blocks in a number of cities.

| 1840 | 1845 | 1850 | 1855 | 1860 | 1865 | 1870 | 1875 | 1880 | 1885 |

1860–1890
Plains Indians Forced onto Reservations
The government relocates Plains Indians onto reservations to make room for continued settlement of the West. Some Indian groups resist and clash with government forces.

1862
Homestead Act
The Homestead Act gives 160 acres of land in the West to settlers willing to work the land.

1869
Transcontinental Railroad Completed
The Transcontinental Railroad is completed, connecting the Atlantic and Pacific coasts and opening the West to further development.

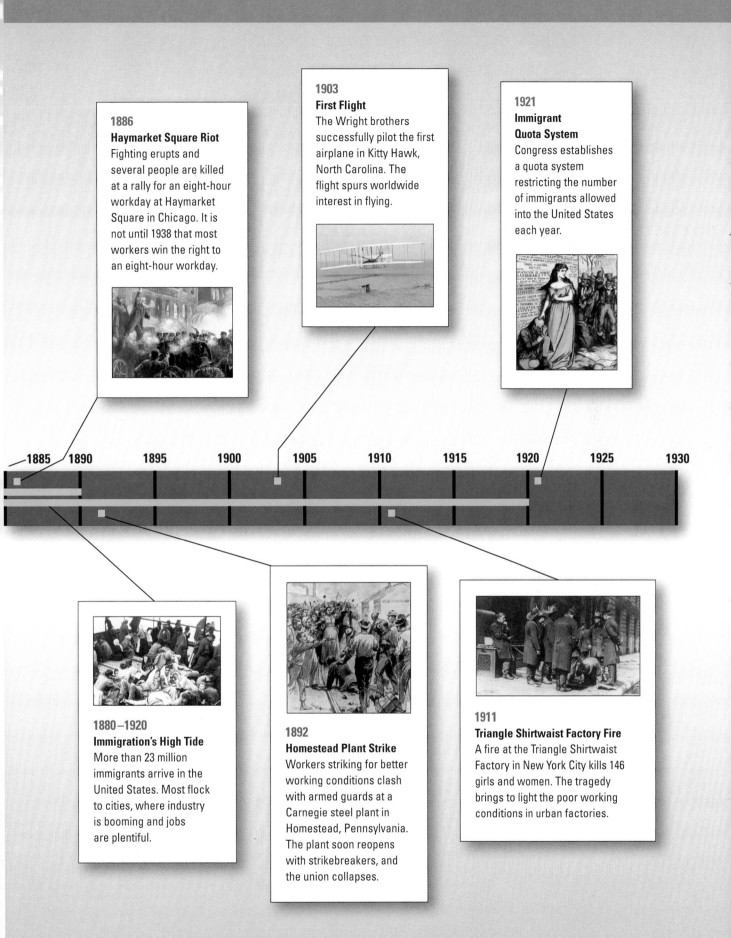

1886
Haymarket Square Riot
Fighting erupts and several people are killed at a rally for an eight-hour workday at Haymarket Square in Chicago. It is not until 1938 that most workers win the right to an eight-hour workday.

1903
First Flight
The Wright brothers successfully pilot the first airplane in Kitty Hawk, North Carolina. The flight spurs worldwide interest in flying.

1921
Immigrant Quota System
Congress establishes a quota system restricting the number of immigrants allowed into the United States each year.

1885 1890 1895 1900 1905 1910 1915 1920 1925 1930

1880–1920
Immigration's High Tide
More than 23 million immigrants arrive in the United States. Most flock to cities, where industry is booming and jobs are plentiful.

1892
Homestead Plant Strike
Workers striking for better working conditions clash with armed guards at a Carnegie steel plant in Homestead, Pennsylvania. The plant soon reopens with strikebreakers, and the union collapses.

1911
Triangle Shirtwaist Factory Fire
A fire at the Triangle Shirtwaist Factory in New York City kills 146 girls and women. The tragedy brings to light the poor working conditions in urban factories.

Chicago in the early 1900s was a bustling city, filled with people, cars, streetlights, and skyscrapers. The Majestic Theater, shown here, was located in Chicago's tallest building at the time.

A Modern Nation Emerges

The United States grew dramatically in the decades after the Civil War. In this unit, you will learn about American expansion overseas and reforms at home that resulted, in part, because of that growth.

The map below shows the places that came under U.S. control following the Civil War. By the late 1800s, American companies were seeking new markets for their products and new sources of raw materials. That quest was connected to the Pacific islands highlighted on the map. It was also related to a massive engineering project that took place far from the United States—the digging of the Panama Canal in the Central American country of Panama.

If U.S. expansion in the Pacific can be linked to trade, in the Caribbean it can be linked to democratic ideals. In this unit, you will read how Americans' call for self-government for the people of Cuba drew the United States into a war with Spain. However, as you will also learn, those ideals were dashed by events following the war.

U.S. Territorial Expansion, 1867–1903

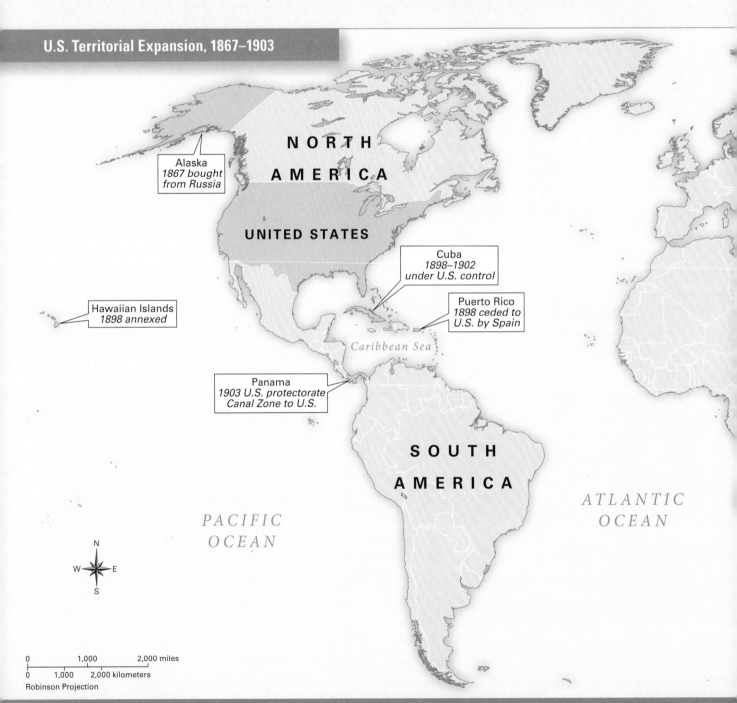

Alaska
1867 bought
from Russia

NORTH AMERICA

UNITED STATES

Cuba
1898–1902
under U.S. control

Puerto Rico
1898 ceded to
U.S. by Spain

Hawaiian Islands
1898 annexed

Caribbean Sea

Panama
1903 U.S. protectorate
Canal Zone to U.S.

SOUTH AMERICA

ATLANTIC OCEAN

PACIFIC OCEAN

N
W   E
S

0   1,000   2,000 miles
0   1,000   2,000 kilometers
Robinson Projection

As the nation was expanding its territories in other parts of the world, some Americans were working to improve life at home. By 1900, much of the work that fueled the nation's industrial growth was performed by young children for low pay. Half of American citizens still could not vote, and those who could had to choose between candidates picked by political party leaders. By 1920, great progress had been made in all three areas. As you read this unit, you will learn how these and other important reforms were achieved.

Reforms in 1900 and 1920

	1900	1920
States that allowed women to vote	4	all
States that allowed voters to choose nominees for presidential office	0	20
States that set minimum age limits for child workers in factories	24	all

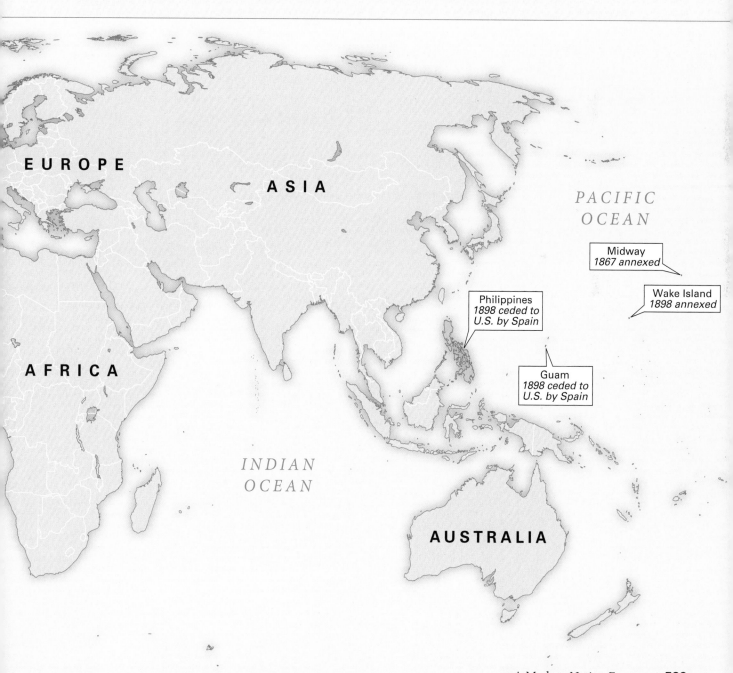

EUROPE

ASIA

PACIFIC OCEAN

Midway
1867 annexed

Wake Island
1898 annexed

Philippines
*1898 ceded to
U.S. by Spain*

Guam
*1898 ceded to
U.S. by Spain*

AFRICA

INDIAN OCEAN

AUSTRALIA

Chapter 27

The Progressive Era

Did the progressives improve life in the United States?

27.1 Introduction

"The men who start the great new movements in the world," said Samuel McClure at his college graduation, "are enthusiasts whose eyes are fixed upon the end they wish to bring about."

Some of his fellow students may have brushed off McClure's words as mere speech making. They shouldn't have. This immigrant from Ireland was serious about starting what he called "great new movements." In 1893, McClure began publishing a journal called *McClure's Magazine*. McClure prided himself on knowing what people wanted to read about. "If I like a thing," he said, "then I know that millions will like it."

In 1900, McClure decided that Americans wanted to know the truth about trusts—gigantic business monopolies that worked to reduce competition. He hired a reporter named Ida Tarbell to write a history of Standard Oil, one of the biggest trusts in the country. Starting in 1902, McClure ran Tarbell's report as a serial, printing one part at a time in issue after issue. The report told about unfair pricing that was putting Standard Oil's competitors out of business.

McClure began hiring more journalists for his magazine. Some people called his journalists *muckrakers* because they "raked up" or exposed corruption in business and society. Writers like Tarbell adopted this name with pride.

Samuel McClure and Ida Tarbell were part of a larger reform effort known as the Progressive movement. Progressives did not work as a single group. Some fought railroad monopolies, while others focused on the problem of child labor. Some worked for equal rights for African Americans, and others worked to protect forests. Whatever their cause, most progressives wanted government to play a larger role in helping to cure the nation's ills. They believed that ordinary people could start "great new movements" that would improve life in the United States.

Samuel McClure (top) published articles by Progressive-era writers such as Ida Tarbell (bottom). Both were part of a movement that focused on social and economic problems created by industrialization.

◀ By the early 1900s, many children worked in factories, mills, and mines. These "breaker boys" were photographed at a coal mine in 1911.

27.2 Sowing the Seeds of Reform

The **Progressive movement** of the early 20th century focused on economic and social injustice, the power of big business, and political corruption. But progressives were not the first to criticize these conditions and to propose far-reaching reforms.

Industrialization began remaking American society shortly after the Civil War. To some, the rise of big industry meant endless progress and prosperity. Other people, however, felt left behind. As early as the 1870s, some of these "have-nots" began organizing mass movements to work for political and social change.

The National Grange Organized protests against the power of big business began on the farms of the Midwest. After the Civil War, many midwestern farmers were caught between rising costs and falling prices for their crops. Farmers felt victimized. Banks made it hard for people to get cash loans to keep their farms going in lean times. Grain storage companies and railroads charged high rates to store and transport crops. And merchants paid too little for what farmers produced.

In 1867, Oliver Kelley, a clerk at the U.S. Department of Agriculture, began organizing self-help clubs for farmers called the National Grange of the Patrons of Husbandry. The movement spread rapidly through the Midwest. By the mid-1870s, the **National Grange** had grown into a political force. Farmers used the National Grange to protest unfair practices by the railroads. Grangers banded together

In the 1870s, angry farmers attacked the power of the railroads to set whatever rates they wanted. This cartoon shows wealthy "rail barons" carving up the country for their own profit.

to negotiate better prices and to start their own banks. They campaigned for political candidates and worked for such reforms as an income tax and laws against trusts.

Pressure from the National Grange led some states to pass laws that limited railroad shipping rates and prices for grain storage. Big businesses protested this interference. In 1877, the Supreme Court sided with the Grangers. In a series of cases, the Court said that states have the right to regulate private property when it is used in the public interest. The National Grange had won a key victory for the idea that government has a responsibility to help protect the common good.

Membership in the National Grange dropped in the 1880s as conditions improved for midwestern farmers. The farmers' revolt continued, however, in the South and West, where organizations called Farmers' Alliances took up the cause of reform.

The Farmers' Alliances angrily challenged the influence of eastern bankers and industrialists. A favorite target was Wall Street in New York City, the nation's financial capital. Mary Elizabeth Lease of Kansas charged,

It is no longer a government of the people, by the people, and for the people, but a government of Wall Street, by Wall Street, and for Wall Street. The great common people of this country are slaves and monopoly is the master.

The Populist Party In 1892, leaders of the Farmers' Alliances founded a new organization that came to be called the **Populist Party**. The organization worked to build an alliance between farmers and industrial workers. Such a mass movement, they believed, could break the power of big business to **dictate** government policy.

That same year, the Populist Party adopted a **platform** calling for such reforms as an eight-hour workday and government ownership of railroads. That fall, Populist candidates won election to hundreds of state and local offices. The Populist candidate for president, James B. Weaver of Iowa, received over a million votes, winning six of the Mountain and Plains states. But that was the high point for the Populist Party.

Four years later, the Democratic Party adopted some Populist ideas as part of its platform. The Populists decided to support the Democratic presidential candidate, William Jennings Bryan. The Republican candidate, William McKinley, drew heavy support from business and financial interests. The battle lines were drawn between eastern capitalists and reform-minded farmers of the South and West.

McKinley won the election handily. His victory was a triumph for those who were opposed to **radical** change. The Populist Party, which had lost its identity after fusing with the Democrats, soon dissolved.

For the moment, big business and its allies reigned supreme. It would be up to other reformers to continue the fight begun by the Grangers and the Populists.

Wealthy industrialists gave huge sums of money to help elect Republican William McKinley to the presidency in 1896.

Populist Party a political party, organized in 1892 by leaders of the Farmers' Alliances, that supported such reforms as an eight-hour workday and government-owned railroads

platform a statement of the policies favored by a political party or candidate

27.3 Andrew Carnegie and John D. Rockefeller: Captains of Industry

When business leaders like Andrew Carnegie and John D. Rockefeller looked at the United States in 1900, they saw progress everywhere. Railroads linked towns and cities across the nation. The increased ease of delivering goods by rail had nourished countless new industries, including their own. Both men were proud to be "captains of industry," leading the way in this growth. "Mere money-making has never been my goal," wrote Rockefeller. "I had an ambition to build."

Andrew Carnegie made a huge fortune in the steel industry. When he retired, he began to give away most of his money. This illustration shows him carrying libraries like gifts, symbolizing the money he gave to thousands of communities for libraries.

Industry Brings Progress New industries meant more jobs for a growing nation. With immigrants pouring into the country, the population of the United States tripled between 1850 and 1900. Every new factory or mill created jobs for the newcomers. Carnegie Steel alone employed more than 20,000 workers, many of them immigrants.

The nation's new industries turned out a wealth of new products at prices ordinary Americans could afford. "The home of the laboring man of our day boasts luxuries which even in the palaces of monarchs as recent as Queen Elizabeth were unknown," wrote Carnegie. "What were the luxuries," he noted, "have become the necessaries of life."

The Benefits of Bigness According to business leaders, the growth of big business made progress possible. Only big business enterprises could deliver quality goods at prices everyone could afford. As Carnegie explained in an article defending big business to its critics,

> [The] cheapness [of goods] is in proportion to the scale of production . . . The larger the scale of operation the cheaper the product . . . Instead of attempting to restrict [growth], we should hail every increase as something to be gained, not for the few rich, but for the millions of poor.

In Carnegie's view, the growth of big business was the expected result of competition. According to this view, when many small companies compete in the same industry, some are more likely to do well than others. Those that are run most efficiently will grow larger.

Those that are not well run will perish. "The law of competition," Carnegie argued, "may be sometimes hard for the individual, [but] it is best for the race, because it ensures the survival of the fittest in every department."

When Carnegie wrote about "the law of competition" in business, he was borrowing an idea from the British naturalist Charles Darwin. Darwin had observed that, in nature, animals and plants compete for food and living space. Those that are best adapted to their environments are the most likely to survive. This idea was popularized as "survival of the fittest."

Before long, some people began to apply Darwin's idea to human society. The result was **social Darwinism**. According to this theory, people and societies compete for survival just as plants and animals do. The most fit become wealthy and successful. The least fit struggle just to survive.

Social Darwinism seemed to provide a "scientific" justification for huge differences in people's wealth and power. It also lent support to the economic concept of laissez-faire, the idea that businesses should operate with a minimum of government interference. The best possible economy will then emerge naturally. By this line of thinking, it is misguided for government to try to correct such problems as child labor, poor working conditions, and unfair business practices.

social Darwinism the theory that people and societies compete for survival, with the fit becoming wealthy and successful while the weak struggle to survive

John D. Rockefeller's Standard Oil Company controlled 90 percent of the oil refined in the United States at the start of the 20th century. His business methods were considered ruthless by his critics and brilliant by his supporters.

Giving Away Wealth In 1901, Andrew Carnegie sold his steel company for $250 million. Then he retired to devote his life to philanthropy, or generosity to charities. Carnegie believed that rich people have a responsibility to use their wealth to help others. "He who dies rich," he wrote, "dies disgraced."

Carnegie used his wealth to build concert halls, universities, and hospitals. Most of all, however, he loved building libraries. A library, he said, "outranks any other one thing that a community can do to benefit its people." Before 1880, few Americans had access to free public libraries. Just one generation later, 35 million people a day were using libraries that Carnegie had helped to build.

"Your example will bear fruits," John D. Rockefeller wrote to Carnegie. "The time will come when men of wealth will more generally be willing to use it for the good of others."

Rockefeller used his own fortune to fund universities, medical research, the arts, and education for all. During his lifetime, he contributed about $182 million to the Rockefeller Foundation, a charitable organization he established to promote "the well-being of mankind throughout the world."

The Granger Collection, New York

Teddy Roosevelt is shown here vigorously shaking the railroad trust. Roosevelt tried to break up monopolistic trusts to make American business fair for all.

regulation the enforcement of laws that control conduct or practices; for example, government regulations control the way goods, food, and drugs are produced and sold to the public

27.4 Theodore Roosevelt: Trust-Busting President

Not everyone admired big business the way Rockefeller and Carnegie did. Many thought big businesses took unfair advantage of workers and consumers. In 1890, Congress passed the Sherman Antitrust Act to prohibit any form of business monopoly. The law was so **vague** and big business so powerful, however, that for years the law was not enforced. The Sherman Antitrust Act got its first real test only after Theodore Roosevelt became president in 1901.

Breaking a Railroad Trust Roosevelt came into the White House with a reputation as a reformer. As president, he attacked business monopolies with great energy. "We do not want to destroy corporations," he assured the public, "but we do wish to make them [serve] the public good."

Roosevelt's first target was a railroad monopoly called the Northern Securities Company. This company controlled nearly every rail line between Chicago and the Pacific Northwest. Roosevelt had the Justice Department sue Northern Securities for violating the Sherman Antitrust Act. The Supreme Court ordered the monopoly to be broken up into smaller railroad companies.

Trust-Busting Expands Just after Roosevelt filed suit against Northern Securities, *McClure's Magazine* began publishing Ida Tarbell's history of the Standard Oil Trust. In her report, Tarbell documented how Rockefeller had driven his competitors out of business. She told about secret deals he had made with railroads to ship his oil at lower prices than other oil companies paid. She explained how Rockefeller had cut his oil prices below what the oil cost to produce. This attracted customers away from other oil companies. After his competitors went out of business, Rockefeller raised prices again.

A shocked public demanded action. Roosevelt filed suit against not only Standard Oil, but against 44 other trusts as well. In 1911, Standard Oil was "busted"—broken up into five major oil companies and several smaller ones.

President Roosevelt thought that government **regulation,** or enforcement of laws, was a good long-term solution to bad business behavior. "The great development of industrialism," he said, "means that there must be an increase in the supervision exercised by the Government over business enterprise."

27.5 Robert La Follette: Fighter for Political Reform

In 1890, Robert La Follette of Wisconsin ran for reelection to Congress and lost. Still a young man, he returned to his work as a lawyer. Then, in 1891, Senator Philetus Sawyer, a powerful Republican Party boss, reportedly offered La Follette a bribe to "fix" a court case. Sawyer thought that he could pay La Follette to guarantee that he would win the case. An insulted La Follette reported the bribery attempt to the newspapers.

An equally insulted Sawyer decided to crush La Follette. But "Fighting Bob" was not an easy man to put down. Sawyer had made him so mad that La Follette decided to run for governor of Wisconsin. As governor, he could work to put the party bosses out of business.

In Wisconsin and other states, political machines, or groups run by party bosses, controlled local and state governments. To make sure their candidates were elected, corrupt bosses were known to bribe voters and "stuff" ballot boxes with fake votes.

Thus, the bosses—not the people—chose each party's candidates for office. The candidates, men like lumber millionaire Sawyer, usually represented powerful business interests. Without the party's support, upstart reformers like La Follette had little chance of reaching voters. La Follette was defeated twice by Wisconsin's powerful Republican "machine" but finally won election as governor in 1900.

Once he took office, La Follette pushed reforms that put the people in charge of politics. Wisconsin became the first state to adopt the direct primary. This election system allowed party members, not bosses, to choose party candidates. By 1916, more than half the states had adopted the "Wisconsin idea." With the people choosing their leaders in primary elections, reform governors were swept into office across the nation.

Oregon introduced three other reforms that put political power into the hands of the people. The *initiative* allowed citizens to enact laws by a popular vote. The *referendum* allowed voters to overturn an existing law. The *recall* allowed voters to remove an elected official from office.

What all these reforms had in common, wrote La Follette, was a belief that each state could become a place where "the opportunities of all its people are more equal . . . [and] human life is safer and sweeter."

Robert La Follette

Party bosses controlled the U.S. political system through a corrupt system of bribery. Reformers like Robert La Follette sought to take power out of the hands of the bosses and return it to the people.

Mother Jones

27.6 Mother Jones: Champion of Workers' Rights

In 1903, labor leader Mary Harris Jones—known as Mother Jones—went to Pennsylvania to support a strike by 75,000 textile workers. About 10,000 of the strikers were children. Jones wrote of these young workers,

Every day little children came into Union Headquarters, some with their hands off, some with the thumb missing, some with their fingers off at the knuckle. They were stooped little things, round shouldered and skinny. Many of them were not over ten years of age.

Child Labor Laws The situation Mother Jones found in Pennsylvania was not unusual. In the early 1900s, more than 1 million children under the age of 16 worked in mines and factories for up to 13 hours a day. To publicize their plight, Jones led a "March of the Mill Children" from Pennsylvania all the way to Oyster Bay, New York, to petition President Roosevelt to support child labor laws.

The children's march prompted stories and photographs of child workers in newspapers and magazines. Across the country, reformers demanded an end to child labor. Employers claimed that abolishing child labor would produce "a nation of sissies." By 1909, however, 43 states had passed laws that outlawed the hiring of children.

Improving Work Conditions Progressive reformers also worked to improve the lives of adult workers. In 1903, for example, Oregon passed a law that limited women workers to a ten-hour workday. Maryland set up a program to assist workers who had been injured on the job.

New York responded to the tragic 1911 Triangle Shirtwaist Factory fire by setting up a state committee to investigate conditions in factories. Based on the committee's work, the state legislature passed 56 worker-protection laws. Many of these laws called for improvements in factory safety. One permitted women workers to take pregnancy leaves. (A leave is time away from work.) Another required employers to provide garment workers with chairs that had backs, rather than simple stools.

Mother Jones saw progress for the worker in such reforms. "Slowly his hours are shortened, giving him leisure to read and to think," she wrote. "Slowly the cause of his children becomes the cause of all."

At the turn of the century, school-age children worked long hours for meager wages in America's mines and factories.

27.7 John Muir: Protector of the Environment

John Muir was so clever with machines that he might have been a great inventor. But one day in 1867, a file slipped from his hand and hit him in the eye. This accident sent Muir's life down a different path.

After recovering from his injury, Muir decided to spend his life roaming wild places. "I might have become a millionaire," he said. "I chose to become a tramp."

Muir found his wilderness home in Yosemite Valley, a place of great natural beauty in California's Sierra Nevada. "God himself seems to be always doing his best here," he wrote of Yosemite.

Humans, in contrast, seemed to be doing their worst. Loggers were cutting down Yosemite's ancient redwood trees. Herds of sheep were stripping its meadows and hillsides bare. "To let sheep trample so divinely fine a place seems barbarous!" wrote Muir.

Yosemite was not the only wild place threatened by human activity. Rapid industrial growth and urbanization were causing massive environmental changes. Loggers were felling the nation's forests at an alarming rate. Miners were scarring mountains and polluting rivers. Many species of birds and animals were near extinction or already lost forever.

Concerns over such changes had given birth to a small but growing **conservation** movement. Some conservationists worried most about dwindling natural resources. They **advocated** careful development of the wilderness. Others, like Muir, wanted to preserve wonders like Yosemite in their natural state.

To rally the public to his cause, Muir started publishing articles urging the passage of laws to protect wilderness areas. By 1890, his writings had attracted enough support to convince Congress to create Yosemite National Park.

Conservationists found an ally in President Theodore Roosevelt. While Roosevelt was in office, he increased the amount of land set aside as national forest from 47 million to 195 million acres. He also doubled the number of national parks. To Muir's delight, the president also prohibited logging and ranching in Yosemite and other national parks.

"Wilderness is a necessity," said Muir. "Mountain parks and reservations are useful not only as fountains of timber and irrigating rivers, but as fountains of life."

Theodore Roosevelt (left) and John Muir (right) are pictured high on a cliff in Yosemite National Park. Muir founded the Sierra Club, an organization committed to the preservation of the environment.

conservation preservation and protection of a natural resource to prevent overuse, destruction, or neglect

W. E. B. Du Bois

In 1917, the NAACP, which W. E. B. Du Bois helped form, organized this silent protest parade against lynching.

27.8 W. E. B. Du Bois: Spokesman for Equal Rights

In 1897, a black sociologist named W. E. B. Du Bois joined the faculty of Atlanta University. His plan was to study social problems "in the light of the best scientific research."

Everywhere he looked, Du Bois saw the terrible effects of racism on African Americans. In the South, Jim Crow laws segregated schools, trains, parks, and other public places. These laws also banned blacks from voting in most states. Blacks in the North were not legally segregated, but they still faced discrimination, particularly in housing and jobs.

African Americans who fought these injustices risked being lynched, or brutally attacked and killed. Between 1892 and 1903, almost 3,000 African Americans were lynched across the South. "One could not be a calm, cool, and detached scientist," Du Bois found, "while Negroes were lynched, murdered, and starved."

Du Bois wanted to do something, but what? Booker T. Washington, the best-known black leader of the time, advised African Americans to make the best of segregation. Washington was a former slave who had founded the Tuskegee Institute, a vocational school for blacks. He believed that job skills for African Americans would lead to economic progress and eventual acceptance. "The wisest among my race understand that the agitation of questions of social equality is the extremest folly," he said.

Du Bois could not accept such thinking. In 1905, he gathered influential African Americans at Niagara Falls to push directly for voting rights. He wanted to see an end to discrimination.

This group of African Americans became known as the Niagara Movement. They continued to meet each year. In 1909, they joined a group of white reformers who were also dissatisfied with Booker T. Washington's cautious approach. Together, they formed the National Association for the Advancement of Colored People. The new organization pledged to work for equal rights and opportunities for all African Americans.

By 1920, the NAACP had over 90,000 members. Their goal was to make 11 million African Americans "physically free from peonage [servitude], mentally free from ignorance, politically free from disenfranchisement [denial of rights], and socially free from insult."

27.9 Upton Sinclair: Truth Writer

When Upton Sinclair wrote a novel about the horrors of slavery, few people bought his work. Then a publisher asked if Sinclair would write a book about factory workers who were treated like slaves. Sinclair jumped at the chance. Workers at a Chicago meatpacking plant had just been brutally defeated in a labor dispute. Sinclair decided to write about them.

Upton Sinclair

Meatpacking Horrors In 1900, Chicago was the home of the nation's biggest meatpacking companies. Disguised as a worker, Sinclair spent seven weeks in the slaughterhouses in 1904. There he observed how cattle and hogs became steaks and sausages. He saw employees with missing thumbs, and others whose fingers had been eaten away by acid. He heard stories of deadly falls into cooking vats.

Based on his research, Sinclair wrote a tragic story of poor immigrants trapped in poverty by greedy business owners. In his 1906 novel *The Jungle,* he described the horrors of meatpacking plants in great detail. He told of sick animals being processed into food. He described sausage made from old, rotten meat mixed with everything from sawdust to rodents. "Rats were nuisances," he wrote, "and the packers would put poisoned bread out for them; they would die, and then rats, bread, and meat would go into the hoppers together."

The Jungle became the nation's biggest best seller since the Civil War–era's *Uncle Tom's Cabin.* But readers were more upset about the contents of their sausage than the treatment of the "wage slaves." "I aimed at the public's heart," said Sinclair, "and by accident I hit it in the stomach."

Safer Food and Drugs After reading *The Jungle,* President Roosevelt ordered an investigation of the meatpacking industry. When his investigators confirmed that conditions were as bad as Sinclair had claimed, Congress passed the Meat Inspection Act in 1906. This established health standards for the meatpacking industry and federal inspection of meat.

Other muckrakers revealed similar problems in the food-canning and drug industries. Also in 1906, Congress passed the Pure Food and Drug Act. This law requires manufacturers to use safe ingredients in their products and to advertise them truthfully. Future decades would bring more laws protecting American consumers.

Upton Sinclair shocked readers with his description of conditions inside meatpacking plants like this one. The unsanitary conditions prompted the government to begin meat inspections.

Alice Paul

27.10 Alice Paul: Women's Rights' Hero

By 1900, women had won their fight for **suffrage,** or the right to vote, in four western states. Elsewhere, the drive for voting rights seemed stalled. The Progressive movement, however, breathed new life into the campaign begun at Seneca Falls in 1848. Many progressives believed that their reforms would be adopted more quickly if women had the right to vote.

A New Suffrage Movement In 1916, a young reformer named Alice Paul formed what came to be known as the National Woman's Party. Older women's groups had worked to win the right to vote state by state. Paul and her supporters were determined to win the vote by a constitutional amendment.

To build momentum for a suffrage amendment, Paul organized a parade in Washington, D.C. More than 5,000 women marched amidst jeers and insults from onlookers. Newspapers applauded the courage of the "suffragettes," as the activists came to be known.

Passing the Nineteenth Amendment By 1918, women could vote in 12 states, but they had made little progress on the suffrage amendment. The National Woman's Party began holding silent vigils outside the White House. The protesters held banners that read, "Mr. President, What Will You Do for Woman Suffrage?" and "How Long Must Women Wait for Liberty?"

Police arrested 200 women for blocking the sidewalk. While in jail, Paul and her supporters went on a hunger strike. When the jailers tried to force-feed them, the public became enraged. The women were released to a hero's welcome.

Less than two months later, a suffrage amendment was approved by the House of Representatives by just one vote more than the two-thirds majority required. The amendment had been introduced by Jeanette Rankin of Montana, the first woman elected to Congress.

suffrage the right to vote

Suffragettes in the National Women's Party, along with women across the country, made banners, marched, and banded together to demand the right to vote.

Senate approval took another 18 months. The states finally ratified the Nineteenth Amendment on August 26, 1920. That year, women across the country voted in their first national election.

Paul went on to draft another amendment guaranteeing equal rights to women. "I never doubted that equal rights was the right direction," she said, even though the amendment was never ratified. "Most reforms, most problems are complicated. But to me there is nothing complicated about ordinary equality."

Chapter Summary

In this chapter, you learned about the Progressive movement of the early 20th century.

Sowing the Seeds of Reform As early as the 1870s, farmers organized to protest the government's laissez-faire policies and the growing power of big business. The Granger and Populist movements championed the cause of the common man and helped sow the seeds of Progressive reform.

Andrew Carnegie and John D. Rockefeller To men of industry like Carnegie and Rockefeller, calls for reform were misguided. All of America, they argued, had benefited from industrialization. The country was growing in wealth, and ordinary Americans enjoyed luxuries that were previously unheard of.

Theodore Roosevelt and Robert La Follette Unlike industrialists, many people thought big businesses took unfair advantage of workers and consumers. As president, Roosevelt broke up business monopolies, including the Northern Securities Company railroad monopoly and the Standard Oil monopoly. As governor of Wisconsin, La Follette helped put party bosses out of business by pushing reforms that put people in charge of politics.

Mother Jones Labor leader Mary Harris Jones—known as Mother Jones—fought hard to end child labor. Because of her influence, 43 states passed laws by 1909 outlawing the hiring of children.

John Muir Naturalist John Muir spurred on the growing conservation movement. His writings called for laws to protect wilderness and helped convince Congress to create Yosemite National Park.

W. E. B. Du Bois Sociologist W. E. B. Du Bois fought racism and discrimination against blacks. He helped to form the National Association for the Advancement of Colored People, which pledged to work for equal rights and opportunities for all African Americans.

Upton Sinclair In his 1906 novel *The Jungle,* Upton Sinclair described the horrors of meat-packing plants. The best seller prompted a federal investigation of the meatpacking industry and led to new laws protecting American consumers: the Meat Inspection Act and the Pure Food and Drug Act.

Alice Paul In 1916, Alice Paul formed what came to be known as the National Woman's Party. Her work led to the ratification of the Nineteenth Amendment in 1920, giving women across the country the vote.

Children at Work

The rise of industry changed the lives of even the youngest members of American society. In the late 1800s and early 1900s, children—some as young as four—worked in mines and factories. They worked on city streets and in tenement rooms. It would take decades of struggle to outlaw this kind of child labor.

These Pennsylvania breaker boys worked in the coal mine for 10 to 12 hours a day, six days a week.

Rows of boys—some only five years old—sat on wooden planks that lay across long chutes. High above the boys, huge carts dumped tons of coal into the chutes. As the coal came tumbling down, the boys sorted it, removing pieces of slate and stone.

The coal came from deep in the earth, where older boys and men had mined it. The boys who sat on the planks were called "breakers," because it was their job to break up the coal and remove the impurities.

Work was hard and days were long. Lewis Hine, a photographer, described a typical workday for the breaker boys. As part of a campaign against child labor, Hine was taking pictures of children at work.

Foremen—breaker bosses—kept watch as the boys toiled at the chutes. Boys who were not working hard enough or carefully enough soon felt a sharp rap on the neck from the breaker boss's stick.

The pieces [of coal] rattled down through long chutes at which the breaker boys sat. It's like sitting in a coal bin all day long, except that the coal is always moving and clattering and cuts their fingers. Sometimes the boys wear lamps in their caps to help them see through the thick dust. They bend over the chutes until their backs ache, and they get tired and sick because they have to breathe coal dust instead of good, pure air.

The boys got to work at 7:00 in the morning (many of their mothers walked them to the mine) and did not go home until 6 or 6:30 at night. At best, the work was uncomfortable. The boys were not allowed to wear gloves because doing so could make them less efficient. So their fingers would swell, crack, and bleed until they hardened after a few weeks on the job. At worst, the work was dangerous. A breaker boy who leaned too far over might fall into a chute and be crushed or smothered to death. Boys who caught their fingers in the conveyers might get them cut off.

When the boys turned 12, they moved to jobs in the mine itself. One such job was "door boy." The door boy sat 500 feet below ground. He listened for the coal cars coming from the mine and opened the door for them when they arrived. Lewis Hine described the lonely job, explaining that the door boy was "by himself nine or ten hours a day in absolute darkness save for his little oil lamp." The boy could not fall asleep, though. If he did, a cart filled with tons of coal might smash through the closed door and crush him.

An 1885 law in Pennsylvania, the site of many coal mines, said that breaker boys had to be at least 12 years old. A 1902 law raised the age to 14. But the law was never enforced. Fake birth certificates were easy to come by. They cost only a quarter, and so a little boy might be identified as "small for his age" in order to pass for 12 or 14.

The 1900 census reported that 1.75 million children under the age of 16 were working in jobs in the United States. Considering how easy it was for underage children to get jobs, that figure is probably lower than the actual number of working children.

During the Progressive era—the first two decades of the 1900s—reformers like Lewis Hine exposed the terrible conditions that children endured in industrial workplaces. They wanted to see child labor outlawed. But it would take until the 1930s for their efforts to win out. In the meantime, children labored at terrible jobs to make money that would help their families survive.

Working at Home and on the Streets

Coal mines were not the only place where children worked. They worked in mills where cloth was made, in factories where glass was made, and in canneries where fish was packaged. On farms, they picked crops and hoed fields.

This boy's job was to open the mine door for the full carts of coal. Lewis Hine wrote about the picture, "Owing to the intense darkness of the mine, I didn't notice the chalk drawings on the door until I had developed the photographic plate. These drawings tell the tale of the boy's loneliness underground."

Many children also worked at home, but they did far more than help with household chores. In the early 1900s, many adults brought work to their homes and did it there. This work was called "piece-work," because workers were paid for each piece they completed, no matter how long the work took.

One reformer described four-year-old Anetta Fachini working with her mother late into the night.

> *The frail little thing was winding green paper around wires to make stems for artificial flowers to decorate ladies' hats. Every few minutes her head would droop and her weary eyelids close, but her little fingers still kept moving—uselessly, helplessly, mechanically moving. Then the mother would shake her gently, saying . . . "Sleep not, Anetta! Only a few more—only a few more."*
> —John Spargo, *The Bitter Cry of the Children*, 1906

Lewis Hine photographed this mother and her children making flowers at home in New York. Together, they earned only about 50 cents a day.

In the "home industries," he continued, "the kindergartens are robbed to provide baby slaves."

Children also worked on the city streets. Some boys worked as "bootblacks," polishing men's shoes for a fee. Others delivered telegrams. The most common job for boys was selling newspapers. In 1899, "newsies," as they were called, could buy 100 newspapers from the publishers for 50 cents. Then they sold the papers for one cent apiece. If they sold all their papers, they made a profit.

Selling newspapers was hard work. The boys waited outside the newspaper offices in the early morning hours to get their papers. Then they rushed out to sell their papers, using whatever skills and tricks they could come up with.

Most children who sold newspapers were boys between 8 and 15 years old. Very few girls worked on the streets. Most helped their mothers at home with ironing, laundry, sewing, and cooking.

Selling newspapers could also be dangerous. Newsies who jumped on and off streetcars might slip and have an arm or leg run over. When a reformer raised money to buy wooden limbs for the injured boys, the boys refused to wear them. They preferred to get the sympathy of potential buyers.

Reformers worried about the newsies. The boys knew their way around the cities—including the saloons, the gambling houses, and other unsavory places. But the boys themselves often liked their work. They felt proud and independent.

Fighting Back

Neither children nor reformers simply accepted child labor. The kids themselves fought for higher pay and better working conditions. For example, some frustrated Pennsylvania breaker boys fought back against one of the foremen who was particularly mean to them. They decided not to go to work one day. Instead, they went to a local swimming hole to play. When the nasty foreman came to get them, the boys pushed him into the water and dunked him. Eventually, another company man rescued him, but the boys won their case. They got a new foreman.

Children also followed the lead of older workers and went on strike. In the summer of 1899, the newsies struck against the *New York Journal* and the *New York World*. The papers' publishers had raised the price they charged newsies to 60 cents for 100 papers.

The boys decided to boycott the two papers. As the boys' leader, Kid Blink, said, "I'm trying to figure out how ten cents on a hundred can mean more to a millionaire than it does to a newsboy. I can't see it." After a two-week strike, the boys accepted a deal. They would pay the 60 cents, but they would be able to return their unsold papers.

Child workers improved their own situations, but reformers wanted to outlaw child labor entirely. Photographers like Lewis Hine and Jacob Riis showed the plight of working children. Their images helped change public opinion. Union organizers like Mother Jones led protest marches. Her efforts pressured employers and politicians. Groups like the National Consumers' League and the National Child Labor Committee lobbied to end child labor. They wanted children to be required to go to school.

Change happened slowly, one state at a time, until 1938. That year, the federal government passed the Fair Labor Standards Act. The law restricted what it called "oppressive child labor." Today, the Fair Labor Standards Act restricts the hours that children under 16 can work. And it prevents children under 18 from doing dangerous jobs. The days of breaker boys and newsies are long gone in the United States.

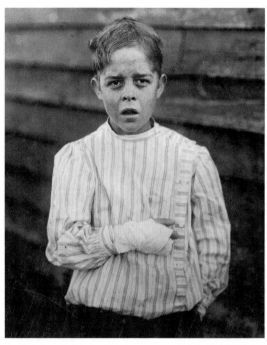

Reformers worked to outlaw child labor. They pointed out that children worked in dangerous conditions in many industries. Children who worked in textile mills, for example, sometimes had fingers cut off by the machines they tended.

Keppler

Chapter 28

The United States Becomes a World Power

Should U.S. actions in world affairs around the turn of the 20th century be praised or condemned?

28.1 Introduction

William McKinley owed Theodore Roosevelt a big favor. Roosevelt had just helped him get elected president. Roosevelt had spoken all over the United States in 1896, promoting McKinley's support of business and industry. With energy and inspiration, he attacked McKinley's opponents. These were Democrats who had adopted some Populist ideas. With the nation in the midst of an economic depression, Roosevelt feared political instability. He cried that McKinley's opponents planned nothing less than "revolution."

Now Roosevelt wanted McKinley to appoint him to be assistant secretary of the navy. McKinley, who favored peace, feared that Roosevelt was too warlike. Still, he gave Roosevelt the job. As he took office, Roosevelt said, "No triumph of peace is quite so great as the supreme triumphs of war . . . It is through strife, or the readiness for strife, that a nation must win greatness."

Some newspapers called Roosevelt patriotic. Others worried that he would push the country into war. Americans had mixed feelings about getting involved in international affairs. Expanding across the continent had given the United States territory to move into for decades to come. Recovery from the Civil War, followed by industrial expansion, had also given Americans plenty to focus on at home.

Now the West was more settled, and the United States was an industrial and agricultural leader. To keep the economy growing, business leaders wanted to market and sell products overseas. The national pride that had inspired Manifest Destiny was calling for new challenges.

Theodore Roosevelt agreed. He allied himself with expansionists—people who wanted to extend the nation's power within the Western Hemisphere and around the world. In this chapter, you will learn how expansionists achieved their goals. As it flexed its muscles overseas, the United States gained new territories and became a world power.

When Theodore Roosevelt became president in 1901, he carried out foreign policies that expanded U.S. involvement around the world—giving the United States a greater role in world affairs.

◀ The American eagle spreads its wings over a canal zone in Panama, the Philippines, and Puerto Rico, all under U.S. control by 1903.

PREPARING FOR THE HEATED TERM.

King Andy and his man Billy lay in a great stock of Russian ice in order to cool down the Congressional majority.

In this political cartoon, Secretary of State William Seward pulls a wheelbarrow containing a block of ice. President Andrew Johnson is pushing the wheelbarrow. What did this cartoonist think about the purchase of Alaska?

imperialism the policy of extending a nation's power by gaining political and economic control over other countries

28.2 The Nation Stretches Its Wings

In 1867, Secretary of State William Seward arranged for the United States to purchase Alaska from Russia. At the time, few people thought that acquiring this vast wilderness was a good idea. Even at a price of just two cents an acre, many labeled the deal "Seward's Folly."

But the "arctic wasteland" turned out to have thick forests, plentiful fish and wildlife, and mild coastal climates. Eventually, settlers would discover gold, copper, coal, and other minerals there. With such natural resources at stake, expansionists felt that the United States should gain control over other areas of the world as well.

In addition to arranging the purchase of Alaska, Seward also secured the rights to the Midway Islands. Located in the Pacific Ocean between California and Asia, the Midway Islands were annexed by the United States in 1867.

Rise of Expansionism Some Americans objected to expansionism, saying that it was contrary to American values. Taking over other lands, declared former senator Carl Schurz, would mean that "our old democratic principle that governments **derive** their just powers from the consent of the governed will have to go overboard."

Others warned that such takeovers would cause revolutions abroad. Some raised racist objections, arguing that nonwhites in other countries could never learn American values.

William Jennings Bryan, who had run for president against McKinley, believed that the United States could be powerful without taking over other lands. He said that the nation "has **exerted** upon the human race an influence more potent for good than all the other nations of the earth combined, and it has exerted that influence without the use of the sword or Gatling [machine] gun."

By the 1890s, however, American business leaders were eager to dig mines and establish plantations in new places. Others wanted new markets for finished products. For years, European countries had been practicing **imperialism,** building empires by taking control of the governments and economies of other countries. U.S. expansionists wanted to follow their example. Senator Henry Cabot Lodge declared, "Commerce follows the flag . . . As one of the great nations of the world, the United States must not fall out of the line of march."

Annexing Hawaii Commerce drove U.S. expansionists to develop an interest in Hawaii, a group of islands located in the Pacific Ocean. Americans had first come to these islands in the 1820s as missionaries. Their goal was to convert the native Hawaiians to Christianity. The Hawaiians, whose ancestors had come from the South Pacific, had lived on these islands for more than a thousand years. They were ruled by their own kings and queens.

In 1835, a Boston merchant established a large sugar plantation in Hawaii. Before long, American-owned sugar and pineapple plantations dotted the islands. The planters brought laborers to Hawaii from China and Japan to work in their vast fields. Under pressure from the planters, the Hawaiians agreed in 1887 to let the United States establish a naval base at Pearl Harbor, on the island of Oahu (oh-AH-hoo). The planters also persuaded Congress to allow Hawaiian sugar to be imported into the United States without paying any tariff (import tax).

U.S. sugar growers objected that the law now favored Hawaiian sugar over domestically grown sugar. They convinced Congress to give a bonus to growers in the United States. Hawaiian planters wanted that bonus, too. So they asked the United States to annex Hawaii.

Meanwhile, native Hawaiians increasingly resented being pushed around by Americans. When Queen Liliuokalani (lee-LEE-uh-woh-kuh-LAH-nee) took the throne in 1891, people rallied around her call of "Hawaii for Hawaiians." Americans in Hawaii feared that they would lose their land. With help from U.S. marines in 1893, sugar planters forced Queen Liliuokalani to give up her throne. Now in control, the planters established a new government for the islands.

Despite the planters' wishes, President Grover Cleveland refused to support the annexation of Hawaii. Cleveland, who opposed imperialism, said that Hawaii should be ruled by Hawaiians. But in 1898, under President McKinley, the United States did annex Hawaii.

Queen Liliuokalani, the last reigning monarch of Hawaii, insisted that native Hawaiians should control the islands. American planters organized a revolt that dethroned her.

U.S. Interest in Japan and China In the mid- to late 1800s, the United States turned its attention to Japan and China. The U.S. government signed a trade treaty with Japan in 1858. Several European countries had made efforts to control trade with China. The United States wanted to maintain its own access to Chinese markets. In 1899 and 1900, the U.S. government issued what became known as the Open Door Policy. It called on foreign nations to allow free trade in China.

28.3 "A Splendid Little War"

Closer to the United States, Americans established huge sugar plantations on the Caribbean island of Cuba, only 90 miles from Florida. Like nearby Puerto Rico, Cuba was still a Spanish colony.

By the 1890s, U.S. expansionists wanted to annex both of these islands. To support their ambitions, they argued that it was time for the United States to enforce the Monroe Doctrine. No European country, they said, should control territory in the Western Hemisphere.

When an explosion sunk the battleship USS *Maine* and killed 260 men, Americans accused Spain of causing the tragedy and demanded war. In 1976, Admiral H. G. Rickover, acting for the U.S. Navy, presented evidence that the explosion was probably caused by spontaneous combustion in one of the coal containers.

Cubans Struggle for Independence The Cubans themselves had staged an unsuccessful revolt against Spain in 1868. In 1895, under the leadership of José Martí (ho-ZAY mar-TEE), Cubans again tried to win their independence.

To crush this movement, the Spanish herded men, women, and children into "reconcentration camps." Forced to live with inadequate food and medical care, tens of thousands of people died.

U.S. newspapers jumped at the chance to report stories of Cuban suffering. Competing fiercely for customers, some newspapers resorted to **yellow journalism,** offering sensational and shocking reports. Some of these stories were based on rumors and untruths. One said that a Spanish general was "feeding prisoners to sharks."

As sympathy for Cubans grew, more and more Americans were willing to go to war for Cuba. To help Americans in Cuba in case of trouble, President McKinley sent the new battleship USS *Maine* to the island's capital city, Havana, in January 1898.

The Spanish-American War Trouble soon erupted in Havana. About three weeks after the *Maine* arrived, an explosion destroyed the battleship, killing 260 U.S. sailors. No one knew whether the explosion was caused by an accident, a mine, or a bomb. But many Americans were quick to blame Spain.

Young men rushed to join the army, raising the battle cry "Remember the *Maine*!" Senators shouted, "Free Cuba!" Hoping to avoid war, McKinley offered to work out a solution between the Spanish and Cubans. But the Spanish did not respond.

Under pressure from newspapers and members of Congress calling him a coward, McKinley asked Congress to declare war. Congress quickly agreed and, in April 1898, voted to go to war with Spain. At the same time, Congress approved a resolution stating that the United States intended "to leave the government and control of the Island [Cuba] to its people."

The Spanish-American War in the Caribbean, 1898

UNITED STATES

Tampa

Gulf of Mexico

Florida

ATLANTIC OCEAN

30°N

BAHAMAS (British)

Tropic of Cancer

USS Maine sunk February 1898

Havana

CUBA

San Juan Hill July 1898

Santiago

DOMINICAN REPUBLIC

20°N

HAITI

80°W

JAMAICA (British)

PUERTO RICO

Caribbean Sea

70°W

→ U.S. forces

✳ U.S. victory

▮▮▮ U.S. naval blockade

☐ Spanish possession

• City

0   250   500 miles

0   250   500 kilometers

Albers Conic Equal-Area Projection

When Spain refused to grant Cuba independence, the United States declared war on Spain. In July 1898, U.S. forces sank or captured the entire Spanish fleet after the Battle of San Juan Hill. The United States then defeated Spanish troops in Puerto Rico.

The African American Tenth Cavalry supported Roosevelt's Rough Riders as they charged up San Juan Hill. The capture of the hill allowed U.S. guns to bombard Santiago Harbor. When the Spanish fleet attempted to escape, it was completely destroyed.

The U.S. Army quickly grew from 30,000 to over 274,000 men. Roosevelt resigned from his position as assistant secretary of the navy and put together his own regiment. A mixture of powerful, wealthy men and seasoned ranch hands, it came to be called the Rough Riders.

After long preparations, the Rough Riders and 17,000 other Americans arrived in Cuba in June 1898. Seeing that Cuban fighters lacked the strength or weapons to force the Spanish out of fortified cities and harbors, Roosevelt and his Rough Riders decided to capture Santiago, a major city. To do this, they had to capture nearby San Juan Hill, from which Spanish forces were able to defend the city.

The attacking force included the Rough Riders and African American troops from several regiments. Up the hill the troops charged, braving Spanish fire. "They walked to greet death at every step, many of them, as they advanced, sinking suddenly or pitching forward . . . but others waded on, stubbornly, forming a thin blue line that kept creeping higher and higher up the hill," wrote an American reporter. "It was a miracle of self-sacrifice, a triumph of bull-dog courage."

The Americans captured San Juan Hill. Realizing that Santiago was lost, the Spanish tried to save their ships, sending them steaming out of the harbor. But Americans sank or captured every ship. The Spanish soon surrendered.

The Spanish-American War lasted just four months. Only 345 Americans died in combat, although 5,500 died of disease. Many Americans agreed with Secretary of State John Hay that it had been "a splendid little war."

Under the terms of the peace treaty between the United States and Spain, Cuba gained its independence from Spain, and Puerto Rico came under U.S. rule. Spain also ceded Guam, an island in the Pacific Ocean, to the United States. In a 1903 treaty with Cuba, the United States leased land in Cuba to establish a naval base at Guantánamo Bay.

yellow journalism the practice of publishing sensational and often exaggerated news in newspapers in order to attract readers and increase sales

28.4 The Philippines

After the *Maine* exploded in Cuba, Assistant Secretary of the Navy Theodore Roosevelt sent a telegram to Admiral George Dewey, the head of the U.S. fleet in the Pacific. "In the event of declaration of war," the telegram ordered, "[begin] offensive operations in Philippine Islands." The Spanish-American War had expanded to include the Philippine Islands, halfway around the globe from Cuba.

Battle at Manila Bay The Philippines provided Spain's main base in the Pacific. The islands' people, called Filipinos, had tried many times to throw off Spanish colonial rule. In 1898, they were trying again. Led by General Emilio Aguinaldo (ah-ghee-NAHL-doh), they had begun attacking the Spanish army and government officials. Now their struggle was about to become part of the war between the United States and Spain.

Dewey's fleet arrived in Manila, the Philippine capital, just five days after the United States declared war against Spain. At dawn on May 1, 1898, U.S. battleships faced Spanish gunships. As naval bands struck up "The Star-Spangled Banner," sailors stood on deck and saluted the flag. These men were about to engage in what would be the first battle of the Spanish-American War.

By 11 A.M., the entire Spanish fleet was burning, sunk, or sinking. Spain's old wooden ships were no match for the modern steel U.S. ships with well-trained crews. Only one American had died in the battle.

General Emilio Aguinaldo believed that the United States would help the Philippines gain independence from Spain. When the United States annexed the Philippines instead, he fought for Filipino freedom.

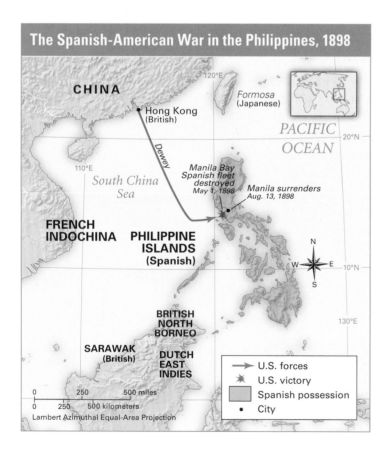

Defeating the Spanish Dewey blockaded Manila's port until U.S. troops could arrive to take over the city. Filipino fighters, allied with Dewey, surrounded Manila. The Filipinos believed that the coming Americans would help them gain independence. While they waited, Aguinaldo issued the Philippine Declaration of Independence, formed a national government, and designed a national flag.

Once U.S. reinforcements showed up, the Spanish agreed to "lose" a fake battle and surrender to the Americans. They didn't want to give themselves up to the Filipinos, who resented Spanish rule so intensely.

The Spanish-American War was fought on two fronts, Cuba and the Philippines. In the Philippines, located south of China, U.S. forces led by Admiral Dewey attacked and destroyed the entire Spanish fleet in Manila Bay.

The Granger Collection, New York

Fighting the Filipinos In a treaty negotiated after the surrender, the United States "bought" the Philippines from Spain for $20 million. Then, in 1899, Congress voted to annex the Philippines.

Aguinaldo's government felt betrayed. Angrily, the Filipino leader called for "war without quarter to the false Americans who have deceived us! Either independence or death!" For three years, more than 80,000 Filipino fighters fought off better-trained and better-armed U.S. troops. Soldiers on both sides tortured prisoners. Americans became increasingly cruel, harming civilians and destroying villages.

Some Americans protested that denying independence to the Philippines violated U.S. ideals. Carl Schurz, a leader among anti-imperialists, said, "We shall, for the first time since the abolition of slavery, again have two kinds of Americans: Americans of the first class, who enjoy the privilege of taking part in the Government . . . and Americans of the second class, who are to be ruled . . . by the Americans of the first class."

But the expansionists won the day. Senator Henry Cabot Lodge argued that "Manila with its magnificent bay . . . will keep us open to the markets of China." President McKinley himself believed that the Philippines could become "a land of plenty."

More than 20,000 Filipinos and about 4,000 Americans died in the struggle. When the revolt was finally put down, the Americans set up a nonmilitary government to "prepare Filipinos for independence." Americans built roads, hospitals, and schools. But the United States did not grant the Philippines independence until 1946.

A long war between the United States and the Filipinos who resisted U.S. control resulted in heavy casualties. More than 20,000 Filipinos were killed before the Philippines became independent in 1946.

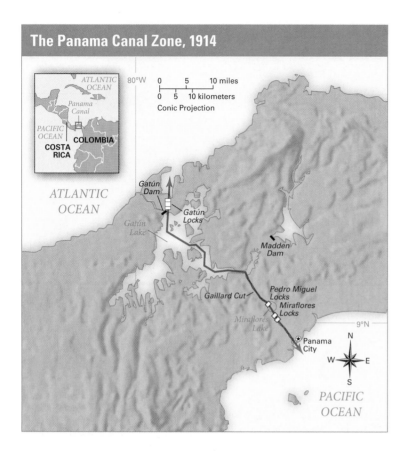

The Panama Canal Zone, 1914

ATLANTIC OCEAN

Panama Canal

PACIFIC OCEAN

COSTA RICA

COLOMBIA

80°W

0   5   10 miles

0   5   10 kilometers

Conic Projection

ATLANTIC OCEAN

Gatún Dam

Gatún Locks

Gatún Lake

Madden Dam

Gaillard Cut

Pedro Miguel Locks

Miraflores Locks

Miraflores Lake

Panama City

9°N

N   W   E   S

PACIFIC OCEAN

The United States took control of the Panama Canal Zone in 1903 and started building the canal the following year. By 1914, the Panama Canal was complete. It provided a shortcut for ships traveling between the Atlantic and the Pacific.

28.5 Panama and the Canal

In 1900, America's favorite hero from the Spanish-American War, Theodore Roosevelt, was elected vice president. "We stand on the threshold of a new century," Roosevelt declared. "Is America a weakling, to shrink from the work of the great powers? No. The young giant of the West stands on a continent and clasps the crest of an ocean in either hand."

Dreaming of a Canal Roosevelt wanted to join the Atlantic and Pacific oceans with a canal. If ships could move quickly between the Atlantic and the Pacific, the navy would be better able to defend the nation's new territories. In addition, businesses would gain from lower shipping costs.

In September 1901, President McKinley was shot and killed by an assassin, and Roosevelt became president. In his first speech to Congress, Roosevelt argued for the canal. "No single great material work which remains to be undertaken on this continent is of such consequence to the American people," he told the lawmakers.

Congress soon approved funding. In 1903, Roosevelt offered Colombia $10 million for land in their province of Panama, the narrowest part of Central America. The Colombian senate refused, believing that the United States was trying to take a weaker country's valuable resources.

Furious, Roosevelt sent a U.S. warship to Panama. Roosevelt knew that Panamanians wanted independence from Colombia. The day after the ship arrived, a revolution started in Panama. With U.S. marines keeping Colombian soldiers from reaching Panama's harbors, the rebels quickly won.

The new country of Panama agreed to accept $10 million in exchange for giving the United States control over a "canal zone" ten miles wide. Some U.S. senators and newspapers—and countries all over the world—objected to America's "gunboat diplomacy." But most of the public supported the president.

Building "The Big Ditch" Construction on the canal began in 1904. Workers faced terrible conditions. "We had to bathe, wash our clothes in the same river; drink the same river water and cook with it," said one. A year later, three-quarters of American workers had quit the project.

The majority of employees were workers from the West Indies who could not afford to go home. To prevent deadly yellow fever and malaria, crews worked to eliminate the mosquitoes that carried these diseases. They drained ditches, spread oil on swamps, and screened doors and windows. Within two years, canal workers were no longer dying from these diseases.

A new chief engineer improved housing and strictly organized the huge project. Using dynamite and huge steam shovels, men made a wide, deep cut through Panama's mountains. The excavated dirt was moved by railroad car to lower elevations. Here, workers created earthen dams to form three giant lakes. Engineers supervised the construction of locks, a type of gate that would allow water levels to be raised and lowered along the canal.

By the time the 51-mile-long canal opened in 1914, Roosevelt had left office. His influence in the Panamanian revolution continued to be controversial. Roosevelt himself admitted, "I took the Canal Zone." In 1921, Congress apologized to Colombia and gave it $25 million. But anti-American feelings remained high in Latin America, and Panamanians increasingly resented U.S. control of the Canal Zone. In 2000, the United States returned the zone to Panama.

The Culebra Cut, shown here, was one of the engineering miracles that allowed engineers to complete the Panama Canal in ten years. Millions of pounds of dynamite blasted apart the mountain. The earth was then used to construct dams to form lakes.

28.6 The Outbreak of World War I

By the time the first ship sailed through the Panama Canal, the world's attention was not on Panama, but on far-off Europe. In August 1914, German troops poured across Belgium, on their way to try to conquer France. Europe was at war.

Tensions in Europe European countries had long competed with each other for colonies, trade, and territory. By the early 1900s, **nationalism** was complicating these rivalries. Austria-Hungry had built an empire by taking over smaller countries in the part of eastern Europe known as the Balkans. Nationalism inspired in the Balkan people a burning desire to be independent of Austrian rule.

As tensions grew, European leaders looked for safety in **militarism,** a policy of glorifying military power and military ideas and values. When Germany built up its navy to challenge Great Britain's fleet, Great Britain constructed more battleships. As Germany's army grew, France built up its own army.

European countries also looked for safety in alliances. In secret treaties, Germany and Austria-Hungary agreed to help each other in case of attack. Great Britain, Russia, and France made similar agreements. Europe was dividing into what amounted to armed camps.

Assassination Leads to War An outburst of nationalism lit the fuse of war. On June 28, 1914, the heir to the Austro-Hungarian throne, Archduke Franz Ferdinand, was visiting the city of Sarajevo in the province of Bosnia. Many Bosnians were Serbs who wanted to be part of nearby Serbia instead of Austria-Hungary. A Serbian nationalist jumped out of a crowd and fatally shot the archduke and his wife.

Outraged, Austria-Hungary accused Serbia of having a hand in the assassinations and pressured Serbia to give up most of its independence. When the Serbs refused, Austria-Hungary declared war. The Russians stepped in to defend the Serbs. The Germans came to the aid of Austria-Hungary by declaring war on Russia. Russia's ally, France, began to prepare for war.

Eventually, more than a dozen countries took sides in the "Great War." Decades later, people called the conflict World War I. Austria-Hungary and Germany headed the Central Powers. France, Russia, and Great Britain led the Allied Powers.

Like most Americans, President Woodrow Wilson wanted to stay out of the war. Declaring that the United States would remain neutral, Wilson begged citizens to be "impartial in thought as well as deed."

nationalism devotion to a national or ethnic identity, including the desire for independence from rule by foreign countries

militarism a policy of glorifying military power and military ideas and values

Archduke Franz Ferdinand and his wife are shown here shortly before being assassinated by a Serbian nationalist. The assassination triggered World War I.

A military tactic called trench warfare was used extensively in World War I. Hundreds of miles of trenches, like this trench for British soldiers, provided protection for soldiers during attacks and allowed supplies and reinforcements to be delivered to the front.

28.7 A New Kind of Warfare

By September 1914, approximately 6 million soldiers were on the march across Europe. On Germany's Eastern Front, German troops fought Russians. On the Western Front, German forces advanced quickly before being stopped by French and British troops at the Marne River, about 40 miles outside the city of Paris. With neither army able to advance, both sides dug long, narrow ditches called trenches to protect their soldiers.

Trench Warfare For the next three years, the war in the west was fought from two parallel lines of trenches. Men ate, slept, fought, and died in these miserable ditches. Eventually, the lines of trenches stretched for 600 miles across France.

Each side protected its front trench with barbed wire and booby traps. The land between opposing trenches was a deadly "no-man's land." Attacking soldiers came under intense fire from the men in the trenches. Thousands upon thousands of soldiers died trying to advance their line of trenches a few yards.

The trenches were wretched places, infested with rats, lice, and disease. "We are not leading the life of men at all," wrote an American who had volunteered to fight with the British forces, "but that of animals, living in holes in the ground, and only showing outside to fight and to feed."

New Weapons New weapons added to the horror of trench warfare. "We never got anywhere near the Germans," one English corporal remembered. "The machine-guns were just mowing the top of the trenches." These new machine guns fired hundreds of bullets a minute. By the end of 1914, the French had lost 300,000 men. Germany lost more than 130,000 soldiers in a single battle.

European Alliances in World War I

ATLANTIC OCEAN

NORWAY

North Sea

SWEDEN

DENMARK

RUSSIA

GREAT BRITAIN

NETH.

GERMANY

BELGIUM

LUX.

AUSTRIA-HUNGARY

SWITZERLAND

FRANCE

ROMANIA

Black Sea

SERBIA

MONTENEGRO

BULGARIA

PORTUGAL

ITALY

OTTOMAN EMPIRE

SPAIN

GREECE

ALBANIA

Mediterranean Sea

AFRICA

Allied Powers
Central Powers
Neutral nations
Farthest advance by Central Powers
Area of German U-boat activity
British blockade

0   250   500 miles
0   250   500 kilometers
Lambert Azimuthal Equal-Area Projection

Tensions in Europe caused by nationalism and a military buildup led to war between two alliances—the Allied Powers and the Central Powers. The Central Powers included Germany. German submarines called U-boats concentrated on attacking ships around Great Britain.

The next spring, a green cloud floated over the Allied lines. Soldiers gasped and died, their throats and noses burning. The Germans had invented poison gas. Soon both sides were using chemical weapons.

The armies' new technology and strategies were effective for defense, but not for decisive attack. At one point, the British tried for six months to advance their lines. They gained only five miles and lost 420,000 men. "The deadlock here is permanent," wrote an American volunteer.

War at Sea To supply soldiers in the trenches with food, ammunition, and other supplies, the warring nations bought goods from neutral countries. Each side tried to cut off the flow of supplies to its enemy.

Most trade, especially with the United States, was by sea. Great Britain had the world's greatest fleet and numerous ocean ports. Germany had a strong navy, but its only access to the ocean was through the North Sea. To close German ports, Great Britain laid mines in the North Sea. This blockade stopped most of the neutral shipping and kept the German fleet bottled up in harbors for most of the war.

Unable to use its surface ships, the German navy tried to blockade Great Britain using submarines, called U-boats (for "underwater boats"). Fearing that the British would try to disguise their ships as neutral, Germany announced that it might sink vessels flying the flags of neutral countries. Because submarines on the surface were easy targets for enemy fire, German submarines began sinking vessels on sight, instead of rising to the surface to give warning, as was expected even in wartime.

Germany Sinks the *Lusitania* The German embassy in the United States placed newspaper ads warning passengers not to sail to Great Britain and specifically not to take the *Lusitania,* a British luxury liner. On May 7, 1915, six days after leaving New York, the *Lusitania* neared the coast of Ireland. Suddenly a ship's lookout shouted, "Torpedo coming on the starboard side!" Within moments, the ship exploded and quickly sank, killing 1,198 people, including 128 Americans.

Americans were outraged. One newspaper called the German attack "wholesale murder." When President Wilson protested, Germany said that the *Lusitania* had been carrying arms. Still, Germany apologized and offered to pay for damages. Hoping to keep the United States out of the war, Germany also promised not to attack merchant and passenger ships without warning in the future.

Protected by this promise, U.S. manufacturers increased their trade with the Allies. Trade with Allied countries swelled to $3.2 billion in 1916, while trade with the Central Powers dropped to $1 million. Americans were not fighting in the war, but they had definitely taken sides.

28.8 To Make the World "Safe for Democracy"

After the sinking of the *Lusitania,* Wilson decided that the United States needed to prepare in case war became necessary. He worked with Congress to get money to improve the army and navy. Still, neither Wilson nor the country wanted war. In 1916, Wilson won reelection under the slogan, "He Kept Us Out of War."

Wilson also tried to start peace talks. But European leaders, having lost so many soldiers, rejected Wilson's call for "peace without victory."

The United States Enters the War The Germans soon risked war with the United States again. Even though U-boats were sinking 50 to 100 British merchant ships per month, enough were getting through to keep the Allies supplied. Desperate to prevent an Allied victory, the Germans decided to cut off British supplies before their own ran out. In February 1917, Germany resumed sinking merchant ships from other countries without warning.

Here, Woodrow Wilson appears before Congress to ask for a declaration of war against Germany. Although Wilson tried to avoid war, he felt that continued U-boat attacks on merchant ships gave him no choice.

In March, U-boats torpedoed three U.S. merchant ships, killing many Americans. In fact, these ships had been carrying weapons to the Allies. The Germans knew that this attack might bring the United States into the war, but they hoped to win before America was ready to fight.

It was a fatal mistake. Addressing a special session of Congress, Wilson urged a declaration of war. America would fight alongside the Allies, he said, not just to protect neutral shipping, but because "the world must be made safe for democracy."

Congress greeted Wilson's speech with applause. Later, Wilson reflected, "My message today was a message of death for our young men. How strange it seems to applaud that."

To recruit the necessary men for an army to send to Europe, the United States resorted to the draft. All men between the ages of 18 and 45 had to register. Within a few months, the army grew from 200,000 men to over 4 million.

Americans Prepare to Fight On April 6, 1917, Congress declared war. The Allies rejoiced, hoping for U.S. supplies—and soldiers. Allied ships were sinking faster than they could be replaced. To get U.S. supplies delivered safely, convoys of U.S. warships started escorting cargo vessels, protecting them from attack. U.S. destroyers also helped the British navy assault U-boats. These strategies dramatically reduced shipping losses.

When the United States entered the war, it had only 200,000 soldiers, and most of those had limited training. Congress quickly authorized a national draft. Soon, 3 million men had been drafted. Another 2 million volunteered.

Fighting and Winning U.S. troops who sailed overseas were called the American Expeditionary Force (AEF). As they began arriving in Europe in June 1917, AEF soldiers soon learned from the Allies about trench warfare. The U.S. commander, General John J. Pershing, hated these terrible conditions for soldiers. He also realized that trench warfare was not winning the war. He worked on a plan for driving the Germans out of the trenches and forcing them to retreat into open country.

Meanwhile, Russia had dropped out of the war. With millions of soldiers dead and starvation spreading across the country, Russians had revolted against their ruler, the czar. Russia's new government made peace with the Germans. This enabled Germany to bring soldiers back from the east, swelling their western forces to 3,500,000 men.

The German forces rushed to capture Paris before large numbers of Americans could arrive from overseas. They pushed quickly through the village of Château-Thierry and a nearby forest called Belleau Wood. They were within 50 miles of Paris when Americans reinforced the exhausted French. Gradually, U.S. machine guns and artillery enabled the Allies to push the Germans back.

By the summer of 1918, more than a million Americans were in Europe. Pershing set his Allied offensive into motion. His plan took advantage of several new technologies that had been developed during the war. Tanks could advance through trenches. Airplanes could deliver machine-gun fire and drop bombs. Carefully **coordinating** huge numbers of soldiers, tanks, airplanes, and artillery, the Allies forced the weakened Germans back to their own border.

To avoid the invasion of their own country, German leaders agreed to an armistice, or cease-fire. On November 11, 1918, for the first time in four years, the guns were silenced.

The costs of the war horrified the world. More than 9 million people had died. Entering the war late, the United States had lost 116,000 lives.

28.9 The Struggle for Peace

Less than two months after the fighting ended in Europe, President Wilson traveled to Paris to take part in peace talks. He was cheered by huge crowds. The United States had saved the French from endless war. And many Europeans welcomed Wilson's eagerness to prevent future wars.

Fourteen Points for World Peace Months earlier, Wilson had presented to Congress a 14-point proposal for a postwar agreement. The first five points aimed to prevent conflict. Nations were asked to avoid secret treaties, to practice free trade, and to reduce their weapon supplies. Wilson asked that new borders be drawn based on self-determination, or the will of the people in each area.

Points 6 through 13 described new boundaries for many European countries. Finally, the ambitious Point 14 called for nations to join a general association of countries to protect each other's independence. Wilson called this organization the League of Nations. With the League of Nations, Wilson believed, the world could achieve a lasting peace.

Germany had surrendered, believing that Wilson's "Fourteen Points" would be the basis for a fair and just peace. But after years of fighting and dreadful losses, some Allied leaders were not satisfied with a just peace.

The Treaty of Versailles On January 18, 1919, delegates from dozens of countries assembled at a French palace outside Paris called Versailles (vehr-SIGH). In addition to Wilson, three Allied leaders dominated the treaty talks. They were David Lloyd George of England, Georges Clemenceau (kleh-mahn-SOH) of France, and Vittorio Orlando of Italy.

The German representatives were not allowed to speak. This reflected the Allies' anger and their determination to punish Germany and remove it as a future threat. They created a treaty that forced Germany to disband almost all of its armed forces, give up its colonies, and surrender territory in Europe. In addition, they called on Germany to pay reparations, or money to make up for damages and war deaths. The amount of these reparations was later set at $33 billion.

This painting shows the signing of the peace treaty that ended World War I. The treaty dealt harshly with Germany and planted the seeds of resentment that would lead to World War II.

Woodrow Wilson toured the country seeking public support for the League of Nations, which Congress opposed. When he suffered a massive stroke, he was unable to continue his fight and the Senate refused to approve the Treaty of Versailles.

President Wilson opposed such harsh treatment of Germany. However, he eventually accepted the Allied leaders' demands for punishment in order to win their support for his Fourteen Points.

The Allies rejected some of Wilson's points, including freedom of the seas. But the peace conference did create new national boundaries in Europe based on self-determination. Most important to Wilson, the Treaty of Versailles established a League of Nations. Wilson thought that this agreement would make the peace treaty successful. The League of Nations, he believed, could fix any problems created by the treaty.

Struggling for Senate Ratification Wilson needed the approval of two-thirds of the U.S. Senate to ratify the peace treaty. He quickly ran into opposition, especially to the League of Nations. Some senators worried that other countries would force U.S. soldiers to fight in international conflicts. They argued that only Congress had the constitutional power to send Americans to war.

The struggle over the treaty became a fight between political parties. Republicans held a majority in the Senate. They felt that Wilson, a Democrat, had made his Fourteen Points a political issue by not appointing any Republicans to his negotiating team.

Anxious to increase public support for the League of Nations, Wilson undertook an intense speaking tour. In 22 days, he toured 29 cities. He spoke up to four times a day, with hardly any rest. Finally, he collapsed with severe headaches. He was rushed back to Washington, D.C., where he suffered a massive stroke.

Recovering slowly, Wilson was less willing or able to compromise with opposition senators. In March 1920, the Senate rejected the Treaty of Versailles.

A Return to Isolationism Once again, the United States was heading toward a policy of isolationism. When the League of Nations opened in Geneva, Switzerland, the United States did not participate. In later years, when crises developed in Europe, the League lacked the power that Wilson hoped it would have.

In Germany, the Treaty of Versailles left a bitter legacy. Germans—notably Adolf Hitler, a corporal who had been temporarily blinded by gas during the war—felt betrayed by the treaty. Hitler's rise to power in the 1930s would pose a fresh challenge to U.S. isolationism. Only after a second world war would the United States take on the role of world power that it continues to fill today.

Chapter Summary

In this chapter, you read about U.S. expansionism and the nation's involvement in World War I.

The Nation Stretches Its Wings The United States' first great expansion after the Civil War was the purchase of Alaska. The nation also expanded westward by annexing the Midway Islands in the Pacific in 1867 and Hawaii in 1898.

The Spanish-American War In 1898, the United States declared war with Spain over the Cuban struggle for independence. As a result of the Spanish-American War, the United States gained two new possessions: Puerto Rico and the Philippines. Although the nation did not take over Cuba, it did, under a treaty made in 1903, lease land in Cuba to establish a naval base.

Panama and the Canal In Central America, the United States encouraged revolution in Panama and then purchased a strip of land from the new country in order to build the Panama Canal. The United States maintained control over the Canal Zone for the rest of the 20th century.

World War I By the time World War I broke out, the United States was becoming a world power. America remained neutral until late in the war, when it entered the conflict on the side of the Allied Powers. President Wilson described the war as a fight to make the world safe for democracy.

A New Kind of Warfare World War I saw great changes in how war was conducted. The war in the west was fought from two parallel lines of trenches that eventually stretched for 600 miles across France. Machine guns and chemical weapons added to the horrors of trench warfare. German U-boats, or submarines, sank vessels on sight.

The Struggle for Peace Americans helped to win the war, but Wilson was unable to get all of his peace plan adopted. The U.S. Senate refused to ratify the peace treaty, preventing the United States from joining the League of Nations. In Europe, the harsh terms imposed by the victorious Allies caused great bitterness in Germany. Meanwhile, the United States turned back toward isolationism.

By the early 1900s, when this photograph was taken, William Randolph Hearst was building the nation's first great media empire. Hearst was just 32 when he bought the *New York Journal* in 1895.

The Yellow Press Goes to War

In the late 1890s, an intense battle raged in New York City. William Randolph Hearst and Joseph Pulitzer waged a "newspaper war" to dominate the city's news business. They relied on yellow journalism, printing sensational stories to attract readers and sell newspapers. In the process, they stirred passions that helped lead to a real war, the Spanish-American War.

William Randolph Hearst needed a good story. His newspaper, the *New York Journal,* was gaining on the city's top paper, the *New York World.* But he needed a spectacular, front-page story to grab readers' attention and sell more papers. In the summer of 1897, he got his break.

On August 17, Hearst's correspondent in Cuba reported that Spanish officials there had thrown a young woman into jail. The story had all the elements Hearst was looking for. The woman, Evangelina Cisneros, was the daughter of a Cuban rebel fighting Spanish rule. She was 18 years old, beautiful, and appeared to be innocent. Now, the correspondent reported, she was being held in a filthy dungeon with hardened criminals. Hearst splashed her story across the front page. He called for an end to Spanish abuses and freedom for the Cuban people.

Hearst went even further. He began a petition drive, calling on women everywhere to protest the Spanish action. Many prominent women signed up, including President McKinley's mother.

Hearst also launched a daring operation to free Cisneros. He sent a reporter to Cuba as a secret agent. In a dramatic, late-night prison break, the agent freed Cisneros and helped her escape to New York. Hearst gave her a thunderous welcome, including a parade down Fifth Avenue and a giant rally at Madison Square Garden. "Evangelina Cisneros Rescued by the Journal," trumpeted the paper's front-page headline.

Hearst's critics accused him of a hoax, saying that Spanish authorities had allowed Cisneros to escape. Meanwhile, Hearst took full advantage of the publicity and his role in making history. He was proud of what he called "journalism that acts." "It does not wait for things to turn up," he bragged proudly. He had a sensational story. Good had triumphed over evil—at least in Hearst's version. Newspaper sales soared.

The Power of the Press

The Cisneros story was typical of Hearst's approach to the news business. Newspapers were very important in the late 1800s. In the days before radio and television, they were the main news medium. They played a key role in making news and influencing public opinion.

New York was the nation's leading newspaper town. With a population of almost 3 million people, it had 15 daily papers with a total circulation of nearly 2 million copies a day. Other cities, such as Boston, Chicago, and Philadelphia, also had a thriving press. But New York papers set the agenda for much of the nation's news.

By 1897, the two most popular papers in New York were Hearst's *Journal* and Joseph Pulitzer's *World.* Locked in a battle for readership, they used a dramatic style of writing called yellow journalism to boost their appeal. In fact, it was their rivalry that gave birth to the term.

The Rise of Yellow Journalism

Hearst, the son of a wealthy mining baron, had bought the *Journal* in 1895. Although it was a small paper at the time, he was determined to make it big. He changed the layout to feature large, catchy headlines and striking illustrations. He filled the pages with society gossip and shocking stories about crime, corruption, and scandal.

The *Journal,* like the *World,* presented itself as a force for truth, justice, and the rights of the common man. It cast its reporters as brave heroes who solved crimes and rooted out corruption. To compete with Pulitzer, Hearst was willing to pay more for good stories. As a result, many journalists left the *World* and came to work for Hearst.

One of those who moved was the cartoonist R. F. Outcault. His popular cartoon "Hogan's Alley" featured a street kid who dressed in a bright yellow nightshirt. The "Yellow Kid's" antics delighted readers and made the cartoon a big hit for the *World.* That is, it did until the Yellow Kid moved to the *Journal.*

To fight back, Pulitzer produced another version of the cartoon. Suddenly, there were two Yellow Kids in the Sunday papers. People began to refer to the *World* and the *Journal* as the "yellow papers." And the style of the papers—brash, bold, and sensational—became known as yellow journalism. Yellow journalism became the style in many papers around the country, but the *Journal* and the *World* set the pattern.

The Yellow Kid played a key role in the newspaper war between Hearst and Pulitzer. As the main character in New York's most popular cartoon, he boosted sales of both the *Journal* and the *World.*

New Yorkers could purchase the city's 15 daily newspapers at newsstands around the city. Americans at the time read newspapers—lots of them. In the late 1800s, about 14,000 weekly and 1,900 daily papers were published in the United States.

The *Journal's* War

New Yorkers could read bulletins about the war's progress on the front of the *Journal's* building as well as in its bold headlines. The *Journal* and other yellow papers helped push the country toward war. But they were just one factor. Many Americans were opposed to colonial rule, and some hoped to annex Cuba to the United States.

In their quest for readers, the *Journal* and the *World* were both drawn to the rebellion in Cuba. Hearst, in particular, used the Cuban conflict to boost sales. He clearly believed in the Cuban cause. But he also saw the conflict as a good story that could help him win his circulation war with Pulitzer.

The *Journal* ran a steady stream of articles that painted the Cuban revolt in black-and-white terms. The Cuban rebels were noble patriots seeking liberty. The Spanish rulers were heartless villains trying to deny Cubans their freedom. In printing these stories, Hearst had one goal in mind: to push the United States into war.

In fact, many of the stories that came out of Cuba were false or exaggerated. Spanish officials allowed reporters little access to the fighting. As a result, many correspondents based their stories on flimsy evidence or on no evidence at all.

In 1897, Hearst published a series of stories that raised the pressure for war. The Cisneros story was one of these. Another concerned a search of three Cuban women on an American ship in Havana harbor. A third reported that a Cuban American doctor had been murdered in a Cuban jail. None of these stories was entirely accurate, but they all raised a storm of protest in the United States.

More stories followed. Early in 1898, the *Journal* reported that a riot in Havana was directed at American citizens, when in fact it was not. Then the paper reported on the contents of a stolen letter from the Spanish ambassador, in which the official called President McKinley "weak." The headline read, "The Worst Insult to the United States in Its History." Again, readers were outraged. But that story was soon pushed aside by a much bigger event.

On February 15, the U.S.S. *Maine* blew up in Havana harbor. Although the cause of the blast was unknown, both Hearst and Pulitzer blamed Spain. "Destruction of the War Ship Maine Was the Work of an Enemy," read the *Journal*'s headline. Other inflammatory stories followed. Hearst even published a card game called "War with Spain."

Two months later, Hearst got his wish. Congress declared war on Spain. On the *Journal*'s front page, Hearst gloated, "How Do You Like the Journal's War?"

Hearst at the Front

Contrary to his claims, Hearst did not cause the Spanish-American War. Although the *Journal* and other yellow papers built public support for the war, they did not make it happen. They were just one factor in a set of circumstances that led to war.

Hearst was brilliant at self-promotion, however, and he knew that war was good for newspaper sales. In fact, circulation figures continued to rise. As the war began, both the *Journal* and the *World* were selling more than a million copies a day.

Hearst made sure his paper was at the center of the action. He sent dozens of correspondents to Cuba to report on the war. He even offered to organize and equip a regiment to fight in Cuba. When President McKinley declined his offer, Hearst proposed sending his own yacht to Cuba as a military vessel. The navy accepted this offer, though it rejected Hearst's request to command the ship.

Denied the chance to fight in Cuba, Hearst went as a reporter. He fitted out a ship with food and medical supplies and sailed to Cuba with some of his staff. There, he filed several stories from the front lines. He took his reporting duties seriously, though he sometimes got in the way of the fighting. At one point, soldiers warned him off the battlefield.

Meanwhile, the *Journal* and the *World* continued their own battle for readership. They sometimes stole each other's stories, rewriting them and claiming them as their own. They also accused each other of publishing false stories. At times, they paid more attention to their own squabbles than to the war itself.

Both papers spent a lot of money on the war, however. In fact, they spent far more than they made back in sales. By the war's end, they were deeply in debt. To cut their losses, Pulitzer and Hearst agreed to cease their newspaper war. They toned down their papers, thus ending the "golden age" of yellow journalism.

The two men continued to leave their mark on the news business. Pulitzer funded the country's first journalism school, at Columbia University. He also lent his name to the Pulitzer Prizes, journalism's top awards. Hearst went on to build a giant media empire, which included radio and film companies. He continued to shape the news for years to come.

Students from Columbia University's School of Journalism, founded by Joseph Pulitzer, celebrate their graduation. Today's journalists work in a wide range of media from television and the Internet to newspapers like Joseph Pulitzer's.

Chapter 29

Linking Past to Present

What changes since 1914 have shaped how we live today?

29.1 Introduction

Henry Ford was a man with a vision. He wanted to build a motorcar "so low in price that no man making a good salary will be unable to own one." The result was the Model T, a car, Ford said, "large enough for the family, but small enough for the individual to run and care for."

To make the Model T affordable, Ford needed a new way to put cars together. At first, workers built Model Ts by hand, a task that took over 12 hours. To reduce this time, Ford designed a moving assembly line. The assembly line moved cars from worker to worker to worker, with each worker adding another part. The time needed to assemble a car dropped to under 6 hours. With this faster assembly time, Ford was able to reduce the price of the Model T from around $850 in 1908 to $360 by 1916.

When Ford unveiled his assembly line in 1914, he made a stunning announcement. He was more than doubling his workers' wages, to $5.00 a day. It was a brilliant move. High pay kept Ford's workers on the job. It also made it possible for them to buy the cars they produced. By 1918, half of all cars sold in the United States were Model T Fords.

Today, the Ford Motor Company is still making "motorcars for the multitudes." But the world in which the company operates is very different. In 1914, the United States was home to just 99 million people. Most people worked on farms or in factories. People moved slowly by foot, horse, or rail. Only the fortunate few earned enough money to afford cars.

In contrast, the United States today has a population of more than 300 million people. Relatively few work on farms or in factories. And most families now consider a car—once a luxury—a necessity. In this chapter, you will learn how changes like these came about and how they have shaped life in the 21st century.

Compare this 1912 photograph of San Francisco with the one on the opposite page. Here we see early cars as well as horse-drawn wagons. Some of these buildings were considered skyscrapers in the early 1900s.

◀ Cars crossing the San Francisco–Oakland Bay Bridge at sunset create a stream of light. How have changes like cars shaped the nation since 1914?

More than 200,000 people heard Martin Luther King's speech during the 1963 March on Washington. "I have a dream that one day this nation will rise up and live out the true meaning of its creed," he said. "We hold these truths to be self-evident, that all men are created equal."

29.2 Securing Equal Rights and Opportunities

Had you been able to visit the Ford Motor Company in 1914, you would have seen a workforce of white men. The same would have been true in most factories. Women might be employed as garment workers or as office help. But the factory floor was a man's world—so long as the men were white.

At a Ford factory today, you would see a far more diverse workforce. Women and men of all races and nationalities now work throughout the company. This change did not just happen. It is the result of a long struggle for equal rights and opportunities.

African Americans Demand Equal Rights For African Americans, the end of slavery had brought freedom, but not equality. During Reconstruction, racial segregation became a way of life in the South. Blacks could not attend the same schools or eat in the same restaurants as whites. Few blacks could vote, much less run for public office. Many African Americans migrated to the North and West to escape such discrimination. However, no part of the country was free from racism.

A major turning point in African American's struggle for equality came in 1954. That year, a lawsuit known as *Brown v. Board of Education of Topeka, Kansas* reached the Supreme Court. The question before the Court was whether segregated schools violated the Fourteenth Amendment. This amendment guarantees all citizens "equal protection of the laws." In a landmark decision, the Court stated that "separate educational facilities are **inherently** unequal."

A second major turning point came in 1955. It was sparked by the arrest of Rosa Parks, a black seamstress who was on her way home from work in Montgomery, Alabama. Parks's crime was refusing to give up her seat on a crowded bus to a white passenger. Montgomery's black residents organized a bus boycott to protest the arrest. They refused to ride city buses until black passengers were treated as the equals of white passengers.

The Montgomery Bus Boycott gave rise to a new civil rights movement. The movement's leader was a young minister named Martin Luther King Jr. King organized marches and protests across the South.

These events awakened the nation to the injustice of both racism and racial segregation.

In 1963, black and white protesters marched on Washington, D.C., to demand action by Congress. Over the next two years, Congress enacted two landmark civil rights laws. The first of these laws, the Civil Rights Act of 1964, banned segregation in public places based on race, gender, religion, or nationality. It also outlawed discrimination in employment based on these same factors.

The second law, the Voting Rights Act of 1965, banned practices that had kept African Americans from voting in many Southern states. In Mississippi, for example, the percentage of black adults registered to vote rose from 7 percent in 1964 to 82 percent by 2008.

Mexican Americans Fight for Economic Justice Mexican Americans also suffered from racism. Many could only find jobs as farmworkers. They worked long hours tending and picking crops for little pay.

Mexican Americans found a champion in César Chávez. In 1962, along with Dolores Huerta, Chávez organized a labor union later known as the United Farm Workers (UFW). In 1968, Chávez called for a nationwide boycott of California table grapes. The boycott put pressure on grape growers to bargain with the UFW. In 1970, the growers agreed to most of the workers' demands for better pay and working conditions. The UFW's success inspired farmworkers to organize in other states.

Civil rights and farm labor leader César Chávez is shown here at a rally in 1966. A migrant farm worker himself, Chávez founded a labor union that later became the United Farm Workers. For his support of working people, Chávez was awarded the Presidential Medal of Freedom.

Women Fight for Equality The 1960s and 1970s saw the rise of a new women's movement. Much of the credit for sparking this movement goes to Betty Friedan. Her 1963 book, *The Feminine Mystique*, challenged the idea that women should be content as stay-at-home wives and mothers. Friedan argued that women should be free to pursue careers outside the home, just as men did.

Friedan and other **feminists** founded the National Organization for Women in 1966. Since then, NOW has worked for the equal treatment of women in all areas of life. For millions of women, equality means the freedom to work at any job. In 1950, women made up about 30 percent of the workforce, but earned only about 60 cents for every dollar that men doing the same work earned. By 2009, women made up nearly half of the workforce, but had yet to close the wage gap. That year, women earned about 80 cents compared to a dollar earned by men in the same jobs.

Women and Minorities Enter Politics Women also began to compete with men in politics. In 1960, no state had a woman governor. By 2010, six states had governors who were women, with that number expected to increase. Women also held a quarter of the seats in state legislatures. African Americans and Latinos saw similar gains. (Latinos are people whose families come from Mexico, Central America, or South America.) In 1971, African Americans and Latinos held only 19 seats in Congress. By 2010, that number had risen to 73.

In 2008, Barack Obama became the first African American nominated to run for president. In his victory speech, Obama said,

If there is anyone out there who still doubts that America is a place where all things are possible, who still wonders if the dream of our founders is alive in our time, who still questions the power of our democracy, tonight is your answer.

On Election Day, more than 69 million Americans cast votes to make Obama the first African American president of the United States.

In 2009, Barack Obama became the nation's first African American president. "Our challenges may be new," he said at his inauguration. "But those values upon which our success depends—honesty and hard work, courage and fair play, tolerance and curiosity, loyalty and patriotism—these things . . . have been the quiet force of progress throughout our history."

29.3 Innovations Change Daily Life

The first Model Ts rolling off Ford's moving assembly line in 1914 were relatively simple machines. The car had a top speed of 45 miles per hour. Its only safety features were headlamps and brakes. Even so, an affordable car was an innovation, or new idea, that would change how Americans lived. Other innovations would soon follow.

Faster, Easier Ways to Travel The Model T ended America's horse-and-buggy era. Cars were faster and easier to manage than horse-drawn buggies. People with cars could travel longer distances to work or shop. This allowed families to move out of crowded cities into suburbs. Cars also changed how people used their leisure time. Families piled into cars to see the country on Sunday drives or to take vacation trips to new places.

The growing popularity of cars gave rise to new industries. Gas stations, repair shops, and tourist stops sprang up along newly paved roads. By the mid-1920s, one out of eight American workers had a job related to the automobile industry. By 2008, that number had dropped only slightly, to about one in ten.

Another innovation, the airplane, cut travel times between distant cities. The world's first scheduled airline service opened in Florida in 1914. The St. Petersburg-Tampa Airboat Line flew passengers between those two cities in 22 minutes. The same journey took 12 hours by train. The Airboat Line flew only 1,205 passengers that first year. Soon, though, more people were traveling by air than rail. In 2008, airlines carried 650 million passengers from one U.S. city to another.

Airplanes dramatically decreased travel time, though passengers may not always feel that way as they move through airport security checkpoints. Terrorist threats in the 21st century have caused airports to tighten security.

New Mass Media Other innovations gave rise to new **mass media**, or means of communicating with large audiences. One form of mass media was the motion picture. In 1914, most Americans had never seen a full-length movie. But during the 1920s, going to the movies became a national pastime. It still is. In 2009, Americans bought 1.47 billion movie tickets.

The next new mass media was radio. The nation's first commercial radio stations began broadcasting in 1920. Families were soon organizing their lives so that they could hear their favorite radio programs. By 1945, nearly every American home had a radio set. But by then, another new media had appeared: television.

In 1946, the first regularly scheduled television programs began broadcasting. The new media offered viewers a window on the world. It also entertained them. By 2010, the average American was watching more than four and a half hours of television a day. Altogether, Americans spend 250 billion hours a year watching TV.

29.4 America's Changing Economy

When the first gas-powered cars appeared in the late 1800s, the United States was still a nation of farms. By the time Model Ts began rolling off Ford's assembly line, the Industrial Revolution had shifted the economy from agriculture to manufacturing. More economic changes lay ahead.

From a Manufacturing to a Service Economy The next major change was a shift from a manufacturing to a service economy. After growing for decades, the number of factory jobs began to shrink after 1960. About 30 percent of the workforce had factory jobs that year. By 2009, only 9 percent of workers were employed in factories.

An assembly line operated by robots puts pickup trucks together at a U.S. auto plant. Automated factories have helped change the way Americans work. Lower labor costs overseas are another factor contributing to the shift from manufacturing to service jobs.

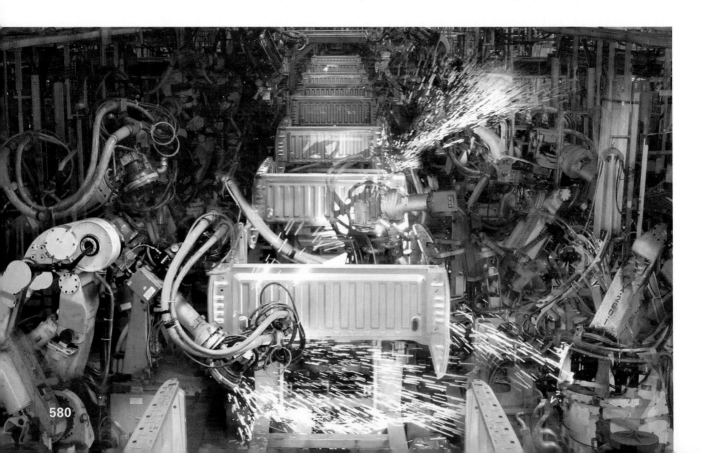

Several factors contributed to this shift. One was automation. **Automation** involves replacing workers with machines. In automobile plants, for example, robots took over jobs once done by people.

A second factor was the growth of worldwide trade, part of a **trend** known as **globalization**. This trend began in 1947 with the General Agreement on Tariffs and Trade (GATT). Over the next half-century, GATT removed trade barriers between nations. As cross-border trade became easier, many U.S. companies moved factories to countries with lower labor costs. This left fewer manufacturing jobs in the United States.

Many workers who lost factory jobs found work in the **service sector,** the part of the economy that provides services rather than goods. Service workers include teachers, doctors, mechanics, and salespeople. By 2010, about 36 percent of the workforce held jobs in the service sector.

The Rise of Knowledge Workers The growing service sector also includes knowledge workers. **Knowledge workers** create and work with ideas and information. Examples include writers, scientists, and engineers. In 1914, knowledge workers were a small part of the workforce. Today, about a third of all workers are knowledge workers.

The rise of knowledge workers was assisted by the invention of the computer. In 1981, the first personal computers (PCs) appeared in offices. PCs put vast amounts of information at a worker's fingertips.

PCs became even more useful in the 1990s when they were linked together via the Internet and World Wide Web. When the Web was opened up to the public in 1991, few U.S. households had Internet access. By 2007, close to two-thirds did. With this shift, the U.S. economy had entered an "information age."

globalization an increase in the flow of people, money, ideas, and trade goods across national boundaries

service sector the part of the economy that provides services instead of producing goods

knowledge worker a person whose main job is working with ideas, information, and technology

Americans born after 1991 have never known a world without the Internet. They consider devices such as computerized phones with Web access and hundreds of thousands of applications a part of everyday life.

29.5 The United States Enters the World Stage

In 1914, war broke out in Europe. The United States entered the war in early 1917. Eight million people would die before the guns finally fell silent in 1918.

Here, U.S. ambassador to the United Nations Susan Rice speaks at the UN. The United Nations was formed in 1945, immediately after World War II, as an international organization dedicated to promoting world peace and security. Today, nearly every country is a member of the UN.

Two World Wars World War I marked America's entry onto the world stage as a major power. When the war ended, Americans hoped it would be the "war to end all wars." These hopes vanished when a second global conflict broke out in 1939.

The United States stayed out of this war for two years. Then, on December 7, 1941, Japanese warplanes attacked a U.S. naval base in Pearl Harbor, Hawaii. The growing conflict soon engulfed most of Europe and Asia. World War II finally ended when the United States dropped atomic bombs on two Japanese cities. After witnessing the destruction caused by this terrifying new weapon, Japan surrendered.

At the war's end, the United States took the lead in founding a new world organization, the United Nations. The primary purpose of the UN is "to maintain international peace." By 2010, the UN had grown from its 51 founding members in 1945 to 192 member nations.

Cold War Conflicts Two nations emerged from World War II as superpowers: the United States and the Soviet Union. By 1947, these two superpowers were locked in a grim struggle for power. Americans saw this struggle as a fight for freedom and democracy. The Soviet Union saw it as a fight to expand communism. **Communism** is an economic or political system in which the government owns all property and controls the economy. Because this struggle was waged without warfare, it is called the Cold War.

The Cold War lasted 44 years. During this time, the United States sent troops to two Asian nations to stop the spread of communism. The Korean War (1950–1953) left the Korean Peninsula divided into two countries, a communist North Korea and a noncommunist South Korea. The Vietnam War (1954–1975) ended with communists taking control of Vietnam.

In 1991, the Soviet Union collapsed, breaking apart to form 15 new nations. This event ended the Cold War and left the United States as the world's sole remaining superpower.

communism an economic or political system in which the government owns all property and controls economic activity

Facing New Global Challenges

Since 1991, the United States has turned its attention to new global challenges. It has, for example, joined with other nations to assist the billion people around the world who live on less than $1.25 a day.

On September 11, 2001, a shocked nation watched as passenger planes hijacked by terrorists flew into the two World Trade Center towers in New York City and the Pentagon in Washington, D.C. In response, President George W. Bush declared a "war on terror." That war has taken U.S. troops into Iraq and Afghanistan. In both countries, U.S. forces have worked to root out groups committed to the destruction of the United States and its allies.

The United States is also working with other nations to deal with climate change. In 1988, the public became concerned about scientists' observations that Earth's climate was growing warmer at an alarming rate. The main reason for this warming, they suggested, is the burning of fuels such as oil, gas, and coal that release carbon dioxide into the atmosphere. As Earth gets hotter, they warned, disasters like hurricanes, floods, and droughts may become more frequent. Preventing such disasters has become one of the greatest global challenges of the 21st century.

A team from the University of Michigan celebrates winning the North American Solar Car Challenge, a cross-country competition to build and race solar-powered cars. Finding new sources of energy is one of the challenges Americans face today.

Chapter Summary

In this chapter, you learned about some of the changes that have shaped life in the United States since 1914.

Securing Equal Rights and Opportunities In 1914, white men dominated the workforce and political life. After much struggle, women and men of all races have won the right to vote and compete as equals in all areas of life.

Innovations Change Daily Life Cars and airplanes made travel faster and easier. Motion pictures created a new form of entertainment. Radio and television brought the world into every home.

America's Changing Economy During the first half of the last century, the United States shifted from an agricultural to an industrial economy. During the second half, it shifted again to a service economy. By the dawn of the 21st century, the economy had entered an information age.

The United States Enters the World Stage In 1914, the United States was just beginning to move onto the world stage. By the turn of the 21st century, it was the world's sole superpower. In the 21st century, new ideas and challenges will continue to change the way we live.

Questions for the Future

Protecting the Earth? Essential. Feeding the people who live here? Also essential. How to do both at the same time is a harder question to answer. Since the 1960s, this challenge has perplexed both the world's most dedicated environmentalists and its best agricultural scientists.

Rachel Carson talked directly to the American people. "We still haven't become mature enough to think of ourselves as only a tiny part of a vast and incredible universe," she cautioned.

Can a book change the world? Rachel Carson did not dare hope that it could. But she wrote *Silent Spring* anyway and crossed her fingers. The book, published in 1962, alerted Americans to the dangers of pesticides. Carson argued that the chemical industry, in their eagerness to stop insects from destroying crops, had exposed plants, animals, and people to poisons. The effects, she warned, would be disastrous.

Carson was a scientist and writer who loved nature. At a time when few women had careers outside the home, Carson earned an advanced degree in marine biology. She went on to write popular books about science.

But *Silent Spring* was unique. In it, Carson criticized the big chemical companies that made pesticides. She also criticized the farmers who used them profusely, as well as the politicians who approved their use to clear public places of bugs. She suggested that by trying to control nature, people risked their own survival.

Carson feared that her position would be very unpopular. In the early 1960s, many Americans put great faith in science. They were likely to accept that whatever scientists thought was a good idea was, in fact, a good idea. Few people thought about protecting the natural environment.

Nonetheless, *Silent Spring* made a huge splash. A lot of Americans were ready for its message, no matter how disturbing it was. The book was a best seller. In just a few months, it had sold 100,000 copies. After its publication, many states introduced bills to regulate pesticides.

Positive reaction to the book was matched by negative reaction, however. Some scientists criticized Carson's lack of objectivity. Many said that chemicals were completely safe and posed no health risks. Some critics even attacked Carson personally and called her a fanatic.

Perhaps Carson's most famous critic was Norman Borlaug. Borlaug, too, was a scientist. He devoted his life to developing crops that could produce more food for people. His plants needed pesticides, but they yielded much more produce than ordinary plants. Borlaug charged that Carson was one of "the people who do not want to eradicate [eliminate] hunger."

For the past 50 years, tensions have simmered between environmentalists like Carson and agricultural scientists like Borlaug. They continue today.

Before *Silent Spring*

Rachel Carson was not the first American to worry about the natural environment. Conservation efforts preceded her by decades. Long before *Silent Spring,* some Americans—even a president—began protecting nature.

Concern about the environment took root as American industry took root. After the Civil War, industrialization began to create the modern world. Factories made products for people to buy. Cities grew. Streetcars, subways, running water—they all got their start as the 19th century ended and the 20th century began.

Progress came at a price, however. Factories put smoke into the air and waste into the water. Cities spread over wilderness or were created on new land that had once been swamps. The need for fresh water sometimes led to drastic action. When Chicago's waste threatened the water supply, for example, engineers reversed the flow of the Chicago River.

These changes alarmed some Americans. They feared that nature would be destroyed if development continued unchecked. President Theodore Roosevelt, a nature lover himself, listened to the fears and took action. In 1905, he created the U.S. Forest Service. The agency set aside large tracts of forest that could not be logged. In addition, a system of national parks gave Americans places to go where they could enjoy nature.

But American industry continued to grow. During and after World War II, the United States led the world in car manufacturing. It took the lead in chemistry and medical research, too. It seemed like Americans could do just about anything.

That was the context in which Rachel Carson wrote and published *Silent Spring.* It is not surprising that the book stirred so much controversy. Many Americans wanted to believe that progress could continue without any negative effects. *Silent Spring* said that simply was not true.

In areas like Silicon Valley in California, cornfields (top) have been replaced by busy industrial centers (bottom). Environmentalists like Rachel Carson worried that people did not take into account the ways that growth affects the natural world.

Researchers came from around the world to study with Norman Borlaug (left front). In this experimental wheat field in Mexico, he spoke about advanced growing techniques. "The three major inputs for raising wheat yields," one farmer said, "are farmers, improved seed and Borlaug."

The Green Revolution Feeds the World

When Rachel Carson began speaking out for nature, Norman Borlaug had already spent nearly two decades looking for ways to feed the hungry. He called Carson an "evil force." He believed that she would rather protect nature than make sure people had enough to eat.

Borlaug spent his whole life developing high-yield crops. *High-yield* refers to crops that are designed to produce more on less land than ordinary crops. In the 1940s, Borlaug learned about a type of high-yield wheat, called dwarf wheat. Dwarf wheat produced more edible grain than other types of wheat. It was also easier to harvest. Borlaug crossed it with a strain of wheat that resists harmful fungus. Borlaug's dwarf wheat was a high-yield crop that changed the world.

In addition to contributing to the science of ending hunger, Borlaug contributed to the politics. He used his status to encourage governments around the world to use high-yield farming techniques. The effects of his work are impressive. In 1950, the world produced 692 million tons of grain on 1.7 billion acres of land. In 1992, 1.9 billion tons of grain were grown on 1.73 billion acres. That means that with a little more than 1 percent more land, production increased 170 percent.

For his efforts, Borlaug is known as the father of the Green Revolution. In 1970, he won the Nobel Peace Prize for his work. Borlaug and his supporters said that the Green Revolution prevented as many as a billion people from starving. Some people have said that Borlaug "saved more lives than any other person who has ever lived."

Borlaug scorned environmentalists. How could they, he wondered, refuse high-yield crops to countries where people were starving? Environmentalists angered him. He said,

> *If they lived just one month amid the misery of the developing world, as I have for fifty years, they'd be crying out for tractors and fertilizer and irrigation canals and be outraged that [people] back home were trying to deny them these things.*

Borlaug believed that the effects of pesticides and chemical fertilizers were minimal. His choice was clear: feed the hungry.

An Ongoing Debate

Now, decades into the Green Revolution, people around the world must wrestle with the same question that haunted Norman Borlaug and Rachel Carson. How can we feed a growing population and at the same time take care of a fragile Earth?

The people who grow food think about this question. Some of them work for agribusiness companies. These companies are large-scale farming outfits. They use pesticides and chemical fertilizers to increase production. Agribusiness leaders say that using less land to produce more will protect forests that would otherwise be cut down to make farmland. They also say their crops are necessary to feed the world's growing population.

Other food growers think about the question differently and support organic farming. Organic farmers use only natural materials to grow crops—no pesticides and no chemical fertilizers. Organic farmers say that high-yield crops are not sustainable. They pollute the land and the water, and they threaten world water supplies. Growing high-yield crops, they say, may make it impossible for future generations to continue farming the land. Organic farmers say their techniques can provide enough food for the people on Earth today—and those who will be here in the future.

But it is not just food growers who need to think about the problems of farming techniques. Everyone who eats—and that means all of us—needs to think about it, too. We address the question of balancing environmental well-being and feeding the world by deciding what kind of food to buy. More and more Americans are choosing locally grown, organic products. Still, most Americans buy food grown with high-yield techniques.

Those of us who live in the United States have the luxury of thinking about how to balance our concern with the environment and our concern with humankind. In other parts of the world, where hunger is a daily problem, it is a question of life and death. People need solutions, and they need them now.

Hunger is not going away. Neither is the need for a healthy Earth. The problem of how to feed people and care for the planet is a problem today and will be one in the future. What is the answer? That remains to be seen. As you get older, you will join in the debates—or you may have already. Perhaps, one day, you will be part of the solution.

Across the United States, farmers' markets make farm-fresh food available in cities. Here, First Lady Michelle Obama and a White House chef shop at a new farmers' market in Washington, D.C.

A Modern Nation Emerges

1867

U.S. Purchase of Alaska

Many Americans originally thought of this acquisition as a "folly," but the nation soon discovered a wealth of resources in Alaska.

1890

Congress Creates Yosemite National Park

The preservation of Yosemite in California is one of the first major victories in a national conservation movement to protect the American wilderness for future generations.

1898

Spanish-American War

The United States enters a four-month-long war with Spain. After a U.S. victory, Cuba declares independence from Spain, and Puerto Rico and the Philippines come under U.S. rule. A revolt against the United States in the Philippines lasts three more years. The Philippines become independent in 1946.

| 1860 | 1865 | 1870 | 1875 | 1880 | 1885 | 1890 |

1870s

The Grange Promotes the Farmers' Cause

This self-help organization for farmers becomes a major force in politics and reform during the 1870s.

1898

U.S. Annexation of Hawaii

After years of debate, the United States makes Hawaii a territory with the support of President McKinley. Queen Liliuokalani is the last Hawaiian monarch to rule the islands.

1901
Andrew Carnegie Becomes Philanthropist
Andrew Carnegie sells his steel company for $250 million and retires to a life of philanthropy. He and other industrialists, like John D. Rockefeller, use their fortunes to build universities, hospitals, libraries, and concert halls to benefit the American people.

1909
Child Labor Draws to a Close
By year's end, 43 of the nation's 46 states outlaw child labor.

1911
U.S. Government Breaks Up Standard Oil
President Roosevelt has John D. Rockefeller and his company investigated for unfair practices. The company's monopoly of the oil industry ends, and many other companies' monopolies over other industries are investigated.

1920
Nineteenth Amendment Ratified
Ratification of the Nineteenth Amendment grants women the right to vote.

| 1890 | 1895 | 1900 | 1905 | 1910 | 1915 | 1920 |

1903
United States Takes Over Canal Zone

Panama cedes a 10-mile-wide "canal zone" to the United States. During the next two decades, the United States oversees the construction of the Panama Canal, which opens in 1921.

1909
Founding of the NAACP

W. E. B. Du Bois and other civil rights activists found the National Association for the Advancement of Colored People to ensure equal rights and opportunity for all African Americans.

1917
United States Enters World War I
U.S. forces side with and ultimately bring victory for the Allied powers. Three years later, the U.S. Senate tries to avoid involvement in future wars by rejecting the Treaty of Versailles, pushing the nation once again toward isolationism.

Resources

This replica of an 1800s one-room schoolhouse
is in Sacramento, California.

The Declaration of Independence

In Congress, July 4, 1776
The unanimous Declaration of the thirteen united States of America

When in the Course of human events it becomes necessary for one people to dissolve the political bands which have connected them with another, and to assume among the powers of the earth, the separate and equal station to which the Laws of Nature and of Nature's God entitle them, a decent respect to the opinions of mankind requires that they should declare the causes which impel them to the separation.

We hold these truths to be self-evident, that all men are created equal, that they are endowed by their Creator with certain **unalienable** Rights, that among these are Life, Liberty and the pursuit of Happiness. —That to secure these rights, Governments are instituted among Men, deriving their just powers from the consent of the governed, —That whenever any Form of Government becomes destructive of these ends, it is the Right of the People to alter or to abolish it, and to institute new Government, laying its foundation on such principles and organizing its powers in such form, as to them shall seem most likely to effect their Safety and Happiness. **Prudence**, indeed, will dictate that Governments long established should not be changed for light and **transient** causes; and accordingly all experience hath shewn, that mankind are more disposed to suffer, while evils are sufferable, than to right themselves by abolishing the forms to which they are accustomed. But when a long train of abuses and **usurpations**, pursuing invariably the same Object **evinces** a design to reduce them under absolute **Despotism**, it is their right, it is their duty, to throw off such Government, and to provide new Guards for their future security. —Such has been the patient sufferance of these Colonies; and such is now the necessity which **constrains** them to alter their former Systems of Government. The history of the present King of Great Britain is a history of repeated injuries and usurpations, all having in direct object the establishment of an absolute **Tyranny** over these States. To prove this, let Facts be submitted to a **candid** world.

He has refused his **Assent** to Laws, the most wholesome and necessary for the public good.

He has forbidden his Governors to pass Laws of immediate and pressing importance, unless **suspended** in their operation till his Assent should be obtained; and when so suspended, he has utterly neglected to attend to them.

The Declaration begins by explaining the document's purpose and setting a principled tone. The idea that people had the right to rebel against an oppressive government was not new. The Declaration's purpose was to show the world that Americans were justified in exercising this right.

Statement of Human Rights
The section presents a logical argument. It begins with what it calls "self-evident truths" and proceeds systematically to the need for revolution. Jefferson's forceful and eloquent words still stand as an enduring statement of America's founding ideals.

unalienable: undeniable

prudence: common sense

transient: passing, fleeting

usurpations: unlawful power grabs

evinces: shows evidence of

despotism: rule by a dictator

constrains: forces, compels

tyranny: unjust government

candid: honest, open

Statement of Charges Against the King
To persuade undecided colonists to support independence, Jefferson lists more than 20 grievances as proof of the king's unjust treatment of the colonies.

assent: approval

suspended: temporarily stopped

He has refused to pass other Laws for the accommodation of large districts of people, unless those people would relinquish the right of Representation in the Legislature, a right **inestimable** to them and **formidable** to tyrants only.

He has called together legislative bodies at places unusual, uncomfortable, and distant from the **depository** of their Public Records, for the sole purpose of fatiguing them into compliance with his measures. He has **dissolved** Representative Houses repeatedly, for opposing with manly firmness his invasions on the rights of the people.

He has refused for a long time, after such dissolutions, to cause others to be elected, whereby the Legislative Powers, incapable of **Annihilation,** have returned to the People at large for their exercise; the State remaining in the mean time exposed to all the dangers of invasion from without, and **convulsions** within.

He has **endeavoured** to prevent the population of these States; for that purpose obstructing the Laws for **Naturalization** of Foreigners; refusing to pass others to encourage their migrations hither, and raising the conditions of new **Appropriations** of Lands.

He has **obstructed** the Administration of Justice, by refusing his Assent to Laws for establishing **Judiciary Powers**.

He has made Judges dependent on his Will alone, for the **tenure** of their **offices,** and the amount and payment of their salaries.

He has erected a multitude of New Offices, and sent hither swarms of Officers to harass our people and eat out their substance.

He has kept among us, in times of peace, Standing Armies without the Consent of our legislatures.

He has affected to render the Military independent of and superior to the Civil Power.

He has **combined with others** to subject us to a **jurisdiction** foreign to our constitution, and unacknowledged by our laws; giving his Assent to their Acts of pretended Legislation:

For **Quartering** large bodies of armed troops among us:

For protecting them, by a **mock** Trial, from punishment for any Murders which they should commit on the Inhabitants of these States:

For cutting off our Trade with all parts of the world:

For imposing Taxes on us without our Consent:

For depriving us in many cases, of the benefit of Trial by Jury:

For transporting us beyond Seas to be tried for pretended offences:

inestimable: invaluable

formidable: alarming

depository: storage site

dissolved: disbanded, broken up

annihilation: destruction

convulsions: disturbances

endeavoured: tried

naturalization: becoming a citizen

appropriations: distributions

obstructed: blocked

judiciary powers: courts of law

tenure: right to hold

offices: government jobs

combined with others: worked with Parliament

jurisdiction: authority

quartering: housing

mock: fake

For abolishing the free System of English Laws in a **neighbouring Province,** establishing therein an **Arbitrary** government, and enlarging its Boundaries so as to render it at once an example and fit instrument for introducing the same absolute rule into these Colonies:

For taking away our Charters, abolishing our most valuable Laws, and altering fundamentally the Forms of our Governments:

For suspending our own Legislatures, and declaring themselves invested with power to legislate for us in all cases whatsoever.

He has **abdicated** Government here, by declaring us out of his Protection and waging War against us.

He has plundered our seas, ravaged our Coasts, burnt our towns, and destroyed the lives of our people.

He is at this time transporting large Armies of foreign **Mercenaries** to compleat the works of death, desolation and tyranny, already begun with circumstances of Cruelty & **perfidy** scarcely paralleled in the most barbarous ages, and totally unworthy the Head of a civilized nation.

He has constrained our fellow Citizens taken Captive on the high Seas to bear Arms against their Country, to become the executioners of their friends and Brethren, or to fall themselves by their Hands.

He has excited domestic **insurrections** amongst us, and has endeavoured to bring on the inhabitants of our frontiers, the merciless Indian Savages, whose known rule of warfare, is an undistinguished destruction of all ages, sexes and conditions.

In every stage of these Oppressions We have **Petitioned** for **Redress** in the most humble terms: Our repeated Petitions have been answered only by repeated injury. A Prince whose character is thus marked by every act which may define a Tyrant, is unfit to be the ruler of a free people.

Nor have We been wanting in attentions to our British brethren. We have warned them from time to time of attempts by their legislature to extend an **unwarrantable** jurisdiction over us. We have reminded them of the circumstances of our emigration and settlement here. We have appealed to their native justice and **magnanimity,** and we have **conjured** them by the ties of our common **kindred,** to **disavow** these usurpations, which, would inevitably interrupt our connections and correspondence. They too have been deaf to the voice of justice and

neighbouring province: Canada

arbitrary: with unlimited power

abdicated: abandoned

mercenaries: hired soldiers

perfidy: deceit, treachery

insurrections: rebellions

The Government's Failure to Answer the Colonists' Complaints
In this section, Jefferson denounces the British people for their indifference to the colonists' plight. American leaders had petitioned the king and Parliament, but their efforts to advance their cause had met with little sympathy among their "British brethren."

petitioned: asked in writing

redress: the righting of wrongs

unwarrantable: unjustified

magnanimity: generosity

conjured: pleaded with

kindred: family relationships

disavow: publicly condemn

of **consanguinity**. We must, therefore, **acquiesce** in the necessity, which **denounces** our Separation, and hold them, as we hold the rest of mankind, Enemies in War, in Peace Friends.

We, therefore, the Representatives of the united States of America, in General Congress, Assembled, appealing to the Supreme Judge of the world for the **rectitude** of our intentions, do, in the Name, and by Authority of the good People of these Colonies, solemnly publish and declare, That these United Colonies are, and of Right ought to be Free and Independent States; that they are **Absolved** from all Allegiance to the British Crown, and that all political connection between them and the State of Great Britain, is and ought to be totally dissolved; and that as Free and Independent States, they have full Power to levy War, conclude Peace, contract Alliances, establish Commerce, and to do all other Acts and Things which Independent States may of right do. —And for the support of this Declaration, with a firm reliance on the protection of divine Providence, we mutually pledge to each other our Lives, our Fortunes and our sacred Honor.

The foregoing Declaration was, by order of Congress, **engrossed** on parchment, and signed by the 56 members.

New Hampshire
Josiah Bartlett, William Whipple, Matthew Thornton

Massachusetts
John Hancock, Samuel Adams, John Adams, Robert Treat Paine, Elbridge Gerry

Rhode Island
Stephen Hopkins, William Ellery

Connecticut
Roger Sherman, Samuel Huntington, William Williams, Oliver Wolcott

New York
William Floyd, Philip Livingston, Francis Lewis, Lewis Morris

New Jersey
Richard Stockton, John Witherspoon, Francis Hopkinson, John Hart, Abraham Clark

Pennsylvania
Robert Morris, Benjamin Rush, Benjamin Franklin, John Morton, George Clymer, James Smith, George Taylor, James Wilson, George Ross

Delaware
Caesar Rodney, George Read, Thomas McKean

Maryland
Samuel Chase, William Paca, Thomas Stone, Charles Carroll of Carrollton

Virginia
George Wythe, Richard Henry Lee, Thomas Jefferson, Benjamin Harrison, Thomas Nelson Jr., Francis Lightfoot Lee, Carter Braxton

North Carolina
William Hooper, Joseph Hewes, John Penn

South Carolina
Edward Rutledge, Thomas Heyward Jr., Thomas Lynch Jr., Arthur Middleton

Georgia
Button Gwinnett, Lyman Hall, George Walton

consanguinity: blood ties

acquiesce: agree

denounces: formally announces

Statement of Independence
In the conclusion, Congress formally declares independence on behalf of the people of the colonies. The signers' final pledge of their "sacred Honor" was a most solemn vow at a time when honor was highly prized.

rectitude: righteousness

absolved: released

engrossed: copied in large, clear handwriting

Delegates to the Constitutional Convention, 1787
John Hancock, a revolutionary leader from Massachusetts, was the first person to sign the engrossed Declaration of Independence. His bold signature is so widely known that when people today sign a document, they are said to be adding their "John Hancock."

The Constitution of the United States

This version of the Constitution retains the original text, spellings, and capitalizations. Parts of the Constitution that have been changed through amendment have been crossed out.

We the People of the United States, in Order to form a more perfect Union, establish Justice, insure domestic Tranquility, provide for the common defence, promote the general Welfare, and secure the Blessings of Liberty to ourselves and our Posterity, do ordain and establish this Constitution for the United States of America.

ARTICLE I.
Section 1.
All legislative Powers herein granted shall be vested in a Congress of the United States, which shall consist of a Senate and House of Representatives.

Section 2.
The House of Representatives shall be composed of Members chosen every second Year by the People of the several States, and the Electors in each State shall have the Qualifications requisite for Electors of the most numerous Branch of the State Legislature.

No Person shall be a Representative who shall not have attained to the Age of twenty five Years, and been seven Years a Citizen of the United States, and who shall not, when elected, be an Inhabitant of that State in which he shall be chosen.

Representatives and ~~direct Taxes~~ shall be apportioned among the several States which may be included within this Union, according to their respective Numbers, ~~which shall be determined by adding to the whole Number of free Persons, including those bound to Service for a Term of Years, and excluding Indians not taxed, three fifths of all other Persons.~~ The actual Enumeration shall be made within three Years after the first Meeting of the Congress of the United States, and within every subsequent Term of ten Years, in such Manner as they shall by Law direct. The Number of Representatives shall not exceed one for every thirty Thousand, but each State shall have at Least one Representative; and until such enumeration shall be made, the State of New Hampshire shall be entitled to chuse [choose] three, Massachusetts eight, Rhode Island and Providence Plantations one, Connecticut five, New York six, New Jersey four, Pennsylvania eight, Delaware one, Maryland six, Virginia ten, North Carolina five, South Carolina five, and Georgia three.

These annotations will help you understand the Constitution.

Preamble
The Preamble states that the federal government gains its power from the people, not the states, and lists the purposes of the government.

ARTICLE I: LEGISLATIVE BRANCH
Section 1: Two-Part Congress
The power to make laws is granted to Congress, which consists of the Senate and the House of Representatives.

Section 2:
House of Representatives
Clause 1: Election Members of the House of Representatives are elected by the people every two years. *Electors* refers to voters.

Clause 2: Qualifications A member of the House must be at least 25 years old, an American citizen for seven years, and live in the state he or she represents.

Clause 3: Apportionment The number of Representatives from each state is based on the state's population. An *enumeration,* or census, must be taken every 10 years to determine that population. The total number of Representatives in the House is now fixed at 435.

When vacancies happen in the Representation from any State, the Executive Authority thereof shall issue Writs of Election to fill such Vacancies.

The House of Representatives shall chuse [choose] their Speaker and other Officers; and shall have the sole Power of Impeachment.

Section 3.

The Senate of the United States shall be composed of two Senators from each State, chosen by the Legislature thereof, for six Years; and each Senator shall have one Vote.

Immediately after they shall be assembled in Consequence of the first Election, they shall be divided as equally as may be into three Classes. The Seats of the Senators of the first Class shall be vacated at the Expiration of the second Year, of the second Class at the Expiration of the fourth Year, and of the third Class at the Expiration of the sixth Year, so that one-third may be chosen every second Year; and if Vacancies happen by Resignation, or otherwise, during the Recess of the Legislature of any State, the Executive thereof may make temporary Appointments until the next Meeting of the Legislature, which shall then fill such Vacancies.

No Person shall be a Senator who shall not have attained to the Age of thirty Years, and been nine Years a Citizen of the United States, and who shall not, when elected, be an Inhabitant of that State for which he shall be chosen.

The Vice President of the United States shall be President of the Senate, but shall have no Vote, unless they be equally divided.

The Senate shall chuse [choose] their other Officers, and also a President pro tempore, in the Absence of the Vice President, or when he shall exercise the Office of President of the United States.

Clause 4: Vacancies If a representative resigns or dies in office, the governor of that state can issue a "Writ of Election," calling for a special election to fill the vacancy.

Clause 5: Officers and Impeachment Power The House elects a speaker, who normally comes from the majority party. Only the House has the power to impeach, or accuse, a federal official of wrongdoing.

Section 3: Senate
Clause 1: Election Each state is represented by two senators, who serve six-year terms. Until 1913, state legislatures elected senators. Since the passage of the 17th Amendment, people now directly elect their senators.

Clause 2: Terms and Classification To ensure continuity in the Senate, one-third of the senators run for reelection every two years.

Clause 3: Qualifications A senator must be at least 30 years old, an American citizen for nine years, and must live in the state he or she represents.

Clause 4: President of the Senate The vice president presides over the Senate but votes only in event of a tie.

Clause 5: Other Officers The Senate selects its other leaders and may also select a temporary ("pro tempore") president if the vice president is absent.

The Senate shall have the sole Power to try all Impeachments. When sitting for that Purpose, they shall be on Oath or Affirmation. When the President of the United States is tried, the Chief Justice shall preside: And no Person shall be convicted without the Concurrence of two thirds of the Members present.

Judgment in Cases of Impeachment shall not extend further than to removal from Office, and disqualification to hold and enjoy any Office of honor, Trust or Profit under the United States: but the Party convicted shall nevertheless be liable and subject to Indictment, Trial, Judgment and Punishment, according to Law.

Section 4.

The Times, Places and Manner of holding Elections for Senators and Representatives, shall be prescribed in each State by the Legislature thereof; but the Congress may at any time by Law make or alter such Regulations, except as to the Places of chusing [choosing] Senators.

The Congress shall assemble at least once in every Year, ~~and such Meeting shall be on the first Monday in December~~, unless they shall by Law appoint a different Day.

Section 5.

Each House shall be the Judge of the Elections, Returns and Qualifications of its own Members, and a Majority of each shall constitute a Quorum to do Business, but a smaller Number may adjourn from day to day, and may be authorized to compel the Attendance of absent Members, in such Manner, and under such Penalties as each House may provide.

Each House may determine the Rules of its Proceedings, punish its Members for disorderly Behaviour, and, with the Concurrence of two thirds, expel a Member.

Each House shall keep a Journal of its Proceedings, and from time to time publish the same, excepting such Parts as may in their Judgment require Secrecy; and the Yeas and Nays of the Members of either House on any question shall, at the Desire of one fifth of those Present, be entered on the Journal.

Clause 6: Impeachment Trials Only the Senate has the power to put impeached federal officials on trial. When an impeached president is tried, the chief justice of the Supreme Court acts as the trial judge. A two-thirds vote of the senators present is required to convict. Congress has used its impeachment power sparingly.

Clause 7: Penalty Upon Conviction A federal official convicted by the Senate is removed from office. The Senate may bar him or her from future office but may not impose further punishment.

Section 4: Elections and Meetings
Clause 1: Elections States regulate their own congressional elections, but Congress may make laws changing the regulations.

Clause 2: Sessions Congress must meet at least once a year. The Twentieth Amendment (1933) moved the opening day of Congress to January 3.

Section 5:
Congressional Proceedings
Clause 1: Attendance Each house judges whether its members are qualified and have been elected fairly. A majority of members of either house must be present for that house to conduct legislative business. This minimum required number is called a *quorum*.

Clause 2: Rules Each house makes its own rules of conduct for its members.

Clause 3: Records Both houses keep a journal of their proceedings. It is published as the *Congressional Record*.

Neither House, during the Session of Congress, shall, without the Consent of the other, adjourn for more than three days, nor to any other Place than that in which the two Houses shall be sitting.

Section 6.

The Senators and Representatives shall receive a Compensation for their Services, to be ascertained by Law, and paid out of the Treasury of the United States. They shall in all Cases, except Treason, Felony and Breach of the Peace, be privileged from Arrest during their Attendance at the Session of their respective Houses, and in going to and returning from the same; and for any Speech or Debate in either House, they shall not be questioned in any other Place.

No Senator or Representative shall, during the Time for which he was elected, be appointed to any civil Office under the Authority of the United States, which shall have been created, or the Emoluments whereof shall have been encreased during such time; and no Person holding any Office under the United States, shall be a Member of either House during his Continuance in Office.

Section 7.

All Bills for raising Revenue shall originate in the House of Representatives; but the Senate may propose or concur with Amendments as on other Bills.

Every Bill which shall have passed the House of Representatives and the Senate, shall, before it become a Law, be presented to the President of the United States; If he approve he shall sign it, but if not he shall return it, with his Objections to that House in which it shall have originated, who shall enter the Objections at large on their Journal, and proceed to reconsider it. If after such Reconsideration two thirds of that House shall agree to pass the Bill, it shall be sent, together with the Objections, to the other House, by which it shall likewise be reconsidered, and if approved by two thirds of that House, it shall become a Law. But in all such Cases the Votes of both Houses shall be determined by Yeas and Nays, and the Names of the Persons voting for and against the Bill shall be entered on the Journal of each House respectively. If any Bill shall not be returned by the President within ten Days (Sundays excepted) after it shall have been presented to him, the Same shall be a Law, in like Manner as if he had signed it, unless the Congress by their Adjournment prevent its Return, in which Case it shall not be a Law.

Clause 4: Adjournment During a session, neither house can close down or hold meetings elsewhere for a period of more than three days without the approval of the other house.

Section 6: Compensation, Immunity, and Restrictions
Clause 1: Salaries and Immunity Members of Congress set their own pay and are paid out of the U.S. Treasury. Legislators may not be sued or prosecuted for their speeches and actions on the floor of Congress.

Clause 2: Employment Restrictions To ensure separation of powers, members of Congress may not hold any other federal office during their terms as legislators.

Section 7: Making Laws
Clause 1: Revenue Bills Only the House can propose a law raising taxes, though the Senate can offer changes. This provision ensures that people are not taxed without their consent.

Clause 2: Submitting Bills to the President A *bill* is a proposed law. A bill that has been passed by both houses of Congress must be sent to the president. The president can sign the bill, which makes it a law. The president may veto the bill, which returns it to the house where it was first drafted. The president may allow the bill to become law without signing it, by not taking any action on it within 10 days of getting it from Congress, not counting Sundays. But if Congress ends its session during those 10 days, the bill does not become law and the president is said to have used the "pocket veto." Congress may overrule a veto by a two-thirds vote in each house.

Every Order, Resolution, or Vote to which the Concurrence of the Senate and House of Representatives may be necessary (except on a question of Adjournment) shall be presented to the President of the United States; and before the Same shall take Effect, shall be approved by him, or being disapproved by him, shall be repassed by two thirds of the Senate and House of Representatives, according to the Rules and Limitations prescribed in the Case of a Bill.

Section 8.
The Congress shall have Power

To lay and collect Taxes, Duties, Imposts and Excises, to pay the Debts and provide for the common Defence and general Welfare of the United States; but all Duties, Imposts and Excises shall be uniform throughout the United States;

To borrow Money on the credit of the United States;

To regulate Commerce with foreign Nations, and among the several States, and with the Indian Tribes;

To establish an uniform Rule of Naturalization, and uniform Laws on the subject of Bankruptcies throughout the United States;

To coin Money, regulate the Value thereof, and of foreign Coin, and fix the Standard of Weights and Measures;

To provide for the Punishment of counterfeiting the Securities and current Coin of the United States;

To establish Post Offices and post Roads;

To promote the Progress of Science and useful Arts, by securing for limited Times to Authors and Inventors the exclusive Right to their respective Writings and Discoveries;

Clause 3: Submitting Other Measures Other measures approved by Congress also require the president's approval or may also be passed over the president's veto.

Section 8: Powers of Congress Congress has the specific powers listed in this section.

Clause 1: Taxation Congress has the power to levy taxes.

Clause 2: Borrowing Congress issues bonds to borrow money, creating a debt to be repaid.

Clause 3: Trade Regulation Congress regulates foreign trade and interstate commerce.

Clause 4: Naturalization and Bankruptcy Congress makes naturalization and bankruptcy laws. *Naturalization* is the process by which an immigrant becomes a U.S. citizen. *Bankruptcy* applies to individuals or companies that are unable to pay their debts.

Clause 5: Currency Congress establishes the national *currency,* or system of money.

Clause 6: Punishment for Counterfeiting Congress punishes counterfeiting, or the making of imitation money.

Clause 7: Postal Service Congress sets up the mail system.

Clause 8: Copyrights and Patents Congress passes *copyright* laws to protect authors and *patent* laws to protect inventors from theft of their work.

To constitute Tribunals inferior to the supreme Court;

To define and punish Piracies and Felonies committed on the high Seas, and Offences against the Law of Nations;

To declare War, grant Letters of Marque and Reprisal, and make Rules concerning Captures on Land and Water;

To raise and support Armies, but no Appropriation of Money to that Use shall be for a longer Term than two Years;

To provide and maintain a Navy;

To make Rules for the Government and Regulation of the land and naval Forces;

To provide for calling forth the Militia to execute the Laws of the Union, suppress Insurrections and repel Invasions;

To provide for organizing, arming, and disciplining, the Militia, and for governing such Part of them as may be employed in the Service of the United States, reserving to the States respectively, the Appointment of the Officers, and the Authority of training the Militia according to the discipline prescribed by Congress;

Clause 9: Court System Congress has the power to create a federal court system. *Inferior* means lower.

Clause 10: Crimes at Sea Congress punishes crimes at sea. Piracy was a key concern when the Constitution was written.

Clause 11: Declaring War Congress declares war. World War II was the last time Congress formally declared war. Since then Congress has usually passed resolutions giving the president the authority to use military force where necessary. Letters of Marque and Reprisal authorize *privateers,* or private ships, to attack and seize enemy vessels during times of war. The United States ceased issuing such letters during the Civil War.

Clause 12: Raising an Army Congress *appropriates*, or sets aside, funds for the military, usually on a yearly basis but never for more than two years. It also regulates the armed forces.

Clause 13: Maintaining a Navy

Clause 14: Regulating Armed Forces

Clause 15: Calling Up the Militia Congress has the power to call up *militias,* or armies of citizen soldiers, in times of emergency. Each state has its own militia, known today as the National Guard.

Clause 16: Regulating the Militia Congress regulates militias but leaves training to the states, under federal guidelines.

To exercise exclusive Legislation in all Cases whatsoever, over such District (not exceeding ten Miles square) as may, by Cession of particular States, and the Acceptance of Congress, become the Seat of the Government of the United States, and to exercise like Authority over all Places purchased by the Consent of the Legislature of the State in which the Same shall be, for the Erection of Forts, Magazines, Arsenals, dock-Yards and other needful Buildings;—And

To make all Laws which shall be necessary and proper for carrying into Execution the foregoing Powers, and all other Powers vested by this Constitution in the Government of the United States, or in any Department or Officer thereof.

Section 9.

The Migration or Importation of such Persons as any of the States now existing shall think proper to admit, shall not be prohibited by the Congress prior to the Year one thousand eight hundred and eight, but a Tax or duty may be imposed on such Importation, not exceeding ten dollars for each Person.

The Privilege of the Writ of Habeas Corpus shall not be suspended, unless when in Cases of Rebellion or Invasion the public Safety may require it.

No Bill of Attainder or ex post facto Law shall be passed.

No Capitation, or other direct, Tax shall be laid, unless in Proportion to the Census or Enumeration herein before directed to be taken.

No Tax or Duty shall be laid on Articles exported from any State.

Clause 17: Control of Federal Property Congress controls the District of Columbia and all other federal land. Congress governed Washington, D.C., until 1973, when an elected municipal government was established.

Clause 18: Elastic Clause This "necessary and proper" clause is known as the "elastic clause" because it gives Congress the flexibility to pass laws to carry out its functions and deal with new problems as they arise.

Section 9:
Limits on the Power of Congress
Clause 1: Slave Trade This clause became obsolete after 1808, when the Constitution permitted Congress to outlaw the slave trade.

Clause 2: Writ of Habeas Corpus A writ of *habeas corpus* gives prisoners the right to challenge their imprisonment in court. Congress may not suspend this right except in extreme emergencies. Habeas corpus has been suspended only rarely in the nation's history.

Clause 3: Unfair Laws This clause protects individuals from unfair laws. Congress cannot pass a law declaring a person or group guilty of a crime *(bill of attainder),* nor can it pass a law making an act illegal after it has been committed *(ex post facto law).*

Clause 4: Individual Taxes This clause banning direct taxes on individuals was voided by the Sixteenth Amendment, which permits Congress to tax individuals.

Clause 5: Taxes on Exports This clause prohibits the taxation of exported goods.

No Preference shall be given by any Regulation of Commerce or Revenue to the Ports of one State over those of another; nor shall Vessels bound to, or from, one State, be obliged to enter, clear, or pay Duties in another.

No Money shall be drawn from the Treasury, but in Consequence of Appropriations made by Law; and a regular Statement and Account of the Receipts and Expenditures of all public Money shall be published from time to time.

No Title of Nobility shall be granted by the United States: And no Person holding any Office of Profit or Trust under them, shall, without the Consent of the Congress, accept of any present, Emolument, Office, or Title, of any kind whatever, from any King, Prince, or foreign State.

Section 10.

No State shall enter into any Treaty, Alliance, or Confederation; grant Letters of Marque and Reprisal; coin Money; emit Bills of Credit; make any Thing but gold and silver Coin a Tender in Payment of Debts; pass any Bill of Attainder, ex post facto Law, or Law impairing the Obligation of Contracts, or grant any Title of Nobility.

No State shall, without the Consent of the Congress, lay any Imposts or Duties on Imports or Exports, except what may be absolutely necessary for executing its inspection Laws: and the net Produce of all Duties and Imposts, laid by any State on Imports or Exports, shall be for the Use of the Treasury of the United States; and all such Laws shall be subject to the Revision and Control of the Congress.

No State shall, without the Consent of Congress, lay any Duty of Tonnage, keep Troops, or Ships of War in time of Peace, enter into any Agreement or Compact with another State, or with a foreign Power, or engage in War, unless actually invaded, or in such imminent Danger as will not admit of delay.

ARTICLE II.
Section 1.

The executive Power shall be vested in a President of the United States of America. He shall hold his Office during the Term of four Years, and, together with the Vice President, chosen for the same Term, be elected, as follows:

Clause 6: Trade Preferences Congress may not favor one port over another and must ensure free trade between the states.

Clause 7: Spending The government cannot spend public money unless Congress has passed a law appropriating it. Congressional "power of the purse" acts as a check on the executive branch by controlling how much it can spend.

Clause 8: Titles of Nobility Congress may not establish titles of nobility, nor may federal officials accept such titles, or any gifts, from a foreign nation without congressional approval.

Section 10:
Limits on the Power of the States
Clause 1: Forbidden Actions The states cannot exercise certain powers granted to Congress or the president. These include negotiating treaties with foreign nations and creating their own money. They also may not tax imports or maintain armies without Congress's approval.

Clause 2: Prohibition on Taxing Trade

Clause 3. Prohibition on Foreign Relations

ARTICLE II: Executive Branch
Section 1:
President and Vice President
Clause 1: Term of Office The power to carry out laws passed by Congress rests with the president. A president and vice president are elected every four years.

Each State shall appoint, in such Manner as the Legislature thereof may direct, a Number of Electors, equal to the whole Number of Senators and Representatives to which the State may be entitled in the Congress: but no Senator or Representative, or Person holding an Office of Trust or Profit under the United States, shall be appointed an Elector.

The Electors shall meet in their respective States, and vote by Ballot for two Persons, of whom one at least shall not be an Inhabitant of the same State with themselves. And they shall make a List of all the Persons voted for, and of the Number of Votes for each; which List they shall sign and certify, and transmit sealed to the Seat of the Government of the United States, directed to the President of the Senate. The President of the Senate shall, in the Presence of the Senate and House of Representatives, open all the Certificates, and the Votes shall then be counted. The Person having the greatest Number of Votes shall be the President, if such Number be a Majority of the whole Number of Electors appointed; and if there be more than one who have such Majority, and have an equal Number of Votes, then the House of Representatives shall immediately chuse by Ballot one of them for President; and if no Person have a Majority, then from the five highest on the List the said House shall in like Manner chuse the President. But in chusing the President, the Votes shall be taken by States, the Representation from each State having one Vote; A quorum for this Purpose shall consist of a Member or Members from two thirds of the States, and a Majority of all the States shall be necessary to a Choice. In every Case, after the Choice of the President, the Person having the greatest Number of Votes of the Electors shall be the Vice President. But if there should remain two or more who have equal Votes, the Senate shall chuse from them by Ballot the Vice President.

The Congress may determine the Time of chusing the Electors, and the Day on which they shall give their Votes; which Day shall be the same throughout the United States.

No Person except a natural born Citizen, or a Citizen of the United States, at the time of the Adoption of this Constitution, shall be eligible to the Office of President; neither shall any person be eligible to that Office who shall not have attained to the Age of thirty five Years, and been fourteen Years a Resident within the United States.

Clause 2: Electoral College This clause establishes the Electoral College, which elects the president and vice president. The Electoral College is a group of citizens, called electors, chosen from each state, which gets as many electors as it has members of the House and Senate combined. Before 1800, electors were usually elected by state legislatures. Today electors are chosen by the voters of each state.

Clause 3: Method of Election The original electoral method described here was modified by the Twelfth Amendment (1804). The revised method, which still operates today, calls for each elector to cast one vote for president and one vote for vice president. Most states give their entire slate of electoral votes to whichever candidate wins the most popular votes in the state. If no candidate for president gets a majority of electoral votes, then the House of Representatives chooses the president.

Clause 4: Time of Elections Presidential elections are held on the Tuesday that follows the first Monday in November, every four years. Electors cast their votes more than a month later, on the Monday following the second Wednesday in December.

Clause 5: Qualifications The president must have been a born citizen of the United States, at least 35 years old, and have resided in the United States for 14 years.

In Case of the Removal of the President from Office, or of his Death, Resignation, or Inability to discharge the Powers and Duties of the said Office, the Same shall devolve on the Vice President, and the Congress may by Law provide for the Case of Removal, Death, Resignation or Inability, both of the President and Vice President, declaring what Officer shall then act as President, and such Officer shall act accordingly, until the Disability be removed, or a President shall be elected.

The President shall, at stated Times, receive for his Services, a Compensation, which shall neither be increased nor diminished during the Period for which he shall have been elected, and he shall not receive within that Period any other Emolument from the United States, or any of them.

Before he enter on the Execution of his Office, he shall take the following Oath or Affirmation:—"I do solemnly swear (or affirm) that I will faithfully execute the Office of President of the United States, and will to the best of my Ability, preserve, protect and defend the Constitution of the United States."

Section 2.

The President shall be Commander in Chief of the Army and Navy of the United States, and of the Militia of the several States, when called into the actual Service of the United States; he may require the Opinion, in writing, of the principal Officer in each of the executive Departments, upon any Subject relating to the Duties of their respective Offices, and he shall have Power to grant Reprieves and Pardons for Offenses against the United States, except in Cases of Impeachment.

He shall have Power, by and with the Advice and Consent of the Senate, to make Treaties, provided two thirds of the Senators present concur; and he shall nominate, and by and with the Advice and Consent of the Senate, shall appoint Ambassadors, other public Ministers and Consuls, Judges of the supreme Court, and all other Officers of the United States, whose Appointments are not herein otherwise provided for, and which shall be established by Law: but the Congress may by law vest the Appointment of such inferior Officers, as they think proper, in the President alone, in the Courts of Law, or in the Heads of Departments.

The President shall have Power to fill up all Vacancies that may happen during the Recess of the Senate, by granting Commissions which shall expire at the End of their next Session.

Clause 6: Presidential Succession If the president dies or leaves office before the end of his or her term, the vice president becomes president.

Clause 7: Salary Congress sets the president's salary and cannot change it during a presidential term. The president cannot accept *emoluments*, or other compensation, while in office.

Clause 8: Oath of Office The oath taken by the president is administered by a judicial officer, typically the chief justice of the Supreme Court.

Section 2: Powers of the President
Clause 1: Military and Executive Powers The president is commander-in-chief of the armed forces of the United States. This means the military is under civilian control. The president can grant pardons for federal crimes, except in cases of impeachment.

Clause 2: Treaties and Appointments The president has the power to make treaties with other nations, but the Senate must approve them by a two-thirds vote. The "advice and consent" of the Senate act as a check on presidential power. The president can name certain officials and federal judges, but a majority of the Senate must approve the president's choices.

Clause 3: Temporary Appointments If the Senate is not in session, the president can make short-term appointments without Senate approval.

Section 3.

He shall from time to time give to the Congress Information of the State of the Union, and recommend to their Consideration such Measures as he shall judge necessary and expedient; he may, on extraordinary Occasions, convene both Houses, or either of them, and in Case of Disagreement between them, with Respect to the Time of Adjournment, he may adjourn them to such Time as he shall think proper; he shall receive Ambassadors and other public Ministers; he shall take Care that the Laws be faithfully executed, and shall Commission all the Officers of the United States.

Section 4.

The President, Vice President and all civil Officers of the United States, shall be removed from Office on Impeachment for, and Conviction of, Treason, Bribery, or other high Crimes and Misdemeanors.

ARTICLE III.

Section 1.

The judicial Power of the United States, shall be vested in one supreme Court, and in such inferior Courts as the Congress may from time to time ordain and establish. The Judges, both of the supreme and inferior Courts, shall hold their Offices during good Behaviour, and shall, at stated Times, receive for their Services a Compensation, which shall not be diminished during their Continuance in Office.

Section 2.

The judicial Power shall extend to all Cases, in Law and Equity, arising under this Constitution, the Laws of the United States, and Treaties made, or which shall be made, under their Authority; —to all Cases affecting Ambassadors, other public Ministers and Consuls; —to all Cases of admiralty and maritime Jurisdiction; —to Controversies to which the United States shall be a Party; —to Controversies between two or more States, —between a State and Citizens of another State; — between Citizens of different States, —between Citizens of the same State claiming Lands under Grants of different States, and between a State, or the Citizens thereof, and foreign States, Citizens or Subjects.

In all Cases affecting Ambassadors, other public Ministers and Consuls, and those in which a State shall be Party, the supreme Court shall have original Jurisdiction. In all the other Cases before mentioned, the supreme Court shall have appellate Jurisdiction, both as to Law and Fact, with such Exceptions, and under such Regulations as the Congress shall make.

The Trial of all Crimes, except in Cases of Impeachment; shall be by Jury; and such Trial shall be held in the State where the said Crimes shall have been committed; but when not committed within any State, the Trial shall be at such Place or Places as the Congress may by Law have directed.

Section 3.

Treason against the United States, shall consist only in levying War against them, or in adhering to their Enemies, giving them Aid and Comfort. No Person shall be convicted of Treason unless on the Testimony of two Witnesses to the same overt Act, or on Confession in open Court.

The Congress shall have Power to declare the Punishment of Treason, but no Attainder of Treason shall work Corruption of Blood, or Forfeiture except during the Life of the Person attainted.

ARTICLE IV.
Section 1.

Full Faith and Credit shall be given in each State to the public Acts, Records, and judicial Proceedings of every other State; And the Congress may by general Laws prescribe the Manner in which such Acts, Records and Proceedings shall be proved, and the Effect thereof.

Section 2.

The Citizens of each State shall be entitled to all Privileges and Immunities of Citizens in the several States.

A Person charged in any State with Treason, Felony, or other Crime, who shall flee from Justice, and be found in another State, shall on Demand of the executive Authority of the State from which he fled, be delivered up, to be removed to the State having Jurisdiction of the Crime.

No Person held to Service or Labour in one State, under the Laws thereof, escaping into another, shall, in Consequence of any Law or Regulation therein, be discharged from such Service or Labour, but shall be delivered up on Claim of the Party to whom such Service or Labour may be due.

Section 3.

New States may be admitted by the Congress into this Union; but no new State shall be formed or erected within the Jurisdiction of any other State; nor any State be formed by the Junction of two or more States, or Parts of States, without the Consent of the Legislatures of the States concerned as well as of the Congress.

Clause 3: Trial by Jury
All defendants accused of a federal crime, except in cases of impeachment, have the right to a jury trial.

Section 3: Treason
Clause 1: Definition Treason, the only crime defined in the Constitution, is described as waging war against the United States or aiding its enemies.

Clause 2: Punishment Congress has the power to decide how to punish convicted traitors. Punishment cannot be directed at the guilty person's relatives or friends.

ARTICLE IV:
Relations Among the States
Section 1: Full Faith and Credit
Each state must honor the laws and authority of other states.

Section 2: Treatment of Citizens
Clause 1: Equal Privileges States may not discriminate against citizens of other states.

Clause 2: Extradition States must honor extradition orders. *Extradition* is the return of a suspected criminal or escaped convict to the state where he or she is wanted.

Clause 3: Fugitive Slaves This clause required states to return runaway slaves to their owners in other states.

Section 3:
New States and Territories
Clause 1: New States A new state cannot be carved out of an existing state or formed by the merger of existing states without the consent of the states and of Congress.

The Congress shall have Power to dispose of and make all needful Rules and Regulations respecting the Territory or other Property belonging to the United States; and nothing in this Constitution shall be construed as to Prejudice any Claims of the United States, or of any particular State.

Section 4.

The United States shall guarantee to every State in this Union a Republican Form of Government, and shall protect each of them against Invasion; and on Application of the Legislature, or of the Executive (when the Legislature cannot be convened), against domestic Violence.

ARTICLE V.

The Congress, whenever two thirds of both Houses shall deem it necessary, shall propose Amendments to this Constitution, or, on the Application of the Legislatures of two thirds of the several States, shall call a Convention for proposing Amendments, which, in either Case, shall be valid to all Intents and Purposes, as Part of this Constitution, when ratified by the Legislatures of three fourths of the several States, or by Conventions in three fourths thereof, as the one or the other Mode of Ratification may be proposed by the Congress; Provided that no Amendment which may be made prior to the Year One thousand eight hundred and eight shall in any Manner affect the first and fourth Clauses in the Ninth Section of the first Article; and that no State, without its Consent, shall be deprived of its equal Suffrage in the Senate.

ARTICLE VI.

All Debts contracted and Engagements entered into, before the Adoption of this Constitution, shall be as valid against the United States under this Constitution, as under the Confederation.

This Constitution, and the Laws of the United States which shall be made in Pursuance thereof; and all Treaties made, or which shall be made, under the Authority of the United States, shall be the supreme Law of the Land; and the Judges in every State shall be bound thereby, any Thing in the Constitution or Laws of any State to the Contrary notwithstanding.

The Senators and Representatives before mentioned, and the Members of the several State Legislatures, and all executive and judicial Officers, both of the United States and of the several States, shall be bound by Oath or Affirmation, to support this Constitution; but no religious Test shall ever be required as a Qualification to any Office or public Trust under the United States.

Clause 2: Federal Territory
Congress has power over all federal territories and property. This means that it can regulate public lands and make laws for overseas possessions.

Section 4: Protection of States
Known as the "guarantee clause," this provision ensures that each state has a representative democratic government. The federal government is obliged to protect the states from invasion and from internal, or *domestic,* violence.

ARTICLE V:
Amending the Constitution
The Constitution can be *amended,* or changed. Amendments must first be proposed either by a two-thirds vote of both houses of Congress or by a national convention of two-thirds of the states. A proposed amendment must then be ratified by three-quarters of the states, either in special conventions or in the state legislatures.

ARTICLE VI: National Supremacy
Clause 1: National Debts This clause recognizes debts incurred by the previous government under the Articles of Confederation.

Clause 2: Supremacy of National Law The so-called "supremacy clause" makes the Constitution and federal law the supreme, or highest, law of the land. If a state law and a federal law conflict, the federal law takes precedence. Federal courts can overturn state laws deemed to be unconstitutional or in conflict with federal law.

Clause 3: Oaths of Office Federal and state officials must swear allegiance to the Constitution. Public officials cannot be required to adopt or practice any religion.

ARTICLE VII.

The Ratification of the Conventions of nine States, shall be sufficient for the Establishment of this Constitution between the States so ratifying the Same.

Done in Convention by the Unanimous Consent of the States present the Seventeenth Day of September in the Year of our Lord one thousand seven hundred and Eighty seven and of the Independence of the United States of America the Twelfth In Witness whereof We have hereunto subscribed our Names.

AMENDMENTS

The Bill of Rights, or first 10 amendments, was passed by Congress on September 25, 1789, and ratified on December 15, 1791. Later amendments were proposed and ratified one at a time. The year of ratification appears in parentheses.

First Amendment

Congress shall make no law respecting an establishment of religion, or prohibiting the free exercise thereof; or abridging the freedom of speech, or of the press, or the right of the people peaceably to assemble, and to petition the Government for a redress of grievances.

Second Amendment

A well regulated Militia, being necessary to the security of a free State, the right of the people to keep and bear Arms, shall not be infringed.

Third Amendment

No Soldier shall, in time of peace be quartered in any house, without the consent of the Owner, nor in time of war, but in a manner to be prescribed by law.

ARTICLE VII:
Ratification of the Constitution
To take effect, the Constitution had to be ratified by nine of the original 13 states. On June 21, 1788, the ninth state (New Hampshire) ratified. New York and Virginia ratified soon afterward. Rhode Island and North Carolina waited until the Bill of Rights was added to ratify. The Constitution went into effect on April 30, 1789.

First Amendment (1791)
Basic Freedoms
This amendment protects five freedoms that lie at the heart of American democracy: freedom of religion, speech, the press, and assembly, and the freedom to *petition,* or ask, the government to correct wrongs.

Second Amendment (1791)
Right to Bear Arms
The right to bear arms guaranteed in this amendment is controversial. The courts have ruled that individuals do have the right to bear arms, but that it is not an unlimited right. The Supreme Court has upheld some federal gun control laws, such as those requiring gun registration and waiting periods, but has ruled that other gun control measures should be left to the states.

Third Amendment (1791)
Quartering of Soldiers
Before the American Revolution, American colonists had to *quarter,* or house, British soldiers in their homes. This amendment bars the government from using private homes as military quarters, except in wartime and in a lawful way.

Fourth Amendment

The right of the people to be secure in their persons, houses, papers, and effects, against unreasonable searches and seizures, shall not be violated, and no Warrants shall issue, but upon probable cause, supported by Oath or affirmation, and particularly describing the place to be searched, and the persons or things to be seized.

Fifth Amendment

No person shall be held to answer for a capital, or otherwise infamous crime, unless on a presentment or indictment of a Grand Jury, except in cases arising in the land or naval forces, or in the Militia, when in actual service in time of War or public danger; nor shall any person be subject for the same offence to be twice put in jeopardy of life or limb; nor shall be compelled in any criminal case to be a witness against himself, nor be deprived of life, liberty, or property, without due process of law; nor shall private property be taken for public use, without just compensation.

Sixth Amendment

In all criminal prosecutions, the accused shall enjoy the right to a speedy and public trial, by an impartial jury of the State and district wherein the crime shall have been committed, which district shall have been previously ascertained by law, and to be informed of the nature and cause of the accusation; to be confronted with the witnesses against him; to have compulsory process for obtaining witnesses in his favor, and to have the Assistance of Counsel for his defence.

Fourth Amendment (1791)
Search and Seizure

Government officials cannot search citizens or their property, or seize citizens or their belongings, without good reason. Searches and seizures generally require a *warrant,* or written order approved by a judge.

Fifth Amendment (1791)
Rights of the Accused

This amendment guarantees basic rights to people accused of crimes. A *capital* crime is punishable by death. *Infamous* crimes are punishable by imprisonment. A *grand jury* is a group of citizens who hear evidence of a crime and decide if the evidence warrants a trial. An *indictment* is their formal accusation. In addition, accused persons cannot be tried twice for the same crime, known as *double jeopardy.* They cannot be forced to *testify,* or give evidence, against themselves. They cannot be jailed or have their property taken without *due process of law,* or a fair court hearing or trial. The government cannot take away private property without paying a fair price for it.

Sixth Amendment (1791)
Right to a Fair Trial

A citizen accused of a crime has the right to a jury trial that is both public and "speedy," or that takes place as quickly as circumstances allow. An *impartial* jury does not favor either side. An accused person has the right to question witnesses and has the right to a lawyer. Both federal and state courts must provide a lawyer if the accused cannot afford to hire one.

Seventh Amendment

In Suits at common law, where the value in controversy shall exceed twenty dollars, the right of trial by jury shall be preserved, and no fact tried by a jury shall be otherwise re-examined in any Court of the United States, than according to the rules of the common law.

Eighth Amendment

Excessive bail shall not be required, nor excessive fines imposed, nor cruel and unusual punishments inflicted.

Ninth Amendment

The enumeration in the Constitution, of certain rights, shall not be construed to deny or disparage others retained by the people.

Tenth Amendment

The powers not delegated to the United States by the Constitution, nor prohibited by it to the States, are reserved to the States respectively, or to the people.

LATER AMENDMENTS

Eleventh Amendment

The Judicial power of the United States shall not be construed to extend to any suit in law or equity, commenced or prosecuted against one of the United States by Citizens of another State, or by Citizens or Subjects of any Foreign State.

Seventh Amendment (1791)
Civil Trials
Citizens have the right to a jury trial to settle lawsuits over money or property worth more than $20. *Common law* refers to rules of law set by previous judicial decisions.

Eighth Amendment (1791)
Bail and Punishment
Bail is money that an accused person pays to get out of jail while awaiting trial. The money is returned when the accused appears at trial; it is kept if he or she doesn't appear. Bail and fines set by a court must be reasonable. Punishments for crimes cannot be "cruel and unusual"— punishment considered too harsh for a particular crime.

Ninth Amendment (1791)
Rights Retained by the People
Americans have fundamental rights beyond the rights listed in the Constitution. The government cannot deny these rights just because they are not specified. This amendment was added so that the Bill of Rights would not be interpreted as limiting people's rights to those listed.

Tenth Amendment (1791)
States' Rights
This amendment attempts to balance power between the federal government and the states. It gives to the states and to the people any powers not specifically granted to the federal government.

Eleventh Amendment (1795)
Lawsuits Against States
People cannot sue a state in federal court if they are citizens of a different state or of a foreign country. The courts have interpreted this to mean that states may not be sued in federal courts without their consent.

Twelfth Amendment

The Electors shall meet in their respective states, and vote by ballot for President and Vice President, one of whom, at least, shall not be an inhabitant of the same state with themselves; they shall name in their ballots the person voted for as President, and in distinct ballots the person voted for as Vice President, and they shall make distinct lists of all persons voted for as President, and of all persons voted for as Vice President, and of the number of votes for each, which lists they shall sign and certify, and transmit sealed to the seat of the government of the United States, directed to the President of the Senate;—The President of the Senate shall, in the presence of the Senate and House of Representatives, open all the certificates and the votes shall then be counted;—The person having the greatest number of votes for President, shall be the President, if such number be a majority of the whole number of Electors appointed; and if no person have such majority, then from the persons having the highest numbers not exceeding three on the list of those voted for as President, the House of Representatives shall choose immediately, by ballot, the President. But in choosing the President, the votes shall be taken by states, the representation from each state having one vote; a quorum for this purpose shall consist of a member or members from two-thirds of the states, and a majority of all the states shall be necessary to a choice. And if the House of Representatives shall not choose a President whenever the right of choice shall devolve upon them, before the fourth day of March next following, then the Vice President shall act as President, as in the case of the death or other constitutional disability of the President. The person having the greatest number of votes as Vice President, shall be the Vice President, if such number be a majority of the whole number of Electors appointed, and if no person have a majority, then from the two highest numbers on the list, the Senate shall choose the Vice President; a quorum for the purpose shall consist of two-thirds of the whole number of Senators, and a majority of the whole number shall be necessary to a choice. But no person constitutionally ineligible to the office of President shall be eligible to that of Vice President of the United States.

Thirteenth Amendment

Section 1.

Neither slavery nor involuntary servitude, except as a punishment for crime whereof the party shall have been duly convicted, shall exist within the United States, or any place subject to their jurisdiction.

Twelfth Amendment (1804)
Presidential Elections
This amendment modifies the electoral process so that the president and vice president are elected separately. In the original Constitution, the candidate who finished second in the voting for president automatically became vice president. In 1800, this resulted in a tie for president between Thomas Jefferson and Aaron Burr. It took the House of Representatives 36 ballots to elect Jefferson president and Burr vice president. The Twelfth Amendment was added to prevent another tie vote.

Thirteenth Amendment (1865)
Abolition of Slavery

Section 1: Abolition
Slavery is banned throughout the United States. *Involuntary servitude* is work done against one's will. No person can be forced to work against his or her will except as punishment for a crime.

Section 2.

Congress shall have power to enforce these articles by appropriate legislation.

Fourteenth Amendment

Section 1.

All persons born or naturalized in the United States, and subject to the jurisdiction thereof, are citizens of the United States and of the State wherein they reside. No State shall make or enforce any law which shall abridge the privileges or immunities of citizens of the United States; nor shall any State deprive any person of life, liberty, or property, without due process of law; nor deny to any person within its jurisdiction the equal protection of the laws.

Section 2.

Representatives shall be apportioned among the several States according to their respective numbers, counting the whole number of persons in each State, excluding Indians not taxed. But when the right to vote at any election for the choice of electors for President and Vice President of the United States, Representatives in Congress, the Executive and Judicial officers of a State, or the members of the Legislature thereof, is denied to any of the male inhabitants of such State, being twenty-one years of age, and citizens of the United States, or in any way abridged, except for participation in rebellion, or other crime, the basis of representation therein shall be reduced in the proportion which the number of such male citizens shall bear to the whole number of male citizens twenty-one years of age in such State.

Section 3.

No person shall be a Senator or Representative in Congress, or elector of President and Vice President, or hold any office, civil or military, under the United States, or under any State, who, having previously taken an oath, as a member of Congress, or as an officer of the United States, or as a member of any State legislature, or as an executive or judicial officer of any State, to support the Constitution of the United States, shall have engaged in insurrection or rebellion against the same, or given aid or comfort to the enemies thereof. But Congress may by a vote of two-thirds of each House, remove such disability.

Section 2: Enforcement

Fourteenth Amendment (1868)
Rights of Citizens
This amendment was originally designed to resolve issues that arose after the Civil War ended and slavery was abolished.

Section 1: Citizenship
By defining as a citizen anyone born in the United States, this section extends citizenship to blacks. It prohibits the states from denying rights, due process, and equal protection of the law to their citizens.

Section 2:
Representation and Voting
This section nullifies the "three-fifths clause" of the original Constitution. It guarantees equal representation to all citizens. The reference to "male inhabitants" upset women's rights leaders who felt that equality for women was being pushed aside in favor of equality for blacks. In time, the "equal protection" provision would be expanded to include women, minorities, and noncitizens.

Section 3:
Former Confederate Leaders
Any member of government who took an oath to uphold the Constitution before the Civil War and who then joined the Confederate cause cannot be elected to any federal or state office.

Section 4.

The validity of the public debt of the United States, authorized by law, including debts incurred for payment of pensions and bounties for services in suppressing insurrection or rebellion, shall not be questioned. But neither the United States nor any State shall assume or pay any debt or obligation incurred in aid of insurrection or rebellion against the United States, or any claim for the loss or emancipation of any slave; but all such debts, obligations and claims shall be held illegal and void.

Section 5.

The Congress shall have the power to enforce, by appropriate legislation, the provisions of this article.

Fifteenth Amendment

Section 1.

The right of citizens of the United States to vote shall not be denied or abridged by the United States or by any State on account of race, color, or previous condition of servitude

Section 2.

The Congress shall have the power to enforce this article by appropriate legislation.

Sixteenth Amendment

The Congress shall have power to lay and collect taxes on incomes, from whatever source derived, without apportionment among the several States, and without regard to any census or enumeration

Seventeenth Amendment

Section 1.

The Senate of the United States shall be composed of two Senators from each State, elected by the people thereof, for six years; and each Senator shall have one vote. The electors in each State shall have the qualifications requisite for electors of the most numerous branch of the State legislature.

Section 2.

When vacancies happen in the representation of any State in the Senate, the executive authority of such State shall issue writs of election to fill such vacancies: Provided, That the legislature of any State may empower the executive thereof to make temporary appointments until the people fill the vacancies by election as the legislature may direct.

Section 4: Public Debts
By voiding all Confederate debts, this section ensured that people who had lent money to Confederate states would not be paid back, nor would former slave owners be paid for the loss of their freed slaves.

Section 5: Enforcement
Congress can make laws to enforce this amendment.

Fifteenth Amendment (1870)
Voting Rights
Section 1: The Right to Vote
States cannot deny voting rights to citizens on the basis of race, color, or previous enslavement.

Section 2: Enforcement

Sixteenth Amendment (1913)
Income Tax
The income tax amendment allows Congress to tax the earnings and income of individuals.

Seventeenth Amendment (1913)
Election of Senators
Section 1: Elections
This amendment provides for the direct election of senators by popular vote. Previously, senators were elected by state legislatures, but deadlocked votes in state legislatures left many Senate seats remaining vacant for long periods.

Section 2: Vacancies
If a Senate seat becomes vacant, and if the legislature of that state approves, the governor of that state may appoint a replacement senator until an election can be held.

Section 3.

This amendment shall not be so construed as to affect the election or term of any Senator chosen before it becomes valid as part of the Constitution.

Eighteenth Amendment
Section 1.

~~After one year from the ratification of this article, the manufacture, sale, or transportation of intoxicating liquors within, the importation thereof into, or the exportation thereof from the United States and all territory subject to the jurisdiction thereof for beverage purposes is hereby prohibited.~~

Section 2.

~~The Congress and the several States shall have concurrent power to enforce this article by appropriate legislation.~~

Section 3.

~~This article shall be inoperative unless it shall have been ratified as an amendment to the Constitution by the legislatures of the several States, as provided in the Constitution, within seven years from the date of the submission hereof to the States by the Congress.~~

Nineteenth Amendment
Section 1.

The right of citizens of the United States to vote shall not be denied or abridged by the United States or by any State on account of sex.

Section 2.

Congress shall have power to enforce this article by appropriate legislation.

Section 3: Previously Elected Senators

Eighteenth Amendment (1919) Prohibition of Liquor

Section 1: Ban on Alcohol
This amendment outlawed the production, sale, and transport of alcoholic beverages within the United States. It was the culmination of a decades-long reform effort to end the problems associated with alcohol abuse. This sweeping ban proved impossible to enforce.

Section 2: Enforcement

Section 3: Ratification

Nineteenth Amendment (1920) Women's Suffrage
Section 1: Right to Vote
This amendment guaranteed women the right to vote. The women's suffrage movement had sought this right since 1848. Although some western states already allowed women to vote, activists argued that a constitutional amendment was needed to guarantee the vote to all women.

Section 2: Enforcement

Twentieth Amendment

Section 1.
The terms of the President and Vice President shall end at noon on the 20th day of January, and the terms of Senators and Representatives at noon on the 3d day of January, of the years in which such terms would have ended if this article had not been ratified; and the terms of their successors shall then begin.

Section 2.
The Congress shall assemble at least once in every year, and such meeting shall begin at noon on the 3d day of January, unless they shall by law appoint a different day.

Section 3.
If, at the time fixed for the beginning of the term of the President, the President elect shall have died, the Vice President elect shall become President. If a President shall not have been chosen before the time fixed for the beginning of his term, or if the President elect shall have failed to qualify, then the Vice President elect shall act as President until a President shall have qualified; and the Congress may by law provide for the case wherein neither a President elect nor a Vice President shall have qualified, declaring who shall then act as President, or the manner in which one who is to act shall be selected, and such person shall act accordingly until a President or Vice President shall have qualified.

Section 4.
The Congress may by law provide for the case of the death of any of the persons from whom the House of Representatives may choose a President whenever the right of choice shall have devolved upon them, and for the case of the death of any of the persons from whom the Senate may choose a Vice President whenever the right of choice shall have devolved upon them.

Section 5.
Sections 1 and 2 shall take effect on the 15th day of October following the ratification of this article.

Section 6.
This article shall be inoperative unless it shall have been ratified as an amendment to the Constitution by the legislatures of three-fourths of the several States within seven years from the date of its submission.

Twentieth Amendment (1933)
Terms of Office
Section 1: Beginning of Terms
The president and vice president take office on January 20. Members of Congress begin their terms on January 3. Prior to this amendment, these terms of office began on March 3. These calendar changes shortened the period during which a "lame duck"—an incumbent who was not reelected or did not run for reelection—remained in office.

Section 2: Congressional Session

Section 3: Presidential Succession
This and Section 4 provide for succession if a newly elected president should die or be unable to take office before the start of his or her term.

Section 4: Congress Decides Succession

Section 5: Date of Implementation

Section 6: Ratification

Twenty-first Amendment

Section 1.

The eighteenth article of amendment to the Constitution of the United States is hereby repealed.

Section 2.

The transportation or importation into any State, Territory, or Possession of the United States for delivery or use therein of intoxicating liquors, in violation of the laws thereof, is hereby prohibited.

Section 3.

This article shall be inoperative unless it shall have been ratified as an amendment to the Constitution by conventions in the several States, as provided in the Constitution, within seven years from the date of the submission hereof to the States by the Congress.

Twenty-second Amendment

Section 1.

No person shall be elected to the office of the President more than twice, and no person who has held the office of President, or acted as President, for more than two years of a term to which some other person was elected President shall be elected to the office of the President more than once. But this Article shall not apply to any person holding the office of President when this Article was proposed by Congress, and shall not prevent any person who may be holding the office of President, or acting as President, during the term within which this Article becomes operative from holding the office of President or acting as President during the remainder of such term.

Section 2.

This article shall be inoperative unless it shall have been ratified as an amendment to the Constitution by the legislatures of three-fourths of the several States within seven years from the date of its submission to the States by the Congress.

Twenty-third Amendment

Section 1.

The District constituting the seat of government of the United States shall appoint in such manner as the Congress may direct:

Twenty-first Amendment (1933)
End of Prohibition
Section 1: Repeal
This amendment ended national prohibition, leaving it to states to ban alcohol if they wished.

Section 2: State Laws
Alcoholic beverages may not be brought into a state where they are still banned.

Section 3: Ratification
This amendment was the only one ratified by special state conventions rather than state legislatures. Most Americans were eager to end prohibition, and this method was quicker.

Twenty-second Amendment (1951)
Term Limits for the Presidency
Section 1: Two-Term Limit
The Constitution did not limit the number of presidential terms. Presidents followed George Washington's example of two terms, until Franklin D. Roosevelt was elected four times during the Great Depression and World War II. After his death in 1945, Congress proposed limiting future presidents to two terms.

Section 2: Ratification

Twenty-third Amendment (1961)
Electors for Washington, D.C.
Section 1: Number of Electors
This amendment gives the citizens of Washington, D.C., the right to vote in presidential elections. It allots to the District of Columbia the same number of presidential electors it would have if it were a state. Until this amendment was enacted, District of Columbia residents could not vote for president.

A number of electors of President and Vice President equal to the whole number of Senators and Representatives in Congress to which the District would be entitled if it were a state, but in no event more than the least populous State; they shall be in addition to those appointed by the States, but they shall be considered, for the purposes of the election of President and Vice President, to be electors appointed by a State; and they shall meet in the District and perform such duties as provided by the twelfth article of amendment.

Section 2.
The Congress shall have power to enforce this article by appropriate legislation.

Twenty-fourth Amendment
Section 1.
The right of citizens of the United States to vote in any primary or other election for President or Vice President, for electors for President or Vice President, or for Senator or Representative in Congress, shall not be denied or abridged by the United States or any State by reason of failure to pay any poll tax or other tax.

Section 2.
The Congress shall have power to enforce this article by appropriate legislation.

Twenty-fifth Amendment
Section 1.
In case of the removal of the President from office or of his death or resignation, the Vice President shall become President.

Section 2.
Whenever there is a vacancy in the office of the Vice President, the President shall nominate a Vice President who shall take office upon confirmation by a majority vote of both Houses of Congress.

Section 3.
Whenever the President transmits to the President pro tempore of the Senate and the Speaker of the House of Representatives his written declaration that he is unable to discharge the powers and duties of his office, and until he transmits to them a written declaration to the contrary, such powers and duties shall be discharged by the Vice President as Acting President.

Section 4.

Whenever the Vice President and a majority of either the principal officers of the executive departments or of such other body as Congress may by law provide, transmit to the President pro tempore of the Senate and the Speaker of the House of Representatives their written declaration that the President is unable to discharge the powers and duties of his office, the Vice President shall immediately assume the powers and duties of the office as Acting President.

Thereafter, when the President transmits to the President pro tempore of the Senate and the Speaker of the House of Representatives his written declaration that no inability exists, he shall resume the powers and duties of his office unless the Vice President and a majority of either the principal officers of the executive department or of such other body as Congress may by law provide, transmit within four days to the President pro tempore of the Senate and the Speaker of the House of Representatives their written declaration that the President is unable to discharge the powers and duties of his office. Thereupon Congress shall decide the issue, assembling within forty-eight hours for that purpose if not in session. If the Congress, within twenty-one days after receipt of the latter written declaration, or, if Congress is not in session, within twenty-one days after Congress is required to assemble, determines by two-thirds vote of both Houses that the President is unable to discharge the powers and duties of his office, the Vice President shall continue to discharge the same as Acting President; otherwise, the President shall resume the powers and duties of his office.

Twenty-sixth Amendment

Section 1.

The right of citizens of the United States, who are eighteen years of age or older, to vote shall not be denied or abridged by the United States or by any State on account of age.

Section 2.

The Congress shall have power to enforce this article by appropriate legislation.

Twenty-seventh Amendment

No law, varying the compensation for the services of the Senators and Representatives, shall take effect, until an election of Representatives shall have intervened.

Section 4: Vice President as Acting President
This section spells out the process by which the vice president takes over as president if the president is unconscious or unable or unwilling to admit that he or she is incapacitated.

Twenty-sixth Amendment (1971) Voting Age
Section 1: The Right to Vote
This amendment lowered the voting age to 18. Previously, the voting age was 21. The amendment was passed and ratified during the Vietnam War, when Americans questioned the fairness of drafting 18-year-olds to fight a war, but not allowing them to vote for the leaders who make decisions about war.

Section 2: Enforcement

Twenty-seventh Amendment (1992) Congressional Pay
If members of Congress vote to raise their own pay, the pay increase cannot go into effect until after the next congressional election.

Presidents of the United States

1.	George Washington	1789–1797	no party
2.	John Adams	1797–1801	Federalist
3.	Thomas Jefferson	1801–1809	Democratic-Republican
4.	James Madison	1809–1817	Democratic-Republican
5.	James Monroe	1817–1825	Democratic-Republican
6.	John Quincy Adams	1825–1829	Democratic-Republican
7.	Andrew Jackson	1829–1837	Democrat
8.	Martin Van Buren	1837–1841	Democrat
9.	William Henry Harrison	1841	Whig
10.	John Tyler	1841–1845	Whig
11.	James Knox Polk	1845–1849	Democrat
12.	Zachary Taylor	1849–1850	Whig
13.	Millard Fillmore	1850–1853	Whig
14.	Franklin Pierce	1853–1857	Democrat
15.	James Buchanan	1857–1861	Democrat
16.	Abraham Lincoln	1861–1865	Republican
17.	Andrew Johnson	1865–1869	Democrat/National Union
18.	Ulysses Simpson Grant	1869–1877	Republican
19.	Rutherford Birchard Hayes	1877–1881	Republican
20.	James Abram Garfield	1881	Republican
21.	Chester Alan Arthur	1881–1885	Republican
22.	Grover Cleveland	1885–1889	Democrat
23.	Benjamin Harrison	1889–1893	Republican
24.	Grover Cleveland	1893–1897	Democrat
25.	William McKinley	1897–1901	Republican
26.	Theodore Roosevelt	1901-1909	Republican
27.	William Howard Taft	1909–1913	Republican
28.	Woodrow Wilson	1913–1921	Democrat
29.	Warren Gamaliel Harding	1921–1923	Republican
30.	Calvin Coolidge	1923–1929	Republican
31.	Herbert Clark Hoover	1929–1933	Republican
32.	Franklin Delano Roosevelt	1933–1945	Democrat
33.	Harry S Truman	1945–1953	Democrat
34.	Dwight David Eisenhower	1953–1961	Republican
35.	John Fitzgerald Kennedy	1961–1963	Democrat
36.	Lyndon Baines Johnson	1963–1969	Democrat
37.	Richard Milhous Nixon	1969–1974	Republican
38.	Gerald Rudolph Ford, Jr.	1974–1977	Republican
39.	James Earl Carter	1977–1981	Democrat
40.	Ronald Wilson Reagan	1981–1989	Republican
41.	George Herbert Walker Bush	1989–1993	Republican
42.	William Jefferson Clinton	1993–2001	Democrat
43.	George Walker Bush	2001–2009	Republican
44.	Barack Obama	2009–	Democrat

The Pledge
of Allegience

I pledge allegience to the Flag
of the United States of America,
and to the Republic
for which it stands,
one Nation under God, indivisible,
with and liberty and justice for all.

The Star Spangled Banner

September 20, 1814
By Francis Scott Key

Oh, say can you see, by the dawn's early light,
What so proudly we hailed at the twilight's last gleaming?
Whose broad stripes and bright stars, through the perilous fight,
O'er the ramparts we watched, were so gallantly streaming?
And the rockets' red glare, the bombs bursting in air,
Gave proof through the night that our flag was still there.
O say, does that star-spangled banner yet wave
O'er the land of the free and the home of the brave?

On the shore, dimly seen through the mists of the deep,
Where the foe's haughty host in dread silence reposes,
What is that which the breeze, o'er the towering steep,
As it fitfully blows, now conceals, now discloses?
Now it catches the gleam of the morning's first beam,
In full glory reflected now shines on the stream:
'Tis the star-spangled banner! O long may it wave
O'er the land of the free and the home of the brave.

And where is that band who so vauntingly swore
That the havoc of war and the battle's confusion
A home and a country should leave us no more?
Their blood has wiped out their foul footstep's pollution.
No refuge could save the hireling and slave
From the terror of flight, or the gloom of the grave:
And the star-spangled banner in triumph doth wave
O'er the land of the free and the home of the brave.

Oh! thus be it ever, when freemen shall stand
Between their loved homes and the war's desolation!
Blest with victory and peace, may the heaven-rescued land
Praise the Power that hath made and preserved us a nation.
Then conquer we must, for our cause it is just,
And this be our motto: "In God is our trust."
And the star-spangled banner forever shall wave
O'er the land of the free and the home of the brave!

Physical Features of the World

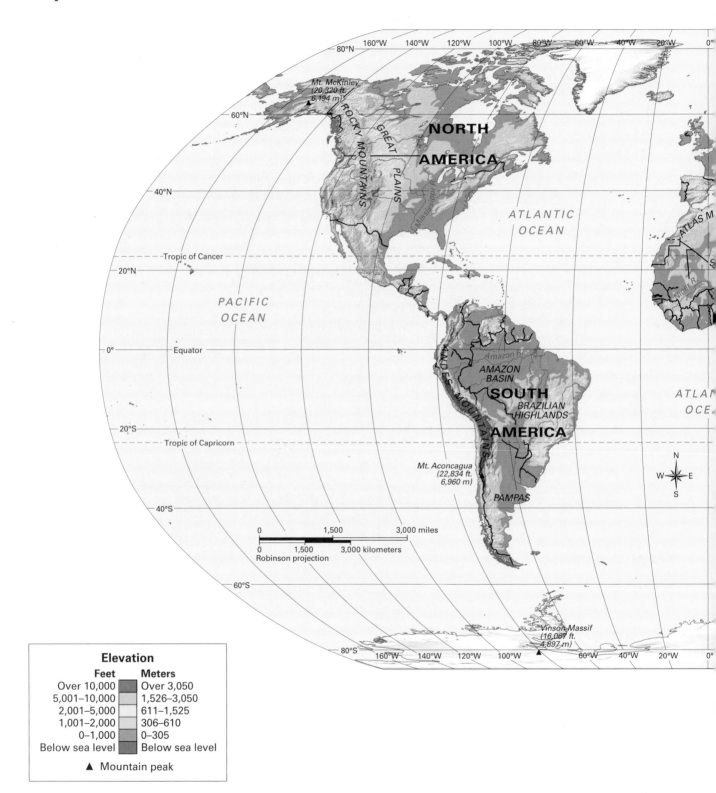

Mt. McKinley
(20,320 ft.
6,194 m)

ROCKY MOUNTAINS

GREAT PLAINS

NORTH

AMERICA

Mississippi R.

ATLANTIC
OCEAN

ATLAS M

PACIFIC
OCEAN

Tropic of Cancer

Equator

Amazon R.

AMAZON
BASIN

SOUTH

BRAZILIAN
HIGHLANDS

ATLAN
OCEA

Tropic of Capricorn

ANDES MOUNTAINS

AMERICA

Mt. Aconcagua
(22,834 ft.
6,960 m)

PAMPAS

Niger R.

N
W E
S

0	1,500	3,000 miles

0	1,500	3,000 kilometers

Robinson projection

Vinson Massif
(16,067 ft.
4,897 m)

Elevation

Feet	Meters
Over 10,000	Over 3,050
5,001–10,000	1,526–3,050
2,001–5,000	611–1,525
1,001–2,000	306–610
0–1,000	0–305
Below sea level	Below sea level

▲ Mountain peak

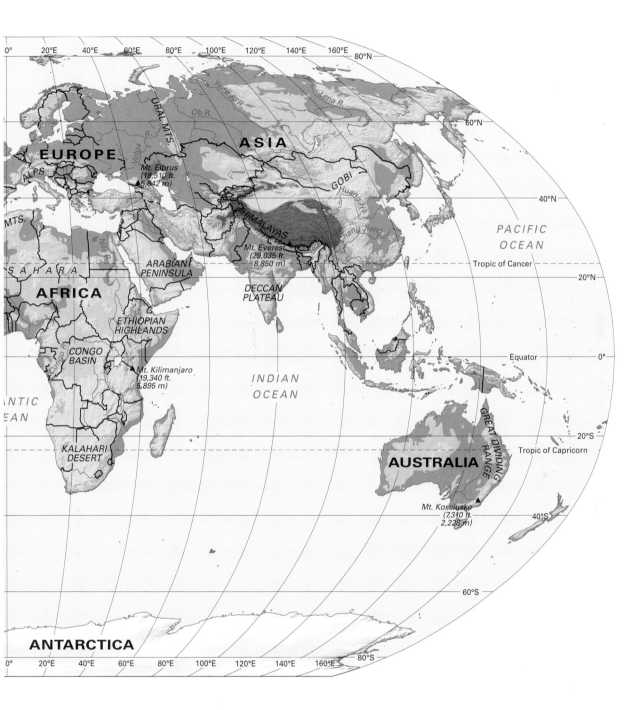

EUROPE

ASIA

ALPS

Mt. Elbrus
(18,510 ft.
5,642 m)

URAL MTS.

Volga R.

Ob R.

Yenisey R.

Lena R.

GOBI

Huang He

Chang Jiang

HIMALAYAS

Mt. Everest
(29,035 ft.
8,850 m)

DECCAN
PLATEAU

ARABIAN
PENINSULA

MTS.

Nile R.

S A H A R A

AFRICA

ETHIOPIAN
HIGHLANDS

CONGO
BASIN

Congo R.

Mt. Kilimanjaro
(19,340 ft.
5,895 m)

INDIAN
OCEAN

PACIFIC
OCEAN

ATLANTIC
OCEAN

KALAHARI
DESERT

AUSTRALIA

GREAT DIVIDING RANGE

Mt. Kosciusko
(7,310 ft.
2,228 m)

ANTARCTICA

80°N

60°N

40°N

Tropic of Cancer

20°N

Equator

0°

20°S

Tropic of Capricorn

40°S

60°S

80°S

0°   20°E   40°E   60°E   80°E   100°E   120°E   140°E   160°E

0°   20°E   40°E   60°E   80°E   100°E   120°E   140°E   160°E

Political Boundaries of the World

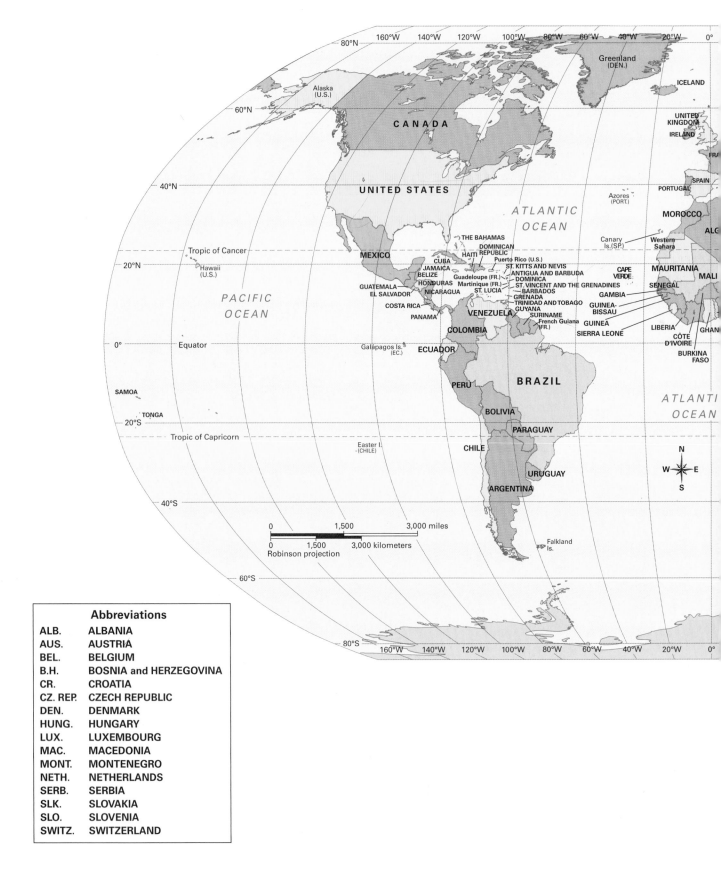

- Independent nations are printed in bold capital letters: **FRANCE**.
- Nations whose independence or governing rule is in dispute are printed in bold type: **Taiwan**.
- Territories, provinces, and the like governed by an independent nation are printed in bold type, with an abbreviation for the ruling nation: **French Guiana (FR.)**.
- Areas whose governing rule is in dispute are printed in nonbold type: Falkland Islands.
- Areas that are part of an independent nation but geographically separated from it are printed in nonbold type, with an abbreviation for the ruling nation: Hawaii (U.S.).

Physical Features of the United States

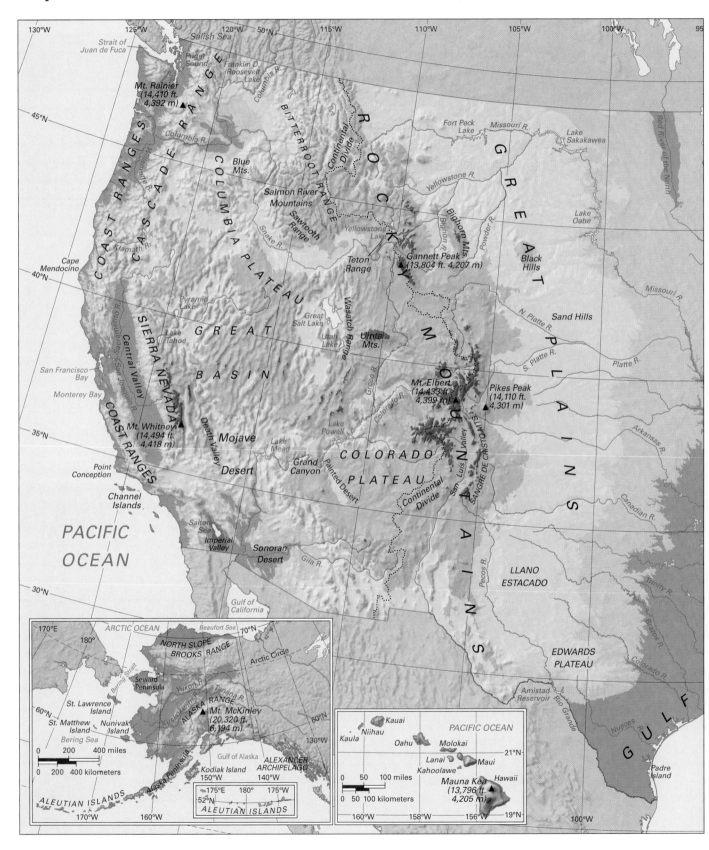

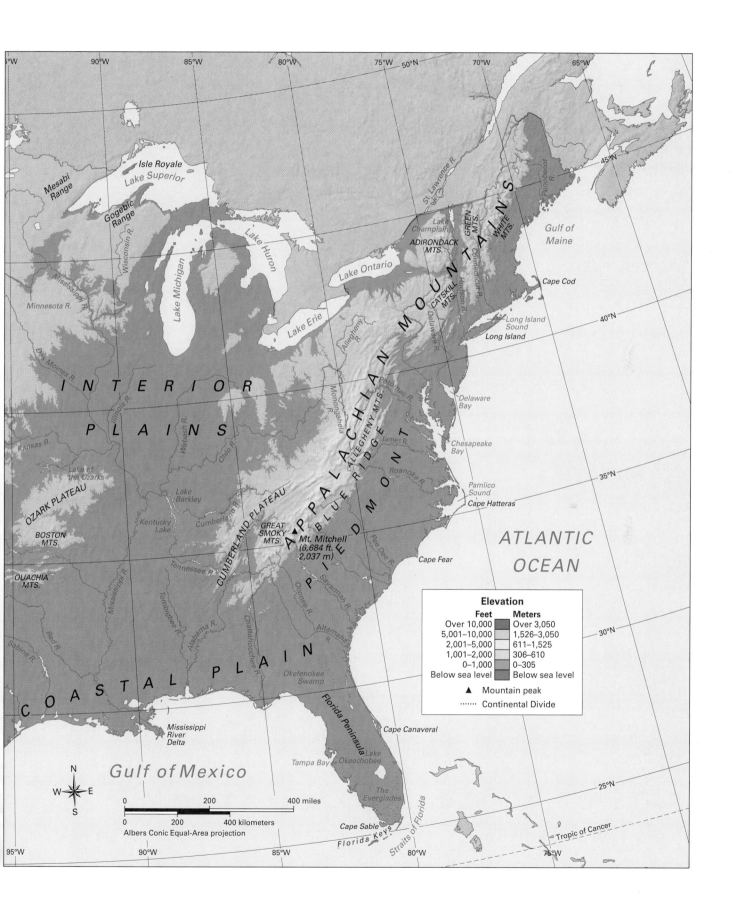

Mesabi Range

Gogebic Range

Isle Royale

Lake Superior

Wisconsin R.

Lake Michigan

Lake Huron

Minnesota R.

Mississippi R.

Des Moines R.

I N T E R I O R

P L A I N S

Illinois R.

Wabash R.

Ohio R.

Kansas R.

Lake of the Ozarks

OZARK PLATEAU

BOSTON MTS.

Lake Barkley

Kentucky Lake

Cumberland R.

Tennessee R.

OUACHIA MTS.

Mississippi R.

Red R.

Sabine R.

Tombigbee R.

Alabama R.

Chattahoochee R.

C O A S T A L   P L A I N

Okefenokee Swamp

Mississippi River Delta

Gulf of Mexico

Tampa Bay

Lake Okeechobee

Florida Peninsula

The Everglades

Cape Sable

Florida Keys

Straits of Florida

Lake Erie

Lake Ontario

St. Lawrence R.

Lake Champlain

ADIRONDACK MTS.

GREEN MTS.

WHITE MTS.

Connecticut R.

Penobscot R.

Gulf of Maine

Cape Cod

Long Island Sound

Long Island

CATSKILL MTS.

Hudson R.

Delaware R.

Allegheny R.

Monongahela R.

Potomac R.

ALLEGHENY MTS.

BLUE RIDGE

A P P A L A C H I A N   M O U N T A I N S

P I E D M O N T

Delaware Bay

Chesapeake Bay

James R.

Roanoke R.

Pamlico Sound

Cape Hatteras

CUMBERLAND PLATEAU

GREAT SMOKY MTS.

▲ Mt. Mitchell (6,684 ft. 2,037 m)

Pee Dee R.

Savannah R.

Oconee R.

Altamaha R.

Cape Fear

ATLANTIC OCEAN

Cape Canaveral

N
W E
S

0   200   400 miles
0   200   400 kilometers
Albers Conic Equal-Area projection

Elevation

Feet	Meters
Over 10,000	Over 3,050
5,001–10,000	1,526–3,050
2,001–5,000	611–1,525
1,001–2,000	306–610
0–1,000	0–305
Below sea level	Below sea level

▲ Mountain peak

······· Continental Divide

95°W 90°W 85°W 80°W 75°W 70°W 65°W

50°N 45°N 40°N 35°N 30°N 25°N

Tropic of Cancer

Political Boundaries of the United States

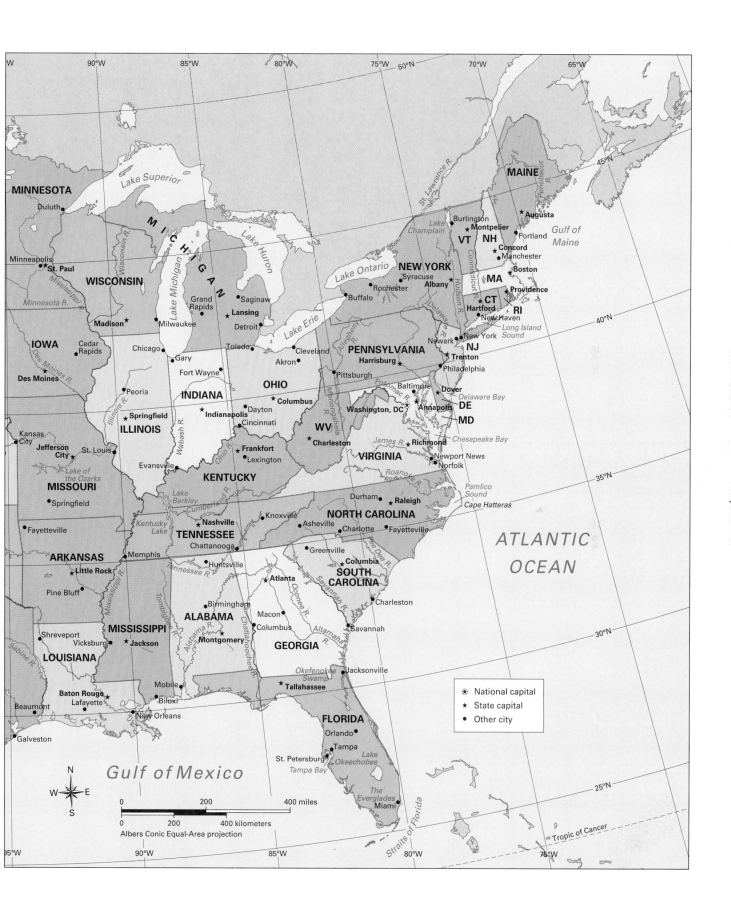

MINNESOTA

Duluth

Lake Superior

MICHIGAN

Minneapolis
St. Paul

Wisconsin R.

WISCONSIN

Minnesota R.

Madison

Milwaukee

Lake Michigan

Grand Rapids

Saginaw

Lansing

Detroit

Lake Huron

Lake Erie

MAINE

Augusta

Burlington

Montpelier

VT NH

Concord

Manchester

Portland

Gulf of Maine

Penobscot R.

St. Lawrence R.

Lake Champlain

NEW YORK

Syracuse

Albany

Boston

Rochester

Buffalo

Lake Ontario

MA

Providence

RI

CT

Hartford

New Haven

Long Island Sound

IOWA

Cedar Rapids

Des Moines R.

Des Moines

Chicago

Gary

Fort Wayne

Toledo

Cleveland

Akron

Illinois R.

Peoria

Springfield

INDIANA

OHIO

Columbus

Dayton

Indianapolis

Cincinnati

PENNSYLVANIA

Harrisburg

Pittsburgh

Allegheny R.

Monongahela R.

Newark

New York

NJ

Trenton

Philadelphia

Delaware R.

Hudson R.

ILLINOIS

Wabash R.

Ohio R.

Frankfort

Lexington

Baltimore

Dover

Delaware Bay

Washington, DC

Annapolis

DE

MD

Kansas City

Jefferson City

St. Louis

Evansville

KENTUCKY

Lake Barkley

Cumberland R.

Kentucky Lake

WV

Charleston

Potomac R.

Chesapeake Bay

MISSOURI

Lake of the Ozarks

Springfield

VIRGINIA

James R.

Richmond

Newport News

Norfolk

Roanoke R.

Pamlico Sound

Cape Hatteras

Fayetteville

Nashville

TENNESSEE

Knoxville

Chattanooga

Durham

Raleigh

NORTH CAROLINA

Asheville

Charlotte

Fayetteville

ARKANSAS

Memphis

Little Rock

Pine Bluff

Huntsville

Tennessee R.

Greenville

Columbia

SOUTH CAROLINA

Charleston

Pee Dee R.

Atlanta

Birmingham

Macon

Columbus

Savannah

Shreveport

Vicksburg

MISSISSIPPI

Jackson

ALABAMA

Montgomery

GEORGIA

Mississippi R.

Tombigbee R.

Alabama R.

Chattahoochee R.

Oconee R.

Savannah R.

Altamaha R.

Sabine R.

LOUISIANA

Baton Rouge

Lafayette

Mobile

Biloxi

Tallahassee

Okefenokee Swamp

Jacksonville

Beaumont

New Orleans

FLORIDA

Orlando

Galveston

Tampa

St. Petersburg

Tampa Bay

Lake Okeechobee

ATLANTIC OCEAN

Gulf of Mexico

The Everglades

Miami

Straits of Florida

N
W E
S

0   200   400 miles

0   200   400 kilometers

Albers Conic Equal-Area projection

Tropic of Cancer

⊛ National capital
★ State capital
• Other city

45°N

40°N

35°N

30°N

25°N

90°W   85°W   80°W   75°W   50°N   70°W   65°W

95°W   90°W   85°W   80°W   75°W

Atlas **629**

Glossary

Some words in this book have been respelled to help you pronounce them. Respelled words have been adapted from *Merriam-Webster's Collegiate Dictionary, Eleventh Edition; The American Heritage Dictionary of the English Language, Fourth Edition;* and *Random House Dictionary.*

Blue words are defined in the margins.

Black words are Academic Vocabulary terms.

A

abolitionist a person who supported abolition, or the ending of slavery

accompaniment a musical or vocal background that supports a piece of music

accumulate to increase in quantity or size over time

acknowledge to recognize; to show that something is seen or accepted

adapt to change in order to adjust to a new condition or environment

advocate to support an interest or a cause

agrarian a person who favors an agricultural way of life and government policies that support agricultural interests

ally a nation that joins another nation in some common effort, such as fighting a war

American Revolution the struggle of the colonies in North America to gain their independence from Great Britain

American System a proposal to the government that called for taxes on imports, federally funded transportation projects, and a new national bank

annex to add a territory to a country. Such an addition is called an annexation.

Appomattox Court House a village in Virginia that was the site of the Confederate surrender to Union forces under the command of General Ulysses S. Grant

Articles of Confederation the first written plan of government for the United States. A confederation is an association of states that cooperate for a common purpose.

assert to state firmly

assimilation the process by which immigrants or other newcomers acquire the attitudes, behaviors, and cultural patterns of the society around them

authority the power or right to control or command

authorize to grant permission for something

automation the process of making something automatically, by mechanical means

B

Bill of Rights a formal listing of the basic rights of U.S. citizens

black codes laws passed in 1865 and 1866 in the former Confederate states to limit the rights and freedoms of African Americans

blockade a closing off of an area to keep people or supplies from going in or out

boycott to refuse to buy one or more goods from a certain source. An organized refusal by many people is also called a boycott.

C

capitalism an economic system based on the private ownership of farms and businesses

cash crop a crop, such as tobacco, sugar, and cotton, raised in large quantities and sold for profit

cease to stop doing something

charter a formal document issued by the king that outlined a colony's geographic boundaries and specified how it would be governed

checks and balances the system that allows each branch of government to limit the powers of the other two branches

civil rights the rights guaranteed by the Constitution to all people as citizens, especially equal treatment under the law

civil servant an employee of the government

civil war a war between opposing groups of citizens from the same country

civilized well organized and socially developed

colony a new settlement or territory established and governed by a country in another land

Columbian Exchange the exchange of plants, animals, diseases, and people across the Atlantic Ocean between Europe and the Americas

committed to agree or pledge to support someone or something

Common Sense a pamphlet published in 1776 by Thomas Paine that persuaded many American colonists to support independence

communism an economic or political system in which the government owns all property and controls economic activity

compensation payment given to someone to offset, or make up for, a loss or injury

Compromise of 1850 the agreements made in order to admit California into the Union as a free state. These agreements included allowing the New Mexico and Utah territories to decide whether to allow slavery, outlawing the slave trade in Washington, D.C., and creating a stronger fugitive slave law.

Confederacy another name for the Confederate States of America, made up of the 11 states that seceded from the Union

conform to obey established rules and patterns

confront to meet, especially in a challenge

conquistadors Spanish soldier-explorers, especially those who conquered the native peoples of Mexico and Peru

conservation preservation and protection of a natural resource to prevent overuse, destruction, or neglect

constitution a written plan that provides the basic framework of a government

Constitutional Convention a meeting held in Philadelphia in 1787 at which delegates from the states wrote the U.S. Constitution

Continental army the American army during the American Revolution

contract a written agreement signed by two or more parties, which binds those parties to do what is stated in the agreement

contradiction a difference between two statements or situations that means they cannot both be true

controversial when many people have strong opinions on a subject, causing conflict and disagreement

convert to change a person's religious beliefs so they accept a different or new religion

coordinate to organize things or people so they work well together

corporation a business that is owned by many investors

cotton gin a hand-operated machine that cleans seeds and other unwanted material from cotton

coureurs de bois French fur trappers who learned many skills from the American Indians with whom they worked and lived

crisis a dangerous moment with a high chance of an unwanted result

crucial very important or necessary

cultural region an area in which a group of people share a similar culture and language

culture a people's way of life, including beliefs, customs, food, dwellings, and clothing

D

debate to formally discuss an issue

Declaration of Independence the document written to declare the American colonies as an independence nation, free from British rule

Declaration of Sentiments a formal statement of injustices suffered by women, written by the organizers of the Seneca Falls Convention. Sentiments means "beliefs" or "convictions."

defendant a person who is required to defend himself or herself in a legal action. An example is an accused person who is put on trial for a crime.

deforestation the clearing away of forests

democracy a system of government in which the power to govern belongs to the people

democratic ruled by the people. In a democracy, citizens elect representatives to make and carry out laws.

deprive to withhold or take away something

derive to get from

devote to give time, money, or effort to help a person or cause

dictate to control, or order how something should be done

dictator someone who rules with absolute power, often harshly

diplomacy the art of conducting negotiations with other countries

discriminate to treat a person or group unfairly

discrimination unequal treatment based on a person's race, gender, religion, place of birth, or other arbitrary characteristic

dispute a strong disagreement

distinct noticeably different

diverse a group of people or things with obvious differences among them

divine heavenly or godlike

domestic relating to issues within a country

domesticated plants or animals that live and breed in a human environment; tame

dominate to be most noticeable within a group

double jeopardy putting a person on trial more than once for the same crime

drastically extreme or sudden

Dred Scott decision a Supreme Court decision in 1857 that held that African Americans could never be citizens of the United States and that the Missouri Compromise was unconstitutional

due process the concept that the government must follow clear rules and act reasonably as it carries out the law

E

economy the way a society organizes the manufacture and exchange of things of value, such as money, food, products, and services

Electoral College the group established by the Constitution to elect the president and vice president. Voters in each state choose their electors.

eloquent to express ideas or feelings in a way that is moving and well-spoken

Emancipation Proclamation an order issued by President Lincoln on January 1, 1863, declaring slaves in the Confederate states to be free

embargo a government order that forbids trade with another country

emerge to come into existence or become more noticeable

English Bill of Rights an act passed by Parliament in 1689 that limited the monarch's power by giving certain powers to Parliament and listing specific rights of the citizens

Enlightenment the "Age of Reason" in 17th- and 18th-century Europe. Enlightenment thinkers emphasized using rational thought to discover truths about nature and society.

enrich to make richer; enhance

ensure to make sure or certain

entrepreneur a person who assembles and organizes the resources necessary to produce goods and services. Entrepreneurs are willing and able to take the risks involved in starting and managing a business.

environment all of the physical surroundings in a place, including land, water, animals, plants, and climate

evident easily seen or understood

executive branch the part of government that carries out, or executes, the laws

exert to put out effort to make something happen

F

faction a group of people within a larger group who have different ideas from the main group

federalism the constitutional system that shares power between the national and state governments

The Federalist Papers a series of essays written by James Madison, Alexander Hamilton, and John Jay in support of the ratification of the Constitution by the states

feminist a person who supports the equality of women with men

Fifteenth Amendment a change to the Constitution, ratified in 1870, declaring that states cannot deny anyone the right to vote because of race or color, or because the person was once a slave

finances the money that a person, company, or nation has, and how it is managed

folk art art made by ordinary people (as opposed to trained artists) using traditional methods

forty-niners the people who joined the rush for gold in California in 1849

Fourteenth Amendment a change to the Constitution, ratified in 1868, granting citizenship to anyone born in the United States and guaranteeing all citizens equal protection of the law

framework a basic set of ideas used to develop a larger plan

Freedmen's Bureau an agency established by Congress at the end of the Civil War to help and protect newly freed black Americans

frontier unexplored wilderness at the edge of the country

fugitive a person who flees or tries to escape (for example, from slavery)

function the use or purpose of something

fundamental basic

G

Gettysburg Address a speech by President Abraham Lincoln in 1863 at the site of the Battle of Gettysburg in memory of the Union soldiers who had died trying to protect the ideals of freedom upon which the nation was founded

globalization an increase in the flow of people, money, ideas, and trade goods across national boundaries

Great Awakening a revival of religious feeling and belief in the American colonies that began in the 1730s

Great Compromise the plan of government adopted at the Constitutional Convention that established a two-house Congress. In the House of Representatives, representation from each state is based on state population. In the Senate, each state is represented by two senators.

guarantee to make something sure or certain

H

habeas corpus the right of an accused person to appear in court so a judge can determine whether he or she is being imprisoned lawfully

homesteader a farmer who is given a plot of public land, or homestead, in return for cultivating it

hostility unfriendly or angry feelings or behavior

I

ignorant lacking knowledge

immigrant a person who moves from one country to another. Such a movement is called immigration.

impact to have a direct effect on a person or thing

imperialism the policy of extending a nation's power by gaining political and economic control over other countries

impose to put in place by authority, such a law, tax, or punishment

independence freedom from control by another government or country

individualism to act based on one's own beliefs

industrialist a person whose wealth comes from the ownership of industrial businesses and who favors government policies that support industry

Industrial Revolution the dramatic change in economies and cultures brought about by the use of machines to do work formerly done by hand

inferior of less importance, value, or quality

ingenious an especially original, intelligent, or clever idea

inherent related to the essential or natural character of something

initial at the beginning

innovation a new idea, method, or invention

interest group an organization that actively promotes the view of some part of the public on specific issues in order to influence government policy

internal inside or within

interstate commerce trade and other business dealings between two or more states

intuition to know or understand based on feeling, not fact

invest to give money to a company or bank, or to buy something, in order to make a profit later

irrigation a system for bringing water to farmland by artificial means, such as using a dam to trap water and ditches to channel it to fields

isolated separated or set apart from other people or things

isolationism a policy of avoiding political or military agreements with other countries

issue to supply or make available

J

Jacksonian Democracy the idea that the common people should control the government

Jim Crow laws laws enforcing segregation of blacks and whites in the South after the Civil War

judicial branch the part of government, consisting of the Supreme Court and lower federal courts, that interprets the laws

judicial review the power of the Supreme Court to decide whether laws and acts made by the legislative and executive branches are unconstitutional

justifiable done for a good reason

K

Kansas-Nebraska Act an act passed in 1854 that created the Kansas and Nebraska territories and abolished the Missouri Compromise by allowing settlers to determine whether slavery would be allowed in the new territories

knowledge worker a person whose main job is working with ideas, information, and technology

L

labor union an organization that brings together workers in the same trade, or job, to fight for better wages and working conditions

laissez-faire a theory that economies work best when there is minimal involvement from government

legacy a person's or a group's impact on future generations

legislative branch the lawmaking part of government, called the legislature. To legislate is to make a law.

leisure time spent not working

Lewis and Clark expedition a journey made from 1804 to 1806 by Meriwether Lewis and William Clark to explore the territory gained in the Louisiana Purchase

liberal not limited to or by established or traditional views; broad-minded

liberate to free

Lincoln-Douglas debates a series of political debates between Abraham Lincoln and Stephen Douglas, who were candidates in the Illinois race for U.S. senator, in which slavery was the main issue

loose construction a broad interpretation of the Constitution, meaning that Congress has powers beyond those specifically given in the Constitution

M

Magna Carta an agreement made in 1215 listing the rights granted by King John to all free men of the kingdom

majority rule a basic principle of democracy that says laws are passed by majority vote and elections are decided by a majority of the voters

manifest destiny the belief that it was America's right and duty to spread across the North American continent

manual using human effort, not electricity or other power

mass media forms of communication that reach large audiences

mass production the use of interchangeable parts and assembly lines to make large quantities of identical goods

Mayflower Compact an agreement that Pilgrims wrote and signed describing how they would govern themselves in the Americas

mercantilism an economic policy in which nations tried to gain wealth by controlling trade and establishing colonies

Mexican-American War the war with Mexico from 1846 to 1847 that resulted in Mexico ceding to the United States a huge region from Texas to California

Mexicano Spanish-speaking people who, in the 1800s, lived in parts of the United States that previously belonged to Mexico

migrate to move from one place and establish a home in a new place. A move of a large number of people is called a migration, and the people are called migrants.

militarism a policy of glorifying military power and military ideas and values

militia a small army made up of ordinary citizens who were trained to fight in an emergency

missionary a person who travels to a territory or community in order to make converts to his or her religion

Missouri Compromise an agreement made by Congress in 1820 under which Missouri was admitted to the Union as a slave state and Maine was admitted as a free state

monopoly a company that controls all production and sales of a particular product or service

Monroe Doctrine President James Monroe's declaration in 1823 that the Western Hemisphere was no longer open to European colonization

Mormons members of the church of Jesus Christ of Latter-Day Saints, founded by Joseph Smith in 1830

motive a reason for doing something

mutual shared

N

Nat Turner's Rebellion a slave rebellion led by Nat Turner that took place in Virginia in 1831

National Grange an agricultural organization formed in 1867 and committed to the economic and political interests of farmers

nationalism devotion to a national or ethnic identity, including the desire for independence from rule by foreign countries

nativism an attitude of resentment and superiority toward foreign-born people

natural resource useful material found in nature, including water, vegetation, animals, and minerals

natural rights rights common to everyone, as opposed to those given by law

neutrality a policy of not choosing sides in a dispute or war between other countries

Northwest Ordinance a law passed by Congress in 1787 that specified how western lands would be governed

Northwest Territory a region of the United States bounded by the Ohio and Mississippi rivers and the Great Lakes. The region was given to the United States by the Treaty of Paris in 1783.

nullify to refuse to recognize a federal law. This action by a state is called nullification.

O

oppression the feeling of being weighed down or held back by severe and unfair force

Oregon Trail an overland route that stretched about 2,000 miles from Independence, Missouri, to the Columbia River in Oregon

P

Parliament the lawmaking body of England, consisting of representatives from throughout the kingdom

passive not active

passport a document issued by a citizen's home government that identifies a person and permits travel to other countries

perpetual continuing forever

persecute to cause a person or group to suffer

petition a formal, written request made to an official person or organization

plantation a large area of privately owned land where crops were grown through the labor of workers, especially enslaved people, who lived on the land

platform a statement of the policies favored by a political party or candidate

pogrom an organized and violent persecution of a minority group

policy a course of action taken by a government

popular sovereignty the idea that the government's authority comes from the people

Populist Party a political party, organized in 1892 by leaders of the Farmers' Alliances, that supported such reforms as an eight-hour workday and government-owned railroads

procession a group of people moving in an slow, orderly way

proclaim to announce publicly

Progressive movement a social and political movement in the early 1900s that focused on improving conditions in American life

proprietor owner

prospect the chance that something will happen

prosperous wealthy

pursue to follow, as in a goal or purpose

Q

quota a limit based on numbers or proportions, such as the proportion of a country's population allowed to immigrate to the United States

R

racism the belief that one race is superior to another

radical relating to or supporting extreme change

rancho a land grant made by the Mexican government, used mostly for raising cattle and crops

ratify to formally approve a plan or an agreement. The process of approval is called ratification.

rebel to fight against a government or another authority

rebellion a violent attempt to resist or overthrow the government or another authority

Reconstruction the period of time after the Civil War in which Southern states were rebuilt and brought back into the Union

reform to make change in order to bring about improvement, end abuses, or correct injustices

reformer someone who works to make change in order to bring about improvement, end abuses, or correct injustice

refugee a person who flees his or her home or country to escape war, persecution, or other dangers

regulation the enforcement of laws that control conduct or practices; for example, government regulations control the way goods, food, and drugs are produced and sold to the public

reinforce to use additional support to make something stronger

reinforcement something that increases strength with additional support

reluctant to have hesitation or an unwillingness to do something

repeal to take back, or to cancel, a law

republic a country governed by elected representatives

reservation an area of land set aside by the federal government for the use of an American Indian tribe

resolution a statement of a formal decision agreed on by a group

resolve to find a solution for

resourceful good at finding ways to solve problems

restore to make something as it was before

restricted controlled or limited

retain to continue to keep

revise to change in order to improve

revolt a violent action in opposition to a government or law

rights powers or privileges that belong to people as citizens and that cannot or should not be taken away by the government

rural relating to the country, as opposed to the city

S

secede to withdraw from an organization or alliance

Second Great Awakening a revival of religious feeling and belief from the 1800s to the 1840s

sedition the crime of encouraging rebellion against the government

segregation the social separation of groups of people, especially by race

self-incrimination giving testimony that can be used against oneself

Seneca Falls Convention the gathering of supporters of women's rights in July 1848 that launched the movement for women's right to vote

service sector the part of the economy that provides services instead of producing goods

signify to mean or represent

slavery the treatment of people as property. People who are denied freedom in this way are said to be enslaved.

slave trade the business of capturing, transporting, and selling people as slaves

so-called commonly described as

social Darwinism the theory that people and societies compete for survival, with the fit becoming wealthy and successful while the weak struggle to survive

spiritual a religious folk song of African American origin

spoils system the practice of rewarding political supporters with government jobs

states' rights theory the theory that rights not specifically given to the federal government by the Constitution remain with the states

status the position of a person, either socially or professionally

stereotype to characterize someone based on a group they belong to

stimulate to encourage activity or growth

strategy an overall plan, such as for winning a war

strict construction a narrow interpretation of the Constitution, meaning that Congress has only those powers specifically given in the Constitution

subsidy money or other things of value, such as land, that a government contributes to an enterprise considered to benefit the public

suffrage the right to vote

sympathetic understanding or agreeing with the feelings or situation of another person

T

tariff a tax imposed by the government on goods imported from another country

technique a specialized method used to achieve a desired result

technological resulting from improvements in knowledge, equipment, or methods

temporary for a limited, often short-term, period of time

territory a region of land; also, a region designated by Congress and organized under a governor

Texas War for Independence the 1836 rebellion of Texans against Mexican rule that resulted in Texas becoming an independent nation

Three-Fifths Compromise an agreement made at the Constitutional Convention stating that enslaved persons would be counted as three-fifths of a person when determining a state's population for representation in the House of Representatives

Thirteenth Amendment a change to the Constitution, ratified in 1865, abolishing slavery in the United States

tolerate to put up with

tradition an inherited or customary pattern of thought, action, or behavior

Trail of Tears the removal of Cherokee Indians from Georgia to Indian Territory in 1838 and 1839

transcendentalism a philosophy emphasizing that people should transcend, or go beyond, logical thinking to reach true understanding, with the help of emotions and intuition

transcontinental railroad a railroad that crosses a continent

trend a line of general direction or movement

trust a group of corporations that unite in order to reduce competition and control prices in a business or an industry

tyranny the unjust use of government power. A ruler who uses power in this way is called a tyrant.

U

Underground Railroad a secret network of free blacks and whites who helped thousands of slaves escape to free states and Canada

Union the United States as one nation united under a single government. During the Civil War, "the Union" came to mean the government and armies of the North.

urban relating to cities

urbanization the growth of cities

V

vague not clearly defined

violation to break an established rule or law

vital necessary for the existence of something

voluntarily done willingly, without being forced

W

warrant an order from a judge that authorizes police or other officials to take a certain action, such as searching someone's property

Washington's Farewell Address George Washington's parting message to the nation, given in 1796, in which he warned of threats to the nation's future

Whiskey Rebellion a revolt by farmers in 1794 against an excise tax on whiskey

Wilmot Proviso a proposal made in 1846 to prohibit slavery in the territory added to the United States as a result of the Mexican-American War

Y

yellow journalism the practice of publishing sensational and often exaggerated news in newspapers in order to attract readers and increase sales

Index

Ostend Manifesto, 409
O'Sullivan John, 279
Outcault, R. F., 571

P

Pacific Railway Act (1862), 472–473
padrone, 514
Paine, Thomas, 110, 114–117, 124
Panama, 552–553, 560–561
Panama Canal Zone (1914), 560m
Pang Houa (Hmong immigrant), 526–527
Paris, France, 567–568
Parker, John, 99–101
Parks, Rosa, 576
Parliament, **68**
    Intolerable Acts, 97–98
    Quartering Act, 92
    Stamp Act, 91
    Tea Act, 95
    Townshend Acts, 92–93
passport, **520**
Paterson, William, 150–151
Patriarca, John, 331
Patriots (Whigs)
    about, 85, 87
    African Americans, 122
    Boston Massacre, 93–95
    Boston Tea Party, 95–97
    boycotts, 92
    formation of militias, 98
    response to Stamp Act, 91
Pattillo, Melba, 458
Pauketat, Tim, 20–23
Paul, Alice, 546–547
"Paul Revere's Ride" (Longfellow), 102–105, 250
Pawnee people, 294
Pearl Harbor naval base, 555, 582
Pee Dee River, NC, 128
Penn, William, 55
Pennsylvania
    child workers, 542, 548
    coal mining, 356

population statistics (1790), 151c
profile of colony, 55c
ratification of U.S. Constitution, 183
slavery ended, 122
Underground Railroad, 390–391
Pennsylvania Magazine, 115
Pérez Rosales, Vicente, 314–315
Perry, Jim, 478
Perry, Oliver Hazard, 233
Pershing, John J., 566
personal computers (PCs), 581
Peru, Spanish exploration, 29
pesticides, 584
Peters, Matthew H., 443
Petersburg, VA, 435, 437
petitions, **110**
    First Amendment rights, 187
Philadelphia (warship), 229, 231
Philadelphia, PA
    in colonial America, 65, 75, 114–115
    Constitutional Convention, 148, 160
    First Continental Congress, 98
    immigrants, 368
    Independence Hall, 113
    meaning of name, 55
    population statistics, 67, 114, 161, 367
    Revolutionary War battles, 127
    street grid, 50
    Underground Railroad, 391, 393
philanthropy, 539
Philippine Islands, 552–553, 558–559
phonographs, 506–507
Pickett, George, 430–431
piece work, 550
Pierce, Franklin, 409
Pike, Zebulon, 299
Pikes Peak, 299
Pilgrims, 47, 51, 60
Pinckney, Charles, 155, 217, 218c

pioneers
    African Americans, 484–487
    women, 304–306
Pioneers, The (Cooper), 250, 254–255
pirates and piracy, 69, 230–231, 234
Pizarro, Francisco, 29
Plains Indians, 474, 477, 480–481
plantations and plantation owners, **358**
    in Hawaii, 555
    slavery and, 376, 380, 382, 384–385
    in Southern colonies, 50, 59
    in Southern states, 358–359, 365–366
Plateau cultural region, 14
platform, **537**
Plessy, Homer, 255
Plessy v. Ferguson (1896), 255
Plimoth Plantation, xxii–1
Plymouth, MA, 47, 51, 60
Pocahontas, 37
pogrom, **516**
Poland, in American Revolutionary War, 130
political activities, 578
political parties, 156, 176
political reforms, 541
Polk, James K., 283–290, 285, 287
poll tax, 454, 460
Polo, Marco, 25
polygamy, 306
Ponce de León, Juan, 30
Poor Richard's Almanac (Franklin), 65
popular participation in government, 176–177
popular sovereignty, **166**
population statistics. *See also under specific cities*
    African Americans (mid-1800s), 375
    free population in U.S. (1790), 143m, 153c

slavery in U.S. (1790), 143m,
153c
in 13 colonies, 85m
in U.S. (21st century), 575
in U.S. (1790), 142m, 151c, 153c
in U.S. (1790–1840), 203c
in U.S. (1860), 277m
Populist Party, **537**
Porter, David, 433
Porter, Lavinia, 304
Portsmouth, RI, 52
post-Reconstruction Era, 454–457
Pottawatomie, KS, 411
Powers, Harriet, 374–375, 387–388
Powhatan, 37
Preamble (U.S. Constitution), 166
Prescott, Samuel, 105
president (U.S.)
checks and balances, 172
decisions of Constitutional
Convention, 155–156, 163
impeachment and removal, 170
powers of, 168c, 169–170
qualifications for office, 169
veto power, 168
Presidential Medal of Freedom,
577
president's cabinet (advisers),
169–170, 172, 206, 261
president's house (White House),
220–223
presidios, 31
press, First Amendment rights,
186–187
Preston, Thomas, 94
Princeton, NJ, Revolutionary War
battles, 124
prison reform, 341–342
privacy, right to, 189, 192
Proclamation of 1763, 90
Progressive Era
about, 535
captains of industry, 538–539
child labor, 548–551
environmental protection, 543

equal rights for African
Americans, 544
health and food safety reforms,
545
political reforms, 541
seeds of reform, 536–537
trust busting, 540
women's rights, 546–547
workers' rights, 542
Progressive movement, **536**
Prophet, the (Lalawethika,
Tenskwatawa), 232, 240
Prophetstown, 240–241
Protestant religion, 56, 368, 522
Providence, RI, 52
public gatherings
Earth Day demonstration, 187
equal rights marches, 459–460,
576–577
farmers' protests, 536
First Amendment rights, 186,
187
Free Speech Movement, 186
suffragettes march, 546
public prayer, 194, 197
public schools, 342–343
Pueblo Indians, 32, 322
pueblos, 15, 31
Puerto Rico, 552–553, 556–557
Pulitzer, Joseph, 570–573
Pulitzer Prizes, 573
Pure Food and Drug Act (1906),
545
Puritans, 51–53, 69, 71
Putnam, Israel, 108

Q

Quaker religion (Society of
Friends), 50, 55
Quartering Act, 92
Quebec, 33–34
Quetzalcoatl, 28
quilts and quilting, 374–375,
386–388
quota system, **522**

R

racism, **376,** 456, 544, 577
Radical Republicans, 448
radio, 580
radiocarbon dating, 22, 156
rail barons, 473, 536
railroads
construction process, 473–475
extermination of buffalo and,
477
industrial development and,
364, 467
map (1860), 364m
map (1870–1890), 467m
Mexico-U.S. connections, 520
Pacific Railway Act (1862),
472–473
rate and price limitations, 537
in southern states, 365
steel industry and, 492–493
trust busting, 540
Raleigh, NC, 437
Raleigh, Sir Walter, 35, 57c
rancheros, 319–320
ranchers, 477–479
ranchos, **300**–301, 320
Randolph, Edmund, 151, 155,
158, 161–162
Rankin, Jeanette, 546
Raphael, Ray, 105
ratify, **157**
reapers (farm machinery), 362
rebellion, 122, 384
recall, 541
Reconstruction, **446**
Reconstruction Era
about, 445
black codes, 447
Congressional actions, 448
end of era, 452–453
Freedmen's Bureau, 446–448
Johnson's goals and plan, 446
military reconstruction
districts (1870), 448m
reversals, 454–457

S

Sac and Fox people, 265
Sacagawea, 298–299
Sacramento, CA, 312
Safran, Rose, 502
St. Augustine, FL, 31
St. Lawrence River, 33
Salem, MA, 69
Salomon, Haym, 120
Salt Lake City, UT, 307
San Antonio, TX, 284–285, 327, 521
San Francisco, CA
    Chinatown, 310, 511, 519
    earthquake (1906), 518
    impact of gold rush, 314–315
    past and present pictured, 574–575
San Jacinto River, 285
San Juan Bautista, CA, 330
San Martín, José de, 235
San Salvador, 26–27
Santa Anna, Antonio López de, 284–285, 289
Santa Fe, NM, 295
Santa Fe Independent School District v. Doe (2000), 197
Santa Fe Trail, 277, 292–295, 299
Sarajevo, Bosnia, 562
Saratoga, NY, Revolutionary War battles, 125–126
Savannah, GA, 128, 365, 436–437
Sawyer, Philetus, 541
Scarlet Letter, The (Hawthorne), 350
Schneiderman, Rose, 502–504
school prayer, 194, 197
schools. *See* education and schools
Schulyer, Catherine, 125
Schulyer, Philip, 125
Schurz, Carl, 554, 559
Schuyler, Elizabeth (Mrs. Alexander Hamilton), 209
Scott, Winfield, 289, 426

search and seizure, Fourth Amendment protections, 189
secede, **262**
secession of Southern states, 416, 423
Second Amendment, 188
Second Continental Congress, 108, 110, 112–113
Second Great Awakening, **340,** 405
Secotan people, 19
Sedgwick, Theodore, 178
sedition, **215**
segregation, **377,** 454–459
self-incrimination, **189**–190
Selma, AL, 460–461
Seminole people, 264, 266, 282
Seneca Falls Convention, **347**–348
Senate (U.S.)
    African American members, 451
    Constitutional provisions, 167–168
    impeachment of president, 170, 449
    Louisiana Purchase ratified, 281
    Mexican Cession ratified, 290
    Oregon treaty ratified, 287
    qualifications for office, 167
    Radical Republican members, 448
    Tallmadge Amendment, 403
    Treaty of Versailles ratification, 568
"separate but equal" doctrine, 459
Separatists, 51, 60
September 11 terrorist attacks (2001), 525, 583
Sequoyah (Cherokee Indian), 264
Serbia, 562
Serra, Junipero, 300
service economy, 580–581
service sector, **581**
Seven Cities of Cíbola, 30
Seventh Amendment, 191
Seward, William, 554

Seward's Folly, 554
sewing machines, 361, 494–495
Seymour, Horatio, 450
sharecropping, 449
Shaw, Robert Gould, 434
Shawnee people, 232–233, 238–241
Shays, Daniel, 147
Shays's Rebellion, 147
sheep raising, 321
Sheridan, Philip, 435–436, 477
Sherman, Roger, 152, 155
Sherman, William Tecumseh, 435–437
Sherman Antitrust Act (1890), 540
ships and boats, 363–365, 432, 514, 564–565
Shoshone people, 298–299
Sierra Club, 543
Silent Spring (Carson), 584–585
Silicon Valley, CA, 585
silver mining, 318, 476–477
Sinclair, Upton, 545
Singleton, Benjamin "Pap," 485
"Sinners in the Hands of an Angry God," 79
Sioux people, 481–482
Sitting Bull (Sioux leader), 481
Sixth Amendment, 190–191
skyscrapers, 499, 575
slave breakers, 382
slave catchers, 383, 391
slave trade, **52,** 70, 112m, 336m, 344
slavery, **27**
    abolition of, 325, 344–345, 446
    in Boston, 418–421
    builders of president's house, 222
    churches and religion, 387
    controlling slaves, 382
    cotton production and distribution, 355, 358, 365, 370, 374–375, 378–379
    counting slaves for representation in Congress, 153–154
    culture of, 388–389

strategy, **125**
street grid (in cities), 50
strict construction, **213**
Stuart, Gilbert, 248
Stuyvesant, Peter, 39–40
subsidy, **472**
Sudanese immigrants, 524–525
suffrage, **546**
Sumner, Charles, 411, 448
Supreme Court (U.S.)
    Brown v. Board of Education of Topeka, Kansas (1954), 459, 576
    Constitutional powers, 171
    District of Columbia v. Heller (2008), 188
    Dred Scott decision, 412–414
    Engle v. Vitale (1962), 197
    Everson v. Board of Education of the Township of Ewing 1947), 197
    Gibbons v. Ogden (1824), 247
    Gregg v. Georgia (1976), 192
    Gregory v. Chicago (1969), 187
    Lee v. Weisman (1992), 197
    Lemon v. Kurtzman (1971), 185
    Marshall era, 246–247
    McCulloch v. Maryland (1819), 247
    Plessy v. Ferguson (1896), 255
    Santa Fe Independent School District v. Doe (2000), 197
    Texas v. Johnson (1989), 187
survival of the fittest, 539

T

Taino people, 26, 42
"taking the Fifth," 190
Talleyrand, 228, 280
Tallmadge, James, 402, 404
Taney, Roger, 412–413
Tarbell, Ida, 535, 540
tariffs, **262,** 490
tattoo mural, 329

taxes and taxation
    American System, 246
    in colonial America, 91–93
    excise taxes, 203, 207
    poll tax, 454, 460
    Reconstruction Era, 451, 452
    religion teachers, payment for, 185
Taylor, Zachary, 289
Tea Act, 95–96
tea taxes, 93, 95–96
technology, 492–495, 563–564, 566, 579–580
Tecumseh (Shawnee leader), 232–233, 238–241
Tejanos, 283–284, 319
telegraph machinery, 506–507
telephones, 494, 581
television, 580
tenements, 498–499
Tennessee
    as Confederate state, 423
    Reconstruction Era, 448
    statehood, 402
Tenochtilán, 28–29
Tenskwatawa (Lalawethika, the Prophet), 232, 240
Tenth Amendment, 192–193
Tenth Cavalry Regiment, 456, 557
Tenure of Office Act, 449
territories, 146, **280**
terrorist attacks (2001), 525, 583
Tex-Mex cooking, 323
Texas
    battle at the Alamo, 284–285
    community property law, 325
    independence and statehood, 285
    Mexican-American War, 288
    Mexican colonies, 283
    Spanish exploration, 30, 283
    War for Independence, **285,** 317
Texas v. Johnson (1989), 187
textile machinery and mills, 360–361, 370–373, 454, 542

Thanksgiving holiday, 51
theater, El Teatro Campesino, 330
theocracy, 50
Third Amendment, 188
Thirteenth Amendment, 173, **446**
Thomas, Cyrus, 20
Thoreau, Henry David, 341, 352
three branches of government.
    See Congress (U.S.); courts; president (U.S.)
Three-Fifths Compromise, **154**
Three Forks, MT, 298
Tilden, Samuel J., 453
Tillman, Ben, 453
Tito (Mexican immigrant), 527
tobacco, 37, 50, 57, 70
Tocqueville, Alexis de, 243, 245, 250
tools
    California cultural region, 12
    colonial American farmers, 66
    Eastern Woodlands cultural region, 17
    farm machinery, 362
    Great Basin cultural region, 13
    Great Plains cultural region, 16
    Northwest Coast cultural region, 11
    Plateau cultural region, 13
    Southeast cultural region, 18
tortillas, 323
total war, 439
Townshend, Charles, 92–93
Townshend Acts, 92–93
townships, 146
toys and games, in colonial America, 74
trading and traders
    China, 555
    commercial trading in New Amsterdam, 61
    fur traders, 33–34, 301–302
    globalization of, 581
    Japan, 555
    on Santa Fe Trail, 293

California History–Social Science Standards, Eighth Grade

Standards	Where Standards Are Addressed
8.1 Students understand the major events preceding the founding of the nation and relate their significance to the development of American constitutional democracy.	
1. Describe the relationship between the moral and political ideas of the Great Awakening and the development of revolutionary fervor.	pp. 71, 76–79
2. Analyze the philosophy of government expressed in the Declaration of Independence, with an emphasis on government as a means of securing individual rights (e.g., key phrases such as "all men are created equal, that they are endowed by their Creator with certain unalienable Rights").	pp. 110–111, 592–593
3. Analyze how the American Revolution affected other nations, especially France.	pp. 117, 126, 133
4. Describe the nation's blend of civic republicanism, classical liberal principles, and English parliamentary traditions.	pp. 88, 148–150 Enrichment Resources: Ch. 8 Enrichment Essay
8.2 Students analyze the political principles underlying the U.S. Constitution and compare the enumerated and implied powers of the federal government.	
1. Discuss the significance of the Magna Carta, the English Bill of Rights, and the Mayflower Compact.	pp. 51, 68
2. Analyze the Articles of Confederation and the Constitution and the success of each in implementing the ideals of the Declaration of Independence.	pp. 145–147, 159
3. Evaluate the major debates that occurred during the development of the Constitution and their ultimate resolutions in such areas as shared power among institutions, divided state-federal power, slavery, the rights of individuals and states (later addressed by the addition of the Bill of Rights), and the status of American Indian nations under the commerce clause.	pp. 149–159, 162–163, 165–177, 183, 193
4. Describe the political philosophy underpinning the Constitution as specified in the Federalist Papers (authored by James Madison, Alexander Hamilton, and John Jay) and the role of such leaders as Madison, George Washington, Roger Sherman, Gouverneur Morris, and James Wilson in the writing and ratification of the Constitution.	pp. 148–163
5. Understand the significance of Jefferson's Statute for Religious Freedom as a forerunner of the First Amendment and the origins, purpose, and differing views of the founding fathers on the issue of the separation of church and state.	pp. 185, 194–196
6. Enumerate the powers of government set forth in the Constitution and the fundamental liberties ensured by the Bill of Rights.	pp. 166–171, 174–175, 184–197
7. Describe the principles of federalism, dual sovereignty, separation of powers, checks and balances, the nature and purpose of majority rule, and the ways in which the American idea of constitutionalism preserves individual rights.	pp. 166–177, 178–181

Standards	Where Standards Are Addressed
8.3 Students understand the foundation of the American political system and the ways in which citizens participate in it.	
1. Analyze the principles and concepts codified in state constitutions between 1777 and 1781 that created the context out of which American political institutions and ideas developed.	p. 150 Enrichment Resources: Ch. 8 Enrichment Essay
2. Explain how the ordinances of 1785 and 1787 privatized national resources and transferred federally owned lands into private holdings, townships, and states.	pp. 146–147
3. Enumerate the advantages of a common market among the states as foreseen in and protected by the Constitution's clauses on interstate commerce, common coinage, and full-faith and credit.	pp. 174–175
4. Understand how the conflicts between Thomas Jefferson and Alexander Hamilton resulted in the emergence of two political parties (e.g., view of foreign policy, Alien and Sedition Acts, economic policy, National Bank, funding and assumption of the revolutionary debt).	pp. 209–209
5. Know the significance of domestic resistance movements and ways in which the central government responded to such movements (e.g., Shays' Rebellion, the Whiskey Rebellion).	pp. 147, 207–208
6. Describe the basic law-making process and how the Constitution provides numerous opportunities for citizens to participate in the political process and to monitor and influence government (e.g., function of elections, political parties, interest groups).	pp. 167–168, 176–177
7. Understand the functions and responsibilities of a free press.	p. 186
8.4 Students analyze the aspirations and ideals of the people of the new nation.	
1. Describe the country's physical landscapes, political divisions, and territorial expansion during the terms of the first four presidents.	pp. 202–203, 205–219, 226–234 (landscapes, political divisions) 276–277, 279–281 (expansion)
2. Explain the policy significance of famous speeches (e.g., Washington's Farewell Address, Jefferson's 1801 Inaugural Address, John Q. Adams's Fourth of July 1821 Address).	pp. 208 (Washington) Enrichment Resources: Ch. 11, 12 Enrichment Essays
3. Analyze the rise of capitalism and the economic problems and conflicts that accompanied it (e.g., Jackson's opposition to the National Bank; early decisions of the U.S. Supreme Court that reinforced the sanctity of contracts and a capitalist economic system of law).	pp. 263–264 (Jackson and National Bank), 246–247 (Supreme Court decisions)
4. Discuss daily life, including traditions in art, music, and literature, of early national America (e.g., through writings by Washington Irving, James Fenimore Cooper).	pp. 248–251 Enrichment Resources: Ch. 13 Enrichment Essay

Standards	Where Standards Are Addressed
8.5 Students analyze U.S. foreign policy in the early Republic.	
1. Understand the political and economic causes and consequences of the War of 1812 and know the major battles, leaders, and events that led to a final peace.	pp. 232–234
2. Know the changing boundaries of the United States and describe the relationships the country had with its neighbors (current Mexico and Canada) and Europe, including the influence of the Monroe Doctrine, and how those relationships influenced westward expansion and the Mexican-American War.	pp. 235–237, 276–277, 279–291
3. Outline the major treaties with American Indian nations during the administrations of the first four presidents and the varying outcomes of those treaties.	pp. 238–241, 264–266, 268–271 Enrichment Resources: Ch. 14, 15 Enrichment Essays
8.6 Students analyze the divergent paths of the American people from 1800 to the mid-1800s and the challenges they faced, with emphasis on the Northeast.	
1. Discuss the influence of industrialization and technological developments on the region, including human modification of the landscape and how physical geography shaped human actions (e.g., growth of cities, deforestation, farming, mineral extraction).	pp. 356, 360–364, 367–368, 370–373 Enrichment Resources: Ch. 19 Enrichment Essay
2. Outline the physical obstacles to and the economic and political factors involved in building a network of roads, canals, and railroads (e.g., Henry Clay's American System).	pp. 244–247, 292–295, 363–365
3. List the reasons for the wave of immigration from Northern Europe to the United States and describe the growth in the number, size, and spatial arrangements of cities (e.g., Irish immigrants and the Great Irish Famine).	pp. 367–368
4. Study the lives of black Americans who gained freedom in the North and founded schools and churches to advance their rights and communities.	pp. 367–368, 376–377, 390–393
5. Trace the development of the American education system from its earliest roots, including the roles of religious and private schools and Horace Mann's campaign for free public education and its assimilating role in American culture.	pp. 72–73, 342–343 Enrichment Resources: Ch. 18 Enrichment Essay
6. Examine the women's suffrage movement (e.g., biographies, writings, and speeches of Elizabeth Cady Stanton, Margaret Fuller, Lucretia Mott, Susan B. Anthony).	pp. 180–181, 346–349, 546–547 Enrichment Resources: Ch. 18 Enrichment Essay
7. Identify common themes in American art as well as transcendentalism and individualism (e.g., writings about and by Ralph Waldo Emerson, Henry David Thoreau, Herman Melville, Louisa May Alcott, Nathaniel Hawthorne, Henry Wadsworth Longfellow).	pp. 248–249, 250–255, 341, 350–353 Enrichment Resources: Ch 13 Enrichment Essay

Standards	Where Standards Are Addressed
8.7 Students analyze the divergent paths of the American people in the South from 1800 to the mid-1800s and the challenges they faced.	
1. Describe the development of the agrarian economy in the South, identify the locations of the cotton-producing states, and discuss the significance of cotton and the cotton gin.	pp. 355, 358–359, 365, 366
2. Trace the origins and development of slavery; its effects on black Americans and on the region's political, social, religious, economic, and cultural development; and identify the strategies that were tried to both overturn and preserve it (e.g., through the writings and historical documents on Nat Turner, Denmark Vesey).	pp. 55, 70, 153–154, 342–345, 358–359, 366, 375–393 Enrichment Resources: Ch. 19, 20 Enrichment Essays
3. Examine the characteristics of white Southern society and how the physical environment influenced events and conditions prior to the Civil War.	pp. 357–359, 365, 366
4. Compare the lives of and opportunities for free blacks in the North with those of free blacks in the South.	pp. 376–377
8.8 Students analyze the divergent paths of the American people in the West from 1800 to the mid-1800s and the challenges they faced.	
1. Discuss the election of Andrew Jackson as president in 1828, the importance of Jacksonian democracy, and his actions as president (e.g., the spoils system, veto of the National Bank, policy of Indian removal, opposition to the Supreme Court).	pp. 257–266, 268–271
2. Describe the purpose, challenges, and economic incentives associated with westward expansion, including the concept of Manifest Destiny (e.g., the Lewis and Clark expedition, accounts of the removal of Indians, the Cherokees' "Trail of Tears," settlement of the Great Plains) and the territorial acquisitions that spanned numerous decades.	pp. 203, 264–266, 268–271, 276–277, 279–290, 293, 297–315, 469–482, 483–487 Enrichment Resources: Ch. 14, 15 Enrichment Essay
3. Describe the role of pioneer women and the new status that western women achieved (e.g., Laura Ingalls Wilder, Annie Bidwell; slave women gaining freedom in the West; Wyoming granting suffrage to women in 1869).	pp. 292–295, 304–306, 312–313 Enrichment Resources: Ch. 16 Enrichment Essay
4. Examine the importance of the great rivers and the struggle over water rights.	pp. 325, 365 Enrichment Resources: Ch. 17 Enrichment Essay
5. Discuss Mexican settlements and their locations, cultural traditions, attitudes toward slavery, land-grant system, and economies.	pp. 283–285, 300–301, 317–327
6. Describe the Texas War for Independence and the Mexican-American War, including territorial settlements, the aftermath of the wars, and the effects the wars had on the lives of Americans, including Mexican Americans today.	pp. 283–285, 288–290, 317, 328–331

Standards	Where Standards Are Addressed
8.9 Students analyze the early and steady attempts to abolish slavery and to realize the ideals of the Declaration of Independence.	
1. Describe the leaders of the movement (e.g., John Quincy Adams and his proposed constitutional amendment, John Brown and the armed resistance, Harriet Tubman and the Underground Railroad, Benjamin Franklin, Theodore Weld, William Lloyd Garrison, Frederick Douglass).	pp. 153, 181, 344–346, 382–384, 390–393, 405–406, 414–415, 418–421 Enrichment Resources: Ch. 20 Enrichment Essay
2. Discuss the abolition of slavery in early state constitutions.	pp. 178, 399 Enrichment Resources: Ch. 8 Enrichment Essay
3. Describe the significance of the Northwest Ordinance in education and in the banning of slavery in new states north of the Ohio River.	pp. 147, 402
4. Discuss the importance of the slavery issue as raised by the annexation of Texas and California's admission to the union as a free state under the Compromise of 1850.	pp. 285, 398–399, 406–407
5. Analyze the significance of the States' Rights Doctrine, the Missouri Compromise (1820), the Wilmot Proviso (1846), the Compromise of 1850, Henry Clay's role in the Missouri Compromise and the Compromise of 1850, the Kansas-Nebraska Act (1854), the *Dred Scott v. Sandford* decision (1857), and the Lincoln-Douglas debates (1858).	pp. 216, 246, 262, 401–417
6. Describe the lives of free blacks and the laws that limited their freedom and economic opportunities.	pp. 178, 181, 376–377, 418–421
8.10 Students analyze the multiple causes, key events, and complex consequences of the Civil War.	
1. Compare the conflicting interpretations of state and federal authority as emphasized in the speeches and writings of statesmen such as Daniel Webster and John C. Calhoun.	pp. 246, 262 Enrichment Resources: Ch. 21 Enrichment Essay
2. Trace the boundaries constituting the North and the South, the geographical differences between the two regions, and the differences between agrarians and industrialists.	pp. 355–368
3. Identify the constitutional issues posed by the doctrine of nullification and secession and the earliest origins of that doctrine.	pp. 216, 262, 402–405
4. Discuss Abraham Lincoln's presidency and his significant writings and speeches and their relationship to the Declaration of Independence, such as his "House Divided" speech (1858), Gettysburg Address (1863), Emancipation Proclamation (1863), and inaugural addresses (1861 and 1865).	pp. 401, 414–417, 423–443, 445 Enrichment Resources: Ch. 22 Enrichment Essay
5. Study the views and lives of leaders (e.g., Ulysses S. Grant, Jefferson Davis, Robert E. Lee) and soldiers on both sides of the war, including those of black soldiers and regiments.	pp. 424–443 Enrichment Resources: Ch. 22 Enrichment Essay

Standards	Where Standards Are Addressed
6. Describe critical developments and events in the war, including the major battles, geographical advantages and obstacles, technological advances, and General Lee's surrender at Appomattox.	pp. 417, 423–443
7. Explain how the war affected combatants, civilians, the physical environment, and future warfare.	pp. 423–443
8.11 Students analyze the character and lasting consequences of Reconstruction.	
1. List the original aims of Reconstruction and describe its effects on the political and social structures of different regions.	pp. 445–457
2. Identify the push-pull factors in the movement of former slaves to the cities in the North and to the West and their differing experiences in those regions (e.g., the experiences of Buffalo Soldiers).	pp. 456–457
3. Understand the effects of the Freedmen's Bureau and the restrictions placed on the rights and opportunities of freedmen, including racial segregation and "Jim Crow" laws.	pp. 445–448, 454–458, 544 Enrichment Resources: Ch. 23 Enrichment Essay
4. Trace the rise of the Ku Klux Klan and describe the Klan's effects.	pp. 452–453
5. Understand the Thirteenth, Fourteenth, and Fifteenth Amendments to the Constitution and analyze their connection to Reconstruction.	pp. 173, 197, 446–461, 484–487, 576
8.12 Students analyze the transformation of the American economy and the changing social and political conditions in the United States in response to the Industrial Revolution.	
1. Trace patterns of agricultural and industrial development as they relate to climate, use of natural resources, markets, and trade and locate such development on a map.	pp. 466–467, 476–480, 490–493, 496–499
2. Identify the reasons for the development of federal Indian policy and the wars with American Indians and their relationship to agricultural development and industrialization.	pp. 264–266, 268–271, 469–482
3. Explain how states and the federal government encouraged business expansion through tariffs, banking, land grants, and subsidies.	pp. 472–473, 479–480, 490–491 Enrichment Resources: Ch. 24 Enrichment Essay
4. Discuss entrepreneurs, industrialists, and bankers in politics, commerce, and industry (e.g., Andrew Carnegie, John D. Rockefeller, Leland Stanford).	pp. 472–474, 490–497, 506–509, 538–540
5. Examine the location and effects of urbanization, renewed immigration, and industrialization (e.g., the effects on social fabric of cities, wealth and economic opportunity, the conservation movement).	pp. 489–509, 511–523, 543, 584–587 Enrichment Resources: Ch. 27 Enrichment Essay
6. Discuss child labor, working conditions, and laissez-faire policies toward big business and examine the labor movement, including its leaders (e.g., Samuel Gompers), its demand for collective bargaining, and its strikes and protests over labor conditions.	pp. 489–504, 535, 542, 548–551

Standards	Where Standards Are Addressed
7. Identify the new sources of large-scale immigration and the contributions of immigrants to the building of cities and the economy; explain the ways in which new social and economic patterns encouraged assimilation of newcomers into the mainstream amidst growing cultural diversity; and discuss the new wave of nativism.	pp. 511–527 Enrichment Resources: Ch. 26 Enrichment Essays
8. Identify the characteristics and impact of Grangerism and Populism.	pp. 536–537
9. Name the significant inventors and their inventions and identify how they improved the quality of life (e.g., Thomas Edison, Alexander Graham Bell, Orville and Wilbur Wright).	pp. 492–495, 506–509 Enrichment Resources: Ch. 25 Enrichment Essays

Historical and Social Science Analysis Skills

Chronological and Spatial Thinking

1. Students explain how major events are related to one another in time.

2. Students construct various time lines of key events, people, and periods of the historical era they are studying.

3. Students use a variety of maps and documents to identify physical and cultural features of neighborhoods, cities, states, and countries and to explain the historical migration of people, expansion and disintegration of empires, and the growth of economic systems.

Historical Research, Evidence, and Point of View

1. Students frame questions that can be answered by historical study and research.

2. Students distinguish fact from opinion in historical narratives and stories.

3. Students distinguish relevant from irrelevant information, essential from incidental information, and verifiable from unverifiable information in historical narratives and stories.

4. Students assess the credibility of primary and secondary sources and draw sound conclusions from them.

5. Students detect the different historical points of view on historical events and determine the context in which the historical statements were made (the questions asked, sources used, author's perspectives).

Historical Interpretation

1. Students explain the central issues and problems from the past, placing people and events in a matrix of time and place.

2. Students understand and distinguish cause, effect, sequence, and correlation in historical events, including the long- and short-term causal relations.

3. Students explain the sources of historical continuity and how the combination of ideas and events explains the emergence of new patterns.

4. Students recognize the role of chance, oversight, and error in history.

5. Students recognize that interpretations of history are subject to change as new information is uncovered.

6. Students interpret basic indicators of economic performance and conduct cost-benefit analyses of economic and political issues.

Notes

Chapter 1

10: Chief Luther Standing Bear, in Valerius Geist, *Buffalo Nation: History and Legend of the North American Bison* (Stillwater, MN: Voyageur Press, 1998). Kenneth Cooper, in Kari Berger, "Walking with Nature: The Native Americans' Age-Old Spiritual Ties with Nature Endure," *In Context: A Quarterly of Humane Sustainable Culture,* Late Winter, 1990, at www.context.org. Wintu woman, in Norbert S. Hill, ed., *Words of Power: Voices from Indian America* (Golden, CO: Fulcrum Publishing, 1999). **15:** Indian song, in David Hurst Thomas, Betty Ballantine, and Ian Ballantine, *The Native Americans: An Illustrated History* (Atlanta, GA: Turner Pub., 1993).

Chapter 2

25: "Marco Polo," Microsoft® Encarta® Online Encyclopedia 2009, at encarta.msn.com, ©1997–2009 Microsoft Corporation. All Rights Reserved. **26:** Christopher Columbus, in Charles W. Eliot, ed., *The Harvard Classics: American Historical Documents 1000–1904,* Vol. 43 (New York: P. F. Collier and Son, 1910), at www.books.google.com. Ibid. **28:** Bernal Diaz del Castillo, *The Discovery and Conquest of Mexico, 1517–1521,* trans. Alfred P. Maudslay (Cambridge, MA: Da Capo Press, 2003). **31:** Francisco Vásquez de Coronado, *The Journey of Coronado 1540–1542,* trans. and ed. George Parker Winship (New York: A. S. Barnes and Co., 1904), at www.books.google.com. Ibid. **34:** Samuel de Champlain, *Voyages of Samuel de Champlain,* Vol. 2, *1604–1610,* trans. Charles Pomeroy Otis, ed. Edmund F. Slafter (Boston: The Prince Society, 1878), at www.books. google.com. **35:** Lorenzo Pasqualigo, in G. E. Weare, *Cabot's Discovery of North America* (Philadelphia: J. B. Lippincott, 1897), at www.books.google.com. **37:** John Smith, The *Generall Historie of Virginia, New England and the Summer Isles,* Vol. 1 (Glasgow: James MacLehose and Sons, 1907). John Smith, "John Smith's 1616 Letter to Queen Anne of Great Britain" at www.digitalhistory. uh.edu. John Rolfe, in Charles E. Hatch Jr., *The First Seventeen Years, Virginia, 1607–1624* (Charlottesville, VA: University of Virginia Press, 1957). **38:** Dutch West India Company, in Division of Historical Studies, "Explorers and Settlers: Historical Background," National Park Service, at www.nps.gov. **42:** Christopher Columbus, *The Log of Christopher Columbus,* trans. Robert S. Fuson (Camden,

ME: International Marine Publishing, 1987). **43:** Christopher Columbus, in Kirkpatrick Sale, *The Conquest of Paradise* (New York: Knopf, 1991). Bartolomé de Las Casas, *The Devastation of the Indies: A Brief Account,* trans. Herma Briffault (Baltimore, MD: John Hopkins, 1992). **44:** Washington Irving, *The Life and Voyages of Christopher Columbus* (New York: Harper and Brothers, 1855), at www.books.google.com. Samuel Eliot Morison, *Christopher Columbus, Mariner* (Boston: Little, Brown, 1955). Samuel Eliot Morison, *Admiral of the Ocean Sea* (Boston: Little, Brown, 1942). Howard Zinn, *A People's History of the United States 1492–Present* (New York: HarperCollins, 2003). **45:** John Noble Wilford, *The Mysterious History of Columbus: An Exploration of the Man, the Myth, the Legacy* (New York: Knopf, 1991).

Chapter 3

47: Gottlieb Mittelberger, *Gottlieb Mittelberger's Journey to Pennsylvania in the Year 1750 and Return to Germany in the Year 1754,* trans. Carl T. Eben (Philadelphia: J. Y. Jeanes, 1898), at www.books.google. com. **51:** John Winthrop, in "A **Modell of Christian Charity" discourse,** at www. bartleby.com. **52:** Roger Williams, in James D. Knowles, *Memoir of Roger Williams: The Founder of the State of Rhode-Island* (Boston: Lincoln, Edmands, and Co., 1834), at www.books.google.com. Cotton Mather, in William G. McLoughlin, *Rhode Island: A History* (New York: W. W. Norton and Co., 1986). **53:** Thomas Hooker, in John Fiske, *The Beginnings of New England or The Puritan Theocracy in Its Religious to Civil and Religious Liberty* (Boston: H. Mifflin, 1892), at www.books.google.com. **54:** James, Duke of York, in John Romeyn Brodhead, *History of the State of New York,* Vol. 2 (New York: Harper and Brothers, 1871), at www. books.google.com. **55:** Gabriel Thomas, in Albert Cook Myers, *Narratives of Early Pennsylvania, West New Jersey and Delaware 1630–1707* (New York: Barnes and Noble, 1959). **56:** George Calvert, in Nan Hayden Agle, *The Lords Baltimore* (New York: Holt, 1962). Cecil Calvert, in Lucian Johnston, *Religious Liberty in Maryland and Rhode Island* (Brooklyn: International Catholic Truth Society, 1903 [in a letter to Leonard Calvert, 1633]), at www.books.google. com. **60:** William Bradford, *Of Plymouth Plantation* (New York: Knopf, 1999). Ibid. **62:** Olaudah Equiano, *Equiano's Travels: The Interesting Narrative of the Life of Olaudah

Equiano or Gustavus Vassa, the African, ed. Paul Edwards (Portsmouth, NH: Heinemann, 1996). Ibid.

Chapter 4

65: Benjamin Franklin, in William Makepeace Thayer, *From Boyhood to Manhood: The Life of Benjamin Franklin* (New York: Hurst and Co., 1889), at www. books.google.com. Benjamin Franklin, *Poor Richard's Almanack* (Waterloo, IA: U. S. C. Publishing Co., 1914), at www.books. google.com. **68:** Anonymous, in Albert S. Bolles, *Pennsylvania Province and State: A History from 1609 to 1790* (Philadelphia: John Wannamaker, 1899), at www.books. google.com. **70:** Olaudah Equiano, *The Life of Olaudah Equiano or Gustavus Vassa, The African* (Boston: Isaac Knapp, 1837), at www. books.google.com. **71:** Benjamin Trumbull, *A Complete History of Connecticut, Civil and Ecclesiastical* (New London, CT: H.D. Utley, 1898), at www.books.google.com. Benjamin Franklin, William Temple Franklin, and William Duane, *Memoirs of Benjamin Franklin,* Vol. 1 (New York: Derby and Jackson, 1859), at www.books.google.com. **73:** Abigail Adams, in Laura E. Richards, *Abigail Adams and Her Times* (New York: D. Appleton and Co., 1917), at www.archive.org. Anonymous, in Arthur W. Calhoun, *A Social History of the American Family from Colonial Times to the Present,* Vol. 1 (Cleveland, OH: The Arthur H. Clark Company, 1917). **76:** Nathan Cole, in "The Great Awakening Comes to Weathersfield, Connecticut: Nathan Cole's Spiritual Travels," at www. historymatters.gmu.edu [first published in George Leon Walker, *Some Aspects of the Religious Life of New England* (New York: Silver, Burnett, and Company, 1897)]. Ibid. **78:** George Whitefield, in Edwin S. Gaustad and Mark A. Noll, eds., *A Documentary History of Religion in America to 1877,* 3rd ed. (Grand Rapids, MI: Wm. B. Eerdmans, 2003). Jonathan Edwards, in Alan Taylor, *American Colonies* (New York: Penguin, 2001). **79:** Jonathan Edwards, in George Marsden, *Jonathan Edwards: A Life* (New Haven, CT: Yale, 2003). Ibid. Isaac Backus, in Taylor, *American Colonies.*

Chapter 5

88: George Washington, in George Thornton Fleming, *History of Pittsburgh and Environs* (New York: American Historical Society, 1922 [first quoted in *London Magazine,* Vol. 13 (1754)]). **89:** George Washington, in a letter to Mary Washington, July 18, 1755, at www.nationalcenter.org. **90:** John H. Plumb, *Men and Places* (London: Cresset Press, 1963). **91:** *The Pennsylvania Journal, in* Nicole Eustace, *Passion Is the Gale: Emotion, Power, and the Coming of the American Revolution* (University of North Carolina Press, 2008). **92:** Quartering Act, in Page Smith, *A New Age Begins: A People's History of the American Revolution* (New York: McGraw-Hill, 1976). Charles Townshend, in ibid. Francis Bernard, in John Adams and Charles Francis Adams, *The Works of John Adams: Second President of the United States,* Vol. 2 (Boston: Little, Brown, and Co., 1865), at www.books.google.com. **92–93:** *Virginia Gazette,* in John Chester Miller, *Origins of the American Revolution* (Stanford, CA: Stanford University Press, 1959). **93:** Charles Townshend, in George Thomas, *Memoirs of the Marquis of Rockingham and His Contemporaries,* Vol. 1 (London: Bentley, 1852). King George, in Marie Louise Herdman, *The Story of the United States* (New York: Frederick A. Stokes Co. Publishers, 1916), at www.archive.org. **94:** Thomas Gage, in Smith, *A New Age Begins.* George Bancroft, *History of the United States: From the Discovery of the Continent,* Vol. 3 (New York: D. Appleton and Co., 1890), at www.books.google.com. Samuel Adams, in Massachusetts Historical Society, *Collections of the Massachusetts Historical Society Volume 1: Warren-Adams Letters* (Boston: The Society, 1917). **95:** Adams, *The Works of John Adams,* Vol. 2. **96:** George Hewes, in John Warner Barber, *The History and Antiquities of New England, New York, New Jersey, and Pennsylvania* (Hartford, CT: Allyn S. Stillman and Son, 1856), at www.books.google.com. **97:** Adams, *The Works of John Adams,* Vol. 2. King George, in H. T. Dickinson, *Britain and the American Revolution* (New York: Longman, 1998). Boston Patriots, in John Chester Miller, *Origins of the American Revolution* (Stanford, CA: Stanford University Press, 1959). **98:** Virginians, in Erik A. Bruun and Jay Crosby, *Our Nation's Archive: The History of the United States in Documents* (New York: Black Dog and Leventhal Pub., 1999). Patrick Henry, speech at the Virginia Convention, Sept. 1774, at www.bartleby.com. **99:** King George, in John R. Alden, *A History of the American Revolution* (Cambridge, MA: Da Capo Press, 1989). **100:** John Parker, speech to troops at Lexington, MA, Apr. 19, 1775, at www.bartleby.com. Captain Isaac Davis, in

Allen French, *Old Concord* (Boston: Little, Brown, and Co., 1915), at www.archive.org. **101:** Hugh Earl Percy, in Charles Knowles Bolton, ed., *Letters of Hugh Earl Percy from Boston and New York, 1774–1776* (Boston: Charles E. Goodspeed, 1902). **102:** Warren G. Harding, in David Hackett Fischer, *Paul Revere's Ride* (New York: Oxford University Press, 1994). **103:** Henry Wadsworth Longfellow, "Paul Revere's Ride," at www.bartleby.com. **104:** Ibid. **105:** Harding, in Fischer, *Paul Revere's Ride.* John Train, in Fischer, *Paul Revere's Ride.* Ray Raphael, *Founding Myths: Stories that Hide Our Patriotic Past* (New York: New Press, 2004). Fischer, *Paul Revere's Ride.*

Chapter 6

107: Joseph Warren, in Christopher Hibbert, *Redcoats and Rebels: The American Revolutions Through British Eyes* (New York: W. W. Norton and Co., 2002). Patrick Henry, "Give Me Liberty or Give Me Death" speech, May 23, 1775, at www.bartleby.com. **108:** John Adams autobiography, part 1, "John Adams," through 1776, sheet 18 of 53 [electronic edition], *Adams Family Papers: An Electronic Archive,* Massachusetts Historical Society, at www.masshist.org. Israel Putnam, in Ernie Gross, *This Day in American History* (New York: Neal-Schuman Pub., 1990). **109:** George Washington, in Paul Leicester Ford, *The True George Washington* (Philadelphia: Lippincott, 1911). William Emerson, in John Frederick Schroeder and Benson J. Lossing, *Life and Times of Washington,* Vol. 2, introduction by Edward C. Towne (Albany, NY: M. M. Belcher Pub., 1903). **110:** John Adams and Charles Francis Adams, *The Works of John Adams: Second President of the United States,* Vol. 1 (Boston: Little, Brown, and Co., 1856), at www.books.google.com. King George, "A Proclamation for Suppressing Rebellion and Sedition," Aug., 23, 1775, at www.masshist.org. Charles Lee and Sir Henry Edward Bunbury, *The Lee Papers, 1754–1776,* Vol. 1 (New York: New York Historical Society, 1872), at www.books.google.com. Thomas Paine, *Common Sense,* 1776, at www.bartleby.com. **112:** John Adams, in a letter to Abigail Adams, July 3, 1776, at www.masshist.org. **113:** Benjamin Franklin, at the signing of the Declaration of Independence, July 4, 1776, at www.bartleby.com. **114:** Benjamin Franklin, in Scott Liell, *46 Pages: Thomas Paine,* Common Sense, *and the Turning Point to Independence* (Philadelphia: Running Press, 2003). **116:**

Thomas Paine, in Craig Nelson, *Thomas Paine: Enlightenment, Revolution, and the Birth of Modern Nations* (New York: Viking, 2006). Ibid. Thomas Paine, in Liell, *46 Pages.* Anonymous, in Eric Foner, *Tom Paine and Revolutionary America* (New York: Oxford University Press, 1976). **117:** Nelson, *Thomas Paine.* Thomas Paine, in Foner, *Tom Paine.* Thomas Paine, in Samuel Edwards, *Rebel! A Biography of Tom Paine* (New York: Praeger, 1974). Thomas Paine, in Foner, *Tom Paine.* Ibid. Benjamin Rush, in Liell, *46 Pages.*

Chapter 7

119: Joseph Plumb Martin, *A Narrative of a Revolutionary Soldier: Some of the Adventures, Dangers, and Sufferings of Joseph Plumb Martin,* introduction by Thomas Fleming (New York: Penguin Group, 2001). Ibid. Isaac Bangs, in Thomas J. Fleming, *Liberty! The American Revolution* (New York: Viking, 1997). **123:** Thomas Mifflin and George Washington, in Gregory T. Edgar, *Campaign of 1776: The Road to Trenton* (Bowie, MD: Heritage Books, 1995). George Washington, *The Writings of George Washington,* Vol. 5, ed. Worthington Chauncey Ford (New York: G. P. Putnam's Sons, 1890), at www.books.google.com. **124:** Worthington Chauncey Ford, *George Washington,* Vol. 1 (New York: Charles Scribner and Sons, 1900). Thomas Paine, *The Crisis,* 1776, at www.bartleby.com. George Washington, in Henry P. Johnston, *The Campaign of 1776 Around New York and Brooklyn* (Brooklyn, NY: Long Island Historical Society, 1878), at www.gutenberg.org. George Washington, in James O'Boyle, *Life of George Washington, the Father of Modern Democracy* (New York: Longmans, Green, and Co., 1915). Anonymous, in Fleming, *Liberty!* **126:** Marquis de Lafayette, in Charlemagne Tower, *The Marquis de La Fayette in the American Revolution,* Vol. 1 (Philadelphia: J. B. Lippincott, 1895), at www.books.google.com. Martin, *A Narrative of a Revolutionary Soldier.* George Washington, in Henry Cabot Lodge, *George Washington,* Vol. 1 (Echo Library, 2007), at www.books.google.com. **127:** Martin, *A Narrative of a Revolutionary Soldier.* Anonymous, in Bruce Chadwick, *George Washington's War: The Forging of a Revolutionary Leader and the American Presidency* (Naperville, IL: Sourcebooks, Inc., 2005). Marquis de Lafayette, in Thomas J. Fleming, *Liberty! The American Revolution* (New York: Viking, 1997). Marquis de Lafayette, in George

Washington Parke Custis, *Recollections and Private Memoirs of Washington* (Philadelphia: J. W. Bradley, 1861), at www.books.google.com. George Washington, *The Writings of George Washington,* Vol. 6 (Boston: Russell, Odiorne, and Metcalf, 1834), at www.books.google.com. **128:** Nathanael Greene in Henry Cabot Lodge, *The Story of the Revolution* (New York: Charles Scribner's, 1903), at www.books.google.com. Charles Cornwallis, *Correspondence of Charles, First Marquis Cornwallis,* Vol. 1, ed. Charles Ross (London: John Murray, 1859), at www.books.google.com. **129:** Martin, *Narrative of a Revolutionary Soldier.* **130:** Smith, *A New Age Begins.* Charles Cornwallis, in James Thacher, *Military Journal, During the American Revolutionary War, from 1775 to 1783* (Hartford, CT: Silas, Andrus, and Son, 1854), at www.books.google.com. Martin, *Narrative of a Revolutionary Soldier.* **132:** Charles Cornwallis, in Henry Phelps Johnston, *The Yorktown Campaign and the Surrender of Cornwallis, 1781* (New York: Harper and Brothers, 1881), at www.books.google.com. **133:** A. J. R. Turgot, in Stanley J. Idzerda and Roger Everett Smith, *France and the American War for Independence* (Scott Limited Editions, 1975). **134:** George Washington, in Saxe Commins , ed., *Basic Writings of George Washington* (New York: Random House, 1948). George Washington, "On His Appointment as Commander-in-Chief," 1775, in www.bartleby.com. George Washington, in Saul K. Padover, ed., *The Washington Papers: Basic Selections from the Public and Private Writings of George Washington* (New York: Harper and Brothers, 1955). **135:** Joseph Plumb Martin, *A Narrative of Some of the Adventures, Dangers and Sufferings of a Revolutionary Soldier,* ed. George F. Scheer (Manchester, NH: Ayer Company Publishers, 1998). George Washington, in Padover, *The Washington Papers.* **136:** Ibid. George Washington, in Frank Donovan, ed., *The George Washington Papers* (New York: Dodd, Mead and Co., 1964). **137:** George Washington, in Padover, *The Washington Papers.* Martin, *A Narrative of Some of the Adventures, Dangers and Sufferings of a Revolutionary Soldier.* George Washington, in Donovan, *The George Washington Papers.* George Washington, in John A. Stevens, et al., *The Magazine of American History with Notes and Queries,* Vol. 6 (New York: A. S. Barnes and Col., 1881), at www.books.google.com. George Washington, in James Thomas Flexner,

ed., *George Washington in the American Revolution (1775–1783)* (Boston: Little, Brown and Co., 1968). Ibid.

Chapter 8

145: James Madison, *The Writings of James Madison,* Vol. 1, 1769–1783, ed. Gaillard Hunt (New York: G. P. Putnam's Sons, 1900), at www.books.google.com. **147:** James Madison, *The Writings of James Madison,* Vol. 2, 1783–1787, ed. Gaillard Hunt (New York: G. P. Putnam's Sons, 1901), at www.books.google.com. James Madison, *Journal of the Federal Convention,* ed. E. H. Scott (Chicago: Albert, Scott, and Co., 1893), at www.books.google.com. "Report of Proceedings in Congress: February 21, 1787," at Yale Law School: The Avalon Project, www.avalon.law.yale.edu. **148:** Thomas Andrew Bailey, *Voices of America: The Nation's Story in Slogans, Sayings, and Songs* (Free Press, 1976). **149:** James MacGregor Burns, *The Vineyard of Liberty* (New York: Knopf, 1982). Thomas Jefferson, *Memoirs, Correspondence, and Private Papers of Thomas Jefferson: Late President of the United States,* Vol. 2, ed. Thomas Jefferson Randolph (London: H. Colburn and R. Bentley, 1829), at www.books.google.com. William Pierce in John F. Jameson, Henry E. Bourne, and Robert L. Schuyler, eds., *The American Historical Review,* Vol. 3 (New York: The Macmillan Company, 1898), at www.books.google.com. Benjamin Franklin, in Buckner, F. Melton, ed., *The Quotable Founding Fathers: A Treasury of 2,500 Wise and Witty Quotations* (Dulles, VA: Brassey's, 2004). George Washington, in Washington Irving, *The Life of George Washington,* Vol. 4 (New York: Cosimo, 2005). **150:** William Paterson, in John R. Vile, *The Constitutional Convention of 1787: A Comprehensive Encyclopedia of America's Founding,* Vol. 2 (Santa Barbara, CA: ABC-CLIO, 2005). **151:** Ibid. **152:** James Wilson, in Ellen Frankel Paul and Howard Dickman, *Liberty, Property, and the Foundations of the American Constitution* (Albany, NY: SUNY Press, 1989). Gunning Bedford, in Max Ferrand, ed., *The Records of the Federal Convention of 1787,* Vol. 1 (New Haven, CT: Yale University Press, 1911). Rufus King, in James Madison, *Journal of the Federal Convention,* ed. E. H. Scott (Chicago: Scott, Foresman, and Co., 1898), at www.books.google.com. **153:** Gouverneur Morris, in George Bancroft, *History of the Formation of the Constitution of the United States of America,* Vol. 2 (New York: D. Appleton

and Co., 1889), at www.books.google.com. Elbridge Gerry, in Max Ferrand, ed., *The Records of the Federal Convention of 1787,* Vol. 1 (New Haven, CT: Yale University Press, 1911). Gouverneur Morris, in Bancroft, *History of the Formation.* **155:** Charles Pinckney, in John R. Vile, *The Constitutional Convention of 1787: A Comprehensive Encyclopedia of America's Founding,* Vol. 2 (Santa Barbara, CA: ABC-CLIO, 2005). Benjamin Franklin, in Vile, *Constitutional Convention of 1787.* Gouverneur Morris, in Thomas J. Fleming, *Liberty! The American Revolution* (New York: Viking, 1997). **157:** James Madison, *The Writings of James Madison,* Vol. 4, ed. Gaillard Hunt (New York: G. P. Putnam's Sons, 1903), at www.books.google.com. Benjamin Franklin, *The Works of Dr. Benjamin Franklin,* Vol. 5 (Philadelphia: Duane, 1809), at www.books.google.com. **158:** Benjamin Franklin, at the Constitutional Convention," Sept. 17, 1787, at www.bartleby.com. **162:** James Madison, in Richard B. Morris, *Witnesses at the Creation: Hamilton, Madison, Jay and the Constitution* (New York: Holt, Rinehart, and Winston, 1985). Edmund Randolph, in Carol Berkin, *A Brilliant Solution: Inventing the American Constitution* (New York: Harcourt, 2002). **163:** James Madison, *Debates of the Adoption of the Federal Constitution in the Convention Held at Philadelphia in 1787,* Vol. 5, ed. Jonathan Elliot (New York: Burt Franklin, 1888), at www.books.google.com.

Chapter 9

172: George Mason, in John R. Vile, *The Constitutional Convention of 1787: A Comprehensive Encyclopedia of America's Founding,* Vol. 2 (Santa Barbara, CA: ABC-CLIO, 2005). **173:** Thomas Jefferson, *Memoirs, Correspondence, and Private Papers of Thomas Jefferson: Late President of the United States,* Vol. 3, ed. Thomas Jefferson Randolph (London: H. Colburn and R. Bentley, 1829), at www.books.google.com. **177:** Carl Van Doren, *The Great Rehearsal* (New York: Viking Press, 1948). **180:** Abigail Adams, in a letter to John Adams, Mar. 31, 1776, at www.thelizlibrary.org. Ibid. John Adams, in a letter to Abigail Adams, Apr. 14, 1776, at www.thelizlibrary.org. **181:** Benjamin Banneker, in a letter to Thomas Jefferson, at www.pbs.org. Ibid. Thomas Jefferson, in a letter to Benjamin Banneker, Aug. 30, 1791, at www.pbs.org.+

Chapter 10

183: James Madison, in "Outline" notes, Sept. 1829, at www.bartleby.com. Gordon Lloyd and Margie Lloyd, *The Essential Bill of Rights: Original Arguments and Fundamental Documents* (Lanham, MD: University Press of America, 1998). **184:** Thomas Jefferson, in Fred R. Shapiro, ed., *The Yale Book of Quotations* (R. R. Donnelley and Sons, 2006). Pierce Butler, in Robert Allen Rutland, in *James Madison: The Founding Father* (Columbia: University of Missouri Press, 1987). James Madison, in Robert A. Goodwin, *From Parchment to Power* (La Vergne, TN: American Enterprise Institute, 1997). Ibid. **185:** Thomas Jefferson, in a letter to the Danbury Baptists, Jan. 1, 1802, at www.loc.gov. **186:** Andrew Hamilton, in James Alexander, *A Brief Narrative of the Case and Trial of John Peter Zenger, Printer of the New York Weekly Journal,* ed. Stanley Nider Katz (Cambridge, MA: Belknap Press of Harvard University, 1963). Justice Oliver Wendell Holmes, in U.S. Supreme Court, *United States Supreme Court Reports,* Vol. 63 (Rochester, New York: The Lawyers Co-operative Pub., 1920). **187:** Supreme Court decision, *Texas v. Johnson,* at www.britannica.com. **188:** Joseph Story, *Commentaries of the Constitution of the United States,* Vol. 2 (Boston: Little, Brown, and Co., 1873), at www.books.google.com. **191:** Thurgood Marshall, in Wallace D. Loh, *Social Research in the Judicial Process: Cases, Readings, and Text* (Russell Sage Foundation, 1984). **192:** Cornell University Law School, Supreme Court Collection, *Gregg v. Georgia,* at www.law.cornell.edu. **194:** Marian Ward, in Peter Irons, *God on Trial* (New York: Viking, 2007). Amanda Bruce, in Peter Irons, *God on Trial.* **195:** Thomas Jefferson, in E. M. Halliday, *Understanding Thomas Jefferson* (New York: Harper Collins, 2001).

Chapter 11

205: George Washington, in a letter to Henry Knox, Apr. 1, 1789, at www.consource.org. **206:** George Washington, First Inaugural Address, 1789, at www.bartleby.com. **207:** Decree by the French Directory, in Robert Debs Heinl, *Dictionary of Military and Naval Quotations* (Annapolis, MD: United States Naval Institute, 1966). **208:** Fisher Ames, in Francis D. Cogliano, *Revolutionary America, 1763–1815: A Political History* (New York: Routledge, 2000). George Washington, Farewell Address, 1796, at www.bartleby.com. **209:** Alexander Hamilton, *The Works of Alexander Hamilton Comprising His Correspondence and His Political and His Official Writings, Exclusive of The Federalist, Civil and Military,* Vol. 2, ed. John C. Hamilton (New York: John F. Trow, 1850), at www.books.google.com. Alexander Hamilton, *The Works of Alexander Hamilton,* Vol. 6, ed. John C. Hamilton (New York: Charles S. Francis and Co., 1851), at www.books.google.com. **210:** John Jay, at www.brainyquote.com. **211:** Alexander Hamilton, in John Chester Miller, *Alexander Hamilton and the Growth of the New Nation* (New Brunswick, NJ: Transaction Pub., 2004). **212:** Thomas Jefferson, at www.encarta.msn.com. ©1993–2009 Microsoft Corporation. Thomas Jefferson, in a letter to Comte Diodati, 1789, at www.etext.virginia.edu. Thomas Jefferson, *Memoirs, Correspondence, and Private Papers of Thomas Jefferson: Late President of the United States,* Vol. 2, ed. Thomas Jefferson Randolph (London: H. Colburn and R. Bentley, 1829), at www.books.google.com. **213:** Thomas Jefferson, *The Jeffersonian Cyclopedia: A Comprehensive Collection of the Views of Thomas Jefferson,* ed. John P. Foley (New York: Funk and Wagnalls, Co. 1900), at www.books.google.com. **214:** Federalist newspaper, quoted in Louis Edward Ingelhart, *Press Freedoms: A Descriptive Calendar of Concepts, Interpretations, Events, and Court Actions, from 4000 BC to the Present* (Westport, CT: Greenwood Press, 1987). John Adams, *The Works of John Adams, Second President of the United States,* Vol. 10, ed. Charles Francis Adams (Boston: Little, Brown, and Co., 1856), at www.books.google.com. Thomas Jefferson, in Samuel Mosheim Smucker, *The Life and Times of Thomas Jefferson* (Philadelphia: J. W. Bradley, 1859), at www.books.google.com. **215:** John Adams, *The Works of John Adams, Second President of the United States,* Vol. 9, ed. Charles Francis Adams (Boston: Little, Brown, and Co., 1854), at www.books.google.com. Sedition Act, July 14, 1798, at www.constitution.org. Benjamin Bache, in Donald Henderson Stewart, *The Opposition Press of the Federalist Period* (Albany: State University of New York Press, 1969). **216:** Abigail Adams, in a letter to Mary Cranch, Nov. 21, 1800, at www.whitehousehistory.org. **217:** Thomas Jefferson, in a letter to Elbridge Gerry, Jan. 26, 1799, at www.jeffersontoday.org. William Linn, *Serious Considerations on the Election of a President: Addressed to the Citizens of the United States* (New York: John Furman, 1800), at www.books.google.com. Oliver Wolcott, *Memoirs of the Administrations of Washington and John Adams,* Vol. 2, ed. George Gibbs (New York: William Van Norden, 1846), at www.books.google.com. **219:** Alexander Hamilton, *The Works of Alexander Hamilton,* Vol. 10, ed. Henry Cabot Lodge (New York: G.P. Putnam's Sons, 1904), at www.books.google.com. **220:** John Adams, in a letter to Abigail Adams, Nov. 2, 1800, at www.ourwhitehouse.org. Abigail Adams, in Betty C. Monkman, *The Living White House* (Washington, DC: WHHA, 2007). **221:** Thomas Jefferson, in Robert P. Watson, ed., *Life in the White House: A Social History of the First Family and the President's House* (Albany: State University of NY Press, 2004). **223:** Anonymous, in Betty C. Monkman, *The Living White House.* John Adams, at www.ourwhitehouse.org.

Chapter 12

226: George Washington, Farewell Address, 1796, at www.bartleby.com. **228:** Robert Goodloe Harper, at www.bartleby.com. **229:** John Adams, *The Works of John Adams, Second President of the United States,* Vol. 10, ed. Charles Francis Adams (Boston: Little, Brown, and Co., 1856), at www.books.google.com. **230:** Thomas Jefferson, in Albert Marrin, *1812, the War Nobody Won* (New York: Atheneum, 1985). Robert Goodloe Harper, at www.bartleby.com. **233:** Thomas Jefferson, *The Writings of Thomas Jefferson,* Vol. 6, ed. H. A. Washington (Washington, DC: Taylor and Maury, 1854), at www.books.google.com. **234:** Edward Channing, *The United States of America 1765–1865* (New York: Macmillan and Co., 1896), at www.books.google.com. **235:** Marion Florence Lansing, *Liberators and Heroes of Mexico and Central America* (Boston: L. C. Page, 1941). Simón Bolívar, in John A. Crow, *The Epic of Latin America,* 4th ed. (Berkeley: University of California Press, 1992). **236:** Thomas Jefferson, *Memoirs, Correspondence, and Private Papers of Thomas Jefferson: Late President of the United States,* Vol. 4, ed. Thomas Jefferson Randolph (London: H. Colburn and R. Bentley, 1829), at www.books.google.com. John Quincy Adams, *Memoirs of John Quincy Adams, Comprising Portions of His Diary from 1795 to 1848,* Vol. 6, ed. Charles Francis Adams (Philadelphia: J. B. Lippincott and Co., 1875), at www.books.google.com. Monroe Doctrine, Dec. 2, 1823, at www.ushistory.org. Ibid. **238:** Tecumseh, in John Sugden, *Tecumseh: A Life* (New York: Henry Holt, 1997).

Tecumseh, in Zoe Trodd, ed., *American Protest Literature* (Cambridge, MA: Belknap Press, 2006). William Henry Harrison, in Sugden, *Tecumseh*. **240:** Tecumseh, in Trodd, *American Protest Literature*. **241:** Tecumseh, in *Ohio History Central*, "Tecumseh," at www.ohiohistorycentral.org.

Chapter 13
243: George Armistead, at www.usflag.org. Alexis de Tocqueville, *Democracy in America*, ed. and trans. Harvey C. Mansfield and Delba Winthrop (Chicago: University of Chicago Press, 2000). **245:** Alexis de Tocqueville, at www.tocqueville.org. **246:** Daniel Webster, *The Works of Daniel Webster*, Vol. 1 (Boston: Little, Brown, and Co. 1890), at www.books.google.com. **249:** Thomas Dartmouth Rice, in W. T. Lhamon, *Jump Jim Crow: Lost Plays, Lyrics, and Street Prose of the First Atlantic Popular Culture* (Cambridge, MA: Harvard University Press, 2003). **250:** Sydney Smith, in William B. Cairns, *British Criticisms of American Writings, 1815–1833* (Madison: University of Wisconsin, 1922). Davy Crockett, in Constance Rourke, *Davy Crockett* (New York: Harcourt, Brace and Co., 1934). Alexis de Tocqueville, in George Wilson Pierson, *Tocqueville in America* (Baltimore, MD: Johns Hopkins University Press, 1996 [first published 1938 by Oxford University Press]). Henry Wadsworth Longfellow, "The Building of the Ship," at www.bartleby.com. **252:** Washington Irving, in Nina Baym, ed., *The Norton Anthology of American Literature 1820–1865* (New York: W.W. Norton, 2008). Ibid. Ibid. Ibid. Ibid. **253:** Ibid. Ibid. **254:** James Fenimore Cooper, *The Pioneers* (BiblioBazaar, 2008 [first published 1823]). Ibid. **255:** Ibid. Ibid.

Chapter 14
257: Anonymous, in Dick Stoken, *The Great Game of Politics: Why We Elect Whom We Elect* (New York: Forge, 2004). **258:** Anonymous, in Hendrik Booraem, *Young Hickory: The Making of Andrew Jackson* (Dallas, TX: Taylor Trade Pub., 2001). Andrew Jackson, in James Parton, *Life of Andrew Jackson*, Vol. 1 (New York: Mason Brothers, 1860), at www.books.google.com. Anonymous, in Parton, *Life of Andrew Jackson*, Vol. 1. Charles Dickinson, in Parton, *Life of Andrew Jackson*, Vol. 1. **260:** Daniel Webster, in James Parton, *General Jackson* (New York: D. Appleton and Co., 1893), at www.books.google.com. Margaret Bayard

Smith, in a letter to Mrs. Kirkpatrick, Mar. 11, 1829, at www.whitehousehistory.org. Ibid. **261:** Henry A. Wise, in Alfred Steinberg, *The First Ten: The Founding Presidents and Their Administrations* (Garden City, NY: Doubleday, 1967). Andrew Jackson, in Marquis James, *Portrait of a President* (New York: Bobbs-Merrill Co., 1937). **262:** Andrew Jackson, in Frederic Austin Ogg, *The Reign of Andrew Jackson* (Bibliobazaar, 2008 [first published 1919 by U.S. Publishers Assoc.]), at www.books.google.com. **265:** Black Hawk, in Page Smith, *The Nation Comes of Age: A People's History of the Ante-Bellum Years* (New York: McGraw-Hill, 1981). Anonymous soldier, in James Mooney, *Myths of the Cherokee* (Washington: G. P. O., 1902). **268:** John G. Burnett, in Thomas Bryan Underwood and Moselle Stack Sandlin, *Cherokee Legends and the Trail of Tears* (Knoxville, TN: S. B. Newman Printing, 1956). Ibid. Ibid. Ibid. **270:** Anonymous, in Theda Perdue and Michael D. Green, *The Cherokee Nation and the Trail of Tears* (New York: Viking, 2007). Ibid. **271:** Ibid. Martin Davis, in Vicki Rozema, ed., *Voices from the Trail of Tears* (Winston-Salem, NC: J. F. Blair, 2003). Anonymous, in Perdue and Green, *The Cherokee Nation and the Trail of Tears*. Chad Smith, in ibid.

Chapter 15
279: John O'Sullivan, in Albert Katz Weinberg, *Manifest Destiny: A Study of Nationalist Expansionism in American History* (Chicago: Quadrangle Books, 1935). Ibid. **280:** James Madison, *The Writings of James Madison*, Vol. 6, 1790–1802, ed. Gaillard Hunt (New York: G. P. Putnam's Sons, 1906), at www.books.google.com. **281:** Talleyrand, at www.lpb.org. Fabricus, in *Jefferson and the Press: Crucible of Liberty* (Columbia: University of South Carolina Press, 2006 [first published July 13, 1803, in the *Columbian Centinel*]). Anonymous, in Thomas A. Bailey, *A Diplomatic History of the American People* (New York: F. S. Crofts, 1940). Anonymous, in Alexander DeConde, *This Affair of Louisiana* (New York: Scribner, 1976). **282:** *Louisiana Advertiser*, in Thomas A. Bailey, *A Diplomatic History of the American People* (New York: F. S. Crofts, 1940). **284:** Antonio López de Santa Anna, in Mary Deborah Petite, *1836 Facts About the Alamo and the Texas War for Independence* (Cambridge, MA: Da Capo Press, 1999). William Travis, in *The National Cyclopædia of American Biography*, Vol. 4 (New York:

J. T. White, 1892), at www.books.google.com. **285:** Antonio López de Santa Anna, in Petite, *1836 Facts*. Sam Houston's troops, in John Holmes Jenkins, ed., *The Papers of the Texas Revolution, 1835–1836*, Vol. 6 (Austin, TX: Presidial Press, 1973). Henry Clay, *The Papers of Henry Clay, Candidate, Compromiser, Elder Statesman, January 1, 1844–June 29, 1852*, Vol. 10, ed. Melba Porter Hay (Lexington: University Press of Kentucky, 1991). **286:** Meriwether Lewis et al., *Original Journals of the Lewis and Clark Expedition 1804–1806*, Vol. 7, ed. Reuben Gold Thwaites (New York: Dodd, Mead, and Co., 1905), at www.books.google.com. **287:** Anonymous, in Ray Allen Billington, *The Far Western Frontier, 1830–1860* (New York: Harper, 1956). Ibid. Anonymous, in Oregon Historical Society, *The Oregon Historical Quarterly*, Vol. 3, ed. Frederic George Young (Salem, OR: W. H. Leeds, 1902), at www.books.google.com. Senators, in "A Disciple of the Washington School," *Oregon: The Cost, and the Consequences* (Philadelphia: 1846), at www.books.google.com. **288:** James K. Polk, in a message to Congress, May 11, 1846, at www.pbs.org. James K. Polk, *The Diary of James K. Polk During His Presidency, 1845–1849*, Vol. 2, ed. Milo Milton Quaife (Chicago: A. C. McClurg, 1910). **289:** Antonio López de Santa Anna, in *The Gentleman's Magazine*, Jan.–June 1847, 182, at www.books.google.com. Mexican officer, in Mark Crawford, *Encyclopedia of the Mexican-American War* (Santa Barbara, CA: ABC-CLIO, 1999). **290:** Anonymous, in *The United States Magazine and Democratic Review* 24 (1849). **292:** Susan Shelby Magoffin, *Down the Santa Fe Trail and into Mexico: The Diary of Susan Shelby Magoffin, 1846–1847*, ed., Stella M. Drumm (New Haven, CT: Yale University Press, 1962). **293:** Anonymous, in Marc Simmons, *Along the Santa Fe Trail* (Albuquerque, NM: UNM Press, 1986). Josiah Gregg, *Commerce of the Prairies: The Journal of a Santa Fe Trader* (Dallas, TX: Southwest Press, 1933 [first published 1844]). **294:** Magoffin, *Down the Santa Fe Trail*. Ibid. Ibid. Ibid. Henry Inman, in Special Publications Division of the National Geographic Society, *Trails West* (National Geographic Society, 1979). **295:** Magoffin, *Down the Santa Fe Trail*.

Chapter 16
297: Horace Greeley, in James Parton, *The Life of Horace Greeley, Editor of the New York Tribune* (New York: Mason Brothers, 1855),

at www.books.google.com. **298:** Meriwether Lewis et al., *History of the Expedition Under the Command of Lewis and Clark,* Vol. 1, ed. Elliott Coues (New York: Francis P. Harper, 1893), at www.books.google.com. **299:** Meriwether Lewis and William Clark, *The Journals of Lewis and Clark,* ed. Frank Bergon (New York: Penguin Books, 1989). Ibid. Meriwether Lewis, et al., *Original Journals of the Lewis and Clark Expedition, 1804–1806,* Vol. 7, ed. Reuben Gold Thwaites (New York: Dodd, Mead and Co., 1905), at www.books.google.com. Zebulon Pike, in "Zebulon Pike: Hard-Luck Explorer or Successful Spy?" at www.nps.gov. **300:** Guadalupe Vallejo, in Elizabeth Smith Brownstein, *If This House Could Talk: Historic Homes, Extraordinary Americans* (New York: Simon and Schuster, 1999). **302:** James O. Pattie, *The Personal Narrative of James O. Pattie, of Kentucky,* ed. Timothy Fint (Chicago: R. R. Donnelly and Sons, 1930), at www.books.google.com. James P. Beckwourth and T. D. Bonner, *The Life and Adventures of James P. Beckwourth, Mountaineer, Scout, Pioneer, and Chief of the Crow Nation of Indians,* ed. Charles G. Leland (London: T. Fisher Unwin, 1892), at www.books.google.com. **303:** Narcissa Whitman and Eliza Spalding, *Where Wagons Could Go,* ed. Clifford Merrill Drury (Arthur H. Clark Co., 1963 [first published 1963 as Vol. 1 of *First White Women over the Rockies: Diaries, Letters, and Biographical Sketches of the Six Women of the Oregon Mission Who Made the Overland Journey in 1836 and 1838*]). Marcus Whitman, in William A. Mowry, *Marcus Whitman and the Early Days of Oregon* (New York: Silver, Burdett, and Co., 1901), at www.books.google.com. Whitman and Spalding, *Where Wagons Could Go.* **304:** Helen Carpenter, in Keith Heyer Meldahl, *Hard Road West* (Chicago: University of Chicago Press, 2007). Lavinia Porter, in Meldahl, *Hard Road West.* **305:** Mary Ellen Todd, in Elliott West, *Growing Up with the Country: Childhood on the Far Western Frontier* (Albuquerque: University of New Mexico Press, 1989). **306:** Brigham Young, in Milton R. Hunter, *Brigham Young the Colonizer,* 3rd ed. (Independence, MO: Zion's Printing and Pub. Co., 1945). Orson F. Whitney, *Popular History of Utah* (Salt Lake City, UT: The Deseret News, 1916). Harriet Young, in Milton R. Hunter, *Brigham Young the Colonizer.* Brigham Young, in Ernest Henry Taves, *This Is the Place: Brigham Young and the New Zion* (Buffalo, NY: Prometheus Books, 1991). Anonymous,

in Ray Allen Billington, *The Far Western Frontier, 1830–1860* (New York: Harper, 1956). **308:** James Marshall, in Gary Noy, ed., *Distant Horizon: Documents from the Nineteenth-Century American West* (Lincoln: University of Nebraska Press, 1999). Walter Colton, in Federal Writers Project, *California: A Guide to the Golden State* (New York: Hastings House Pub., 1939). Luzena Wilson, in Fern Henry, *My Checkered Life: Luzena Stanley Wilson in Early California* (Nevada City, CA: Carl Mautz Pub., 2003). **309:** Ibid. Ibid. Louise Clappe, *The Shirley Letters: Being Letters Written in 1851–1852 from the California Mines* (San Francisco: T. C. Russell, 1922). Anonymous, in Walker Demarquis Wyman, *California Emigrant Letters* (New York: Bookman Associates, 1952). Chinese circular, in Xiao-huang Yin, *Chinese American Literature Since the 1850s* (Urbana: University of Illinois Press, 2000). **310:** Lai Chun-Chuen, at www.museumca.org. John McDougal, in Xiao-huang Yin, *Chinese American Literature.* William Kelly, *A Stroll Through the Diggings of California* (Oakland, CA: Biobooks, 1950). Anonymous, in Donald Dale Jackson, *Gold Dust* (New York: Knopf, 1980). William Shaw, in J. A. G. Roberts, *China to Chinatown: Chinese Food in the West* (London: Reaktion Books, 2002). **311:** Rolander Guy McClellen, *The Golden State: A History of the Region West of the Rocky Mountains* (Philadelphia: William Flint and Co., 1876), at www.books.google.com. **312:** Luzena Stanley Wilson, in "Luzena Stanley Wilson '49er: Her Memoirs as Taken Down by her Daughter in 1881," at www.pbs.org. Ibid. Ibid. **313:** Thomas Kerr, in California Historical Society, "An Irishman in the Gold Rush: The Journal of Thomas Kerr and Charles L. Camp," *California Historical Society Quarterly* 8, no. 2 (June 1929). Ibid. **314:** Vicente Pérez Rosales, in Edwin A. Beilharz and Carlos U. López, eds., *We Were 49ers: Chilean Accounts of the California Gold Rush* (Pasadena, CA: Ward Ritchie Press, 1976). Ibid. Ibid. **315:** Alvin Coffee, in Rudolph M. Lapp, *Blacks in Gold Rush California* (New Haven, CT: Yale University Press, 1977). Vicente Pérez Rosales, in Beilharz and López, eds., *We Were 49ers.*

Chapter 17

317: David J. Weber, *Foreigners in Their Native Land: Historical Roots of the Mexican Americans* (Albuquerque: University of New Mexico Press, 2003). **318:** Anonymous, in

Dan De Quille, *A History of the Comstock Silver Lode and Mines* (Virginia, NV: F. Boegle, 1889), at www.books.google.com. **321:** Anonymous, in "Sheep Ranching," at www.tshaonline.org. **323:** William Heath Davis, *Sixty Years in California: A History of Events and Life in California* (San Francisco: A. J. Leary, Pub., 1889), at www.books.google.com. **324:** Anonymous, in Karen J. Weitze, *California's Mission Revival* (Los Angeles: Hennessey and Ingalls, 1984). **326:** Davis, *Sixty Years in California.* **328:** Judith F. Baca, "About the Great Wall of Los Angeles: A Personal Message from Judy Baca," at www.sparcmurals.org. **329:** *BorderLore,* "The Ins and Outs of a 'Tatoo' Mural in Tucson," interview with Alex Garza, at www.borderlore.com. Alex Garza, in Arizona Public Media, *Las Artes,* at www.azpm.org. **330:** Carl Heyward, "El Teatro Campesino: An Interview with Luis Valdez," interview with Luis Valdez, *The Community Arts Network,* September 2002 [first published in *High Performance* 32, no. 4 (1985)], at www.communityarts.net. **331:** John Patriarca, in Charro Days Fiesta "2008 Parades and Dances Highlight 71st Fiesta," at www.charrodaysfiesta.com.

Chapter 18

339: Sojourner Truth, in Maurianne Adams, et al., eds., *Readings for Diversity and Social Justice* (New York: Routledge, 2000). Frances Dana Gage, in Kai Wright, ed., *The African-American Experience: Black History and Culture Through Speeches, Letters, Editorials, Poems, Songs, and Stories* (New York: Black Dog and Leventhal Pub., 2001). **340:** Rev. Charles G. Finney, *Lectures on Revivals of Religion* (Oberlin, OH: E. J. Goodrich, 1868), at www.books.google.com. **341:** Henry David Thoreau, *Walden; or, Life in the Woods* (New York: E. P. Dutton and Co., 1912). **342:** Dorothea Dix, in Erik Bruun and Jay Crosby, eds., *Our Nation's Archive: The History of the United States in Documents* (New York: Black Dog and Leventhal Pub., 1999). **343:** Horace Mann, *Annual Reports on Education* (Boston: Lee and Shepard Pub., 1872), at www.books.google.com. Horace Mann, in *Life and Works of Horace Mann,* at www.bartleby.com. **344:** Philip Bell, in Jacqueline Bacon, *Freedom's Journal: The First African-American Newspaper* (Lanham, MD: Lexington Books, 2007). **345:** William Lloyd Garrison, "Salutory of the Liberator," Jan. 1, 1831, at www.bartleby.com. William Lloyd Garrison, in William S. McFeely, *Frederick*

Douglass (New York: W. W. Norton and Co., 1991). Frederick Douglass, in "Biographies: Frederick Douglass," at www.pbs.org. **346:** Angelina Grimke, in Rosemary Skinner Keller and Rosemary Radford Ruether, eds., *Encyclopedia of Woman and Religion in North America* (Bloomington: Indiana University Press, 2006). **347:** Lucy Stone, in Elizabeth Cady Stanton, et al., eds., *History of Woman Suffrage,* Vol. 1, 2nd ed. (Rochester, NY: Charles Mann, 1889), at www.books.google.com. Elizabeth Cady Stanton, *Elizabeth Cady Stanton: As Revealed in Her Letters Diary and Reminiscences,* Vol. 1, eds. Theodore Stanton and Harriot Stanton Blatch (New York: Harper and Brothers, 1922), at www.books.google.com. **348:** Elizabeth Cady Stanton, et al., in Erik Bruun and Jay Crosby, eds., *Our Nation's Archive.* Charlotte Woodward, in Diane Balser, *Sisterhood and Solidarity: Feminism and Labor in Modern Times* (Boston: South End Press, 1987). Lucretia Mott, in Gail Collins, *America's Women: Four Hundred Years of Dolls, Drudges, Helpmates, and Heroines* (New York: HarperCollins, 2003). **349:** Elizabeth Cady Stanton, in Karen Gibson, "A Powerful Partnership," at www.britannica.com. **350:** Nathaniel Hawthorne, in Leland S. Person, *The Cambridge Introduction to Nathaniel Hawthorne* (Cambridge, NY: Cambridge University Press, 2007). Nathaniel Hawthorne, in Lindsay Swift, *Brook Farm: Its Members, Scholars, and Visitors* (New York: Macmillan, 1900). **351:** George Ripley, in Philip F. Gura, *American Transcendentalism: A History* (New York: Hill and Wang, 2007). Ibid. **352:** Anonymous, in Gura, *American Transcendentalism.* Marianne Dwight, *Letters from Brook Farm, 1844–1847* (Poughkeepsie: Vassar, 1928). Ibid. John Codman, in Sterling F. Delano, *Brook Farm: The Dark Side of Utopia* (Cambridge, MA: Belknap Press, 2004). **353:** Nathaniel Hawthorne, Delano, *Brook Farm.*

Chapter 19

355: Eli Whitney, in J. Franklin Jameson, ed., *The American Historical Review,* Vol. 3 (New York: The Macmillan Co., 1898), at www.books.google.com. **357:** Anonymous, in John Brickell, *The Natural History of North Carolina* (Raleigh, NC: Trustees of the public libraries, 1911), at www.books.google.com. **358:** Eli Whitney, in Karen Gerhardt Britton, *Bale O' Cotton: The Mechanical Art of Cotton Ginning* (College Station: Texas A&M Univ.). **359:** Anonymous, in William

C. Davis, *Brother Against Brother: The War Begins* (Time-Life Books, 1983). **360:** Anonymous, in Hannah Josephson, *The Golden Threads: New England's Mill Girls and Magnates,* Vol. 2 (New York: Duell, Sloan and Pearce, 1949). **363:** John C. Calhoun, in David E. Nye, *America as Second Creation: Technology and Narratives of New Beginnings* (MA: MIT, 2003). Robert Fulton, in Mabel B. Casner and Ralph Henry Gabriel, *The Story of American Democracy* (New York: Harcourt, Brace, and Co., 1950). Anonymous, in Douglas Brinkley, *American Heritage History of the United States* (New York: Viking, 1998). **366:** Anonymous, in Alan Brinkley, *The Unfinished Nation: A Concise History of the American People* (New York: A. A. Knopf, 1997). **367:** William Newnham Blane, *Travels Through the United States and Canada* (London: Baldwin and Co., 1828), at www.books.google.com. **370:** Clementine Averill, in Harriet Jane Hanson Robinson, *Loom and Spindle: Or, Life Among the Early Mill Girls* (Kailua, HI: Press Pacifica, 1976 [first published 1898]). **371:** Sally Rice, in Thomas Dublin, *Women at Work: The Transformation of World and Community in Lowell, Massachusetts, 1826–1860* (New York: Columbia University Press, 1979). **372:** Mary Paul, in Mary S. Page and Larry Metzer, *Voices and Masks: The Experience of Nineteenth Century Mill Girls and Enslaved Women from Primary Sources* (Concord, MA: Wayside Publishing, 2000). Anonymous, in Thomas Dublin, *Women at Work.* **373:** Robinson, *Loom and Spindle.* Lucy Larcom, in Dublin, *Women at Work.*

Chapter 20

375: W. E. B. Du Bois, "The Sorrow Songs," at www.bartleby.com. **376:** Frederick Douglass, *My Bondage and My Freedom* (New York: Miller, Orton, and Mulligan, 1855), at www.books.google.com. Frederick Douglass, *Narrative of the Life of Frederick Douglass: An American Slave* (Cambridge, MA: Belknap Press, 2009 [first published 1845, by the Anti-slavery Office]). **377:** Douglass, *My Bondage and My Freedom.* Anonymous, in Alfred Abioseh Jarrett, *The Impact of Macro Social Systems on Ethnic Minorities in the United States* (Westport, CT: Greenwood Pub., 2000). Anonymous, in Charles Robert Crowe, *The Age of Civil War and Reconstruction, 1830–1900: A Book of Interpretive Essays* (Homewood, IL: Dorsey Press, 1966). Douglass, *My Bondage and My Freedom.* Frederick Douglass, et

al., in Richard Newman, Patrick Rael, and Phillip Lapansky, eds., *Pamphlets of Protest: An Anthology of Early African American Protest Literature, 1790–1860* (New York: Routledge, 2001). **378:** Robert William Fogel, *The Rise and Fall of American Slavery: Without Consent or Contract* (New York: W. W. Norton and Co., 1989). **380:** Anonymous, in William Loren Katz, *Eyewitness: A Living Documentary of the African American Contribution to American History* (New York: Simon and Schuster, 1995). Anonymous, in William Maxwell, ed., *The Virginia Historical Register, and Literary Companion,* Vol. 5 (Richmond: Macfarlane and Fergusson, 1852), at www.books.google.com. Sara Grudger, in John Michael Vlach, "Back of the Big House: The Cultural Landscape of the Plantation Exhibition," at www.gwu.edu. Ira Berlin, Marc Favreau, and Steven Miller, eds., *Remembering Slavery: African Americans Talk About Their Personal Experiences of Slavery and Emancipation* (New York: The New Press, 1998). Anonymous, in Meg Greene, *Slave Young, Slave Long: The American Slave Experience* (Minneapolis, MN: Lerner Pub., 1999). **381:** Josiah Henson, *Father Henson's Story of His Own Life* (Boston: John P. Jewett and Co., 1858). Douglass, *Narrative of the Life of Frederick Douglass.* Georgia Baker, in Ira Berlin, et al., eds., *Remembering Slaves: African Americans Talk About Their Personal Experiences of Slavery and Freedom* (New York: New Press, 1998). Douglass, *Narrative of the Life of Frederick Douglass.* Ibid. **382:** Ibid. Douglass, *My Bondage and My Freedom.* Ibid. Ibid. Harriet A. Jacobs, *Incidents in the Life of a Slave Girl: Written by Herself,* ed. Jean Fagan Yellin (Cambridge, MA: Harvard University Press, 1987). **383:** Douglass, *Narrative of the Life of Frederick Douglass.* Ibid. **384:** Anonymous, in William Loren Katz, *Eyewitness.* Anonymous, in Philip Sheldon Foner, *History of Black Americans: From the Emergence of the Cotton Kingdom to the Eve of the Compromise of 1850,* Vol. 2 (Westport, CT: Greenwood Press, 1975). **385:** Alonzo Pondley, in Andrew Waters, ed., *On Jordan's Stormy Banks: Personal Accounts of Slavery in Georgia* (Winston-Salem, NC: John F. Blair, 2000). Booker T. Washington, *Up from Slavery: An Autobiography* (New York: Doubleday, Page, and Co., 1902). Elijah Marrs, in Andrew Ward, *The Slaves' War: The Civil War in the Words of Former Slaves* (New York: Houghton Mifflin, 2008). William Webb, in

Ruth Tucker, *The Family Album: Portraits of Family Life Through the Centuries* (Victor Books, 1994). Frederick Douglass, *Life and Times of Frederick Douglass* (Hartford, CT: Park Pub., 1882), at www.books.google.com. **386:** Anonymous, in Lerone Bennett Jr., "Behind the Cotton Curtain," *Ebony* 17, no. 3(Jan. 1962). Rachel Cruze, in Ira Berlin, et al., eds., *Remembering Slavery*. John Cole, in Work Projects Administration, *Slave Narratives*, Vol. 4, *Georgia Narratives*, Part 1 (BiblioBazaar, 2008 [original copyright 1941]). **387:** Cornelius Garner, in William E. Montgomery, *Under Their Own Vine and Fig Tree: The African-American Church in the South 1865–1900* (Baton Rouge: Louisiana University Press, 1993). Wash Wilson, in Julius Lester, *To Be a Slave* (New York: Dial Press, 1968). James L. Smith, in Albert J. Raboteau, *Slave Religion: The "Invisible Institution" in the Antebellum South* (New York: Oxford University Press, 1978). Anonymous, in Anne Devereaux Jordan and Virginia Schomp, *Slavery and Resistance* (Tarrytown, NY: Marshall Cavendish Benchmark, 2007). **388:** Frederick Douglass, in Page Smith, *The Nation Comes of Age: A People's History of the Ante-Bellum Years* (New York: McGraw-Hill, 1981). Robert Anderson, in David Kenneth Wiggins, ed., *Sport in America: From Wicked Amusement to National Obsession* (Champaign, IL: Human Kinetics, 1995). **390:** Harriet Tubman, in Catherine Clinton, *Harriet Tubman: The Road to Freedom* (Boston: Little, Brown, 2004). **391:** Harriet Tubman, adapted from Sarah Bradford, *Scenes in the Life of Harriet Tubman* (Auburn, NY: W. J. Moses, 1869). Ibid. **392:** R.C. Smedley, *History of the Underground Railroad* (Lancaster, PA: John A. Hiestand, 1883), at www.books.google.com. **393:** Harriet Tubman, in Judith Bentley, *Harriet Tubman* (New York: Franklin Watts, 1990). Joe Bailey, in ibid. Harriet Tubman, in Clinton, *Harriet Tubman*.

Chapter 21

401: Abraham Lincoln, in Michael S. Green, *Freedom, Union, and Power: Lincoln and His Party During the Civil War* (New York: Fordham University Press, 2004). Abraham Lincoln, in a letter to Albert G. Hodges, at www.loc.gov. **402:** Anonymous, in Stephen Ambrose and Douglas Brinkley, eds., *Witness to America: An Illustrated Documentary History of the United States from the Revolution to Today* (New York: HarperCollins, 1999). **403:** Arthur Livermore, in Marion Mills Miller, ed., *Great Debates in American History: Slavery from 1790 to 1857*, Vol. 4 (New York: Current Literature Publishing Co., 1913). **404:** Thomas Cobb, in Stephen B. Oates, *The Approaching Fury: Voices of the Storm, 1820–1861* (New York: HarperCollins, 1997). James Tallmadge, in ibid. **405:** John Quincy Adams, *Memoirs of John Quincy Adams: Comprising Portions of His Diary from 1795 to 1848*, Vol. 5, ed. Charles Francis Adams (Philadelphia: J. B. Lippincott and Co., 1875), at www.books.google.com. Mississippi state legislature, in Page Smith, *The Nation Comes of Age: A People's History of the Ante-Bellum Years* (New York: McGraw-Hill, 1981). **406:** The Wilmot Proviso, 1846, at www.ushistory.org. **407:** Daniel Webster, in Miller, *Great Debates in American History*, Vol. 4. **408:** Jarmain Loguen, in Howard Zinn, *A People's History of the United States: 1492–Present* (New York: HarperCollins, 2003). Ralph Waldo Emerson, in Stephen B. Oates, *Approaching Fury*. Anonymous, in Smith, *Nation Comes of Age*. Harriet Beecher Stowe, *Uncle Tom's Cabin* (Philadelphia: Henry Altemus Co., 1900). **410:** Horace Greeley, *Horace Greeley: Voice of the People* (New York: Harper, 1950). Anonymous, in Geo. W. Martin, ed., *Collections of the Kansas State Historical Society*, Vol. 10 (Topeka: State Printing Office, 1908). **411:** Charles Sumner, *Charles Sumner: His Complete Works* (Boston: Lee and Shepard, 1900). Henry Wadsworth Longfellow, in Smith, *Nation Comes of Age*. **412:** Anonymous, in David Herbert Donald, *Charles Sumner and the Coming of the Civil War* (Naperville, IL: Sourcebooks, 1960). Roger Taney, in Smith, *Nation Comes of Age*. **413:** *The New York Tribune*, "Editorial on the Dred Scott Supreme Court Decision," March 11, 1857, at www.politicalquotes.org. *The New York Independent*, in David M. Potter, *The Impending Crisis, 1848–1861*, ed. Don Edward Fehrenbacher (New York: Harper and Row, 1976). **414:** Massachusetts convention, in Smith, *Nation Comes of Age*. Abraham Lincoln, in Marion Mills Miller, ed., *Life and Works of Abraham Lincoln: Speeches and Debates, 1856–1858*, Vol. 3 (Rahway, NJ: The Quinn and Boden Co., 1907). Abraham Lincoln, in the "Last Joint Debate, at Alton," at www.bartleby.com. **415:** John Brown, in Fred R. Shapiro, ed., *The Yale Book of Quotations* (R. R. Donnelley and Sons, 2006). *Charleston Mercury*, in Kenneth M. Stampp, ed., *The Causes of the Civil War* (New York: Simon and Schuster, 1991 [first published Oct. 11, 1860]). **416:** Abraham Lincoln, in Stephen B. Oates, *With Malice Toward None: A Life of Abraham Lincoln* (New York: HarperCollins, 1977). Charleston Mercury, Dec. 1860, at www.americanhistory.si.edu. Abraham Lincoln, First Inaugural Address, 1861, at www.bartleby.com. **417:** *The New York Tribune*, in Horace Greeley, *The American Conflict: A History of the Great Rebellion in the United States of America 1860–64*, Vol. 1 (Hartford: O. D. Case and Co., 1866 [first published Apr. 15, 1861]), at www.books.google.com. **418:** Anonymous, in Albert J. Von Frank, *The Trials of Anthony Burns: Freedom and Slavery in Emerson's Boston* (Cambridge, MA: Harvard University Press, 1998). **421:** William Llyod Garrison, in Wendell Phillips Garrison, *William Llyod Garrison*, Vol. 2 (New York: The Century Co., 1885), at www.books.google.com. Maria Weston Warren, in Benjamin Quarles, *Black Abolitionists* (New York: Oxford University Press, 1969). "Great Massachusetts Petition," in Donald M. Jacobs, ed., *Courage and Conscience: Black and White Abolitionists in Boston* (Bloomington: Indiana University Press, 1993).

Chapter 22

423: Stephen Douglas, in James McPherson, *Battle Cry of Freedom: The Civil War Era* (New York: Oxford University Press, 1988). **425:** Abraham Lincoln, "First Inaugural Address," 1861, at www.bartleby.com. Jefferson Davis, in William J. Cooper, ed., *Jefferson Davis: The Essential Writings* (New York: Modern Library, 2003). **426:** Bernard Bee, in Thomas L. Preston, "General Hill's Article on Stonewall Jackson," *The Century* 48, no. 1 (May 1894). Thomas Jackson, in R. L. Dabney, *Life and Campaigns of Liet-Gen. Thomas J. Jackson* (New York: Blelock and Co., 1866), at www.books.google.com. **429:** M. F. Roberts, in Bob Blaisdell, ed., *The Civil War: A Book of Quotations* (Mineola, NY: Dover Pub., 2004). J. W. Love, in ibid. **430:** Abraham Lincoln, in Ronald C. White, *A. Lincoln: A Biography* (New York: Random House, 2009). **431:** Abraham Lincoln, Lincoln's Gettysburg Address, Nov. 19, 1863, at www.bartleby.com. **433:** David Porter, in Nathan Miller, *The U.S. Navy: A History*, 3rd ed. (US Naval Institute Press, 1997). Anonymous, in David S. Heidler and Jeanne T. Heidler, eds., *Encyclopedia of the American Civil War: A Political, Social, and Military History* (Santa Barbara, CA:

ABC-CLIO, 2000). Mary Boykin Chesnut, in Mary A. DeCredico, *Mary Boykin Chesnut: A Confederate Woman's Life* (Lanham, MD: Rowman and Littlefield Pub., 2002). Anonymous, in La Salle Corbell Pickett, *Pickett and His Men* (Atlanta, GA: Foote and Davies, 1899), at www.books.google.com. **434:** James Henry Gooding, in Herbert Aptheker, *A Documentary History of the Negro People in the United States* (New York: Citadel Press, 1969). **435:** Ulysses S. Grant, in Peter G. Tsouras, ed., *The Book of Military Quotations* (St. Paul, MN: Zenith Press, 1992). Ulysses S. Grant, in Ernie Gross, *This Day In American History* (New York: Neal-Schuman Pub., 1990). Ulysses S. Grant, in David Macrae, *The Americans at Home: Pen-and-Ink Sketches of American Men Manners and Institution,* Vol. 1 (Edinburgh: Edmonston and Douglas, 1870), at www.books.google.com. **436:** Ulysses S. Grant, in E. B. Long, ed., *Personal Memoirs of U. S. Grant* (Cambridge, MA: Da Capo, 1982). William Tecumseh Sherman, in Shelby Foote, *The Civil War: A Narrative* (New York: Random House, 1974). **437:** Robert E. Lee, in McPherson, *Battle Cry of Freedom.* **438:** Ulysses S. Grant, in ibid. Oliver Wendell Holmes, in Hugh Tulloch, *The Debate on the American Civil War Era* (New York: Manchester University Press, 1999). **440:** Abraham Lincoln, "A House Divided Against Itself Cannot Stand" speech, 1858, at www.nationalcenter.org. Benjamin Hardin Helm, in Stephen Berry, *House of Abraham: Lincoln and the Todds, A Family Divided by War* (New York: Houghton Mifflin Co., 2007). Ibid. Ibid. **441:** Robert E. Lee, in ibid. **442:** Abraham Lincoln, in ibid. Ibid. John J. Crittenden, in ibid. Robert Breckenridge, in ibid. Robert J. Breckenridge, in ibid. Henry Lane Stone, in Amy Murrell Taylor, *The Divided Family in Civil War America* (Chapel Hill: University of North Carolina Press, 2005). **443:** James Campbell, in William J. Hamilton III, "Brother Against Brother at Secessionville," at www.civilwar.org. Matthew H. Peters, "My Brother and I," *Blue and Gray: The Patriotic American Magazine,* June 1893. David Davis, in Berry, *House of Abraham.*

Chapter 23

445: Abraham Lincoln, Second Inaugural Address, 1865, at www.bartleby.com. **446:** Frederick Douglass, *Life and Times of Frederick Douglass* (Hartford, CT: Park Pub., 1882), at www.books.google.com.

George P. Sanger, ed., *The Statutes at Large, Treaties, and Proclamations, of the United States of America,* Vol. 13 (Boston: Little, Brown, and Co., 1866), at www.memory.loc.gov. **447:** Randy Finley, *From Slavery to Uncertain Freedom* (Fayetteville: University of Arkansas Press, 1996). **449:** House of Representatives, in Benjamin Perley Poore, ed., *Trial of Andrew Johnson, President of the United States, Before the Senate of the United States, on Impeachment by the House of Representative for High Crimes and Misdemeanors,* Vol. 1 (Washington: Government Printing Office, 1868), at www.books.google.com. Lyman Trumbull, in Benjamin Perley Poore, ed., *Trial of Andrew Johnson,* Vol. 3. **451:** Anti-Slavery Society, in Page Smith, *Trial by Fire: A People's History of the Civil War and Reconstruction* (New York: McGraw-Hill, 1982). Georgia Reconstruction Constitution, in W. E. B. Du Bois, *Black Reconstruction in America 1860–1880* (New York: The Free Press, 1935). James G. Blaine, in Cathy E. Dubowski, *Andrew Johnson: Rebuilding the Union* (Englewood Cliffs, NJ: Silver Burdett Press, 1991). **453:** Benjamin Tillman, in *Congressional Record,* 59th Congress, 2nd Session, Jan. 21, 1907. Henry Adams, in *Reports of Committees of the Senate of the United States for the First and Second Sessions of the Forty-Sixth Congress 1879–80* (Washington: Government Printing Office, 1880). **454:** Frederick W. M. Holliday, in Edgar W. Knight, *Public Education in the South* (Boston: Ginn and Co., 1922). **455:** *Charleston News and Courier* editorial, in Sacvan Bercovitch, ed., *The Cambridge History of American Literature,* Vol. 5 (New York: Cambridge University Press, 2003). John Marshall Harlan, in Christine Compston and Rachel Filene Seidman, *Our Documents: 100 Milestone Documents from the National Archives* (New York: Oxford University Press, 2003). **456:** Anonymous, in Eric Foner, *Forever Free: The Story of Emancipation and Reconstruction* (New York: Vintage Books, 2006). **458:** Ernest Green, in Juan Williams, *Eyes on the Prize: America's Civil Rights Years, 1954–1965* (New York: Viking, 1987). Melba Pattillo, in ibid. Dwight Eisenhower, in ibid. **460:** Martin Luther King Jr., "I Have a Dream" speech, Aug. 28, 1963, at www.mlkonline.net. Martin Luther King, Jr., "Give Us the Ballot, We Will Transform the South" speech, May 17, 1957, at www.pbs.org. **461:** John Lewis, in Williams, *Eyes on the Prize.* Joe Smitherman, in ibid. Lyndon Johnson, in ibid.

Chapter 24

469: Kipkapalikan, in E. Jane Gay, *With the Nez Perces: Alice Fletcher in the Field 1889–1892* (Lincoln: University of Nebraska Press, 1981). **470:** Chief Joseph, in Peter Cozzens, *Eyewitness to the Indian Wars 1865–1890: Wars for the Pacific Northwest,* Vol. 2 (Stackpole Books, 2002). James Snell, in Alvin M. Josephy, *The Nez Perce Indians and the Opening of the Northwest* (New Haven, CT: Yale University Press, 1965). **471:** Chief Joseph, in Bob Blaisdell, ed., *Great Speeches by Native Americans* (Mineola, NY: Dover Pub., 2000). Dr. Latham, in Helen Addison Howard, *Saga of Chief Joseph* (Caldwell, ID: Caxton, 1965). **474:** Henry Stanley, in Stephen E. Ambrose, *Nothing Like It in the World: The Men Who Built the Transcontinental Railroad 1863–1869* (New York: Touchstone, 2001). **476:** J. Ross Browne, "A Tour Through Arizona," *Harper's New Monthly Magazine,* Nov. 1864, 29. **477:** Ibid. Philip Sheridan, in Thomas Dionysius Clark, *Frontier America: The Story of the Westward Movement* (New York: Scribner, 1959). **478:** *Evening Star,* in Clark, *Frontier America.* **479:** Colorado newspaper, in Keith Wheeler, *The Railroaders* (New York: Time-Life Books, 1973). **481:** Sitting Bull, in Robert M. Utley, *Sitting Bull: The Life and Times of an American Patriot* (New York: Holt Paperbacks, 1993). George Crook, in Page Smith, *The Rise of Industrial America: A People's History of the Post-Reconstruction Era* (New York: McGraw-Hill, 1984). **482:** Wolf Necklace, in Virginia Irving Armstrong, *I Have Spoken: American History Through the Voices of the Indians* (Chicago: Sage Books, 1971). **484:** C. P. Hicks, in Nell Irvin Painter, *Exodusters: Black Migration to Kansas After Reconstruction* (Lawrence: University Press of Kansas, 1986). **485:** Anonymous, in ibid. Benjamin Singleton, in William Loren Katz, *The Black West: A Documentary and Pictorial History of the African American* (New York: Simon and Schuster, 1996). **486:** John Solomon Lewis, in Painter, *Exodusters.* Williana Hickman, in Katz, *The Black West.* **487:** Ava Speese Day, in Frances Jacob Alberts, ed., *Sod House Memories* (Hastings, NE: 1964).

Chapter 25

489: Rosey Safron, "The Washington Place Fire," *The Independent,* Jan.–June 1911, 70. **491:** William Makepeace Thayer, *Marvels of the New West: A Vivid Portrayal of the Stupendous Marvels in the Vast Wonderland West of the Missouri River* (Norwich,

CT: Henry Bill Pub., 1890). **492:** Andrew Carnegie, *The Empire of Business* (New York: Doubleday, Page and Co., 1902). Ibid. **493:** Thomas Edison, in Paul Israel, *Edison: A Life of Invention* (New York: John Wiley, 1998). **494:** Alexander Graham Bell, in his journal, at the Library of Congress, http://memory.loc.gov/mss/magbell/253/25300201/0022. **497:** *Chicago Tribune,* in Wayne Moquin and Charles Van Doren, eds., *The American Way of Crime: A Documentary History* (New York: Praeger, 1976). **498:** Anonymous, in James R. Green, *The World of the Worker: Labor in Twentieth-Century America* (New York: Hill and Wang, 1980). Joseph Asch, in Leon Stein, *The Triangle Fire* (Ithaca, NY: Cornell University Press, 2001). **499:** Hamlin Garland, *A Son of the Middle Border* (New York: Macmillan Co., 1917). Anonymous, in Doreen Rappaport, ed., *American Women: Their Lives in Their Words: A Documentary History* (New York: T.Y. Crowell, 1990). **500:** Pauline Newman, in Barbara Mayer Wertheimer, *We Were There: The Story of Working Women in America* (New York: Pantheon Books, 1977). **501:** *Labor Standard,* in William L. Abbott, *The American Labor Heritage* (Honolulu: University of Hawaii, 1967). *People v. Harris,* 168, Supp. 134 (Gen. Sess., 1911). **502:** Rose Schneiderman, in Leon Stein, ed., *Workers Speak: Self Portraits* (New York: Arno, 1971). Rose Safron, in Leon Stein, *The Triangle Fire.* Oliver Mahoney, in ibid. Anonymous, in ibid. Anonymous, in "141 Men and Girls Die in Waist Factory Fire" *New York Times,* March 26, 1911, at www.law.umkc.edu. **503:** Uriah Stephens, in Philip Sheldon Foner, *History of the Labor Movement in the United States,* Vol. 1 (New York: International Pub., 1947). The Labor Publishing Co., *Labor: Its Rights and Wrong: Statements and Comments by the Leading Men of Our Nation* (Washington, DC: Labor Pub., 1886), at www.books.google.com. Anonymous, in Edward Robb Ellis, *The Epic of New York City: A Narrative History* (New York: Carroll and Graf Pub., 2005). Rose Schneiderman, in Leon Stein, *The Triangle Fire.* **504:** Rose Schneiderman, in Stein, ed., *Workers Speak: Self Portrait.* **506:** W. G. Lathrop, in a letter to Thomas Edison, Mar. 5, 1921, at www.memory.loc.gov. Thomas Edison, in Neil Baldwin, *Edison: Inventing the Century* (Chicago: University of Chicago Press, 1995). **507:** Edward Johnson, in Randall Stross, *The Wizard of Menlo Park: How Thomas Alva Edison Invented the Modern World* (New York: Crown Pub., 2007). **508:** Thomas Edison, at www.quotationsbook.com. Marshall Fox, in Stross, *Wizard of Menlo Park.* Thomas Edison, in Stross, *Wizard of Menlo Park.* **509:** Ibid.

Chapter 26

511: Emma Lazarus, "The New Colossus," at www.jwa.org. **513:** Pascal D'Angelo, *Pascal D'Angelo, Son of Italy* (New York: Macmillan, 1924). **514:** Pascal D'Angelo's father, in ibid. **516:** Mary Antin, *The Promised Land* (New York: Houghton Mifflin, 1912). Ibid. Ibid. Ibid. Anonymous, in Ronald Sanders, *Shores of Refuge: A Hundred Years of Jewish Emigration* (New York: Holt, 1988). **517:** Mary Antin, *Promised Land.* Anonymous, in *Review Journal of Philosophy and Social Science,* Vol. 1 (Anu Prakashan, 1976). **518:** Lee Chew, "The Biography of a Chinaman," *The Independent,* Jan.–Dec. 1903, 102. Anonymous, in Barbara Lee Bloom, *The Chinese-Americans* (San Diego, CA: Lucent Books, 2002). Anonymous, in Ruthanne Lum McCunn, *An Illustrated History of the Chinese in America* (San Francisco: Design Enterprises of San Francisco, 1979). **519:** Lee Chew, "The Biography of a Chinaman," *The Independent,* Jan.–Dec. 1903, 102. **520:** Pablo Mares, in Albert Camarillo, *Chicanos in California: A History of Mexican Americans in California* (San Francisco: Boyd and Fraser Pub., 1984). Anonymous, in Ricardo Romo, *East Los Angeles: History of a Barrio* (Austin: University of Texas Press, 1983). *El Labrador,* in David J. Weber, ed., *Foreigners in Their Native Land: Historical Roots of the Mexican Americans* (Albuquerque: University of New Mexico Press, 1973). **521:** Anonymous, in Albert Camarillo, *Chicanos in a Changing Society: From Mexican Pueblos to American Barrios in Santa Barbara and Southern California, 1848–1930* (Cambridge, MA: Harvard University Press, 1979). Anonymous, in Robert J. Lipshultz, *American Attitudes Toward Mexican Immigration, 1924–1952* (San Francisco: R and E Research Associates, 1971). Anonymous, in Mark Reisler, *By the Sweat of Their Brow: Mexican Immigrant Labor in the United States, 1900–1940* (Westport, CT: Greenwood Press, 1976). Anonymous, in Paul Schuster Taylor, *An American-Mexican Frontier: Nueces County* (Chapel Hill: University of North Carolina Press, 1934). Isidro Osorio, in Manuel Gamio, *The Life Story of the Mexican Immigrant: Autobiographic Documents* (Mineola, NY: Dover Pub., 1971). **522:** John Mitchell, in The United States Immigration Commission, *Reports of the Immigration Commission: Statements and Recommendations Submitted by Societies and Organizations Interested in the Subject of Immigration* (Washington, DC: Government Printing Office, 1911). **525:** Manyang, in Susan Buckley and Elspeth Leacock, *Journeys for Freedom: A New Look at America's Story* (Boston: Houghton Mifflin, 2006). Ibid. **527:** Yulia, in Marina Tamar Budhos, *Remix: Conversations with American Teenagers* (New York: Holt, 1999). Tito, in Janet Bode, *New Kids in Town: Oral Histories of Immigrant Teens* (New York: F. Watts, 1989).

Chapter 27

535: Samuel Sidney McClure, *My Autobiography* (New York: Frederick A. Stokes, 1914). Ibid. Samuel Sidney McClure, in Lincoln Steffens, *The Autobiography of Lincoln Steffens* (Berkeley, CA: Heyday Books, 2005 [first published 1931 by Harcourt, Brace, and Co.]). **537:** Mary Elizabeth Lease, in Howard Zinn and Anthony Arnove, *Voices of a People's History of the United States* (New York: Seven Stories Press, 2004). **538:** John D. Rockefeller, in John T. Flynn, *God's Gold: The Story of Rockefeller and His Times* (John T. Flynn, 1932). Andrew Carnegie, *The Gospel of Wealth and Other Timely Essays* (BiblioBazaar, 2009). Andrew Carnegie, "Popular Illusions About Trusts," *The Century,* May.–Oct. 1900, 60. Andrew Carnegie, *The Gospel of Wealth.* **539:** Ibid. Andrew Carnegie, in Joseph Frazier Wall, *Andrew Carnegie* (New York: Oxford University Press, 1970). John D. Rockefeller, in Raymond B. Fosdick, *The Story of the Rockefeller Foundation* (New Brunswick, NJ: Transaction Pub., 1989). Ibid. **540:** Theodore Roosevelt, in Ruth Wood Gavian and William Albert Hamm, *The American Story* (Lexington, MA: D. C. Heath, 1947). Theodore Roosevelt, in Henry F. Pringle, *Theodore Roosevelt: A Biography* (New York: Cornwall Press, 1931). **541:** Robert M. La Follette, *La Follette's Autobiography: A Personal Narrative of Political Experiences,* 3rd ed. (Madison, WI: Blied Printing, 1919). **542:** Mary Harris Jones, *Autobiography of Mother Jones* (Mineola, NY: Dover Pub., 2004 [first published 1925 by Charles H. Kerr and Co.]). Ibid. **543:** John Muir, *The Wilderness World of John Muir,* ed. Edwin Way Teale (New York: First Mariner Books, 2001). John Muir, *Nature Writings* (New York: The Library of America, 1997). Ibid. Ibid.

544: W. E. B. Du Bois, *On Sociology and the Black Community,* eds. Dan S. Green and Edwin D. Driver (Chicago: University of Chicago Press, 1978). Ibid. Booker T. Washington, in Richard D. Heffner, *A Documentary History of the United States,* 7th ed. (New York: New American Library, 2002). NAACP, in *W. E. B. Du Bois: A Reader,* ed. David Levering Lewis (New York: Henry Holt, 1995). **545:** Upton Sinclair, *The Jungle,* introduction by Jane Jacobs (New York: Random House, 2006 [first published 1906 by Upton Sinclair]). Ibid. **547:** Alice Paul, The Alice Paul Institute, at www.alicepaul.org. **548:** Lewis Hine, in Russell Freedman, *Kids at Work: Lewis Hine and the Crusade Against Child Labor* (New York: Clarion, 1994). **549:** Ibid. Ibid. **550:** John Spargo, *The Bitter Cry of the Children* (New York: Johnson Reprint Corporation, 1969) **551:** Kid Blink, in Susan Campbell Bartoletti, *Kids on Strike!* (New York: Houghton Mifflin Co., 1999).

Chapter 28

553: Theodore Roosevelt, *The Wisdom of Theodore Roosevelt,* ed. Donald J. Davidson (New York: Kensington Pub., 2003). **554:** Carl Schurz, "Thoughts on American Imperialism," *The Century,* May–Oct. 1898, 56. William Jennings Bryan, *Speeches of William Jennings Bryan,* Vol. 2 (New York: Funk and Wagnails Co., 1913). Henry Cabot Lodge, "Our Blundering Foreign Policy," The Forum, Mar.–Aug. 1895, 19. **556:** *Journal, in James Satter, Journalists Who Made History* (Minneapolis, MN: The Oliver Press, 1998). Teller Amendment, 1898, at www.

loc.gov. **557:** Richard Harding Davis, "The Battle of San Juan," *Scribner's Magazine,* July–Dec. 1898, 24. **558:** Theodore Roosevelt, *Autobiography of Theodore Roosevelt* (Forgotten Books, 2008), at www.books. google.com. **559:** Emilio Aguinaldo, in Lyman Abbott, "International Brotherhood Applied to the Conduct of the United States in the Philippines," *The Outlook,* Jan.–Apr. 1899, 61. Carl Schurz, *Speeches, Correspondence, and Political Papers of Carl Schurz,* Vol. 6 (New York: G. P. Putman's Sons, 1913). Henry Cabot Lodge, *The Retention of the Philippine Islands: Speech of Hon. Henry Cabot Lodge* (Washington: 1900). William McKinley, *Speeches and Addresses of William McKinley: From March 1, 1897– May 30, 1900* (New York: Doubleday and McClure, 1900). **560:** Theodore Roosevelt, in Tom Lansford, *Theodore Roosevelt in Perspective* (New York: Nova Science Publishers, 2005). Theodore Roosevelt, *Address and Presidential Messages of Theodore Roosevelt 1902-1904,* introduction by Henry Cabot Lodge (New York: G. P. Putman's Sons, 1904). Anonymous, in *Panama Canal: Gateway to the World* (New York: Putnam, 1989). **561:** Theodore Roosevelt, in Henry F. Pringle, *Theodore Roosevelt: A Biography* (New York: Cornwall Press, 1931). **562:** Woodrow Wilson, in Gregory J. W. Urwin, *The United States Infantry: An Illustrated History, 1775-1918* (Norman: University of Oklahoma Press, 2000). **563:** Alan Seeger, in Zachary Kent, *World War I: The Way to End Wars* (Hillside, NJ: Enslow Pub., 1994). Anonymous, in ibid.

564: Alan Seeger, *Letter and Diary of Alan Seeger* (New York: Charles Scribner's Sons, 1917). Leslie Morton, in Kent, *World War I.* **565:** *The Independent,* "The 'Lusitania' Case," Apr.–June 1915, 82. Woodrow Wilson, in Robert Torricelli and Andrew Carroll, eds., *In Our Own Words: Extraordinary Speeches of the American Century* (New York: Kodansha America, 1999). Ibid. **570:** William Randolph Hearst, in W. A. Swanberg, *Citizen Hearst: A Biography of William Randolph Hearst* (New York: Scribner, 1961). **573:** Ibid.

Chapter 29

575: Henry Ford, *My Life and Work* (Garden City, NY: Doubleday, Page, and Co., 1923). Ibid. Nathan Miller, *New World Coming: The 1920s and the Making of Modern America* (New York: Scribner, 2003). **576:** Martin Luther King Jr., "I Have a Dream" speech, Aug. 28, 1963, at www.mlkonline.net. *Brown v. Board of Education,* 347 U.S. 483 (1954). **578:** Barack Obama, "Change Has Come to America: Election Night Victory Speech," at www.america.gov. Barack Obama, "President Barack Obama's Inaugural Address," at www. whitehouse.gov. **582:** United Nations, "The United Nations: Organization," at www.un.org. **584:** Rachel Carson, in Mark H. Lytle, *The Gentle Subversive: Rachel Carson, Silent Spring, and the Rise of the Environmental Movement* (New York: Oxford University Press, 2007). Norman Borlaug, at www.globalrust.org. **586:** Ibid. Anonymous, in ibid. Anonymous, at www.worldfoodprize.org. Norman Borlaug, at www.nationalcenter.org.

Credits

Photographs

Front Cover
Greg Pease/Getty Images

Title Page
Greg Pease/Getty Images

Table of Contents
v: Library of Congress **vi:** Library of Congress **ix:** Library of Congress **xi:** Library of Congress **xiii:** RF/Dean Biriny/iStockphoto.com **x:** RF/Picture Research Consultants & Archives **xii:** Library of Congress **vii:** RF/scounting-stock/Shutterstock **viii:** RF/cascoly/Big Stock Photo

Unit 1 Opener
1: Lisa Poole/AP Photo **4:** RF/Alamy

Chapter 1
5: Werner Forman/Art Resource, NY **7:** Corbis **10:** "She Walks with Spirits" by Merlin Little Thunder/Oklahoma Indian Art Gallery **11:** RF/Aypril Porter/Shutterstock **12:** RF/PhotoDisc **13:** RF/Pauline Walton/Alamy **14:** RF/jeffzenner/Shutterstock **15:** RF/Digital Stock/Corbis **16:** RF/PhotoDisc **17:** RF/Digital Stock/Corbis **18:** RF/PhotoDisc **19:** Library of Congress **20:** Richard A. Cooke/Corbis **21:** Cahokia Mounds Historic Site **22:** Cahokia Mounds Historic Site **23 T:** Cahokia Mounds Historic Site **23 B:** Cahokia Mounds Historic Site

Chapter 2
24: Bettmann/Corbis **25:** RF/SuperStock **26:** Library of Congress **27:** The Granger Collection, New York **28:** The Granger Collection, New York **30:** Library of Congress **31:** RF/Henryk Sadura/Shutterstock **32:** Mission San Carlos Del Rio Carmelo, late 19th century, by Oriana Day. Oil on canvas, 20 x 30. Fine Arts Museums of San Francisco. Gift of Mrs. Eleanor Martin, 37556 **33:** New York Public Library **34:** Library of Congress **35:** The Granger Collection, New York **36:** The Granger Collection, New York **37:** Library of Congress **38:** The Granger Collection, New York **40:** Library of Congress **41:** The Granger Collection, New York **42:** Erich Lessing/Art Resource, NY **43 T:** Arxiu Mas, Biblioteca Colombina, Sevilla **43 B:** Library of Congress **44:** The Granger Collection,

New York **45 R:** Mark Leffingwell/AFP/Getty Images **45 L:** Spencer Platt/Getty Images

Chapter 3
46: Library of Congress **47:** Library of Congress **48:** Tim Wright/Corbis **50:** Library of Congress **51:** North Wind Picture Archives **52:** North Wind Picture Archives **53:** Burstein Collection/Corbis **54:** Library of Congress **55:** Library of Congress **56:** The Granger Collection, New York **57:** The Granger Collection, New York **58:** Library of Congress **59:** Library of Congress **60:** RF/Private Collection/Picture Research Consultants & Archives **61:** RF/Picture Research Consultants & Archives **62 T:** Royal Albert Memorial Museum, Exeter, Devon, UK/The Bridgeman Art Library **62 B:** Courtesy, American Antiquarian Society **63:** Granger Collection

Chapter 4
64: Marston, James Brown (1775–1817). "Old State House". Oil on canvas, 1801. MHS image number 71. Courtesy of the Massachusetts Historical Society. **65:** Library of Congress **66:** Library of Congress **67:** Library of Congress **68:** The Granger Collection, New York **69:** The Granger Collection, New York **70:** The Granger Collection, New York **71:** Library of Congress **72:** The Granger Collection, New York **73:** North Wind Picture Archives **74 T:** The Granger Collection, New York **74 B:** Library of Congress **75:** Library of Congress **76:** RF/Picture Research Consultants & Archives **77:** The Bridgeman Art Library **78:** © Bettmann/CORBIS **79:** Library of Congress

Unit 1 Timeline
80 BC: Library of Congress **80 T:** Library of Congress **80 BR:** RF/Picture Research Consultants & Archives **80 BL:** RF/Wikimedia **81 BM:** Library of Congress **81 TL:** RF/Picture Research Consultants & Archives **81 BL:** RF/Private Collection/Picture Research Consultants & Archives **81 TC:** Library of Congress **81 TR:** RF/Wikimedia **81 BR:** Library of Congress **81 BR:** RF/Wikimedia

Unit 2 Opener
83: Joe Raedle/Getty Images

Chapter 5
86: Library of Congress **87:** Library of Congress **88:** Bettmann/Corbis **89:** The Granger Collection, New York **91L:** Library of Congress **91R:** Courtesy of the Massachusettes Historical Society **93:** Courtesy, Winterthur Museum **94:** Library of Congress **95:** Library of Congress **96:** The Granger Collection, New York **98:** The Granger Collection, New York **99:** Doolittle engraving, Battle of Lexington. The Connecticut Historical Society, Hartford, Connecticut **100 T:** Doolittle engraving, Engagement at North Bridge. The Connecticut Historical Society, Hartford, Connecticut. **100 C:** RF/Dan Tobin/iStockphoto.com **101:** David Muench/Corbis **102 T:** Miriam and Ira D. Wallach Division of Art, Prints and Photographs, The New York Public Library. Astor, Lenox and Tilden Foundations **102 B:** Courtesy of Lou Sideris/Minute Man National Historical Park **103:** The New York Public Library for the Performing Arts/Music Division **104:** RF/Picture Research Consultants & Archives **105:** The Granger Collection, New York

Chapter 6
106: The Granger Collection, New York **107:** Library of Congress **108:** The Granger Collection, New York **109:** Library of Congress **110:** Library of Congress **111:** Library of Congress **113:** Library of Congress **114:** Library of Congress **115:** The Free Library of Philadelphia **116:** The Granger Collection, New York **117:** Colonia Williamsburg Foundation

Chapter 7
118: The Granger Collection, New York **119:** Library of Congress **120:** Getty Images **121:** The Granger Collection, New York **122:** Getty Images **123:** "Advance of the Enemy" by Alfred W. Thompson 1885. Oil on canvas. 25 ¼ x 45 ¼ in. The Connecticut Historical Society: Hartford Connecticut. **124:** Library of Congress **125:** Library of Congress **126:** Library of Congress **127:** The Granger Collection, New York **128:** Library of Congress **130:** The Granger Collection, New York **132:** Gianni Dagli Orti/Corbis **133:** Library of Congress **134:** RF/Picture Research Consultants & Archives **135:** Bettmann/CORBIS **136:** North Wind Picture Archives **137:** The Granger Collection, New York

270 T: Library of Congress 270 B: "Trail of Tears" by Brummet Echohawk: Gilcrease Museum: Tulsa: Oklahoma: 271: Copyright © Jeff Greenberg/Photo Edit:

Unit 4 Timeline
272 TC: Library of Congress 272 TR: Library of Congress 272 BC: Library of Congress 272 TR: Allyn Cox/Architect of the Capitol 272 BR: Library of Congress 272 BL: The Granger Collection, New York 273 TC: Library of Congress 273 TR: Library of Congress 273 BR: RF/Picture Research Consultants & Archives: 273 TL: RF/Hulton Archive/istockphoto.com 273 BL: Library of Congress 273 BC: Library of Congress

Unit 5 Opener
275: RF/Visions of America, LLC/Alamy

Chapter 15
278: Library of Congress 280: Library of Congress 281: The Granger Collection, New York 282: Corbis 283: Texas State Library 284: Fall of the Alamo by Robert Jenkins Onderdonk, courtesy of the Friends of the Governor's Mansion, Austin. 285: Oldest Known Lone Star Flag, Republic Period. Collection of the Star of the Republic Museum. Gift of Cletus Brown, Jr. 286: Approaching Chimney Rock by William Henry Jackson, Scotts Bluff National Monument. 288: E. Punderson, Exeter, N.H. [Exeter, New Hampshire, volunteers leaving for the Mexican War], c. 1846. Daguerrotype, ¼ plate. P1979.33. Amon Carter Museum, Fort Worth, Texas 289: The Granger Collection, New York 291: Library of Congress 292 T: Missouri Historical Museum 292 B: Yale Collection of American Literature, Beinecke Rare Book Room and Manuscript Library, Yale University 293: RF/Picture Research Consultants & Archives 294: Bent's Old Fort National Historic Site 295: New Mexico Museum of Art

Chapter 16
296: The Granger Collection, New York 297: RF/Nicolay Stanev/Shutterstock 298: Edgar S. Paxon, "Lewis and Clark at Three Forks." Oil on canvas, 1912, Mural in the Montana State Capitol. Courtesy of the Montana Historical Society. Don Beatty, photographer 299: Library of Congress 300: Carlos Nebel,

"Hacendado y Su Mayordomo "(Museum Collection Number 980). History Collections, Los Angeles County Museum of Natural History 301: The Granger Collection, New York 302: Arthur Fitzwilliam Tait, "Trappers at Fault - Looking for the Trail." The Anschutz Collection. 303: Corbis 304: Library of Congress 305: Nebraska State Historical Society, Digital ID nbhips 12377 307: C.C.A. Christensen, "Handcart Pioneers", 1900. © by Intellectual Reserve Inc. Courtesy of the Museum of Church History and Art. 308: Charles Christian Nahl (1818–1878) and Frederick August Wenderoth (1819–1884), "Miners in the Sierras", 1851–1852. Oil on canvas, 54 ¼ x 67 in. Smithsonian American Art Museum, Washington, DC/Art Resource, NY 309: California State Library 310: Bettmann/Corbis 312: Library of Congress 313: Courtesy of the California History Room, California State Library, Sacramento, California 314: Miriam and Ira D. Wallach Division of Art, Prints and Photographs, The New York Public Library. Astor, Lenox and Tilden Foundations. 315 T: Courtesy of the California History Room, California State Library, Sacramento, California

Chapter 17
316: USC Digital Library/California Historical Society, CHS-5162 317: USC Digital Library/California Historical Society, CHS 326 318: Courtesy of the Arizona Historical Society, AHS# 14546 319: Bancroft Library, University of California, Berkeley. 320: "California Vaqueros" by James Walker/The Anschutz Collection. 321: Mission San Gabriel Arcangel by Oriana Day/Fine Arts Museums of San Francisco/Gift of Eleanor Martin, DY37556. 322: Courtesy of the Arizona Historical Society, AHS# 3767. 323: Mariana Coronel Grinding Corn by A. Harmer, Museum Collection Number 1000. History Collections, Los Angeles County Museum of Natural History. 324: RF/Michelle Marsan/Shutterstock 325: Ramona Martinez Cruz & Carlos Cruz: Museum Collection Number 3875. History Collections: Los Angeles County Museum of Natural History. 326: New York Public Library 327: Hulton Archive/Getty Images 328 B: "Great Wall of Los Angeles: Division

of the Barrios and Chavez Ravine" 328 T: Photography by Edgar Hoill 329: M. Alvarez: 330 T: Benson Latin American Collection,University of Texas at Austin 330 B: Bradley Stuart/Indybay.org 331: Lindsay Hebberd/CORBIS

Unit 5 Timeline
332 TL: Library of Congress 322 TC: RF/Picture Research Consultants & Archives 332 BC: Approaching Chimney Rock by William Henry Jackson, Scotts Bluff National Monument. 332 BR: Library of Congress 332 BL: Library of Congress 332 TR: Library of Congress 333 BL: California State Library 333 TC: Franklin D. Roosevelt Library 333 BR: Library of Congress 333 BC: Library of Congress 333 TL: RF/Brandon Seidel/123RF

Unit 6 Opener
335: Museum of the City of New York/ Corbis

Chapter 18
338: Library of Congress 339: State Archives of Michigan 340: Library of Congress 341: Library of Congress 342: Library of Congress 343: The Granger Collection, New York 344 B: Massachusetts Historical Society/Bridgeman Art Library 344 T: Library of Congress 345: Art Resource: 346: "Pic Nick Camden Maine" by Jerome B. Thomson/Museum of Fine Arts: Boston. Gift of Maxim Karolik for the M and M Karolik Collection of American paintings. 1815–1865. 347 L: Library of Congress 347 R: Bettmann/Corbis 348: Library of Congress 350: RF/Picture Research Consultants & Archives: 351: RF/Private Collection/ Picture Research Consultants & Archives 352 T: RF/Picture Research Consultants & Archives: 352 B: Brooklyn Museum/ Corbis 353: Oneida Community Mansion House 354 T: The Granger Collection, New York

Chapter 19
354 B: Library of Congress 355: Library of Congress 356: Todd Gipstein/Getty Images 357: RF/iStockphoto 358: The Art Archive 360: Corbis 361: Bettman/ Corbis 363: Decker, Herman. Lonsdale Wharf, Providence RI, 1878. Gouache, 24 x 38 in. Museum of Art, Rhode Island School of Design/Mary B. Jackson Fund

486: Nebraska State Historical Society.
487 T: Nebraska State Historical Society
487 B: Photo by Cotton Coulson/National Geographic/Getty Images)

Chapter 25
488: UNITE ARCHIVES, Kheel Center, Cornell University, Ithaca, NY 489: Underwood & Underwood/Corbis 490: The Granger Collection, New York 491: Photo courtesy of The Preservation Society of Newport County, Rhode Island 493: Broadway and Maiden Lane, lithograph by J.J. Fogerty, negative number 2946. The Collection of the New York Historical Society. 495 B: Library of Congress 495 T: Library of Congress 496: Library of Congress 497: Library of Congress 498: Bettmann/Corbis 499: Library of Congress 500: Library of Congress 501: Bettmann/Corbis 502: Library of Congress 503: UNITE Archives, Kheel Center, Cornell University, Ithaca, NY. 504: Brown Brothers 505: UNITE Archives, Kheel Center, Cornell University, Ithaca, NY. 506: Bettmann/CORBIS 507 B: Bettmann/CORBIS 507 T: Bettmann/CORBIS 508: The Granger Collection, New York 509 R: Library of Congress 509 L: Library of Congress

Chapter 26
510: Getty Images 511: New York Public Library 512: Bettmann/Corbis 514: Library of Congress 515: Library of Congress 516: Library of Congress 517: Library of Congress 518: Philip Gould/Corbis 519: Library of Congress 520: Bettmann/Corbis 521: Courtesy of the Arizona Historical Society, Tucson, AHS #64323 522: Library of Congress 523: BettmannCorbis 524: Karen Blier/AFP/Getty Images 525: Courtesy Paul and Carl Jean Brown 526: Alain Nogues/Sygma/Corbis 527: Larry Downing/Reuters/Corbis

Unit 8 Timeline
528 TC: Library of Congress 528 BL: Library of Congress 528 TL: RF/Picture Research Consultants & Archives: 528 TR: U.S. Department of the Interior, National Park Service, Edison National Historic Site 528 BC: RF/Jason Yoder/123RF 528 BR: Library of Congress 529 TL: Library of Congress 529 BL: Library of Congress 529 TC: Library of Congress 529 TR: Library of Congress 529 BC: Library of Congress 529 BR: Library of Congress

Unit 9 Opener
531: Bettmann/Corbis

Chapter 27
534: Library of Congress 535 T: The Granger Collection, NY 535 B: Library of Congress 536: Culver Pictures Inc. 537: Library of Congress 538: Bettmann/Corbis 539: Library of Congress 540: The Granger Collection, New York 541 B: Photo courtesy of The Newberry Library, Chicago 541 T: Library of Congress 542 B: Library of Congress 542 T: Library of Congress 543: Library of Congress 544 B: Library of Congress 544 T: Library of Congress 545 B: Corbis: 545 T: Library of Congress 546 B: Library of Congress 546 T: Library of Congress 548 B: RF/Picture Research Consultants & Archives: 548 T: Library of Congress 549: Library of Congress 550 B: Library of Congress 550 T: Library of Congress 551 Library of Congress

Chapter 28
552: The Granger Collection, New York 553: Library of Congress 554: Library of Congress 555: Bettmann/Corbis 556: Corbis: 557: The Granger Collection, New York 558: The Granger Collection, New York 559: The Granger Collection, New York 561: Library of Congress 562: Bettmann/Corbis 563: Getty Images 565: Library of Congress 566: Library of Congress 567: The Signing of Peace in the Hall of Mirrors, Versailles, 28th June, 1919 by Sir William Orpen/Imperial War Museum, London. 568: Library of Congress 570: Library of Congress 571 T: The Granger Collection, New York 571 B: Library of Congress 572 L: The Granger Collection, New York 572 R: Library of Congress 573: James Leynse/Corbis

Chapter 29
574: RF/Dean Birinyi/iStockphoto.com 575: Library of Congress 576: Bettmann/Corbis 577: Ted Streshinsky/Corbis 578: Reuters 579: Chris Rank/Corbis 580: Car Culture/Corbis 581: AP Photo: 582: Shen Hong/Xinhua Press/Corbis 583: Todd Korol/Reuters 584: Photo by Alfred Eisenstaedt/

Time Life Pictures/Getty Images 585 T: Bob Sacha/Corbis 585 B: Proehl Studios/Corbis 586: Ted Streshinsky/CORBIS 586: RF/Ellen Isaacs/Alamy 587: Photo by Win McNamee/Getty Images

Unit 9 Timeline
588 TL: Library of Congress 588 BL: Library of Congress 588 TC: Library of Congress 588 TR: National Archives 588 BR: Library of Congress 589 TL: Library of Congress 589 BL: RF/Picture Research Consultants & Archives: 589 TC: Library of Congress 589 BR: National Archives 589 BC: Library of Congress 589 TC: RF/Wikimedia 589 TL: Library of Congress

Resources Opener
591: RF/Ellen Isaacs/Alamy

Art

Chapter 8
151: QYA Design Studio 153: QYA Design Studio

Chapter 9
172–173: QYA Design Studio 175: QYA Design Studio

Chapter 16
315: Gary Undercuffler

Chapter 20
379: QYA Design Studio

Chapter 26
513: QYA Design Studio